NEW TESTAMENT WORDS
IN TODAY'S LANGUAGE

WAYNE A. DETZLER

VICTOR

BOOKS a division of SP Publications, Inc.
WHEATON, ILLINOIS 60187

Offices also in
Whitby, Ontario, Canada
Amersham-on-the-Hill, Bucks, England

Unless otherwise noted, Scripture quotations are from the *New American Standard Bible* (NASB), © the Lockman Foundation 1960, 1962, 1963, 1968, 1971, 1972, 1973, 1975, 1977. Other quotations are from the *King James Version*; the *Holy Bible, New International Version* (NIV), © 1973, 1978, 1984, International Bible Society. Used by permission of Zondervan Bible Publishers; the *American Standard Version* (ASV).

Recommended Dewey Decimal Classification: 225.4
Suggested Subject Heading: REFERENCE BOOK, GREEK WORD STUDIES

Library of Congress Catalog Card Number: 85-062710
ISBN: 0-89693-528-0

To our children

Mark and Cathy Detzler
Scott and Carol Samuelson

with deep thanks
for the love, joy, and companionship
which they bring into our lives

FOREWORD

The best thing about this book is its balance, and that comes because of the life and ministry of the author, my longtime friend, Wayne Detzler.

He is first of all a careful student of the Word of God. He has taught in Bible school and in seminary and he has the solid credentials that are needed. But he is also a pastor and a preacher. He not only knows the Word, but he also knows how to apply it to needy hearts. There is nothing "academic" about his ministry, and that includes this book. It will speak to your heart's needs.

Dr. Detzler has served faithfully as a missionary. He has a wide view of ministry and of what God wants to accomplish in this world. He writes and preaches from a burning heart and a burdened heart, and this compassion is contagious.

There are numerous books available on the key words of the Greek New Testament, but this one is exceptional because of this balance. Pastors, Sunday School teachers, and all Christians who are serious about Bible study will find these word studies a source of spiritual wisdom and power. They are a joy to read! They will enrich your life!

Warren W. Wiersbe
Back to the Bible Broadcast
Lincoln, Nebraska

PREFACE

This volume has been prepared to better equip Bible students and teachers for the task of communicating divine truth in human language. To that end 200 Greek Bible words have been studied, and the individual articles contain historical, linguistic, biblical, and illustrative material.

Several basic tools have been helpful in preparing this volume. To determine the basic meaning of each Greek word I have turned to F. Wilbur Gingrich and Frederick W. Danker's translation of Walter Bauer, *Greek-English Lexicon of the New Testament and other Early Christian Literature*, 2nd edition (Chicago: University of Chicago Press, 1979).

The theological and literary use of these words has been studied with the help of Colin Brown, editor, *The New International Dictionary of New Testament Theology* (Grand Rapids: Zondervan, 1975) and Gerhard Kittel, editor, *Theological Dictionary of the New Testament*, translated by Geoffrey W. Bromiley (Grand Rapids: Eerdmans, 1964-75).

In illustrating the various words, many illustrations have been gleaned from personal ministry. Literary illustrations have been found in several collections, including the following: *The Concise Oxford Dictionary of Quotations* (New York: Oxford University Press, 1964), Laurence J. Peter, *Peter's Quotations* (New York: Bantam Books, 1977), Lloyd Cory, *Quotable Quotations* (Wheaton, Ill.: Victor Books, 1985), I.D.E. Thomas, editor, *A Puritan Golden Treasury* (Chicago: Moody Press, 1975), and Sherwood Eliot Wirt and Kersten Beckstrom, editors, *Living Quotations for Christians* (London: Hodder and Stoughton, 1974).

A special word of thanks is due to my mother, Edwina Detzler, for her patient proofreading of the manuscript. She brought all of her experience as an English teacher to bear on the improvement of the text.

Wayne A. Detzler
1986

ABIDE

MEANING

The basic Greek word for "abide" is *meno*. Occurring 112 times in the Greek New Testament, this word is found 66 times in the writings of the Apostle John. It is translated with such words as "abide," "continue," "remain," "live," "lodge," and "dwell."

Though the word is relatively frequent in its appearances, its related forms are even more popular. By adding a prefix to the root word we have *epimeno* (to live in), *katameno* (to wait), *parameno* (to stay near), *prosmeno* (to continue), *perimeno* (to expect), and *hupomeno* (to stand fast, persevere). Indeed it is the last of these which is most significant, because we draw our entire doctrine of perseverance from its wellspring. The noun form of the word *hupomeno* means perseverance, patience, endurance, steadfastness, and fortitude. This concept is the major focus of our biblical study.

BIBLE USAGE

The word *meno* functions on two levels of meaning in the Bible. First, it relates to rather common concepts of life. Living in a house (John 1:38) is described by the word. It is used of Jesus' visit to Zaccheus (Luke 19:5) and Peter's presence at Simon's tannery (Acts 9:43). It also referred to the place where Paul was held under house arrest (28:16), known in Latin as *custodia libera*, literally, "free custody."

A second slant takes the word into the realm of the spiritual. Christians are urged to make the Lord their place of abode, to persevere. In fact the Greek word for perseverance is *hupomeno*, a combination of the prefix *hupo* (under, as in under the rule or sovereignty of someone) and *meno* (to remain). So the combination word conveys the concept of continuing under the rule or sovereignty of the Lord. That is biblical steadfastness or perseverance. Now let us explore the biblical connections of this word.

By its primary form of *meno* (to remain) Christians are instructed to remain in "the teaching" (2 John 9), Christ's word (John 8:31), and in the love of the Lord (15:9). This continuance is related to Christ (15:4-5), the Father (1 John 2:24), and the Holy Spirit (John 14:17) who remain with us. In the Apostle Paul's great "Psalm of Love" (1 Cor. 13), we are told that faith, hope, and love remain (13:13). Steadfast staying power is part and parcel of biblical Christian living.

It is, however, in the combination form of *hupomeno* that our little word comes into its fullest development. James loved it, and he urged his fellow believers to stand firm or persevere in persecution and trial (James 1:12). In fact the very heat of harassment refines the Christian and increases his durability (James 1:2-4).

In Hebrews the same truth is hammered home. In fact it frames the gallery of godly greats. Faithful followers of the Lord endured suffering (Heb. 10:32). This truth is expounded in the Westminster Abbey of Bible heroes (chap. 11). Then in the very next chapter we are urged to run with endurance (12:1) as we fix our gaze on God.

When the Apostle Paul neared his end, he likewise urged Christians to continue. He prodded Timothy to pursue perseverance (1 Tim. 6:11). In Paul's final letter the dying apostle praised Timothy for imitating his perseverance (2 Tim. 3:10).

Predictably the climax of Christian teaching on endurance is in the Book of Revelation. There the resurrected Redeemer is the paragon of perseverance (Rev. 3:10). John, the exiled prince of Christians, is also one who persevered (1:9).

Eternity will reveal the reward of the redeemed who persevere under persecution (13:10; 14:12). So there is no doubt that perseverance is a high priority in the plan of God for Christians, both individually and collectively.

ILLUSTRATIONS

Charles Haddon Spurgeon said: "By perseverance the snail reached the ark." Another great Britisher, Samuel Johnson, claimed: "Great works are performed not by strength but by perseverance." "Triumph," added an anonymous wit, "is just umph added to try."

William Wilberforce, a 19th-century parliamentarian, was moved by the Lord to oppose the slave trade. In 1807 he brought about the banning of the slave trade in England. But not until 1833 was slavery as an institution abolished, and the news reached Wilberforce on his deathbed.

Nature also illustrates perseverance. "Today's mighty oak is just yesterday's little nut that held its ground," someone said. Another statement is attributed to Coleman Cox: "Even the woodpecker owes his success to the fact that he uses his head and keeps pecking away until he finishes the job he starts."

No one group of writers and preachers said more about perseverance than the Puritans of the sixteenth and seventeenth centuries. Thomas Watson wrote: "God's decree is the very pillar and basis on which the saints' perseverance depends. That decree ties the knot of adoption so fast that neither sin, death, nor hell can break it asunder." His companion in conflict was William Secker who put it profoundly: "Though Christians be not kept altogether from falling, yet they are kept from falling altogether."

True Christian perseverance is not tied to tenacity. It is rather the work of God the Holy Spirit in a believer's life. The starch in a saint's spine is shown by Scripture to be nothing less than the sanctifying work of the Holy Spirit. Only in this way can one explain the work of Gladys Aylward, a London parlor maid. Societies scorned her missionary application. She seemed too dull to master Chinese and fulfill her vision of serving in China. Realizing this, she scoured up her own fare to China and sailed in 1930. After slogging her way across Siberia she reached her field in remote Yangcheng.

When the Japanese invaded in 1940 she led 100 children on an epic journey that caught the imagination of Hollywood. In 1947 failing health forced her back to England where she crusaded for missions until her death in 1970. That was tenacity, not just British grit. It is God's persevering grace.

In his famous poem, "Perseverance Conquers All," Henry W. Austin summarized the essence of perseverance: "Genius, that power which dazzles mortal eyes, is oft but perseverance in disguise." In a similar vein Thomas Edison said: "Genius is five percent inspiration and ninety-five percent perspiration."

ACKNOWLEDGE

MEANING

A word which is sometimes translated "acknowledge" in the New Testament is a combination of two Greek words. The prefix *epi* means upon, and in this case it is attached to the main verb *ginosko* (to know). When the prefix is added it sometimes intensifies the verb. Here the simple verb "to know" is intensified to mean "to perceive," "to observe," or "to confirm and affirm." In its basic meaning the word means "to recognize a thing for what it is." Thus we find it translated with such terms as "to know exactly (or thoroughly)," "to recognize," and "to acknowledge."

BIBLE USAGE

There appear to be three aspects of knowing expressed in our Greek verb. First, it is an exact knowledge. Under the inspiration of the Holy Spirit, Dr. Luke undertook exhaustive explorations before writing his wonderful Gospel and the Book of Acts. His method of research is outlined in the prologue of Luke's Gospel and again in Acts. He wrote so that subsequent generations might know the truth about Christ exactly (Luke 1:4). This exact knowledge is our Greek word. Luke again employed this word when describing a man healed at the temple gate (Acts 3:10) and the Jewish perception of the apostles (4:13).

Paul also employed this word in the introduction to his great theological treatise, the Book of Romans. People who suppressed the truth did so despite the fact that they knew about the revelation of God in His Creation. This knowledge is described with our word in Romans 1:32.

Again in the Book of Colossians Paul uses the word. The evangelistic conquest of Colossae is stated in terms of knowledge. Paul prompts them to remember the day when they came to a full understanding *(epiginosko)* of God's gracious truth (Col. 1:6).

A second slant to this word is recognition, usually the recognition of a person. For instance, the disciples who plodded from Jerusalem to Emmaus after the Crucifixion failed to recognize the risen Lord (Luke 24:16). Only when He switched on the light of revelation did they recognize Him (24:31).

Another incident is almost humorous. The Apostle Peter had been divinely released from prison by an angel. When the rather bewildered apostle appeared at the door of Mary's home, he was not expected. (After all, they were busy praying for his release.) The Acts record uses our word when it recounts that the servant girl Rhoda recognized Peter's voice (Acts 12:14). Incidentally, she was so shocked that she forgot to let Peter into the prayer meeting.

The third aspect of the word is acknowledgment or recognition. The Prophet Malachi promised that an Elijah would precede the coming of Christ as Messiah (Mal. 4:5). On the slopes of the Mount of Transfiguration Jesus took up that prophecy and identified John the Baptist as that Elijah (17:12). Then Jesus rebuked the religious Jews because they did not acknowledge John the Baptist for who he was.

Paul urged the Corinthian Christians to receive his friends when they came. Since Corinthians were not known for their hospitality, spirituality, or humility, Paul urged them to acknowledge the godly Greeks who had helped him on his way (1 Cor. 16:18).

In his pastoral epistles Paul employed the word to connote Christian discernment. Paul taught Timothy how to school straying saints in the spiritual art of discernment (2 Tim. 2:25). When writing about the moral and spiritual chaos of

Crete, Paul described himself as one who had discerned true godliness (Titus 1:1).

ILLUSTRATIONS

Karl Marx defended what some consider a strange view of truth. Truth, according to him, was not only to be believed; it was to be acted out. Actually this is a Jewish concept of truth, and a Christian concept also. Knowing without doing is unthinkable. No wonder the Talmud asserts: "He who adds not to his learning diminishes it." This is the heart of our word.

My elderly uncle illustrates this from his school days in Indiana. "It is not for the teacher, but for life that we learn," insisted his schoolmistress in the early days of our century. Learning without living was libel in her eyes.

A spiritual twist to that truth is given by many famous preachers and writers. The great prophetic preacher of mid-century Chicago, A.W. Tozer, made this point when he wrote his famous book, *The Knowledge of the Holy*. A more modern but no less significant book is J.I. Packer's *Knowing God*. These writers approach the subject from vastly different viewpoints, but their emphases are complementary.

John Bunyan, the bard of Bedford jail, knew a thing or two about spiritual knowledge. He is reputed to have said: "There is knowledge and knowledge: knowledge that resteth in the bare speculation of things, and knowledge that is accompanied with the grace of faith and love, which puts a man upon doing even the will of God from the heart." This is the exact knowledge conveyed by our word.

Such depth of knowledge is often seen by its contrast with ignorance. A German proverb proclaims: "He that boasts of his own knowledge proclaims his own ignorance." Someone said: "The little I know I owe to my ignorance." Another added: "The person who knows everything has a lot to learn."

A partially humorous twist to this knowledge is the story about a young boy watching his grandfather religiously read the Bible. "What are you doing, Grandpa?" the child queried.

The old man's reply was direct: "I am preparing for my final examinations."

Tozer, mentioned earlier, wrote: "To know God is at once the easiest and the most difficult thing in the world. It is easy because the knowledge is not won by hard mental toil. . . . But this knowledge is difficult because there are conditions to be met and the obstinate nature of fallen man does not take kindly to them."

The penetrating nature of this knowledge can be seen in an experience common to most of us. One enters a church, or a store, or a school and sees someone who is vaguely familiar. Conversation ensues, and soon one determines that the familiar face belongs to a friend from college days. Then recognition comes and reminiscence takes over. It is this sort of recognition and discernment which our word contains. However, in the spiritual realm we are not cast on aging memories but on the Holy Spirit's illumination.

True spiritual insight is a by-product of the Holy Spirit living in a believer. Many brilliant people are blind to spiritual truth. They can analyze, categorize, and synthesize facts, but they ignore the most basic fact of all human existence: God. (See: *Knowledge*.)

ADOPTION

MEANING

The Greek word translated "adoption" is a combination of two words. The basic term is *huios* (son), and to it is added the word *thesia* (placing). Thus the compound word *huiothesia* means "adoption," or literally, "placing one as a son."

"No word is more common to Greek inscriptions," according to one commentator. Throughout the Greek world the wealthy and influential practiced adoption. Sometimes just a simple declaration in the marketplace turned a slave into a son. It was an ancient remedy used when a marriage failed to produce a male heir. No change in name came, but the adopted son immediately became heir to the entire wealth and position of his adoptive family. Conversely the adopted son also assumed responsibility for the parents in their time of need. Adoption in the Greek and Roman world was a beautiful picture.

His contemporary culture gave the Apostle Paul this word, but he gave the word a new, Holy Spirit-inspired meaning. (Only Paul uses this word to describe the relationship of believers to their Heavenly Father.)

No concept is more meaningful to a believer. For adoption deposits everything that God owns to the accounts of His sons and daughters. Adoption is all about position and privilege.

BIBLE USAGE

Adoption is important not because of its numerous appearances in the New Testament. It is rather important because of the greatness of its meaning. To take a hopeless sinner and elevate him to become a hopeful son requires a miracle, a miracle which the Apostle Paul calls adoption. Actually, adoption has three phases to its meaning.

First, adoption refers to a past event. Paul reached back across the millennia to the point where God "adopted" Israel (Rom. 9:4). Jehovah had declared Israel to be His son (Ex. 4:22). Like adoption in the Greek world, this declaration had far-reaching effects. Despite Israel's unlikelihood, Jehovah declared that nation to be His sons. Though Christ had called a whole new generation of faith-children for Abraham, Israel remained as the adopted son of God, who never cheats on a covenant. In the past God adopted Israel.

In the present, adoption describes the tie which binds believers to their Lord. The roots of this relationship reach far back before the world was. God settled the aim of our adoption before He made a world for us to live in (Eph. 1:4-5). What a comfort that is! Before God raised up the Rockies He raised up sons and daughters, and they had future believers' names on them.

At the point of our conversions, God gives us the Holy Spirit, who kindles the fire of assurance in our souls. He lets us know that we have been adopted as God's children (Rom. 8:15). He even teaches us to call God "Abba," literally, "Daddy." It is the very name which Christ used when speaking to His Father (Mark 14:36).

The present priority of adoption is seen in the great Galatians passage which deals with Christ's coming to earth. After describing the detailed plan of God (Gal. 4:4), the Apostle Paul puts a point on the whole idea in the next verse. Christ came to buy (redeem) us out of bondage and make us children through adoption (4:5).

Adoption has a further future meaning also. It is seen in Romans 8:23. Christians are not at home in this world. The Holy Spirit has borne fruit in their lives and they cannot wait to go home to glory. Then "adoption" will take on an added meaning. Our bodies will be adopted and we shall have a whole new home in which to live. In the ancient world adoption had two stages. At the declaration the child was declared adopted into his new family. Then when the father died, the son's or daughter's adoption was fulfilled as the child inherited the entire estate. So it is with a Christian. At conversion God makes every believer His child. In the glory God gives all His riches to the sons and daughters of His love. Now that is some adoption.

ILLUSTRATIONS
Walking down the dusty streets of Nazareth one summer afternoon I was almost run over by a racing boy. As he charged past me the little lad caught sight of his father. In a shrill, childish voice he screamed: "Abba, Abba!" Then I began to understand the intimacy of relationship which God sustains to us. What wonderful, God-ordained words to use in prayer: "Abba, Father."

The Puritans again illustrate this word. Thomas Watson, one of the most prolific Puritan writers, put it this way: "A man adopts one for his son and heir that does not at all resemble him; but whosoever God adopts for His child is like Him; he not only bears his Heavenly Father's name, but His image."

A lesser-known Puritan writer was Thomas Gataker. His comment on adoption was more theological, but nonetheless practical: "The least degree of sincere sanctification . . . is a certain sign of adoption, a sure argument to [the Christian] that he has it, that he is the adopted child of God."

Dr. John Evans wrote the Romans section of Matthew Henry's monumental commentary. In discussing the future adoption of Romans 8:23, Dr. Evans' eloquence showed through: "Now are we the sons of God, but it does not yet appear; the honor is clouded; but then God will publicly own all His children. The deed of adoption which is now written, signed, and sealed, will then be recognized, claimed, and published" (*Matthew Henry's Commentary*, VI, p. 421).

George Whitefield, a great revival preacher of the 18th century, was one day at dinner with Lady Huntington, a patroness of the awakening. The preacher had boldly declared that "Christ would receive even the devil's castaways." While dining with the Countess of Huntington, Whitefield was summoned to meet two street women who had been born again. These proved the propriety of the preacher's claim, as they demonstrated the doctrine of adoption.

Adoption can best be illustrated from a common experience. When entering upon a pastoral ministry in Bristol, England I met various families. Each time we tried to link the children with their parents. One strapping six-footer told me his name. Soon thereafter, I met his parents, neither of whom topped five feet. Perplexed, I asked the mother about her sizable son. She answered that her son was adopted. We may not look like our Heavenly Father yet, but someday we shall. (See: *Child, Son.*)

ADORN

MEANING

The word translated "to adorn" is the Greek word *kosmeo*. In literature it referred to setting an army in order, and one can picture the ranks of Greeks in glittering array ready for battle. Homer made frequent use of this picture in his writings.

The word is also related to a well-known noun, *kosmos*, which is usually translated "world." To the Greek it meant the sum total of everything here and now, the orderly universe. The word *kosmos* occurs 187 times in the New Testament, and it is treated elsewhere in this book. (See: *World*.)

Returning to the original verb *kosmeo*, we see a remarkable relative in the English language. It is our word "cosmetic," to adorn or to make more attractive. This is the aspect here under consideration.

BIBLE USAGE

The word *kosmeo* has four shades of meaning in the New Testament. First, it speaks of putting something in order. The word occurs in Christ's Parable about the Wise and Foolish Virgins (Matt. 25). The wise virgins were prepared to greet the groom, and their lamps were "trimmed." To put it another way, their lamps were in working order. It is important for us to have the instruments of our service for God in working order. The reason is stated in Christ's parable: we never know when Christ is coming.

A second aspect of the word has close connections to "cosmetics," the adornment or decoration of people or things. Women were instructed by Paul through Timothy in the basics of beauty. Christian women were not to rely on fancy hair arrangements, costly clothes, and luxurious jewelry. True adornment was spiritual and internal. True beauty is really deeper than the skin (1 Tim. 2:9).

Lest the ladies bear the brunt of this word, Paul also applied it to the men. When laying down ground rules for godly elders, Paul instructed Timothy to seek men with various characteristics. One of these is "respectability" (NIV), "prudence" (NASB), or "good behavior" (KJV) as seen in 1 Timothy 3:2. So spiritual beauty in a woman is counterbalanced by respectable behavior in a man.

The Apostle Peter struck the same chord. When he described the true beauties in God's eyes, he also referred to this word. Such ladies were not marked by outward "adornment" (1 Peter 3:3), but rather by hope which enhanced their beauty (3:5). Who has not seen an elderly saint who simply radiates the Lord, her very face adorned by the hope of the Lord.

When Christ comes to call for His bride, the whole church will be thus adorned. In the final pages of history we see the Holy City as a bride on her wedding day, adorned for her husband (Rev. 21:2). As the hymn-writer put it: "Oh, that will be glory for me."

A third turn to our word is decoration, usually applied to buildings. In His parabolic preaching Christ spoke of a house which was swept and garnished (Matt. 12:44). In the overture to the Olivet Discourse the disciples remarked on the temple at Jerusalem. It was described as being "adorned" with beautiful stones which had been dedicated to God (Luke 21:5). This decorative adornment is also seen in the revelation of heaven (Rev. 21:19).

A final feature of the word is more abstract. This is the credit brought upon a nation by its citizens. An ambassador is said to be a credit to his country. In the same way a Christian is called on to be a credit to the cause of Christ. To put it in Paul's words, a Christian should "adorn the doctrine" (Titus 2:10).

ILLUSTRATIONS

The word *kosmeo* links two strong ideas: order and beauty. In the Greek mind order was the essence of true beauty. Aristotle said it eloquently: "Beauty is a gift of God." The 19th-century Scottish novelist and poet George MacDonald rephrased the same idea: "God's fingers can touch nothing but to mold it into loveliness." When God produces order, or adorns something or someone, the inevitable result is beauty.

This is seen in the world of literature. Samuel Johnson was a great luminary of literature in 18th-century England. When called on to frame an epitaph for Oliver Goldsmith, his friend, Samuel Johnson wrote: "To Oliver Goldsmith, a Poet, Naturalist, and Historian, who left scarcely any style of writing untouched, and touched none that he did not adorn" (*Boswell's Life of Johnson*, II, p. 82). Here the word "adorn" comes to its full fruition. Goldsmith made all writing beautiful.

Another side of the story is found in the writings of Rudyard Kipling. In his elegant "Tree Song," Kipling used the word: "Of all the trees that grow so fair, / Old England to adorn, / Greater are none beneath the Sun, / Than Oak, and Ash, and Thorn." Here adornment is attributed to nature with the sentimentality of an Englishman abroad.

Nowhere in common usage is our Greek word used more frequently than in the field of cosmetics, or cosmetology. This is the science that strives to spruce up fading beauty.

A homespun illustration relates to a little boy. He happened to notice his grandmother putting cosmetics on her face.

"What are you doing?" he badgered her.

"I'm making myself beautiful," she half jested.

A few moments later the grandmother emerged from her bedroom to face the scrutiny of the eager-eyed youngster. His comment: "It didn't work, did it, Grandma?"

The practical point of the word "adorn" is this: Christians are called and commissioned by Christ to make the Gospel more beautiful. As God creates order out of the chaos of a life, true beauty emerges and the Gospel is enhanced.

This idea is seen in the Gospel chorus:

Let the beauty of Jesus be seen in me,
All His wonderful passion and purity;
Oh, Thou Spirit divine,
All my nature refine
Till the beauty of Jesus be seen in me.
                                    T.M. Jones

ANGEL

MEANING

"Angel" is almost a direct copy of the Greek word *angelos*. In its elemental form this word means simply a messenger, one who is sent, an errand boy. The word *angelos* is seen in our word "*evangel*ism." (Of course, this does not mean that angels can evangelize. Rather it speaks of a person sent with good news.)

A messenger in biblical terms can be sent by a human, God, or even Satan. For the purposes of this study we shall concentrate on angels who are sent by God to carry out His commands. Elsewhere perverted angels, devils, and demons will be discussed. (See: *Demon, Devil.*)

BIBLE USAGE

Billy Graham wrote a book titled, *Angels: God's Secret Agents.* In it he sought to squelch the skepticism which surrounds angels. They really do exist, and they are active in the seen and unseen worlds. For the purposes of this study we shall consider some biblical facts about angels.

First, there was a day when angels were created. So there was a time when they were not in existence. They owe their lives to God's creative act. This fact is seen in the Book of Revelation. As the climax drew near, the Apostle John was carried away, and bowed before the revealing angel. The angelic reaction was instinctive. Immediately the heavenly herald forbade John to worship him. Then the angel explained that he was a creature, just as John was (Rev. 22:8-9).

Second, angels are social creatures. They love company. Jesus knew that the Father commanded multitudes, "legions" of angelic beings. These were also at the command of the Lord Jesus Christ (Matt. 26:53). Another picture of angelic assembly comes from the penman of Hebrews. He speaks of thousands of angels in joyful assembly (Heb. 12:22). In fact, angels seldom go out alone.

Third, angels are not supermen. They are spirit beings, not physical creatures (1:14). Because of their spiritual nature, they are also not sexual beings (Matt. 22:30). They appear in four distinct ranks: angels (Luke 2:12-13), cherubs (Gen. 3:24), seraphs (Isa. 6:2, 6), and archangels (1 Thes. 4:16). Though they occupy the unseen world, they also take on themselves human forms (Heb. 13:2).

Fourth, angels have limitations. As creatures they are less than God but more than men. They do not know everything (Matt. 24:36; 1 Peter 1:12). Neither can they do everything (Ps. 103:20-21). Furthermore, they are not sinlessly perfect (1 Cor. 6:3; 2 Peter 2:4).

Fifth, angels are endlessly busy. To paraphrase an old adage: "An angel's work is never done." In heaven they worship and serve God (Heb. 1:6). On earth they attend personally to children, and many think each Christian has a "guardian angel" (Matt. 18:10). Angels sometimes guide God's people through difficult times (Acts 12:8-9). They also lift the saints' sinking spirits (27:23-24). Sometimes we mistake angels for human strangers, and only in heaven will we know how many times we have encountered them.

Sixth, angels made special appearances during Christ's earthly life. When He was conceived, the Archangel Gabriel announced it to Mary (Luke 1:26-38). At His birth in Bethlehem's cave, a whole host of angelic creatures accompanied His coming (2:9-10, 13). After Jesus' devilish temptation abated, angels were on hand to comfort Him (Matt. 4:11). In the Garden of Gethsemane angels strengthened the Saviour (22:43). The heralds of the Resurrection were also angels (Matt. 28:2-7). His return will likewise be ushered in by an angelic announcement (1 Thes. 4:16).

From the Scriptures we can make a few generalizations. Angels were created. They are limited in other ways than we are, but they are still finite creatures. Nonsatanic angels are obedient to God and carry out His will completely. No new angels are being born. (They do not marry or evangelize other angels.) But new Christians are being born every day.

ILLUSTRATIONS

No characters from Christian history are more misunderstood than angels. They are often trivialized. Cupid is seen as a mini-angel flying all over, shooting painless love arrows at unsuspecting humans.

As teenagers we had a silly joke about angels. Our driving habits were often more dictated by risk than by reason. "Watch out," we would say, "your guardian angel will bail out if you break the speed limit." Of course, this showed both a grave misunderstanding of angels, and the folly of tempting God.

Angels were subjected to a nationalistic twist in the writings of James Thompson, an 18th-century British poet:

When Britain first, at heaven's command,
  Arose from out the azure main,
This was the charter of the land,
  And guardian angels sung this strain:
"Rule, Britannia, rule the waves;
Britons never will be slaves."

Another inadequate application of angels is this: Often angels are used to account for human goodness. Benjamin Disraeli, the Prime Minister of England, reacted to the theory of evolution with this phrase: "Is man an ape or an angel? Now I am on the side of the angels." Actually, man is no more related to angels than he is to apes.

Another famous British literary man was Lord Byron. He also made the mistake of aligning angels with human perfections when he wrote: "Though women are angels, yet wedlock's the devil."

A more biblical picture of angels is seen in the experience of believers. Dale Evans Rogers, a western movie actress, is a sincere Christian. When a child with Down's syndrome was born to her and her husband, Roy Rogers, they discovered delight and deep affection. After the child died Dale Evans wrote a little book titled, *Angel Unaware*. She took her title from Hebrews 13:2, which says that some who care for the needy entertain angels unawares. The book is sentimental, but it is also scriptural.

ANOINT

MEANING

The word for "anoint" in the Greek Testament is *chrio*. Though this simple root word occurs only five times in the New Testament, its relatives occupy a prominent place in the Bible.

For instance, in Israel marked men were anointed for God's special service. Samuel anointed Saul and David to be the first kings over God's people. Prior to that time the high priests were likewise anointed. Prophets also were acknowledged by God in the ceremony of anointing.

In the New Testament the idea of anointing takes on titanic significance for Scripture. The name Christ is derived from the Greek verb *chrio*, "to anoint." Christ, or literally "the Anointed One," appears 529 times in the New Testament. No fewer than 379 of these occurrences flowed from Paul's pen.

Closely connected to Christ is the name Christian, in Greek *christianos*. This word means "little Christs" or, more likely, "followers of Christ." Christians should be Christlike in their attitudes and actions.

Several negative words also spring from our verb "to anoint." There is the false Christ, literally *pseudochristos*, about whom Christ warned His followers. In the Apostle John's letters, the antichrists, *antichristoi*, who oppose Christ at every turn, are targeted.

So the word "anoint" is most strategic to the New Testament. Its major implications appear in the study which follows.

BIBLE USAGE

An unusual trail of topics is laid down by the term "to anoint." The first one arises out of the Old Testament, where the coming Messiah is identified as "the Anointed." Three office-bearers in Israel were anointed. In order of their appearance, they are priest, king, and prophet. At the birth of the levitical priesthood, the service of recognition and consecration was characterized by anointing (Ex. 29:29; Lev. 4:3, 5). When Samuel set out to select a king for Israel, he took the anointing oil along (1 Sam. 16:1-13). Finally, the prophets' power also flowed from their anointing (1 Kings 19:16).

In the same context the coming Messiah would be known as "the Anointed One" (Ps. 2:2; Isa. 61:1-2). This name is carrried over into the New Testament, especially in the writings of Luke. In his Gospel, Dr. Luke quotes directly the prophecy from Isaiah 61:1-2 (Luke 4:18-19). In Acts, Jesus is equated with the Anointed One (Acts 4:26-27; 10:38).

The name of Christ, which means anointed, is then a logical extension of the messianic teaching of God's Anointed One. This powerful proclamation ties Jesus of Nazareth to the Messiah. It is seen in His Gospel: the Good News "of Christ" (Rom. 1:16, KJV), the testimony about Christ (1 Cor. 1:6), Christ's coming in God's grace to defeat death (Rom. 14:9), and the satisfaction of the Law by Christ's sacrifice (Gal. 3:13).

Out of this all-embracing name of the Lord Jesus is drawn a new name for His disciples. At first the pagans flung a supposed insult at the disciples when they called them Christians (Acts 11:26). A spiritually insensitive King Agrippa chided the Apostle Paul with this taunt: "Will you try to make me a Christian?" (26:28) But by the time Peter wrote his first letter, the name Christian had taken on an aura of honor (1 Peter 4:16).

Moving from the exalted experience of anointing in the Old Testament through the glorious name of Christ, a Christian comes finally to a tremendous truth. Now the Christian has an anointing, *chrisma* (1 John 2:20, 27). This enables every Christian to cope with the conflict against Satan. Anointing has become the privilege of every possessor of Christ.

ILLUSTRATIONS

In *King Richard the Second* William Shakespeare, the bard of Avon, depicted the popular perception of anointing:

> Not all the rough rude sea
> Can wash the balm from an anointed head.

Here was the prevailing opinion of divine anointing, an opinion still sanctioned by the rite of coronation in many lands.

However, it is not an earthly king who commands our interest, but the heavenly Monarch. Puritan penman William Dyer did justice to Christ's reign when he wrote: "Jesus Christ is threefold King. First, His enemies' King; secondly, His saints' King; thirdly, His Father's King. . . . Well may He be our King, when He is God's King. But you may say, how is Christ the Father's King? Because He rules for His Father." Who better bears the royal anointing than King Jesus, the Christ?

He is also our High Priest, and was thus anointed. He now intercedes for us constantly. No poet of praise put this more beautifully than Charles Wesley:

> The Father hears Him pray, His dear anointed One;
> He cannot turn away the presence of His Son:
> His Spirit answers to the blood,
> And tells me I am born of God.
>
> My God is reconciled, His pardoning voice I hear;
> He owns me for His child, I can no longer fear;
> With confidence I now draw nigh,
> And Father, Abba, Father! cry.

Finally Christ is also the Prophet. He warned about false prophets and condemned them. He painted a prophetic picture yet to come true. He knew that no prophet was honored in his hometown. But this anointed Prophet proclaimed truth which makes even our enlightened age gasp in disbelief.

His experience was echoed by the otherwise unknown writer Benjamin N. Cardozo: "The prophet and the martyr do not see the hooting throng. Their eyes are fixed on eternities." Whom does this describe better than the anointed Prophet?

An anointing announced the Christ. In turn the Christ commits this anointing to us (1 John 2:20, 27). Commenting on this divine anointing, the venerable John Reynolds of Shrewsbury wrote: "This sacred chrism [anointing] or divine unction, is commended on these accounts: (1) It is durable and lasting. . . . (2) It is better than human instruction. . . . (3) It is a sure evidence of truth" (*Matthew Henry's Commentary*, VI, p. 1072).

Here in 1 John 2:20 is a perfect contrast. The antichrists with their false anointings are countered by the Holy Spirit's true anointing. Every true Christian has this anointing.

(See: *Antichrist, Christ, Christian.*)

ANTICHRIST

MEANING

Well known in English, this word is a combination of two Greek words. The prefix *anti* meant originally "instead of." Later it took on the meaning of "in opposition to." It is visible in such English words as "antidote" (to counter poison), "antiseptic" (to combat infection), and "antifreeze" (to resist freezing).

In the title of *Antichrist* the prefix *anti* combines two basic ideas. First, it refers to the adversary of Christ who opposes Him in every way. Second, it refers to the rival of Christ, who seeks to supplant the Saviour in world domination. Thus the idea of opposition: *anti* is combined with the name of Christ to portray the arch-villain of the end times.

The Antichrist is found only in the writings of the Apostle John. Furthermore, he is confined to Christian writings, with no reference in contemporary literature. He is an apocalyptic figure, limited to the last times. As this brief study develops, the disreputable demeanor of this demonic demagogue emerges.

BIBLE USAGE

As the adversary of Christ, the Antichrist is foretold by the Apostle John. He is a liar who unleashes libel against the Lord Jesus Christ (1 John 2:22). During the last decade of the first century his deceptive dealings were directed mainly against the embryonic groups of Christians who were fighting for survival (2 John 7).

Though not mentioned by name, the Antichrist appears elsewhere in the New Testament. Paul pointed out this purveyor of spiritual stagnation when he spoke of "the man of lawlessness . . . the son of destruction" (2 Thes. 2:3). The Apostle John was moved by the Holy Spirit to discuss the Antichrist in detail. In the Revelation John described the Antichrist as a beast, blasphemer, a human being, and the bearer of the number 666 (Rev. 13:4-18).

Jesus seems to align the Antichrist with the "Abomination of Desolation" (Mark 13:14-27). He will unleash a time of tribulation unparalleled in human history. At the same time he will strut his stuff as a false christ. In fact, he will seek to seduce the very elect of God.

Though the Antichrist refers to one dominant demon-controlled dictator in the last times, there are other applications of the word. Some people are called "antichrists" (1 John 2:18). The earmarks of these antichrists are clearly set down. They hide in the fellowship without accepting the lordship of Christ. When discovered they storm out of the assembly of believers. Their doctrinal deviation is a denial of Christ's incarnation (2:19; 4:3). Such devious disciples are under the control of the "spirit of the Antichrist" (4:2-3).

The Apostle John laid down three basic beliefs of Antichrist and all his henchmen. First, they deny that Christ is God's Son, which implies a disregard for the deity of Christ (2:22; cf. 4:15; 5:5). Second, they also reject the Incarnation, claiming that God never became man in Christ. This was the error which John attacked most vigorously (2:22; 4:1-3; 2 John 7). Third, the messiahship of Christ was also discarded by these deviants. They rejected the role of Christ as Messiah (1 John 2:22; 4:1-3). In short, their attack concentrated on Christ's person and work. Small wonder that they were called "antichrists."

Though one grand Antichrist is expected at the end of this age, there are many lesser antichrists along the way. It is therefore realistic to assume that there are antichristian people in the world today, and they are moved by the spirit of the Antichrist. In fact, they are preparing the way for the Antichrist.

ILLUSTRATIONS

Throughout the centuries antichrists have been confused with *the* Antichrist. In fact, this has been true from Old Testament times onward. King Antiochus IV Epiphanes (the manifested god) of Syria ruled from 164-75 B.C. He destroyed Jerusalem and desecrated the temple by erecting a high altar to Zeus and sacrificing a pig on it. He is referred to as "the Abomination of Desolation." In some senses he was a pre-Christian antichrist. Similar traits were manifested in the Roman Emperor Caligula (41-37 B.C.) who sought to set up a statue of himself in the temple at Jerusalem. Herod the Great was also lumped together with these antichrists, because of his opposition to Christ.

Obviously the antichrist mentality became more clear after Christ's time. Cerinthus died in Asia Minor at the end of the first century. He claimed Jesus was the son of Joseph and Mary, that at His baptism the Christ came upon Him, and Christ left Him at the Crucifixion. For this the early church fathers called Cerinthus the Antichrist.

Midway through the first century Nero came to the Emperor's throne (A.D. 54-68). In his insanity he unleashed a horrible and general persecution against Christians. He slew them and used their bodies as grotesque lanterns for his garden parties. Augustine and Jerome identified Nero with the 666 figure in Revelation 13:18. In their eyes he was the Antichrist.

Another persecutor of the church was the Emperor Domitian, who reigned from A.D. 81-86. Demanding that all worship him, he declared himself *Dominus et Deus* (Lord and God). When Christians and Jews refused to worship him, he slew them. In fact, it was probably Domitian who exiled John to the island of Patmos. It is small wonder that many people called him the Antichrist.

As the Reformation era dawned many marked out the pope or the papacy as the Antichrist. This viewpoint was held by such divergent characters as Dante, Wycliffe, Huss, and even Nietzsche, an ungodly atheist. Nietzsche called this antichrist "the madman."

Jumping into our century, there have also been many presumed Antichrist models. Lutheran commentator Richard Lenski identified the Antichrist with such characters as Charles Taze Russell (founder of the Jehovah's Witnesses), Mary Baker Eddy (mother of Christian Scientists), and liberal theology as a school of thought (*The Interpretation of the Epistles of St. Peter, St. John and St. Jude*, p. 432).

During the dark days of World War II several men were called the Antichrist. One recalls the mathematical gymnastics of prophetic preachers to calculate that Adolf Hitler was the Antichrist. Still others identified the Antichrist with Benito Mussolini, the Italian dictator. Obviously these satanically controlled dictators passed from the scene without ushering in the Great Tribulation. There have been many antichrists, but *the* Antichrist is still to come.

(See: *Anoint, Christ, Christian.*)

APOSTLE

MEANING

The English word "apostle" is almost a direct transliteration of the Greek word *apostolos*. Literally it means "sent one." This Greek word occurs 79 times in the New Testament. The root which gives rise to our word is a verb, *apostello*, "to send away." This simple verb shows up no fewer than 131 times in the New Testament, and it is found 119 times in the Gospels and Acts. So its basic idea is that of mission, one who is sent to do a job.

Secular literature sheds further light on the subject. Demosthenes, a famous Athenian orator of pre-Christian times, used "apostle" to describe a cargo ship sent out with a load. He also spoke of a naval fleet as "apostles" sent out to accomplish a mission. In the same vein colonists were sent out as "apostles," people with a purpose.

This New Testament word associates authority with assignment. The person sent represents fully the Sender. Apostles were men with a magnificent obsession, and the fulfillment of their charge was never in doubt.

BIBLE USAGE

"Apostle" has several meanings in the New Testament. First, it signifies simply an envoy or delegate. Titus and his companions were "messengers" sent by Paul to check up on a church (2 Cor. 8:23). By the same token the Philippian church sent Epaphroditus and his colleague to comfort Paul. These benevolent brothers were likewise "apostles" (Phil. 2:25).

A second slant shows apostles in a place of equality with the prophets. In fact the Septuagint, the Greek Old Testament, uses the word more than 700 times to describe the delegates of the Lord. Luke links apostles with prophets (Luke 11:49), as does the Apostle Paul (Eph. 3:5).

The third aspect of apostleship involves the Lord Jesus Christ. The author of Hebrews, in one of his divinely creative choruses of praise, speaks of Christ as "the Apostle and High Priest of our confession" (Heb. 3:1). No truth is more eternally eloquent than this. Jesus Christ was sent by the Father, and He brought the definitive revelation of God (John 17:3).

Obviously the most common concept of apostle in the New Testament relates to the Twelve. Matthias was chosen by lot to replace Judas Iscariot (Acts 1:15-26). Later Paul was added to this number. The usual apostolic greeting called attention to apostleship (Rom. 1:1; 1 Cor. 1:1; Eph. 1:1, etc.). Peter fell in line with this practice also (1 Peter 1:1; 2 Peter 1:1). Thus their main claim to fame was being sent as apostles by the Lord Jesus Christ, who designated His disciples as apostles (Matt. 10:2; Luke 11:49; Acts 14:14).

Added to the Twelve and Paul were other less likely apostles. In concluding Romans, Paul put Junias and Andronicus into the apostolic rank (Rom. 16:7). Barnabas likewise achieved apostleship (Acts 14:14). Also James, Jesus' half brother, was seen as apostolic in importance (Gal. 1:19).

In 1 Corinthians Paul presented some startling facts about apostles. First, apostles had an assured role. They knew they were apostles (1 Cor. 9:1). Second, they each had a specific personal ministry (9:2). Third, apostleship allowed for marriage (9:5). Fourth, there was a special gift of apostleship (12:28-29). Fifth, the apostles testified to a personal encounter with the Lord (15:7). Sixth, the apostolic office was plagued by counterfeits (2 Cor. 11:13). Finally, the apostles had a proven ministry, confirmed by miracles (12:12).

ILLUSTRATIONS

Apostles demonstrated the dominion of Christ over His church. No local church was a law unto itself, but rather a part of the body of Christ, controlled by the Head Himself. The first apostles were not a lordly class that controlled the church for their own ends. Neither was there any sense in which the apostolic office was passed on to bishops or popes.

By the second century, however, an apostolic succession had developed. Both Tertullian (170-220) and Cyprian (200-258) claimed that priests stood in succession to Christ's apostles. The Church of England and the Roman Catholic Church affirm this belief in their rites of episcopal ordination.

The New Testament apostles were not officials building a dynasty, but rather missionaries mandated by the Master. Therefore we look to missions for illustrations of apostolic activity. According to Gerhard Kittel's word studies: "The missionary element is something which radically distinguishes the NT [New Testament] apostolate from the Jewish institution" (*Theological Dictionary of the New Testament*, I, p. 432).

The perfect picture of apostolic mission is Christ. "The Bible is a missionary book," wrote Harold Lindsell in his introduction to missions. Then he added: "Jesus Christ is the Father's Missionary to the lost world."

David Livingstone put it even more simply: "God had an only Son, and He was a Missionary and a Physician." A contemporary of Livingstone was Henry Martyn, a pioneer preacher in India. Martyn laid down an axiom of missions when he wrote: "The Spirit of Christ is the spirit of missions, and the nearer we get to Him the more intensely missionary we must become."

Doubtless the Lord is the leading Light of apostolic missions, but He commissioned His apostles to carry on the task. Swiss theologian Emil Brunner brought this truth home when he wrote: "A church exists by mission as fire by burning."

The same emphasis is seen in the writings of two famous Scottish missionaries. John A. Mackay was uncompromising in his conviction: "The whole church must become a mobile missionary force, ready for a wilderness life. It is a time for us all to be thinking of campaign tents rather than cathedrals."

From the same standpoint another Scottish missionary, James S. Stewart, wrote from South Africa: "There is no argument for missions. The total action of God in history, the whole revelation of God in Christ—this is the argument."

Contemporary missions men echo similar sentiments. George Verwer, who founded Operation Mobilization, often says: "We must mobilize for missions or fossilize." Though Ralph Winter belongs to an older generation, he sounds the same call when he speaks of abandoning our easy lifestyle and adopting a "wartime" lifestyle.

(See: *Disciple*.)

APPEARING

MEANING

The word translated "appearing" commands two strong verbs in Greek. They are *phaino* and *phaeroo*. Both speak of an appearance. One aspect of the words is "to shine," as the shining of the sun. The emphasis here falls on the light source. The sun does not reflect: it shines. Another slant is the idea of "appearance": how something seems to be. Far and away the most important picture conjured up by these words is the sudden appearance of a person.

One is reminded of the old theater billboards. They trumpeted such phrases as, "Coming Soon," or "Now Appearing." It is exactly this expectant emphasis that the Greek word carries, which is demonstrated later.

The Greek word has several reflections in English. It is seen in the liturgical and theological term, "epi*phany*." "Epiphany" marks the manifestation of Christ to the wise men, an event that is celebrated on January 6th in some churches. (How that date was chosen is shrouded in the mists of history.)

Another related English word is "*pheno*menon." This word is really just a Greek participle taken letter for letter into English. A literal translation would be "the thing which appears."

BIBLE USAGE

Our Greek word refers to the appearance of people. Pharisees were compared in appearance with whitewashed tombs (Matt. 23:27). They appear clean on the outside, but inside they are rotten. Thus appearances and actuality do not always agree.

Paul was concerned for the appearance of his spiritual offspring. He prayed that the Corinthian Christians might appear before God in a good light (2 Cor. 13:7). In fact, Paul was quite concerned about the appearance of all Christians at Christ's coming (5:10).

Life itself is defined in terms of an appearance. Shakespeare caused Macbeth to say:

> Life's but a walking shadow, a poor player,
> That struts and frets his hour upon the stage,
> And then is heard no more; it is a tale
> Told by an idiot, full of sound and fury,
> Signifying nothing.
> (*Macbeth*, v, iii, 16)

Though Shakespeare did not intend it, he echoed a biblical idea. Human life is like a puff of smoke that appears and then drifts away (James 4:14).

Though the appearance of people is as limited as life itself, the appearance of Christ is monumental in its meaning. Like a light He shone in the world. The word for "shines" is *phaino* (John 1:5).

Christ's miraculous works were phenomenal in the basic sense of the word. Nothing like them had ever "appeared" in Israel before. This in itself was a large signpost signaling His deity (Matt. 9:33).

Another aspect of Christ's first appearance focuses on His resurrection. The disciples, like other disillusioned followers, had seen Him die. They had heard about His burial. They had viewed the sealed tomb guarded by Roman soldiers. Then He "appeared" again, and that was as revolutionary in the first century as it would be today (Mark 16:9).

When John wrote his epistles he undertook a Holy Spirit-inspired attempt to prop up the faith of the faithful. One of his primary points was the fact that Christ was still shining. The Sun of Righteousness still blazes brightly in the sky of human history (1 John 2:8).

Predictably the final "appearance" of our word deals with Christ's second coming. He referred to His coming appearance. He will appear in the sky! (Matt. 24:30) The same use of this word is seen in other New Testament passages. When Christ's glory appears, the believers will share that glory (Col. 3:4). In fact, the Apostle John revealed that Christ's appearance will transform Christians into Christ's likeness (1 John 3:2).

"Appearance" is brimming with meaning in the New Testament. The main focus of this word is not the appearance of angels or men. It is the first and second appearances of Christ Himself.

ILLUSTRATIONS

Two appearances of Christ convey meaning to an otherwise meaningless world. The first appearance was His birth at Bethlehem. Of this event the Victorian prince of preachers, Charles Haddon Spurgeon, wrote: "Christ is the great central fact in the world's history. To Him everything looks forward or backward. All the lines of history converge upon Him. All the great purposes of God culminate in Him. The greatest and most momentous fact which the history of the world records is the fact of His birth."

Spurgeon sympathized with the Puritans theologically, and they shared his unrestrained regard for the event of Christ's birth. William Bridge caught the shining rays of Christ's coming when he wrote: "God is best known in Christ; the sun is not seen but by the light of the sun."

To this Stephen Charnock added a similar statement: "In nature, we see God, as it were, like the sun in a picture; in the Law, as the sun in a cloud; in Christ we see Him in His beams; He being 'the brightness of His glory, and the exact image of His person.'"

If Christ's first appearing was bright, His second coming will be glorious. The Reformers were not famous for their doctrine of the last times, but they did savor the Saviour's appearing. John Calvin wrote, "Our Lord will come at last to break through all the undertakings of men and make a passage for His Word."

Though Luther and Calvin disagreed on some things, they agreed fully on Christ's coming appearance. Luther taught the imminency of Christ's coming: "Christ designed that the day of His coming should be hid from us, that being in suspense, we might be, as it were, upon the watch."

To this Archbishop Richard Trench of Dublin added: "The Second Advent is possible any day, impossible no day." A Scottish expositor of note was Alexander Maclaren, and he sustained the statement of Archbishop Trench. As Maclaren put it: "The primitive church thought more about the second coming of Jesus Christ than about death or heaven. The early Christians were looking not for a cleft in the ground called a grave, but for a cleavage in the sky called glory. They were watching not for the 'undertaker' but for the 'Uppertaker.'"

The church of Jesus Christ seems to thrive when there is a clear conscious-ness of His coming. In the turbulent years around World War II Christians concentrated on Christ's coming, and there was an evangelistic zeal which swept thousands into the kingdom. Since then there has been an apathy toward His coming in many circles.

ARISE (See: *Resurrection.*)   **25**

ARMOR

MEANING

The Greek word for "armor" is *panoplia*. It takes no imagination to see the English equivalent "panoply." Panoply means simply a complete suit of armor, or a splendid array. The word is a combination of two Greek words: *pan* means "all," "every," "entirety." One sees it in such English words as "*Pan*american," pertaining to North and South America. Another example of *pan* is "*pan*orama," the overall view of a scene. The second word in *panoplia* is *oplon*, meaning "arms," "weapons," or "equipment." So *panoplia* is armor which protects every part of a person.

The New Testament was written in Roman times, so the idea of armor was meaningful to most people. Everywhere the apostolic writers saw Roman soldiers suited up in their full panoply. Thus armor was an easily understood picture word for New Testament readers. Josephus wrote of the soldiers of Titus (about A.D. 70) whose equipment consisted of helmet, shield, sword, dagger, javelin, and tools to entrench themselves.

BIBLE USAGES

The word for armor occurs only twice in the New Testament. When describing the devil's devices, Jesus spoke of a soldier whose armor is taken away. As a result he is plundered (Luke 11:22) and dealt a deathblow. The armor could have protected him, but without it he was vulnerable.

It was the Apostle Paul who portrayed armor as a source of spiritual protection. The apostle described the armor in detail (Eph. 6:13-17). He employed the picture of the Roman legionnaires. By comparing Paul's panoply with first-century Roman references we gain a remarkable biblical picture.

The "belt of truth" (6:14) was first. A Roman soldier's vitals were protected by this belt, which also served to hold his sword. A Christian's spiritual vitals are protected by truth. He not only speaks the truth, but he also lives the truth. Truth is an essential spiritual element and the sole support against hypocrisy.

Second, Paul mentioned "the breastplate of righteousness" (6:14). This was called the *thorax*, because it protected the chest region, which we now medically call the thorax. Our heart is protected by God's righteousness. In Christ God makes us righteous. Thus we are enabled to live righteous lives before other people. This protects our hearts from Satan's spears.

Third, feet were shod with the Gospel of peace (6:15). Caesar's troops were successful in their military prowess, partly because of their strong footwear. This enabled them to undertake long treks and fight when they arrived. Christians are at peace with God and man, and this enables them to march on, overcoming obstacles. God's peace protects us against the stress that saps our strength.

Fourth, the shield of faith deflects the devil's darts (6:16). There were two types of shields in the Roman ranks. The *thureos* was used by combat soldiers in the ranks, and the *aspis* was used by the general's guard. It is the combat shield that Paul presents in the Christian's armor. When enemy forces shot flaming arrows at the army, they were fended off by their shields. Thus a Christian deflects the missiles of Satan with the faith God gives.

Fifth, Christians wear the helmet of salvation (6:17). The Greek word for this helmet is *perikaphalaia*, literally, "surrounder of the head." (*Peri* means around, and *kephale* refers to head, as in "tephalic.") A Roman helmet was impregnable, except when struck on the main seam with a battle ax. In a spiritual sense salvation protects us from the doubts which bombard our minds.

Sixth, the single offensive weapon is "the sword of the Spirit," the Word of God (6:17). This was a large dagger, *machaira*, a short sword used in hand-to-hand combat. The Scriptures are the weapon which a Christian wields in close combat with the forces of evil. When liberal theological thought first threatened the Bible, Dwight L. Moody said: "A mutilated Bible is a broken sword."

As the Roman legions were the best-protected army in the ancient world, so a Christian's spiritual armor (if he wears it) amply guards him in the conflict with sin.

ILLUSTRATIONS

Metal armor is unknown to us, except in museums. However, there are some striking parallels in modern society. A hockey goalie is completely covered with a panoply of padding. Similarly a football player wears much padding, to soften the blows of body contact.

In England the police are traditionally unarmed, except for nightsticks. When a riot breaks out they are issued riot shields. These large rectangles of tough plastic shield the policemen from bottles, bricks, and bullets. This is an excellent picture of the protection afforded by the armor of God.

Literature abounds with examples of armor. In describing a truly happy man, 17th-century writer Sir Henry Wotton wrote:

How happy is he born and taught
  That serveth not another's will;
Whose armor is his honest thought,
  And simple truth his utmost skill.
("Character of a Happy Life")

A resigned regard for armor is found in the writings of James Shirley, who said in dismay: "There is no armor against fate; death lays his icy hand on kings" (*The Contention of Ajax and Ulysses*). Though no one can be shielded against death, the shield of faith protects one in death.

A third literary reference to armor is found in the sayings of Horace, who lived in the century before Christ's birth. In lamenting the passing of life he wrote: "Now my armor and lute, whose campaigns are over, will hang here on yonder wall." Again a tone of depression characterizes the use of armor.

How different it is when the Christian's armor is arrayed. In *Pilgrim's Progress* John Bunyan introduces Mr. Great-Heart. Clad in the full panoply of spiritual armor he leads Pilgrim straight to the Celestial City, pausing only to slay a giant.

In the writings of the Wesleys spiritual armor is seen in all its glistening glory. Nowhere is this more true than in Charles Wesley's hymns. One of the best known is:

Soldiers of Christ, arise
And put your armor on.
And take to arm you for the fight,
The panoply of God.

AUTHORITY

MEANING

"Authority" represents the Greek word *exousia*. The noun is related to the verb *existi*, which refers to something that is permitted, possible, or proper. Again the connection to English is easily seen. It is our word "exist," which is taken directly from the Latin word, *existere*. To summarize, authority speaks of the permissible, the proper, and the possible.

In the Greek mind, authority found expression in relationships. It spoke of the relationship of government over subjects. The rulers determined the limits of action within society. From another angle authority was exercised by slave masters over their slaves. The authority of a master was absolute. A final Greek example was found in the family. Though it flies in the face of freedoms known to us, Greek parents held absolute authority over their children. There were no two ways about it; authority was written large in Greek culture.

As it is with other words, the New Testament sanctifies terms and spiritualizes them. The word *exousia* appears more than 100 times in the New Testament. It ranges in use from authority, through power, to privilege. In its New Testament contexts the word takes on a whole new family of meanings.

BIBLE USAGE

Authority in the New Testament is seen in its exercise. To use an old phrase, "Authority is as authority does." Though it defies categories to some extent, authority relates biblically to at least six different subjects.

First, God has absolute authority to act. His sovereignty by sheer definition knows no bounds. This word is wrapped in the language of omnipotence. Even the closest companions of Christ were barred from knowing the future. This was God's purview alone (Acts 1:7). Like a potter God had made men and women, and He can determine their roles in the world (Rom. 9:21). The very existence of Creation cries out in praise of the Creator who has all authority.

Second, authority is seen in the natural order. In many cases the created order exercises complete control. Nature itself is an ordered entity. The Book of Revelation demonstrates this. Locusts have authority to destroy (Rev. 9:3). Scorpions have authority to sting (9:10). God's authority overarches all created authority (16:9), and He uses angels to display that authority (18:1).

A third level of authority relates to Satan. He has a sphere of authority which God has allowed him (Luke 4:6). But Satan's dominion is vulnerable, because Christ is forever snatching sinners away from His diabolical foe (Acts 26:18). Satan is even called "the prince of the power of the air" (Eph. 2:2). Satan's authority has God-defined limits, beyond which he cannot go.

Fourth, authority is epitomized in Christ. He had authority to lay down His life and take it up again (John 10:18). God gave Christ authority over all the human race (17:2). After His resurrection the Lord introduced His missionary mandate by revealing that He had all authority in heaven and in earth (Matt. 28:18). Christ's commands are without limits. His authority is all-embracing.

Fifth, the Christian community also exercises authority. Those who believe in Jesus Christ are delegated authority to become the children of God (John 1:12). This authority is then concentrated in the Christian church. The apostles exercised their authority to build up believers (2 Cor. 10:8). This authority was constantly under control of the Holy Spirit, to avoid abuse by the apostles who bore it (13:10). Finally this authority will open the gates of glory to the Christian community (Rev.

22:14).

Sixth, a final use of authority is supernatural. God allows authorities to exist which are above and beyond our world. These supernatural powers will someday be terminated by God (1 Cor. 15:24). God has ordained the church to demonstrate His dominion to these rulers and authorities in heavenly places (Col. 2:10).

To summarize, wherever authority is found, it flows from God Himself. Whether it is above the earth in the heavenlies, or below the earth in the spheres of Satan, or upon the earth in the natural order, all authority comes from God. He sets the limits, and He will someday shut them down. Before Creation all authority resided in God's hands, and the day is coming when His authority will again reign unchallenged.

ILLUSTRATIONS

Authority and power are different. Here is a simple illustration. A policeman has authority but he may not have power. He has the authority to stop a car by raising his hand, but he does not have the physical power to stop it with his hand. Thus a Christian does not have the psychological or mental power to confront Satan, but he has the spiritual authority in Christ's name.

Reformed theologian Klaas Runia summarized the issue of authority: "All authority ultimately comes from God and is rooted in God Himself. But how are we to handle it? What is the norm? For the Christian there is only one answer: the norm is found in Scripture. Being the Word of God, Scripture is the highest norm for all authority, because it deals with the basic questions of life."

Billy Graham said the same thing in fewer words: "I am convinced that people are open to the Christian message if it is seasoned with authority and proclaimed as God's own Word."

Authority goes beyond this, however. Several times in our missionary career we experienced the authority of Christ. When we faced demonic forces, we discovered that authority was inherent in the name of the Lord Jesus Christ. This is substantiated by a noted authority, Dr. Timothy Warner of Trinity Evangelical Divinity School.

Many examples of this authoritative work occurred in church history. In the year 724 "the Apostle to Germany" Boniface confronted the priests of Thor at Geismar. There he chopped down the sacred oak, which was supposedly the seat of Thor's power. To the amazement of Thor's priests and the people, nothing happened. They saw that the God of the Bible had authority over the mythological god Thor. Boniface then hewed the wood and made a chapel for the Lord. What an example of biblical authority that was.

One time a student came to say that he was plagued by his past sin. After a prolonged session of counseling I showed him that the sacrifice of Christ was adequate to cover all his sin. He there and then claimed the assurance of forgiveness. Several years have passed, and as far as is known he is still living in the freedom Christ gives. The authority of God's Word made that young man aware of God's cleansing power.

(See: *Power.*)

BABY: (See: *Infant.*)   29

BAD

MEANING

"Bad" and "evil" represent two different Greek words. The first of these is *kakos*. It is seen in several English words, such as *"caco*phony" (a discordant, bad sound), *"caco*graphy" (illegible writing), and *"caco*demon" (an evil demon—as if there were "good" demons). This word *kakos* speaks of a lack of goodness. It occurs about 50 times in the New Testament.

The second word relating to evil is *poneros*. In its various forms this word occurs about 75 times in the New Testament. It often refers to evil persons, or to the evil one, Satan. Here the emphasis is on doing evil acts. Just as Satan is the source of evil, so he moves people to commit evil deeds. He is not just lacking in goodness, but rather absolutely without goodness. To say there is "a little good in everyone" ignores the existence of Satan in whom there is no good whatever.

BIBLE USAGE

In surveying the Scripture we shall separate our two words. The first one, *kakos*, speaks of a lack of moral virtue. Jesus Christ in His Olivet Discourse discussed the "evil slave" who ignored his master's coming (Matt. 24:48). The slave made the wrong moral choice. The Apostle Paul warned against "evil workers" when writing to the Philippians (Phil. 3:2).

A second aspect of this word relates to the emotions. Christ condemned those who entertain "evil thoughts" (Matt. 15:19). To the Colossians Paul challenged Christians to consider themselves dead to evil desires, to banish evil desires from their brains (Col. 3:5).

Third, there is a lack of legal righteousness which is also identified here. Jesus challenged His accusers to demonstrate how He had broken the Old Testament Law (John 18:23). Paul lamented that lust for the illegal still lingered in his heart (Rom. 7:21). A Spirit-filled saint is filled with the love of God, and is progressively freed from selfish desires (1 Cor. 13:5). In fact, a large part of spiritual maturity is distinguishing between good and evil (Heb. 5:14).

A fourth and final use of this word is social evil, evil which affects others. Jesus spoke of the rejection which the beggar Lazarus experienced as being evil (Luke 16:25). God gave us government to restrain the rampant ragings of social evil (Rom. 13:3-4). Without God every society is capable of becoming like Crete, which Paul portrayed as a population of "evil beasts" (Titus 1:12).

The first word, *kakos*, speaks of a lack of goodness. The second word, *poneros*, presents evil acts and their perpetrators. Christ condemned bad men in His preaching, and He will finally condemn them in judgment (Matt. 22:10, 13). There is no sense in which they are misguided or mistaken. These people are intrinsically evil, because they are motivated by the evil one.

Christ called Satan the evil one. He is the source of all evil (John 8:44). It is this evil one who snatches the seed of the Gospel from many hearers (Matt. 13:19). There is even a hint of him in the Lord's Prayer. Literally the Lord instructed His disciples to pray: "Deliver us from the evil one" (6:13, NIV).

In some cases the word *poneros* speaks of the principle of evil in the world. An evil person cannot help but speak and do evil (Luke 6:45). The Apostle Paul is insistent in urging Christians to abstain from every form or appearance of evil (1 Thes. 5:22).

In summarizing the two words which signify evil, certain spiritual lessons may be drawn. First, evil is not eternal. It entered the human scene when Satan stripped

Adam and Eve of their innocence. Second, evil is not inevitable. God can and does enable trusting Christians to combat the power of Satan. Third, evil is not acceptable to God. In His holiness God is completely cut off from evil in every shape and form. Fourth, evil is not triumphant. At Calvary Christ crushed the head of Satan and defeated evil once for all (Gen. 3:15).

ILLUSTRATIONS

The conflict with evil has absorbed a good deal of energy since the time of Christ. Martin Luther tackled the issue when he spoke of temptation. "It is not wrong to allow birds to fly over your head," the popular preacher proclaimed, "but it is wrong to let them nest in your hair." In other words, no one can avoid temptation, but every true Christian can avoid giving in to it.

Thomas Adams was known as "the prose Shakespeare of Puritan theologians." He paraphrased Luther's lines on temptation: "We cannot keep thieves from looking in at our windows, but we need not give them entertainment with open doors. 'Wash thy heart from iniquity, that thou mayest be saved; how long shall thy vain thoughts lodge within thee?' They may be passengers, but they must not become sojourners."

Temptation is not sin, and it can be prevented from becoming sin. The secret is to resist it in the power of Christ. In fact, the Bible assures us that there is always an escape hatch out of every temptation (1 Cor. 10:13).

Charles Haddon Spurgeon made this point with typical eloquence. When faced with a choice, he gave this advice: "Of two evils, choose neither." A lesser-known writer, Samuel Sewall, struck the same chord as Spurgeon: "Evil must not be done that good may come of it."

During a recent winter, Chicago was plunged into a deep freeze. On a sunny Sunday afternoon a father and his little lad went sledding by the shore of Lake Michigan. Though he saw it coming, the father was unable to prevent his four-year-old from falling into the icy water. The boy had played too near the edge, and months passed before he finally recovered from being submerged.

That incident is typical of evil. People play near the edge. In an unguarded moment they slip into sin. Despite the goodness of God, our Father, they fall beneath the ice, and recovery takes weeks, months, or even years.

A Jewish author applies the same spiritual truth. Abraham Jeschel wrote: "There is an evil which most of us condone and are even guilty of: indifference to evil. We remain neutral, impartial, and not easily moved by the wrongs done unto other people. Indifference to evil is more insidious than evil itself; it is more universal, more contagious, more dangerous."

Another homespun story summarizes the danger of sin. Suppose that a bullfrog were put into a pan of cool water, and that pan was then placed on the stove. By heating the pan slowly the frog would be deceived into staying until the water boiled. Similarly sin can deceive us into indifference and defeat.

BAPTIZE

MEANING

The Greek word for "baptize" is nearly identical to the English word; it is spelled *baptizo*. This is a remarkable word, however, because it has several interesting meanings. The most elementary meaning is to soak, plunge, drench, or sink in water. It is in this context that it appears no fewer than 74 times in the New Testament.

But the word has other meanings. These are seen in Greek literature. The most picturesque is taken from the seaman's world. *Baptizo* also means to suffer shipwreck, to sink, or to perish in the water. The story is told of a Greek sea captain who was torpedoed. He broadcasted this mayday message: "Baptizo! Baptizo!" (literally, "I'm sinking! I'm sinking!")

A final twist to the word is taken from the emotions. One who is under severe pressure speaks of being overwhelmed. This too may be signified by the word *baptizo*.

BIBLE USAGE

In the Scriptures there are several distinct "baptisms." They begin in the Old Testament. There the priests were charged with certain ceremonial washings. Both priest and people had to wash themselves before engaging in worship (Lev. 15:11, 13). When proselytes or converts came into the Jewish community they underwent a ceremonial washing. The first use of baptism is this ceremonial washing and it is referred to in the New Testament, where it is called (lit.) a "baptism" (Mark 7:4; Luke 11:38; Heb. 9:10).

The second reference to baptism concerns the work of John the Baptist. This was a pre-Christian baptism. It was the outward symbol of a repentant heart. The connection between John's baptism and Jewish ceremonial cleansing seems quite close (Matt. 3:6; John 1:25). It was noted by the Apostle Paul, however, that John's baptism was not Christian baptism. In fact, the Ephesian believers were rebaptized after they came into a full knowledge of Christ (Acts 19:3-4). This incident has implications for people who underwent either infant or adult baptism before believing in Christ.

Far and away the most common use of baptism in the New Testament is the third form, Christian baptism. After Jesus Christ had been raised from the grave He appeared to His disciples. In His final charge, known as "the Great Commission," Jesus included a command to baptize. Not only was the act commanded, but also its form. It was to be in the Triune name (one single name and three Persons) of the Father, the Son, and the Holy Spirit. This was not the cause of one's conversion, but a mark of his discipleship (Matt. 28:19).

That the Christians took this seriously is seen in Acts. As soon as the church was born, about 3,000 new believers were baptized (Acts 2:41). When the imperial treasurer of Ethiopia responded to Philip's evangelistic effort, the converted crown servant was likewise baptized (8:36-38). At the other end of the social scale was a jailer in Philippi. His conversion was linked to an earthquake which leveled his establishment. Immediately thereafter, the apostolic band baptized the jailer and his family. Incidentally, this is often used to justify infant baptism. But if there were children in the jailer's family, they were old enough to understand the teaching and believe (16:31-34). It would appear that belief and baptism went hand in hand, and that they occurred in that order.

The remaining appearances of baptism are typological. In this fourth category are some unusual expressions. Baptism, by or in the Holy Spirit, is closely identified with conversion (1:5; 11:16). Every believer appears to have experienced this, though there is a good deal of discussion among biblical students concerning the time and effect of Spirit baptism.

Another typological baptism is martyrdom. Jesus spoke of His death as a "baptism" (Mark 10:38; Luke 12:50). This seems strange at first, but it does have a parallel idea in English. We may speak of a difficult experience as "a baptism of fire."

Yet another unusual, typological baptism is the passage of the Children of Israel through the Red Sea. The unifying effect of that experience is emphasized, though Paul declares that they were "baptized into Moses." It seems to mean that they came under Moses' leadership (1 Cor. 10:2).

One final use of the word "baptism" also appears in 1 Corinthians. In speaking of the Resurrection Paul speaks of baptism "for the dead" (15:29). This is not an easy passage, but it seems to refer to baptism on behalf of the dead. It is as though a believer died before being baptized. The relative could then be baptized in the name of the deceased disciple. (This is not a license for a similar doctrine espoused by Mormons.)

ILLUSTRATIONS

Baptism of believers is a beautiful experience. The leader of the Slavic Mission in Stockholm once invited me to view a remarkable film. A group of Russian Christians filtered through the forest to the water's edge. Then one by one believers strode into the stream and were baptized. This flickering amateur film left an indelible mark on my memory. For those Christians the confession of baptism was tantamount to ostracism from Soviet society.

Once in Germany I shared in another baptism service. Afterward I asked the candidate what this event meant to him. His answer was astonishing. "It probably means I shall lose everything, my job, my friends, and my family." That public profession was a break with his past life, and that too is part of Christian baptism.

Martin Luther expressed the meaning of baptism powerfully: "[Baptism] signifies that the old Adam in us is to be drowned by daily sorrow and repentance, and perish with all sins and evil lusts; and that the new man should daily come forth again and rise, who shall live before God in righteousness and purity forever."

Another Lutheran was Ole Hallesby, who lived, wrote, and taught in his native Norway. He too saw deep significance in baptism. He contrasted baptism with the promises of God. "The promises of God are never spoken to the individual alone, but to all at one time," he wrote. Then he added: "Baptism, on the contrary, is something that God does to the individual."

The practical aspect of baptism was demonstrated by a former colleague of mine in England, J.A. Motyer. Writing from the Anglican tradition, Motyer put it succinctly: "Baptism points back to the work of God, and forward to the life of faith."

In a similar strain a little-known German named Friedrich Rest wrote: "In baptism, the direction is indicated rather than the arrival." This reminds me of a friend and elder with whom I served in England. He always exhorted baptismal candidates to stand firm, and warned them that Satan would oppose this step of obedience.

BEAR, BIRTH, BORN

MEANING

Obviously this word deals mainly with biology. It represents the Greek word *gennao* from which we derive such English words as "*gene*ration," "*gene*tic," "*gene*," and even the Bible book which deals with the birth of the world and all its inhabitants, "*Gene*sis." Where the little word *gene* occurs, it always reflects on birth, and usually in a biological connection.

In the Bible our word *gennao* also has a spiritual significance. Here too it speaks of the commencement of life where none existed before. In the Jewish world it referred to the relationship between a master and his disciple. Entering upon that relationship was likened to rebirth. Therefore "birth" had both a physical and a spiritual meaning.

BIBLE USAGE

Starting with simple physical birth, one notices a breadth of meaning in the word *gennao*. When a father "begat" a son, this word was used. This is evident in the long genealogies of the Old and New Testaments (Gen. 11; Matt. 1; Luke 3). It is set off in bold contrast with spiritual birth in such verses as John 1:13; 3:3. (A later article deals with the Greek word for "born again.")

Predictably the word *gennao* refers most directly to the physical birth by a mother. This is seen in the great nativity passages of Luke. Elizabeth would bear a son in her old age. The completely natural concept of birth takes on a miraculous meaning in this case (Luke 1:13). The spectacular size of this miracle is multiplied in the virgin birth of the Lord Jesus, as it is announced to an astonished Mary (1:26-38).

In our day of easy abortion, birth is particularly important. When speaking of the coming Christ, the angelic announcement employs this word to describe the fetus. The Greek New Testament uses the word *gennao* (to bear) when referring to the conception of Jesus (Matt. 1:20; Luke 1:35). (*Note:* These texts equate "birth" with "conception.") A similar identification of conception with birth is found in a dialogue between Jesus and some Pharisees (John 9:34). Whether one considers the Old Testament (Ps. 139:13-16; Jer. 1:5; Ps. 51:5) or the New Testament, the Bible paints a picture of personality which commences at conception. Thus abortion is a crime against a real person.

The word *gennao* also refers to spiritual birth in many places. In fact, of the 80 or more appearances in the New Testament, many describe spiritual rebirth. The vast majority of these occur in the writings of John. Most notable among these are the statements in John 1:13; 3:1-7. This birth issues in a righteous life (1 John 2:29). It also produces an antipathy to sin (3:9). By the same token it causes twice-born people to love each other (4:7). A proper perception of the incarnation of Christ comes with this spiritual birth also (5:1). Such a spiritual birth is attributable solely to the Spirit of God (John 3:5).

Satan also has spawned spiritual progeny. They have the same habits as their father. Even a religious exterior cannot hide their true, sinister natures. Jesus developed this idea when He confronted the Pharisees. They claimed kinship with Abraham, but Christ called them sons of Satan (8:38-47).

An interesting aspect of our word is found in Pauline writings. The Apostle Paul tried to establish contact with the rebellious Christians of Corinth. His claim of influence over them was a previous relationship. In fact, the apostle asserted that he had fathered them as a father produces children. The word used is the physical word, *gennao* (1 Cor. 4:15). What a remarkable assertion!

A final, fascinating occurrence of the word applies to the relationship between God the Father and God the Son. In a missionary context the Apostle Paul preached at Pisidian Antioch. He quoted to the Jews the famous statement from Psalm 2:7, that God had begotten the Son. This Davidic declaration was given an entirely new meaning here. For Paul said that God the Father brought the Son to birth when He raised Jesus from the grave. The Resurrection was for Jesus a "new birth" (Acts 13:33-34).

Therefore our word is capable of many interpretations. The Holy Spirit sanctioned a mind-boggling array of uses for this common word. It embraced everything from the normal birth of a child to the remarkable resurrection of the Lord Jesus Christ.

ILLUSTRATIONS

"Birth" conjures up a question of significance in our day. It is about the whole matter of abortion. As a pregnant woman said recently, "Abortion would be out of the question, if the womb had windows." In the light of the above discussion of birth it would also seem to be out of the question.

In discussing the subject, a *New York Times* writer boldly asserted, "The onset of individual life [at conception] is not a dogma of the church but a fact of science" (June 8, 1981). About the same time another article appeared in *Time* magazine which stated: "Abortion. It is, without question, the most emotional issue of politics and morality that faces the nation today" (April 6, 1981).

In 1973 the Supreme Court ruled, in *Roe vs. Wade* and *Doe vs. Bolton*, that abortion should be offered on demand. In the following decade more than 12.5 million lives were snuffed out, before they even saw the light of day. More than 98 percent of these lives were terminated simply because they were inconvenient, despite the fact that 77 percent of Americans questioned felt this flimsy reason was inadequate, and 65 percent believed that abortion was morally wrong (*Life*, November 1981).

In 1980 the *British Medical Journal* carried an article, "The First Year of Life." It demonstrated that during pregnancy the fetus feels pain, hears sounds, sees light, and experiences much of life. He is not an "it" but a living being with all the senses of a newborn (*British Medical Journal*, January 26, 1980).

From the first, Christians have condemned this intrusion into the birth process. In the year 197 Tertullian put it this way: "For us murder is once for all forbidden; so even the child in the womb . . . it is not lawful for us to destroy."

In his 1984 "State of the Union Address," President Ronald Reagan identified abortion as one of the great scourges of our time. He said it was more damaging to public morality than almost any other practice. During the same week more than 25,000 concerned citizens, many of them Christians, marched on Washington, D.C. to call for an end to abortion on demand.

As Thomas Jefferson said: "The care of human life and happiness and not their destruction is the first and only legitimate object of good government."

BEHOLD

MEANING

In the New Testament three main words speak of seeing, and each one has a distinctive flavor. The most common is the word *horao*. It appears more than 350 times in the New Testament. It means to have personal experience of something or someone. Its emphasis falls on participation.

A second word is *blepo*, which appears about 137 times in the Greek New Testament. In the case of *blepo* the main thrust concerns the ability to see, sight in contrast with blindness. Other related concepts are reading, the perception of a truth, and a prophetic vision.

There is a third word which is used only 58 times. This is *theoreo*. The English reader can easily see that this word is related to "theory." Here the viewer is a spectator enjoying the spectacle and theorizing about its meaning.

All three of these words occur in the New Testament, and each of them has a distinctive role. Together they give a picture of sight and vision in the Greek New Testament.

BIBLE USAGE

First we shall survey the verb *horao*. From a physical standpoint, this word speaks of "catching sight" of someone or something. On the first Easter Sunday morning an angel assured the disciples that they would "behold" (*horao*) the Lord (Matt. 28:7, 10).

In the same vein the disciples had seen the miracles that Jesus did. They were not just figments of their fertile imaginations (John 4:45). Indirectly Jesus claimed, to the amazement and anger of the Pharisees, that He had seen Abraham's days (8:57). This word relates to the experience of seeing, to physical vision.

Horao also expresses spiritual vision. Jesus warned the disciples to "Watch out," to be on their guard and not be taken in by the Pharisees (Matt. 16:6). The same word was used in a totally different context when Judas rued his treachery against Christ, and the Jewish authorities told him to look out for himself (27:4). So in a figurative sense this word means to look out for dangers.

The second Greek word for seeing is *blepo*. Here is the elementary ability to see. Jesus employed this word when He spoke of seeing a speck of dust in your brother's eye, while ignoring a log in your own eye (7:3). Many believe this was a humorous exaggeration by the Lord to make the point that legalism is hypocritical. At any rate, the Lord dealt here with the basic ability to see.

Another related use is the appearance of this word in contrast with blindness. Perhaps the best-known instance is the story of a man born blind. His eloquent testimony is this: "Whereas I was blind, now I see" (John 9:25).

The same word applies also in a figurative, abstract sense. The disciples discerned that Jesus did not see one man above another (Matt. 22:16). This truth is revolutionary, for it meant that Jesus did not prefer one disciple above the other. Neither did He prefer Jews above Gentiles, who were generally hated.

Another figurative aspect of *blepo* is to see trouble coming. In His Olivet Discourse, Jesus warned the disciples about coming events. Especially He pointed out the danger of false prophets and false Christs. In this connection He said, "See to it that no one misleads you" (24:4).

The third word for seeing is *theoreo*, and it combines ideas from the other two words. In fact, its basic meaning seems to be prolonged contemplation. When Jesus was being crucified, many of the women who followed Him gazed at the spectacle of His crucifixion (27:55). This verse brings up a thorny issue. Why is it that women often demonstrated a greater fidelity in following the Lord than men did?

The same word is used by Christ in describing devotion to Himself. Contemplation is seen as essential to discipleship. Followers are ones who behold the Lord, who do not lose sight of Him (John 6:40).

Just as it is with the other words, *theoreo* has a figurative meaning. The Samaritan saw that Jesus was a Prophet (4:19). In the same way Paul saw through the religious practices of the Athenians (Acts 17:22).

Therefore the words used for sight in the New Testament are similar to their English counterparts. All three have a physical application, what one sees with his eyes. They also have a figurative usage, that which is seen by mental perception.

ILLUSTRATIONS

Children in Sunday School may sing the chorus: "Be careful, little eyes, what you see." The tune may be trite, but the message is profound. A Christian should guard his vision. Prolific Puritan writer William Gurnall summarized this significant teaching: "Set a strong guard about thy outward senses: these are Satan's landing places, especially the eye and the ear."

Nowhere is this more applicable than in modern society. Through television a veritable smorgasbord of scenes are shown in our living room. A concerned Christian recently said: "Did you ever notice what we watch on television today that we would have switched off ten years ago?" This points up the priority of guarding our vision.

In God's eyes vision is of utmost importance. Yet vision is a rare commodity today. The *Indianapolis Times* is quoted as having said: "It would be easier to develop great statesmen if vision were as available as television."

Another author, B.C. Forbes, put a spiritual point on that statement: "The Bible says, 'Where there is no vision, the people perish.' Have you a vision? And are you undeviatingly pressing and pushing toward its accomplishment? Dreaming alone will not get you there. Mix your dreaming and determination with action." Occupational and Christian counselors now conclude that most people have some sort of a vision of their lives. But true satisfaction only comes when reality and vision coincide.

One of the great hymn-writers of our century was Katherine A.M. Kelly, who died in 1942. She epitomized the importance of spiritual vision:

Give me a sight, O Saviour,
Of Thy wondrous love to me,
Of the love that brought Thee down to earth,
To die on Calvary.

Oh, make me understand it,
Help me to take it in,
What it meant to Thee, the Holy One,
To bear away my sin.

BELIEF, BELIEVE

MEANING

Few words in the Bible carry as much meaning as "believe" and "belief." They are related to such words as "trust," "confidence," and "faith." The Greek words are *pisteuo*, "I believe," *pistis*, "faith," and *pistos*, "faithful."

Something of the significance of these words can be seen in the numbers of their occurrences. For instance, the verb "to believe" shows up no fewer than 233 times in the New Testament. Though it occurs only 10 times in Matthew and Mark and 9 times in Luke, this little verb dominates John's Gospel with 99 appearances. It is no wonder that Dr. Merrill C. Tenney called John "the Gospel of faith."

The noun form, "faith," is equally as compelling in its frequency. It occurs 239 times in the New Testament. The adjective which is translated "faithful" or "believing" appears 52 times. On the average, this word in one of its forms appears twice in every single chapter of the New Testament.

BIBLE USAGE

In order to round out our understanding of faith, we shall first look at some of its near neighbors. A fairly close connection exists between faith and *trust*. Trust speaks of confidence in a word, fact, or person. The apostles put their trust in the name of the Lord Jesus Christ, and thus they performed miracles of healing (Acts 3:16; 14:9). Great men and women of faith, as Abraham and Sarah, put their trust completely in the promises of God. They did not waver in this faith (Rom. 4:17-20). This unshakable trust was and is a product of the Holy Spirit's work in a believer's life (1 Cor. 12:9).

Also closely connected with faith is the word *obey*. Early Christians were characterized not only by their trust, but also by their obedience to the message of the Gospel (Rom. 1:5, 8). This arose out of a clear comprehension of the Gospel as spread by the apostles (10:16-17). In the great "Westminster Abbey of Faith" (Heb. 11) a close link exists between belief and obedience. From Abel right up through Abraham and even today, belief begets obedience (11:4, 17).

A third close relative of faith is *hope*. It is seen in the triplet of faith, hope, and love (1 Cor. 13:13; 1 Thes. 1:3). Another confirmation of the close ties between faith and hope is found in the above-mentioned faith chapter, Hebrews 11. Both Noah and Abraham placed their hope in God, though they had no visible basis for belief (11:10, 27). A parallel passage is Romans 4:18.

Finally, faith is allied to *perseverance*. In the listing of men and women of faith, there is a close connection between perseverance and the motivation of faith (Heb. 11:32-40). In writing to the persecuted Thessalonians, Paul equated perseverance with faith (2 Thes. 1:4). This was likewise Peter's theme in his first epistle (1 Peter 1:5, 7, 9).

Thus faith is known by its friends, but faith is also seen in every dimension of a believer's life. First, faith speaks of a *past commitment*. As a Christian believes "in" [lit., into] the Lord's "name," he becomes a child of God (John 1:12). Paul reminded the Corinthian Christians of their commitment to the Gospel as a past, completed event (1 Cor. 15:3-4, 11, 14). Throughout the known world the Romans' reliance on the Lord was known (Rom. 1:8). The same was true of the Thessalonians (1 Thes. 1:8). Faith, then, is a past commitment with continuing effects.

Second, faith is a *present conduct*. Perhaps the most well-known biblical slogan of the Reformation was Luther's life verse: "The just shall live by [or through] faith" (Rom. 1:17, KJV). Faith is not just a one-time event at salvation; it is a constant corrective of our conduct. This great principle was first enunciated in the Old Testament (Hab. 2:4). Then it was repeated three times in the New Testament (Rom. 1:16-17; Gal. 3:11; Heb. 10:38). The point is strengthened by repetition: the Christian lives as he came to life, by faith alone. *Sola Fide* (faith alone), as Luther put it!

Third, faith also fixes our gaze on *future confidence*. In fact, the biblical definition of faith focuses on "the substance of things hoped for, the evidence of things not seen" (11:1, KJV). For this reason Paul put forward the earthshaking statement: "We walk by faith, not by sight" (2 Cor. 5:7). As a runner looks to the finish line, we keep our eyes on the glorious goal of Christian living. From start to finish the Christian life is all by faith.

ILLUSTRATIONS

A Bible translator was working on John 3:16. Each word came to mind with one exception: faith. This robbed that key verse and indeed John's Gospel of its meaning. As the missionary worked, a runner dashed into his tent, muttered a few words, and collapsed on a cot. "What did he say?" demanded the translator.

His informant explained that the runner had exclaimed: "I will throw my whole weight on this cot!"

"That's my word," the translator said. Then he translated the verse: "For God so loved the world, that He gave His only begotten Son that whoever 'throws his whole weight' on Him, will not perish but have everlasting life."

Faith is eulogized by every believer. Dr. V. Raymond Edman, a former President of Wheaton College, said: "Faith makes the uplook good, the outlook bright, the inlook favorable, and the future glorious." He also reminded his students: "Never doubt in the dark what God told you in the light."

The great hero of faith Martin Luther loved to sing its virtues. He said: "Faith is a living, daring confidence in God's grace. It is so sure and certain that a man could stake his life on it a thousand times."

Even the American patriot Patrick Henry went on record regarding his faith: "The most cherished possession I wish I could leave you is my faith in Jesus Christ," he told his loved ones. "For with Him and nothing else you can be happy, but without Him and with all else you'll never be happy."

Thomas Watson, a Puritan writer, likewise spoke of faith's rewards: "Faith is seated in the understanding, as well as the will. It has an eye to see Christ, as well as a wing to fly to Christ." To this he added: "Faith, though it hath sometimes a trembling hand, it must not have a withered hand, but must stretch." Another Puritan, John Flavel, insisted, "The soul is the life of the body. Faith is the life of the soul. Christ is the life of faith."

Concerning faith A.W. Tozer said: "Faith first comes to the hearing ear, not to the cogitating mind." Elsewhere Tozer added: "To seek proof is to admit doubt, and to obtain proof is to render faith superfluous."

BELOVED (See: *Love.*)
BIND (See: *Chain.*)

BISHOP

MEANING

The English word "bishop" derived from the Greek *episkopos*. It is seen in such English words as *"episcop*ate" (the position of being bishop), *"episcop*alian" (a church ruled by bishops), and *"episcop*acy" (the rule of a church by bishops). The English word "bishop" arises from Latin slang, as the Romans corrupted *episkopos* and made it *biscopus*.

The root word *episkopos* means literally "to oversee," "to look over," "to care for someone." Thus the Bible translates it with such words as "visitation," "concern," "protection," "oversee," and "watch out." The word was commonly used in the Greek Old Testament, the Septuagint, to describe God and His prophets and kings, who cared for the people of Israel.

BIBLE USAGE

The words for "bishop" and "overseer" are used quite specifically in the New Testament. They have both a divine and a human frame of reference.

In agreement with the Old Testament, the words refer first to *God*. When Christ raised the son of the widow of Nain from the dead, the people of that Galilean village said: "God has visited ['cared for,' NASB marg.] His people" (Luke 7:16). Here the verb is translated to visit, or to care for. In other words, a bishop visits and cares for people, as God does.

Another reference to God's visitation is connected with the birth of John the Baptist. Twice Zacharias praised God, because God visited His people in the birth of the forerunner (1:68, 78).

Not only did God thus visit and care for His chosen people. At the Council of Jerusalem the early church discovered that God had a wider embrace. He "concerned Himself" with the Gentiles and also called out of their ranks a people for Himself (Acts 15:14).

The coming of Christ is seen as a special visitation of God. He is concerned with the human race and sent His Son to care for them. This truth is demonstrated in Hebrews 2:6, where a quotation is extracted from the Greek version of Psalm 8:4.

God is the first One to bear the name of "Bishop." Predictably the second bearer is the Lord Jesus Christ. In common with references to God, the first appearance of this idea is in the Gospel of Luke. There the Lord speaks of His presence in Jerusalem as a day of visitation (Luke 19:44). His gracious revelation to Jerusalem is rejected, so she is judged by God.

Peter applied the word to Christ in another way. Peter described His second coming as a "day of [God's] visitation" (1 Peter 2:12).

Later in 1 Peter Christ is called "the Shepherd and Guardian [Bishop] of our souls" (2:25). What a beautiful picture this is. Jesus Christ is not only our Redeemer, but He continually oversees our souls to protect them from the vicious attacks of the evil one.

Of course there is a third aspect to our word. People are also described as "bishops, overseers." In the Gospels only One is Bishop, Christ. Already in Acts, however, we find the term applied to the successor of Judas (Acts 1:20, NASB marg.). Paul and Barnabas exercised oversight over the missionary churches (15:36). Paul solemnly charged the elders of Ephesus to oversee and care for the congregation under their charge (20:28).

In Paul's epistles the name of "bishop" or "overseer" is given to all the elders. It is treated as a title in his greetings to the church at Philippi (Phil. 1:1). In writing to Timothy, Paul described the office of a "bishop" as something to be desired (1 Tim. 3:1). Specific requirements were laid down for the overseer, as in Paul's Epistle to Titus (Titus 1:5-9). Throughout the New Testament there seems to be a complete identification of elder with bishop. A bishop was not a special person in charge of several churches, but rather the pastor (or *a* pastor) of one congregation.

Peter concurs with this understanding of the overseer/bishop. Elders should "shepherd" the flock of Christ and exercise oversight (1 Peter 5:2). Their model is the Lord who is the Chief Shepherd (5:4).

Thus we have come full circle. God is the "Overseer" in the fullest sense of the word. He sent His Son Jesus Christ to carry out that role in the earth. Out of those whom the Lord oversees some are called to exercise the same function in their churches. The emphasis is not on position (as a bishop), but rather on service to the body of Christ.

ILLUSTRATIONS

The word for "bishop" is seen in two connections today. First it is seen in the assemblies known as the Christian (or Plymouth) Brethren. Their elders are called out by the church to serve the Lord. These men become the "oversight," the "bishops," of the church. In Baptistic churches (Baptists, Bible Churches, etc.) the same role is fulfilled by the pastor and elders.

The second use of the word "bishop" is taken from "episcopal" churches, such as the Episcopal Church, the United Methodist Church, and the Roman Catholic Church. Often official bishops are little more than bureaucrats. But some of them exercise real spiritual oversight over the clergymen in their care.

Some years ago I first heard Bishop Festo Kivengere of Uganda. Coming from the Anglican (Episcopal) Church, he had a large diocese in that tortured land. In fact, the Bishop became a refugee and fled from the murderous dictator Idi Amin. As soon as it was safe he returned to his post. Both his life and his ministry have left an indelible mark on our age.

Another Ugandan bishop studied in a college where I taught. His presence in class was a constant reminder of the persecuted church, and his strong spiritual life was a testimony to professors and students alike.

Bishop J.C. Ryle was an Anglican Bishop of Exeter and later Winchester. His preaching and writing have left a legacy of biblical study. Someone said Bishop Ryle's Gospel sermons were "wonderfully simple and simply wonderful." He was a true, biblical bishop—overseer.

The biblical bishop is a pastor who cares for his people. He visits them and exercises godly oversight of their spiritual health. This sort of ministry is exemplified in Richard Baxter's excellent book, *The Reformed Pastor* (Carlisle, PA: The Banner of Truth Trust, 1974). As a mentor in the ministry told me: "A home-going pastor makes a churchgoing people."
(See: *Elder*.)

BLASPHEMY, BLASPHEME

MEANING
The words "blaspheme," "blasphemy," and "blasphemer" are direct transliterations of the Greek words *blasphemeo, blasphemia,* and *blasphemos*. In their various forms they appear 55 times in the New Testament.

Though one usually imagines that blasphemy is directed against God, it can also be aimed at people or things. In essence the word "blaspheme" means to "slander, revile, defame, or malign." It is a most serious sin. In fact, the Law of Moses decreed that anyone who blasphemed the name of Jehovah God should be stoned (Lev. 24:10-16). This law even included foreigners who were guests in the camp of Israel.

BIBLE USAGE
During Old Testament times God treated blasphemy as being a matter of life and death. Much of this serious approach is also revealed in the New Testament treatment of blasphemy. Actually, in the New Testament there are at least five objects of blasphemy, all of which are prohibited.

The foremost object of blasphemy is *God*. This was one charge which Jewish authorities laid against Jesus. They accused Him of committing blasphemy against God when He declared Himself to be the Son of God and Messiah (John 10:36). The same charge was leveled at Him when He forgave sins (Mark 2:7). The truth is profound. Christ claimed to be God incarnate. His enemies understood this, and they slew Him for it. (How odd it is that some contemporary theologians deny His deity.)

Actually, by rejecting the Messiah and playing fast and loose with the Law of God, the Jews were blaspheming both the name of God and the Law among the Gentiles (Rom. 2:24). Behavior can be blasphemous as well as speech.

Women who are shrews at home and abroad are likewise accused of blaspheming or dishonoring the Word of God (Titus 2:5). People who opposed the apostolic ministry and disrupted the church life were also guilty of blasphemy (1 Tim. 1:20).

The ultimate blasphemy of God will appear in the last times. The beast of Revelation will go throughout the known world. His main mission will be to blaspheme God, His people, and His heavenly home (Rev. 13:6). Thus God is the primary object of blasphemy.

By extension blasphemy is also directed against *Christ*. At the Crucifixion Jews and Romans "heaped abuse" (lit., blasphemed) on the crucified Christ. This was part of the whole mockery which characterized that event (Matt. 27:39; Mark 15:29; Luke 23:39).

Of special significance is blasphemy against the *Holy Spirit*. In the Gospels this is referred to as the sin which is not forgiven (Mark 3:29; Luke 12:10). As Kittel eloquently says "This can hardly refer to the mere utterance of a formula in which the word *pneuma* [Spirit] appears. It denotes the conscious and wicked rejection of the saving power and grace of God toward man" (*Theological Dictionary of the New Testament,* I, p. 624).

Angels are a further object of blasphemy. Peter speaks scathingly of the moral and spiritual degeneracy of the last days. He outlines some of the abuses which will arise and includes those who "revile [blaspheme] angelic majesties" (2 Peter 2:10). A similar reference is found in the little Epistle of Jude (v. 8). There the hated false teachers who prey on the church are accused of reviling (blaspheming) angels.

Finally, slander or blasphemy can be directed against *people*. The Apostle Paul and his colleagues were often misunderstood, and sometimes they were misquoted by their enemies. This practice was slander or blasphemy against them and their teaching (Rom. 3:8). Paul and his friends were also slandered personally, and this carried the same label as blasphemy (1 Cor. 4:13; 10:30). In fact, this blasphemy against the good character of Christians is an experience common to many (1 Peter 4:4).

The only good thing to come out of this discussion is seen in the life of the Apostle Paul. Blasphemy is subject to God's forgiveness, with the exception of the above-mentioned rejection of the Holy Spirit's work. The Apostle Paul stated that he had been a blasphemer, but God in His grace sought and saved him (1 Tim. 1:13, 15).

ILLUSTRATIONS

Blasphemy is slandering or defaming God or a human. The catalog of slander against God provides us with some particularly evil examples. Ludwig Feuerbach, a German philosopher and atheist, said that God is a figment of man's imagination. The American atheist Robert Ingersoll echoed these sentiments: "An honest God is the noblest work of man."

A similarly slanderous statement came from the pen of Jules Renard: "We must be greater than God," he bragged, "because we have to undo His injustice." A 19th-century English editor, John Collier, concurred with these malignant assessments of God: "I've steered clear of God. He was an incredible sadist." But such blatant blasphemy is no more destructive than the teaching of critical theologians.

During the '60s a movement emerged in America under the slogan, "God is dead." This phrase appeared on the cover of *Time* magazine. The proponents of this demonic doctrine were Thomas Altizer and W. Hamilton. Meanwhile other theologians, such as Paul Tillich, tried to shape God according to their own designs, which is also a form of blasphemy.

Most of the cults also slander the God of the Bible. Mormonism insists on more than one god. Hare Krishna says that God is in everything, which is pantheism. The Children of God (or the Family of Love) try to enlist God's support for their pornographic activities. Transcendental Meditation encourages its followers to fall down before an idol. These are some of the religious blasphemies which are committed against the God of the Bible in our day.

Communism in its various forms also blasphemes God. God is seen as irrelevant to modern man. Karl Marx wrote off religion (and by association God) as an "opium of the people." Churches are desecrated, worship is disrupted and disbanded, Christians are persecuted, and God is blasphemed.

A further final expression of blasphemy is seen in the lives of Christians who do not conform to God's standards. One recalls a man who claimed to be a Christian but lived like one who did not know the Lord. His hypocritical lifestyle persisted over a period of years, and many knew about it. Some were hindered from believing because of his blatant inconsistency. One day the Lord took him and ended his blasphemous life.

BLIND

MEANING

The Greek word for "blind" is *tuphlos*. It is related to the verb *tuphoo*, which speaks of one who is mentally beclouded, foolish, or stupid. Lest an unfortunate connection be formed, it must also be noticed that the word for blind or blindness arises from another Greek verb, *tupho*, meaning "to give off smoke." In other words, a blind persons's sight is beclouded, as if by a haze of smoke. Perhaps this arose from the milky appearance of the eye pupil in some blind people.

Though blindness today indicates a large degree of lost vision, in ancient times it usually referred to complete loss of sight. Aristotle indicated that blindness was a hereditary disease in the Mediterranean basin. Sometimes blindness was inflicted by a conquering general on the vanquished. In all cases blindness was presumed to be incurable.

BIBLE USAGE

Because blindness was presumably incurable, the ministry of Christ in healing the blind was most significant. In fact it was seen by some contemporary observers as a mark of the Messiah (Matt. 11:5; cf. Isa. 29:18; 35:5). Only Jehovah God was capable of giving sight to the blind.

The remarkable aspect of Jesus' healing the blind is seen in the methods He employed. Jesus at one time encountered two blind men. These He healed by simply touching their eyes and letting in the light (Matt. 9:27:31). A similar incident occurred in Jericho, and there too He touched eyes and healed the blind (20:29-34).

In Bethsaida a blind man was led to Jesus. Having heard of the other incidents, the man asked Jesus simply to touch his afflicted eyes. Instead Jesus spat on His hands and then touched the sightless eyes. Soon the man saw the hazy outline of objects, more sight than he had previously enjoyed. As Jesus touched him again, his sight cleared completely (Mark 8:22-25). Apparently the man had seen at one time, because he recognized objects by sight. Here then is another method of Jesus, a healing in stages.

At Jericho Jesus met a blind man named Bartimaeus. This event is significant because Jesus was bound for Jerusalem and the Cross. Not shy, Bartimaeus cried out: "Son of David, have mercy on me!" Jesus did just that. When Jesus heard his unqualified request for restoration, He immediately healed Bartimaeus. There is no record of Jesus even touching him. The Master said the word, and the blind man saw (10:46-52). Faith was rewarded.

Winding His way through Galilee, Jesus came to the village of Nain, where He raised a widow's son at the cemetery gate (Luke 7:11-15). Afterward Jesus also gave attention to the infirm. He granted many blind people sight, and He confirmed that this was a messianic sign (7:21-22).

A final incident of healing is found in John's Gospel. Here is a man born blind, whom the Lord healed (John 9:1-34). After covering his eyes with clay, Jesus sent him to wash in the Pool of Siloam. Immediately the young man came back seeing. In his own words: "I was blind, but now I see" (9:25, NIV). The Pharisees were quick to catch the implication, that Jesus was taking a messianic prerogative upon Himself, and they excommunicated the young man from the synagogue.

Of course the Bible uses blindness in another way. In the New Testament there are a dozen references to spiritual blindness. Christ condemned the Jewish leaders who rejected Him. They were, in His eyes, "blind guides of the blind" (Matt. 15:14).

Christ confirmed that His presence in the world would open the eyes of many blind. However, He would also blind the eyes of many who should be able to see. Those who knew the most about Judaism were blind to Gospel truth (John 9:39-40). Those who were blind to Isaiah's prophecy remained blind at Christ's coming (12:40; cf. Isa. 6:10).

Peter prefaced his second epistle with a long list of characteristics that should be common to Christians. In fact, he set them down as the essential marks of a Christian. They include diligence, moral excellence, knowledge, self-control, perseverance, godliness, and brotherly kindness. If these are missing in a Christian's life, Peter says that person is really spiritually blind or shortsighted (2 Peter 1:5-9).

During Jesus' life on earth He healed many people who were blind. Afterward they saw things clearly. Most of those who were spiritually blind, however, simply remained in the dark. This also characterizes many of our contemporaries.

ILLUSTRATIONS

Literature abounds with illustrations concerning blindness. Many of these refer to mental or spiritual blindness. In his *Dialogue* Jonathan Swift wrote: "There's none so blind, as they that won't see." This seems to set the tone for other examples.

Lord Nelson, known for his eye patch, was accused of ignoring a signal and pressing the battle at Copenhagen. He confessed with this great line: "I have only one eye; I have a right to be blind sometimes. . . . I really did not see the signal." He played on the word, claiming he could not see the reason for the signal.

No one made more of this selective blindness than did William Shakespeare. In *The Merchant of Venice* he wrote: "But love is blind, and lovers cannot see the pretty follies that they themselves commit."

Along the same line the Scottish poet Robert Burns expressed Shakespeare's idea in the highland vernacular:

Had we never lov'd sae kindly,
Had we never lov'd sae blindly,
Never met—or never parted,
We had ne'er been brokenhearted.
(*"Ae Fond Kiss"*)

Though blindness is treated lightly by literature, it is a serious matter in real life. Elsewhere Dr. V. Raymond Edman has been mentioned as a late President of Wheaton College. During the '50s he spent several years in virtual blindness. (Some of his most moving devotional literature was written during that time.)

After his sight had been surgically restored he visited missionaries and called at the college where we taught. He spoke to the alumni about his experience of blindness. Honestly he recounted how he had trusted God to heal, but the healing came only after tortuously painful surgery. Still Dr. Edman praised the Lord for the spiritual insights he had "seen" during the dark days of blindness. He could echo the words of Gospel character who said: "I was blind, but now I see."

BLOOD

MEANING
From the time of Creation blood has been identified with life. The Greek word for "blood" is *haima,* and it is seen in several English words. "*Hemo*philia," is a disease in which blood does not clot easily. Similarly "*hemo*rrhage" speaks of an uninterrupted flow of blood, which is life-threatening. On a more cheerful note "*hemo*stat" is an instrument that stops bleeding. The word "blood" appears 97 times in the New Testament.

It is not only the physical necessity of blood which concerns the scriptural writers, but more specifically its spiritual significance. From the start God declared that the shedding of human blood was sinful, because life is inherent in the blood (Gen. 9:4-6). Of course, the main biblical emphasis falls on the blood of Christ, which symbolizes His saving death.

BIBLE USAGE
In the New Testament there are several references to human blood. Jesus was on his way to a miracle and surrounded by a crowd when a woman touched Him. She was healed of a hemorrhage immediately, simply because she believed and touched His robe. Her bleeding literally dried up (Mark 5:25-30).

Another reference to blood is found following Peter's great commission. Jesus assured him that "flesh and blood" had not revealed this to him (Matt. 16:17). This phrase, "flesh and blood," is used elsewhere in the New Testament to describe human life (1 Cor. 15:50; Gal. 1:16; Eph. 6:12).

Another unusual reference to human blood is taken from the Garden of Gethsemane. There Jesus prayed in deep agony. The Scriptures record that His sweat was like drops of blood (Luke 22:44).

In several New Testament contexts blood is declared to be the essence of human life. The believing martyrs in the Old Testament were illustrated by Abel and the priest Zechariah, who was slain between the altar and the temple (11:51). Jesus described the martyrs' history of the Old Testament in this phrase, "from the blood of Abel to the blood of Zechariah."

Paul also noted the significance of blood as the source of life, when he preached to the Athenians. He reminded his pagan audience that God made all nations on earth from one blood (Acts 17:26). This emphasizes the unity of the human race. (Incidentally this teaching did not please either the Jews or the Greeks.)

Obviously the most important references to blood in the New Testament revolve around Christ. He sacrificed His own lifeblood as a ransom for us (Heb. 9:12-14). The contrast is presented between the effect of Christ's blood and the relative ineffectiveness of the Old Testament animal sacrifices (9:12). Here the picture is drawn from the Day of Atonement when a lamb was slain to atone for sin. This legal provision was temporary and thus ineffective. Christ's death was permanent and therefore totally effective (9:20-22).

The blood of Christ is seen as the guarantee of Christian fellowship. Because all Christians are cleansed by Christ's sacrifice, they have fellowship with one another (1 John 1:7). Peter also included all believers in this sacrifice of blood (1 Peter 1:2, 19). Paul likewise described the church in Ephesus as having been purchased by Christ's blood (Acts 20:28). The infinite value of Christ's sacrifice shows the infinite worth of His church.

Nowhere is the central importance of Christ's blood seen more clearly than in the Communion. Before His death Christ converted the cup into a symbol of the New Covenant (Matt. 26:27-28). Because Christ was present when He said, "This is My body," there can be no confusion. The cup of wine is a symbol of His blood, but it is not transformed into real blood. This is especially clear in Paul's presentation of the Communion to the Corinthians (1 Cor. 11:25).

From the original statement that life is in the blood (Gen. 9:4-6) to the institution of the Communion (1 Cor. 11:23-30), blood plays a dominant role in the Scriptures. There is no redemption without the shedding of blood (Heb. 9:22). However, since Christ's blood was shed there is no need for blood to be spilled (9:28).

ILLUSTRATIONS

When writing about the sacrifice of Christ, Mary Baker Eddy displayed her total lack of understanding of biblical truth. She foolishly declared: "The material blood of Jesus was no more efficacious to cleanse from sin when it was shed upon 'the accursed tree,' than when it was flowing in His veins as He went daily about His Father's business" (*Science and Health*, p. 25).

What a contrast there is between Mary Baker Eddy and the teaching of Scripture, and even the hymns of the church. One thinks of William Cowper who wrote from a deep understanding of the sacrifice of Christ:

> There is a fountain filled with blood,
> Drawn from Immanuel's veins;
> And sinners plunged beneath that flood
> Lose all their guilty stains.

The powerful preacher Harry Ironside occupied the pulpit as pastor of Moody Memorial Church in Chicago. At a time when liberal theologians scoffed at the blood of Christ, Ironside said: "The holy walk, the devoted life of our Lord Jesus Christ, could not avail to put away sin. It was life poured out in death that saved. Apart from His death, His life could only bring out in bold relief our exceeding sinfulness. But His blood shed for us was life given up, poured out in death that we might live eternally."

Chinese Bible teacher Watchman Nee took up the same idea and gave it an unusual twist: "The blood [of Christ] deals with what we have done, whereas the Cross deals with what we are. The blood disposes of our sins, while the Cross strikes at the root of our capacity to sin." As always, Watchman Nee makes fine distinctions, but his emphasis on the blood of Christ is worth noting.

Another important exposition of this great theme came from Marcus Rainsford: "The blood is the poured-out life of the Son of God, given as a price, the atonement, the substitute, for the forfeited life of the believer in Jesus Christ. Any sinner who receives Christ as God's gift is cleansed from all sin by His blood."

Another beautiful expression of the sacrifice of the Lord is found in the hymns of Robert Lowry, a 19th-century American hymn-writer. One of his most powerful stanzas is this:

> What can wash away my sin?
> Nothing but the blood of Jesus;
> What can make me whole again?
> Nothing but the blood of Jesus.

BODY

MEANING

In the New Testament the word for body is *soma*. It appears in various connections throughout the Greek text, and there are 147 occurrences in the New Testament. The body covers a wide range of concepts, from the physical part of people (dead or alive) to the invisible church of Jesus Christ.

The Greek word *soma* is not unknown in the English language. For instance, a "psycho*soma*tic" illness is a malady which has physical symptoms and a psychological cause. In science the term "*soma*tology" refers to basic body structure. The adjective "*soma*tic" refers to anything relating to the body.

The understanding of the body has changed over the centuries. In the pre-Christian days philosophers such as Plato and Aristotle spread the word that the body was inherently evil, and the mind was good. When Christ came into this world clothed in a human body, He gave it a new dignity. In our day of physical fitness, health food, and professional sports, the body is almost exalted to an unrealistic position.

BIBLE USAGE

The Greek word for body has several meanings in the Bible. Most obviously it refers to the human body, the material part of a person. According to Christ, it is better for one's body to perish than for his soul to be lost (Matt. 5:29). In Christ's miracles one sees that the body is subject to all sorts of sickness (Mark 5:29). Though the body is not sinful, it can be used by Satan to lead one into sin (1 Cor. 6:18). Therefore each Christian is commanded to reject the rule of sin in his body (Rom. 6:12).

Because one's physical body is so important, a Christian is urged to commit it to God for His service (12:1-2). The Apostle Paul further asserted that our bodies are the temples of the Holy Spirit, a concept which unconverted people cannot understand (1 Cor. 6:19-20).

Not only does the body speak of a living organism in the New Testament, but the same word is used to describe a corpse. When Jesus was buried, He was described in all four Gospels as a dead body (Matt. 27:58-59; Mark 15:43; Luke 23:55; John 19:31).

Beyond the grave there is an existence of the body. The Scriptures speak of a resurrection body. As the Holy Spirit raised Jesus from the dead, so He will breathe life into our dead bodies (Rom. 8:11). In Paul's classical study of the Resurrection he dwells long on this resurrection body which will never again succumb to decay (1 Cor. 15:35-44). Just how it will be identified with the Lord's resurrection body is not completely clear.

In the New Testament the body has a further meaning. This is a spiritual meaning, and it refers to the invisible church of Jesus Christ. All the believers of all places and all times are collected together in the mystical body of Christ. This body is amply equipped to serve the Lord (Rom. 12:5). The unity of this body exists despite diversity (1 Cor. 10:17; 12:27).

The Ephesians epistle has the most references to the body of Christ. The church expresses all the fullness of Christ (Eph. 1:23). All nations and many notions are reconciled in His body (2:16). The body of Christ is His means of working in our world (4:12, 16). A further reference to the church as Christ's body is seen in the beautiful analogy of a bride and groom. Paul wrote that a husband cares for his bride as he would his own body (5:28-29).

In the parallel Epistle to the Colossians, Paul returned to the theme of the church as Christ's body. Christ directs His body, the church, as a head gives orders to a human body. By the same token, one's body responds to its head and carries out actions (Col. 1:18).

The final reference to the body is sacramental. When Christ instituted the Last Supper, He declared that the bread was a symbol of His broken body. The emphasis is on the word "broken," because Christ was sacrificed for our redemption (Matt. 26:26-29; Mark 14:22-25). Later the Apostle Paul explained that the symbols of bread and cup were a reminder of the death of Christ, which reminders should be perpetuated until He returns (1 Cor. 11:23-26).

Therefore the body takes on deep significance in the Scriptures. It is sanctified in the Christian's life, and it is the picture of the church of Jesus Christ on earth. In some ways, the church is the incarnation of Christ on earth. This has given rise to so-called "incarnational theology."

ILLUSTRATIONS

In pre-Christian times the body was misunderstood by the greatest brains. According to Plato, who lived about 400 years before Christ, the mind was trapped in the body, as an oyster is a captive of its shell. A hundred years later Aristotle was still asserting that the mind was superior to the body.

In literature the body bears some remarkable references. Queen Elizabeth I said: "I know I have the body of a weak and feeble woman, but I have the heart and stomach of a King, and of a King of England too." What a picture that is. Christians have the bodies of mere mortals, but within them beat hearts of eternal life.

The body plays an important part in the marriage ceremony. In the venerable old *Book of Common Prayer* the marriage ceremony is picturesque. The couple make this vow in giving the ring: "With this ring I thee wed, with my body I thee worship, and with all my worldly goods I thee endow." In these quaint words the truth is seen that the body is part of one's marital commitment.

But it is well to remember that the body is not completely determinative. Both Milton and Homer were blind. The famous composer Beethoven was deaf. President Franklin Roosevelt, the only four-term President of the United States, governed from a wheelchair. The body is not in control of the mind, and for the most successful people it is "mind over matter."

At death the body and soul separate. In poetic form Shakespeare included this in *King Richard II*:

And there at Venice gave
His body to that pleasant country's earth,
And his pure soul unto his Captain Christ,
Under whose colors he had fought so long.

Though Shakespeare was making more of a poetic point than a spiritual one, he did emphasize a profound spiritual truth. It is more clearly stated in the familiar words of committal: "We therefore commit his body to the ground; earth to earth, ashes to ashes, dust to dust; in the sure and certain hope of the resurrection to eternal life." For the Christian, the body is important. It is the temple of the Holy Spirit. His indwelling sanctifies it. However, our earthly bodies will someday give way to glorious resurrection bodies.

BORN AGAIN

MEANING
"Born again" is taken from a Greek word, *anagennao*. The prefix *ana* means "again," and it is found in such English words as "*ana*baptist" (to be baptized again), "*ana*logy" (to state things again in other words), "*ana*glyph" (to emboss a design so it stands out in low relief).

The second half of our word is *gennao*, which we discussed under the heading, *BEAR, BIRTH, BORN*. Thus the Greek word is translated into English quite literally: "born again." Other variants on the same idea are found in John 3 where Jesus instructs Nicodemus, that he must be "born from above" (*gennesthe anothen;* John 3:3, 7, marg.). Another aspect of the same idea is the statement of Paul that one must be "regenerated," a Latin version of the same word (Titus 3:5).

BIBLE USAGE
The word *anagennao* occurs only twice in the New Testament, both times in the writings of Peter. In the first case God has given new birth unto a living hope, which attaches to the resurrection of Christ (1 Peter 1:3). The early church father Chrysostom, writing in the fourth century, observed that being born to new life was like resurrection from the dead. Much as Christ came alive to new life after the Crucifixion, so a Christian is born again to new life through conversion.

The second appearance of our word speaks of the means of effecting the new birth. A Christian is born again by the Word of God. Like a seed, the Word of God works to produce new life. Unlike a seed, which ultimately dies, the Word of God lives forever (1:23).

A related concept is found elsewhere in Peter's epistle. Here a Christian is portrayed as a "newborn" baby. The Greek word is *artigennao: arti* means "immediately, at once." Here is a baby who has been born "immediately." According to Peter this sort of baby should have an insatiable thirst for genuine milk (2:2-3). Put in the spiritual context, an immediately born Christian cannot survive without the genuine milk of the Word. This is the sole means of spiritual growth.

The whole concept of "rebirth" or "regeneration" is often misunderstood. Some think one is "born again" by the sacramental act of a clergyman. But whether one is baptized as an infant or an adult, baptism cannot make him a child of God.

The new birth is also not a matter of maturity. Horace Bushnell, in his book *Christian Nurture,* sees a child growing up as a Christian. By sending or taking a child to church, the child would realize that he or she is a Christian. But the new birth is not a matter of growth. Neither is the new birth a matter of turning over a new leaf. Every day thousands start to diet, thousands more quit smoking, and thousands start to exercise. They usually start these good practices many times, but that is not like the biblical new birth.

The new birth is worked by the Holy Spirit (Titus 3:5). Only the Holy Spirit can so work upon a mortal as to make him eternally alive. No human procedures can produce the new birth. That is God's business. God, who works the new birth in a person's life, does so in response to faith, which draws a clear line of distinction between a once-born and a twice-born individual (1 John 5:1, 4-5).

ILLUSTRATIONS
In the mid-'70s the term "born again" received an unexpected boost. Charles Colson had been a close adviser of President Richard Nixon and, like Nixon, Colson fell from power through the Watergate affair. As a result of this crisis Colson came

to personal faith in Jesus Christ, and he wrote a book titled *Born Again*.

At the same time an evangelical renaissance was sweeping the United States. The national magazines reported it. Both *Time* and *Newsweek* carried cover stories concerning "born-again" Christians. Some estimated that the born-again minority comprised one-third of America's population.

Though no one would claim that a third of all Americans were biblical Christians, there is certainly a large and vocal minority of people who have experienced the new birth. Ironically the advocates of Communism have revived Karl Marx's teaching about "the new man," who is a product of socialistic indoctrination.

Literature has many excellent examples to illuminate the concept of the new birth. In describing his conversion, Richard Knill wrote: "Clang! Clang! went every bell in heaven, for Richard Knill was born again."

The great evangelical awakening in England in the 18th century had an impact on the American colonies. One of the major preachers was George Whitefield, a sometime colleague of John Wesley. As Whitefield attempted to win people to Christ, one of his evangelistic letters was directed to the American patriot Benjamin Franklin. To Franklin, Whitefield wrote these powerful lines: "As you have made a pretty considerable progress in the mysteries of electricity, I would now honestly recommend to your diligent unprejudiced pursuit and study the mysteries of the new birth."

Another approach to the same subject emerged in the preaching of Bob Pierce, founder and first president of World Vision. In speaking of salvation he said: "There are too many grandchildren of Christ in the world, those whose parents were Christians but they aren't. Nowhere in the Bible does God claim grandchildren—just children, born again by faith in Christ."

Though the Puritans were much more restrained in their discussion of conversion, they sometimes put it quite plainly. One of the most notable Puritan authors was Thomas Adams, a refugee during the Civil War in England. In writing concerning conversion Adams said: "Repentance is a change of the mind, and regeneration is a change of the man." Then he added concerning the new birth: "The Creation of the world is a shadow of the regeneration of a Christian. . . . Adam was created after the image of God, and placed in Paradise; so the new man is confirmed to the image of Christ, and shall be reposed in the paradise of everlasting glory."

Even Horace Bushnell, who was negatively quoted earlier, sometimes wrote quite acceptable theology. Especially did he say some straight things concerning the new birth. "There could be no growth if there were not something planted. . . . Until the new man is born, or begotten, the soul abideth in death, and therefore cannot grow."

An anonymous writer summarized the truth concerning this new birth, or regeneration. He wrote: "To be highborn is nice, but to be newborn is necessary!"

BREAD

MEANING

The Greek word for "bread" is *artos*, which appears almost 100 times in the New Testament. It is important, because it was the staple of Palestinian meals in the first century. Usually bread was baked on a griddle, which produced a flat loaf about one inch thick and twenty inches in diameter. In other words, a loaf of bread looked like a large pancake. Sometimes it had a hole in the middle to aid in tearing it apart.

The main ingredient of bread was barley, but it also contained beans or lentils to add nourishment. Such a loaf of bread was accepted as food for a day's journey (Mark 6:8). Also its price was a standard for comparison (John 6:7). Bread played a big part in the average Jewish family's financial reckoning and dietary planning.

BIBLE USAGE

Bread in the Bible refers most frequently to the flat loaf which was as common as our sandwich. When Jesus was fasting in the desert, Satan urged Him to turn stones into bread. The Lord answered, from the Old Testament, that man needs more than bread to live (Matt. 4:4, quoting Deut. 8:3).

When Jesus was left with a large crowd on His hands, He took a boy's lunch to provide barley bread and fish for everyone to eat (John 6:8-12). However, Jesus also reminded them that bread was not enough to give eternal satisfaction (6:49-50). Jesus drew a close connection between the bread He gave and the manna that the Israelites ate in the desert. In both cases the people enjoyed God's provision, but that did not guarantee them eternal life.

Another reference to bread equates it with all of our physical needs. In the Sermon on the Mount Jesus taught His disciples to pray. Part of that model prayer was this sentence: "Give us this day our daily bread" (Matt. 6:11).

When the Prodigal Son in Jesus' parable realized his state, he remembered that his father's servants had bread enough to spare. In other words, all of their physical needs were provided. Here bread stands for the sum total of one's nourishment (Luke 15:17).

In setting down a Christian work ethic, Paul told the Thessalonians that each person should earn his own bread (2 Thes. 3:8). Here too bread is seen as the symbol of all our physical requirements.

Bread in the New Testament also has spiritual significance. Jesus described Himself as "the Bread of Life" (John 6:48-50). Here Christ compared Himself to the manna which God rained on the Jews in the desert (Ex. 16:4; Ps. 78:24).

Jesus used the simple picture of bread to teach three profound spiritual lessons: Bread is necessary to life, and He is necessary to spiritual life (John 6:50-51, 58). Bread must be broken to extract the nourishment, and Jesus' body was broken for our salvation (6:51). Bread must be eaten personally if we are to gain from it, and Christ also must be received personally (6:35, 47, 50).

The Communion adds yet another dimension to the concept of spiritual bread. Jesus declared that the bread symbolized His body which was broken for us (Matt. 27:26). From that point onward Christians remembered the Lord's death by breaking bread (Acts 2:42; 20:7). In writing to Corinthian Christians, Paul instructed them to approach this Christian remembrance with utmost sincerity. Anyone who treats the broken bread lightly is guilty of disrespect for the broken body of the Lord Jesus Christ (1 Cor. 11:23-31). In fact, this violation of a sacred symbol may be punished by sickness or death.

One final expression of spiritual bread is found in the Gospels. Jesus referred to a feast in the kingdom of God (Luke 14:15). At the institution of the Lord's Supper He mentioned that He would eat again with the disciples in the kingdom glory (22:18). Perhaps this means that the symbolic supper will be fulfilled in glory, but it will be celebrated once again in its fulfilled form.

Bread is a most meaningful concept in the New Testament. It speaks of sustenance. The most elemental food in Scripture seems to be bread. Therefore it is an ideal symbol for the Lord Himself, the Bread of Life.

ILLUSTRATIONS

Bread is not only a biblical staple. It is also found in most societies today in one form or another. As Americans we are used to sandwiches. This is seen in hamburgers, hot dogs, lunch sandwiches, and even toasted sandwiches.

The Scandinavians produce wonderful trays of open-faced sandwiches. These may be decorated with caviar, fish, vegetables, fruit, egg, or almost anything else. Together a collection of such sandwiches makes up a smorgasbord.

French bread is shaped somewhat like a baseball bat. It can be transported easily, and tastes delicious, if it is eaten when fresh. Nowadays one often slices a loaf of French bread and makes it into a submarine sandwich.

Bread is also an important part in the diet of most nations. Malcolm Muggeridge tells of visiting an American televison studio with Mother Theresa of Calcutta. As she listened to the advertisements for diet, low calorie bread, she shook her head in disbelief. Her energies are devoted to increasing the dietary intake of Indian people.

Bread was basic in the declining Roman Empire. Around the time of the apostles Juvenal wrote that the Roman people "limit their anxious longings to two things only—bread and circuses" (*Satires*). Seventeen centuries later Edmund Burke applied the principle to the British people: "And having looked to government for bread, on the very first scarcity they will turn and bite the hand that fed them" (*Thoughts and Details on Scarcity*).

Nursery rhymes abound with references to bread. "The Queen was in the parlor, eating bread and honey." "Little Tommy Tucker sings for his supper; What shall we give him? White bread and butter." Incidentally, that last one reflects the life of a child in 18th-century England (*Tommy Thumb's Pretty Song Book*, 1744).

In the ancient Jewish community a host would lift the loaf from the table and say: "Blessed be the Lord our God, the King of the universe, who has caused bread to spring out of the earth." To which the guests would answer, "Amen." Whereupon the host would give each guest a piece of bread and eat one himself. This is the beautiful historical and cultural root for the Lord's Supper and the feeding of the 5,000 (*The New International Dictionary of New Testament Theology*, I, p. 250).

BROTHER

MEANING

The Greek word for "brother" is *adelphos*. In this basic form it occurs 346 times in the New Testament. (The feminine version, *adelphe*, is found 24 times.) It is significant to notice that "brother" is usally found within the Christian church. For instance, the Book of Acts uses the word 30 times, and Paul in his church-related epistles mentions it 130 times.

There are several interesting combination words which include *adelphos*. The most familiar one to us is "phil*adelphia*," taken from the word *phileo* for love and *adelphos* for brother. This word means "brotherly love," a phrase used frequently by Peter.

The Greeks used this word mainly to indicate a family relationship, and its most common use pertained to "blood brothers." However, sometimes it was broadened out to include other male relatives, such as cousins.

Another use of *adelphos* was for military honor. Alexander the Great, who lived and died 300 years prior to Christ's coming, helped give shape to the Greek language of New Testament times. When Alexander wished to honor a soldier, he bestowed on him the title of "brother." This indicated that the Emperor regarded him as a brother.

Likewise the rabbis called their fellow Jews brothers. This was a common occurrence, and it was expanded to include proselytes, people who had been converted to Judaism. This gives a precedent for a later Christian practice, in which true believers called each other "brothers."

BIBLE USAGE

First of all the word "brother" meant sons of the same parents. In the genealogy of Matthew there are frequent references to "brothers." Among the brothers mentioned are the sons of Jacob (Matt. 1:2) and the sons of Josiah (1:11). In each case it obviously refers to the sons of one father.

Two sets of brothers were part of the apostolic band. Soon after Andrew came to Christ he recruited his brother, Simon Peter (John 1:41). Another set of brothers were James and John, sons of Zebedee (Matt. 10:2).

The New Testament also speaks of the brothers of Jesus, half brothers with the same mother, Mary (12:46; John 2:12; Acts 1:14). Catholic doctrine has traditionally claimed that Mary was a perpetual virgin, and that these "brothers" were really cousins of Jesus (*Theological Dictionary of the New Testament*, I, p. 145). However, as early as the second century after Christ's birth, the church father Tertullian spoke of later children of Joseph and Mary (*Dictionary of New Testament Theology*, I, p. 256).

The word, "brother" also refers to brothers in the faith. Jesus called every faithful follower a brother or sister (Matt. 12:50; 28:10). The writer of the Book of Hebrews emphasizes an honor, that Jesus is not ashamed to call Christians His brothers (Heb. 2:11-12).

Early in the life of the church "brother" became a term of address. After Saul of Tarsus had been converted he went into Damascus in a state of temporary blindness. Ananias, despite deep fears, went to find and welcome the new convert. Ananias' initial greeting was magnificent, for he called the erstwhile persecutor of the church "Brother Saul" (Acts 9:17).

In the early churches the term "brother" was used to describe the relationship of Christians to one another. This is seen in the apostolic greeting (1 Cor. 1:1;

2 Cor. 1:1; Col. 1:1). Paul in each case introduced his coworkers as brothers.

The word "brother" had one further meaning in New Testament Greek. It also referred to countrymen. Thus Jews called each other brothers (Acts 2:29; 3:17; Rom. 9:3).

In the same manner the word for sister, *adelphe*, is capable of both literal and spiritual meanings. It is used for physical sisters such as Mary and Martha (John 11:1, 3, 5). Also it speaks of spiritual sisterhood, such as the renowned Phoebe (Rom. 16:1). Another reference is found in the small Book of Philemon, where Paul sends greetings to Apphia, "our sister" (Phile. 2).

No doubt the greatest bearer of the name "brother" is the Lord Jesus Christ. He fulfills the picture of the "friend who sticks closer than a brother" (Prov. 18:24).

ILLUSTRATIONS

As with many other biblical concepts, brotherhood is open to misinterpretation. This can be seen in the writings of famous people. One of the great Russian writers of the last century, Feodor Dostoevski, sang the praises of brotherhood: "Until you have become really in actual fact a brother of everyone, brotherhood will not come to pass. Only by brotherhood will liberty be saved."

A similar approach to brotherhood characterized the author of *The French Revolution*, Thomas Carlyle. When he came to discuss brotherhood, he eloquently wrote: "The mystic bond of brotherhood makes all men one." To him brotherhood was a fact of life.

Another British writer saw the dark side of brotherhood. In his aptly titled book *1984* Eric Blair, alias George Orwell, coined the phrase: "Big brother is watching you." Well, 1984 has come and gone, and so has Orwell.

Both the benevolent and the malevolent analysis of brotherhood disagree with the biblical approach. Christian brotherhood is the product of common parentage. Only those who are born again of God are spiritual brothers and sisters.

In 1953 I was an exchange student in Germany. One Sunday I attended a small evangelical church in Osnabrück. Not understanding much German, I tried to catch the spirit of the service. My delight was real when I heard the pastor welcome me as "Bruder [brother] Detzler." Despite language and cultural barriers, we were brothers.

Years later I was pastor of a small church near Manchester, England. As part of our witness we contacted a lovely fashion model and her successful husband. The model was reticent to receive Christ, lest she be thrown together with less sophisticated folks. However, after she believed in the Lord she became a warm, loving member of the Lord's family. She was united with her brothers and sisters by the common bond of Christ.

Early Christians were accused of many things by the Romans. One of the most frequent accusations was that of incest. The Romans knew Christians called each other brother and sister, and brother often married sister. This was a convenient, grossly inaccurate, criticism against Christ's family.

BUILD

MEANING

The idea of building plays a large part in biblical literature. In the Greek New Testament, words pertaining to building are usually constructed from the Greek word *oikodomeo*. In its various forms, this word appears about 50 times.

The verb *oikodomeo* has two parts. *Oikia* means a house. This root is seen in several English words, such as *"economy"* (which originally meant the law of the house) and *"ecology"* (study of the house or living environment). The second half of our word is *domeo*. This refers to a roof. We see it in such English words as *"dome"* (a rounded roof), *"domestic"* (what happens at home under the roof), and *"domicile"* (a place of residence). So quite literally our word *oikodomeo* means "to build a place of residence."

BIBLE USAGE

Like many words in the New Testament, "build" has two levels of meaning. First, it refers to common construction projects. In the Sermon on the Mount Jesus told a story familiar to many children. He spoke of a man who built his house on a sandy foundation. When the storms came that house was swept away. Another man built his house on a big rock, and his dwelling withstood the storms and winds (Matt. 7:24-27). The spiritual point was this: only a person who builds his life on the Word of God has a firm foundation.

Jesus also told about a man who laid out a vineyard and built a watchtower as protection against bandits (21:33). Here too our word is used for simple masonry construction.

Another example of literal building is Jesus' discussion of the magnificent temple of Herod. This temple had been erected on a smaller scale than Solomon's temple, but it was nonetheless grand. In fact, all who saw it were impressed. The stones were cut so carefully that a perfect fit was insured. The Olivet Discourse was introduced by a discussion of the temple's construction (24:1; Mark 13:1-2; Luke 21:5-6).

The spiritual meaning of our word "build" revolves around what used to be called "edification." To edify someone means to build him up. ("Edifice" means building.) By fellowship with other believers Christians are personally edified, built up. Paul trusted that the Christians would also be built up by the Word of God (Acts 20:32).

Writing to his problem children, the Corinthians, Paul emphasized the need of their being built up. They could not be edified by enormous knowledge, but rather by a loving relationship (1 Cor. 8:1). In discussing practices and programs Paul urged the Christians to devote themselves only to those which edify (10:23).

In his final instructions to the Thessalonian Christians Paul returned to the theme of edification. When Christians encourage one another, they build one another up (1 Thes. 5:11). In contemporary conversation edification would probably be called discipleship.

Not only are individuals built up in the faith, but the church of Jesus Christ is corporately constructed in this way. When Jesus introduced the term "church," He indicated that He would build His church. Nothing and no one, even Satan, can thwart this construction project (Matt. 16:18).

When Saul of Tarsus was converted from a persecutor to a preacher, he immediately started declaring the deity of Christ. His initial ministry in Damascus was effective, which resulted in the church being built up (Acts 9:31).

In teaching the Corinthian church Paul referred to his job as an "architect" (Greek *architekton*) or "master builder." He laid Christ as the Foundation of the church. This was essential in Paul's plans for the church (1 Cor. 3:10). Sound spiritual materials had to be used in this construction (3:12). Only in this way would the church survive into eternity (3:14). The church of Jesus Christ will outlast any of the world's great cathedrals, because its Builder is Christ, not an earthly builder.

As the church is being built it all fits together. Christ takes care of this when He calls people to become Christians. As they mature in the faith, they grow together like a magnificent church, more glorious than any on earth (Eph. 4:16, 29).

Peter also picked up the idea and wrote under the inspiration of the Holy Spirit about the construction of Christ's church. Christ is the Cornerstone, and we are all stones in the building. Peter calls us living stones (1 Peter 2:4-7).

The comfort of all Christian workers is this: we are working on the biggest building project ever. As "coworkers" with God we are building the church of Jesus Christ. But only when we arrive in heaven will we see the finished project.

ILLUSTRATIONS

Building is hard work. Some years ago I helped a Bible college in England expand its facilities. From the first drawings by the architect to the final paint on the finished walls, the project took thousands of hours and dollars. When finished it was still a very modest structure.

The building of great cathedrals is much more expensive in terms of manpower and money. In Europe we toured many of these magnificent structures. Westminster Abbey in London took a total of more than 500 years to finish. It was started in 1245 and finally completed in 1750.

In Rome St. Peter's Basilica was built during the 16th century. In fact, financing that cathedral was one of the causes of the Reformation, because the Vatican sapped the church all over Europe in an effort to procure funds. But even with that large financial base it took 120 years to finish St. Peter's.

Compared with Westminster Abbey and St. Peter's, the construction of St. Paul's Cathedral in London was accomplished quickly. Sir Christopher Wren set about to build a monument to his name, as well as to St. Paul's. Starting in 1675, the great cathedral was completed only 35 years later, in 1710.

George Bancroft, who was Dean of St. Paul's, saw the significance of Christ's church. He drew this pointed comparison: "Where Christ erecteth His church, the devil in the same churchyard will have his chapel."

In the church of Jesus Christ every true believer is an important building block. Puritan writer Joseph Hall said, "There is no place for any loose stone in the edifice." So every time a Christian is built up in faith, the church of Jesus Christ is built more solidly, and that is a building that will stand forever.

CALL, CALLING

MEANING

One of the most frequently used words in the Bible is this one. In the Greek version of the Old Testament, the Septuagint, the word for "call" appears more than 300 times. The same word shows up 148 times in the New Testament. The Greek word for "call" is *kaleo.*

Kaleo is used in several interesting and fairly familiar combinations. One of the names of the Holy Spirit is the *Paraclete.* This name comes from two Greek words: *para,* "alongside" and *kletes,* taken from our verb *kaleo.* Thus *paraclete* means "one who is called alongside." The word also means to comfort, exhort, and admonish, all of which are roles of the Holy Spirit.

A second combination word is *ecclessia,* the Greek word for church. Literally this means "called-out ones." The church of Jesus Christ is composed of people who are "called out" of the world and "called to" serve the Lord.

The word for call occurs in almost all New Testament books. Its concept is fundamental, both to the Christian church and to the nation of Israel. Both believers and Jews were called of God to a special status as His chosen children.

BIBLE USAGE

To survey the biblical uses of this word is almost beyond the scope of one article, but we shall notice briefly the ways in which our word is used. Like its English equivalent this word means to call someone a name and also to invite or summon someone.

The Gospels relate "call" to the Lord Jesus Christ and His work. When the announcement of Christ's birth came, Mary and Joseph were told to call His name Jesus (Matt. 1:21). Because He lived in the town of Nazareth, He was also called a Nazarene (2:23). In Luke's account of Christ's birth, where more detail is given, Jesus is called "the Son of the Most High" (Luke 1:32).

Jesus also gave people special names. To Simon he gave the name Cephas or Peter (John 1:42). Christ's forerunner was given the name John (Luke 1:59-60). Saul of Tarsus received the new name of Paul (Acts 13:9, 13). Every believer is given a new name; he or she is called a child of God (1 John 3:1-2).

A second meaning of our word relates to an invitation. In a parable Jesus told about a banquet to which guests had been invited (Luke 14:16-24). When the invited guests were called to come, they all made excuses. Then the host threw the invitation open to the common people, and they came gladly. (Incidentally, this biblical priority for common people is often a forgotten emphasis in our evangelism.)

Third, the word *kaleo* relates to legal proceedings. The early apostles were called before the council to be tried for their supposedly seditious acts. This was a legal summons (Acts 4:18).

Fourth, the Bible lays heavy emphasis on the call of God to His people. Christians are called to fellowship with God's Son (1 Cor. 1:9). When God calls someone he is drawn into an earthly fellowship of the church (Eph. 4:1-4). Those who share this calling have also been ushered into a peaceful relationship (Col. 3:15). The call to Christ also involves receiving eternal life (1 Tim. 6:12). Holy living is also an expected result of this call (2 Tim. 1:9). Though it be through suffering, every Christian is also called to eternal glory (1 Peter 5:10). Finally, the Christian's call leads us out of darkness into God's marvelous light (2:9).

The call of God should totally transform a Christian. He is drawn out of the chaos and confusion of his sin into the beauty of God's glory. When God claims a person, He creates a whole new person and a new environment to match. What a great call!

ILLUSTRATIONS

The Reformers such as Martin Luther spoke often of "vocation," which is a Latin word for call. They spoke of a call to conversion. John Calvin put it this way: "There is a universal call by which God, through the external preaching of the Word, invites all men alike. . . . Besides this there is a special call which, for the most part, God bestows on believers only."

On the same subject the Westminster Shorter Catechism states: "Effectual calling is the work of God's Spirit, whereby, convincing us of our sin and misery, enlightening our minds in the knowledge of Christ, and renewing our wills, He doth persuade and enable us to embrace Jesus Christ, freely offered to us in the Gospel."

Both Calvin and the Catechism speak here of the call to conversion, but the Scriptures also contain a call to service. Even secular literature refers to this aspect of a calling or vocation. Oliver Wendell Holmes, a chief justice of the Supreme Court, explained a calling: "Every calling is great when greatly pursued."

From another generation scientist and educator James Bryant Conant wrote about the same subject: "Each honest calling, each walk of life, has its own elite, its own aristocracy, based upon excellence and performance."

J.W. Hyde was a missionary in India, where he founded the Punjab Prayer Union. In fact prayer so marked his life that he was known as "Praying Hyde." Of his vocation he wrote: "No other organization on the face of the earth is charged with the high calling to which the church is summoned: to confront men with Jesus Christ."

A great theologian of vocation was Martin Luther. He often spoke and wrote of the Christian's calling to serve the Lord. His view in a nutshell is this: "How is it possible that you have not been called? . . . Nobody is without comand and calling. . . . God's eyes look not upon the works, but on the obedience in the work."

Robert R. Calhoun summarized the topic admirably: "We still speak of our daily pursuits as vocations and callings, being [an] unconscious witness to the permeation of ordinary speech by a once novel and daring theological usage. But the words have gone stale."

Hymnology is full of references to this subject of call. Fanny Crosby was blind, but her spiritual vision was bright when she wrote:

Jesus is tenderly calling thee home
    Calling today, Calling today;
Why from the sunshine of love wilt thou roam
    Farther and farther away?

Similar sentiments are expressed in a hymn by Cecil F. Alexander:

Jesus calls us! O'er the tumult
    Of our life's wild, restless sea.
Day by day His sweet voice soundeth,
    Saying, Christian, follow Me.

CARNAL

MEANING

The word "carnal" in the *King James Version* is translated "fleshly" in the *New American Standard Version* and "worldly" in the *New International Version*. The Greek word at the root of these English terms is *sarkikos* or *sarkinos,* which comes from the Greek noun *sarx,* meaning "body."

In English the word occurs in some rather interesting forms. For instance, the word *"sarc*asm" means literally to tear flesh (a sarcastic remark rips at one's heart). Another related word is *"sarc*ophagus," which refers to a stone coffin, and the word means "flesh-eater." In Greek society coffins were often made from limestone. These dissolved corpses, or ate them away. Though this is a bit gruesome, it does reveal the true nature of our word. A rare English word is *"sarc*ous," used to describe anything composed of muscle or flesh.

The noun *sarx* and its related adjectives appear about 160 times in the New Testament. Predominantly they refer to the flesh in contrast with the spirit, which is seen in the following analysis of biblical references.

BIBLE USAGE

In some cases the word "fleshly or worldly" is morally neutral. It simply describes the difference between the material and immaterial parts of a person. Because Gentile Christians shared in the spiritual blessings of Israel, Paul argued that they should share their material blessings with the Jews (Rom. 15:27). This is an interesting and biblically valid view of stewardship, and it could be used in teaching Christian responsiblity. Indeed Paul often used it to urge Christians to be generous.

In writing to the Corinthian Christians Paul applied this principle to himself and to them. Since Paul and his colleagues sowed spiritual seed among the Greeks, they should produce material fruit for Paul and his coworkers in evangelism (1 Cor. 9:11). Here material things seem to refer to the necessities of life, as food and clothing.

An extention of this illustration is found in Paul's second letter to the Corinthians. Paul viewed new Christians as living letters of commendation. God had written spiritual truths on their "fleshly" hearts, so they displayed the validity of his apostolic mission (2 Cor. 3:3).

Though these examples portray "flesh" as being neutral, Paul also saw the flesh as the enemy of the spirit. His most direct discourse on this is found in 1 Corinthians 3:1-3. Paul declared that the Corinthians were "carnal" (KJV), or "fleshly" (NASB), and did not serve spiritual ends. In fact, they argued and bickered like babies in the faith. "Fleshly" behavior here describes the way in which some people claim to be Christians but live like the world.

As an example Paul declared that he operated according to spiritual wisdom, not along the lines of worldly wise men (2 Cor. 1:12). Because he was moved by the grace of God and not worldly wisdom, Paul professed and possessed a clear conscience toward God.

Continuing in the same vein, Paul described his methods of work. He did not rely on human devices to demonstrate the power of God. It was God's own strength which demolished the bastions of evil. Fleshly arms cannot fight spiritual battles, according to the Apostle Paul (10:4). The apostle here established a principle: Spiritual struggles require spiritual methods. We could save ourselves much grief and defeat if we learned this basic lesson.

On a more personal level the Apostle Paul described the battle raging within himself. His spiritual aspirations were constantly under threat from his physical drives. An entire section of Romans is devoted to this, and the issue came to a point in Romans 7:14.

The Apostle Peter was likewise concerned with a Christian's combat against fleshly lusts (1 Peter 2:11). Though a Christian is not liberated from the world's lusts, he can be victorious in his conflict against them. He lives in his flesh, but he does not have to be dominated by his flesh and its pleasures (4:2-3). This is a picture of the Christian whom Christ prayed for in His high-priestly prayer (John 17:15-17).

The Scripture is clear. Christians constantly have conflict with their "carnal" natures. However, no Christian need be defeated, because Christ has guaranteed victory to those who obey Him.

ILLUSTRATIONS

The pleasures of the flesh are a source of constant comment among the writers of history. About the time of Christ Ovid wrote: "There is no such thing as pure pleasure; some anxiety always goes with it." Rabindranath Tagore represented a similar viewpoint when he concluded: "Pleasure is frail like a dewdrop; while it laughs it dies."

Lust for pleasure has been condemned by God from the first. The Ten Commandments forbid stealing, coveting, false witness, and adultery. All of these are rooted in fleshly lust. According to Puritan writer Thomas Watson, the Greeks held their funerals at the temple of Venus, because lust was the cause of so much disease.

Professor Ian Donald addressed a class of nursing students. He warned them against lustful men in strong terms: "Girls should be taught to value themselves more and not to enslave themselves to the 'lusts and deceptions of male chauvinist pigs' " (*Daily Telegraph,* November 7, 1977).

Another form of lust is covetousness. According to LeRoy Eims: "Covetousness accuses God of mismanagement." It accuses God of not giving me my fair share. Or as another writer summarized it, "Covetousness is the desire to get what we have not earned."

Puritan Thomas Watson wrote a great book on the Ten Commandments. In it he stated his conclusions concerning carnal Christianity: "All the danger is when the world gets into the heart. The water is useful for the sailing of the ship; all the danger is when the water gets into the ship; so the fear is when the world gets into the heart. 'Thou shalt not covet.' "

Indeed this tendency toward fleshly lusts can paralyze an entire generation of Christians. A.W. Tozer struck at this mentality when he wrote: "I think the church *has* failed, not by neglecting to provide leadership but by living too much like the world. . . . The world wants the church to add a dainty spiritual touch to its carnal schemes, and to be there to help it to its feet and put it to bed when it comes home drunk with fleshly pleasures" (*Man: The Dwelling Place of God,* pp. 138-139).

CAST (See: *Throw.*)   **61**

CHAIN

MEANING

The Bible refers often to both physical prison and spiritual bondage. Two separate words are used in the Greek New Testament to describe bondage in chains. The most common verb is *deo*. Its meanings include the binding of weeds in bundles, imprisonment, legal constraints, and tying up an animal. In all, this adaptable little verb appears 45 times in the Greek New Testament.

A second word translated "chains" is the Greek word *desmos*. In various other forms it refers to a bundle, a prisoner and his prison, and also to a jail-keeper. A further example of this word is a physical handicap. *Desmos*, in all its forms, occurs about 40 times in the New Testament.

These words are not important because of their frequency. Their significance lies in their spiritual meanings. Jesus Christ repeatedly loosed the bonds that bound people and then bound them to Himself with the bonds of love.

BIBLE USAGE

The most common word, *deo*, speaks of a durable connection. This word is used to describe the close bond of love which joins husband and wife, a tie which is also legally binding (Rom. 7:2; 1 Cor. 7:27).

The verb is also used to describe the bondage of prison. When Herod seized John the Baptist and bound him, our word was used (Matt. 14:3). The same fate befell Jesus when a temple guard bound Jesus and delivered Him to a mock trial (27:2).

Saul of Tarsus had similar plans for the Christians in Damascus, and set out with a commission from the Jewish leaders to bind and imprison them (Acts 9:2). After Saul of Tarsus became Paul the apostle, he too was subjected to such treatment and binding (Col. 4:3). The Gospel occasioned his imprisonment.

Another use of the word is seen in Jewish funeral customs. A corpse was prepared for burial by being bound with tight cloths interlaced with spices. When Lazarus was raised from the dead, these bindings had to be loosed (John 11:44). Jesus' body was prepared for burial in the same way after Joseph of Arimathea and Nicodemus secured it (19:40).

Binding also has a spiritual significance. Satan is portrayed as one who binds people. He ties them up in such a way that they cannot respond to God's gracious call (Luke 13:16).

One further unusual appearance of the word is in an often-debated statement of Christ: Whatever disciples bind on earth is bound in heaven, and whatever they loose on earth is loosed in heaven (Matt. 16:19; 18:18). This seems to refer to church discipline (Gerhard Kittel, *Theological Dictionary of the New Testament*, II, p. 61).

The lesser-used word, *desmos*, refers to prison and prisoners in most cases. It is used of a demon-possessed man who was bound with chains to control him (Luke 8:29). The apostles were often imprisoned for their missionary activites, and thus they are most often the objects of this word (Acts 16:25-27; Phil. 1:13; Col. 4:18; Phile. 10).

The word is also employed to describe physical handicaps of whatever source. It refers to the tongue of a dumb person being bound (Mark 7:35). Likewise it is taken to describe the binding of a cripple by disease (Luke 13:16).

One of the most beautiful wordplays in the New Testament centers around our word. The Apostle Paul claimed that he was in bondage because of the grace of

God. He wore his prison chains as chains of honor. Though Paul was a prisoner, the Word of God is never bound. It still revolutionizes the world (2 Tim. 2:9).

ILLUSTRATIONS
Bondage is always negative. We use similar phrases in daily life. Someone is nervous and says, "I am all tied up in knots." A particularly picturesque word picture is, "He has all sorts of hang-ups." A similar metaphor is a situation where a person claims to be "all strung out." My favorite description of stress is this: "He is as tight as a piano string." One can almost hear the twang!

Literature is likewise full of references to the bondage of fear and stress. In the 17th century Richard Lovelace wrote some rather exquisite poetry. One poem was titled, "To Althea, from Prison." In this otherwise unknown poem he wrote the famous lines:

> Stone walls do not a prison make
>   Nor iron bars a cage;
> Minds innocent and quiet take
>   That for a hermitage;
> If I have freedom in my love,
>   And in my soul am free;
> Angels alone, that soar above,
>   Enjoy such liberty.

Obviously Richard Lovelace knew something of true soul-freedom, which is oblivious to physical bondage. This is the experience of every true Christian, in or out of prison.

In her remarkable book *Vanya*, Myrna Grant recounted the story of a young Russian believer drafted into the mililtary. Despite unspeakable persecution, his soul was free. Though his body was tortured, his spirit sang. Finally in desperation his persecutors drowned him in an icy lake, but he never capitulated. Here again, a bodily bondage could not fetter a free spirit indwelt by the Holy Spirit.

Christians of every age have learned the lessons of bondage and freedom. During the Puritan period of English church history lived a great Welsh preacher named Vavasor Powell. After initial service in his homeland he went to London where he became a courageous spokesman for biblical truth. After the Civil War he was captured and died in prison in 1670. Despite these experiences Powell wrote: "There is no real bondage, but what is either *from,* or *for* sin."

John Bunyan was a contemporary of Powell. Like the Welshman, Bunyan was jailed for his faith. While living in England, I visited the sites of Bunyan's life, in and around Bedford. Despite imprisonment, or perhaps because of it, Bunyan wrote the classic *Pilgrim's Progress*. He framed his emancipation proclamation in the song of the shepherd boy:

> I'll fear not what men say,
> I'll labor night and day
>   To be a pilgrim.

The last word on freedom from bondage comes from the pen of Charles Wesley:
> My chains fell off, my heart was free;
> I rose, went forth, and followed Thee.

CHASTEN, CHASTISEMENT

MEANING

Depending on which Bible version one uses, the word "chasten" may be translated "discipline," "educate," or "train." It is really the Greek word *paideuo*. As such, this word is related to the noun *paidon* which means a very young child, or an infant.

The Greek word is reflected in several English terms. The science of teaching is called "*peda*gogy." A "*peda*gogue" is a schoolteacher, which literally means "one who leads children." In a negative sense a "*ped*ant" is one who overrates his educational importance.

Learning played an important role in Greek culture. Under the Stoics it became a dominant drive of civilization. Government was duty-bound to educate the children, a specific emphasis in the classical era of Greek history.

The Jews saw education as a spiritual matter. Children were bound to master the Law. Jehovah God was the great Educator, and piety was the primary emphasis of education. Both the family and later the synagogue had this as their chief object.

BIBLE USAGE

In the New Testament *paideuo* has several aspects. It means to instruct or train. In his final (and only recorded) address, Stephen remarked that Moses was trained in all the wisdom of Egypt (Acts 7:22). Paul asserted that he was trained at the feet of the great teacher of the Law, Gamaliel (22:3). The role of human education is thus emphasized.

Another side of the same term is the role of the Scriptures in spiritually educating people. Paul described the Mosaic Law as a "pedagogue" to lead the Jews to Christ. In other words, Jews who knew the Law should have been prepared for Christ's coming (Gal. 3:24).

Indeed the whole of Scripture has the function of instructing in righteousness (2 Tim. 3:16). The end result of this instruction is the spiritual maturity of Scripture students. Consequently they can do every good work. Study of Scripture helps one grow up spiritually, which is seen in a changed lifestyle.

Not only does the Bible speak of education, but it also adds the concept of correction. A father should guide and correct his child. As a ship's captain keeps his vessel on course, so a father is charged to keep his son on course (Eph. 6:4; Col. 3:21). Children should be brought up in the "discipline and instruction" of the Lord.

Such discipline is also appropriate in a church. When Christians commence to deviate from doctrinal truth, the pastor and elders are charged with gently correcting the errant members. This correction is another expression of our word for discipline (2 Tim. 2:25).

Indeed every Christian should be disciplined by the coming of Christ. As he looks forward to Christ's coming, it should have a chastening and disciplinary effect on his life. Paul urged Titus to teach this principle to a most undisciplined people, the Cretes (Titus 2:12).

Our word moves from education to correction and finally embraces the concept of punishment. This idea is quite unpopular, because many Christians confuse salvation with sentimentality. God does not tolerate sin among Christians, but rather disciplines them as a good father would (Heb. 12:5-11). In fact, if a Christian is comfortable and undisciplined, there is cause to doubt that he truly is a believer.

In explaining the serious nature of Communion, Paul warns most strongly against participation by sinning saints. Such looseness has caused some to fall ill, and others have died as a result of this sacrilege. Such punishment is the discipline of the Lord (1 Cor. 11:30-31).

The punishment of the Lord is not designed to kill Christians. Rather it is an instrument of God to draw back deviating children from the errors of their ways. Corrected saints are used by God to demonstrate His glory in the world (2 Cor. 6:9).

ILLUSTRATIONS

Eighteenth-century British statesman and orator Edmund Burke emphasized the essential nature of discipline in public life. He said: "Men are qualified for civic liberties in exact proportion to their disposition to put moral chains upon their appetites."

This idea has persisted throughout history. In the 19th century American Congregationalist pastor Austin Phelps said: "Character is, by its very nature, the product of probationary discipline." Almost 500 years before Christ, the Greek philosopher and mathematician Pythagoras put it in similar form: "No man is free who cannot command himself."

In an extended statement Mrs. Gladys Brooks said: "Discipline is demanded of the athlete to win a game. Discipline is required for a captain running his ship. Discipline is needed for a pianist to practice for the concert. Only in the matter of personal conduct is the need for discipline questioned. But if parents believe standards are necessary, then discipline certainly is needed to attain them."

Such discipline is part and parcel of the Christian faith. According to James Alexander: "The study of God's Word, for the purpose of discovering God's will, is the secret discipline which has formed the greatest characters."

Though not as eloquent as Alexander, Coach Tom Landry of the Dallas Cowboys football team shares the same opinion: "To live a disciplined life, and to accept the result of that discipline as the will of God—that is the mark of a man." Coach Landry's public image and coaching results prove the wisdom of this statement.

Many Puritan writers referred to the discipline of the Lord. Some of them were rather graphic in their descriptions. William Gurnall is best known for his classic treatment of the Christian's spiritual warfare (Eph. 6). When he turned to the discipline of the Lord, Gurnall wrote: "God's wounds cure; sin's kisses kill."

Another Puritan writer was John Trapp, whose main fame rests on his Bible commentary. He used an agricultural picture to demonstrate the discipline of the Lord. After a farmer prunes the vines, they grow and produce a crop of grapes. By the same token according to Trapp: "Better be pruned to grow than cut up to burn."

The same sentiment is expressed by Abraham Wright: "We may feel God's hand as a Father upon us when He strikes us as well as when He strokes us."

CHIEF (HIGH) PRIEST

MEANING

The word translated "chief priest," *archierus,* is found more than 120 times in the Greek New Testament. This word is reflected in English. The prefix *arch* is seen in *"arch*bishop," and it means "to rule." In other words, an *"arch*bishop" is a ruling bishop. The second part of the word is *hierus,* and it is seen in the word *"hier*archy," which speaks of a priestly order.

The high priests in Judaism were united by blood, as all of them were descendants of Aaron. The high priests were drawn from the adult male members of that line. By the time of Jesus these high priests were very political. They ruled the temple with a rod of iron. From their ranks came the captain of temple police and the treasurer. One of them presided over the Sanhedrin, an eminent collection of 71 priests, scribes, and elders.

BIBLE USAGE

There is nothing in the New Testament to commend the high priests. Three high priests are mentioned in the New Testament. Caiaphas served from about A.D. 18-37. It was he who tried Jesus in the religious court (Matt. 26:57-65).

Another high priest mentioned in the New Testament was Annas. He preceded Caiaphas in office, and was Caiphas' father-in-law (John 18:13, 24). Even as a retired high priest Annas had the opportunity of hearing Jesus before sending Him on to Caiaphas.

A third high priest in the New Testament was Ananias. He was in office at Jerusalem when Paul was arrested. Though this high priest ordered Paul to be struck, the apostle still showed grudging respect to his office (Acts 23:1-5). It was Ananias who pressed charges against Paul and thus sent him to the governor (24:1).

The political aspect of the high priests is seen in their associations. The chief priests were among the rulers of the people (Luke 23:13). As such they brought charges against Jesus after His arrest. Indeed Luke held them primarily responsible for the Crucifixion (24:20).

In the same connection the high priests were numbered among the scribes, the legal experts of Jewish laws. These too were collaborators in the crucifixion of Christ (Matt. 16:21; Mark 8:31). Together with the scribes and elders the chief priests dogged the steps of the Lord and sought to trip Him up (11:18, 27). Their opposition was seen even in the nativity story of Christ, for the high priests and scribes subscribed to Herod's hateful act (Matt. 2:4).

The high priests occupied prominent places in the Sanhedrin. In this capacity they managed the betrayal and trial of Jesus. Finally they falsely charged Jesus by fabricating evidence (26:59-63).

The high priests were scarcely more friendly to Christians than they were to Christ. When Saul of Tarsus set out to ensnare the saints at Damascus, he did so with the expressed permission and authority of the high priests (Acts 9:1, 14). They persisted in persecuting Christians, and later their most public attack was directed against Paul (22:30—23:5).

The New Testament contains a remarkable contrast in the term "high priest." The Book of Hebrews gives an entirely new meaning to this awesome title. Here Christ is seen as the great High Priest of our confession (Heb. 3:1).

He is aware of our needs. Indeed Christ is one with us in our needs. He has experienced all the temptations we shall ever bear, and withstood them triumphantly (4:15).

Human priests sometimes get in the way and hinder the access between God and man. But Christ our High Priest paves the way for us to enter into meaningful prayer with His Heavenly Father (4:14, 16).

The Old Testament tells of a shadowy figure, the priest-king of Salem (Jerusalem), Melchizedek. He is seen as an entirely new kind of priest, and Christ is consecrated a High Priest after the order of Melchizedek (5:10).

Christ is able to mediate between the holy God and the unholy human race because He is absolutely sinless, a perfect High Priest (7:26-28). Furthermore, His term of office never runs out; He is the eternal High Priest.

Christ is not only the Bearer of a sacrifice for us, but He is the sacrificial Lamb for our sin. This sets Him apart further as the perfect High Priest (9:26-27).

ILLUSTRATIONS

The office of high priest is so unfamiliar to us that we must seek out illustrations in antiquity. In fact the Bible gives us the best sermonic illustrations for this great concept. By way of illustration we may compare Christ with the high priests of Judaism.

First, the Jewish high priests were essentially political power brokers who exploited the common people for their own advantage. But Christ was a spiritual Leader who enriched every life He touched.

Second, the high priests of Judaism were functionaries of the Old Testament Law who rigorously enforced the minutest statutes to keep the people in their place. But Christ came as the Messenger of grace who fulfilled the Law and gave grace to His people.

Third, the chief priests' jobs were hereditary, and they boasted of their lineal descent from Aaron, though they had long since departed from Aaron's faith. But Jesus Christ is unique. In fact God the Father referred to Him as the "only [uniquely] begotten Son."

Fourth, once a year the high priests performed a sacramental function when they went into the holy of holies on the Day of Atonement. Christ on the other hand was sacrificial, for He died once to provide atonement for our sins.

Fifth, in the same connection the high priests of Judaism had an annual role, and they served only for a prescribed time. But Jesus Christ was appointed by God the Father as a perpetual High Priest, so we can count constantly on His mediation.

The high priestly office of the Lord Jesus Christ is expounded in the Book of Hebrews. This is seen in a beautiful summary included in the *Westminster Shorter Catechism:* "Christ as our Redeemer executeth the offices of a Prophet, of a Priest, and of a King both in the estate of humiliation and exaltation."

As John Bunyan put it: "As a sacrifice, our sins were laid upon Him, [Isa. 53]; as a Priest, He beareth them, [Ex. 28:38]; and as an Advocate, He acknowledges them to be His own" [Ps. 69:5].

(See: *Priest.*)

CHILD

MEANING

Three basic words in the Greek New Testament describe children. The first of these is *pais*, which appears 25 times and describes a young child. It also denotes the paternal relationship between a master and his servant, the servant being treated as if he were a child. In fact, in the Greek Old Testament (the Septuagint) the word *pais* is used 341 times to speak of a slave. It is from this word that we derive our words for children, "pediatrics," "pediatrician," and even "pedobaptism" (infant baptism).

Arising out of the first word is a second, *paidion*. This is a diminutive version of *pais* and refers to a smaller child, or even an infant. This word appears 51 times in the New Testament, and is often translated "child." Sometimes, however, it is translated "young child," or even "newborn baby."

The third common word for child is *teknon*. Coming from the verb *tikto* (to beget), this word emphasizes a child's origin. It speaks of physical ancestry, or even spiritual fatherhood and sonship. The word *teknon* occurs 98 times in the New Testament. Usually it is translated "child," but about one-fifth of its references deal specifically with a son.

BIBLE USAGE

Though some Bible students have tried to make these three Greek words denote different age-groups, that distinction is somewhat blurred. What can be said, however, is that *pais* usually refers to a small child. It is the word to describe the childhood of Jesus (Luke 2:43). At that time Jesus was a Boy of twelve. Children of similar age were described by the word *pais* in other passages (Matt. 17:18; Luke 9:42). Eutychus, who fell asleep during Paul's sermon at Troas, was also called by the same term (Acts 20:12). In another situation the word referred to a son (John 4:51). Because of the paternal relationship sustained by masters and servants, the word was also used to describe a servant (Luke 7:7; 12:45).

Like similar words, this one has a spiritual side to it. Israel is declared to be God's servant or child (Luke 1:54), as is David (1:69; Acts 4:25). This is the term used to refer to Christ as the Servant of God in certain passages (Matt. 12:18; Acts 3:13; 4:27).

The diminutive version of *pais* is *paidion*, which refers usually to small children or newborn infants. When Jesus was eight days old, this word was applied to Him (Luke 2:21). It also was used to represent Jesus when the wise men sought Him as a slightly older infant (Matt. 2:8-9). When Jesus fed the 5,000 the children were described as *paidion* (14:21). Such infants were used by Jesus as models of repentance and faith (18:2). Moses was also portrayed by this word before his rescue by Pharaoh's daughter (Heb. 11:23).

The final major New Testament word is *teknon*. Here the emphasis falls on the relationship between parent and child. Elizabeth and Zacharias were without a child when John was conceived (Luke 1:7). Jesus used this word in describing the divisions which would result between His followers and their parents (Matt. 10:21; Mark 13:12). Descendants are also described with this word (Matt. 2:18; 27:25; Acts 2:39).

Here too there is a spiritual aspect. Paul speaks of Timothy as his child in the faith (1 Tim. 1:2; 2 Tim. 1:2). The Scriptures refer to believers as children of God, and this term is used (John 1:12; Phil. 2:15). When John wrote his second epistle, church members were called children (2 John 1, 4, 13). Children of Abraham were denoted by this word (Matt. 3:9; Luke 3:8; John 8:39), as were the daughters of Sarah (1 Peter 3:6).

Though the age differences in our three Greek words are somewhat debatable, the dual usage of these words is clear. They refer both to physical and spiritual children. The Lord Jesus Christ as well as His followers used the terms to describe committed believers.

ILLUSTRATIONS

Children have been a subject of lively discussions for centuries. Like many of his 16th-century contemporaries, Francis Bacon regarded children as a burden. He said: "Wife and children are a kind of discipline of humanity."

A century later Bishop Jeremy Taylor took a more positive view: "He that loves not his wife and children feeds a lioness at home and broods a nest of sorrow."

The Puritans took a predictably moralistic view of the family. Jeremiah Burroughs said, "There is little hope of children who are educated wickedly. If the dye has been in the wool, it is hard to get it out of the cloth." To this opinion is added that of John Flavel: "What a mercy was it to us to have parents that prayed for us before they had us, as well as in our infancy when we could not pray for ourselves."

At the end of the 19th century Leo Tolstoy addressed the subject of the family in *Anna Karenina:* "All happy families resemble one another; every unhappy family is unhappy in its own way."

A more recent view of children is expressed by contemporaries. Randolph Miller wrote: "By the time children are five, their parents will have done at least half of all that can ever be done to determine the children's future faith."

Kenneth Taylor who has a large family and translated his *Living Bible* to be read to them, feels strongly about discipline: "A father's task is many-sided, but the most important part of his work is to fit himself and his children into God's plan of family authority. . . . To refuse to discipline a child is to refuse a clear demand of God, for a child who doesn't learn to obey both parents will find it much harder to learn to obey God."

Robert Holmes takes another angle on the same subject. "True parenthood is self-destructive. The wise parent is one who effectively does himself out of his job as a parent. The silver cord must be broken. It must not be broken too abruptly, but it must be broken. The child must cease to be a child. . . . The wise parent delivers his child over to society.

The *Sinai Sentry* contained a long list of rules about children, and some of them are the following:

If a child lives with criticism, he learns to condemn.
If a child lives with hostility, he learns to fight.
If a child lives with fear, he learns to be apprehensive.
If a child lives with tolerance, he learns to be patient.
If a child lives with encouragement, he learns to be confident.
If a child lives with acceptance, he learns to love.

(See: *Infant.*)

CHOOSE

MEANING

The word "to choose" has a wide span of meaning in the Bible. The Greek word *eklegomai* is translated by various English words ranging from "selecting" or "choosing" to the biblical doctrine of election. Two roots make up this word. They are *ek*, meaning "out of," and *lego*, "to speak." The rudimentary idea is to select someone or something out by means of speaking. In the New Testament the verb "to choose" occurs 21 times, and the noun for "choice" shows up 30 times.

The Septuagint Greek Old Testament contains the word more than 108 times. In Jehovah's economy of things this divine selection includes objects (the tabernacle), people (Jeremiah, Isaiah, David), places (Jerusalem), and nations (Israel).

BIBLE USAGE

Like a precious stone, God's choosing or electing has several facets. First, He chooses one alternative from many possibilities. When the Lord called out His disciples, He declared that they were selected especially out of the world. This drew a line of demarcation between the disciples and the world around them.

Early in His ministry the Lord Jesus Christ spent an entire night in prayer. On the next day He chose the Twelve. They were to have a double function. As disciples they were to learn from the Lord, and as apostles they were to declare His name (Luke 6:13).

A similar incident of selection from among possibilities was the appointment of Matthias to fill the place vacated by Judas. Joseph and Matthias were put forward for the apostolic vacancy, and the lot fell on Matthias (Acts 1:23-26).

Simple selection from a range of options is the first meaning of our word. The second meaning involves selection for a personal possession. It is like a person who has a custom-tailored suit or shirt. In the same manner the Lord chooses people as His own personal possessions (John 15:16).

Following His resurrection the Lord met with the disciples, apparently on a frequent basis. Their final meeting concluded with His ascension, after He had given them instructions concerning the coming Holy Spirit's power (Acts 1:2).

In speaking at the synagogue in Pisidian Antioch, the Apostle Paul presented a summary of Jewish history. A strong point in his argument was the fact that God chose the Hebrew "fathers" and prospered them despite imprisonment in Egypt (13:17).

Both Israel and Christians are marked out as God's special possession. In this sense the concept of election and selection is similar in both the Old and New Testaments.

A third meaning of the word relates to the purposes for which one is chosen. In discussing the subject with His disciples, Jesus emphasized that He called them all, including Judas Iscariot, whom He called "a devil" (John 6:70). In other words, Judas was chosen with God's full purpose in mind.

The concept of purpose is seen much more clearly in Acts. Peter knew he was chosen by God to proclaim the Gospel to Gentiles, especially to Cornelius. Peter took this choosing seriously and built an entire doctrine on it (Acts 15:7).

When writing to the Corinthian Christians, Paul added to the whole idea. He taught them that God has chosen them despite their obvious inabilities and inadequacies. Their weakness stood out in bold contrast with God's glory (1 Cor. 1:27-31).

A fourth aspect to the concept of choosing is the election of Christians to be saved. Paul taught that God's elect were set aside and separated from the world (Rom. 8:33). They were solidly the Lord's.

As the "elect" or chosen ones, Christians are urged to live lives which show the sanctifying work of the Holy Spirit (Col. 3:12). They are to display godly characteristics in their communications with others. These marks are expected of every Christian, not just the apostles (Titus 1:1; 2 John 1, 13).

Peter harked back to the Book of Exodus in explaining election. Israel was a chosen priesthood and a royal people (Ex. 19:5-6). By the same token the church is likewise a select group set apart for special service to God (1 Peter 2:9). Here rests the exciting doctrine of the priesthood of all believers, for which every Christian has been chosen.

ILLUSTRATIONS

Few Bible teachings have been more misunderstood than election or predestination. Some feel it cuts the nerve of human responsibility. Others see it as fatalism. A third group find in this teaching great comfort and glory. Four truths need to be seen, if one is to understand election.

First, God is eternally just. We are all sinners by birth and by choice, and God could justly condemn us all. However, He chooses to reach out and draw in some of us. His justice is not tarnished by this. Puritan penman Elnathan Parr derived comfort from this: "This doctrine [of election] affords comfort; thy unworthiness may dismay thee, but remember that thy election depends not upon thy worthiness but upon the will of God."

Second, man is responsible to obey God's call. The responsibility of man and the sovereign call of God are like two sides of the same coin. We cannot blame someone else for our sin. Reently I saw a T-shirt with these words scrawled on it: "The devil made me do it." But God holds us responsible, and we cannot blame the devil, or society, or our upbringing.

Third, evangelism is essential to Christian living. God commands us to proclaim the Good News of Jesus Christ. God's sovereign election does not water down that imperative. Farmers know their crops are at the mercy of the elements, but they still cultivate them. So we devote our best efforts to evangelism. Charles Haddon Spurgeon believed in both election and evangelism. He reconciled them in this prayer: "Lord, save Thine elect, and then elect some more."

Fourth, faith supercedes logic. This great biblical truth is accepted by faith, not reason. Who can comprehend how a black and white cow eats green grass and gives white milk which is churned into golden butter, or even curdles into blue cheese? But we believe it and we enjoy the benefits.

English divines caught the majesty of this teaching when they compiled *The Westminster Confession of Faith*. One article describes the doctrine of election in these terms: "All those whom God hath predestined unto life . . . He is pleased, in His appointed and accepted time, effectually to call by His Word and Spirit."

CHRIST

MEANING

To most of us "Christ" is simply another name for the Lord Jesus. But to a first-century believer the name was heavily loaded with meaning. "Christ" is taken directly from the Greek *christos,* and that word is taken from the verb *chrio* (to anoint). Therefore the title "Christ" means the Anointed One. This title is used 529 times in the New Testament, 379 times in the writings of Paul.

The entire concept is taken from the Old Testament. There anointing was a sign of special divine approval. When Samuel was commissioned to crown a king for Israel, he anointed Saul and later David.

Another anointed office in the Old Testament was that of priest. Who can forget that picture in the Psalms of the anointing oil flowing down Aaron's head and cascading over his beard? (Ps. 133)

Though it never became a standard initiation into the prophetic office, Elisha was anointed as successor to Elijah (1 Kings 19:16). The Old Testament writers understood that the abiding of the Holy Spirit on a prophet was a spiritual anointing. (See: *Anoint.*)

BIBLE USAGE

All the other meanings of this word are dwarfed by its application to Jesus the Messiah. In fact every major event and expression of Jesus' earthly life was marked by references to the Christ.

His birth ushered in the messianic title. Matthew described the birth of Jesus by ascribing to Him the name of Christ (Matt. 1:16-18). When the angel announced the birth to shepherds in the fields, the Baby was introduced as "Christ the Lord" (Luke 2:11).

Jesus took His disciples up into the hills to a small town called Caesarea Philippi. There He asked them who people thought He was. All sorts of answers came: Jeremiah, Elijah, John the Baptist. Then Jesus asked the disciples, and Peter answered: "Thou art the Christ, the Son of the living God" (Matt. 16:14-16). To Peter and the disciples Messiah meant Christ.

The Lord refers to Himself as Christ. He even compares Himself to the Messiah who was predicted by Davidic psalms and prophetic preaching. This identification confirmed the believers and inflamed the opposers (Mark 12:35; Ps. 110:1).

The trial of Jesus was liberally punctuated with references to His deity. Whether His accusers used it in mockery or sincerity, they understood that He was called the Christ. The Sanhedrin threw this up as a charge against Him (Luke 22:67). Christ's accusers presented this as the cause for Jesus' trial (23:2). As He hanged on the cross they sneered at Him and mocked Him as the Christ (23:35).

In His resurrection Jesus reconfirmed the correct claim that He is Christ. Walking back to Emmaus He intercepted two disconsolate disciples, perhaps a husband and wife. To them Jesus opened the Scriptures and showed that He, the Christ, was the pivotal point of all biblical revelation (24:25-26).

The Gospel message centers mainly around the name of Christ. Paul presented this in his great Resurrection chapter (1 Cor. 15:12). He likewise showed how Christ had become our Substitute, paying our penalty on the cross (Gal. 3:13). In fact the name of Christ becomes the focal point of all Gospel declaration in the writings of Paul (Rom. 1:16; 1 Tim. 1:15).

The church is identified completely with its Head, Christ. All believers are called the people of Christ (1 Cor. 15:23). In Him there are no distinctions of race, economic status, or gender (Gal. 3:27-28). In fact, the Apostle Paul loved to refer to the church universal as the body of Christ (Rom. 12:5; 1 Cor. 12:12). Lest anyone become possessive of the church, Paul repeatedly taught that the church is Christ's alone (Rom. 16:16).

Thus Christ is not only a descriptive title, portraying Him as the Anointed One of God. It is far more; it is the personal name forever linked to the Lord Jesus. Under this name is gathered a body of believers, spanning centuries and continents. This body's magnitude will only be measured in glory.

ILLUSTRATIONS

Literature abounds with references to Christ. Predictably the most eloquent statements come from clergymen. American Presbyterian Archibald Alexander said: "All my theology is reduced to this narrow compass—Christ Jesus came into the world to save sinners."

Along a similar line English clergyman George Bancroft added: "I find the name of Jesus Christ written on the top of every page of modern history." To this the historian Will Durant would add: "Caesar hoped to reform men by changing institutions and laws: Christ wished to remake institutions, and lessen laws, by changing men."

A Free Church of Scotland divine, James Denney, was as famous in the pulpit as he was in print. Of Christ he wrote: "No man can give at one and the same time the impression that he himself is clever and that Jesus Christ is mighty to save."

From among the classical Puritan writers came Samuel Rutherford, a man who knew fame and infamy because of his belief. In early life he was jailed for two years, during which time he wrote his *Letters* to former parishioners. To them he wrote: "Jesus Christ came into my prison cell last night, and every stone flashed like a ruby."

One of the most famous 19th-century American clergymen was Phillips Brooks, an Episcopal Bishop of Boston. On the person of Christ he said: "Jesus Christ [is] the condescension of divinity and the exaltation of humanity."

From the early church came a most quotable father, Bishop Augustine of Hippo in North Africa. In speaking of the sanctified Christian life, Augustine made this famous remark: "Jesus Christ will be Lord of all or He will not be Lord at all."

No less quotable was a Victorian Baptist preacher of London, Charles Haddon Spurgeon. Though his statements were often profound, they were almost always simple. Of Christ Spurgeon said: "I have a great need for Christ; I have a great Christ for my need."

From a similar doctrinal viewpoint came the great London preacher of our generation, Dr. Martyn Lloyd-Jones. Like Spurgeon he loved to preach the Gospel simply and clearly. "The Doctor," as he was affectionately known, once said: "You cannot receive Christ in bits and pieces."

J.W. "Praying" Hyde, a missionary statesman, summarized his message in these words: "If every person in the world had adequate food, housing, income; if all men were equal; if every possible social evil and injustice were done away with, men would still need one thing: Christ."

CHRISTIAN

MEANING

Taken from the Greek word *Christos* (see: *Christ*) the word Christian comes directly from the Greek word *christianos*. It seems to mean "an adherent of Christ." Some think this is a diminutive form of *Christos*, meaning "little Christ." Either way it is a flattering term, because it connects a believer with his Lord. In a real sense being a Christian means bearing the name of Christ. Since Christians bear the name of Christ, they should strive to be like Christ (John 8:46; 2 Cor. 5:21).

There are some parallel constructions in the ancient language. Followers of Herod were known as "Herodians." Likewise those loyal to Caesar were known as "Caesarians." This appears to be the model on which the name "Christian" was formed.

In ancient literature the name of Christian had several meanings. It meant membership in a community, the community of believers. Another implication was agreement with the apostles' doctrinal teaching. Also there is implicit in this word a statement concerning lifestyle, as Christians lived like Christ. All in all this word had significant meaning for a New Testament believer. Being a Christian gives a believer the responsibility to live up to the name.

BIBLE USAGE

In the New Testament the word "Christian" appears only three times. First it was the response of a pagan society to the rapid growth of the Christian community. In Syrian Antioch the church grew quickly, and it was clearly distinguished from the Jewish synagogue. Through the yearlong teaching of Paul and Barnabas these Christians coalesced into a community. Therefore "the disciples were first called Christians at Antioch" (Acts 11:26).

The second occurrence is in a similar vein. Herod Agrippa had heard Paul's defense, in which the apostle declared the Gospel of Christ and the duty of his commitment to Christ. In a parting remark Agrippa retorted, "Will you make me a Christian with so little effort?" (26:28, author's paraphrase) Many have felt that Agrippa was close to commitment. But the Greek text seems to show that the King was simply frustrated by his inability to refute Paul's proclamation.

The third and final appearance of our word in the New Testament is found in Peter's writings. Here too the emphasis falls on public persecution of believers. Peter says it is worthwhile to suffer "as a Christian" (1 Peter 4:16). Here the emphasis seems to fall on persecution for the name of Christ, which is part and parcel of a Christian's life. Jesus had warned of this many times (Matt. 13:21; John 15:20; 16:33).

The opposers of Christians applied several nicknames to believers. Jewish persecutors of Paul spoke of Christians as "the sect of the Nazarenes" (Acts 24:5). This focused on the fact that Jesus came from Nazareth, a rather unprepossessing village in Galilee. In fact, people did not believe that a spiritual leader could come from Nazareth (John 1:46).

A second nickname for the Christians was used in the early church. During his days as a persecutor Paul, then Saul, diligently sought out any who were of "the way" (Acts 9:2). This seems to refer to the saying of the Lord Jesus Christ, that He is the way, the truth and the life (John 14:6). Another acceptable translation of John 14:6 shows the prominence of this term: "I am the true and living way" (author's paraphrase). Thus believers were accused of setting Jesus Christ up as the exclusive way. But in reality He made that claim for Himself.

ILLUSTRATIONS

The Christian life has drawn comments from almost every major and minor thinker who ever lived. Therefore selecting illustrations is difficult. The father of the Reformation, Martin Luther, said: "I am to become a Christ to my neighbor and be for him what Christ is for me."

In our century A.W. Tozer fulfilled a prophetic role to the urban society. Of Christians he said: "There is nothing so refreshing as to watch a new Christian before he has heard too many sermons and watched too many Christians." In other words, new Christians are often more Christlike than older ones.

The Christian life is all about witness. In *The Interpreter's Bible* Albert George Butzer said: "Some Christians are not only like salt that has lost its savor, but like pepper that has lost its pep." On the same subject, well-known Baptist pastor David Otis Fuller posed this question: "If you were arrested for being a Christian, would there be enough evidence to convict you?"

The Christian life is also a life of holiness. When a Christian fails to maintain a biblical standard of conduct, the Lord is displeased and the non-Christian world is deluded. On the priority of Christian living, the gifted evangelist and professor Paul Little concluded: "Collapse in the Christian life is seldom a blowout; it is usually a slow leak."

Pursuing the same topic the Presbyterian clergyman and evangelist J. Wilbur Chapman added: "Anything that dims my vision of Christ, or takes away my taste for Bible study, or cramps my prayer life, or makes Christian work difficult, is wrong for me, and I must, as a Christian, turn away from it."

Another aspect of Christian living is the responsibility of citizenship. Concerning this the statesman Daniel Webster commented aptly: "Whatever makes men good Christians makes them good citizens."

Another large aspect of the Christian life is fellowship. The Christian is seen in company with others. T.J. Bach, a missionary statesman, saw the need for fellowshp and said: "When a Christian is in the wrong place, his right place is empty."

On the same subject of Christian fellowship John Nelson Darby, founder of the Christian (Plymouth) Brethren, wrote: "Remember that you are nothing and nobody except Christians, and on the day you cease to provide an available amount of communion for every recognized believer in the Lord Jesus, you will become sectarian, and merely add, by your meetings, to the disorder and ruin of Christendom."

A famous and telling proponent of Christianity in our age was C.S. Lewis, an Oxford don. In his simple and striking way he summarized the genius of Christianity: "Christianity, if false, is of no importance, and, if true, of infinite importance. The one thing it cannot be is moderately important."

The Christian life is aptly summarized by an anonymous writer: "Faith makes a Christian. Life proves a Christian. Trial confirms a Christian. Death crowns a Christian." Another anonymous writer phrased it: "The Christian life doesn't get easier; it gets better."

CITY, CITIZEN

MEANING

The Greek word for "city" is *polis*. It is reflected in such English terms as *"politics"* (the art of compromise, as someone said), *"polity"* (the form or process of government), *"police"* (the enforcers of public order), and *"policy"* (the standard of order).

To the ancient Greeks the word *polis* had several connotations. First, it marked the contrast between city and village. Second, it gave the social and geographic flavor to an entire region, such as Galatia. Third, it identified a unit of population, as seen in the statement, "The whole city went out to see Jesus" (Matt. 8:34). The word *polis* appears no fewer than 160 times in the New Testament.

Greeks regarded a city highly. To them it was the primary building block of society, and cities were often independent states with their own democratic, popular governments. The *polis*, or small Greek state, has been described as "the most typical phenomenon in ancient Hellenic [Greek] culture" (Gerhard Kittel, *Theological Dictionary of the New Testament*, VI, p. 520). To the Greeks it meant a fortified town such as the Athenian *"acropolis."* Related to the word *polis* is *polites*, the word for "citizen."

BIBLE USAGE

In common with many other biblical words, the word "city" has both literal and figurative meanings. Jesus spoke of a city set on a hill (Matt. 5:14). Present-day tourist guides in the Holy Land identify that city as Sefad, a picturesque place in the Galilean uplands.

Another literal meaning of the word pertains to the population. When Jesus liberated a demon-possessed man and sent the demons into a herd of swine, "the whole city" came out to Jesus. Their purpose was not to welcome Him, but rather to plead with Him to flee from their city (8:34).

Cities could be placed under spiritual bondage. When a city refused the apostolic message, its messenger was free of obligation. However, Jesus taught that such a city would suffer a worse fate than Sodom and Gomorrah (10:14-15). This raises questions concerning the eternal fate of today's sinful cities. Conversely a city which responded to the Gospel would be blessed. This was true of some pagan cities in Asia Minor (Acts 14:20-21), especially Corinth (18:10).

Sometimes cities were famous because of outstanding residents. Perhaps the most well-known example of this is Bethlehem, the birthplace of the Lord Jesus. Before His birth it was known as the City of David (Luke 2:4, 11). Someone has tabulated that more than half of all references in the New Testament to cities are in the writings of Luke. Could this be because Luke, a Greek physician, shared the Greeks' love for cities?

Just as the literal meaning of "city" is full of meaning, so is its figurative meaning. Predictably the most prominent use pertains to the Holy City, Jerusalem. In chronicling the temptation of the Lord, Matthew refers to "the holy city," Jerusalem (Matt. 4:5). This seems to be a phrase taken from Nehemiah, who had a deep affection for the restored city of Jerusalem and called it "the holy city" (Neh. 11:1). Perhaps this phrase first appeared after the Babylonian Captivity, when the Jews fully appreciated their birthright to Jerusalem (Dan. 9:24-25).

A second figurative city is the New Jerusalem, the heavenly Jerusalem. Abraham, the roaming tent dweller, looked for such a permanent city, but he knew it would only be found in heaven (Heb. 11:10). When the Revelation reaches its magnificent climax there is the vision of a New Jerusalem, a heavenly holy city, as splendid as a bride on her wedding day (Rev. 21:2, 10).

Also in the Book of Revelation is a third, figurative city. This one is marked by its evil and is a mirror image of ancient Babylon which hated God's elect people. In fact, this evil city of the end times is called Babylon (16:19; 17:18; 18:10).

ILLUSTRATIONS

The greatest literary exposition of the spiritual city was written by Augustine about A.D. 413-427. In *The City of God* he wrote a masterful interpretation of history. The city of man is earthly and controlled by Satan, but the city of God is heavenly and ruled by the Lord. Sometimes these cities conflict, but ultimately the city of God will triumph. To this eternal city the Christian owes his allegiance.

Incidentally Rome is nicknamed "the eternal city." Augustine knew that the eternal city was not Rome, which had fallen in 410 to the vicious attack of the barbarians from northern Europe. In the wake of this horrendous event Augustine wrote his *City of God.*

Christian writers picked up the phrase from Augustine, and references have dotted Christian literature ever since. For instance, John Newton, a slave-ship captain turned hymn-writer, picked up the phrase in his famous hymn: "Glorious things of Thee are spoken, Zion, city of our God."

Matthew Arnold was a clergyman who became professor of poetry and later professor of modern history at Oxford in 1841. He wrote of "That sweet city with her dreaming spires, / She needs not June for beauty's heightening" (*Thrysis*, I, 19). His theology was liberal, but his writings were beautiful.

In his poem "The Seekers," John Masefield likewise returned to the theme. He wrote longingly of the world to come:

> Friends and loves we have none,
>   nor wealth nor blessed abode,
> But the hope of the city of God
>   at the other end of the road.

This emphasis on a brighter, better city to come is common to Christian writers.

A century ago John Neale translated a hymn from the seventh century and titled it "Christ Is Made the Sure Foundation." One stanza refers to the heavenly city:

> All that dedicated city
> Dearly loved of God on high,
> In exultant jubilation
> Pours perpetual melody,
> God the One in Three adoring
> In glad hymns eternally.

As the word "city" has rich meaning, so has the word "citizen." American humorist Clifton Fadiman said, "We are all citizens of history." Socrates put it another way: "I am a citizen, not of Athens or Greece, but of the world." A Christian knows he is neither a citizen of his homeland nor of the world, but rather of heaven (Phil. 3:20). Life on earth is only an exile, and someday saints will return home to live forever.

CLEAN

MEANING

The concept of cleansing and cleanness appears frequently in the Scriptures, and in the New Testament it is usually represented by the Greek words *katharos* (clean) or *katharizo* (to cleanse). The connections with English words are quite obvious. Some examples are *"cathar*sis" (an emotional or physical purging), *"cathar*tic" (any substance used to induce a purging), and *"Cathar"* (a member of a medieval sect which sought the purging of evil from its members).

From a biblical standpoint the concept of cleansing is deeply rooted in both the Old and the New Testaments. Under the levitical laws heavy emphasis was placed on ceremonial cleansing. This forbade contact with any unclean animal, substance, person, or place. By the time Christ came this preoccupation with ceremonial cleanness had partially displaced true worship of the Lord. Thus the New Testament focuses mainly on a clean conscience, rather than on ceremonial cleanness.

BIBLE USAGE

There are three levels of cleanness in the New Testament. The first is physical cleansing. Jesus used this as an example when Peter was reluctant to have Jesus wash his feet. Jesus reminded Peter that one who has bathed is clean all over and requires only to have his feet washed (John 13:10). This seems to have spiritual implications also. One who has been cleansed by conversion requires only daily cleansing from the sins of that day.

Another instance of physical cleansing is a reference to funeral practices. When Joseph of Arimathea and Niocodemus prepared the body of Jesus for burial they wrapped it in "clean" linen as they followed the embalming procedures (Matt. 27:59).

In another sense leprous people were considered to be cleansed when Christ healed them. Though this has ceremonial overtones, the New Testament focuses on the physical cleansing from the marks and the contamination of leprosy (8:3).

Though the line of demarcation is not always clear, the second aspect of cleanness is ceremonial. Here too we discover references to lepers. The apostolic commission included cleansing lepers (10:8). When a leper begged for cleansing, Jesus' answer was magnanimous: "I am willing; be cleansed" (Luke 5:13).

Another aspect of this ceremonial cleansing is the reference to "clean foods." In a dream the Lord used this example to show Peter that nothing was ceremonially unclean (Acts 10:15). Therefore Peter could evangelize the Roman officer Cornelius with a clear conscience. Later Peter taught this same lesson to leaders of the Jerusalem church (11:9).

In the final facet of this concept of cleansing we come to a distinctively New Testament teaching, namely moral or spiritual cleansing. Jesus set the tone for this in the Sermon on the Mount. There He instructed His followers to be pure, or clean, in heart (Matt. 5:8). Literally Jesus said: "Blessed are the pure in [clean of] heart, for they shall see God."

The Apostle Paul presented an elaborate comparison between Christ's church and His bride in Ephesians. There Paul proclaimed that Christ has cleansed His bride through the process of sanctification by the Word. Therefore the church will appear spotless in eternity (Eph. 5:27). What a marvelous prospect! It accords with other biblical statements along the same line (2 Peter 1:9; Jude 24).

This principle of moral and spiritual cleansing is described in many phrases.

According to James we should have clean hands and pure hearts to serve the Lord (James 4:8). In the Book of Hebrews we are seen as having clean consciences (Heb. 9:14; 1 Tim. 1:5). Peter describes Christians as people with clean souls (1 Peter 1:22).

In fact the Apostle John devotes a good deal of space to the concept of spiritual cleansing. Every Christian stands in need of it, and every Christian can obtain it on a daily basis (1 John 1:7, 9). This becomes a dominant characteristic of Christians in Paul's pastoral epistles, and the whole church is seen as a purified, cleansed people who are distinctively the Lord's (Titus 2:14; 3:5).

Thus in the New Testament cleansing comes into its own. We are no more bound to the regimentation of ritual washings. Now Christians are cleansed from the inside out by the blood of Christ.

ILLUSTRATIONS

In every generation faithful preachers of God's Word have spoken of the need for spiritual cleansing. John Donne, born a Catholic (1573) but in his late years Protestant Dean of St. Paul's Cathedral in London, was renowned for his poetry. On the subject of spiritual cleansing he said: "Sleep with clean hands, either kept clean all day by integrity or washed clean at night by repentance."

A leader in the great East African revival was Roy Hession, author of *The Calvary Road* (Christian Literature Crusade, 1950). One of the dominant themes of that awakening was constant cleansing from sin. No wonder Roy Hession said: "We do not lose peace with God over another person's sin, but only over our own. Only when we are willing to be cleansed, will we have His peace."

From a completely different background comes Dale Evans Rogers, wife and costar of Roy Rogers. Though her life has been spent in the unreal atmosphere of Hollywood, her faith is realistic. She described spiritual cleansing in these words: "Just as Jesus found it necessary to sweep the money changers from the temple porch, so we ourselves need a lot of housecleaning."

Literature is full of references to cleansing. Perhaps Shakespeare's *Macbeth* contains the most powerful pleas for moral cleansing. Macbeth says to a physician:

Canst thou not minister to a mind diseas'd,
Pluck from the memory a rooted sorrow,
Raze out the written troubles of the brain,
And with some sweet oblivious antidote
Cleanse the stuff'd bosom of that perilous stuff
Which weighs upon the heart?

To this the doctor replies:

Therein the patient
Must minister to himself (V, iii, 22).

It is strange that one of the greatest minds of all time had to admit utter despair when it came to moral cleansing. Nowadays some psychiatrists try to explain away guilt. An entertainer tries to charm a gawking generation out of its guilt. Sociologists seek to exorcise guilt from our society. But only God can cleanse people from the guilt which drove Macbeth mad.

CLOTHE

MEANING

The word "clothe" comes from the Greek term *enduo*. Literally it means "to draw on," but in the Greek New Testament it always refers to clothing oneself. An interesting English relative is the word "endue" (to bring in or to put on), an exact transliteration of the Greek word.

Pythagoras used this word in his teaching about the transmigration of the soul. One person "put on" the soul of another person, which is similar to the Hindu view of reincarnation.

In the Bible the word is always used to indicate putting on either clothes or characteristics. Thus in the Septuagint, the Greek Old Testament, writers spoke of putting on the Holy Spirit (Jud. 6:34), righteousness (Job 29:14), strength (Isa. 52:1), and salvation (Isa. 61:10). This is also the pattern of use in the New Testament.

BIBLE USAGE

As is true of many New Testament words, the word "clothe" has both a literal and a figurative meaning. Literally it refers to putting on clothes, but its contexts are fascinating. The Lord spoke of the flowers of the field as models of the Creator's provision. God clothes them in unimaginable beauty; therefore He will also take care of His people (Matt. 6:25-30). This same liberating message was given to the disciples before their first missionary journey. They were to leave the matter of clothing to the Lord and not worry about taking along extra garments (Mark 6:9).

Another interesting example is found in the Parable of the Wedding Feast. There the oriental custom of providing a wedding garment is described, and those who lack the appropriate attire are excluded from the feast (Matt. 22:11-13).

At the trial of Jesus soldiers stripped Him of His own garment. Then they threw a scarlet robe on Him. This was a prelude to their cruel mockery of the King of kings (27:28, 31). Afterward they taunted and poked Him, shouting all the while, "Hail, King of the Jews!"

Another example of clothing is the Pauline passage on the Resurrection. In 1 Corinthians 15 the Apostle Paul presents the fullest teaching on the resurrection of the body. Part of that teaching is the truth that in the Resurrection we shall put on new bodies which are not subject to decay (15:53-54; 2 Cor. 5:2-3). Because the Bible views the Resurrection as literal, we include this concept as a literal clothing.

But the New Testament also contains many figurative references to clothing. The most general statements are found in writings of Paul. He describes the Christian life as being clothed with Christ (Rom. 13:14; Gal. 3:27). In another connection Paul speaks of putting on the new self (Eph. 4:24; Col. 3:10). The idea seems to be this: when one believes in the Lord Jesus Christ, he receives the nature of Christ. Thus He becomes the very atmosphere and appearance of a Christian. When people see us, they see Christ. This is known by some as "incarnational theology," because we are identified with the Lord Jesus Christ.

As in the Old Testament, so the New Testament speaks of putting on certain characteristics. Christians put on compassion, kindness, humility, gentleness, and patience (3:12). This is proof that they are God's elect, "holy and beloved." In the same vein, Christians are clothed with spiritual power by the Holy Spirit's presence in their lives (Luke 24:49).

Paul took a cue from the Roman soldiers who surrounded him and spoke of spiritual armor which a Christian should put on. In the face of spiritual darkness,

Paul urged the Romans to put on the armor of light (Rom. 13:12). Because the Ephesians were in the midst of a pagan society they were vulnerable to attacks by Satan, so they needed "the full armor of God" (Eph. 6:11). Here again the idea is to put on the characteristics of a spiritual person. (See: *Armor.*)

The word "clothe" is clad in beautiful imagery. It speaks of an inseparable bonding to the Lord Jesus Christ. But it also speaks of the spiritual qualities which are part and parcel of a believer's life. As "clothes make the man," so our spiritual clothes make our spiritual lives.

ILLUSTRATIONS
Clothes are a subject of fascination. Jonathan Swift's satire was unleashed on a hapless lady. After asserting that "she's no chicken; she's on the wrong side of thirty," he added insult to injury. Of her appearance he said: "She wears her clothes as if they were thrown on her with a pitchfork" (*Polite Conversation,* Dialogue 1).

When I was a boy we lived in a large industrial city. Some people had only one suit, which they wore to worship on Sunday. This was known colloquially as "a Sunday-go-to-meeting suit." Spiritual clothing is not "Sunday-go-to-meeting" but everyday work clothes.

The Bible has an interesting contrast on the subject of clothing. We are instructed to take off certain things such as: the old (preconversion) habits (Col. 3:9), the old selfishness which was corrupted by lusts (Eph. 4:22), anger, wrath, malice, slander, abusive speech, and lies (Col. 3:8-9).

After taking off this sinful lifestyle, a Christian is to put on a whole new lifestyle. It is the exact opposite of the old habits which have been shed like a snakeskin. We are to put on every Christian virtue which will make us appear like the Lord Jesus. Otherwise we shall be like the poor unfortunate wretch Benjamin Franklin King wrote about in "The Pessimist":

Nothing to do but work,
Nothing to eat but food,
Nothing to wear but clothes,
To keep one from going nude.

This is a particularly pointed picture of modern people who have turned their backs on God, and now find life meaningless.

By contrast the hymn-writer Edward Mote took a positive stance in the final stanza of his hymn, "The Solid Rock":

When He shall come with trumpet sound,
Oh, may I then in Him be found;
Dressed in His righteousness alone,
Faultless to stand before the throne.

Ancient Jewish scholars used to debate the question of what people would wear in the Resurrection. Finally Rabbi Eliezer put their minds at ease. He concluded that resurrected bodies would be clothed in shrouds. A Christian knows, however, that he will wear a robe of Christ's righteousness.

COME

MEANING

As in English, so the word for "come" in Greek is as common as dust. In fact, in its elemental form it occurs 609 times in the Greek New Testament. The Greek word under study is *erchomai* and is translated with both "come" and "go." Its meaning is implied by its context.

In addition to the root word, *erchomai* is combined with many prefixes which change its meaning. When the verb is preceded by *dia* (through or throughout), it speaks of the universal spread of something. An example is Paul's statement that death spread throughout the whole human race (Rom. 5:12).

When the preposition *eis* (into) is added to our basic word, the meaning becomes "to go into." Sometimes it refers to an actual entrance, as when a healed man entered the temple (Acts 3:8). It can also refer to the spiritual reality of entering into the kingdom (Mark 10:15).

Add to our word the prepositon *ex* (which means "out of" in Greek as in Latin and English), and the verb takes on the meaning of an "exit." Lazarus exited from the grave, after Christ called him back to life (John 11:44). When Christ was raised many people left their tombs and walked around Jerusalem (Matt. 27:53).

Another combination includes the preface *peri* (around, as in *peri*meter). This changes the basic word to mean "wander around." According to the "Westminster Abbey of the faithful," many serious saints "wandered about" in sheepskins, goatskins, and destitution (Heb. 11:37, KJV).

When the prepositon *pros* (toward) is added to our basic verb, the word becomes "to come toward," or "to devote oneself." Thus a woman with an hemorrhage drew near to Jesus (Matt. 9:20), as did a centurion in Capernaum (8:5).

A final combination includes the preposition *sun* ("with" or "together"), which changes the verb to mean "to come together" or "congregate." The church in Corinth came together, but not always for mutual benefit (1 Cor. 11:17).

Thus the basic word "to come" is embellished by its combinations with many other words. They give a variety of flavors to our basic word.

BIBLE USAGE

Though we have surveyed combinations, it is fitting that we should also consider the biblical contexts of our basic word *erchomai* ("to come" or "to go").

The most significant coming in the New Testament is the coming of Jesus to people. He came to proclaim the kingdom of God (Mark 1:38). He also came calling sinners to repentance (2:17; Luke 5:32). He came in God's will as the Messiah (John 8:42), and this means salvation for many in a doomed world (12:47). After Zaccheus was turned around by the Lord, Jesus asserted that He had "come to seek and to save the lost" (Luke 19:10).

Closely connected with Christ's coming to people is the coming of people to Him. At His birth the shepherds came to worship Him (2:16). Later the wise men also came (Matt. 2:2). Throughout the Gospels people were always coming to Jesus, just to be near Him and be helped by Him (8:2; 9:18; 15:25; Mark 5:33). Coming to Jesus marks the beginning of a life of discipleship (Matt. 16:24; Luke 9:23). The greatest decision in human life is seen in the experience of the Prodigal Son who got up and came to his father (Luke 15:20). Thus the Lord is a Host, bidding guests to come to His richly laden table (14:17).

The coming of the Lord to people is important, and the coming of people to the Lord is a matter of life and death. There is a third emphasis in the New

Testament, the second coming of Christ. Connected with it are a myriad of meanings. He will come in power and glory (Matt. 16:27). The agenda for His coming is hidden in the councils of God, and it will occur when no one expects it (24:42). For the Christian this coming is a personal hope, for he shall be snatched away to be with the Lord (John 14:2-3). (See: *Appearing; Coming, Second.*)

ILLUSTRATIONS
At the 1984 Democratic Party Convention black leader Jesse Jackson spoke. His address was electric, because of his powerful speaking style. He represented a "rainbow coalition" of political minorities, and his message was presumptuous: "Our time has come." But only the Lord can say truthfully, "My time has come."

The time of His first advent came when the world was ready (Gal. 4:4). Charles Haddon Spurgeon, a great Victorian preacher, put the coming of Christ into context: "Christ is the great central fact in the world's history. To Him everything looks forward or backward. All the lines of history converge upon Him. All the great purposes of God culminate in Him. The greatest and most momentous fact which the history of the world records is the fact of His birth."

A contemporary of Spurgeon was a Scottish writer, Thomas Carlyle. His view of Christ's coming was more cynical than Spurgeon's. Carlyle said: "If Jesus Christ were to come today people would not crucify Him. They would ask Him to dinner and hear what He had to say, and make fun of it."

The coming of Christ into a person's life is eternally significant. Southern evangelist Sam Jones said: "Christ always lives where there is room for Him. If there is room in your heart, He lives there; if there is room in a law office for Christ, He lives there; if there is room on a locomotive engine, He will be there."

The same truth of Christ coming into a life was emphasized by John Henry Jowett, who gained fame as a preacher on both sides of the Atlantic. He spoke of Christ's coming this way: "We get no deeper into Christ than we allow Him to get into us."

Though the second coming of Christ will be handled later, a few illustrations highlight our word "to come." Andrew Blackwood, a professor of preaching, pointed to Christ's return with these words: "He may come any time. He's sure to come sometime. Let's be ready when He does come."

The contagiously optimistic Dutch missionary Corrie ten Boom loved to talk about the return of Christ. Someone asked her about the generation in which we live, and her answer was wonderful: "We are not a postwar generation but a pre-peace generation. Jesus is coming."

Though separated by half a millennium from Andrew Blackwood and Corrie ten Boom, Martin Luther had the same hope: "Christ designed that the day of His coming should be hid from us, that being in suspense, we might be, as it were, upon the watch."

COMFORTER

MEANING

The term "comforter" relates mainly to the Holy Spirit, and it is the title given Him by the Lord Jesus Christ. The Greek word which is translated comforter is *parakletos*. It is seen in our English word "paraclete," which literally means "one who is called alongside."

In secular Greek the term "paraclete" had several interesting uses. Most basically it meant one who is called to someone's aid, as one today would call a mechanic to fix a car. This gave way to a more specific meaning, one who appears on behalf of another person, as a lawyer in a court case. Finally the word came to mean an intercessor, mediator, or helper.

Christian writers under the inspiration of the Holy Spirit (the Paraclete) gave the word a full range of new meanings. In its Christian use the word means one who encourages, exhorts, appeals, or gives comfort or consolation. It is used mainly, though not exclusively, in the writings of the Apostle John.

BIBLE USAGE

Most notably the word Paraclete is used by the Lord Jesus as a name of the Holy Spirit. As such He is the Successor to the Lord Jesus, another Comforter (John 14:16). It is important to notice that the coming of the Holy Spirit at Pentecost as "another Comforter" did not herald the end of the Lord Jesus' work. They are not mutually exclusive in ministry.

The Holy Spirit stands in close trinitarian connection with the Father and the Son. He is sent by the Father and the Son into the world, and He bears constant witness to the Lord Jesus Christ (15:26). Furthermore, the Holy Spirit stands as our personal Advocate at the court of God's justice, as is emphasized in the parting teaching of the Lord (16:7-11). Therefore the term Paraclete primarily points to the Holy Spirit.

Christ too is called the Paraclete. The most outstanding reference to Christ as the Paraclete is also found in John's writings. In his first epistle he instructs Christians about coping with sin in their lives. They are not to be surprised when they fall into sin, but neither should they linger in the limbo of sin. They are to seek immediate cleansing from the Lord (1 John 1:7-10). The availability of this cleansing is related to the finished work of the Lord Jesus Christ, who now is our Advocate (Paraclete) before the throne of God's justice (2:1). Here the concept of advocacy is stressed.

In Philippians another aspect of Christ's role as Paraclete is shown. Philippians 2 is known mainly as a teaching section about the deity of Christ (Phil. 2:5-11). However, it is intended in the first instance as a practical injunction to humility. For that reason Paul starts by reminding the Christians of the "encouragement" (*paraklesis*) of Christ (2:1). Christ encourages His people to live humbly. From Christ Christians have received eternal comfort and grace (2 Thes. 2:16).

The Holy Spirit is the Paraclete, and Christ fulfills that role in believers' lives also, but God the Father is also referred to in the same terms. In exhorting the Roman Christians to steadfastness, Paul reminded them that God gives them perseverance and encouragement (Rom. 15:5). A similar turn of phrase appears in Hebrews, where the sheer integrity of God is seen as a source of encouragement (Heb. 6:18).

The term paraclete is also applied to people. In the Septuagint, the Greek Old Testament, Job laments that his friends are "poor comforters" (Job 16:2).

The New Testament introduces many true comforters. The Jerusalem church nicknamed Barnabas "the son of consolation" (Acts. 4:36, marg.). After the leaders hammered out a basis for receiving Gentiles into the church, the Bible records that the believers at Antioch found great consolation in this (15:31, KJV).

The Apostle Paul often referred to Christians as a source of encouragement or comfort. Because Christians had found comfort from the Lord, they were in a position to comfort persecuted brothers and sisters (2 Cor. 1:5-7). When Paul wrote to the church at the home of Philemon, the apostle thanked God for the comfort those Christians had been to him (Phile. 7).

Thus a word which is related mainly to the Holy Spirit and His ministry has a much broader impact in the New Testament. It embraces all three Persons of the Trinity, and it also describes the attitude and affection of Christians toward one another.

ILLUSTRATIONS

"Comforter" meant one thing to me, when I was a boy. It was what my grandmother called that wonderful feather-filled quilt on her big bed. I used to love to be tucked in under the "comforter." As we have seen, however, the New Testament has a much broader definition of the term.

Professor C.R. Vaughan, a Southern Presbyterian theologian, wrote an excellent book, *The Gifts of the Holy Spirit* (Edinburgh: Banner of Truth, 1975). In describing the comfort of the Holy Spirit, Vaughan uses these words: "The sources of comfort employed by the Holy Ghost are varied by the evils which it is designed to qualify. . . . To comfort one who is weak, he must be strengthened, or help must be found for him. To comfort one who is afraid, his fears must be qualified or removed. To comfort one in distress, some source of easement must be found" (p. 353).

Nineteenth-century Baptist theologian A.H. Strong quoted his contemporary A.A. Hodge in writing on the comfort of the Holy Spirit: "The Roman 'client,' the poor and dependent man, called in his 'patron' to help him in all his needs. The patron thought for, advised, directed, supported, restored, comforted his client in all his complications. The client, though weak, with a powerful patron was socially and politically secure forever" (A.H. Strong, *Systematic Theology* [Old Tappan, N.J.: Fleming H. Revell], p. 323).

In its poetic version of the Twenty-third Psalm, the Anglican Book of Common Prayer contains a beautiful line about the comfort of the Lord:

> The Lord is my Shepherd:
> therefore can I lack nothing.
> He shall feed me in a green pasture:
> and lead me forth beside the waters of comfort.

A contemporary Christian can enjoy this comfort because of the indwelling Holy Spirit in his life. It is no wonder that Professor Vaughan concluded his discussion on the Comforter with these lines: "The Holy Spirit as a Comforter is a power practically available and in the reach of every Christian" (p. 362).

COMING, SECOND

MEANING

Though the second coming of Christ has been discussed in the articles on Appearing and Coming, there is a distinctive Greek work which relates almost solely to His second coming. That word is *parousia*. It is therefore essential to give specific consideration to this most important event in God's prophetic plan, the second coming of Christ.

In secular Greek literature the word *parousia* often referred to the visit of a ruler. When its reigning emperor came to visit, a whole city was turned on its head. Streets were repaired, delicacies were provided for the emperor to eat, donkeys were found for celebrities to ride on, and there were interminable flattering speeches. (This sounds familiar, because dignitaries in our country are treated similarly.) This visit was known as *parousia*.

In Old Testament times the concept of *parousia* referred to the presence of Jehovah God. He was present in dreams and angelic appearances. His power was revealed in military victory and the establishment of the monarchy. His Spirit lived permanently in the place of worship, and thus the tabernacle was known as "the tent of meeting [presence]." In the Greek Old Testament *parousia* referred mainly to the coming Messiah, and no clear distinction was made between His first and second comings.

BIBLE USAGE

The New Testament sharpens the concept of *parousia* to a fine point. It is employed mainly to describe the second coming of Christ. When the Lord sat on the Mount of Olives He explained coming events to His disciples. The centerpiece of coming history would be His return (*parousia*; Matt. 24:3, 27).

Frequent references to the coming of Christ appear in Paul's letters. The grand assurance of our resurrection is the coming of Christ (1 Cor. 15:23). Because of the anxiety of Thessalonian Christians about the state of departed believers, Paul placed heavy emphasis on the coming of Christ in his letters to them. Paul looked to Christ's coming as a time of reward for service (1 Thes. 2:19). The sanctification of saints will be complete when Christ comes back (3:13). When a loved one dies, our hope is the return of Christ (4:13-18). The ultimate benediction and blessing given to Christians is the coming of Christ (5:23). Again in his second letter Paul returned to the theme of Christ's coming (2 Thes. 2:1, 8).

James' epistle is practical in its directions to the church. However, he too turned to the Second Coming to reinforce his teaching. Christians should be patient and persistent in their service because of the coming of the Lord Jesus (James 5:7).

Peter likewise referred to the coming of Christ in his second epistle. In proving the truth of his Gospel message, Peter referred to the first coming of Christ, which he had seen firsthand (2 Peter 1:16). Later Peter warned of those who do not believe in the second coming of Christ, calling them scoffers or mockers (3:4). In Peter's writings the coming of Christ is the same as the coming of God (3:12). This only proves the firm conviction which the disciples held concerning Christ's return. After all, they had an angelic promise to prove it (Acts 1:10-11).

The Apostle John regarded the coming of Christ in the same way as Peter, Paul, and James. For John, the Lord's return was an inspiration to faithful service. John was greatly concerned that Christians not be ashamed when Christ comes back (1 John 2:28). Though the Greek word is different, the concept is the same in the last verses of Revelation. There the Apostle John records this sincere prayer:

"Come, Lord Jesus" (Rev. 22:20). This should be the daily prayer of sincere believers now and in every age, until the Lord returns.

ILLUSTRATIONS

The coming of the Lord finds a practical picture in the visit of an important person. When we were living in Bristol, England the beautiful young Princess Diana came to our city. She toured the Bristol Children's Hospital and spoke personally with dozens of patients and their parents, nurses, and doctors. It was amazing to see how hard-bitten old reporters went soft when faced with Princess Diana. The whole city was enchanted by her coming.

If the coming of a princess has that impact, think of the infinite significance of the Saviour's return. Billy Graham says about the Lord's return: "Our world is filled with fear, hate, lust, greed, war, and utter despair. Surely the second coming of Jesus Christ is the only hope of replacing these depressing features with trust, love, universal peace, and prosperity. For it the world wittingly or inadvertently waits."

Renowned New Testament scholar and archbishop Richard Trench wrote about the return of the Lord. He emphasized the imminence of Christ's coming when he said, "The Second Advent is possible any day, impossible no day." (Incidentally, this imminent view of the Lord's coming seems to characterize most serious Bible students.)

William Gurnall was a famous Puritan writer, whose most outstanding book was a large volume dealing with the saint's spiritual armor. When Gurnall turned to the Second Coming, he was full of hope and urgency, for he said: "Christ hath told us He will come, but not when, that we might never put off our clothes."

A contemporary author is J. Oswald Sanders, who has devoted his life to the ministry of the Overseas Missionary Fellowship. Recently he produced a fine little survey of teaching concerning Christ's coming under the title, *Certainties of Christ's Second Coming* (Eastbourne, England: Kingsway, 1982). Sanders quoted several creeds concerning Christ's return. The Apostles' Creed claims that "Christ ascended into heaven; and sitteth at the right hand of God the Father Almighty; from thence He shall come to judge the quick and the dead" (p. 16).

The importance of Christ's coming is not to fuel foolish discussion, but rather to spur us into action in evangelizing our world. J. Hudson Taylor, founder of the Overseas Missionary Fellowship, said concerning the return of the Lord: "If the Lord is coming soon, is it not a very practical motive for greater missionary effort? I know of no other that has been so stimulating to myself."

Another great missionary, Robert Jaffray, said: "I am convinced that the one thing of first importance for which the Lord is waiting ere He can return is the preaching of the Gospel to every nation."

COMMON

MEANING

In English the word "common" has two basic meanings. First, it describes those things which are shared by a group of people, what is held by a "community." Second, it refers to things which are unimportant because of their "commonness," as common as an "old shoe." Both of these meanings are embraced by the Greek word *koinos*.

Plato projected a day when the common good would dominate all decisions. Guardians and soldiers would be fed communally from a vast storehouse. Their wives and children would likewise form a "commune." Aristotle even advocated a common ownership of wealth.

In the New Testament the word *koine* takes on further significance, because it speaks of the common interest of all Christians. Like many other words, the word *koinos* has other connections. A companion is called a *koinonos,* and the fellowship of believers is *koinonia* (see: *Fellowship*). A partner in business is called *sugkoinonos* (combining *sun,* "together," with *koinonos,* "companion").

Incidentally, the Greek language of the New Testament is called *koine* Greek. This was the "common" language spoken on the streets of the Roman Empire. The Holy Spirit "put the Bible on the lower shelf," so many people could read it.

BIBLE USAGE

In the New Testament the word *koinos* refers first of all to things held in common. The Lord challenged His disciples to share their possessions and thus build up treasure in heaven (Matt. 6:20; Luke 12:33; 14:33). Jesus was sustained by the generosity of women, who contributed to support Him and His disciples (8:1-3). Jesus taught, "It is more blessed to give than to receive" (Acts 20:35), a statement not recorded in the Gospels.

The early church understood generosity to mean community of goods. At Pentecost a large group of visitors were swept into the church by the Holy Spirit, 3,000 in one day. Many of them were immediately without work, simply because they were religious pilgrims celebrating Pentecost in Jerusalem. This created an immediate need for community of goods, and the Christians shared their wealth (2:44-45; 4:32). Barnabas even sold a plot of land to give for the needs of other Christians (4:37). Some think that faithful Jews had burial plots in Jerusalem, so they would be there when the Messiah appeared. But after they believed that Jesus is Messiah, the need for these burial plots was gone. So they sold them to alleviate a more real need.

Another shared possession was the common faith of all believers. Paul reminded Titus of the faith which they all held to be true, their common faith (Titus 1:4). A reflection of this idea is seen in the short Epistle of Jude, where the author speaks of our common salvation (Jude 3).

There is no difficulty in understanding the use of *koinos* to refer to wonderful things held in common, but a problem comes with its second meaning. "Common" also means something which is ordinary, low-class, or vulgar. Could the explanation be that some things are owned by so many people that they lose their value and become ordinary? This might explain the second meaning of common, a meaning which is also found in Greek.

Peter referred to ceremonially unclean meat as being "common or profane" (Acts 10:14, marg.). Then the Lord taught him that no meat is "common or profane" (11:9, marg.). This was an object lesson the Lord used to compel

Peter to evangelize the Roman Centurion Cornelius. Here too is a wonderful lesson: no one is ordinary in God's eyes.

A second reference to this meaning of "common" is found in Paul's writings. Here too the teaching is tremendous, that no food is unclean in God's eyes (Rom. 14:14).

In Hebrews we learn of people who pervert the Cross of Christ and thus make it common or ordinary. They do this by sinning willfully against the Lord after hearing the Gospel (Heb. 10:29). This elicits from the inspired writer a warning of judgment which will be swift and severe (10:30-31). There is nothing "common" about the Cross of Christ.

Though God rejected the Pharisees' views of things which are ceremonially clean or unclean, the Revelation warns that certain people are unclean, and they will never be tolerated in heaven. What makes them unclean? They have rejected the Lord Jesus Christ, and their names are not in the Lamb's Book of Life. These are unclean in God's eyes (Rev. 21:27).

Thus the two meanings of *koinos* come together. Christians are people who hold all things in common, and they meet one another's needs. They also share a "common" salvation and hope. Nothing is ceremonially "common" or unclean, except those who treat the Cross of Christ as common or unclean, and they will never enter heaven.

ILLUSTRATIONS

Because early Christians had things in common and shared their possessions, many have mistakenly concluded that Communism is correct. They ignore three basic facts about this early Christian phenomenon. It was temporary, voluntary, and Christian. Communism in the Soviet sense is permanent, enforced, and atheistic.

True sharing is seen best in marriage. The old wedding ceremony included this as part of the vows. As the couple exchanged rings they said: "With this ring I thee wed, and with all my worldly goods I thee endow." Now that quaint saying is seldom used, but the community of property is still a legal (and loving) fact of life.

The same care for others is seen in the Christian church. One church on the west coast of America was known for the loving care which Christians exhibited toward each other. At one stage the pastor said: "When the offering plate is passed, if you wish to give, do so. If you have a need of $10 or less, please feel free to take from the offering plate." Because of abuse, this had to be suspended, but the idea was good.

On the subject of giving, Richard Braunstein said: "It is possible to give without loving, but it is impossible to love without giving." Peter Marshall, a late chaplain of the United States Senate, said: "Let us give according to our incomes, lest God make our incomes match our gifts."

One evening a church member telephoned me in Bristol, England. "Pastor, what do you think of tithing?" he asked.

Amazed by his question, I hastened to affirm that this was both a good idea and God's plan for our giving. A few weeks later the eager Christian told me that he and his family learned an age-old lesson: the Lord can make 90 percent go farther than we could ever make 100 percent go. You cannot out-give the Lord! (See: *Fellowship.*)

CONDEMNATION (See: *Judgment.*)   89

CONSCIENCE

MEANING

The Greek word translated "conscience" is a combination of two words: *sun*, "with" and *eidesis* from *oida* "to know." The same idea is seen in the Latin word *conscientia*, meaning literally "to know with." The Christian conscience compares our behavior with the standard of the Scriptures, so our conscience is clear only when it concurs with the Word of God.

The Greek idea of conscience grew slowly prior to New Testament times. Socrates (469-399 B.C.) said that conscience evaluated our actions. However, the idea of a standard by which to judge people's behavior was basically a Christian idea and is foreign to the best of Greek philosophy.

Even liberal writers agree that the conscience is most finely developed in the writings of Paul. The New Testament makes conscience an awareness of self and an awareness of sin. The Bible is the standard and the Holy Spirit is the Source of our conscience.

BIBLE USAGE

In the New Testament there are two aspects of conscience. The first is general awareness, or consciousness. It is this which gives one a consciousness of sin (Heb. 10:2). Likewise this is a consciousness of God, an awareness of His existence (1 Peter 2:19). In discussing the eating of meat offered to idols, Paul also mentioned the awareness, or consciousness, that such an offering had been made (1 Cor. 8:7). In its basic form, the word means an awareness, a consciousness. Nothing is implied about one's reaction to the knowledge.

Another closely related meaning is the moral aspect of conscience, the awareness of right and wrong. No matter where a person was born he has a God-implanted conscience (Rom. 2:15; 9:1). This is true of Christians and non-Christians. According to the New Testament conscience is an extremely personal matter, and no one should dare to bind another person's conscience (1 Cor. 10:29).

The Apostle Paul relied on the reality of conscience when he proclaimed the Gospel. He trusted God to speak through people's consciences and convince them that the apostolic message was true. Thus Paul called his hearers' consciences to witness in support of his ministry (2 Cor. 1:12; 4:2; 5:11). According to John this conscience-awareness is reinforced by the Holy Spirit's anointing (1 John 3:19-22).

At salvation one's conscience is cleansed by the blood of Christ, and this deals effectively with past sin (Heb. 9:14). This clean conscience becomes the most valuable possession of a Christian (13:18). Conversely a non-Christian has a defiled conscience, which no amount of human activity can make clean (Titus 1:15).

In the pastoral epistles Paul made much of the conscience. Those who denied the truth had a "seared" conscience, which could not respond to revelation (1 Tim. 4:2). Church leaders were supposed to have clear consciences (3:9), and this was applied specifically to Timothy (1:19). Paul himself was an example of a clear conscience, which gave credibility to his ministry (2 Tim. 1:3). The Apostle Peter placed equal emphasis on the need for a clear conscience (1 Peter 3:16).

A careful study of the New Testament reveals the absolute importance of a clear conscience. This is true of our relationships with other people in the world and in the church. Most important is a clear conscience toward God.

ILLUSTRATIONS

Often conscience has been trivialized. According to Franklin P. Jones: "Conscience is a small, still voice that makes minority reports." To this someone added: "Conscience is also what makes a boy tell his mother before his sister does."

Christopher Morley said about conscience: "Pop used to say about the Presbyterians, 'It don't prevent them committing all the sins there are, but it keeps them from getting any fun out of it.'"

The late General Omar Bradley was more serious in commenting on conscience: "The world has achieved brilliance without conscience," he conceded. "Ours is a world of nuclear giants and ethical infants."

On the subject of conscience Martin Luther declared before the court of the Roman Empire at Worms in 1521: "My conscience is captive to the Word of God. . . . I am more afraid of my own heart than of the pope and all his cardinals. I have within me the great pope, Self."

When a person comes to faith in Christ, his conscience becomes acutely sensitive to sin. No longer as a Christian can he sin with impunity. The story is told about an old Indian chief who was converted. Later a missionary asked him: "Chief, how are you doing spiritually? Are you experiencing victory over the devil?"

"It's like this," the chief replied. "I have two dogs inside me: a good dog and a bad dog. They are constantly fighting with each other."

"Which dog wins?" asked the puzzled missionary.

"Whichever one I feed the most," retorted the wise old man. His conscience was being shaped by the Scriptures.

As a young missionary I taught at a small Bible institute. As we surveyed the Old Testament I taught students about the danger of tolerating unforgiven sin. One young man came after class and confessed having stolen a piece of equipment from his employer. That same day he wrote to his former boss and made it right. The result was not just a good grade in the course, but also a clear conscience, which is worth much more.

It is important to have a conscience sensitive to others. When we moved to England, I carried on with many practices which were acceptable to American Christians. Soon a British brother mentioned to me that English evangelicals did not go to restaurants to eat on Sunday. This was strange to me, but for the sake of my English friends I stopped eating out on Sunday. This protected my conscience and our fellowship.

In his usual practical way Billy Graham set out the importance of a clear conscience: "To have a guilty conscience is a feeling. Psychologists may define it as a guilt complex, and may seek to rationalize away the sense of guilt, but once it has been awakened through the application of the law of God, no explanation will quiet the insistent voice of conscience."

COUNCIL

MEANING

The word for "council" is specialized in the New Tesament. In Greek it is spelled *sunedrion,* from which we have the word Sanhedrin. Literally it means, "to sit together." Originally it identified a place where a council met; later it came to be the title for the chief council in Israel. From the Greek word comes the Latin term *senatus* and the English derivative "senate."

In the New Testament the main use of the word is in connection with the Sanhedrin, which is a Hebrew form of the Greek *sunedrion.* It was the chief council of Israel during the period of Roman occupation. It was comprised of 71 "elders," drawn from religious and secular spheres of influence. This council gained influence after the Babylonian Exile, and gained authority as the guardian of Jewish customs and rites. But its jurisdiction was limited by the Roman occupational forces.

BIBLE USAGE

In the New Testament the Sanhedrin has almost uniformly negative connotations. The Gospels use the term to refer to the meeting of the council (John 11:47), but the word also refers to the place where it met (Luke 22:66). The limits of the Sanhedrin were mentioned in the account of Jesus' trial. Apparently they could recommend the death sentence, but it had to be confirmed by the Romans (John 18:31).

The most prominent trial held before the Sanhedrin was that of Jesus Christ. The Gospels present a mosaic of information which can be combined to give a picture of the Sanhedrin's role in this miscarriage of justice. When He was taken before the court and they found no evidence for His guilt, the council paid false witnesses to testify against our Lord (Matt. 26:59).

Mark mentioned, in his account of the trial, that the testimony against Jesus was conflicting (Mark 14:55-56). Despite this fabricated evidence, the council arrived at a guilty verdict and had Jesus taken away to Pilate (15:1). The record of council interrogation in Luke's Gospel conveys the impression of desperation. They were at their wits' end as they sought to convict Jesus of blasphemy (Luke 22:66-71).

The experience of Jesus was duplicated in the disciples' lives. After healing a lame man at the temple gate, Peter and John were hauled before the Sanhedrin. Here the Sanhedrin is called "the Senate of the sons of Israel" (Acts 5:21). The high priest harangued at Peter and John, because they had acted in the name of the Lord Jesus (5:27-28). Despite the reasonable suggestion of Gamaliel (5:34-39), Peter and John were beaten and warned (5:40). But bearing a beating for the Lord was a badge of honor to the disciples (5:41).

The next disciple called before the Sanhedrin was Stephen. He was likewise interrogated and beaten. They could not comprehend the peace which Stephen displayed, as his face looked like that of an angel (6:12-15). Despite his piety and eloquent speech the Sanhedrin had him stoned, probably without Roman approval (7:54-60).

With the full concurrence of the council, Saul of Tarsus set out to imprison and kill Christians at Damascus. On the way he met Jesus, and that persecutor became a preacher. When he returned to Jerusalem after his missionary journeys, the council put him on trial (22:30). Despite the explanation of his conversion, Paul was accused. He responded by pitting the miracle-believing Pharisees against the secular-minded Sadducees (23:6-7). When a plot to murder Paul was hatched (23:15), he was quickly sent back to Roman jurisdiction (23:26-30).

Though the Sanhedrin opposed Jesus Christ and His apostles, some members were friendly. As mentioned, Gamaliel urged the council to spare John and Peter from death (5:34-39). Another friendly face in the Sanhedrin was Nicodemus, who became a secret disciple (John 19:39-42).

ILLUSTRATIONS
Persecution has always been part of the Christian life. The English reformer Hugh Latimer, who was burned to death at Oxford in 1555, said: "Wherever you see persecution, there is more than a probability that truth is on the persecuted side."

Born soon after the death of Latimer was the Puritan preacher John Penry, who was also executed for his faith. He warned his persecutors with these solemn words: "He that liveth the life of the persecutor dieth also the death of the bloody man."

In our century Christians have been persecuted worldwide. From the death of John and Betty Stam in China to the martyrdom of Nepalese pastors in the 1980s, there has been a steady stream of blood flowing for the faith in Christ.

One of the most valued members of our church in Bristol, England was a Chilean pastor. He had been hounded out of his homeland by the authorities, and lived in England as an exile. His presence in our fellowship was a constant reminder of the price of faithfulness to the Lord.

Since 1960 persecution has been intensified in the Soviet Union. About that time Nikita Khruschev launched a five-year program designed to wipe out religion. Children under the age of 18 were barred from worship. Parents were forbidden to give religious instruction at home. More than 10,000 churches were closed to worshipers.

In 1976 the *Daily Telegraph* of London carried this editorial comment: "Never before has the assault by an intolerant and almighty secular power on religious faith and observance been so sustained, scientific, and insidious as during the past 60 years in Russia" (December 1, 1976).

One of the most vehemently antireligious periodicals in the Soviet Union is *Science and Religion*. Its editors painted a powerful picture of Christians under fire. "Religion is like a nail," they wrote. "If you hit it on the head, it will go deeper." The proposed solution was more picturesque than it was practical: "We must surround religion, squeeze it from the bottom, and pull it up" *Sparks* (May, 1976).

In his famous 1972 Lenten letter, Aleksandr Solzhenitsyn spoke out against the Soviet repression of religion. "A church dictatorially directed by atheists is a spectacle that has not been seen for 2,000 years."

A fourth-century bishop of Constantinople, John Chrysostom, saw persecution as part of the Christian life. As such it should not be shunned. He wrote: "It behooves thee not to complain, if thou endurest hardness, but to complain, if thou dost not endure hardness."

CROSS

MEANING

In many ways the Cross is the crux of the New Testament. On it turns the whole of the Gospel message and the entirety of the Christian life. The Greek word for cross is *stauros*. We see this word in such technical terms as *"stauro*lite" (a cross-shaped crystal in a mineral) and *"stauro*scope" (a device to find planes of light in crystals). For a Christian, however, the Cross relates solely to the Saviour.

In Roman times a cross meant one thing: execution. It was the lowest form of capital punishment, reserved for slaves and non-Roman citizens. A condemned man was forced to carry his cross through the streets. At the place of execution he was nailed to his cross or bound to it with thongs; then it was hoisted into place. Usually the victim died of circulatory collapse, but sometimes his bones were broken to hasten his death.

According to Jewish Law crucifixion was a cursed death (Gal. 3:13; Deut. 21:23). Therefore the marauding Roman soldiers under Titus (A.D. 70) humiliated the Jews by crucifying thousands of them. According to Josephus' *Wars of the Jews:* "So the soldiers, out of the wrath and hatred they bore the Jews, nailed those they caught, one after another, to the crosses, by way of jest; then their multitude was so great, that room was wanting for crosses, and crosses were wanting for bodies" (Book 5, Chap. 11).

BIBLE USAGE

The Cross of Christ is most significant in this consideration. Not only was the death of Christ part of God's eternal plan (Phil. 2:5-8; Rev. 13:8), but it was also a marked departure from the usual Roman execution. As He hung on the cross a sponge soaked in wine and myrrh was offered Him, which was a particularly Jewish custom (Mark 15:23). Furthermore, His body was removed from the cross on Friday evening in accordance with levitical Law (John 19:31; Deut. 21:23).

In other ways the crucifixion of Christ was that of a common criminal. Before He was put on the cross He carried it until its weight became too much, and Simon of Cyrene took over (Matt. 27:32; Mark 15:21; Luke 23:26). Then He was nailed to the cross, the most painful means of attaching a victim (24:39; John 20:25). No foot rest was provided (contrary to many artists' drawings of the Crucifixion).

The Cross is also important because of its value in teaching the spiritual life. The Apostle Paul saw it as the centerpiece of the Gospel, because it provides forgiveness for our sins (1 Cor. 1:17-18). The Cross becomes the point of commitment for a Christian, and commitment to the message of Christ's Cross sets us apart from all other religions (Gal. 6:12-14). This commitment to the Cross unites believers of various backgrounds (Eph. 2:16; Col. 1:20).

Not only does the Cross carry theological significance, but it also gives us an example of godly living. Jesus called His disciples to "take up" their crosses, which meant to commit themselves fully to following Him (Matt. 16:24; Mark 8:34; Luke 9:23). It involved learning from Him in every aspect of life (Matt. 11:29). The writer of the Book of Hebrews sees the Cross of Christ as the model for Christian living (Heb. 12:2).

Thus the Cross has three significances in the New Testament. First, the Cross of Christ speaks of a historical event. Jesus actually died in my place, and this is as true as the existence of the Roman Empire and the hill called Calvary. Second, the Bible teaches that the sacrifice of Christ fulfilled all the Jewish sacrifices. From that point onward, only one sacrifice had any validity in dealing with sin, and that was the once-for-all sacrifice of Christ (9:28). Third, the Cross of Christ defines a disciple's lifestyle. We should be dead to our desires and alive to God's will because Christ is at work in us (Gal. 2:20).

ILLUSTRATIONS

The Cross is the symbol of Christianity. It is seen in all sorts of connections. In 1859 the Swiss layman Henri Dunant founded a society for the aid of people in distress; its symbol was a red cross, in memory of Christ's cross.

Soaring above Fleet Street in London at the top of Ludgate Hill is St. Paul's Cathedral. As one walks along Fleet Street, where all of the world's sordid news is printed daily, one looks up to the dome of St. Paul's. That dome is crowned by a glistening golden cross. Christ's Cross stands above the chaos of our world.

Many years ago an article was written by Dr. Vernon Grounds, former President of Denver Seminary. The content of the article and its title are long forgotten, but one line has given guidance to all my preaching. Dr. Grounds said to young preachers: "Pick any text in the Bible and head straight cross country to Calvary." This is an excellent rule for anyone who preaches or teaches the Bible.

Concerning the significance of the Cross, Jansenist preacher Louis Bourdaloue (1632-1704) said: "In the Cross of Christ excess in men is met by excess in God; excess of evil is mastered by excess of love." Bourdaloue was known as "the king of orators and the orator of kings."

Along the same line Puritan preacher John Owen said: Jesus "suffered not as God, but He suffered who was God." A colleague in the Puritan struggle, John Bunyan, explained the significance of Christ's Cross: "As a sacrifice, our sins were laid on Him [Isa. 53]; as a Priest, He beareth them [Ex. 28:38]; and as an Advocate, He acknowledges them to be His own [Ps. 69:5]."

Several generations later a noted South African preacher, Andrew Murray, became famous for his writings. Among his 250 published works was his most famous one, *Abide in Christ.* Of the Cross Murray said: "The Cross of Christ does not make God love us; it is the outcome and measure of His love for us."

Two writers can be selected to emphasize the practical aspect of the Cross. The first is Thomas à Kempis (1380-1471), a Spanish Carmelite monk known for his *Imitation of Christ.* Of the Cross Thomas à Kempis said: "Jesus now has many lovers of His heavenly kingdom, but few bearers of His Cross."

The second writer was separated by half a millennium from Thomas à Kempis. Furthermore, he is a staunch son of the Reformation. Still this writer had the same burden as the Spanish Carmelite. He was A.W. Tozer, who spoke as a prophet to the great city of Chicago in the mid-20th century. Concerning the Christian life Tozer said, "To be crucified means, first, the man on the cross is facing only one direction; second, he is not going back; and third, he has no further plan of his own."

CROWD

MEANING

The Greek word for "crowd," "throng of people," and "the common people" is *ochlos*. Predictably this word occurs frequently in the New Testament, in fact 174 times. Interestingly it is found mainly in the Gospels and in the Book of Acts.

This common Greek word has an interesting linguistic development. In its original form it referred to a crowd of people milling about, sort of an ancient version of a "mob scene." Later it came to mean a military troop, a lightly armed cavalry, platoon, or even a pack train. A further development gave the meaning to the word of a population, or the general populace. One thing is common in these varied usages: they all refer to a group of people.

In the New Testament the word *ochlos* always refers to a crowd of people. Sometimes they sided with Jesus against the Pharisees and Sadducees. But other times they were found in fickle opposition to the Lord.

BIBLE USAGE

Throughout the Gospels the crowd was usually on the side of Christ. His followers came from every part of Palestine, Galilee, Decapolis, Jerusalem, Judea, and the Transjordan (Matt. 4:25). Once along the Sea of Galilee a crowd forced Jesus to board a small boat in order to address them on the subject of the kingdom (13:2). Sometimes a crowd even prevented Him from eating (Mark 3:20).

It was the miraculous aspect of Jesus' ministry which attracted the crowds to Him. This moved multitudes to glorify God (Matt. 9:8). They viewed Jesus as a unique appearance in Israel (9:33). Not only did they marvel at His miracles, but they also understood and appreciated His teaching, that it too was unique in Israel (Mark 11:18). Wherever Jesus taught, multitudes came to hear Him (Matt. 7:28).

He extended His healing ministry to the multitudes, as there was no sense of elitism in Christ's compassion (12:15). In fact, Jesus was moved with compassion for the crowds around Him (9:36; Mark 6:34). He looked on them as if they were sheep without a shepherd, and extended to them the care of the Good Shepherd.

Another expression of the compassion of Christ toward a multitude came at the feeding of the 5,000 (Matt. 14:13-22; Mark 6:32-44; Luke 9:10-17; John 6:1-13). He saw to it that every individual was fed; there was no "mass movement mentality" in Jesus. Only after He had provided for them did He send the multitudes away (Matt. 14:22).

Jesus frequently contrasted the attitude of the multitudes with that of the Pharisees. The people received Him warmly, but the religious leaders were vicious in their opposition to Him. The Apostle John drew this contrast most plainly in his Gospel (John 7:11, 43-45; 12:12-13, 19).

But the crowds were not always favorable toward Jesus. Pilate perceived the condemnation of Christ to be the will of the crowd (Mark 15:15). At the beginning of Passion Week a crowd cried out, "Hosanna! [salvation is of Jehovah]" (John 12:12-13). But in the same city of Jerusalem a similar crowd shouted one week later, "Crucify Him! Crucify Him!" (Luke 23:4, 21; John 19:15)

Not only were the Jewish crowds fickle, for the same phenomenon is seen in the missionary journeys of the Apostle Paul. At Lystra in Asia Minor Paul and Barnabas healed a man. Immediately the people fell down and worshiped the missionaries, calling them Zeus and Hermes (Acts 14:13). But after Barnabas and Paul denied that they were deity the crowd turned on them and stoned them, leaving them for dead (14:19).

Popularity is pretty fragile. In fact it is a mixed blessing. The "darling" of the crowd today may easily become the "dunce" of the crowd tomorrow. This was the experience of Jesus and His apostles, and it is the experience of the church today. It is good for Christians to pledge sole allegiance to the Lord, and not to any crowd.

ILLUSTRATIONS

In the year 800 Alcuin, an English scholar from York, was serving at the court of Charlemagne. When Charlemagne accepted the crown of empire, Alcuin wrote the emperor this famous line: "The voice of the people is the voice of God."

Five hundred years later Archbishop Walter Reynolds preached at the ascension of Edward III to the throne of England. Here the Archbishop repeated Alcuin's line: "The voice of the people, the voice of God." Both Alcuin and the archbishop asserted that the popular acclaim of their respective rulers was the will of God. (Alas, the crowd is not always correct, and it does not often speak with divine insight.)

This reliance on the reason of the common man has been variously stated. Comedian George Burns said: "Too bad that all the people who know how to run the country are busy driving cabs and cutting hair." Simon Strunsky said: "If you want to understand democracy, spend less time in the library with Plato, and more time in the buses with people."

Before his election to the White House Abraham Lincoln said: "You can fool all the people some of the time, and some of the people all the time, but you cannot fool all of the people all of the time." Later he gave a specific example: "This country, with its institutions, belongs to the people who inhabit it. Whenever they grow weary of the existing government they can exercise their constitutional right of amending it, or their revolutionary right to dismember or overthrow it."

George Washington held to the same principle, but appended a qualifying statement when he said: "It is only after time has been given for cool and deliberate reflection that the real voice of the people can be known."

During the heyday of the Roman Empire the same idea was stated by Cicero, a philosopher-politician (106-43 B.C.): "The good of the people," he warned, "is the chief law."

Early students of business said, "Management is getting things done through people." Jesus did not see people as objects manufactured for manipulation, but rather as creatures capable of re-creation through God's grace. Swedish hymnwriter Carolina Sandell Berg saw this clearly and she wrote:

> Children of the Heavenly Father
> Safely in His bosom gather
> Nestling bird nor star in heaven
> Such a refuge ere was given.

CROWN

MEANING

The Greek word for crown is *stephanos*, which is reflected in our English names "Stephen" and "Stephanie." The word comes from the verb *stepho* which means "to encircle." A crown encircles a head. In Bible times these crowns were made out of laurel leaves, palm leaves, or sometimes metal.

Many dignitaries wore crowns. In paganism the priests were crowned as a badge of office. Similarly the religious oracles, such as the oracle of Delphi, were crowned as a mark of authority. Children marching in a religious procession wore crowns. Politicians also bore crowns, a foretaste of the royal crowns of Europe. From about 800 B.C. onward Olympic victors were crowned with laurel wreaths. Soldiers in ancient Sparta likewise were distinguished by crowns. On her wedding day a bride wore a crown. Sometimes even corpses were crowned. Thus a crown was a common symbol in the ancient world.

Though the predominant term for crown was *stephanos*, another crown was used to mark royalty. It was known as *diadema*, or "diadem." The *stephanos* marked achievement, but the *diadema* signified position. Both are found in the New Testament, though *stephanos* is much more common.

BIBLE USAGE

In the Gospels one crown stands out above all others. It is the crown of thorns which mocking soldiers pushed down on the brow of the Lord (Matt. 27:29; Mark 15:17; John 19:2). Palestinian thorns are not short, little, prickly briars such as we know. They are stiff, wooden spikes up to two inches long, which cut deeply into the flesh. The New Testament portrays this grotesque coronation as part of Christ's sacrifice on our behalf. He was crowned with thorns, in order that we may be crowned with glory.

A second usage of the word *stephanos* in the New Testament relates to heaven. The Book of Revelation carries several references to crowns. The 24 elders who surround the throne of God all wear golden crowns and white robes as a mark of the honor God confers upon them (Rev. 4:4).

The greatest crowned head in Revelation is the Lord Jesus Christ as He appears as Judge (14:14). He has earned the crown through His triumph over Satan. In another place Jesus is seen wearing many diadems, because He is entitled to the position of King of kings (19:12). Thus Jesus wears both the *stephanos*, because of His achievement on the cross, and also the *diadema*, because of His position in God's economy of the world.

It is also interesting that the Antichrist wears a diadem (12:3; 13:1). This is puzzling, but it need not worry us. The crowns which the Antichrist wears indicate that he is the titular head of Satan's kingdom on earth, a kingdom doomed to destruction.

Not only does the Lord Jesus wear a crown, but His triumphant servants will also be crowned. The Apostle Paul was pleased with the prospect of a crown, as is any serious saint. Spiritual victory earns for a victor an imperishable laurel wreath (1 Cor. 9:25). At the end of his earthly life Paul spoke of the "crown of righteousness" which was waiting for him and every other Christian (2 Tim. 4:7-8).

James wrote to Christians under attack. He promised them that their troubles would be crowned with eternal life when the Lord returns (James 1:12). This crown is a special reward for fidelity, according to the glorified Lord's message to the church at Smyrna (Rev. 2:10).

There is an unusual reference to the crown in the New Testament. Paul referred to converts through his ministry as his crown (Phil. 4:1). When the Lord returns, our crown and joy will be those we have won for Him (1 Thes. 2:19). Thus the old hymn is biblically correct when it asks, "Will there be any stars in my crown?" Something will be missing when the Lord evaluates the works of those who have never won souls for Him.

ILLUSTRATIONS

In the original Olympic games the winners of the races and contests were awarded laurel wreaths. Contemporary olympians win gold, silver, and bronze medals. There is one remnant of the ancient custom, however. Gold-medal winners of boxing events are crowned with gold laurel wreaths. This is the picture of the crown in the New Testament.

Another picture from the sporting world comes from horse racing. The winner of a horse race is often given a large wreath of flowers. This also pictures a winner's crown.

In the 17th century Francis Quarles (1592-1644) was a poet and chronicler of London. He wrote in his meditation on *Esther*: "He that had no cross deserves no crown." In 1669 William Penn wrote a pamphlet titled, "No Cross, No Crown." Both Quarles and Penn took the idea from the Lord Jesus, whose cross was a prerequisite for His crown.

The best-known hymn concerning the crowning of Christ was written by George Elvey (1816-93) in 1868. All stanzas start with "Crown Him": "Crown Him with many crowns. . . . Crown Him the Son of God. . . . Crown Him the Lord of life. . . . Crown Him the Lord of love." The entire hymn is a coronation anthem to the Lord Jesus Christ.

Thomas Kelly (1769-1854) wrote a meaningful hymn on the subject, one verse reading:

> The head that once was crowned with thorns
>   Is crowned with glory now;
> A royal diadem adorns
>   The mighty Victor's brow.

Other hymns speak of the crown which Christians earn by enduring hardships. One such hymn was written by John Samuel Bewley Monsell (1811-75). The first stanza of that hymn reflects the theme:

> Fight the good fight with all thy might,
> Christ is thy strength, and Christ thy right;
> Lay hold on life, and it shall be
> Thy joy and crown eternally.

Heads of state are still crowned. The coronation of Queen Elizabeth II of Great Britain took place in 1953. The Archbishop of Canterbury placed the coronet on her head as a symbol of her position under God.

But Christ needs no human dignitary or church official to crown Him. He is crowned by God as King of kings and Lord of lords. At his feet every knee shall bow and every tongue confess His lordship.

CURSE

MEANING

The Greek word for curse is *anathema*, and is transliterated in the English word "anathema" (a curse, or a statement of excommunication). Actually, the word comes from the Greek verb *anathemi*, "to set or place." It originally described an offering to God, but later took on the meaning of handing someone over to God for judgment.

In Oriental and Latin cultures the curse is still practiced. In them a gesture or formula is used to inflict harm on someone, or to wish someone harm. The procedure can vary from a mild questioning of character to a wish for damnation. In our language it is seen in profanity when someone is "damned" or "condemned to hell," though the speaker seldom intends that his curse should be carried out.

BIBLE USAGE

In the New Testament the word *anathema* is used sparingly. In fact there are only about a dozen occurrences. In each case the concept of a curse is used seriously, and thus clear insight into its importance can be deduced from surveying the texts.

The first appearance is found in the story of Christ's trial and crucifixion. When Peter was asked about his connection with Jesus, he denied it and cursed (Matt. 26:74; Mark 14:71). Peter called down a curse on himself in insisting that he did not know Jesus. It was something like this: "May I be accursed if I know this Man!" No wonder Peter was overcome with grief afterward (14:72).

The second appearance of the word is in the story of Paul's final arrest. He was being held in prison at Jerusalem, and a fanatical few took an oath and vowed to kill Paul. They called down a curse on themselves, if they ate before they killed Paul (Acts 23:14).

In Romans there is a moving mention of the word. The Apostle Paul was so burdened for his people, the Jews, that he could wish himself accursed, if by so doing the Jews could be saved (Rom. 9:3). This is an exact parallel to a prayer of Moses for Israel (Ex. 32:32).

In teaching about the Holy Spirit, Paul mentioned that nobody led by the Holy Spirit says that Christ is accursed (1 Cor. 12:3). By contrast he shows that the devil continually calls down curses on the Lord Jesus Christ. Therefore, anyone who curses Christ is moved by a satanic spirit, not by the Holy Spirit.

When Paul concluded his first Corinthian letter he mentioned another curse. Anyone who does not love the Lord is accursed (16:22). This curse is reinforced by the use of "Maranatha" ("O Lord come"). The apparent meaning is that the return of the Lord will reveal the curse which rests on those who do not love Him.

Not only are all accursed who do not love the Lord, but those who preach a false gospel are under a special curse. Paul aimed part of his Galatian letter at counterfeiters of the Christian message. Anyone who does not preach the same Gospel as Paul is accursed (Gal. 1:8-9). In this day of wildly divergent theologies, it is good to remember how important Gospel purity is.

As may be expected, the Book of Revelation also contains references to curses. In fact the final book of the New Testament explains the fate of all those who are previously cursed in the Scriptures. When Christ comes to reign in His kingdom the curses will be over. Christ bore our curse for us (3:13), so the new heaven and new earth will be free from the curse which sin brought on our earth (Rev. 22:3).

It is good to know that curses will come to an end when Christ comes to **100** reign. But until that time Satan spreads the virus of curses throughout the world.

Only when he is finally defeated will curses be condemned with him to the lake of fire.

ILLUSTRATIONS

Curses have become popular in our day. Whether on television or on the street, conversations are often peppered with curses. Increasingly even Christians are using curse words. Many years ago Dr. V. Raymond Edman, then president of Wheaton College, wrote a small tract with the title, "Minced Oaths." In it he reminded Christians of the danger of verbal carelessness. He emphasized the origins of such words as "golly" and "gosh" (God), and "gee" (Jesus). Alas, today many Christians are much more careless than Dr. Edman could have imagined.

As a boy I often went to hardware stores with my father. One of them had an intriguing sign next to the cash register. "Please don't swear," the sign said, "because profanity is a feeble mind trying to express itself forcefully." Anyone who has listened to the mindless repetition of profanity can understand the thinking behind that sign.

When the Revolutionary Army was being trained, General Washington heard some of his troops swearing. He immediately ordered the men to watch their language. His order is worth quoting: "The General is sorry to be informed that the foolish and wicked practice of profane cursing and swearing, a vice heretofore little known in the American army, is growing into fashion. He hopes the officers will, by example as well as influence, endeavor to check it, and that both they and the men will reflect that we can have little hope of the blessing of heaven on our arms, if we insult it by our impiety and folly. Added to this, it is a vice so mean and low, without any temptation, that every man of sense and character detests and despises it."

Perhaps the popularity of profanity can be seen in another incident. When General Von Steuben, a Prussian military genius, was training the American Army, he became very angry. In a rage he called to his aid: "Come here and swear at them for me in English."

Cursing and swearing are signs of a careless attitude toward God. As Christopher Morley put it: "To many people, the word 'God' is a formula on Sundays and an oath on weekdays."

In the Hebrew Old Testament the name Jehovah is represented by four letters, YHWH. It was so sacred that Jews would not throw away a piece of paper carelessly, lest the name of Jehovah might be written on it. Though this name appears more than 6,000 times in the Old Testament, a Jew never took it upon his lips. He thought it was too sacred a name to be profaned by speech.

The second commandment warns: "You shall not take the name of the Lord your God in vain" (Ex. 20:7). As one commentator put it: "To use God's name and to fail to perform one's oath is to call into question in reality the existence of God." Thus believers are warned not to play with the name of God.

DAY

MEANING

The Greek word for "day" is *hemera*. It is common in the New Testament, appearing about 360 times. In the Hebrew Old Testament "day" embraced both day and night. In New Testament times the Greeks calculated a day from sunrise to sunrise. (They did not have the benefit of modern clocks and watches.)

In the Scripture, as in our common use, the word "day" has several meanings. First, it refers to a normal 24-hour period, though it was measured according to the sun. Second, it refers to special days, such as our Sunday or Lord's Day, a day devoted to serving the Lord. Third, it may refer to a coming event, such as the Day of the Lord, when judgment will be meted out. Finally, "day" may also speak of a period of time, such as the "day of grace."

BIBLE USAGE

As mentioned above, the word "day" is capable of several interpretations in the New Testament. The following selection of Scriptures demonstrates the diversity in this common little term. Most frequently the word speaks of a calendar day: the disciples of John spent the day with Jesus (John 1:39). What an inestimable privilege that would be. A similar experience was shared by the Christians at Ptolemais (or Acre), when the Apostle Paul visited their otherwise undistinguished church (Acts 21:7). Jesus seems to have spent the early hours of many days in communion with His Father (Luke 4:42). In Acts we read of a daybreak which brought consternation to Roman guards, for they saw that Peter had escaped (Acts 12:18). Many and perhaps most of the references to "day" in the Scriptures deal with everyday affairs made extraordinary by the coming of the Lord.

There is also a figurative use of the word. Jesus referred to His earthly life as His day (John 9:4). Christians are known as "sons of the day," because their lives have been enlightened by the Lord (Rom. 13:12; 1 Thes. 5:5). The idea of summarizing life with a day is seen in today's language too: "In my day things were different."

The word is also used to connote special days, such as holidays. Though Jesus infused it with an entirely new meaning, the early Christians did observe the Jewish Sabbath Day. The Gospel narrative is often measured by weeks which began and ended with the Sabbath (Luke 4:16; John 19:31). After the resurrection of the Lord, Christians celebrated the first day of the week as the Lord's Day (Acts 20:7; Rev. 1:10).

Another usage of this word is the coming day of judgment. Jesus compared judgment day to the destruction of Sodom and Gomorrah (Luke 17:29-30). That day will be accompanied by a general resurrection (John 6:39-40). According to Paul, on the day of judgment, Christ will "judge the secrets of men" (Rom. 2:16). However, Christians will have confidence on that day (2 Thes. 2:2), though the earth will be dissolved by fire (2 Peter 3:12).

A day can also describe a longer period of time. "Days" can refer to the reign of a king (Matt. 2:1; Luke 1:5). Jesus and Peter mentioned the "days of Noah" (17:26; 1 Peter 3:20). Paul spoke of a day of salvation (2 Cor. 6:2) and an evil day (Eph. 6:13).

The most common use of the word "day" is the simple passing of time. Days are a yardstick by which we measure our lives. Jesus spent 40 days in the desert, being tempted by the devil (Matt. 4:2). People spent many days listening to Him speak (15:32). For Lot, days dragged by as he lived in the sinful city of Sodom

(2 Peter 2:8).

Days mark the divisions of our lives on earth. They are a concession to our captivity in time and space. When we live in eternity there will be no further need for days. Meanwhile we live by the alarm clock and the time clock.

ILLUSTRATIONS

"Time and tide wait for no man," according to an old English proverb. Living near the sea in England, we often experienced the truth of this statement. I can well remember one frustrating afternoon when the tide went out and left our little boat on a sandbank. We waited for the tide to refloat us, but the tide was in no hurry.

Jeremy Taylor (1613-67), Anglican bishop and prolific author, commented on time: "Enjoy the blessings of this day, if God sends them; and the evils of it bear patiently and sweetly: for this day only is ours; we are dead to yesterday, and we are not yet born to tomorrow." Time is precious and we must use it wisely.

What Taylor said eloquently others have said also. An anonymous writer said: "Our days are identical suitcases—all the same size—but some can pack more into them than others." Always a quick wit, Benjamin Franklin commented: "Dost thou love life? Then do not squander time, for that is the stuff life is made of." Another noted communicator, Jean-Jacques Rousseau, said: "The moment passed is no longer; the future may never be; the present is all of which man is the master."

There seems to be no end to comments on time. Abraham Lincoln said: "The best thing about the future is that it comes only one day at a time." Samuel Taylor Coleridge added: "In today already walks tomorrow."

Kay Lyons said: "Yesterday is a canceled check; tomorrow is a promissory note; today is the only cash you have—so spend it wisely." In the same vein John Wayne commented: "Tomorrow is the most important thing in life. Comes into us at midnight very clean. It's perfect when it arrives and it puts itself in our hands. It hopes we've learned something from yesterday."

Hendrik Willem Van Loon wrote this intriguing parable about time: "High up in the North in the land called Svithjod, there stands a rock. It is one hundred miles high and one hundred miles wide. Once every thousand years a little bird comes to this rock to sharpen its beak. When the rock has thus been worn away, then a single day of eternity will have gone by."

A great English pulpit orator, Joseph Parker, wrote a haunting hymn, because it speaks of the truth that our times are in God's hands. The first two stanzas set time in its proper place:

> God holds the key to all unknown
>   And I am glad;
> If other hands should hold the key
> Or if He trusted it to me,
>   I might be sad.

> What if tomorrow's cares were here
>   Without its rest!
> I'd rather He unlocked the day,
> And, as the hours swing open, say,
>   My will is best.

DEACON

MEANING

The Greek word for "deacon," *diakonos,* is similar to its English word. In its basic form the word means "servant." However, it also came to mean a church official, or "deacon." A similar word is *doulos,* which is translated "slave" or "bondslave," though this distinction is not rigorously observed.

The whole idea of serving was repugnant to the Greeks. It was simply not a dignified occupation for them. Plato asserted that ruling, not serving, is proper for a man. He reasoned, "How can a man be happy when he has to serve someone?" (Gerhard Kittel, *Theological Dictionary of the New Testament,* II, p. 82)

On the other hand, Jews found nothing inherently disdainful in service. They regarded service to a great master as a position of honor. Every rabbi had to learn one artisan's craft.

BIBLE USAGE

Christ lifted service to an entirely new level. To Him service was greatness, and He exemplified this in His earthly life. This too He taught His followers. The key New Testament text is Mark 10:45, which asserts that Christ came not to be served, but to serve, and to sacrifice Himself as a ransom for us.

In His Olivet Discourse the Lord equated service to others with service to Himself (Matt. 25:42-45). When the disciples sought to understand spiritual greatness, He pointed to service (20:26-28).

Service in the New Testament has many interesting connections. First, it refers to serving tables, which was probably the basic meaning of the word. Martha of Bethany was often serving tables (Luke 10:40; John 12:2). It is also mentioned in the story of the marriage at Cana (John 2:5, 9). In the early church this task was taken up by the first deacons (Acts 6:1-5).

A second aspect of the word is service to royalty. In the Parable of the Wedding Feast mention is made of the king's servants. They did the master's bidding without doubt or delay (Matt. 22:13).

The apostles considered themselves servants, and the word is often translated with "minister" in their epistles. For instance, Paul explained that he was a "minister" or "servant" to the church at Ephesus (Eph. 3:7). In writing to the Colossians Paul referred to himself as "a minister" of the Gospel (Col. 1:23). This has taken on a formal meaning since Paul's time.

Throughout the New Testament many were known as servants of the church, either local or universal. In Jerusalem the first deacons were servants of the church at Jerusalem (Acts 6:1-5). They took care of the needs of Hellenistic widows and guaranteed fairness in the distribution of food.

In writing to the troublesome church at Corinth, Paul singled out Stephanas as a servant of the church. The apostle urged Christians to be subject to such servants (1 Cor. 16:15-16). This is ironic, because the servant appeared to be a leader in that church.

Paul saw service to the church as preaching the Gospel and teaching Christians (Col. 1:25). This matches the statement he made earlier (1:23), and it also parallels the practice of modern ministers who serve their churches.

In his first epistle Peter likewise mentioned service to the church. Christians have spiritual gifts to help them serve one another. These gifts may be specific works or specific words of encouragement (1 Peter 4:10-11).

On a higher level Christians are called to serve God. No matter how important a preacher is, he is nothing more or less than a servant of God (1 Cor. 3:5). In the final analysis God should get the glory for all that is accomplished.

Similarly we are servants of the Lord Jesus. This is the basic work of every Christian, according to Paul (2 Cor. 11:23). Every believer is charged with serving the Lord (Eph. 4:11-12). For faithfulness in service Paul noted Epaphras of Colossae (Col. 1:7). The Apostle Paul knew that simple acts of service were top priority for all Christian workers (1 Tim. 4:6).

The word "deacon" crept into the New Testament as the church gained shape organizationally. When Paul wrote to the Philippians he distinguished between "overseers" (or "bishops" or pastors) and "deacons" (Phil. 1:1). In writing to Timothy Paul urged him to set high standards for deacons (1 Tim. 3:8, 12). Apparently women also fulfilled this role, for Phoebe is mentioned as a deaconess (Rom. 16:1).

ILLUSTRATIONS

The impact of the word "deacon" is simple. It is service. In "Pippa Passes" Robert Browning said: "All service ranks the same with God." (The truth of the statement could be questioned theologically, but it is good sense practically.)

Calvin, who was concerned with service to God, wrote: "No one gives himself freely and willingly to God's service unless, having tasted His Fatherly love, he is drawn to love and worship Him in return."

Luther expressed a similar sentiment about service: "A Christian man is the most free lord of all, and subject to none; a Christian man is the most dutiful servant of all, and subject to everyone." The paradox was more apparent than real, for every Christian is bound to serve others.

A spiritual father of the Reformation was the great mystic Master Eckhart (1260-1327). Of service he said: "If one were in a rapture like St. Paul, and there was a sick man needing help, I think it would be best to throw off the rapture and show love by service to the needy." When one recalls Eckhart's emphasis on ecstatic worship, his injunction to service takes on even more weight.

In the Victorian era there were many great preachers. One of them was the powerful Frederick William Robertson of Brighton, England. Of service he said: "It is not the possession of extraordinary gifts that makes extraordinary usefulness, but the dedication of what we have to the service of God."

Another famous preacher was the Puritan Henry Smith. He said of service: "We should not serve God by fits, as we used to pray when the night comes, to hear when the Sabbath comes, to fast when Lent comes, to repent when death comes; but the service of the heart is a continual service."
(See: *Slave*.)

DEATH

MEANING

The Greek word for death is *thanatos*. This is reflected in the English word, "*thana*tology" (the study of death and dying). The Greeks had a rather shadowy concept of death, that a person passed in some form into Hades. In Homer's writings there is virtue in hazarding death to achieve fame. Pythagoras saw death as the liberation of the soul from the body, a concept similar to Plato's. The Stoics saw death as part of the natural processes of life.

In the New Testament a whole new viewpoint on death emerges. It is seen as part of the Fall and is related to sin. The continuing existence of the soul is presupposed, and this is true of both believers, and unbelievers. Resurrection will usher in a time of judgment for non-Christians, but Christians will enter eternal life in the presence of the Lord. Annihilation is nowhere taught in the New Testament. Death is really the divesting of a decaying body and the entrance into another aspect of life.

BIBLE USAGE

Like a precious stone, the concept of death in the New Testament has many facets. The most fundamental is reference to physical death. In discussing the death of Lazarus, Jesus taught His disciples that death was like sleep (John 11:11-13). Paul perceived that death would never separate a believer from his Lord (Rom. 8:38). In fact for Paul death was an immense gain, because it would usher him into the presence of the Lord (Phil. 1:20-21).

It was among other things the death of Christ that united Him to the human race. After Peter confessed confidence in Christ's deity, Christ told the disciples of His impending death (Matt. 16:21). In the face of Calvary, Christ was grieved. His reaction to death revealed even more of His humanity (26:38). He died on our behalf and for our sins; He was our Substitute (Rom. 5:10). When Adam and Eve fell into sin, the death penalty was passed on them (5:12; 1 Cor. 15:21), and therefore we all need a Saviour to bear that penalty for us. Now we observe the Lord's Supper in remembrance of His death (11:26).

The death of Christ reinforces the connection between death and sin. Jews saw that death was the penalty for blasphemy, and on this basis they slew Jesus (Matt. 26:65-66). This seems to prove that the Jews understood Jesus' claim to divinity, for this is the reason they killed Him (Luke 24:20).

Many Christians have died for their faith in the Lord. They are known as martyrs. (Incidentally the word "martyr" comes from the Greek word for witness, *martureo*, so a martyr bears witness to Christ by his death.) Paul never forgot the martyrdom of Stephen, in which he played a part as Saul of Tarsus (Acts 22:4-5, 20). A special honor attaches to those who die for the Lord (Rev. 2:10; 12:11).

In addition to literal and physical death, the Bible also speaks of death in a figurative sense. The Apostle Paul often portrayed death as a person, an enemy of all people (Rom. 5:14; 6:9; 1 Cor. 15:21). Death is a foe that has been defeated by Christ. Death is a paper tiger with no teeth left.

Jesus often spoke of spiritual death. This means that people without Him are spiritually dead, cut off from God. But people who believe in Jesus are liberated from this spiritual death (John 5:24). Paul picked up this theme of spiritual life and death in his writings too (Rom. 3:23; Eph. 2:1-2). John spoke of conversion and regeneration as passing "out of death into life" (1 John 3:14).

There are in Scripture references to eternal death. This is real. People who ignore the warning of Scripture are destined for death in a spiritual sense (Rom. 1:32; 6:16, 21-23). People who do not repent from their sin will endure eternal death (2 Cor. 7:10). Only Jesus Christ can abolish spiritual death (2 Tim. 1:10; Heb. 2:14).

The logic of Scripture revolves around Jesus Christ. We were all spiritually dead and physically dying because of our sin. Jesus took on Himself a human body to die for us. Those who are attached to Him by faith live eternally. Thus physical death, for a Christian, is entrance into eternal life in a new dimension.

ILLUSTRATIONS

We use death in the same two ways that the Bible does. Obviously we speak of physical death, when a person is separated from his body, his possessions, his family, and his friends. We then give thanks to God for that person in a funeral or memorial service, and we bury or cremate the remains of his body.

We also speak of death in a figurative sense. A "dead end" street leads nowhere. When a telephone is out of service, the line is "dead." A person who sleeps deeply is "dead to the world." In each case life will return, but the appearance of death is there.

For a Christian physical death is no threat. Catherine Booth, the wife of Salvation Army founder General William Booth, said in her last words: "The waters are rising, but I am not sinking."

James Burns echoed the same sentiments when he said: "I have been dying for twenty years. Now I am going to live." George MacDonald added: "I came from God, and I'm going back to God, and I won't have any gap of death in the middle of my life."

The Puritans of the 17th century had a healthy view of death. Richard Baxter, famous Puritan author and pastor, said: "Rebirth brings us into the kingdom of grace, and death into the kingdom of glory."

Another Puritan writer, Thomas Watson, said: "We spend our years with sighing; it is a valley of tears; but death is the funeral of all our sorrows." Richard Sibbes said: "Death is only a grim porter to let us into a stately palace."

A Welshman among the Puritans was Vavasor Powell. Of death he said: "The fear of death is ingrafted in the common nature of all men, but faith works it out of Christians." He is also credited with the statement: "Pray that thy last days, and last works, may be the best; and that when thou comest to die thou mayest have nothing else to do but die."

William Gurnall was a lion among the Puritan preachers and writers. His works are full of the victory of the Lord. He dispelled any talk of fear when he said: "Let thy hope of heaven master thy fear of death. Why shouldst thou be afraid to die, who hopest to live by dying?"

A fitting conclusion to this brief glimpse of death is a statement by George Swinnock, another Puritan: "Death is never sudden to a saint; no guest comes unawares to him who keeps a constant table."

DECLARE

MEANING

"Declare" in the New Testament represents the Greek word, *anaggello*. It is also translated "report," "disclose," "announce," "teach," and "proclaim." We find echoes of this word in such English words as *"angel"* (one who brings a message from God), *"evangel*ism" (a declaration of the Gospel), and *"evangel*ical" (one who believes in the Gospel message). The common root in all these English words is *angel*, which is also the root of our Greek term *ananggello*, which means literally "to tell again."

In Greek society this word was used to describe a royal proclamation. It also came to describe the report of an envoy or ambassador. In pagan Greek religion it was used to characterize the statement of a god or an oracle. In each case there were some common elements. A message was received from a higher authority. That message had to be passed on unchanged. Complete, immediate compliance was expected. The messenger was respected only because of the message he brought.

BIBLE USAGE

It is helpful to see how this word is used in the Septuagint (Greek Old Testament). The Lord declared His message to Isaiah, who was commissioned to pass it on unchanged (Isa. 42:9). However, false gods have no ability to declare a message (44:7).

The greatest proclamation of all times was the coming of Christ. Even a Samaritan woman of poor reputation was aware of this proclamation (John 4:25). Believers are blessed above the angels of heaven, because they have heard the declaration of the Gospel (1 Peter 1:12). For this reason the apostles were eager to announce the coming of Christ and His saving work (1 John 1:5).

Great events in the life of Christ produced their own proclamations. When Jesus restored a lame man's legs, he immediately proclaimed the power of Christ (John 5:15). After Jesus rose from the grave, the grave guards went to "report" the Resurrection to their masters (Matt. 28:11). For the guards and their chiefs this was a disaster, but for believers it was the confirmation of all Christ had said. Now that is something to shout about!

At the end of His earthly ministry the Lord promised "another Comforter," the Holy Spirit. When the Spirit would come He would fulfill many functions, but one of the most significant would be His proclamation of the Lord Jesus Christ (John 16:13). Three times in this connection the Lord says that the Holy Spirit will "disclose," *anayyegello*, the facts of Christ's life and the faith they engender.

As the Apostle Paul toured the ancient world, he constantly declared the Gospel. Near the end of his active life he could say that he had privately and publicly declared all the truth of Christ (Acts 20:20). In the same address to the Ephesian elders Paul without embarrassment explained that he had declared to them "the whole purpose of God" (20:27).

Though the primary use of our word refers to the proclamation of the Gospel, it also refers to reporting on a human level. After conversion people often reported their past sins (Acts 19:18). The apostles reported to the Christians at Antioch that the Lord had drawn Gentiles to Himself (14:27). This was the basis of the discussion at the Council of Jerusalem, where the position of Gentiles in the church was clarified (15:4-21). When the Apostle Paul was cut off from his friends and all alone in Macedonia, Titus came to the lonely apostle and "reported" good news about the

Christians at Corinth (2 Cor. 7:7).

The word sometimes speaks of human reporting. However, the vast majority of appearances in the New Testament point to a proclamation of Jesus Christ. This word was originally used to describe the declaration of an ambassador on behalf of his sovereign. Thus a Christian is an ambassador who declares the glory of his heavenly Sovereign in the earth (2 Cor. 5:20).

ILLUSTRATIONS

In our day there is a great deal of discussion about the proclamation of the Gospel. Some say that we should simply show a Gospel presence in the world. As a battleship steams into troubled waters to show the presence of its nation's flag, so Christians should show their presence in the world. The Scriptures, however, indicate that we must not only show presence but also speak in proclamation of the Gospel.

Men of God in past generations have usually sided with proclamation rather than presence. Dwight L. Moody was known on both sides of the Atlantic as a powerful preacher. He said of proclaiming the Bible: "The best way to revive a church is to build a fire in the pulpit."

Another famous preacher, William A. Quayle, wrote convincingly about potent proclamation: "Preaching is not the art of making a sermon and delivering it. Preaching is the art of making a preacher and delivering that."

Focusing on the purpose of proclamation, Charles C. Colton claimed: "The Christian messenger cannot think too highly of his Prince or too humbly of himself." Here the focus falls on the ambassadorial role of the Christian proclaimer.

Leighton Ford, a contemporary evangelist, wrote the excellent little volume, *The Christian Persuader* (New York: Harper and Row, 1966). Of Christian proclamation Leighton Ford said: "When power goes out of the message it is because the Word has become not flesh, but words." In other words, the Gospel must come alive by the power of the Holy Spirit.

Along the same lines Thomas Betterton said: "Actors speak of things imaginary as if they were real, while you preachers too often speak of things real as if they were imaginary."

The old English Puritans also emphasized the primacy of proclamation. Christopher Nesse attacked the flowery form of preaching in his day. "Rhetorical flowers and flourishes, expressions without impressions in praying or preaching, are not true bread, but a tinkling cymbal to it." How often have young people in the church caused some pompous preacher to see the emptiness of his expressions and the poverty of his pretty prayers.

Thomas Cartwright (1535-1603) was a Reformation hero and a distinguished Cambridge professor of theology. He was thoroughly convinced of the need for proclaiming the Scriptures: "When the fire is stirred up and discovered it giveth more heat than when it is not, so the Word of God by preaching and interpreting maketh a greater flame in the hearts of the hearers than when it is read." (See: *Preach.*)

DEFENSE

MEANING

In the New Testament the word translated "defense" is *apologia*. It gives rise to such English terms as *"apologetic"* (a defense of Christianity), *"apologia"* (a defense of one's position or life), and *"apology"* (a formal excuse). However, "defense" in the Scripture carries no negative feelings of "defensiveness," but is a reasoned presentation of one's case.

In the ancient Greek culture this word spoke of a legal defense in which a defense advocate pleaded his client's case. It means a presentation of legal argument. Flavius Josephus (A.D. 37-100) was a Jewish writer who chronicled the history of the Jewish people. In his history of the Jews he spoke of their legal superiority and their means of substantiating a defense (*Antiquities,* book 4, chap. 8, sec. 15). He used the word "apologia."

BIBLE USAGE

In the New Testament the word "defense" has three distinct meanings. First, it describes a speech in defense of someone's actions. This phrase is most frequently used in the Book of Acts. Perhaps it is connected to Paul's Jewish legal training. When Paul was arrested in Jerusalem and accused of desecrating the temple, he made an eloquent public defense before the people of Jerusalem (Acts 22:1).

Appearing before Portius Festus, the Roman governor of Palestine, Paul gave a cogent defense of his Christian experience and expression (25:8). But though Festus was impressed with Paul, he felt that Paul had a slight case of religious mania, induced by study (26:24). Incidentally, this verse has been used by opposers of academic study among Christians from Paul's day until ours.

The third mention of Paul's defense is in connection with Herod Agrippa, a puppet Roman ruler. Agrippa permitted Paul to defend his actions, though he had no intention of agreeing with Paul. Neither did Agrippa intend to pass judgment on Paul, but rather sent Paul on to appear before Caesar in Rome (26:1, 32).

The second use of our word is action. A prisoner may appear before rulers to make his defense. When Agrippa and Queen Bernice visited Jerusalem, Paul was summoned before them. His appearance had the purpose of a defense (25:16). Such a profound defense of the Gospel seemed almost wasted on such biased judges as Agrippa and his consort.

Another active defense was Paul's appearance before the Emperor. Paul mentioned in the Second Epistle to Timothy his defense before Nero, who ruled (or misruled) in Rome, A.D. 54-68. Actually, during the first period of his reign Nero was quite reasonable, but afterward he became totally insane. Paul said that no one stood with him at his appearance before Nero (2 Tim. 4:16).

There is a third meaning of the word "defense" in the Bible. This is evangelism. Here we must remind ourselves of the basic meaning of the word, a reasoned explanation on behalf of some principle. This is seen especially in the writing of Peter. He urged Christians to always be ready to give an answer when they were questioned concerning their faith (1 Peter 3:15).

Paul likewise described his evangelistic ministry in terms of a defense. In writing to the Philippian Christians he portrayed his preaching as a "defense and confirmation of the Gospel" (Phil. 1:7). This was the primary emphasis of Paul's ministry (1:16).

The Lord instructed His disciples not to panic when they were summoned before rulers. In the very act of defense the Holy Spirit would give them the words to say (Luke 12:11). Some have taken this as an excuse for not preparing to preach. Professor Merrill Tenney used to say, however: "These words were intended not for preachers, but for martyrs."

The defense of the Gospel is not a negative, frightened effort to fend off attackers. It is a reasoned, articulate, Holy Spirit-empowered presentation of God's Gospel. This is the biblical meaning of defense.

ILLUSTRATIONS

There are many reasons why we need to present a reasoned defense of the Gospel. Indeed the Gospel is worth standing up for. We see this in the names of modern martyrs. Throughout the world people are paying for faith with blood. One such was the late Archibishop Luwum of Uganda. When Idi Amin unleashed an insane attack on the church of Christ many clergymen and laymen were slain. None was more notable than the Anglican Archbishop Janani Luwum, who was slaughtered for his faithfulness to the Word of God and the people of God.

Others defend the faith by a reasoned "apology." Clark Pinnock says the Bible idea of a defense is a response to the question: "Why are you a Christian?" We are not pandering to people's intellectual arrogance, but rather we are catering to their intellectual integrity.

According to popular evangelist Josh McDowell, "Some people say the best offense is a good defense, but I say unto you that the best defense is a good offense . . . a clear, simple presentation of the claims of Christ, and who He is" (*Evidence that Demands a Verdict*. San Bernardino: Campus Crusade for Christ, 1972, pp. 1-3).

This was my experience during high school days. Periodically our high school band was invited to play somewhere on Sunday. Each time I would excuse myself on the basis that Sunday is the Lord's Day and as such is set apart for worship. Never did this defense of Christian lifestyle hinder my progress in the band.

Professor Sir Norman Anderson is a distinguished scholar of Oriental law at London University and a former moderator of the General Synod of the Church of England. He is also a devoted disciple of Jesus Christ. He argued, in defense of the Gospel, that "Christianity is based on indisputable facts" (J.N.D. Anderson, *Christianity: The Witness of History*. Downers Grove: InterVarsity, 1970, p. 10).

One of my colleagues was engaged to debate with the head of the humanist society in a western Canadian city. They debated the validity of Christianity against the opposing view of humanism. At the end of the debate the university audience was asked to give their verdict. More than 90 percent voted that Christianity was more believable than humanism.

In a court of law there are three bases for defense. First, the lawyer may plead that his client was temporarily insane when the act was committed. Second, the prosecution may lose a case on a technicality. Finally, the sheer weight of facts may win the case for the defendant. But the best defense of the Gospel is the fact of Christ's life.

DEMON

MEANING

The Greek word *daimon* is similar to its English equivalent, "demon." The Greeks also had a word to describe the state of being demon-possessed, which was *daimonizomai*, "demonized."

As one remembers from the study of Greek mythology, the Greeks were almost obsessed with the idea of demons. To them "demon" meant any deity, any god. Demons were evil spirits who occupied positions between men and God. This equation of demons with deities is most clearly seen in the writings of Homer, where a demon was the human face of a god. Wherever a god meets man, that god was seen as a demon (Gerhard Kittel, ed., *Theological Dictionary of the New Testament*, II, p. 2).

These demons fulfilled three roles in Greek thought. First, they were intermediaries between God and men, sort of cosmic errand boys. Second, they controlled the destiny of people. Third, they possessed people and compelled them to do evil things.

In the New Testament demons are always evil; they are the opposite of angels who are always good. Throughout Scripture demons are actively involved in the affairs of people.

BIBLE USAGE

According to the New Testament demons engage in several injurious activities. First, they are the cause of many illnesses. (Note, however, that they are not the cause of all illness.) A man in the Gerasene cemetery was possessed by a "legion" of demons (Luke 8:27-30). When demons were driven out by the Lord, people were healed (Matt. 7:22; 10:8; Mark 1:24-27; 16:17; Luke 11:14; 13:32).

Second, demons were seen as the cause of unusual behavior. John the Baptist was accused of being controlled by a demon (Matt. 11:18). The same charge was leveled against Jesus by a Jewish crowd (John 7:20). Furthermore the Jewish leaders, especially the Pharisees, accused Him of being demon-possessed (8:48-52).

Third, demons are considered in Scripture to be the source of false doctrine (1 Tim. 4:1). This reveals the influence which demons could and can exert upon the thinking and speech of people. Paul saw this as a particular problem of the last times.

Fourth, demons are known for their many deceptions. They are called "deceitful spirits" by the Apostle Paul (4:1). They even seek to counterfeit miracles (Rev. 16:14).

Fifth, demons seek to rob God of the worship due His name alone. When people offer worship to idols they are actually worshiping demons (1 Cor. 10:20). The risen Lord in His revelation to John emphasizes the danger of worshiping idols and thus giving devotion to demons (Rev. 9:20).

The chief of the demons is a character called Beelzebub or Baal-Zebub. This relates him to Baal, "the lord of flies." He is the prince of demons (Matt. 10:25; 12:24; Mark 3:22; Luke 11:15-19). In the eyes of Jesus he was identical with Satan (Matt. 12:26; Mark 3:23). Thus demons are nothing more or less than Satan's personal emissaries.

In the Bible demons are not explained away as the fantasies of a bygone age. They are real, and their activities are motivated by none other than Satan. They are the cause of much evil in our world, and they also cause much illness. It is good to remember, however, that they do not cause all sickness and death. Some is just the result of the Fall, and some is caused by people's sins. It is also noteworthy that Jesus is far greater than the devil and all his demons (1 John 4:4).

ILLUSTRATIONS

Even the most casual observer of films must conclude that there is box office success to be found in the topic of demons. Several years ago *The Exorcist* and *The Omen* signaled a new trend toward the occult. This theme has been developed and dramatized further in the recent appearance of *The Gremlins,* which portrayed demons as cute and cuddly little animals. Though the films are fictional, their theme is real. The Bible clearly presumes the existence of demons.

Dr. Timothy Warner of Trinity Evangelical Divinity School has broad experience in counseling the "demonized." He prefers the term "demonized" to the less specific "demon-possessed." Dr. Warner speaks of three tiers of reality. The highest level is God. On the second level is a realm called in Scripture "the heavenlies." The third level is the earth. Within the heavenlies are angels (good) and demons (evil). These spiritual creatures influence life on the earth, though their activities are limited by God.

In his counseling with "demonized" people Dr. Warner experiences real confrontations with Satan. He also finds disbelief among some evangelical Christians, who wish to deny the existence of demons and even Satan. There are two major errors concerning the demon world, according to Dr. Warner. The first is to ignore demonic forces. The second mistake is to be paralytically fearful of Satan and satanic forces.

In Europe we discovered many manifestations of demonic power. During the mid-'60s it was estimated that there were 85,000 occultic functionaries in Germany. They outnumbered medical doctors, and were twice as numerous as Protestant pastors. Peter Mayer of Switzerland's Beatenberg Bible Institute claimed that more than 3 million West Germans were involved in occultic activities.

When Teen Challenge began its work among German young people, the leaders found that many of their contacts had been lured into drug dependence by the occult. In fact, addiction often was the external symptom of an occultic connection.

Richard Jensen reported in *The Wall Street Journal* (Dec. 10, 1974) that up to 3 million Britons were involved with the occult. Jensen said that exorcism in England was "quite literally an everyday affair."

During 1975 the Vatican released a major statement on the occult. Pope Paul VI urged Catholics to be vigilant against demonic activity. The Pope pronounced the subject of demons "a very important chapter in Catholic doctrine that ought to be studied again, although this is not being done much today" (*New York Times,* Dec. 18, 1975).

In France there is also a lively interest in things demonic. More than $7.5 million per year is spent on sorcery. One lawyer claimed to have cast spells on the troublesome husbands of wealthy widows. In Paris there is one priest for every 5,000 Parisians, one doctor for every 514, but one sorcerer for every 120. It is small wonder, then, that up to 100,000 Frenchmen per day visit fortune-tellers.

DEPART

MEANING
The Greek word for "depart" is *aperchomai*. It is a combination of two words: *apo* (from or away from) and *erchomai* (to come or go). The combination verb is found 115 times in the Greek New Testament.

One might think that this is just a "secular" word with little spiritual impact, but it is usually connected to "discipleship" in the New Testament. The concept implicit in the word is one of radical separation. Jesus used it in commanding a radical break with sin. It is used to describe the sending away of all which militates against spiritual life. It even describes the disappearance of the first, fallen Creation in the Book of Revelation.

Though this word appears to be a vehicle of history which tells who goes where and when, in practice it describes radical separation as a by-product of discipleship.

BIBLE USAGE
In its most basic form this word means to "go away" or "depart." It speaks of returning to one's home (Matt. 8:21), or of leaving a group of people (16:4). Often the phrase, "he went away" or "departed" is used (Acts 10:7; 28:29). This is simply a statement of fact.

Sometimes the word carries a concept of purpose. Jesus used the examples of one going to gather a harvest (Matt. 13:28), and going to sell one's possessions (13:46). An unfaithful servant went away and hid his talent (25:18, 25). An executioner went away and beheaded John the Baptist (Mark 6:27). On a happier note healed lepers went away and showed themselves to the priest (Luke 5:14).

Another use of the word is in leaving a person. An angel left Mary after making the momentous announcement of Christ's birth (Luke 1:38). Angels also departed after proclaiming Christ's birth to the shepherds in the fields around Bethlehem (2:15). After Jesus healed a demon-possessed man in the region of the Gerasenes, the townspeople begged Him to go away (8:37).

A second major use of the word is figurative, as when a disease "goes away." A leper was cleansed and his leprosy went away miraculously (Mark 1:42; Luke 5:13). The great woes of Revelation likewise will pass away (Rev. 9:12; 11:14).

A third aspect of the word focuses on a destination, the place into which a person "goes away." Jesus often went out into the desert to pray to His Father (Mark 1:35). He also spoke about the crowds which went out into the desert to hear John the Baptist (Luke 7:24).

In speaking of destination the word is also used to describe "going home." A Syrophoenician woman went home and found her daughter healed by Jesus (Mark 7:30). After Zacharias' priestly service he returned to his home (Luke 1:23).

For Jesus home meant Galilee, and He seemed to accomplish most of His ministry there. This becomes obvious to a tourist in Israel, who finds most of the scenes of Christ's life in Galilee. Often He went home to Galilee (John 4:3; Matt. 28:10).

The Apostle Paul was frequently under way during the early years of his ministry. He saw his final trip to Rome as a stage on the journey. In fact as he wrote the Roman epistle he planned on traveling onward to the edges of the Empire in Spain (Rom. 15:28).

A fourth aspect of the word emphasizes one's purpose in going out. A report about Christ's miraculous ministry went throughout all of Roman Syria. This resulted in the people bringing all sorts of invalids to Him for healing (Matt. 4:24). The disciples entered the Gospel story as they went away from their jobs to follow Jesus (Mark 1:20). In fact, the Pharisees lamented, "The world has gone after Him" (John 12:19).

Though the word *aperchomai* is basically a common word which carries forward the narrative of the New Testament, it also has a deeper significance. It often refers to the obedient activities of the disciples of the Lord.

ILLUSTRATIONS
To be separated from sinful practices "is often used as the synonym for discipleship," according to the scholarly *Theological Dictionary of the New Testament* (II, p. 657). In fact, in earlier days people often preached on the subject of "separation" as a means of presenting essentials of discipleship.

Dr. V. Raymond Edman wrote a book titled, *The Disciplines of Life* in which he laid down principles of Christian living. "Discipleship is discipline," he wrote. "The disciple is one who has come with his ignorance, superstition, and sin, to find learning, truth, and forgiveness from the Saviour. Without discipline we are not disciples."

"Attachment to Christ results in detachment from the world," according to Mirmer. In a more picturesque vein the Scottish pastor and theologian Samuel Rutherford wrote: "If you were not strangers here, the hounds of the world would not bark at you."

Dr. Sherwood Wirt worked for many years with Billy Graham as editor of *Decision* magazine. From this evangelistic standpoint Dr. Wirt wrote: "Separation equips the Christian with the weapons of his warfare. Instead of getting him out of the world, it gets him into the world more effectively. The sharper the separation, the greater the dependence upon Christ and the more effective the involvement."

The expression of this separation can be seen in the writings of Malcolm Muggeridge, an elder statesman of British journalism and a free-lance Christian journalist. Concerning separation from the world he wrote: "I have inevitably and increasingly been driven to the conclusion, almost against my own will, that for a West European whose life and background and tradition are in terms of Western European Christian civilization, the only answer lies in the person and life and teaching of Christ."

As one may guess, the Puritans were "experts" in separation. George Swinnock said: "The world is therefore a purgatory, that it might not be our paradise." William Gurnall added to the idea: "Temporal good things are not the Christian's freight, but his ballast, and therefore are to be desired to poise, not load, the vessel."

"Let us use the world, but enjoy the Lord," Thomas Adams wrote.

Hymn-writer James Rowe caught the idea of separation in his familiar hymn:

Earthly pleasures vainly call me; I would be like Jesus;
Nothing worldly shall enthrall me; I would be like Jesus.

He has broken every fetter, I would be like Jesus;
That my soul may serve Him better, I would be like Jesus.

DESTROY

MEANING

The Greek word for "destroy" is *apollumi*, and it appears 90 times in the New Testament. The word *apollumi* comes from a basic Greek word, *ollymi* meaning "to destroy." The word *opollymi* is translated "ruin," "destroy," "kill," "lose," "perish," and "die." It embraces such significant themes as death, lostness, and perishing.

In early Greek writings the word *apollumi* spoke of eternal loss or annihilation, which reflected the Greek concept of the afterlife. Later the word came to mean "violent injury" or "destruction." Finally in the writings of Plato it is mentioned: "Evil is everything that corrupts [*apollyon*] and destroys, and good is that which preserves and strengthens" (*Republic*). Among the destructive forces which Plato mentioned were sickness for the body, rot for wood, and rust in iron (Colin Brown, editor, *Dictionary of New Testament Theology*, I, p. 463).

BIBLE USAGE

The New Testament uses the word in several connections. Most obviously it refers to physical death. Herod planned to kill the Baby Jesus (Matt. 2:13). The Pharisees repeatedly sought an occasion to "destroy" Jesus (12:14; Mark 11:18). Ultimately, of course, they succeeded in their death plot against Jesus (Matt. 27:20), but their victory was temporary for the Resurrection reversed it.

Jesus cast many demons out of possessed people, and some of them begged Him not to "destroy" them (Mark 1:24; Luke 4:34). Apparently demons regarded expulsion from a possessed person to be the end of their earthly existence and activity. In a real sense, then, Jesus partially destroyed the work of the devil (1 John 3:8).

The first meaning is literal death or destruction, whereas a second meaning speaks of figurative loss or death. Jesus told many parables to illustrate the meaning of being lost. Nowhere is this more clearly stated than in Luke 15. First one sheep out of a flock of a hundred is lost, and the shepherd seeks for the sheep until it is found (Luke 15:3-7). Second, a young woman loses one out of ten coins which she has saved as a dowry for her coming marriage, and she seeks the coin until she finds it (15:8-10). Finally, a father loses his son. The "prodigal" squanders his father's money and his own youth and his grieving father considers the boy to be dead (15:24, 32). In this triplet of parables "lost" embraces animals, things, and people. It is a picture of a person without the Lord, and it is a good, biblical word, used to describe an unsaved person.

Closely connected with the second, figurative use of our word is its third meaning. This is the doctrinal teaching that people without Christ are "lost." John made frequent reference to this in his Gospel. He quoted the teaching of Jesus that people without Him are perishing or lost (John 3:16). He recorded Jesus' statement that Judas perished (17:12). However, John placed heavy emphasis on the teaching that no one whom Jesus saves will ever perish (10:28; 17:12).

Paul knew that rejecters of the Gospel are doomed to perish (Rom. 2:12; 1 Cor. 1:18). Those who have rejected Jesus Christ are perishing, and they will be lost as long as they reject the Gospel (2 Cor. 2:15; 4:3). The Antichrist will be doomed to destruction in the last days (2 Thes. 2:8). God is not pleased that any should perish, but those who reject the redemption offered in Jesus will certainly perish (2 Peter 3:9).

It must be noted, however, that perishing in Scripture does not refer to annihilation. A person who rejects Christ will not simply cease to exist. The Bible teaches that he or she will endure eternal, conscious punishment (John 5:29; Rev. 14:9-11).

Peter adds a wonderful truth to our consideration of this sad word. He tells us that our faith is refined by trouble, as gold is refined by fire. The difference is that gold ultimately perishes, but faith survives (1 Peter 1:7).

ILLUSTRATIONS

Literature contains many references to lostness. In *Paradise Lost* John Milton sets the tone of his epic with this beginning strophe:

> Of Man's first disobedience, and the fruit
> Of that forbidden tree, whose mortal taste
> Brought death into the world, and all our woe,
> With loss of Eden. (Book 1, line 1)

The remainder of Milton's work paints in dismal colors the dismal experience of the human race in rebellion against God.

Going from the sublime to the ridiculous an American folk song by Percy Montrose speaks of a lost loved one:

> In a cavern, in a canyon,
> Excavating for a mine,
> Dwelt a miner, Forty-niner,
> And his daughter Clementine.
> Oh, my darling, oh, my darling,
> Oh, my darling Clementine!
> Thou art lost and gone forever,
> Dreadful sorry, Clementine.

Though the lost daughter has been trivialized by generations of school children, her loss was serious to the songwriter.

The biblical concept of man's lostness is captured in the majestic prose of *The Book of Common Prayer*. In the Prayer of General Confession which precedes the celebration of the sacrament, the congregation prays: "We have erred, and strayed from Thy ways like lost sheep."

One of the most famous literary pictures of lost mankind was written by Alighieri Dante (1265-1321) in his famous treatise, *The Inferno*. He affixed the following inscription above the gates of hell: "All hope abandon, ye who enter here."

The Scriptures always connect sin with lostness and destruction. Even Benjamin Franklin caught this when he said: "Sin is not hurtful because it is forbidden, but sin is forbidden because it is hurtful." On the same theme, an unknown author paraphrased "The wages of sin is death" (Rom. 6:23) by adding: "Even in this age of inflation, the wages of sin remain the same."

Another description of this lostness comes from the pen of W.R. Matthews: "The essence of hell is complete separation from God, and that is ultimate disaster."

No theme in the Scripture is more difficult to explain than the lostness of people without Christ. An Overseas Missionary Fellowship missionary, Dick Dowsett, wrote a masterful exposition of this truth with the title: *God, That's Not Fair!* (Sevenoaks, Kent: OMF Books, 1982). In his introduction Dowsett said: "People long for the assurance of heaven, but they do not want to face up to the horrors of the alternative destination. But the two stand or fall together" (p. ix).

DEVIL

MEANING

The two biblical words for "devil" are both known to English speakers. The first is *diabolos*, which occurs 37 times in the New Testament. Literally it means "one who throws between," or "the slanderer." The idea of "throwing between" is seen in our idiom of "throwing a monkey wrench in the works." In Greek literature and in the Greek Old Testament the term meant "slanderer."

A second word for the devil is *satanas*, and it is transliterated in our English word "Satan." This name appears 36 times in the New Testament. It is taken directly from Hebrew and refers to a traitor (1 Kings 11:23-25), to an adversary (Zech. 3:1), and to the tempter who moved David to number Israel (1 Chron. 21:1).

BIBLE USAGE

In discussing the biblical references we shall treat the two names, *diabolos* and *satanas*, separately. *Diabolos* speaks most often of "the slanderer." It was he who tempted Jesus in the desert and tried to trip Him up (Matt. 4:1, 5, 8, 11). Hell is his home, and those who reject the Lord will be consigned to the devil's domain. By influencing Judas the devil also organized the betrayal of Jesus (John 13:2).

As the devil dogged the footsteps of the Lord on earth, so he continually opposes the children of God today. He turns anger into sin (Eph. 4:26-27). Likewise he flings the fiery arrows of temptation at Christians (6:11-13). It is his aim to trap Christian leaders and cause them to sin (1 Tim. 3:7). His attacks are especially aimed at weak Christians (2 Tim. 2:26). As a roaring lion he prowls around pouncing on unsuspecting saints (1 Peter 5:8). Those who are unsaved are called "children of the devil" (John 8:44; 1 John 3:10).

In his other guise as Satan, the devil is equally unsavory. He is the enemy of God and all who belong to Him. He incites people to do evil acts (Acts 5:3; 1 Cor. 7:5). He was the motivator of Judas (John 13:27). At his command people fall ill (Luke 13:16). He hindered the Apostle Paul in his work of evangelism (1 Thes. 2:18). Satan sows false beliefs among believers in the Lord (1 Tim. 5:15). It is Satan who spurs on the persecution of Christians (Rev. 2:13). He even manipulated Peter to misunderstand the message of the Cross (Matt. 16:23). In essence this was a satanic effort to turn Jesus aside from the Cross, and thus it was similar to His temptation in the desert.

At the end times Satan will have one last fling. He will send the Antichrist to lead astray as many as possible (2 Thes. 2:9). He will transform himself into an angel of light to deceive Christians and the world (2 Cor. 11:14). During the Millennium Satan will be imprisoned and freed again (Rev. 20:7). Finally Satan will be defeated (Rom. 16:20). The risen Lord identified Satan as the devil (Rev. 20:2).

Satan or the devil has but one aim in the world, to thwart the work of God. In the Old Testament he opposed Israel at every turn. During Christ's time on earth Satan turned his full opposition against Him. He moved the religious Pharisees to reject the Lord. He also sought to turn aside the followers of the Lord whenever possible. He blinds the eyes of people who cannot recognize that Jesus is Lord. Constantly Satan seeks to stir up trouble in the church. The great comfort of Christians, however, is this: Satan is not infinite; he is limited. The Lord Jesus Christ is greater than the adversary, and ultimately Jesus Christ will be triumphant. Furthermore, Christians who resist the devil drive him away in Jesus' name.

ILLUSTRATIONS

Literary warnings against the devil abound. Elizabeth Barrett Browning said, "The devil's most devilish when respectable." Samuel Chadwick, a great English preacher, said, "The one concern of the devil is to keep us from praying." To which the noted Puritan Joseph Hall added, "Satan rocks the cradle when we sleep at our devotions."

One of the most devious devices of Satan is to convince people that he no longer exists, or to trivialize himself as an old goat in a red costume, with a forked tail. Clate Risley, a late Sunday School advocate, said: "God is not dead, but neither is Satan." Ironically, in a particularly satanic attack, Dr. Risley was shot down and killed in front of his office.

Along the same lines Ronald Knox wrote: "It is so stupid of modern civilization to have given up believing in the devil when he is the only explanation of it."

Agnostic philosopher and writer Aldous Huxley said, "Few people now believe in the devil; but very many enjoy behaving as their ancestors behaved when the fiend was a reality as unquestionable as his Opposite Number."

William Shakespeare sprinkled his writings with references to the devil, and surprisingly most of them were biblically acceptable. "The devil can cite Scripture for his purpose," the bard wrote. This surely agrees with the experience of Christ in His temptation. Referring to the deceptive genius of Satan, Shakespeare said, "The devil hath power to assume a pleasing shape."

The Puritans also made frequent reference to the devil. "The devil," according to John Trapp, was "the great peripatetic." To this Thomas Adams added, "Saul has slain his thousands, and David his ten thousands; but Satan his millions." The method of satanic stealth was outlined by John Robinson: "He sometimes slanders God to men, as to Eve. . . . sometimes men to God, as Job. . . . and continually, man to man."

The resistance against Satan is a Christian's primary task. Puritan Arthur Dent said: "The first limit is [Satan's] nature, for he is not able to do anything than that which his natural disposition will permit and suffer. The second limit is the will of God, for he can do nothing against the will of God."

Martin Luther is reputed to have flung an inkwell at the devil and the stain is still shown to tourists at Wartburg Castle. Of combat against Satan, Luther said: "The best way to drive out the devil, if he will not yield to the texts of Scripture, is to jeer and flout him, for he cannot bear scorn."

Remembering that Jesus called Satan the "father of lies" (John 8:44), Paul Matlock framed this telling sentence: "Satan deals with confusion and lies. Put the truth in front of him and he is gone."

"Satan is only God's master fencer to teach us to use our weapons," said Samuel Rutherford. Paul reminds us that our weapons are spiritual and not physical or military, and that by them the strongholds of Satan are smashed (2 Cor. 10:4-5).

DISCIPLE

MEANING

"Disciple" is a word which Jesus attached to His followers. It is a translation of the Greek word *mathetes*. It comes from the root *manathano* meaning "I learn." So a disciple is a learner. The Greek root is seen in our word *"mathe*matics." In essence, then, a disciple is one who learns from another person.

The emphasis on discipleship in Greek is not formal school learning, but rather fellowship with the teacher. It is seen in two situations. First, it refers to the followers of a certain philosopher. They derived not just information from their teacher but also inspiration. Disciples learned the teacher's entire outlook on life, not just the facts which he taught. Second, discipleship had a religious context. It was seen in the pre-Christian mystery religions and in the Greek schools of the Epicureans and Stoics.

Discipleship involved two principles. First, it meant that the disciples had fellowship with their teacher. They lived with him as Jesus' disciples lived with Him. Second, disciples carried on the tradition of their teacher. After he died they taught the same things that he did. Disciples were the main means of perpetuating teaching in the ancient world, since many great teachers wrote no books.

BIBLE USAGE

The most important use of the word "disciple" refers to Jesus; His disciples were collectively called the Twelve. He empowered them and sent them out to preach and heal (Matt. 10:1; 11:1). They were with Him day in and day out, so that sometimes they had to eat on the run (12:1). Jesus had little time without His disciples, because they followed Him nearly everywhere He went (Mark 6:1). They were sometimes contrasted with the Pharisees' followers (Matt. 15:1-2).

Because the disciples of Jesus were learners, they sometimes failed. They did not always comprehend Jesus' sayings (Mark 5:31; 10:24; Luke 8:9). Neither did they realize Jesus' power (Mark 6:35-36, 52). They were not always clear about Christ's role (Mark 8:27), or use the power that was theirs (9:14-18).

Despite their inadequacies, the disciples were chosen by the Lord to carry on His earthly ministry. In fact they were charged with the task of making disciples of all nations (Matt. 28:19). They were not only told to preach the Gospel (Mark 16:15), but also to produce disciples as Jesus had done.

A second group of disciples in the New Testament was the disciples of John the Baptist. As soon as Jesus appeared, some of John's disciples followed Jesus (John 1:35-37). There is no hint of jealousy on John's part, and Jesus assumed that this transferal of allegiance was completely normal.

The disciples of John were more rigorous than those of Jesus, as John's disciples fasted regularly (Matt. 9:14; Mark 2:18). They remained true to John the Baptist after he was imprisoned (Matt. 11:2). They kept John informed concerning the teaching of Jesus (Luke 7:18). They also cared for the burial of John after Herod beheaded him (Matt. 14:12).

Faithful Jews considered themselves to be disciples of Moses (John 9:28). However, Jesus pointed out that true disciples of Moses also followed Him. Some Jews even became disciples of Pharisees (Matt. 22:15-16).

In the Book of Acts the early church is called collectively "disciples." Their number increased markedly after Pentecost, and this put pressure on the relief work of the church (Acts 6:1). After Saul of Tarsus' Damascus Road conversion, he was received into the fellowship of the disciples (9:19). At Antioch the disciples were given a new name, that of "Christians" (11:26). They were noted for the joy which they exhibited to all (13:52).

Throughout New Testament times the followers of Jesus were seen as disciples. This term extended to embrace all who believed in Him. It was not limited to those who had known Jesus during His earthly life, but rather it referred to all who comprised the true church.

ILLUSTRATIONS

"Discipleship" was not always as popular as it is today. This must be remembered in reading the following quotation from G. Campbell Morgan, a pastor of London's Westminster Chapel: "The word 'disciple' signifies a taught or trained one. Disciples are those who gather around this Teacher [Jesus] and are trained by Him. They are seekers after truth, not merely in the abstract, but as a life force. The condition of discipleship was clearly declared by the Lord Himself: 'If ye abide in My Word, then are ye truly My disciples' (John 8:31, ASV)."

Dietrich Bonhoeffer's life was marked by violent times in Nazi Germany. He spoke about discipleship in this moving way: "Happy are they who know that discipleship simply means the life which springs from grace, and that grace simply means discipleship."

The classic book on the subject of discipleship is A.B. Bruce's *The Training of the Twelve* (New Canaan, CT: Keats Publishing, Inc., 1979). Professor Bruce summarized the training of Jesus' disciples in this sentence: "The most important part of the training consisted in the simple fact of being for years with such a One as Jesus" (p. 544).

Dr. Robert Coleman wrote a classic, *The Master Plan of Evangelism* (Old Tappan: Fleming H. Revell, 1963). In summarizing Christ's plan for evangelism, Dr. Coleman refers to discipleship: "Yet we must recognize that the kind of manpower that Christ needs does not happen by accident. . . . Wherever [Christians] are, they must be reached and trained to become effective disciples of our Lord."

A master disciple-maker was Dawson Trotman, founder of the Navigators. In a compendium titled *Discipleship* (Grand Rapids: Zondervan, 1981), Dawson Trotman describes the need of our hour: "I belive it is an army of soldiers, dedicated to Jesus Christ, who believe not only that He is God, but that He can fulfill every promise He has ever made, and that there isn't anything too hard for Him" (pp. 180-181).

Writing from the context of Latin America, Pastor Juan Carlos Ortiz of Buenos Aires said: "Discipleship is not a communication of knowledge or information. It is a communication of life. . . . Discipleship is more than getting to know what the teacher knows. It is getting to be what he is. That's why the Bible says we are to make disciples. That is much more than just talking to them, or winning them, or instructing them. The making of a disciple means the creating of a duplicate" (Juan Carlos Ortiz, *Disciple*. Carol Stream: Creation House, 1975).

DISPENSATION

MEANING
Though the word "dispensation" is somewhat obscure in English, its Greek equivalent is quite common. The Greek word involved is *oikonomia*, which is reflected in our English word "*economics*." Literally, the word "economics" means "law of the house" or "house order." But in recent years it has come to mean the management of money.

Greek writers about the time of the New Testament used *oikonomia* to describe the job of a household manager. In practice Greek slaves often managed the homes of wealthy landowners. Later this term came to describe the general work of administration.

In the New Testament, and later, under the church father Ignatius, the word took on a theological twist. It came to mean the plan of God for redeeming people. The *King James Version* used the word "dispensation," but the best Greek lexicons indicate that the meaning of this word is "administration," "stewardship," "commission," or "management."

BIBLE USAGE
In its basic form *oikonomia* referred to an office of administration. The Apostle Paul spoke of his heavy responsibility because the stewardship of the Gospel had been entrusted to him (1 Cor. 9:17). This conveyed upon him the highly prized title of a minister of the Gospel, which conferred the right to admonish Christians (Col. 1:28). The same idea is emphasized in Ephesians 3:2, where he speaks of the "administration" (NIV) of the grace of God. In declaring the Gospel Paul was administering the grace of God, though he frequently emphasized that God is the sole Source of that grace.

Paul also used the word to describe God's sovereign order of salvation. All of human history found its fulfillment in the coming of Christ, and all of history flows from His coming. This is seen in Christ's creation of His church (1:10). In the same epistle Paul speaks of the "administration of the mystery" of the Gospel (3:9). This means that Paul was trusted with a Gospel message which had been planned in the mind of God and hidden until Christ came. Now it is the glad Gospel proclamation, the open secret of salvation by grace through faith.

The Ephesians passages are the heart of the New Testament teaching about the "dispensations" or "administrations" of the Gospel. They teach the essential fact that Jesus Christ entered the world to bring salvation. His coming introduced a whole new period in human history. The apostolic messengers were thus pioneers and administrators of a new covenant. The emphasis of the New Testament falls not so much on that time period but on the plan of God which was carried out in all history and culminated in Christ's coming.

One further use of our word is found in Paul's first letter to Timothy. There the apostle warns his younger colleague about the dangers the "dead-end streets" of myths, endless genealogies, and speculation. These simply raise more questions than they answer, and furthermore they do not contribute to "the administration [*oikonomia*] of God which is by faith" (1 Tim. 1:4). The danger seems to be that people may become sidetracked with secondary issues, and thus miss the main point of the Gospel.

It is good to remember that "dispensation" or "administration" does not refer in Scripture to a period of time, but rather to God's dealings with people. So a "dispensation" is a building block in God's total structure of salvation.

ILLUSTRATIONS

The study Bible author Dr. C.I. Scofield popularized a scheme of interpretation called "dispensationalism." It presents a helpful breakdown of Bible truth, dividing God's plan of salvation into seven biblically logical periods. Each one is marked by a covenant between God and His people.

The first is the covenant of the Garden of Eden. In Genesis 1:28; 2:15-17 God makes an arrangement with Adam. In exchange for God's blessing Adam is required to do five things: propagate the race, subdue the animals, till the soil, dress the garden, and abstain from eating from the tree of the knowledge of good and evil. This is the dispensation of Innocence.

Second, following the Fall, God establishes the Adamic covenant. Adam is caused to work for his food, and childbearing becomes painful. Satan is cursed and condemned to ultimate defeat. However, God also promises a coming Redeemer (Gen. 3:15), the Lord Jesus Christ. This is the dispensation of Moral Responsibility.

Third, after the Flood God established the Noahic Covenant. God promises that the earth will never be destroyed again by flood (Gen. 9:16). The mechanism for creating order in the world is human government so this is the dispensation of Human Government.

Fourth, God focuses His covenant blessings on one family, that of Abraham (12:1-3). This is the Abrahamic Covenant, which promises blessing on Abraham and his descendants. Here is the dispensation of Promise, for God has promised to use Abraham as a vehicle for worldwide blessing.

Fifth, in the wake of Israel's exodus from Egypt, God establishes a covenant with Moses. The Law of God is given on Mount Sinai, whereby Israel is to be rewarded for obedience and punished for disobedience (Ex. 19:5). Here is the dispensation of Law.

Sixth, God's gracious covenant is established with His people, the church. These have been saved by Jesus Christ, who fulfilled on their behalf all of the demands of the Law (Gal. 3:13). Pentecost, the birthday of the church, ushers in the dispensation of the Church. The Church Age will continue until believers are snatched away in the Rapture (1 Thes. 4:13-18), after which will follow the Great Tribulation (Rev. 7:14), the Millennium (19:11, 17; 20:2-7), and finally God's eternal kingdom (20:4). This ends the dispensation of the Church.

Seventh, when the Lord has defeated Satan and cast him into the lake of fire, the Kingdom Age will dawn. In the kingdom Christ will rule supremely as King of kings and Lord of lords. Here the triumph prophesied in the Garden of Eden after the Fall (Gen. 3:15) will reach its fulfillment.

Dispensationalism is only one of several methods of interpreting the Scriptures and tracing God's plan through the centuries. But it appears to be consistent with the teaching of Scripture and helpful in understanding both the work of God in the past and also in the present and future. No system gives a better interpretation of the prophetic passages of the Old Testament.

DIVORCE

MEANING

"Divorce" seldom occurs in the New Testament, but where it does the Greek words are *apoluo* (to divorce, set free, or dismiss) and *apostasion* (to write a certificate of divorce).

The first word, *apoluo*, is a general word. It is a term also applied to discharge from the military, and thus was meaningful in the military state that was the Roman Empire of the first century. In addition it referred to release from jail, and to setting a debtor free.

The second word, *apostasion*, was a specific word meaning the bill of divorcement, or the decree. The Septuagint Greek Old Testament used this word to describe the document given to a woman when her husband sent her away because of indecency (Deut. 24:1, 3). Throughout the history of Israel such divorces became common, almost as frequent as they are today. But God looked on the practice of easy divorce as being distasteful and dishonoring to His name. Twice God referred to divorce as treachery, and then added through the pen of Malachi: "I hate divorce" (Mal. 2:14-16).

BIBLE USAGE

The words *apoluo* and *apostasion* speak of divorce. In the Jewish-Christian context this usually meant that a man divorced his wife without any recourse on her part. There are three principles involved. First, divorce was permissible when a husband found some natural, moral, or physical defect in his wife. Second, a husband had to give his wife a bill of divorcement, which gave her legal status and protected her position in society. Third, a man who divorced his wife could never marry another (D. Martyn Lloyd-Jones, *Studies in the Sermon on the Mount* [Leicester: InterVarsity Press, 1969-70], pp. 258-259). So this procedure was no license to consecutive polygamy, where one man marries successively younger, or more beautiful, or richer women.

The New Testament gives some rather clear teaching on the subject of divorce. When engaged Mary conceived Jesus, Joseph's immediate reaction was to divorce her (Matt. 1:19, marg.). An angel of the Lord appeared to Joseph in a dream to stop the planned divorce (1:20).

In the Sermon on the Mount Jesus discussed the subject of divorce. It is apparent that Jews had perverted the practice of divorce by sending away a wife for almost any imaginable or unimaginable cause. Jesus warned that free and easy divorce and subsequent remarriage was adultery. In fact, Jesus only allowed divorce if a mate had committed adultery (5:31-32).

The parallel passage in Mark indicates that a woman who divorced her husband and remarried also committed adultery (Mark 10:12). It was almost unheard of for a Jewish woman to divorce her husband, but Salome (the wicked sister of Herod the Great) did so. Divorce was common among Greeks and Romans. This can be deduced from Paul's writing to the Corinthians (1 Cor. 7:10, 13).

In the Sermon on the Mount Jesus taught His standards to His disciples. Later on in His earthly ministry the hardhearted Pharisees asked about divorce. Jesus introduced the exception clause, permitting divorce in the case of adultery. However, He indicated that most divorces arose from the hardheartedness of people (Matt. 19:3, 7-9). From pastoral experience one would have to agree with Jesus. Today many divorces are the result not of adultery, but of hardheartedness embellished with the legal term "incompatibility."

With the exception of adultery (either heterosexual or homosexual), divorce appears to be unacceptable according to New Testament standards. The question of remarriage is even more difficult to answer. Until recent times few Christian churches had given their blessings to the remarriage of divorced people.

ILLUSTRATIONS

Over the past twenty or thirty years divorce has become almost as common as marriage. At first it was a Hollywood fad in which movie stars' lives imitated the films they made. But soon this was seen as the easy answer to the hard questions in marriage. Before long one marriage out of every two or three ended up in the garbage can of divorce.

From the screen and the street, divorce moved into the high offices of government. In the '70s a President's wife had experienced divorce, and by 1980 it was a President who had gone through divorce. Even notable Roman Catholic figures divorced their spouses, contrary to the dictates of their church.

In the '80s it was learned that witches' circles around the world were praying to Satan for the breakdown of Christian marriages. The high incidence of divorce among Christians and even spiritual pacesetters proved the effectiveness of these perverse prayers.

Concerning the subject of divorce Billy Graham said: "Divorce is an easy escape, many think. But, in counseling many divorcees, the guilt and loneliness they experience can be even more tragic than living with their problem."

Walter Wangerin, a Lutheran pastor from Indiana, wrote a perceptive article on divorce for *Christianity Today* (May 18, 1984) under the title, "On Mourning the Death of a Marriage." He began: "The only natural death a marriage may suffer is the natural death of one of its partners. Every other death of a marriage is *un*natural.

"Divorce announces that marriage's unnatural death.

"The divorced marriage was put to death.

"Murdered."

After this startling introduction Wangerin enumerated seven possible contributing factors to such a murder: the starvation of service to one another, suffocation of communication, stab wounds of accusation, poison of unspoken suspicion, plague of adultery, blows of anger, and drowning in alcoholism. Just some of these are sufficient to kill a marriage.

Writing in the *Chicago Tribune* (January 21, 1984) Russell Baker titled his commentary, "Divorce and an early grave." According to Baker, "Divorce seems to cause heart disease, cancer, cirrhosis of the liver, pneumonia, high blood pressure, and accidental death." Then he added: "Every divorce lawyer [should] be tattooed with the words: 'Warning: Divorce is Dangerous to Your Health.'"

Sponsored by the Amherst H. Wilder Foundation, sociologist Daniel P. Mueller examined the long-term effect of living in a one-parent family. Researchers interviewed 1,368 men and women, 19 to 34 years old, in St. Paul, Minnesota. Children of one-parent families were less likely to finish high school than the two-parent offspring. They were also more likely to be divorced, have a child out of wedlock, endure mental or emotional problems, and use hard drugs (*USA Today,* October 1, 1984).

DOCTRINE

MEANING
The Greek word translated "doctrine" or "teaching" is *didache*. It comes from the verb *didasko* (I teach), and is reflected in the English word "didactic" (material or methods used to teach). In fact, the early church called its body of doctrine, "The Didache."

To pre-Christian Greeks *didache* and *didasko* referred to the imparting of information. This was the understanding which Homer placed on the words. Later on, the same word was used to describe the teaching of skills, on-the-job training. Finally it came to mean demonstrating a theory in order to prove its validity. (In earlier times geometry students were compelled to learn the proofs for theorems.)

In the New Testament the word *didache* has a rather specific meaning. It is that body of teaching which Jesus and the apostles passed on to Christians. This is the doctrinal basis of the Christian church.

BIBLE USAGE
Primarily the word *didache* refers to doctrine. In the Gospels heavy emphasis falls on the doctrines, or the teachings, of Jesus. According to Matthew the crowds were amazed when they heard Jesus' teachings (Matt. 7:28; 22:33). In fact, the authority with which Jesus taught set Him off from the Jewish scholars, the scribes (Mark 1:22). A further reason for this distinction lies in the source of Jesus' teaching, as He derived it directly from God the Father (John 7:16). It was this authoritatively distinctive teaching which aroused the anger of the Pharisees (18:19).

Following their Master, the disciples and apostles also provided authoritative teaching. The early church was founded firmly on their teaching, and this built the basis for regular worship (Acts 2:42). Much as Jesus' teaching had angered the Pharisees, so the Sanhedrin forbade the apostles to teach in Jesus' name (5:28). It was this teaching which moved some pagans to ponder the deity of Christ (13:12). Because of this teaching Paul was summoned before the court in Athens (17:19).

Salvation was linked to compliance with this teaching (Rom. 6:17). Consequently the teaching of the apostles became the standard of Christian belief (16:17). Such tenets of teaching were passed on in worship services (1 Cor. 14:26). When Christians lived consistently with their teaching, they "adorned" the doctrine by their very lives (Titus 2:10). The teaching concerning Christ's deity was the benchmark of Christian belief, and whoever denied it was rejected by true Christians (2 John 9).

By the end of the first century certain false teachings had intruded into church life. Earlier the teaching of Balaam had subverted the position of israel and produced treachery against God's people (Rev. 2:14; Num. 31:16). In the same context the risen Lord condemned the teaching of the Nicolaitans, who engaged in idolatry and immorality (Rev. 2:6, 15). Others had embraced the idolatrous and evil teachings of Jezebel, the pagan wife of Israel's King Ahab (2:20-24; 1 Kings 16:31).

Not only did the word *didache* refer to the body of teaching, but also to the act of teaching. Teaching was viewed by Paul as being a gift profitable for the church, more profitable than tongues (1 Cor. 14:6). It was the solemn responsibility of faithful preachers such as Timothy (2 Tim. 4:2).

Teaching plays an important part in the New Testament. This is not because one is saved by learning great masses of teaching. Nor is one necessarily more spiritual because of learning doctrine. However, the teaching of biblical truth should produce a greater appreciation of God's Word and God's way.

ILLUSTRATIONS

The teaching of Jesus is eternally important for us as Christians. Dr. Carl Henry in his delightful way said: "Jesus clothes the Beatitudes with His own life." In other words, what Jesus said and what He did were identical.

The same idea was emphasized by H.G. Taylor, who wrote: "Christ came not to talk about the beautiful light, but to be that light—not to speculate about virtue, but to be virtue." Here again the complete agreement between Christ's teaching and life is emphasized.

Speaking to a group of young people, William Lyon Phelps said: "I call the attention of you . . . to Jesus, the greatest Leader, the most proficient Teacher, the most absolutely right Person the world has ever known. I tell you that the only way this world can be saved is by Jesus." Only by knowing Christ and thus knowing Christ's teaching can one be saved, in the eyes of this great American preacher.

Archibald Alexander, a 19th-century American Presbyterian preacher and theologian concluded: "All my theology is reduced to this narrow compass—Christ Jesus came into the world to save sinners." Again the emphasis falls on the saving nature of Christ's works and words.

In the generations after the ascension of Christ, Christian teaching soon took form. One of the earliest statements of teaching was "The Didache," taken directly from the Greek word here under consideration. Though this document was not found until 1056, its influence was traced as far back as the fourth century. It gave definite Christian teaching on the way of life and the way of death. A concise commentary on baptism, fasting, and the Lord's Supper was included, as was heavy emphasis on the second coming of Christ.

Another early standard of faith was "The Apostles' Creed." Some trace its beginning back to about A.D. 215. It was mainly a commentary on the Trinity and the person and work of Christ. Thus it is an excellent example of Christian teaching (*didache*).

At the time of the Reformation new doctrinal standards came into being. Lutheran beliefs were declared in the "Augsburg Confession," which was written by Luther's friend Philip Melanchton in 1530. The Reformed faith found expression in John Calvin's *Institutes of the Christian Religion* (1536), and later in the Presbyterian "Westminster Confession" (1643).

When liberal theology swept the world, Bible-believing Christians in America published a series of twelve booklets with the overall title, *The Fundamentals* (1910-15). These affirmed faith in essential doctrines of Christianity, including the sinfulness of people, salvation by grace, the atonement of Christ, and the authority of the Bible. The result was the Fundamentalist movement which stood for the Gospel amid the darkness of liberal theology.
(See: *Teach.*)

DOOR

MEANING

The Greek word for "door" is *thura*, and if one pronounces this word correctly it sounds quite close to our word *door*. The relationship becomes even clearer when one considers the German words *tuer* (door) and *tor* (gate). In Old English *tor* meant a rocky peak which served as a lookout for intruders; many such *tors* are still seen in the English counties of Devon and Cornwall.

The Greek word *thura* is so basic that its meanings can almost be assumed. There are five basic uses of this word. First, it refers to the door of a house, though often this was little more than a doorway without any door. Second, it referred to an outer door leading from the street to a courtyard, or even the door of a walled sheepfold. Third, it was the door to a room, or a prison cell. Fourth, the gate to a city or a temple court was often a large wooden door. Finally, the door could mean simply a rough-hewn entrance to a cave.

BIBLE USAGE

In biblical use the door has two distinct emphases. First it is a literal door, fulfilling one of the above-mentioned functions. The whole city gathered at the door to Simon Peter's home when his mother-in-law was healed by Jesus (Mark 1:33). Later a house was so filled that people could not even enter its door to hear or be healed by Jesus (Mark 2:2).

Likewise the outer door to the courtyard is also mentioned in Scripture. After Peter was released from prison he stood at the outer door to the house of Mary, mother of John Mark (Acts 12:13). This is a much more positive picture than the other one, of Peter standing outside the door during the trial of Jesus (John 18:16).

The door to a room is mentioned in the Sermon on the Mount, when Jesus taught that one should go into his closet and close the door so that he could pray secretly (Matt. 6:6). In Jerusalem a prison door or gate was sprung wide open by an angel when Peter was released (Acts 12:6-10).

In Jerusalem the most well-known gate was the entrance to the temple. At the Beautiful Gate John and Peter healed a lame man (3:2). When Paul was arrested and dragged from the temple, the gates were slammed shut (21:30).

There are three "door miracles" in the Book of Acts. Peter and John were released from prison (5:19). Peter was released from jail (12:6-10). And Paul and Silas were freed from prison in Philippi (16:26-31).

The word "door" also has figurative meanings in the New Testament. Jesus taught that entering His kingdom was like passing through a door (Luke 13:24). The same emphasis is found in Revelation 3:8.

Paul spoke of opportunities to serve the Lord as open doors. It reminds one of the inaccurate old saying, "Opportunity knocks but once." At Ephesus Paul found a wide open door of service (1 Cor. 16:9). The same was true of his preaching mission in Troas (2 Cor. 2:12). From his first imprisonment Paul prayed that a door might again be opened to serve the Lord (Col. 4:3).

In John's Gospel Jesus used many word pictures to describe Himself. He said He was the Bread of life (John 6:35, 48), the Light of the world (8:12), the Resurrection and the Life (11:25), the Way, the Truth, and the Life (or the True and Living Way; 14:6), and the Vine (15:5). However, He also called Himself the Door to the sheepfold. As the Good Shepherd He alone grants entrance to eternal life (10:1-2, 7).

The Scriptures speak of opportunity, the occasion of all time which grants entrance to eternal life. Ultimately we who trust Christ shall pass through gates of pearl into heaven, the city which never passes away.

ILLUSTRATIONS

Doors always create the first impression for good or ill. When I became minister of a church in Bristol, England the church was a stately, hundred-year-old stone building with faded purple doors. Few noticed the church, but everyone noticed the doors. Mercifully, the caretaker painted out the purple and covered it with a more suitable shade. Despite their color, those doors have opened to salvation and spiritual fellowship for five generations of people.

Not far from that church was another door. This one had a small brass plaque on it which said: "Her Majesty's Prison." (This did not indicate that it was Queen Elizabeth's personal prison, but that it was one of Britain's top security lockups.) For the inmates and their families, that door meant solitude and shame.

Another famous door was located in Wittenberg, Germany. On October 31, 1517 Martin Luther nailed a list of "Ninety-Five Theses" for debate on the massive doors of Wittenberg Cathedral. This was the blow that began the Reformation and shattered the Roman Catholic Church's unity.

Doors speak of opportunity. Miguel de Cervantes (1547-1616) put this line in the mouth of his tragic character Don Quixote: "When one door is shut, another opens."

The American writer Ralph Waldo Emerson (1803-82) gave the idea a slightly different slant: "If a man can write a better book, preach a better sermon, or make a better mousetrap than his neighbor," theorized Emerson, "though he build his house in the woods, the world will make a beaten path to his door."

For some the word door means not opportunity but death. In *The Duchess of Malfi* John Webster (1580?-1625?) wrote: "I know death hath ten thousand several doors, for men to take their exits."

A similar dismay affects the conclusions of Edward Fitzgerald (1809-83) in his *Rubaiyat of Omar Khayyam:*

> Myself when young did early frequent
> Doctor and Saint and heard great argument
> About it and about: but evermore
> Came out by the same Door as in I went.

What a different tone infuses the Christian's view of a door. A Rector of Bemerton, George Herbert (1593-1633), wrote these lines about worship in the church:

> The church with psalms must shout,
> No door can shut them out:
> But above all the heart
> Must bear the longest part.

Christians throughout the ages have loved singing about heaven. They have woven great hymns around this theme, among which there is none greater than Frederick A. Blom's (1867-1957) glorious Swedish song:

> He the pearly gates will open,
>   So that I may enter in;
> For He purchased my redemption,
>   And forgave me all my sin.

EARTH

MEANING

In Greek the word for the "earth" is *ge*. We see it in many English words such as "geography" (the study of the earth and its inhabitants), "geology" (the science of the earth's crust and all its rocky formations), "geophysics" (the branch of science which deals with the physics of the earth).

In Bible times the word earth had several basic meanings. It was the place where people lived, and thus it was distinguished from the rest of the universe. (Of course, the space programs have enlarged people's living and littering areas.) In the Old Testament the earth was the opposite of the heavens, both of which were created by God. Thus the earth is of spiritual significance only because of its Creator and His concern for its creatures.

BIBLE USAGE

In its most basic form the earth stands for soil. Jesus emphasized this in His Parable of the Sower and the seed which fell onto four different kinds of soil (Matt. 13:3-9, 18-23). He also taught a profound truth, using the soil as an object lesson. When a seed falls into the soil and germinates, its fruitfulness is multiplied (John 12:24). Jesus taught that this is also true of people. Those who sacrifice themselves multiply their spiritual influence.

Not far from the meaning of soil is the second meaning of earth, that of the ground. At the feeding of the 4,000, people sat on the ground (Mark 8:6). Sick people fell to the ground (Luke 9:42). When Jesus prayed in Gethsemane His tears and His sweat dripped on the ground (Luke 22:44). The ground is here the floor of the great outdoors.

From our knowledge of English, we know that "earth" or the "land" also has other implications. The land was the seashore (Mark 4:1), as when one "lands" a boat (John 21:8; Acts 27:39, 43). The "earth" or "land" also has political overtones. The New Testament account speaks of the lands of Judah (Matt. 2:6), Israel (Matt. 2:20), Gennesaret (Matt. 14:34), Judea (John 3:22), and Egypt (Acts 7:36).

Jesus used the Jewish picture of earth as a counterbalance to heaven. He said that heaven and earth would pass away before His word would (Matt. 5:18). In the Lord's Prayer (or the Disciples' Prayer) we are taught to pray that the will of God may be accomplished without resistance on earth (Matt. 6:10). When Christ was born in Bethlehem, both heaven and earth rejoiced (Luke 2:14).

Paul perceived that Jesus Christ was Creator of heaven and earth (Col. 1:16). The same truth is repeated when the writer of Hebrews quoted a psalmist (Heb. 1:10, Ps. 102:25). Peter said that the Lord made the heaven and earth, and He will cause them to be destroyed by fire in final judgment (2 Peter 3:5, 7, 10).

Finally the earth stands for the inhabited globe, which represents the total world population. Christians are the "salt of the earth," and they are here to postpone God's judgment upon the earth (Matt. 5:13). When the Lord judges the earth He will be looking for believers, people of faith (Luke 18:8). As Jesus prayed to His Father, He could declare that He had glorified the Father on the earth (John 17:4).

The apostles likewise focused on the earth as the inhabited globe. Paul saw that his mission embraced the whole inhabited earth, and his enemies knew this too. In fact, they said he had turned the world (earth) upside down (Acts 17:6, KJV). Paul likewise predicted the judgment of the whole earth (Rom. 9:28).

There should be no surprises in this brief survey of passages relating to the earth. In most cases we have the same usages in English. However, it is good to be reminded that the Lord is Lord of the whole earth.

ILLUSTRATIONS
The Christian view of the earth is distinctive, because we believe that the earth was created by God. In fact, an African chief caught this truth and said: "No rain, no mushrooms. No God, no world."

A similar story was told about a Russian farmer. When the commisar came to call, he asked the farmer about the potato crop. "The potatoes reach to the foot of God," declared the farmer proudly.

"Comrade," chided the commisar, "We are Communists and we do not believe in God."

"Right," responded the farmer. "No God, no potatoes."

Louis Pasteur, eminent French scientist and inventor, underscored the importance of God's Creation: "Posterity will someday laugh at the foolishness of modern materialistic philosophy. The more I study nature, the more I am amazed at the Creator."

Augustine, a famous bishop of Hippo, loved to laud the Creator. He said: "Thus does the world forget You, its Creator, and falls in love with what You have created instead of with You."

Like others of his colleagues, former astronaut Frank Borman expressed his belief in God: "The more we learn about the wonders of our universe," he claimed, "the more clearly we are going to perceive the hand of God."

Thomas Carlyle, a historian of the 19th century, shared Borman's view: "I don't pretend to understand the universe," declared the Scottish writer. "It's a great deal bigger than I am."

Leigh Nygard spoke in phrases familiar to our times. He said: "The Engineer of the universe has made me a part of His whole design." Along the same line the German writer Johann Friedrich von Schiller could add: "The universe is a thought of God."

William Francis Gray Swann likewise saw the Creation as a reflection of God's handiwork: "When I view the universe as a whole, I admit that it is a marvelous structure; and what is more, I insist that it is of what I may call an intelligent design."

Copernicus thought that the sun was at the center of the universe. But he *was* right when he wrote: "How could anyone observe the mighty order with which our God governs the universe without feeling himself inclined . . . to the practice of all virtues, and to the beholding of the Creator Himself, the Source of all goodness, in all things and before all things?"

Once I had the privilege of visiting Stuart Hine, translator of the hymn "How Great Thou Art." He told of a life of missionary travel throughout Eastern Europe, and he described the glorious scenery he had seen. As he originally put it in the song's first stanza:

O Lord when I in awesome wonder
Consider all the works Thy hands have made,
I see the stars, I hear the mighty thunder,
Thy power throughout the universe displayed.

EAT

MEANING

The Greek word for "eat" is *esthio*, which in its various forms occurs 65 times in the New Testament. This one word includes everything from taking nourishment to wild, gluttonous feasts.

In ancient literature eating and drinking were glamorized. Even the pagan gods had wild feasts at which they gorged themselves on delicacies. Who can forget the stories of Romans who ate their fill and then vomited to make room for more? Even in Tudor England eating was encrusted with crude customs.

On the other hand, Jews often linked eating to worship. The Jews carefully distinguished between clean and unclean meats (Lev. 11; Deut. 14:3). "Eating" also meant the enjoyment of divine blessings (Job 21:25). To "eat" of the Lord, means to partake in His blessings (John 6:52-57). Therefore "eating" has both a literal and a figurative meaning.

BIBLE USAGE

One of the main emphases of the New Testament is on what people ate. John the Baptist ate locusts and wild honey (Mark 1:6). This was the simple diet of a common person who lived off the land.

Frequent references are also made to the Israelites who ate manna from the Lord (John 6:31, 49). Manna in the New Testament is called "bread out of heaven" to show the miraculous nature of God's provision (6:31, 49).

The most basic source of nourishment was bread, which often symbolized the total nutritional needs of people (6:26; 2 Thes. 3:12). People went out to "earn their bread." The flower children of the 1960s spoke of money as "bread."

There were also people in Bible times who ate nothing but vegetables. Such people often viewed this as a spiritual discipline (Rom. 14:2). But Paul taught that such abstinence did not assure spiritual growth (Rom. 14:20-23).

Eating also has a spiritual significance. Belief in the Lord Jesus is equated with eating the Bread of Life (John 6:53). Christians partook of the Lord's Supper as a sacred act, and there was serious punishment for those who partook of the Lord's Supper while harboring sin (1 Cor. 11:23-30).

To the New Testament writers, eating was basically the satisfying of natural needs, but it also had a social meaning. To eat with someone indicated friendship with him. Jesus ate with turncoat tax collectors who helped the Roman occupying force. For this He was condemned by hidebound Jewish officials (Matt. 9:11; Mark 2:16-17). The Pharisees accused Him of being a friend of sinners and tax collectors, which He was and is.

By the same token, Jesus also ate with some Pharisees (Luke 7:36). While at a Pharisee's table a woman came in and anointed Jesus' feet (7:38), and His host immediately criticized Christ for contact with a sinful woman (7:39). Jesus used this incident to teach the love which arises out of forgiveness (7:40-50).

On the night of His betrayal Jesus ate with His disciples. This meal has become known as the Last Supper. There Jesus shared fellowship with His betrayer, Judas Iscariot (Matt. 26:21). At the same time He also instituted the Lord's Supper, which we still celebrate (Matt. 26:26-30).

Even heaven is compared to the pleasures of eating. In glory we shall eat of the tree of life (Rev. 2:7). When Christ has taken His bride home there will be the marriage feast of the Lamb (Luke 22:30).

Eating, like so many other words in the Bible, has two meanings. First, it refers to the basic act of nourishing our bodies. This is physical eating. Second, it refers to enjoying the pleasures of the Lord. This is spiritual eating.

ILLUSTRATIONS

Soon after the Berlin Wall was built we toured East Berlin. All the way a spy was close on our heels. Late in the afternoon we visited an exhibition of Marxist achievements. The spy leaned over our shoulders as we wrote in the guest book. One of my colleagues summarized the experience thus: "What Communism has achieved is great indeed. However, Jesus said: 'Man shall not live by bread alone, but by every word which proceeds from the mouth of God'" (Matt. 4:4). Our unwanted chaperone disappeared after seeing that sentence.

Eating has been used as a means of withstanding persecution. In some countries where Christians are strictly forbidden to conduct home Bible studies, a group of people sits around a table laden with food. They study their Bibles until a party functionary comes. Then they slip their Bibles into a drawer and start eating.

Another example of a special meal occurred at our first home. We had just purchased a house in Christchurch, on the scenic south coast of England. A group of Swiss students came to spend the weekend with us, almost before we were settled. They were new Christians and we taught them the basics of the Christian life. On one Saturday evening we held a most informal Communion service in our living room. In some ways that event consecrated our home, and untold blessing flowed from it.

Some meals are memorable for other reasons. While teaching at a small Bible college in Germany we were required to eat with the students. As if by design, the cook served raw fish on the evening of my appointment. It was there that I learned the missionary's prayer: "Lord, I'll get it down. You keep it down."

As an evangelistic missionary there were many occasions to test the above-mentioned prayer. One summer we worked in a rural area of Germany. For seven weeks we conducted children's evangelistic meetings, and many came to the Lord. Each evening we greeted the meal with expectation or dread. Dread was reserved for the nights when raw meat (steak tartare) was on the menu. Here again our prayer of thanksgiving was the missionary's prayer.

One other experience lingers from those years overseas. I had been teaching at an Anglican (Church of England) theological college. On one occasion I was asked to preach at the weekly Communion service. Though the liturgical service was foreign to my Baptist background, I enjoyed the beautiful hymns and readings. Then came the time to distribute the elements. Together with a tall, handsome African pastor I helped distribute the wafer and the cup. Finally the beloved principal of the college came to the Communion rail, and I handed him the wafer with the words: "George, Christ's body was broken for you." Then we shared the large chalice in memory of the Lord's shed blood on our behalf.

ELDER

MEANING

In the Greek New Testament the word for "elder" is *presbyteros*. This is seen in the name of the *Presbyter*ian Church, a church led by governing and teaching elders. In the New Testament an "elder" acquired the title by one of two means: either he was older, or he was a recognized leader in the church.

In ancient Greek literature elders were older men, venerated because of their age. This is the use found in Homer. By the time that Sparta developed into a world power, however, an elder was the president of the college of magistrates.

Among the Jews, elders had a twofold meaning. They were community leaders, as Moses informed them before initiating the Exodus (Ex. 3:16-18). During the period of the Judges and the Kings the elders became the political governors of Israel. In New Testament times the Jewish elders were mainly religious leaders, and together they formed the Sanhedrin.
(See: *Council.*)

BIBLE USAGE

In the New Testament the word "elder" has three basic uses. First, it refers to older men. When Peter quoted the Prophet Joel, he referred to "old men," that is, elders (Acts 2:17). Here the emphasis was on age rather than position.

The same emphasis is found in the Pastoral Epistles. Paul urged Timothy to treat older men in the church with respect (1 Tim. 5:1). The same context refers also to older women as *presbytera* (the feminine version of *presbyteros,* 5:2). Quite clearly here the reference is to age rather than office, because the respect is extended to all older men and women in the church.

In the Book of Hebrews much is made of the faith exhibited by previous generations. At the outset of the great Westminster Abbey of Faith in Hebrews 11 the writer refers to "men of old" as elders (Heb. 11:2). In this case, elder means almost the same thing as ancestor.

The Apostle Peter used the term elder to describe spiritual leaders in the local churches (1 Peter 5:1-5). In some cases these elders were recognized spiritual leaders (5:1). In other cases they simply appear to be older men, who commanded respect because of their age (5:5).

A second use of the word elder refers to Jewish leaders. They were the heads of communities (Luke 7:3). In the Gospels there are many negative references to the spiritual elders of Judaism, the Sanhedrin (Matt. 16:21; Mark 8:31; Luke 9:22). These were the officials who plotted to put Christ to death.

In the early Christian church elders were the local leaders. Paul and Barnabas appointed elders in various churches (Acts 14:23). These elders discussed the formulation of doctrine (15:2). They appear to have been paid officials of the local churches (1 Tim. 5:17-22). Also part of their work was the care of the sick (James 5:14). In fact, elder appears to be the title which the early church applied to men who exercised the ministries of pastor and bishop (literally overseer).

The Book of Revelation introduces another group of elders. They sit on thrones around the throne of the Lord (Rev. 4:4). Their primary purpose appears to be worship of the Lord in His glory (5:14; 7:11). Their reverence is both an indication of Christ's glory and also an example of the worship we shall give in heaven (11:16). Again near the end of Revelation the elders are pictured in a posture of worship and adoration (19:4).

In our day elders are set aside to lead the church and to care for it by the teaching and application of God's Word. In the preview of heaven's glory, elders exemplify the worship in which we shall engage throughout all eternity.

ILLUSTRATIONS

The office of elder came to the fore in Reformation days through the writings of John Calvin. In his extensive *Institutes of the Christian Religion* Calvin says this about elders: "In giving the name of bishops, presbyters [elders], and pastors indiscriminately to those who govern churches, I have done it on the authority of the Scripture, which uses the words as synonymous" (*Institutes of the Christian Religion*, book IV, chap. 3).

On the other hand, Baptists have always seen elders to be pastors. There can be more than one elder in a church only if there are assistant pastors. Together with Calvin, Baptists teach that elders are pastors, and that this means the same thing as bishop. Both Calvin and the Baptists believe that there is no essential or class difference between elders and other Christians. All believers are priests (1 Peter 2:9), not just those who have been ceremonially set aside by ordination.

Even the Church of England's Bishop Joseph Barber Lightfoot (1828-89) adopted a similar position on the role of elders. In his commentary on Philippians he wrote: "It is a fact now generally recognized by theologians of all shades of opinion that in the language of the New Testament the same officer in the church is called either 'bishop,' 'elder,' or 'presbyter.'" Many New Testament students see elder as a title for men who fulfilled the ministries of caring (pastors) for and overseeing (bishops) the church.

A modern Church of England writer was the late David Watson (1933-84). In writing about the church he said this concerning elders: "The word 'priest' today has a different connotation from its original meaning. The word itself comes from the Latin *presbyter* and from the Greek *presbuteros*, simply meaning elder—though later it was to describe the leader of a community" (David Watson, *I Believe in the Church* [London: Hodder and Stoughton, 1978], p. 248). Like his famous Anglican predecessor Lightfoot, David Watson played down any distinction between laymen and clergy (elders).

In writing to students, Michael Griffiths made some rather wise observations concerning elders in a local church: "Young people may also need to be reminded that their 'elders' are not just older people who have been a blessing to them. We cannot appoint our own elders from father figures whom we happen to like. Elders are appointed in the local church to which we belong, and we have to accept that congregation as it is, not as we might prefer it to be" (Michael Griffiths, *Cinderella with Amnesia* [London: InterVarsity Press, 1975], p. 114).

While finishing graduate studies I served as assistant pastor of a church near Chicago. Part of the privileges of my position included attendance at elders' meetings. Sometimes I was disturbed by their unwillingness to change, and other times I was frustrated by the narrowness of their viewpoint. But since then I have become thankful for their faithfulness to the Lord and His work.

END

MEANING

In the New Testament the word "end" is a translation of the Greek word *telos*. It is seen in such English combinations as *"tele*graph" (literally distance writing), *"teleol*ogy" (the evidences for purpose, or an end in nature), and *"tele*scope" (an instrument which sees faraway objects).

In ancient Greek literature *telos* meant several things. It referred to achievement of one's ends, or carrying a plan to its conclusion or end. Along the same lines *telos* was used to identify the power to carry out a task, or to determine the outcome of circumstances. Another aspect of the word was perfection or completion of a process, such as the maturity of a person, or the fulfillment of an obligation, or the consummation of a marriage.

The Greek Old Testament, the Septuagint, used the word to speak of the fulfillment of God's plan for human history. Thus it referred to the end times or the latter days. Then the goals of God will have been accomplished in human history.

BIBLE USAGE

In the New Testament there are many facets of meaning in the word *telos*, but they can be reduced to two. First, the word refers to the end of a process or event. All human kingdoms have an end, but God's kingdom knows no ending (Luke 1:33). The splendor of Moses, after he came down from Mount Sinai, ended (2 Cor. 3:13).

Another side to this more general use of the word *telos* is that of fulfillment. Death fulfills the process initiated by sin (Rom. 6:21). Christ was the fulfillment, or the end, of the Mosaic Law (10:4; Gal. 3:24). The end or goal of apostolic teaching is the propagation of love among Christians (1 Tim. 1:5). The removal of Christians from Satan's realm is the end or object of their salvation. The greatest example is the crucifixion of Christ, when He cried, "It is finished" (John 19:30).

The first aspect of *telos* is an end or a termination. Some event, process, or institution comes to an end. The other side to our word is even more common in New Testament writings. For it is also used to describe the end of human history. In this connection the Bible speaks of the "end times" or the "latter days."

In His Olivet Discourse Jesus devoted a large block of teaching to the end times (Matt. 24:6—25:46). The parallel passages are Mark 13:7-37; Luke 21:9-38. Here Jesus described in detail the events which would occur before His coming.

Paul, in writing to his problem children, the Corinthians, referred to the end times. At the end even Corinthians would be fully sanctified (1 Cor. 1:8). The cataclysmic events of the last days should be a warning to Christians (10:11). Paul hoped that the Corinthians would finally, at "the end," understand his teaching (2 Cor. 1:13).

At the end times those who have rejected the Lord will experience a full and final (*telos*) judgment (1 Thes. 2:16). By the same token Christians' hopes will be fulfilled in the end times (Heb. 6:11). The resurrected Christ revealed Himself to the Apostle John, and in so doing He expressed a special reward for those who endure until the end (Rev. 2:26).

The implicit teaching of the word "end" is this: our Lord is in absolute control of human history. As believers we may also trust Him for all our future, right up to and including the end. Even our world will have its ending in the plan of God. The word *telos* speaks of the total control and perfect purposes of God in our lives, our families, our church, and our world.

ILLUSTRATIONS

As the old saying goes, "There is light at the end of the tunnel" of human history. To which a pessimist added, "The light at the end of the tunnel is usually an oncoming express train." Because of Christ, however, a Christian should be more optimistic.

The future and prophecy are closely intertwined in Christian thought. Professor William Sanford LaSor said, "It is an infallible rule of prophetic interpretation that the prophecy becomes fully clear only after it has been fulfilled."

On the same theme of fulfilled prophecy Robert B. Laurin said, "The fulfillments [of prophecy] in Israel were only the beginning phase of God's plan. We are still on the road to final enrichment of that fulfillment, and so can live in trust that God fulfills His promises."

For the Christian the greatest fulfillment will come when Christ returns for His own. In his wise way C.S. Lewis gave good advice concerning the end of our age: "Aim at heaven and you will get earth thrown in," he said. "Aim at earth and you will get neither."

Another typical viewpoint of C.S. Lewis is this one: "Has this world been so kind to you that you should leave it with regret? There are better things ahead than any we leave behind."

Dr. Carl F.H. Henry spoke of God's future when he said: "The final chapter of human history is solely God's decision, and even now He is everywhere active in grace or judgment. Never in all history have men spoken so much of end-time, yet been so shrouded in ignorance of God's impending doomsday."

Along the same lines, British-American broadcaster Alistair Cooke gave this opinion concerning the future of our world: "I'd be astounded if this planet is going by 50 years from now. I don't think that we will reach 2000. It would be miraculous."

At a scientific conference at the Massachusetts Institute of Technology a blue ribbon commission of international experts gathered. They used computers to chart the relationships between population increase, agricultural production, natural resources depletion, industrial output, and the pollution of the world. Their conclusion: "At our present rates of economic and population growth . . . the world will collapse around the year 2100."

The *Southern Baptist Brotherhood Journal* came to a much more optimistic conclusion: "Every tomorrow has two handles; we can take hold by the handle of anxiety or by the handle of faith."

An elderly gentleman stood beside the grave of his beloved wife. As the funeral director offered condolences, the old fellow's eyes brightened. "You don't understand my situation," the old man said to the undertaker. Then he quoted a hymn line: "The sky, not the grave, is our goal." As Christians we are not waiting for the undertaker, but rather the "Upper-taker."

ENEMY

MEANING

Two words are used in Greek to describe an "enemy." The most common is *echthros*, which appears 29 times in the New Testament. The root meaning of *echthros* is "hatred." Thus the enemy is the hated one, or one who shows hostility. In the Septuagint Greek Old Testament this word was used to describe personal enemies (Es. 7:6), as well as national enemies (Josh. 7:8). Often these enemies of Israel were identified as idolaters.

A second word for "enemy" is *antidikos*, which appears only five times in the New Testament. Here the picture is that of an adversary in a lawsuit. In fact, the context is almost always that of legal proceedings. In the Septuagint, Jehovah is seen as the Advocate for His people against their adversaries (Isa. 41:11, 13).

BIBLE USAGE

As one can imagine, the idea of an "enemy" in the New Testament relates mainly to Satan and his people. The most frequently used term, *echthros*, speaks of open hostility and hatred. In the Gospels many references are made to the enemies of Christ. David prophesied that God would subdue Christ's enemies under His feet (Matt. 22:44; Ps. 110:1). The same psalm is applied to Christ in Acts 2:35 and Hebrews 1:13.

Because Jesus had satanic enemies, He warned His disciples that they too would have enemies. Some enemies would be in their own families (Matt. 10:36). In the Parable of the Tares and the Wheat, an enemy of the kingdom secretly sowed bad seed in the field in order to destroy the crop (13:25, 28).

In dealing with human enemies, the Lord urged His disciples to show love. Though Christians can expect persecution, they are instructed by Jesus to love their enemies (5:44). Indeed they should pray for enemies, do good to enemies, bless them, and turn the other cheek (Luke 6:27-29). The Apostle Paul picked up the same idea and instructed Christians to feed their enemies. This would have the effect of melting down their opposition, as if one heaped hot coals on their heads (Rom. 12:20-21).

Jesus explained to His disciples that the source of all such persecution was their main enemy, Satan. In the Parable of the Tares and the Wheat the evil weed-sower was none other than Satan (Matt. 13:39). Jesus claimed power over Satan because He existed before Satan and indeed saw that evil one fall from heaven (Luke 10:18-19).

The second word for "enemy" is *antidikos*, and it too has a double meaning. It speaks of a legal adversary, and urges Christians to "settle out of court" (Matt. 5:25). The same idea is expanded in Luke's Gospel, where Christians are warned that going to court can result in a prison term (Luke 12:58).

In the Parable of the Widow and the Unjust Judge, the widow sued for protection against her opponent (*antidikos*). Finally the judge granted relief because of her persistence (18:2-5). In every case the word *antidikos* is found in a legal context.

The same is true when it is used to label Satan. The main role of Satan is that of a cosmic prosecuting attorney, an accuser of Christians (Rev. 12:10). This role is seen best in the Old Testament. When Satan set his sights on Job, he accused Job of serving God only because God was good to him (Job 1:6-11). Later in Israel's history Satan appeared again to level libelous accusations against the righteous high priest Joshua (Zech. 3:1).

The Apostle Peter specifically warned Christians against the accusations of Satan. He compared Satan to a roaring lion who prowls around seeking to swallow up saints (1 Peter 5:8). If Christians could only see that such devilish attacks are the work of Satan, perhaps they would be more ready to rebuke him in the power of Jesus' name. Unfortunately most Christians turn against fellow believers instead of rebuffing the wretched king of demons.

ILLUSTRATIONS

A well-known Bible teacher once warned Christians against the attacks of Satan and his henchmen. After a particularly blessed Bible conference the speaker admonished his hearers: "Be careful of Satan's attacks, for he always leans against the gate of the garden of prayer."

George Bancroft, a Dean of St. Paul's Cathedral, London, saw Satan realistically. He commented: "Where Christ erecteth His church, the devil in the same courtyard will have his chapel."

Nathaniel Howe caught the same theme in writing, "The way of this world is to praise dead saints and persecute living ones." However, such trouble usually strengthens a Christian. Famous English novelist and educational reformer Hannah More stated this truth: "Outward attacks and troubles rather fix than unsettle a Christian, as tempests from without only serve to root the oak faster."

Such opposition was the theme of the Puritan writer Samuel Rutherford: "You must learn to make your evils your great good and to spin comforts, peace, joy, communion with Christ, out of your troubles. They are Christ's wooers, sent to speak on your behalf to Himself."

Later the great Baptist preacher Charles Haddon Spurgeon spoke of troubles: "If you tell your troubles to God, you put them into the grave; if you roll your burden somewhere else, it will roll back again." One recalls that Spurgeon was criticized, tricked, and driven to a nervous breakdown by trouble.

The therapeutic nature of persecution is seen in the following quote from the *Dresch Messenger:* "If you have some enemies, you are to be congratulated, for no man ever amounted to much without arousing jealousies and creating enemies. Your enemies are a very valuable asset as long as you refrain from striking back at them, because they keep you on the alert when you might become lazy."

Similarly the *Megiddo Messenger* warned of spiritual opposition: "The world is a spiritual jungle in which we all are traveling. In it we find that it is not the big enemies from which we stand in the greatest danger of losing our self-control, but the little things that lurk in the dark recesses of our nature: gossip, the poisoner of the blood, the temper uncontrolled, the unruly tongue which shoots out the venom of bitter words, the lust for forbidden things, the foolish or injurious word, the unholy thought, the wasted moment."

An old Christian Indian was seen taking many gifts to his enemy's teepee. "What are you doing?" asked the missionary.

"I am burning him to the ground," replied the chief, "by heaping coals of fire on his head" (Rom. 12:20).

ENTER

MEANING

The Greek word translated "enter" is the very common compound verb *eiserchomai*. It is composed of two words: *eis* (into) and *erchomai* (I go). The word *eiserchomai* appears 169 times in the New Testament.

In secular Greek *eiserchomai* was the entrance onto a stage, especially when the chorus made its entrance in a Greek drama. It also referred to embarking on a job and entering into an office. Yet another use was commercial, to make demands upon someone, or to come due. In religion this word marked the invocation of a deity, the request that a god might come into his temple.

When the Greek Old Testament was translated, this word represented 19 different Hebrew words. It spoke of Jehovah coming to His people, and to people entering into God's presence. It also described marriage when a man wer.t in to his wife. Thus in ancient Greek writings the word has many meanings, which is also true in the New Testament.

BIBLE USAGE

Predictably the word *eiserchomai* has both literal and figurative meanings. Literally it describes activity. People enter into cities, such as Jerusalem (Matt. 21:10), Capernaum (Matt. 8:5; Mark 2:1), and Caesarea (Acts 10:24; 23:33).

In the same way people enter into places or buildings. Jesus entered into Capernaum and went immediately into the synagogue (Mark 1:21). (Incidentally, archeologists have recently excavated the floor and some walls of the Capernaum synagogue.) Priests also entered into the temple at Jerusalem (Luke 1:9). The disciples entered villages, cities, and houses in their efforts to preach Christ (Matt. 10:11-12).

On a much larger scale, the Bible speaks of Christ entering our world in His incarnation (Heb. 10:5). This is undoubtedly the most significant entrance in human history. It was needed because sin entered the world and brought death with it (Rom. 5:12).

Just as the Greek word describes literal entrances, it also speaks of figurative entrances. In the Gospels reference is made to demons entering people (Luke 8:30). After Jesus expelled the demons from a poor, pathetic man in the region of the Gerasenes, his evil spirits entered into a herd of swine (8:32-33). In the same way Satan entered into people. One such example is Judas Iscariot (John 13:27).

Another form of entrance involves people joining a group. After the ascension of Jesus, steps were undertaken to select an apostolic replacement for Judas. A requirement was that he had gone in and out among the other disciples (Acts 1:21).

A final aspect of entrances is participation in an experience. The aim of believers is entrance into the kingdom of heaven (Matt. 5:20; 7:21; Mark 9:47; 10:15; Luke 18:17; John 3:5). At death a Christian enters into the glory of Christ (Luke 24:26). Christians are instructed to pray, that they may not enter into temptation (Matt. 26:41).

In fact, the whole of the Christian life is compared to entrances. We enter into Christ when we believe on Him. Each day we enter into a growing understanding of His work on our behalf. Service involves entering into the physical and spiritual needs of other people. Christians find that life is one large open door, into which they may enter, serving their Lord. By becoming Christians we also enter into the fellowship of like-minded Christians. Finally we shall enter into His heavenly kingdom, there to stay forever.

ILLUSTRATIONS

People go through many entrances in their lives. As a college student I sang in the men's chorus. Formally, entrance was procured by an audition. Informally, the entrance rite was a frightening and funny initiation. Ever since then there has been a bond among the men who sang in that choir.

On the other hand, entrance into the Christian church is much easier. Wilbur Large said: "The church is the only institution in the world that has lower entrance requirements than those for getting on a bus." Along the same lines Charles Clayton Morrison said: "The Christian church is the only society in the world in which membership is based upon the qualification that the candidate shall be unworthy of membership."

Though a Christian's entrance into the Lord is important, the Lord's entrance into our world is even more significant. As Handel H. Brown put it: "The shepherds did not go to Bethlehem seeking the birth of a great man, or a famous teacher, or a national hero. They were promised a Saviour."

In the great debate between liberalism and fundamentalism, one of the foremost soldiers for scriptural truth was Professor J. Gresham Machen. Speaking of Christ's coming he said: "Theoretically, a man can believe in the Resurrection ... without believing in the Virgin Birth; yet such a halfway conviction is not likely to endure. The Virgin Birth is an integral part of the New Testament witness about Christ, and that witness is strongest when it is taken as it stands."

It is important that Christ came to earth, but His entrance into each believer's life is personally important. This is the theme of William Holman Hunt's (1827-1910) famous painting of "Christ, the Light of the World" in St. Paul's Cathedral, London. Christ is seen standing at a door, holding a lantern. The door is overgrown with vines, but the Saviour still stands, seeking entrance. Thus the painter portrayed Jesus' desire to enter human lives.

Many hymns and choruses have set this theme to music. As small children we learned this chorus:

Into my heart, into my heart,
Come into my heart, Lord Jesus.
Come in today, come in to stay,
Come into my heart, Lord Jesus.

The words and the tune of this simple, old chorus have made a spiritual impact on many children and adults.

More musically acceptable is Emily E.S. Elliott's Christmas hymn, set to the tune "Margaret." In it Emily Elliott paraphrased the statement of John 1:11 in these lovely lines:

Thou didst leave Thy throne and Thy kingly crown
When Thou camest to earth for me;
But in Bethlehem's home there was found no room
For Thy holy Nativity:
O come to my heart, Lord Jesus!
There is room in my heart for Thee.

Heaven's arches rang when the angels sang,
Proclaiming Thy royal degree;
But in lowly birth Thou didst come to earth,
And in great humilty:
O come to my heart, Lord Jesus!
There is room in my heart for Thee!

(See: *Come* and *Depart*.)

ETERNITY

MEANING

The Greek word for "eternity" is *aion*. It is clearly reflected in the English word "aeon" or "eon," which means an indefinite period of time. In geology "aeon" or "eon" refers to a period of 1 billion years.

In ancient Greek philosophy the thinkers drew a clear line between *aion* (eternity) and *chronos* (time). Incidentally, the word for time, *chronos*, is seen in such English words as "*chronology*" (the listing of things or events in order of occurrence) and "*chronicle*" (the record of events as they occurred).

According to Plato, "eternity" (*aion*) was a timeless whole with no divisions such as minutes, hours, and days. On the other hand, "time" (*chronos*) was created to show the relationship of the world to the passing of time.

In the Old Testament "eternity" referred to a prolonged period of time, either in the past or future. When "eternity" as we know it was mentioned in the Old Testament it was usually in the plural form, "eternities." This revealed the greatness of God who is infinitely greater than all time.

BIBLE USAGE

In the New Testament eternity refers both to the past and the future. God spoke through His prophets from eternity past (Luke 1:70). When Jesus healed a man born blind, He broke a precedent which had existed from eternity past (John 9:32; Acts 3:21). The mysteries of redemption were hidden in the wisdom of God from before the eternities (1 Cor. 2:7). When eternity past is mentioned, it usually refers to God's redemptive plan which was revealed in Jesus Christ. In other words, we who live in the age of grace have privileges unknown in eternity past.

Believing on Jesus Christ produces "eternal life" (John 3:16; 6:51, 58). As children of God we remain in His home forever (8:35). The Holy Spirit has come to minister in our hearts forever (14:16). John's Gospel is filled with references to eternity. John's letters also make frequent reference to eternity. He who does the will of God lives eternally (1 John 2:17). The truth of God also is eternal (2 John 2). Thus John's writings give a good study of the word "eternal."

In some cases "eternity" is called "the age to come." Disciples will be rewarded in eternity (Mark 10:30: Luke 18:30). Marriage will not take place in eternity (20:35). The saving work of Christ will be revealed in its fullness only in the ages to come (Eph. 2:7). Salvation itself is called a taste of the ages to come (Heb. 6:5).

The full force of eternity is most clearly seen in the great doxologies of the Bible. The Lord's Prayer concludes with praise that God's kingdom, power, and glory are eternal (Matt. 6:13). Paul's burden for Israel is climaxed with a great doxology: "God blessed forever" (Rom. 9:5). Another doxology states that all of history is in God's hands (11:36). Often Paul ascribed glory to God eternally (Phil. 4:20). In his first epistle to Timothy, Paul praised God as "eternal, immortal, invisible, the only God" (1 Tim. 1:17). Again in his final epistle to Timothy, Paul ascribed praise to God (2 Tim. 4:18). A similar statement concludes the Book of Hebrews (Heb. 13:21). In Peter's epistles he too gave eternal praise to God the Father and God the Son (1 Peter 4:11; 5:11).

When Christians are moved to praise, they focus on the eternity of God. According to Revelation the occupation of heaven is eternal praise for who God is and what He did in Jesus Christ (Rev. 4:9). Though Christians here and now have eternal life (1 John 5:11-12), they will enjoy an entirely new dimension of life in the eternal realms of His glory.

ILLUSTRATIONS
Literature is full of references to eternity. Blaise Pascal (1623-62), a pietistic French scientist and philosopher, wrote in his famous *Pensees:* "The eternal silence of these infinite spaces [heavens] terrifies me" (III, p. 206).

Lord Byron (1788-1824) touched the theme of eternity in his famous *Sonnet on Chillon.* Byron believed that the human spirit was unbreakable, even in prison, and in this vein he wrote:

> Eternal spirit of the changeless mind!
> Brightest in dungeons, Liberty! thou art.

Always interesting are the writings of Alexander Pope (1688-1744). He too spoke of eternity in his *Essay on Criticism.* To Pope hope is eternal, and he wrote:

> Hope springs eternal in the human breast;
> Man never is, but always to be blessed.
> The soul uneasy, and confined from home,
> Rests and expatiates in a life to come.

The Lord Mayor of Dublin, John Philpot Curran (1750-1817), gave another twist to eternity. In his most famous speech he said: "The condition upon which God hath given liberty to man is eternal vigilance; which condition if he break, servitude is at once the consequence of his crime, and the punishment of his guilt."

To a Christian, however, eternity has a far different meaning. The sole source of eternity is God. As the famous Puritan writer John Flavel said, "His sovereignty is gloriously displayed in His eternal decrees and temporal providences." Another Puritan, Christopher Nesse, summed it up more simply: "God is the Cause of causes."

Yet another Puritan, Robert Harris, spoke of God's eternity thus: "He [God] approaches them while gazing on the near prospectus of time, and by raising and extending the point of sight He adds eternity to the view, and leaves them lost in the contemplation of a boundless eternity."

A Christian, by believing in the Lord Jesus Christ, experiences something of eternity here and now. Devotional writer and theologian John Baillie wrote: "I thank Thee, O Lord, that Thou hast so set eternity within my heart that no earthly thing can ever satisfy me wholly."

Robert Murray McCheyne, the great father of Scottish revival, set this standard for his life of faith: "Live near to God, and all things will appear little to you in comparison with eternal realities."

For a Christian, however, eternity also means heaven. Billy Sunday, a baseball player turned evangelist, painted a picture of eternity worth seeing: "I stand on the shores of eternity and cry out, 'Eternity! Eternity! How long art thou?' Back comes the answer, 'How long? When ten thousand times ten thousand times ten thousand years have passed, eternity will have just begun.'"

Jack MacArthur put it briefly: "The choices of time are binding in eternity."

EVERY

MEANING

The Greek word for "every," "all," and "each" is *pas, pasa,* or *pan* depending on the context of the sentence. It is reflected in such English words as *"panacea"* (a remedy for all), *"Pan*-American" (referring to both Americas), and *"panchromatic"* (a sensitivity to light of all colors).

One might expect this word to occur frequently in the Scriptures, and it does. It shows up about 8,000 times in the Greek Old Testament, the Septuagint, and appears 1,228 times in the Greek New Testament.

Often it is used to describe the total control of God over the world. Secular Greek writers did not accept this, for they attributed the world to an impersonal force. Some also advocated *"pan*theism," which sees a god in everything.

On the other hand, Jews regarded God as the Creator of all, and thus the Controller of all. Christians likewise found the source of everything in God and applied the word to God's activities.

BIBLE USAGE

This simple word is best seen in connection with other words. Quite naturally it is related to people, and the Bible makes broad general statements about all people. When Christ came into the world, His appearance was pertinent to all people (John 1:9). All people are on earth because of the creative act of God, and this extends also to all nations (Acts 17:26). The devastating effects of sin likewise extend to all people (Rom. 3:20, 23; 5:12). Christ is the Firstborn of all Creation (Col. 1:15), so all people are thus legitimate objects of evangelism and discipleship (1:28).

The same broad strokes are used to paint a picture of the nations. At Pentecost representatives from every nation under heaven were gathered (Acts 2:5). Christians were charged with the task of making disciples from all nations (Matt. 28:19). The entire Gospel was designated for declaration to all the nations (Luke 24:46-48).

The Lord extended His invitation and His ministry to whole cities. All Jerusalem was in an uproar over the birth of Jesus (Matt. 2:3). John the Baptist reached people from all Judea and all of the Jordan region (3:5). Every creature deserves to hear the Gospel in his own language (Mark 16:15). The lordship of Christ is valid for all of the house of Israel (Acts 2:36). There is a largeness in the expanse of Christ's Gospel, and this is the real reason for missions.

Just as all people are in the purview of divine providence, so all Creation is important in God's plan. In one of his fine doxologies the Apostle Paul presents God as the Source, Sustainer, and Significance of all things (Rom. 11:36). All of Creation holds together only at the express command of Christ the Lord (Col. 1:17; Heb. 1:3). The Redeemer of all the saved is the Creator of all the world, according to a heavenly hymn of praise (Rev. 4:11).

This sovereignty of God over all things is a constant theme in the Bible. All things have been committed to Christ by His Heavenly Father (Matt. 11:27). Christ was the means by which God created all things (John 1:3; 3:35). All of the events in life are woven together for the good of Christians by their loving Father (Rom. 8:28). Indeed, Christ is over all and in command of all that comes to pass (9:5). Spiritual insight is likewise totally within the control of God, the Holy Spirit, and all spiritual truth is communicated by Him (1 Cor. 2:10). Thus the scope of God's control is limitless, and all people and every thing is included in His power.

This means that Christians should be totally at the disposal of the Lord, and here again the word "every" or "all" gives important emphasis. The Apostle Paul said he served the Lord with all good conscience (Acts 23:1). To him this meant that all perseverance (Eph. 6:18) and all boldness (Phil. 1:20) were brought to bear on the apostolic task. Peter urged Christians to serve the Lord with all diligence (2 Peter 1:5), and James told believers to endure trouble with all joy (James 1:2, 12).

The secret of such triumphant Christianity is seen in the final use of our word "all." Before giving His final command to the disciples, Jesus reminded them that He had all authority (Matt. 28:18). This authority embraces heaven and earth, and it enables the broad, general service and worship indicated in the Bible by the words "all" and "every."

ILLUSTRATIONS

"Jesus Christ must be Lord of all, or He is not Lord at all." Some say that this phrase came from Augustine, but it has been used by Christians down through the centuries.

Marcianus Aristides was a pre-Christian Athenian statesman, but he set down a principle worthy of Christian living. According to Aristides, "God is not in need of anything, but all things are in need of Him." Though Marcianus did not speak of the God of the Bible, he did ennunciate a biblical idea.

In *The Brothers Karamazov,* Fyodor Dostoevsky put the following line in the mouth of Father Zossima: "Love all God's Creation, the whole and every grain of sand in it. Love every leaf, every ray of God's light." Thus he captured the biblical emphasis of God's universal domain.

Concerning the all-embracing control of God, E.B. De Condillac concluded: "The most perfect idea of God that we can form in this life is that of an independent, unique, infinite, eternal, omnipotent, immutable, intelligent, and free First Cause, whose power extends over all things." Though his language is complicated, the fact shines through that God is the Creator of everyone and everything we see.

One of the great Christian writers of pre-Reformation times was Lady Julian of Norwich (1342-1413). She wrote the beautiful devotional book, *Revelation of Divine Love.* In it she said: "Some of us believe that God is Almighty and may do all, and that He is All-wisdom and can do all; but that He is All-love and will do all— there we stop short."

Bishop Augustine of Hippo, who turned to Christ after years of vain searching, spent thousands of words describing the greatness of God. One such description of His sovereignty is this: "God is an infinite circle whose center is everywhere and whose circumference is nowhere."

This truth of God's all-encompassing greatness and love drove John Wesley throughout his life. In a letter to Francis Asbury in America Wesley wrote: "Oh, beware! Do not seek to be something! Let me be nothing, and Christ be all in all."

EXALTATION

MEANING

The Greek word which is translated "I exalt" is *hupsoo*. Literally it means, "raise," "elevate," or "lift up." It is seen in technical words such as *"hypso*graphy" (mapping high places in the land) and *"hypso*meter" (an instrument for measuring altitudes).

The word was rarely used in secular Greek. However, it did appear with reference to the elevation of gods, heroes, and mystical experiences. Here the figurative meaning is seen: to emphasize and make something or someone prominent.

In the Greek Old Testament the basic biblical meaning of exaltation is found. Jehovah God is exalted above all other false deities. Worship is seen as the act of lifting up God and making His name great. The Psalms are magnificent expressions of the exaltation of God. In the messianic sections of Isaiah, Christ, the Servant of Jehovah, is exalted. Thus exaltation in the New Testament builds on the ideas of the Old Testament.

BIBLE USAGE

The New Testament word *hupsoo* contains two main meanings. First it emphasizes the physical raising up of someone or something. Christ used this word to explain that He would be lifted up on a cross (John 3:14). Here He drew a comparison with the brass serpent in the wilderness. When it was lifted up by Moses on a pole, it provided healing for the snake-bitten people of Israel (Num. 21:9). On the threshold of His crucifixion, Jesus expanded this idea. If He were lifted up, He would draw all men to Himself (John 12:32).

Another twist to the same truth is found in John 8:28. The Crucifixion would reveal that the message of Christ is true, and this would prove the Pharisees to be false. Here too "lifting up" refers to the Cross.

In condemning Capernaum for its rejection of the Redeemer, Christ warned that its residents would never be elevated to heaven. They would instead be brought down to Hades (Matt. 11:23; Luke 10:15). Here the reference appears to be future; Christ implied that Capernaum would deserve greater judgment than Tyre and Sidon on the final day.

Lifting up is also used to describe the resurrection of the Lord. After being raised from the dead, Jesus was raised to the right hand of God the Father. This elevation was followed by the sending of the Holy Spirit (Acts 2:33). This elevation also resulted in the proclamation of repentance and forgiveness to Israel (5:31).

Not only does exaltation mean physical elevation, but it also means figurative elevation. God exalts, or raises up, one class of people: the humble (Matt. 23:12). When teaching the essentials of effective prayer, Jesus emphasized the need of humility as a prerequisite for prayer (Luke 18:14). Paul humbled himself, even though the Corinthians did not understand it, and he exalted other believers (2 Cor. 11:7). Both James and Peter teach the principle: if we humble ourselves, God will exalt us (James 4:10; 1 Peter 5:6). This truth is so pervasive in the New Testament that it cannot be avoided. Still Christians fall into the trap of pride.

An example of this principle is seen on the national scale. God chose Israel and made them great during the time when they were held prisoner by Egypt (Acts 13:17). The Proverbs teach that only righteous nations will be exalted by God (Prov. 14:34).

Perhaps the greatest text concerning exaltation is the hymn of Philippians, chapter 2. There Jesus Christ is exalted to the highest place by His Father (Phil.

2:9). The same idea is seen in Hebrews 2:9. Jesus Christ is raised from the grave, into heaven, and to the right hand of God. This exaltation is the basis of coming kingdom glory, which we shall share with the Lord.

ILLUSTRATIONS

Exaltation is seen from two standpoints. First, God will exalt believers who truly are humble. Second, in worship believers exalt and raise up the name of their God and Saviour.

William Bridge restated the biblical maxim, that humility leads to exaltation. According to that Puritan writer: "If you lay yourself at Christ's feet He will take you up into His arms."

A similar statement about future exaltation is found in the writings of Richard Sibbes: "There will be a resurrection of credits, as well as bodies," he wrote. "We'll have glory enough by and by." In other words, we can content ourselves here and now with a humble life, because God will pass out glory by and by.

The same idea is seen in the writings of Thomas Manton, another Puritan: "The best of God's people have abhorred themselves. Like the spire of a steeple, we are least at the highest." A little thought shows the profundity of that remark.

Phillips Brooks, an American Episcopalian bishop, was theologically liberal, but he did understand this exaltation. Brooks wrote: "The true way to be humble is not to stoop until you are smaller than yourself, but to stand at your real height against some higher nature that will show what the real smallness of your greatness is." Such is the experience of every true believer in the Lord Jesus Christ.

When we turn our eyes on the Lord Jesus Christ, we see true exaltation. An early Baptist missionary to Burma, George Dana Boardman (1801-31) said: "The Cross [of Christ] is the only ladder high enough to touch the threshold of heaven."

Andrew Murray, noted South African Bible teacher and preacher, said: "Jesus was born twice. The birth at Bethlehem was a birth into a life of weakness. The second time He was born from the grave—'the firstborn from the dead'—into the glory of heaven and the throne of God."

The same truth of Christ's exaltation was stated beautifully by Puritan Henry Bridge: "As Christ ceased not to be King because He was like a servant, nor to be a lion because He was like a lamb, nor to be God because He was made a man, nor to be a judge because He was judged; so a man doth not lose his honor by humility, but he shall be honored for his humility."

Many grand hymns of exaltation were written by Isaac Watts (1674-1748), masterful hymnist of the Puritan era. Most hymnals fittingly set this hymn to a tune titled "Adoration," and the words reveal the reason for this melody:

Join all the glorious names
Of wisdom, love, and power,
That ever mortals knew,
That angels ever bore;
All are too mean [poor] to speak His worth,
Too mean to set my Saviour forth.

As *The Westminster Catechism* says: "The chief end of man is to glorify God and enjoy Him forever." No work is greater than worship.

EXAMPLE

MEANING

The word "example" is a translation of the Greek *tupos*. One can easily see the connection between *tupos* and such English words as "type," "typical," and "typewriting." In its basic form the Greek word *tupos* means to strike, or to make a mark by striking a blow. (One writes on a typewriter by striking a blow on the key which in turn strikes a blow on the paper and makes an impression.)

In secular Greek the word *tupos* retained its original meaning. But though it meant to strike a blow, this was soon changed to include setting a seal in wax and hammering out a mold.

It was the Greek Old Testament, the Septuagint, which gave new meaning to this word. There it was used to describe the model on which the tabernacle was built. Thus it became a pattern, or example, and this meaning dominated in the New Testament.

BIBLE USAGE

After the Resurrection Jesus appeared to His disciples, but Thomas was absent. As a test of Christ's reality Thomas said he wanted to put his fingers in the marks (*tupos*) of the nails in Christ's hands. Jesus offered him that chance (John 20:25, 27), but Thomas was probably convinced by the sight of his Saviour. Thus the nail-prints show the most basic use of this word.

In Stephen's defense of the Gospel, he condemned the Jews for their flirtation with idolatry. They had forged images (*tupos*) to worship Moloch and Rompha (Acts 7:43). This reference to idolatry is close to the basic meaning of our word.

The exemplary use of the word is seen throughout the New Testament. Christ is the example par excellence. After washing the disciples' feet, Christ urged them to follow His example (John 13:15). Peter spoke of Christ as the example of forbearance. His suffering was an example, as was His sinlessness (1 Peter 2:21-22). Furthermore He never struck back either physically or verbally, because He trusted His Father to judge justly (2:23). Peter urged Christians to copy the example of Christ.

Individual Christians were also urged to live exemplary lives. The Apostle Paul instructed his younger colleague Timothy to be an example to other believers (1 Tim. 4:12). As a young person, Timothy was sent as an example to the entire church at Ephesus.

Paul assumed the responsibility of being an example to Christians also. He urged the Philippian Christians to follow his example in living a godly life (Phil. 3:17; 4:9). Paul could instruct Christians to follow his example, because he was faithfully following the example of Christ.

In his brief letter to Titus, Paul made much of the exemplary life. He urged godly women to be examples to younger Christians (Titus 2:1-5). Titus and the other Christian men at Crete were likewise to be examples to newly converted men and boys (2:7). The entire teaching of Titus is build on the imitation of Christian examples.

At the end of Peter's first epistle, he included a long list of instructions for elders. In agreement with other sections of Scripture, Peter urged the elders to follow the example of Christ. The reason for this teaching was that elders should be examples to the Christians (1 Peter 5:3). This rules out all tyrannical domination of the church.

There is one further use of the word *tupos*, and this is the concept of types. Paul saw Adam as the first man, and as such he was a type of Christ (Rom. 5:14). Though Adam fell into sin, he still filled a significant, unique role in human history. Christ, of course, was the uniquely begotten Son of God. In a limited sense, then, the first Adam was a type of the second Adam, Christ.

ILLUSTRATIONS

The famous German philosopher Georg Wilhelm Friedrich Hegel (1780-1831) may have coined the phrase: "The only thing we learn from history is that we learn nothing from history." The same idea was echoed by the Spanish-born American philosopher George Santayana (1863-1952): "Those who forget history are bound to repeat it." The point is this: if we do not learn by the examples of the past, we must learn by trial and error.

Children usually learn by imitation of their parents. As a small boy I saw my dad polish his shoes with his socks. This appeared logical and practical to me, so I did it. Recently I saw my son do the same thing. (Needless to say, we have three generations of slightly disturbed wives, because shoe polish stains socks.)

An elderly pastor friend has in his study the pictures of several famous preachers of the past. I asked him once about this montage of portraits, and he said they represent men who influence his preaching. They are his examples.

To a Christian, however, the Lord Jesus is the primary example. Christian editor and publisher, Philip E. Howard, Jr., explained the example of Christ in these words: "The Lord Jesus Christ is the perfect example for all His followers, for He said: 'I am among you as the One who serves'" (Luke 22:27).

A famous Lutheran confessional theologian was Christoph Ernst Luthardt (1823-1902). He was an influential professor and writer on the Gospel of John. Of Jesus' exemplary life he said: "Jesus is the true prototype of the human race."

The great defender of orthodox Christianity in the fourth century was Athanasius (296-373). He triumphed over the heresy of Arius, who denied the deity of Christ. Of the Lord Athanasius said: "He became what we are that He might make us what He is."

William Arnot expanded on this statement: "The gentleness of Christ is the comeliest ornament that a Christian can wear."

Along the same lines Henry Drummond (1851-97), a Scottish professor and friend of D.L. Moody, wrote: "To become Christlike is the only thing in the whole world worth caring for, the thing before which every ambition of man is folly and all lower achievement vain."

D.W. Lambert added to this remark: "The Christian goal is not the outward and literal imitation of Jesus, but the living out of the Christ life implanted within by the Holy Spirit."

In 1915 the Congregational minister Charles Monroe Sheldon (1857-1946) wrote his famous novel, *In His Steps*. This famous book sold more than 6 million copies. It traced the developments in a small town church, when the members regulated all their actions by this question: "What would Jesus do in this situation?" Needless to say, the results were sensational. Perhaps this is what the Bible means when it sets forth Christ as our example.

FACE

MEANING

The word for "face" in the Greek New Testament is *prosopon*. The dominant idea is the preposition *pros* (toward), so the face is that part which shows toward others. *Prosopon* occurs about 70 times in the New Testament, and appears more than 780 times in the Greek Old Testament.

In ancient secular Greek *prosopon* simply meant the countenance of a person, or the face he presented to the public. But as Greek literature developed, the word came to mean the mask which an actor wore, or the part he played. Arising out of this theatrical aspect of the word was a later meaning, the role which a person played in society. So Greek literature gave a wide and wonderful range of meanings to the word *prosopon*.

In Jewish literature, especially the Old Testament, the word had other meanings. For instance, one "saw the face of the king" when he had an audience with the monarch. When Jacob met God at Bethel, he said he saw the face of God. (Actually, no one could come "face to face" with God and live. For Jacob, a vision of God was like seeing the face of God.)

BIBLE USAGE

The most interesting references to "face" are those which speak of God. In teaching the value of childlike faith, Jesus spoke of the simplicity of children and their importance. Then He added that their guardian angels always behold the face of God in heaven (Matt. 18:10).

In Peter's Pentecost sermon he quoted the Old Testament several times. In quoting Psalm 16:8-11, where David found his highest pleasure in serving the Lord, the psalmist saw his ultimate fulfillment in the presence of God, literally, "before the face of God" (Acts 2:28). Here is the royal concept of an audience with the king, and David described heaven as a prolonged gaze at the face of the King of kings.

The writer of Hebrews portrayed Christ as the great High Priest after the order of Melchizedek. In this capacity Christ now represents us before the throne of God, and the writer said that the Lord entered heaven to appear in the presence (literally "before the face") of His Father and ours (Heb. 9:24). What a comfort we can derive from the intercession of Christ.

Peter also quoted the Old Testament concerning the face of God. Again the psalmist is quoted, to teach concerning the face of God. The righteous live their lives under the watchful eye of God, but the Lord turns His face away from evil persons (Ps. 34:15-16; 1 Peter 3:12).

Heaven is described clearly in Revelation. One of the privileges of glory will be that believers will see the face of the Lord (Rev. 22:4).

The Bible teaches that God is spirit (John 4:24). A spirit has no body, but God is given human characteristics to describe His actions. His hands help us. His ears hear us. His eyes see us. His feet take Him throughout the world. His face is His gracious presence and pleasure.

The New Testament also mentions the face of the Lord Jesus Christ. John the Baptist was the prophesied messenger who was sent before the Lord's face. Before Jesus appeared, His messenger came (Matt. 11:10, quoting Mal. 3:1).

On the Mountain of Transfiguration the face of the Lord glowed with a heavenly light (Matt. 17:2). This was like an incandescent light bulb which shines from within. Thus the divine glory of the Lord shone through His human face. When the time for His crucifixion came, Jesus set His face toward Jerusalem

(Luke 9:51). This meant that He resolutely made up His mind to carry through the redemptive plan of God, including His death on the cross.

The trial of Christ was a cruel mockery of justice. They pressed down a crown of thorns on His forehead. Then the mob humiliated Him, some spitting in His face (Mark 14:65). No greater insult can be imagined than this, and He bore it for us.

The face of God speaks of His presence with us. The infinite God revealed Himself to finite people. The face of Christ speaks of His incarnation. The immortal God was incarnate in mortal man, and His face was marred beyond recognition (Isa. 52:14).

ILLUSTRATIONS
The face of God is often seen in literature and hymnology. In his poem, "Crossing the Bar," poet laureate Alfred Lord Tennyson (1809-92) wrote:

And may there be no sadness of farewell,
When I embark,
For tho' from out our bourne of Time and Place
The flood may bear me far,
I hope to see my Pilot face to face
When I have crost the bar.

A brighter side of God's face is seen in the words of the great 19th-century evangelist, Dwight L. Moody. "To see His star is good," admitted Moody, "but to see His face is far better."

Along the same line, noted Christian educator and writer Arno Gaebelein looked forward to heaven with unmitigated delight. He wrote, "We shall see His face, and His name shall be on our foreheads. We are sons with Him [Jesus], heirs of God, and fellow heirs with our Lord Jesus Christ. The acquired glory of our Lord is the glory which every saved sinner will share with Him."

Hymns have often caused people to reflect on the face of God. As a popular Gospel song of the mid-20th century says:

We shall see His lovely face,
Some bright golden morning,
When the clouds have rifted
And the shades have flown.
Sorrow will be turned to joy,
Heartaches gone forever,
No more night, only light
When we see His face.

An older but no less powerful reminder of the face of God is a hymn which Carrie E. Breck wrote in 1898:

Face to face with Christ my Saviour,
Face to face—what will it be—
When with rapture I behold Him,
Jesus Christ who died for me?
Face to face I shall behold Him,
Far beyond the starry sky;
Face to face in all His glory,
I shall see Him by and by.

FALSEHOOD

MEANING

The Greek word for "falsehood" is *pseudos,* and it is seen in several English words. A *"pseudo*nym" is a false name, *"pseude*pigraphy" means attributing some writing to a false author, and a *"pseudo*sophistication" is acting as though one is sophisticated when he really is not. In English "pseudo" always speaks of a false impression, and this links it to the basic meaning of our Greek word.

In ancient Greek literature this word spoke mainly of lying. The worst possible lie was perjury, when one told a lie about someone else. Another form of lying was deception, when a workman deceived his boss, or a wife deceived her husband. Aristotle is supposed to have said: "No one believes a man who lies" (Gerhard Kittel, *Theological Dictionary of the New Testament,* IX, p. 596).

Of course, the Christian concept of true and false comes from the Old Testament. In the Ten Commandments bearing false witness is condemned as being evil (Ex. 20:16). This pronounced a divine judgment on perjury, slander, and lying. In fact, the integrity and holiness of Jehovah was the guarantee of truth. By the same token, those who bore false witness placed themselves under God's judgment.

BIBLE USAGE

The concept of falsehood in the New Testament is defined by the Lord Jesus Christ. In speaking to the Pharisees He taught that the devil is a liar from the beginning, and is the father of lies (John 8:44). Therefore any falsehood can be traced directly to the evil one. In the New Testament this lying tendency is seen in several connections.

First, there are many references to lying. Ananias and Sapphira were moved by Satan to lie to the Holy Spirit (Acts 5:3). Paul repeatedly stated that he was not lying, but that his teaching came directly from God (Rom. 9:1; 2 Cor. 11:31; Gal. 1:20). Christians were charged by the Apostle Paul to lay aside all lying (Eph. 4:25). Those who persisted in lying were assumed to have "seared" or insensitive consciences (1 Tim. 4:2). Christians who say they belong to the Lord but live in sin are liars (1 John 1:6; 2:4). Thus the liars in the New Testament were hypocrites whose words and works did not agree.

Second, the New Testament speaks of false (lying) prophets. In the Sermon on the Mount Jesus warned His disciples about false prophets. He compared them to wolves in sheep's clothing (Matt. 7:15). Jesus repeated this warning in the Olivet Discourse, and said they would be a sign of the last times (24:11). Paul's first missionary journey was disturbed by Elymas Bar-Jesus, a false prophet (Acts 13:6). Peter likewise warned against the appearance of false prophets in the last days (2 Peter 2:1), as did John (1 John 4:1).

The New Testament refers, thirdly, to false witnesses. Jesus soundly condemned the sin of false witnessing when He repeated the commandments against murder, adultery, stealing, defrauding, and disrespect of parents (Matt. 19:18; Mark 10:19). It is ironic that the Jewish authorities, who paid lip service to the Law, used false witnesses to condemn Christ (14:55-57).

Fourth, another danger confronting the church was that of false teachers. Peter mentioned this in a warning (2 Peter 2:1). Earlier the Apostle Paul had warned Corinthian Christians against the false (lying) apostles who preyed upon the believers (2 Cor. 11:13).

Fifth, Jesus warned in His final address to the disciples against false christs

(Matt. 24:24). They would appear in the last days and pretend to be the Lord Himself. Their deceptive powers would be great, but the Holy Spirit would help believers to discern the danger.

Thus the New Testament contains many warnings against falsity in faith. Every time such falsity is found, it speaks of the influence of Satan, and it should be rebuked and resisted by believers in the Lord.

ILLUSTRATIONS

Every school child has seen a "true or false" test. A long list of statements appears on a paper, and next to each statement are the letters "T" and "F" for true and false. If a statement agrees with what the teacher said, it is true. If it does not fit the facts as the teacher told them, it is false. In many cases it turns into a guessing game.

Most writers and speakers have commented for many centuries on the matter of truth and falsehood. Mark Twain said: "A lie can travel halfway around the world while the truth is putting on its shoes." In other words, people are more eager to believe a lie than the truth.

Winston Churchill also made his share of startling statements. On the subject of truth and falsehood he outshone himself when he said: "There are a terrible lot of lies going about the world, and the worst of it is that half of them are true."

Robert Louis Stevenson (1850-94) had it right when he said: "The cruelest lies are often told in silence." To which Douglas Malloch added: "The biggest liar in the world is 'They Say.'" (Every church member knows the potency of that remark!)

The ancient Romans were likewise bothered by lies. Quintilian, who is supposed to have lived from A.D. 35-95, put it this way: "A liar needs a good memory." To which some later wit added: "If at first you don't succeed, lie, lie again!" Setting this in a political context, another author said: "All political parties die at last of swallowing their own lies." (That statement sounds modern, but it was said by John Arbuthnot [1667-1735].)

Many have emerged in recent history to claim they are liberators. In reality they are false christs. Some of them were Karl Marx, Mary Baker Eddy (of Christian Science fame), Sun Myung Moon (who founded the Unification Church, the Moonies), and the Latin American liberator Che Guevara. No false christ was more devilish than Adolf Hitler, whose deception can be seen in this quote from one of his speeches: "In the size of the lie is always contained a certain factor of credulity, since the great masses of the people . . . will more easily fall victims to a great lie than to a small one." Then he added: "The victor will never be asked if he told the truth."

Thomas Jefferson (1743-1826) realized the danger of lying, and its potential for destruction of a nation, a society, or a person. Therefore he said: "He who permits himself to tell a lie once finds it much easier to do it a second and a third time till at length it becomes habitual." "To an inveterate liar," claimed an anonymous writer, "truth is stranger than fiction." As the Lord Jesus said, the father of lies is Satan (John 8:44).

FATHER

MEANING

The Greek word for father is *pater*. It takes little imagination to see the connection with such English words as *"paternity"* (becoming a father), *"paternalism"* (the fatherly care exercised by governments for those whom they govern), and *"paternoster"* ("our father," as in the Lord's Prayer).

In Greek literature and philosophy the term "father" had many varied meanings. In the time of Homer it referred to the "patriarchal" control of a father over his house and family. This extended not only to his immediate family, but also to his extended family of household slaves. (The same was true in Roman culture.)

The same patriarchal authority was found in Greek religion, where Zeus was regarded as a divine patriarch. In the mystery religions their gods likewise appeared as father figures. According to Plato a good, ultimate, supreme father presided over all things.

To the Jews their King was perceived to be a father. He was supposed to rule over the nation with a loving, benevolent, fatherlike care. As father of the nation, the King ruled in the place of God and at God's behest. In reality Jehovah was seen to be the Creator and Father of all.

BIBLE USAGE

The New Testament presents two streams of understanding concerning "father." First, it speaks of biological fatherhood. Jesus was returned to Palestine when Archelaus received the crown of his evil father, Herod (Matt. 2:22). James and John were known by the name of their father, Zebedee (4:21). Jesus raised a little lass from the dead in the presence of her father and mother (Mark 5:40-41).

The same word, father, is also applied to forefathers or ancestors. Jews claimed that Abraham was their father (Mattt. 3:9; Luke 1:73). Even the Samaritans said that Jacob was their (fore)father (John 4:12). When Jesus was received triumphantly into Jerusalem, the people identified Him with their (fore)father David (Mark 11:10). Father means either a male parent or a male forefather in a biological or national sense.

But father also has figurative meanings. Jews called their rabbis or teachers father, a practice that Jesus forbade (Matt. 23:9). (Many feel that this also prohibits the practice of calling Roman Catholic and Church of England clergymen by the title father.)

The Jews spoke of their spiritual ancestors as fathers in the faith of Judaism (2 Peter 3:4). The same meaning was applied by Paul in writing about the generation which escaped Egypt in the Exodus (1 Cor. 10:1). Here the meaning is almost that of forefathers.

In many cases the New Testament applies the title father to God Himself. He is seen as the Father of spirits (Heb. 12:9). Jesus often referred to God as the Heavenly Father, or literally the Father of heavens (Matt. 5:48; 6:14, 26). As such He is also the Father of glory (16:27; Mark 8:38).

Because God is the Father of the Lord Jesus Christ, He is also the Father of believers. Thus Paul called God "our Father" (Rom. 1:7; 1 Cor. 1:3; Gal. 1:3). In his great praise passage of Ephesians, Paul spoke of God as Father of all believers (Eph. 4:4-6).

It is only because of the reconciling work of Jesus Christ on the cross that Christians enter into the position of children of God. They are thus encouraged by the Scripture to regard God as "Abba [Daddy] Father" (Rom. 8:15). When they pray, their introduction is the phrase: "Our Father, who art in heaven" (Matt. 6:9).

ILLUSTRATIONS

Fatherhood is one of the most elemental facts of life. Most of us are proud of some famous ancestor. Of these John Garland Pollard said: "Genealogy: [is] tracing yourself back to people better than you are." Along the same lines Dean Inge (1860-1954) of St. Paul's Cathedral remarked: "A nation is a society united by a delusion about its ancestry and by common hatred of its neighbors."

On the same subject of fatherhood broadcaster Paul Harvey said: "A father is a thing that is forced to endure childbirth without an anesthetic. . . . A father never feels worthy of the worship in a child's eyes. He is never quite the hero his daughter thinks, never quite the man his son believes him to be, and this worries him, sometimes. . . . Fathers are what give daughters away to other men who aren't nearly good enough, so they can have grandchildren who are smarter than anybody's."

Author Jim Bishop echoed Paul Harvey's sentiments. When his daughter became engaged Jim Bishop said: "This is the third of our four daughters. Every time it happens, I'm obsessed with the feeling I'm giving a million-dollar Stradivarius to a gorilla."

A famous Puritan Nonconformist preacher was John Flavel (died in 1691). His collected writings have been published with great effect. Of Christian fatherhood he once said: "What a mercy was it to us to have parents that prayed for us before they had us, as well as in our infancy when we could not pray for ourselves!"

If finite fathers are so protective of their children, our Heavenly Father must be infinite in His loving care. The Puritans often put pen to paper concerning God's fatherly love. Thomas Watson wrote: "The little word, Father, pronounced in faith, has overcome God." He emphasized the prevailing power of prayer in unleashing God's power. Stephen Charnock (1628-80), a great Presbyterian divine and author of *Existence and Attributes of God,* added: "The word Father is personal; the word God is essential."

Dispelling the dangerous myth that all are the children of God, Louis Everly wrote: "It is only when we are subject to a common father that we are brothers. To become brothers we have only to become sons again."

Professor Merrill Unger of Dallas Theological Seminary concluded regarding the fatherhood of God: "Children of God are only those who are regenerated as a result of faith in Christ. The indwelling Spirit gives to the child of God the realization of his sonship. The popular doctrine of the fatherhood of God and the brotherhood of man is not taught in Scripture. Since man is fallen, a person becomes a child of God only by faith in Christ."

The full import of the fatherhood of God is seen in William Runyan's great hymn:

Great is Thy faithfulness, O God my Father,
There is no shadow of turning with Thee;
Thou changest not, Thy compassions, they fail not;
As Thou hast been Thou forever wilt be.

FEAR

MEANING

The Greek words for fear are *phobos* (fear) and *phobeo* (I fear), and they occur 132 times in the New Testament. One can easily see many connections between the Greek and English words. For instance, "claustro*phobia*" means a fear of small, enclosed places, "agora*phobia*" is a fear of open spaces, and "hydro*phobia*" had as its primary meaning a dread of water. In fact, the word "phobia" means any fear or aversion.

In ancient Greek the word *phobos* came from the word *phebomai* meaning to flee, or to be startled. Thus *phobos* meant flight or terror, and was connected with fear of the unknown, fear of the future, and fear of authorities. It also took on the meaning of fear or reverence for God. This was particularly true in the teaching of Aristotle.

It is the reverential aspect of fear which marked the Old Testament. Israel was commanded to reverence Jehovah. Those who came face to face with an angelic being fell on their faces. Moses was instructed to take off his sandals, when he was in the presence of God on Mount Horeb (Ex. 3:5). Thus the fear of the Lord is reverence (Ps. 111:10).

BIBLE USAGE

As might be expected, there are two basic meanings of fear in the New Testament. First, fear refers to people. Many of Jesus' listeners were afraid of the Jews (John 7:13). At Jesus' trial Pilate also reflected fear of the Jews (19:8). Especially after the Crucifixion the disciples were still afraid of the Jews (20:19). Only the appearance of the resurrected Lord alleviated this fear.

The disciples were plagued by all sorts of fears. They feared the storm on Galilee, though some of them had sailed on it for years (Matt. 14:26). Then they were afraid when they saw that Jesus commanded the storm to stop (Mark 4:40-41).

Even a bold apostle like Paul was not immune from fears. As the enemies of the Gospel closed in, the apostolic band was gripped by fear (2 Cor. 7:5). The Christians at Corinth also showed fear, fear that their testimony might not ring true (7:11).

The Apostle Peter warned Christians of coming trouble. Then he instructed them to resist fear and reject intimidation (1 Peter 3:14). In fact, a Christian should be delivered from the spirit of fear (Rom. 8:15; 2 Tim. 1:7), because the perfect love of God drives away fear (1 John 4:18). Christians who are gripped by the fear of death can be freed by the Lord (Heb. 2:15).

The first meaning of fear is negative, but its second meaning is positive. Godly fear is the reverence which we have toward the Lord. Those who do not know the Lord are characterized as being without fear (reverence) for God (Rom. 3:18). This reverential awe before God motivates Christians to win others (2 Cor. 5:11), and it also moves believers to live godly lives (7:1). In fact, such reverence marks all of the relationships in an obedient Christians's life. Wherever he goes he displays this reverence toward God (Phil. 2:12).

Peter depicted this reverential fear as a part of holiness: as a Christian draws nearer to the Lord his or her life is marked by this reverence or fear (1 Peter 1:16-17). So a Christian's witness is marked by reverence. As we give an answer to those who question our beliefs, we do so in a reverent way, showing that we fear the Lord (3:15).

A third meaning of the word is respect for people. Paul urged the Romans to show respect to all who are in authority (Rom. 13:3, 7). Peter extended this concept to include the respect of employees for their employers (1 Peter 2:18) and the respect of wives for their husbands (3:1).

Thus the word "fear" includes both a negative emotion and a positive attitude. Christians are not to fear people or persecution or even Satan. They are, however, to show reverence toward God and to respect other people.

ILLUSTRATIONS

Many people have spoken about fear, and most have condemned it. Lioyd Douglas said: "If a man harbors any sort of fear, it . . . makes him landlord to a ghost." H.A. Overstreet declared fear to be unnatural: "To hate and to fear is to be psychologically ill . . . it is, in fact, the consuming illness of our time." The German philosopher Heidegger said that ours is an era of "Angst," which means fear in German.

Courageous people from all walks of life have condemned fear. Franklin Delano Roosevelt, who overcame a handicap to serve as President of the United States said: "The only thing we have to fear is fear itself." Along the same lines Henry David Thoreau (1817-62), a transcendentalist writer, wrote: "Nothing is so much to be feared as fear." In the same vein, Arthur Wellesley, a Duke of Wellington (1759-1852) concluded, "The only thing I am afraid of is fear."

As much as fear of people and events is to be disdained, so reverential fear of God is to be cultivated. C. Neil Strait said of this reverential fear: "Not all fears are bad. Many of them are wholesome, indeed, very necessary for life. The fear of God, the fear of fire, the fear of electricity, are lifesaving fears that, if heeded, bring a new knowledge to life."

The stark contrast between fear of man and reverence for God appears in many places. Well-known Puritan penman John Flavel said: "By the fear of the Lord men depart from evil; but by the fear of man they run themselves into evil."

Another famous Puritan writer, William Gurnall, showed that God is the Conqueror of all fear: "Our help is in the name of the Lord, but our fears are in the name of man."

This same liberating reverence for God found expression in the writings of F.B. Meyer, a great pulpit orator in London. He wrote: "God incarnate is the end of fear, and the heart that realizes that He is in the midst, that takes heed to the assurance of His loving presence, will be quiet in the midst of alarm."

Many people have faced frightening experiences, and sometimes nations have passed through times of terror. One such nightmare of human history was the frequent bombing of London and other English cities by Germany during World War II. Many Christians testified that those nighttime attacks were times of great peace because the Lord was with them. In this vein, one London church posted the following sign on its bulletin board: "If your knees knock, kneel on them."

Robert Louis Stevenson gave some advice worth following: "Keep your fears to yourself; share your courage with others."

FELLOWSHIP

MEANING

The word "fellowship" in the New Testament represents a well-known Greek word, *koinonia*. The root meaning of this word is "common," so fellowship is having an experience or possessions in common with someone else. The masculine word *koinonos* means someone who participates or shares in an experience.

In secular Greek the word was used to describe normal human relationships. A business partnership was known by this name. It also referred to marriage, in which people hold things in common. Friendship was also described by this word, and to a Greek person friendship implied the sharing of possessions. But in Greek religion fellowship was applied mainly to sacramental meals.

The Greek Old Testament used this word sparingly. It had both legal and friendly meanings in the Old Testament, but no reference was made to fellowship with God. Jehovah in the Old Testament was far too holy and exalted to be drawn into an intimate fellowship with His people.

BIBLE USAGE

But in the New Testament a whole new concept is developed, that of intimate fellowship between man and man, and between God and man. In fact, this word has several different applications. First, it applies to partnerships in business. According to the Gospel of Luke, James and John, Zebedee's sons, were partners with Simon Peter in the fishing business (Luke 5:10).

Second, the word applies to fellowship with Christ. Salvation calls each Christian into fellowship with Christ (1 Cor. 1:9), so a believer becomes a "fellow partaker" of the Gospel (9:23). The Gospel by which we are saved also becomes the basis of our fellowship (Phil. 1:5).

Third, the Lord's Supper is closely connected with fellowship. In it we remember our sharing in the body and blood of the Lord (1 Cor. 10:16). We share one bread, such as the Jews shared in the offering on one altar (10:17-18). Partaking of the Lord's table precludes any participation in idolatrous feasts (10:21).

Fourth, in a real sense Christians share in Christ's life-experiences. Christians enter into the sufferings of Christ (Rom. 8:17; Phil. 3:10). In dying to themselves they also share in His crucifixion (Rom. 6:6; Gal. 2:20). By the same token believing in Christ gives Christians new life, a share in His resurrection (Col. 2:12-13; 3:1; Eph. 2:5-6). Ultimately Christians will also share with Christ in His glorification (Rom. 8:17).

Fifth, fellowship in the New Testament also links Christians to the Holy Spirit. This is most clearly seen in the apostolic benediction. As Paul pronounced a blessing on the Corinthian Christians, he committed them to the fellowship of the Holy Spirit (2 Cor. 13:14).

Sixth, the church of Jesus Christ is the greatest expression of spiritual fellowship known to people. To the Romans Paul indicated that fellowship included sharing our prosperity and our homes in hospitality (Rom. 12:13). Titus was commended because he shared in the ministry with Paul; he was a "fellow-worker" (2 Cor. 8:23). According to Philippians, the Christians shared with Paul in his suffering and in the great grace of God (Phil. 1:7). In writing to Philemon, Paul requested that Onesimus be accepted as a partner in the Gospel (Phile. 17). Perhaps it was John who made the most of fellowship, as he described Christian fellowship as embracing not only other Christians but also the Lord Himself (1 John 1:3, 7).

Fellowship means sharing. When we share a common faith, we also share a common Lord. Because of this bond we also share our possessions and our homes with one another. In missions we share the Gospel of God's grace with those who have never heard about it.

ILLUSTRATIONS

Fellowship figures largely in the preaching and writing of Christian communicators. A leading light in the Rwanda Revival and a gifted preacher of holiness is Roy Hession. On the subject of fellowship he said: "The only basis for real fellowship with God and man is to live out in the open with both." (Fellowship was one of the primary themes of the Rwanda awakening.)

Thomas Kelly, a Puritan preacher and writer, added to this theme: "The final grounds of holy fellowship are in God. Persons in the fellowship are related to one another through Him, as all mountains go down into the same earth. They get at one another through Him."

From Switzerland the practical Christian psychologist Paul Tournier underscored the essential nature of Christian fellowship with these words: "To satisfy the burning thirst of tormented souls, nothing will do but to take them to the well of living waters, to true fellowship with Christ."

Along the same lines of fellowship with the Lord, the beloved pastor Malcolm Cronk said: "When our fellowship with the Lord is ruptured, our conscience gets dull, we blow our stacks, let the seamy side of life show through, and live like children of the devil."

Concerning the fellowship of the church David Schuller said: "God calls us not to solitary sainthood but to fellowship in a company of committed men."

Also concerning fellowship with others Sydney Harris said: "Searching for oneself within is as futile as peeling an onion to find the core: when you finish, there is nothing there but peelings; paradoxically, the only way to find oneself is to go outward to a genuine meeting with another."

Even the celebrated bishop and theologian Augustine expressed the need for fellowship, when he said: "I loved the talk, the laughter, the courteous little gestures toward one another, the sharing of the study of books of eloquence, the companionship that was sometimes serious and sometimes hilariously nonsensical, the differences of opinion that left no more bad feeling than if a man were disagreeing with his own self, the rare disputes that simply seasoned the normal consensus of agreement."

Elisha Hoffman caught the genius of fellowship with the Lord in this hymn:

> What a fellowship, what a joy divine,
>   Leaning on the everlasting arms;
> What a blessedness, what a peace is mine,
>   Leaning on the everlasting arms.

The heavenly dimension of fellowship was caught by John Sammis in the final stanza of his hymn:

> Then in fellowship sweet we will sit at His feet,
>   Or we'll walk by His side in the way;
> What He says we will do, Where He sends we will go—
>   Never fear, only trust and obey.

FIRST

MEANING

The Greek word for "first" is *protos* or *proton*. It occurs in its various forms more than 220 times in the New Testament. It is also reflected in such English words as "*proto*type" (the original model of an invention), "*proto*plasm" (the stuff from which elementary life forms are made), and "*proto*col" (the order of ranks on formal social occasions).

Just as the word has many combinations in English, so it is found in many different Greek compound words. For instance, *protocathedria* speaks of the place of highest honor (Matt. 23:6; Mark 12:39). Stephen, the first martyr, was called in Greek *protomartus* (Acts 22:20). The first Child of Mary was Jesus, and He is called *prototokos*, the Firstborn (Luke 2:7). He is also known as "the firstborn among many brethren" (Rom. 8:29). The idea of *protos* is first among equals, but Christ was also the *monogenes* (uniquely or only begotten One).

BIBLE USAGE

In Greek the word *protos* or *proton* stands for "first" in three ways. It means first in terms of space, or one who is out in front. Also, it stands for first in terms of time, the earliest one. Finally it speaks of being first in rank or value, the leader of a group. All of these blend in New Testament usage.

The primary use of the word is numerical. In listing the disciples, Peter is first (Matt. 10:2). Because of Moses' role in writing the Pentateuch, he was the first to state some spiritual truths (Rom. 10:19). Paul considered himself to be first in the rank of sinners, because he had persecuted many Christians (1 Tim. 1:15).

Early Christians also had the privilege of priority, as they were the first. Paul commended the Philippian Christians, because they had been with him from the first day of that church (Phil. 1:5). This seems to include Lydia and the Philippian jailer who were converted when Paul visited Philippi (Acts 16). Paul paid the same compliment to the Ephesian Christians who had stood with him from his first mission to Asia (20:18).

The same term was used by Paul to describe his trial before Caesar. In writing to Timothy, Paul lamented that no one stood with him at his first trial (2 Tim. 4:16). In fact Paul's "friends" had abandoned him in the crisis, and this required special forgiveness on Paul's part.

First also has theological implications. The Old Testament is known in the New Testament as the first covenant. The death of Christ was the ultimate Sacrifice paid for the sins committed under the first covenant (Heb. 9:15). Thus the New Covenant of Grace replaces the Old Covenant of Law. The proof of the New Covenant is seen in the fact that Jesus was the first to proclaim light to both Jews and Gentiles (Acts 26:23).

Jesus is known as the First and the Last (Rev. 1:17; 2:8; 22:13). This reflects a similar statement concerning Jehovah God (Isa. 44:6). The corollary of this truth is seen in John the Baptist's statements that Jesus held the preferred position in God's plan. Though Jesus came after John in time, He is before John in preeminence (John 1:15, 30). Indeed, we should all make Christ's glory our top priority (Matt. 6:33).

Another aspect of priority is seen in Jesus' teaching. He quoted the commandment from Deuteronomy 6:5 concerning man's duty to love God with all his heart, soul, and mind. Then Jesus asserted that this is the first commandment (Matt. 22:38). The reason is this, that one who loves God truly also loves others.

A final and important use of the word relates to Jesus' teaching concerning the attitude of His disciples. After talking about the disciples' leaving relatives for His sake, Jesus said that the first shall be last (19:30). Then Jesus followed through on this teaching by asserting that the road to greatness in God's kingdom leads through service. Again the last shall be first and the first last (20:27). This teaching lays down the ground rules for Christian service.

Though the word "first" has some ordinary meanings as a numerical term, it also has some extremely profound spiritual applications. The most meaningful of these is Jesus' teaching that the first shall be last, and the last shall be first.

ILLUSTRATIONS

There is a heartwarming ring to the word "first." For many children, first grade marks the beginning of a marvelous educational adventure. As a child grows up, "first" marks many achievements, everything from first place in a music contest to first place in sports. Entering into the teenage years, first love takes on a poignant meaning. Afterward comes marriage, and the unforgettable first anniversary. Soon comes the first child and a generation later the first grandchild. "First" has an exciting sound to it.

First speaks of priorities in our lives. President Dwight Eisenhower said, "The older I get the more wisdom I find in the ancient rule of taking first things first—a process which often reduces the most complex human problem to a manageable proportion."

The Jansenist philosopher and mathematician Blaise Pascal put a similar idea into fewer words: "The last thing one knows is what to put first."

From the Scripture one sees clearly that Christ should be put first. Christ is top priority because of who He is. George Bancroft, a venerable dean of St. Paul's Cathedral, said, "I find the name of Jesus Christ written at the top of every page of modern history." Jesus Christ is preeminent, or first, in the history of humanity.

From France the famous author Jean Paul Richter wrote: "[Jesus Christ], being the holiest among the mighty, the mightiest among the holy, lifted with His pierced hand empires off their hinges, and the stream of centuries out of its channel, and still governs the ages."

On a more modern theme Donald R. Brown said of Jesus: "When I nominated Jesus as my supreme ecologist, years of inner pollution became instantly biodegradable."

Speaking about the preeminence of Christ, Napoleon Bonaparte said: "Caesar, Charlemagne, and I have built empires on force, and they will decline. Only Jesus Christ, the crucified Nazarene, has built His empire on love, and to this very day millions would die for Him."

Charles W. French spoke along the same lines: "Jesus Christ alone stands at the absolute center of humanity, the only completed harmonious man. He is the absolute and perfect truth, the highest that humanity can reach; at once its perfect image and supreme Lord."

FOLLOW

MEANING

The important New Testament term "to follow" represents the Greek word *akoloutheo*. Its significance in the New Testament can be seen in the fact that it occurs no fewer than 90 times in the New Testament, and 79 of those occurrences are in the Gospels. Thus the term is linked firmly to the life and ministry of Jesus. He is the One to follow.

The basic meaning of "follow" is to go after someone or something. Early in the history of the Greek language, however, it took on another meaning: to imitate or follow someone's example. This dual meaning colored the New Testament use of our word *akoloutheo*.

In the Greek Old Testament, the Septuagint, "following" often had a negative connotation. It spoke of following evil people into the sin of idolatry (Jud. 2:12). Sometimes it spoke of following Jehovah (Deut. 1:36), though the Jews did not sense an intimate relationship between themselves and their exalted God. People followed examples, as Elisha followed Elijah (1 Kings 19:20). Otherwise "following" is largely a New Testament concept.

BIBLE USAGE

The idea of following is usually attached to the Lord Jesus Christ. From the first, large crowds came after Him. Early in His ministry crowds came from Galilee, Jerusalem, and Transjordan to follow Him (Matt. 4:25; Mark 3:7-8; Luke 6:17-18). After Jesus gave the Sermon on the Mount multitudes followed Him (Matt. 8:1). On His final trek to Jerusalem crowds pursued Him (19:2). At the Triumphal Entry into Jerusalem the crowds cried, "Hosanna! [Jehovah save]" (21:9). From the early days of His earthly ministry Jesus was popular with the crowds, not least because of His healing ministry.

The primary party of His followers were the disciples. Wherever Jesus went they accompanied Him. Some others said they would follow, but the price put them off. One example was a man who had family responsibilities (8:18-22), and another was a rich young ruler (Mark 10:17-21; Luke 18:22-23).

The true disciples obeyed Christ's command to follow. Matthew gave up his tax business (Matt. 9:9; Mark 2:14; Luke 5:27). Peter packed in his fishing and followed Jesus (Matt. 4:18-20; Mark 1:16-20). This principal of following Jesus is the cornerstone of true discipleship (Luke 9:23).

However, discipleship is much more than simply strolling with the Saviour. It means following His lifestyle. Following the Lord means alignment with His kingdom (9:61-62). Eternal life is defined as following Jesus (Mark 10:17, 21; John 8:12). In the Revelation triumphant disciples are described as those who "follow the Lamb wherever He goes" (Rev. 14:4).

Jesus placed a high priority on following. Those who do not take up the cross and follow Him are not worthy of Him (Matt. 10:38). This involves counting the cost of discipleship before jumping in at the deep end (Luke 14:27-33).

For the disciples of Jesus' day, following Him meant identification with Him in His entire life. Those who followed Jesus had no secure home; they were "transients" as He was (Matt. 8:19-20). Those who followed Jesus were committed to go forward and never look back (Luke 9:61-62). Following Jesus meant taking the daily risk of losing one's life, or at least losing control over one's life (Mark 8:34). On the verge of His passion Jesus again underlined the total commitment involved in following Him (John 12:25-26).

In writing on the subject of following, the German theologian Gerhard Kittel said: "[Following Jesus] is not in any sense an imitation of the example of Jesus . . . but exclusively a fellowship of life and suffering with the Messiah which arises only in the fellowship of His salvation" (*Theological Dictionary of the New Testament*, I, p. 214).

ILLUSTRATIONS

Following is a common experience for us all. Who has not seen a little lad with short legs trying to keep up with his long-legged daddy? This is most picturesque in the snow, as the small boy tries to tread in his daddy's footsteps. Usually the boy falls face-first in the fluffy white stuff.

When we first started flying, back in the '50s and '60s, the whole air transport industry was more primitive than it is now. As a plane touched down, a little car would position itself in front of the landing aircraft. Atop the car roof was a sign bearing these words: "Follow Me." The driver led the pilot and his passengers to the terminal.

Sometimes it is wrong to follow. Who has not heard of those little Norwegian rodents, the lemmings? Apparently they are so devoted to their pack-mates that when one rushes headlong over the cliff into a fjord, the whole pack follows to their death. This suicide migration is actually a precise picture of the human race in its rebellion against God. A professor recently said: "As I grew up I was promoted from the human race to the rat race."

What a difference there is in following the Lord. Charlene Myhre echoed the experience of many Christians when she said: "Lord, let it not be that I follow You merely for the sake of following a leader, but let me accept You as Lord and Master of every step I take."

William Lyon Phelps echoed this sentiment when he said: "I call the attention of you young people to Jesus, the greatest Leader, the most proficient Teacher, the most absolutely right Person the world has ever known. I tell you that the only way this world can be saved is by Jesus." In other words, "Follow Jesus."

In the Christian context obedience and following lie close together. Puritan writer Thomas Watson warned of the danger of incomplete following: "Some will obey partially, obey some commandments, not others; like a plow which, when it comes to a still piece of earth, makes a balk. But God that spake all the words of the moral law, will have all obeyed." Following by "fits and starts," according to Watson, is not following at all.

Many hymns and songs deal with this subject, none more clearly than this one we learned in England:

> I want to walk with Jesus Christ,
> All the days I live of this life on earth,
> To give to Him complete control
> Of body and of soul.
>
> Follow Him, follow Him; yield your life to Him.
> He has conquered death; He is King of kings.
> Accept the joy which He gives to those
> Who yield their lives to Him.

FOOLISHNESS

MEANING
The Greek word for a "fool" is *moron,* and their word for "foolishness" is *moria.* This root is seen in the English word "moron" (literally, an adult with the intelligence of an average child 8-12 years old).

The Greek words are remnants of even older terms. Some think they are connected to the Sanskrit word *muras,* which means dull-witted. Another possible connection is the Latin term *morus,* meaning absurd.

In secular Greek the word was used to describe insipid, tasteless foods. From a physical standpoint it meant fatigued or dull people. It can refer to the acts of a person who failed to show judgment, or who exhibited a general "deficiency of intellectual and spiritual capacities" (Gerhard Kittel, *Theological Dictionary of the New Testament,* IV, p. 832). The word was even applied to a politically "foolish" decision.

BIBLE USAGE
There are three levels of meaning in the New Testament for this word, *moron.* The first level of meaning is apparent foolishness. Paul said that Christians appear to be foolish (1 Cor. 3:18; 4:10). However, they are spiritually wise.

Closely allied to the first meaning, apparent foolishness, is a second meaning. This might be called theological foolishness. In God's economy some things are right, though they appear foolish by man's standards. To unsaved people the preaching of the Cross appears to be foolish, but Christians find in it eternal strength (1:18). Greek wisdom never solved the deepest problems of people, but the "foolishness" of the Gospel did (1:21).

The same idea is used to describe the apparent "foolishness" of Christians who place Christ above culture (3:18; 4:10). They appear to be foolish by human standards, but by God's measuring stick they are wise. In fact God sometimes uses people who appear foolish to the world to confound the wisest people (1:26-31). The end result of this strange switch is that God is glorified (1:31; 3:19).

Another aspect of this theological foolishness is found in Paul's Letter to the Ephesians. Sinful, filthy talk is ultimately revealed to be foolish (Eph. 5:4). Paul pursued this same idea in his Pastoral Epistles. Timothy was instructed to refute all foolish arguments and petty quarrels (2 Tim. 2:23). The same injunction was delivered to Titus. He was to shun all foolish philosophical debates which detract from the cause of the Gospel and the health of the church of Jesus Christ (Titus 3:9).

A further aspect of foolishness may be called illustrative foolishness. Christ showed the foolishness of all practices which excluded God. This is most clearly seen in the parables. In the Sermon on the Mount, there are several references to foolishness. But it is the height of social sin to call one's brother a fool (Matt. 5:22). On the other hand, it is unadulterated foolishness to ignore the Word of God as a foundation for life. This is compared to building one's house on sand (7:24-27).

To spend all of one's energies in gathering a large harvest and to neglect the spiritual issues of life is likewise foolish. Someday one will have to leave the earth and all one has accumulated here. To trade material prosperity for soul prosperity is foolish in the extreme (Luke 12:13-21).

In His final discourse Jesus told a story about Five Wise and Five Foolish Virgins. The five foolish virgins were not prepared when the bridegroom came to the wedding. By the same token many will not be prepared when Christ returns for

His own. These are seen to be fools forever (Matt. 25:1-13).

To summarize, wisdom is ordering one's life according to God's standards. On the other hand, foolishness is placing any physical or material consideration above spiritual priorities. Eternity will reveal the dimensions of that foolishness.

ILLUSTRATIONS

Literature is full of references to foolishness. President Abraham Lincoln (1809-65) admitted, "You can fool all the people some of the time, and some of the people all of the time, but you cannot fool all of the people all of the time." Foolishness has its limits, and leaders must realize this.

William Shakespeare (1564-1616) alluded to foolishness in his play *King Richard III*: "O," lamented the King, "I am Fortune's fool" (Act III, scene 1). Many of Shakespeare's characters were made fools of by Fortune.

William Butler Yeats (1865-1939) reckoned that love makes a fool of people, as he said in "Down by the Salley Gardens":

She bid me take love easy, as the leaves grow on the tree
But I, being young and foolish, with her would not agree.

Edward Young (1683-1765) caught the same idea in his poem, "Love of Fame": "Be wise with speed," he urged. "A fool at forty is a fool indeed."

Frances Bacon (1561-1626) urged fools to hide their foolishness from the public. It was Bacon who penned the line: "Silence is the virtue of fools."

Martin Luther (1483-1546) is credited with many wise and witty sayings. He is presumed to be the author of great sermons and grand songs, but this statement is also attributed to him: "He who loves not woman, wine, and song / Remains a fool his whole life long." (To be fair, the authorship of that quip is hotly disputed.)

More famous lines underscore the nature of foolishness. Alexander Pope (1688-1744) wrote: "Fools rush in where angels fear to tread." John Lyly (1554-1606) coined the phrase: "There is no fool like an old fool." To which Jacob M. Braude appended: "There's no fool like an old fool—you can't beat experience." The great Oliver Wendell Holmes, Jr. said: "Controversy equalizes fools and wise men—and the fools know it." Edgar Allan Poe (1809-49) wrote: "I have great faith in fools; self-confidence, my friends call it." Returning to the theme of romance Joey Adams said: "Never let a fool kiss you or a kiss fool you."

As in all things, God has the last word on the subject of foolishness. In a great psalm David began by writing: "The fool has said in his heart, 'There is no God'" (Ps. 14:1).

FOREKNOWLEDGE

MEANING

The Greek word represented by "foreknowledge" is *proginosko*. It is reflected in the medical word "prognosis" (a prediction concerning the future course of a disease, based on diagnosis).

In secular classsical Greek the word *proginosko* indicated the ability to discern a coming event, either by wise forethought or by cleverness. There is also an aspect of events foretelling themselves, such as a storm which signals its arrival by dark clouds and strong winds. The Greeks also used the word to describe a medical *prognosis*. Homer warned, however, that any real foreknowledge of destiny is hidden from people.

The word "foreknowledge" is important to Christians, since it expresses an aspect of God's knowing. Because God is infinite, He knows everything. Thus He can foresee events in time and space, and He can also empower prophets to predict the future.

BIBLE USAGE

The word "foreknowledge" appears only seven times in the entire New Testament, and three of these appearances are in the letters of Peter. Foreknowledge is seen as a divine ability, as God foreknows events. Before the dawn of human history and before Adam ate the forbidden fruit, God knew that Jesus Christ would die for our sin (Acts 2:23). Interestingly, the same verse indicates that the people who put Christ to death were responsible. Thus divine sovereignty and human responsibility are placed side by side in Scripture.

Another mention of God's foreknowledge is found in Paul's writings. Here the predestination by which God causes people to be elected for salvation is teamed up with His foreknowledge. God predestined those whom He foreknew would be saved (Rom. 8:29). Some scholars think that foreknowledge limits God's sovereignty. Because He knows something will happen, He is helpless to change the course of events. But nothing can curtail the absolute freedom of God.

In speaking of Israel's history, God foreknew that they would reject Christ as Messiah. Still Jehovah did not reject them (11:2). He will ultimately bring them to a realization that Jesus is Messiah. Thus the infinite God is marked by foreknowledge.

A second application of foreknowledge refers to Jesus, who also exhibited this knowledge of the future. Peter wrote that Christ's coming was foreknown before the foundation of the world (1 Peter 1:20). In fact, God the Father is the One who foreknew. Other portions of Scripture indicate that the decision to sacrifice the Saviour occurred before the commencement of human history (Rev. 13:8).

The third use of "foreknowledge" refers to humans, who do *not* have divine omniscience. Thus for us foreknowledge is either a shrewd guess or a logical deduction. We either speculate that something might occur, or we conclude that something must occur.

In fact Paul used this word to speak of previous knowledge. Jews knew about him for a long time in the past, so they could have testified on his behalf when he came to trial in Jerusalem (Acts 26:5). Of course they did not testify for him, but rather against him. In this verse the word *proginosko* almost means in-depth knowledge, rather than foreknowledge.

The final appearance of "foreknowledge" in the New Testament is found in 2 Peter. Peter urges Christians to be alert to coming events, especially the climax of human history. Because they have received prophetic foreknowledge, they should stand fast against the satanic strokes of the last days (2 Peter 3:17). Here again, it is not the Christians who have foreknowledge; rather they profit from a prophetic vision communicated through the Holy Spirit's inspiration.

Foreknowledge is God's business. Only He knows "the end from the beginning." People are in the dark about the future unless God gives them a prophetic word.

ILLUSTRATIONS

Many women exhibit "a sixth sense." They anticipate events or assess character with uncanny accuracy. This is just sensitivity, and should not be confused with God's foreknowledge.

In business people often make educated guesses. The American car companies guessed that people would ultimately want smaller cars. Based on this analysis and advanced planning, car companies survived the oil crisis of the '70s. This was not foreknowledge, just good business sense.

Every day we see weather people predicting precipitation or a lack of it. They can usually tell us when a cold front will move through our region, and when we will enjoy clear weather and balmy breezes. Unfortunately they are not always completely accurate. Their predictions are only as good as their equipment and the whims of airflow patterns. This is not foreknowledge.

A black preacher was asked to explain God's foreknowledge. He put it quaintly: "God knows what He am doing, and He am doing it."

A world away from that black preacher was the fifth-century Bishop of Hippo, St. Augustine (354-430). He saw the same truth of God's foreknowledge and said to God: "Our knowledge, compared with Yours, is ignorance."

John Milton (1608-74), who wrote the great epics *Paradise Lost* and *Paradise Regained*, also took note of God's foreknowledge. Milton asked, "What can escape the eye of God all-seeing, or deceive His heart omniscient?"

An author of many books on God's sovereignty is James I. Packer, an evangelical Anglican theologian and professor. He wrote *Evangelism and the Sovereignty of God* and more recently *Knowing God.* Of God's foreknowledge Packer wrote: "God knows how the cookie will crumble."

Recently Walter Elwell edited an *Evangelical Dictionary of Theology* (Grand Rapids: Baker Book House, 1984). In it Professor Geoffrey Bromiley wrote an article on "Foreknowledge" (pp. 419-421). He rooted foreknowledge in God's omniscience. God knows what has happened, is happening, and will happen. Furthermore God is eternal, so all events are in the present for Him. Because God is in sovereign control and wills events to happen, He also has foreknowledge, but this does not rob man of his responsibility.

Corrie ten Boom, gifted Dutch missionary-evangelist, told a personal story about the foreknowledge of the Lord. As a small girl she often took train trips. Just before departing, her beloved father would put the necessary ticket into her hand. She had the ticket, just when she needed it. Corrie used this to illustrate the foreknowledge of her Heavenly Father. He never gives us sustaining grace until the crisis arises. Through His all-wise foreknowledge, He knows just when we need it.

FORGIVENESS

MEANING

In the New Testament "forgiveness" comes from the Greek word *aphiemi*. Literally this means to send away, or to put apart. Thus the root meaning of forgiveness is to put away an offense.

In secular Greek literature, this word was fundamental. It was used to indicate the sending away of an object or a person. Later it came to include the release of someone from the obligation of marriage, or debt, or even a religious vow. In its final form it came to embrace the principle of release from punishment for some wrongdoing.

The Greek Old Testament, the Septuagint, contained many of these ideas. In the Old Testament *aphiemi* spoke of releasing a prisoner or remitting a debt, but it also came to mean pardon or forgiveness. The New Testament contains 142 references to this word. Of these, 47 are in Matthew, 34 in Mark, 34 in Luke, and 14 in John. This leave only 13 for the remainder of the New Testament. In other words, forgiveness is tied closely to the life of Christ.

BIBLE USAGE

From a Christian standpoint the most important meaning of *aphiemi* is that of pardon or forgiveness. God is the great Source of forgiveness. In the Lord's Prayer we pray for forgiveness of our sins (Matt. 6:12). When John the Baptist came he proclaimed the necessity for such forgiveness (Mark 1:4). Jesus confirmed His deity by forgiving sins (2:5; Luke 7:47). In His final days on earth Jesus urged His disciples to proclaim forgiveness worldwide (24:47).

Peter's Pentecost sermon ended with an invitation to forgiveness (Acts 2:38), which was part and parcel of apostolic preaching (5:31; 10:43). Paul also emphasized the forgiveness of sin (Eph. 1:7; Col. 1:14). Likewise the Apostle John placed primary emphasis on forgiveness (1 John 1:9; 2:12).

Another aspect is the forgiveness which people show to one another. According to the Sermon on the Mount, we are forgiven as we forgive others (Matt. 6:12-14). Though this is a "hard teaching," it seems that Christians who fail to forgive will not be forgiven.

As already mentioned, the first meaning of our word is forgiveness. However, a second meaning is that of departure. Satan left (*aphiemi*) Jesus after tempting Him in the desert (4:11). Jesus left His disciples and went away to pray (26:44). James and Peter left their father Zebedee and his fishing business to follow Jesus (Mark 1:20). Some Jewish bullies also left Jesus, because the crowd was attached to Him (12:12). In these instances the meaning of the word is departure. It is loosely related to the idea of forgiveness, because it speaks of separation from someone.

The idea of separation also pertains to things. Jesus talked about men who had left their houses (Matt. 23:38; Mark 13:34). The disciples said they had left all to follow Jesus (Matt. 19:27; Mark 10:28). Here again the idea is one of separation: people have separated themselves from certain things or places.

One final aspect of the word shows the basic meaning even more clearly. Jesus left the crowds to have privacy with His disciples (Matt. 13:36). In Paul's teaching mention is also made of divorce, in which a husband sends his wife away (1 Cor. 7:11).

The basic meaning of *aphiemi* is to send away. One sees this in the illustrations from the Gospel narratives. The main meaning, however, is forgiveness, in which one puts away all grudges and forgets the wrong done. This is the majestic spiritual importance of this common Greek word. It is important for every Christian to learn the art of forgiveness, or else his or her relationship with the Lord will remain forever clouded, to say nothing of relationships with other people.

ILLUSTRATIONS

Literature and folklore are full of references to forgiveness. "He who forgives ends the quarrel," according to an African proverb. A comparable English proverb is: "The noblest vengeance is to forgive."

Henry Ward Beecher (1813-87), famous Congregational clergyman, said: " 'I can forgive, but I can't forget,' is just another way of saying, 'I will not forgive.' " In other words, forgiveness entails forgetting.

According to Alice Cary (1820-71), a hymn-writer: "Nothing in this lost world bears the impress of the Son of God so surely as forgiveness." A similar sentiment was expressed by Hannah More (1745-1833), an educator and writer: "A Christian will find it cheaper to pardon than to resent. Forgiveness saves the expense of anger, the cost of hatred, the waste of spirits."

C.S. Lewis (1898-1963) sounded a cautionary note to the subject of forgiveness. "Everyone says forgiveness is a lovely idea," he said, "until they have something to forgive."

In commenting on forgiveness a businessman said: "You won't catch me getting ulcers. For one thing, I just take things as they come. For another, I don't ever hold a grudge, not even against people who have done things to me that I'll never forgive."

It is God's forgiveness which presents a pattern for human forgiveness. Devotional writer Oswald Chambers (1874-1917) said: "Never build your preaching of forgiveness on the fact that God is our Father and He will forgive because He loves us. . . . It is shallow nonsense to say that God forgives us because He is love. The only ground on which God can forgive me is through the Cross of my Lord."

Billy Graham put it even more directly: "If His conditions are met, God is bound by His Word to forgive any man or woman of any sin because of Christ."

Christian film producer Billy Zeoli said, concerning forgiveness, "Our God has a big eraser." Someone else formulated forgiveness this way: "We are most like beasts when we kill. We are most like men when we judge. We are most like God when we forgive."

John Owen (1616-83), a well-known Puritan preacher and writer, commented on forgiveness in this statement: "Poor souls are apt to think that all those whom they read or hear of to be gone to thither [heaven] because they were so good and so holy. . . . Yet no one of them, not any one that is now in heaven [Jesus Christ alone excepted], did ever come thither any other way but by forgiveness of sins."

Thomas Adams, another Puritan, said: "Sins are remitted, as if they had never been committed." To which John Bunyan added: "No child of God sins to that degree as to make himself incapable of forgiveness."

FREE, FREEDOM

MEANING

Though the Greek words for "freedom" are found only about 40 times in the New Testament, their significance outstrips their frequency. The Greek words involved are *eleutheros* (free), *eleutheria* (freedom), and *eleutheroo* (to free someone or something).

In the Greek language these words have an interesting history. In their most basic forms, these words related to a "free man" in contrast with a slave. Such persons were usually born free, but some of them had purchased their freedom.

Later the word came to connote the liberation of a country from a tyrant, or from some external foes. (This is especially seen in the writings of historian Herodotus.) Still later freedom of thought became a focus for the word. As the internal order of Greece declined, the freedom of people to think what they wished was cherished.

In the biblical connection freedom is first and foremost spiritual. People are freed from the bondage of sin by the sacrifice of the Lord Jesus Christ.

BIBLE USAGE

Spiritual freedom is the main focus of the Bible. Through Christ Christians are freed from the constraints of their own sinful natures. Jesus' teaching on this theme is found in John 8:31-36. The truth of God's Word makes us free (8:32). This freedom is not enjoyed by Israel, despite their ancestry (8:33-34). Sin enslaves, but Christ is able to free us (8:36). Without Christ people are bound, like a drug addict. With Him they are liberated like a bird on the wing.

The Apostle Paul presented the same subject from another viewpoint. Christians are freed from the slavery of sin, as Jesus had taught (Rom. 6:17-18). Since that liberation they have become bound by the friendly bonds of God's righteousness (6:19-22). Though they once lived in sin, now their relationship to the Lord binds them to His righteous standard of living.

Not only are Christians free from sin, but they are also free from the Law. Here again Paul sets out the principle that Christians are not bound to pedantically obey the Law. Christ compels them to live a godly life, "free from the Law" (7:3-6).

Nowhere is this teaching concerning freedom from the Law more clear than in the Letter to the Galatians. Christians have been spiritually liberated, which Satan's forces cannot abide (Gal. 2:4). To live under the Law is compared to the life of Ishmael, but living in freedom is compared to the life of Isaac, Abraham's heir by faith (4:21-31). Therefore Christians are enjoined to stand firm in their freedom.

God the Father is the Originator of freedom. When one becomes a child of God, he enters into glorious freedom (Rom. 8:21). Serving God sets one free from bondage to anyone or anything; one is bound only to serve the Lord our God (1 Peter 2:16).

Our spiritual freedom involves the Lord Jesus Christ. He Himself taught that when the Son makes people free, they are really free (John 8:36). This freedom is tied to belief in Him and reception of His truth (8:32). In fact, only the Lord can snap the chains of sin and set people free. Abraham Lincoln was known as "the great emancipator," but Jesus Christ is the greatest Emancipator.

When Christ came to the earth, part of His messianic call was to set captives free (Isa. 61:1; Luke 4:18). As His life invades the heart of a believer, true freedom follows (Rom. 8:2, 21). True spiritual freedom results wherever Christ is owned and adored.

By the same token the Holy Spirit also is the Agent of liberation. Whenever the Holy Spirit is in control of a life, there is true spiritual freedom (2 Cor. 3:17). In fact the Holy Spirit is called "the Spirit of life" (Rom. 8:2).

The principle at stake here is profound. If one is bound by sin or Satan, he is most assuredly not a child of God. When Christ comes into a person's life, it is "independence day." True freedom is spiritual, and all freedom which ignores Christ is only fantasy.

ILLUSTRATIONS

Most great men have at some time commented on freedom, though usually they spoke of political or personal freedom. President Dwight D. Eisenhower pointed out: "If we did not believe in the spiritual character of man, we would be foolish indeed to be supporting the concept of free government in the world."

However, people have always realized that freedom costs dearly. Abraham Lincoln (1809-65) reflected on his role as emancipator of slaves and said: "The shepherd drives the wolf from the sheep's throat, for which the sheep thanks the shepherd as his liberator, while the wolf denounces him for the same act as the destroyer of liberty."

President Thomas Jefferson (1743-1826) said a similar thing in other words: "The tree of liberty must be refreshed from time to time with the blood of patriots and tyrants. It is its natural manure."

If political freedom is costly, the price of spiritual freedom is incalculable. Judge Learned Hand showed that Christ was the cause of true liberty when he said: "The spirit of liberty is the spirit of Him who, nearly 2,000 years ago, taught mankind that lesson it has never learned, but has never quite forgotten: that there is a kingdom where the least shall be heard and considered side by side with the greatest."

Paul E. Sherer, a modern American, caught the same idea when he said: "We find freedom when we find God; we lose it when we lose Him." To which the former editor of Decision magazine Sherwood Wirt appended: "Freedom ranks after life itself as the quintessence [highest expression] of the human experience. Freedom defines the man; it stamps the divine image upon him."

Having telephoned a Christian radio station in Chicago, a woman spoke feelingly about freedom. "People tell me of women's liberation," she said, "but I was totally liberated the day I was saved."

John Bunyan (1628-88), famous author of Pilgrim's Progress, suffered in Bedford jail for his faith. On the subject of freedom he said: "Wherefore, though the Christian, as a Christian, is the only man at liberty, as called thereunto of God; yet his liberty is limited to things that are good: he is not licensed thereby to indulge the flesh."

None of the above quotations come near the hymns of Charles Wesley (1707-88) who wrote these immortal lines:

Long my imprisoned spirit lay
    Fast bound in sin and nature's night;
Thine eye diffused a quickening ray,
    I woke, the dungeon flamed with light;
My chains fell off, my heart was free;
I rose, went forth, and followed Thee.

FRIEND

MEANING

The Greek word for friend is *philos,* and it is related to the word for filial love, *phileo.* This root is seen in such English terms as *"phila*delphia" (brotherly love), *"phil*anthropy" (benevolence or, literally, the love of man), and *"phil*ology" (the love of words). A friend is one for whom you have filial love.

Early Greek literature used the word *philos* to describe the followers of a political leader. Later it came to mean the clients of a wealthy man, or legal assistants. When the Romans embraced the language they extended the word to include friends and relatives. It is much like the "official family" of a political person, governor, or President.

In ancient usage the word "friend" had much deeper implications than our casual usage. Aristotle indicated that a person might be called on to sacrifice his life for that of a friend. According to that famous Greek philosopher: "To a noble man there applies the true saying that he does all things for the sake of his friends" (*Theological Dictionary of the New Testament,* IX, p. 153). This concept of friendship lays the basis for the New Testament use of this word.

BIBLE USAGE

The word *philos* appears 29 times in the New Testament; 17 of these references are in the culturally Greek writings of Luke. He attaches many shades of meaning to this basic word.

First, "friend" speaks of social contact. Jesus was accused of loose behavior, because He ate with tax collectors and sinners (Luke 7:34). When the shepherd of Jesus' parable found his one lost sheep, he summoned his friends to celebrate the event with him (15:6). In Acts, the other book by Luke, he refers to Paul's friends who attempted to save the apostle from a dangerous situation in Ephesus (Acts 19:31).

Second, a friend can also refer to a neighbor. People invited friends and neighbors to their feasts, for this was normal (Luke 14:12). When the Prodigal Son returned home, his overjoyed father fetched his friends and neighbors for a party (15:29). Here again friends are found among one's neighbors. The same truth is seen in the parable of a neighbor who came late at night to ask for help (11:5-8).

Third, friends are a source of genuine joy. In the trilogy of parables found in Luke 15 this is the main theme. A shepherd is joyful when he finds his lost sheep (15:6). A young woman rejoices when she finds her lost coin (15:9). Finally a father is joyful at the return of his wayward son (15:32).

Fourth, allegiance to Christ outweighs fidelity to one's family. Jesus urged His disciples to obey Him, even if they had to leave friends and family (21:16). This is a hard teaching when one considers the depth of feeling attached to oriental friendships.

Fifth, the disciples were called friends by Jesus. The Lord prefaced His most serious teaching about martyrdom by calling the disciples, "My friends" (12:4). A similar preface preceded His injunction to obedience. His "friends" obey Him implicitly, and they also enjoy the Father's favor (John 15:14-15). The most extravagant application of this word is a quotation from 2 Chronicles 20:7. Because of his faithfulness to the Lord, Abraham was given an almost unique title. He was called "the friend of God" (James 2:23).

Sixth, another use of the word is seen in the Jewish wedding customs. A groomsman was called "the friend of the bridegroom" (John 3:29). His function was to accompany the groom as he brought his bride home on the wedding day.

Friendship is seen at different levels. Most of us have many acquaintances, whom we know on a superficial level. Others are friends with whom we have many things in common. Fortunate is the person who has one "bosom friend" who enters into the deepest concerns of his life. Only the Lord is the "Friend who sticks closer than a brother" (Prov. 18:24).

ILLUSTRATIONS
There are two types of friends which require illustration. The first is a human friend. Of friends Charles Colton said: "The firmest friendships have been formed in mutual adversity, as iron most strongly united by the fiercest flame." In other words, "A friend in need is a friend indeed."

Samuel Johnson, noted English author and wit, said concerning friendships: "If a man does not make new acquaintances as he advances through life, he will soon find himself left alone. A man, sir, should keep his friendship in constant repair."

The famous Victorian preacher Charles Haddon Spurgeon counted among his friends George Mueller and Hudson Taylor. On friendship Spurgeon said, "Friendship is one of the sweetest joys of life. Many might have failed beneath the bitterness of their trial had they not found a friend."

Dale Carnegie was famous for his book, *How to Win Friends and Influence People*. Of friendship he said: "You can make more friends in two months by becoming interested in other people than you can in two years by trying to get other people interested in you."

The second main emphasis of the word "friend" is the Lord Himself. Sherwood Wirt confirmed this when he wrote: "After the friendship of God, a friend's affection is the greatest treasure here below."

Charles Andrews referred to the friendship of Christ when he wrote: "The older I grow in years, the more the wonder and the joy increases when I see the power of these words of Jesus—'I have called you friends'—to move the human heart. That one word 'friend' breaks down each barrier of reserve, and we have boldness in His presence. Our hearts go out in love to meet His love."

Giovanni Papini, a biographer of Jesus, wrote: "Jesus' home was the road along which He walked with His friends in search of new friends."

Another magnificent expression of this friendship is in Joseph M. Scriben's (1820-86) famous hymn:

What a Friend we have in Jesus,
    All our sins and griefs to bear!
What a privilege to carry
    Everything to God in prayer!
O what peace we often forfeit!
    O what needless pain we bear!
All because we do not carry
    Everything to God in prayer.

Similar to this hymn is Wilbur Chapman's fine hymn based on Luke 7:34:

Jesus! What a Friend of sinners!
    Jesus! Lover of my soul;
Friends may fail me, foes assail me,
    He, my Saviour, makes me whole.

FRUIT

MEANING

The Greek word for "fruit," which appears 66 times in the New Testament, is *karpos*. A closely related combination word in the New Testament is *karpophoros* (fruit-bearing). However, this article will concentrate on the basic word, *karpos*.

The meanings of our word hold few surprises. From earliest mention it stood for the fruit of a tree, or the crop in farming. Also the offspring of a herd was called its fruit. In another sense fruit was the gain achieved in business.

The Greek Old Testament, the Septuagint, also used the word *karpos* in similar ways. The harvest was the fruit of the earth. Human offspring are the fruit of a person. There was also a spiritual implication, as a person's behavior was considered to be a fruit of his belief.

The spiritual aspect of this word was also seen in Persian literature: "The soul is often described as a tree or plant which is planted by the messenger of life with a view to bringing forth fruit. Paradise is the garden, planted by God, in which the souls of the perfect are plants that bear rich and precious fruits" (*Theological Dictionary of the New Testament*, III, p. 614).

BIBLE USAGE

The most frequent references to "fruit" in the New Testament pertain to natural fruit. Jesus noticed a fig tree which bore no fruit, and caused the tree to wither immediately (Matt. 21:18-19). He also used fruitfulness as an analogy to teach spiritual responsibility (Luke 6:44).

A second type of natural fruit is the grape. Jesus often referred to vines and grapes in His parables (Matt. 21:34; Mark 12:2; Luke 20:10). Fruit is the reward for a person who plants a vineyard (1 Cor. 9:7). The Communion cup is called "the fruit of the vine" (Matt. 26:29).

Another natural use of the word "fruit" (sometimes translated "wheat," "crops," or "produce") is more generic. Christ mentioned it in His Parable of the Sower and the Seed (13:8, 26). Crops are seen as payment for farm labor (2 Tim. 2:6; James 5:7).

A second aspect of fruit is biological. In her welcome of the Virgin Mary, Elizabeth spoke of Jesus as the "fruit" of Mary's womb (Luke 1:42). In Peter's sermon at Pentecost Christ is called the "fruit" of David's line (Acts 2:30, marg.). Here fruit refers to the descendants of important personages, or the important descendants of common people.

The third and final use of the word is spiritual fruit. In the Sermon on the Mount, Jesus spoke of fruit as an aspect of Christian character. People are known by their fruit, just as a tree or vine is. So the injunction of Christ was that His disciples should live godly lives (Matt. 7:15-20).

Again in John's Gospel this concept arises. Here Jesus teaches the disciples that they have a relationship to Him of dependence, as branches do to a vine. They are to bear spiritual fruit which is lasting in its effect (John 15:5, 8, 16). There is some debate whether this fruit refers to Christian character or to souls won for Christ. It seems possible that both meanings are correct.

One final passage of Scripture is significant in this consideration of spiritual fruit. Paul wrote the Galatians and described the evil deeds of the flesh, the natural behavior of unregenerate people. The apostle contrasted that with the spiritual cluster of fruit which results from the indwelling Holy Spirit (Gal. 5:19-23).

174   A Christian bears spiritual fruit not because of effort. This would be as senseless as if a gardener would tie apples onto a pear tree. It is a spiritually natural phenomenon that happens when Christians bear the fruit of godly lives and win souls for the Saviour.

ILLUSTRATIONS
Literature has many references to fruit, and they emphasize various aspects. For instance, John Keats (1795-1821) in "To Autumn," wrote:

> Season of mists and mellow fruitfulness,
>   Close-bosom friend of the maturing sun;
> Conspiring with him how to load and bless,
>   With fruit the vines that round the thatch-eaves run.

That lovely picture of autumn reminds one of many falls in England.

Christina Georgina Rossetti (1830-94) spoke of the fullness of a long life when she penned her poem, "A Birthday." "My heart is like an apple-tree," she wrote, "Whose boughs are bent with thickset fruit." Who of us cannot remember such years, when blessings loaded the branches of our lives.

Thomas Campion (died 1620) spoke of the face of his loved one as a garden of delight in his *Fourth Book of Airs*. Of her face he said: "A heavenly paradise is that place / Wherein all pleasant fruits do flow" (vii).

The Book of Common Prayer paraphrases many truths from the Scriptures. God is praised for "The kindly fruits of the earth, so as in due time we may enjoy them." Of the analogy between children and fruit the book says: "Thy wife shall be as the fruitful vine upon the walls of thy house. Thy children like the olive branches round about thy table."

On the subject of spiritual fruit the gifted Lutheran minister Ross Hidy said, "I do not believe it is possible for the fruits of regeneration to be visible in the unregenerate."

To this statement Friedrich Schleiermacher, a famous German theologian and philosopher, added, "The fruits of the Spirit are nothing but the virtues of Christ."

Roy Gustafson, a delightful Bible teacher from St. Petersburg, Florida, spoke of the fruit of the Holy Spirit in this way: "Regardless of how sincere a soul-winner may be, he cannot add one member to the body of Christ. It would be like putting waxed apples on a tree. The Holy Spirit alone does the work."

Jesus taught us not to judge other Christians. This is His prerogative. However, He gave us a good standard by which to judge whether a person is a believer. The Holy Spirit will produce the fruits of righteousness. Someone said: "We are not called to be judges, but we are called to be fruit inspectors."

Many hymns use the picture of fruit to describe a productive Christian life. In recent years many people have moved away from farms, so these analogies have lost popularity. One such old hymn refers to the time when Jesus curses an unfruitful fig tree:

> Nothing but leaves for the Master,
>   O, how His blessed heart grieves,
> When instead of the fruit He is seeking,
>   We offer Him nothing but leaves.

FULLNESS

MEANING

The Greek word for "fullness" is *pleroma*. It comes from the verb *pleroo*, meaning "to fill up." Together these words are used about 100 times in the Greek New Testament.

Originally the word had several practical meanings in Greek. It spoke of the cargo of a ship. A ship was filled with grain, for instance. On a slightly different tack, the word referred to the crew of a ship: a ship was "fully manned." It is easy to see the literal meaning of "fullness."

This word referred to a full container, but it also had abstract meanings. A person was "full of years," meaning that he was very old. On the other end of the scale a baby was spoken of as being "full term." The sea was "full" of riches, including fish.

The Bible uses both aspects of the word. It speaks of a container or a vessel which is full. The Bible also speaks of fullness in an abstract sense. Both of these focuses appear on these pages.

BIBLE USAGE

In a physical sense, the word "fullness" is easily understood. After Jesus fed the 5,000, twelve baskets were filled with "leftovers" (Mark 6:43). All of the treasures and the peoples of the earth are the Lord's, so Paul claimed that the earth is the Lord's and the fullness of it (1 Cor. 10:26, marg.). A slightly different twist is given to our word in the Parable of the Patched Garment. The word translated "to patch" means to complete or fill out the torn garment (Matt. 9:16; Mark 2:21). These are some of the basic, practical uses of the word.

The spiritual applications of the word "fullness" are actually more interesting in the context of this article. Christ is spoken of as the fullness of grace (John 1:16). The incarnate Lord represented the fullness of the Godhead in human, bodily form (Col. 1:19; 2:9). As Christians mature in the faith, they progress toward the fullness of the image of Christ (Eph. 4:13). Christian maturity is a translation of this same word, as a Christian grows to his or her full potential (Col. 1:28; Heb. 6:1). Jesus Christ fulfilled all righteousness, beginning with His baptism (Matt. 3:15).

In Christ the Scriptures, that is the Old Testament, were fulfilled. As He appeared and began to teach, the prophecies concerning the coming of Messiah began to be fulfilled (Mark 14:49). At the end of His earthly life He revealed Himself to two disillusioned disciples on the Emmaus Road, and told them that His life, death, and resurrection had fulfilled the Law and the Prophets (Luke 24:44). In fact, the coming of Christ fulfilled the time schedule set down in God's sovereign plan of salvation (Gal. 4:4; Eph. 1:10).

The church is portrayed by the Apostle Paul as the fullness of Christ's work on earth. The worldwide church of Jesus Christ is *the* fulfillment of His plan to save people (1:23). Someday the whole number of the people of God will be filled up (Rom. 11:25), and then the Lord will return.

Christians are also described as receptacles. They are urged to be full of the Holy Spirit, and not full of alcoholic spirits (Eph. 5:18-19). John the Baptist was filled with the Holy Spirit before he was born (Luke 1:15). In Christ Christians are enabled to fulfill the righteousness required by the Law of God (Rom. 8:3-4). They consciously fulfill the will of God in what they do (Gal. 6:2). This in turn fulfills the law of love as exemplified in the person and work of the Lord Jesus Christ (Rom. 13:10).

There is something wonderful about the word "fulfillment." It speaks of the completion which alone comes through the Lord Jesus Christ.

ILLUSTRATIONS

Some years ago a documentary film showed the remarkable capabilities of a submarine. When the chambers were filled with water the submarine sank slowly beneath the waves and disappeared. At the command of the skipper the same tanks were filled with air; as air forced out water, the craft surfaced. So it is with Christians. The Holy Spirit forces sin out of our lives as He fills us, and we rise to new levels of spiritual life.

Blaise Pascal, famous French mathematician and philosopher, spoke of the "God-shaped vacuum" in every person. There is a void in the life of every person which can only be filled by God. To attempt to fill it with things, or fame, or even culture, is of no avail. Only when Christ Jesus fills that place is there true satisfaction.

In preaching I am often compelled to fly. Actually it is a very pleasant means of travel. When the pilot takes off from Denver for Chicago, he has a flight plan. During the next two hours he flies exactly according to that plan, and when he has fulfilled it, we arrive safe and sound at O'Hare Field in Chicago. God has a plan for our lives, and He will fulfill it if we allow Him to. At the end we shall arrive safe and sound in heaven.

There is yet another fulfillment of significance to each Christian. This is the fullness of the Holy Spirit. A former president of Wheaton College, V. Raymond Edman, loved to speak about the Holy Spirit. Of Him Dr. Edman wrote: "The Spirit-filled life is no mystery revealed to a select few, no goal difficult of attainment. To trust and to obey is the substance of the whole matter."

Dr. Edman used to put the point simply in this way. "What happens," he would ask, "if you are carrying a cup of water and you are jostled?"

"Well," we would answer, "the water spills."

"Correct," Dr. Edman said. "By the same token, if you are filled with the joy of the Lord and you are jostled, only the joy of the Lord can spill over."

Bible paraphraser J.B. Phillips explained the fullness of the Holy Spirit in another way: "Every time we say, 'I believe in the Holy Spirit,' we mean that we believe that there is a living God, able and willing to enter human personality and change it."

Speaking of the entire church of Jesus Christ, British preacher and writer John Stott said: "Before Christ sent the church into the world, He sent the Spirit into the church. The same order must be observed today."

GENTILES (See: *People.*)

GIFTS (SPIRITUAL)

MEANING

Few words in the Greek New Testament are as well known or as emotive as the word for "spiritual gifts." It is the word *charisma*. In English it speaks of charm or ability, such as the charisma of a politician or preacher. Closely related to this word is "charismatic," which often refers to people who place much emphasis on the gifts of the Spirit. The Greek root behind *charisma* is *charis*, which means "grace." God gives spiritual gifts because of His grace, not our goodness.

So specialized is this word that it is largely unknown in secular Greek. But ancient Greeks did use it in referring to social graces. It spoke of a benefit which one derived from another, and also referred to a gift given as a proof of favor. Nevertheless it was rarely used in ancient Greek literature.

By the same token the Greek Old Testament, the Septuagint, also used the word only sparingly. There it usually was translated with the word "mercy." This reveals the close connection between God's mercy and God's grace. Roger Bacon once said: "In grace God gives us what we do not deserve [salvation]. In mercy God does not give us what we do deserve [judgment]."

BIBLE USAGE

Since the word *charisma* is seldom used in secular Greek and is seldom used in the Greek Old Testament, it is to the Apostle Paul we must look for its use in the Bible. There are actually four distinct uses of the word in the New Testament.

First, it speaks of spiritual privilege. Paul believed that the Jews had been given many spiritual privileges. Because God called them He also gifted them (Rom. 11:29). They were His covenant people (11:27). They were beloved by God because of the patriarchs (11:28). Though most of them rejected the Lord, He did not withdraw all the gifts He had bestowed on them. Thus the spiritual privileges of Israel were characterized by our word *charisma*.

Second, God's grace-gifts were seen in physical preservation. Paul spoke of his deliverance from danger as the "favor" (*charisma*) of God (2 Cor. 1:10-11). The implication is that Paul knew he was preserved not by his wisdom or wit, but by the grace of God. Thus God's grace-gift was seen to be preservation.

Third, salvation is seen in the New Testament as a free grace-gift. God revealed His grace in Jesus Christ, and with Him came the inestimable gift of salvation. In the Book of Romans Paul contrasts the bondage of sin with the grace-gift of salvation through the Lord Jesus Christ. In this case the word *charisma* refers to salvation itself (Rom. 5:15: 6:23).

Fourth, the most common application of the word is with reference to spiritual gifts. Paul saw an apostolic role in passing on spiritual gifts (1:11). These were indispensable for the church of Jesus Christ (12:6).

The most extensive treatment of spiritual gifts is found in the Corinthian letters. It is the teaching of the apostle that every Christian has at least one spiritual gift (1 Cor. 1:7; 7:7). The Holy Spirit is the sole Source of every gift (12:4, 9). These gifts were appointed by God for the sake of the church (12:28). Each gift is important, and various believers have differing gifts (12:30). Still Christians are urged to strive after spiritual gifts, which indicates that they are received on request (12:31).

In the Pastoral Epistles Paul relates gifts to the ministry of the church. Timothy received a spiritual gift when the elders prayed over him, and Paul urged young Timothy to develop that gift (1 Tim. 4:14). Again in his second letter, Paul urged Timothy to fire up the gift which he had received (2 Tim. 1:6). Perhaps the gift was preaching.

Whatever one says about spiritual gifts, they do appear to be given by the Holy Spirit. Their exercise is designed to enhance the ministry of the church. Therefore, an individual Christian should take no credit whatever for his or her gift or gifts.

ILLUSTRATIONS

The subject of gifts is always controversial. The pulpit committee of a certain church was seeking a pastor who could preach, administer, engage in visitation, and inspire the youth. Someone suggested this standard of judgment. If the prospect had one gift, the church would continue at about the same size. Should the candidate have two of the above-mentioned gifts, the church would grow. If he had three of the four gifts, the church might expect to become the largest in town. If he had all four gifts, suggested the adviser, do not touch him with a ten-foot pole. He is a freak. This humorous little story hides a significant truth. Many church people expect their pastor to be a "jack-of-all-trades" and a master of them all.

One of the most provocative writers on the subject of gifts was the late David Watson. Shortly before his untimely death he wrote, *I Believe in the Church* (London: Hodder and Stoughton, 1978). In introducing the subject of gifts, David Watson quoted Dr. Donald Coggan, the Archbishop of Canterbury, who said: "Why is it that the Pentecostal churches are growing at such a phenomenal rate? Is it possible that they have gifts of the Spirit which we have not?"

In another connection David Watson quoted an enthusiastic German pastor, Arnold Bittlinger. He defined spiritual gifts in this pointed phrase: A spiritual gift is "a gratuitous manifestation of the Holy Spirit, working in and through, but going beyond, the believer's natural ability for the common good of the people of God."

David Watson, who enjoyed a thriving pastoral ministry in York, England, suggested three inevitable results if spiritual gifts are employed within a church. First, inferiority and superiority complexes are banished from the church. If one is simply exercising a God-given grace gift, he has nothing of which to be proud or to be ashamed.

Second, Christians should earnestly desire spiritual gifts. A sensitive pastor or leader will seek out spiritual gifts. Then he will suit service to develop and expand those gifts. The end result will be a stronger church fellowship.

Third, we must use the gifts which are available. If we do not, we reduce people to cogs in a wheel. As a keen lay preacher once told me, "Pastor, if I cannot use my gift, I become a dumb priest." (He reflected the priesthood of all believers [1 Peter 2:9; Ex. 19:5-61].)

According to Michael Harper, another Anglican: "No amount of theological training can bestow *charisma* on a person. It is the sole gift of God."

GLADNESS

MEANING

The Greek word for "gladness" is *chara* and is related to the verb "to be glad" (*chairo*). It is translated in the New Testament with many words such as "be glad," "rejoice," "be joyful," "all hail," "farewell," "greetings," and "Godspeed." The reason for this bewildering batch of meanings becomes clear in this article.

The Greek dramatist Aeschylus (525-456 B.C.) concluded, "Joy [is] a beauteous spark divine." To ancient Greeks it was a greeting, a wish for the happiness of one's friend. It was also the object of fellowship, as seen in the festal joy of religion. Greeks spoke, as we do, of "tears of joy." Homer saw joy as being rooted in human passions, as we may "feel" joyful.

On the other hand, the Stoics (who are mentioned in Acts 17:18) were a sour bunch of Greek philosophers. They had no room for joy, which they regarded as a false judgment of reality. If you felt joyful, you must be ignorant of the facts! (Most of us know people like that.)

The Greek Old Testament made much of joy. It referred to weddings as joyful feasts. Joy also characterized Israel when they had a great military victory, and joy was part of the true worship of God.

BIBLE USAGE

There are two broad categories of usage in the New Testament. First, the word is used to describe joyful experiences. Christians share the joy of others. Jesus both taught and exemplified the reality of joy (John 15:11; 16:20-24). He expected His disciples to be joyful people. The Apostle Paul also taught the truth that Christians are joyful, and they can share the joy of others (Rom. 12:15).

In His parables Jesus taught the lesson of spiritual joy. When a shepherd finds his lamb, he rejoices (Luke 15:7). A girl finds her lost coin and rejoices (15:9). By the same token, a father finds his lost son, and this causes joy (15:32). Thus, when a sinner is converted the angels in heaven rejoice (15:10).

Christian friends likewise spread joy to one another. Paul expressed joy because of the faithfulness of Roman Christians (Rom. 16:19). He was also joyful when he learned about the spiritual stability of the Thessalonian believers (1 Thes. 3:8-9).

Even the news of spiritual victories produces joy. This was especially true when the Gentiles began to accept Christ as Lord (Acts 13:48; 15:31). This rejoicing over spiritual victory is seen even in times of persecution. Christians are able to triumph over trouble through Christ (Matt. 5:12; Acts 5:41; 1 Peter 4:13).

The birth and life of Christ were also a source of joy. When John the Baptist came as the forerunner, his parents rejoiced (Luke 1:14). Heaven and some on earth rejoiced at the birth of Christ (2:10). Jesus brought joy when He came into the home of a wicked tax man, Zaccheus (19:6). Even now Christians are joyful because of the Lord and His fellowship (Phil. 3:1; 4:4).

There is a second implication of our word, and this is as a greeting. It was almost equivalent to "hello" when a Greek or a Jew said, "Hail," or "Joy." In most modern translations, this word is translated "greetings" or "hail" (Matt. 26:49; 27:29; 28:9, NIV).

Letters also began with the same word. After the Council at Jerusalem, the apostles sent a letter to the scattered saints, and they began with the word, "Greetings" (Acts 15:23). Together with other apostolic writers James began with the same word, "Greetings" (James 1:1).

By the same token, the word is also translated as a parting greeting. The Apostle John used it in his second epistle, where it is translated "Godspeed" in the *King James Version* (2 John 10). Twice the Apostle Paul used it as a farewell greeting (Phil. 3:1 [translated "rejoice"]; 4:4).

Thus the word "gladness' or "joy" is full of meaning for a Christian. The reason is not just cultural, because many Greeks used the word to greet people. For a Christian there is a true Source of joy, none other than the Lord Himself.

ILLUSTRATIONS

The world has a jaundiced view of joy, gladness, or happiness. Don Marquis caught the common idea of happiness when he wrote: "Happiness is the interval between periods of unhappiness."

President Thomas Jefferson (1743-1826) concluded: "Happiness is not being pained in body or troubled in mind." This was a view similar to that of the sad old Stoics.

The German writer Johann Wolfgang von Goethe (1749-1832) concluded, "The happy do not believe in miracles." Put another way, he said: "Happy the man who early learns the wide chasm that lies between his wishes and his powers."

A contemporary and compatriot of Goethe was Friedrich Schiller (1729-1805). He too had a dismal view of happiness, for he said, "No greater grief [exists] than to remember days of gladness when sorrow is at hand." He echoed the words of the Italian writer Dante Alighieri (1265-1320): "There is no greater sorrow than to recall, in misery, the time when we were happy."

What a change prevails when one turns to Christian concepts of happiness. The famous Austrian composer Franz Joseph Haydn (1732-1809) acclaimed: "When I think of God, my heart is so full of joy that the notes leap and dance as they leave my pen; and since God has given me a cheerful heart, I serve Him with a cheerful spirit."

Claudel, a French poet, listened attentively to Beethoven's magnificent Fifth Symphony, after which he concluded that there must be joy at the heart of the universe.

According to Oswald Chambers, a great devotional writer, "The joy that Jesus gives is the result of our disposition being at one with His own disposition."

Though enduring unspeakable sadness, C.S. Lewis believed that God gave joy. Concerning this, he wrote, "Joy is the serious business of heaven."

The theologian Bernard Ramm came to a similar conclusion when he wrote: "Jesus Christ can put joy into the joyless work of the 20th century." A contemporary of Ramm, Keith Miller, wrote, "Joy seems to be distilled from a strange mixture of challenge, risk, and hope." Yet another modern man, Samuel Shoemaker, said, "The surest mark of a Christian is not faith, or even love, but joy."

A noted preacher of modern England was H.W. Webb-Peploe. In speaking of joy he said: "Joy is not gush; joy is not jolliness. Joy is perfect acquiescence in God's will because the soul delights itself in God Himself."

GLORY

MEANING

In the New Testament the Greek word for "glory" is *doxa,* and the verb form, "to glorify," is *doxazo.* These words are reflected in the English word *"doxology"* (a liturgical formula which ascribes glory to God). Another related word in English is *"orthodoxy"* (this word is taken from two Greek words: *ortho,* "the same," and *doxy,* "opinion"). Thus the basic meaning of "ortho*doxy*" is to be of the same opinion or belief.

In the earliest Greek literature *doxa* referred to one's opinion, what he thinks about any subject. Later it was twisted slightly to mean one's expectation. According to the philosopher Plato, it was halfway between knowledge and certainty.

Later the word came to mean renown or glory. This was seen most clearly in the writings of Philo and Josephus. In fact, Josephus wrote of the glory *(doxa)* or splendor of the Queen of Sheba.

In the Greek Old Testament, the Septuagint, our word meant glory. It was most often used to describe the glory of God, and in this connection it appeared no fewer than 280 times in the Old Testament's Greek version.

BIBLE USAGE

When the New Testament was written, the meaning for glory was taken directly from the Old Testament. In fact, it was seen to be a style of living. God is glory personified, and He revealed this in Jesus Christ, the Son. Those who are connected to God likewise share this glory. This progression can be seen in the following Scriptures.

First and foremost, glory attaches to God's name and person. At the birth of Christ, God's glory shone like the sun around the whole event (Luke 2:9, 14). Jesus Christ quoted Isaiah 6:10 in describing the glory of God (John 12:40-41). To the dismay of Stephen's persecutors, he identified himself with the God of glory (Acts 7:2). At Saul of Tarsus' conversion, he was struck down by the brightness of God's glory (22:11). To ignore or pervert the glory of God is seen as idolatry (Rom. 1:23). The Lord Jesus Christ and the Christians who believe on Him combine to bring glory to God (1 Peter 4:11). This will be clearly evident in eternity (Rev. 15:8).

Second, as God the Father dwells in glory, so Jesus Christ's earthly life was marked by God's glory. This was most clearly seen at His transfiguration, when God's glory shone through His earthly body (Matt. 17:1-7). Here the glory of God is seen as a bright light, like a light bulb which shines from the inside out.

Not only did the Transfiguration reveal the glory of Jesus, but His first miracle at a marriage at Cana also revealed this (John 2:11), as did the raising of Lazarus (11:40). The betrayal and crucifixion of Jesus brought glory to Him (12:23, 28). He emphasized this in His high priestly prayer to the Father (17:1-4). The Christians' work in eternity will be the proclamation of Christ's glory (Rev. 5:12-13).

Stephen saw Jesus standing at the right hand of God's glorious majesty (Acts 7:55). Paul proclaimed the glory of Christ's resurrection (Rom. 6:4), and the glory of His ascension (1 Tim. 3:16). Peter pointed forward to time when Christ will glorify His disciples and reward them for their service (1 Peter 5:1).

Glory originates with God the Father and shines through God the Son. The Scriptures also assert that believers will someday share this glory. After Christians have suffered, they will also share the glory of the Lord in heaven (Rom. 8:17-18, 21; 2 Cor. 4:17). Christ's Holy Spirit living in believers is the Guarantor of this coming glory (Col. 1:27). When Christians arrive in eternal glory, this will be the fulfillment of the call of God (1 Thes. 2:12). The ultimate reward of Christians is to share in Christ's glory (1 Peter 5:4). This is most dazzlingly revealed in the Book of Revelation (Rev. 21:24-27).

Glory cannot be separated from God. Only to the degree that God is glorified is there any glory at all. It follows that in heaven where God is perfectly glorified we shall enjoy the heights of glory.

ILLUSTRATIONS

Literature speaks of two aspects of glory. The first is the fading glory of people. As Thomas à Kempis (1380-1471) put it: "How quickly does the glory of the world pass away!" Three hundred years later Thomas Gray (1716-71) penned his "Elegy Written in a Country Churchyard." It contained this line: "The paths of glory lead but to the grave."

Much of literature underscores this opinion. Shakespeare (1564-1616) put these hopeless words into the mouth of his *King Henry VIII*: "Farewell! A long farewell, to all my greatness. . . . Vain pomp and glory of this world, I hate ye" (III. i. 3).

When Percy Bysshe Shelley (1792-1822) wrote "The Lament," he climaxed it with a dismal assessment of human glory:

O world! O life! O time!
On whose last steps I climb,
Trembling at that where I had stood before;
When will return the glory of your prime?
No more—Oh, never more!

What a difference there is when one contemplates the glory of God! "What is the chief end of man?" begins the *Westminster Shorter Catechism*. The answer shines like sterling: "To glorify God and to enjoy Him forever."

The Society of Jesus, the Jesuits, were founded by Ignatius Loyola. Their motto adorned many books and educational institutions, and it was this: "To the greater glory of God." How wonderful it would be if all our accomplishments were done under that motto.

John Mason Neale (1818-66) translated the Latin hymn of praise, and the English version contains this stanza:

All glory, laud, and honor
  To Thee, Redeemer, King,
To whom the lips of children
  Made sweet Hosannas ring.

One of the most influential Christian women in Germany is M. Basilea Schlink, a brilliant scholar and deeply pious leader of the Protestant Sisters of Mary in Darmstadt. She wrote about Christian service: "If the glory of God is to break out in your service, you must be ready to go out into the night."

Dr. Arno Gaebelein was the founder and headmaster of Stony Brook School on Long Island. His life was marked by a deep devotion to the Lord, concerning whose glory he said: "We shall see His face, and His name shall be on our foreheads. We are sons with Him, heirs of God and fellow heirs with our Lord Jesus Christ. The acquired glory of our Lord is the glory which every saved sinner will share with Him."

J.H. Thornwell said: "If the church could be aroused to a deeper sense of the glory that awaits her, she would enter with a warmer spirit into the struggles that are before her."

GOD

MEANING

One of the best-known Greek words is *theos*, the word for God. In English we see it reflected in such terms as "*theo*logy" (the study of God), "*theo*centric" (a view of life which puts God in the middle of all things), and "*theo*cracy" (a country or people that is governed by God, as Israel was before the anointing of her first King, Saul).

The ancient Greeks had a quite different view of God than the Jews and Christians did. To the Greeks *theos* spoke of an ordered universe. Their gods were sustainers of all that existed and guarantors of natural order. Their gods were assumed to be impersonal forces.

Later, in Homer's time, gods were thought to be eternal, though their actions and reactions were marked by "human" frailties. They were unable to alter the fates of people, and thus they were little more than deified humans. Years later gods were viewed as sources of evil, for when a god was offended he supposedly sent trouble on people. To Aristotle, a god was the final cause of all that exists.

The Jewish-Christian view of the personal God is foreign to Greek mythology. One must turn to the Scriptures to find the God who is personal, eternal, and infinite.

BIBLE USAGE

The Scriptures contain some general references to gods. When King Herod pretended to be a god, the true God punished him with death (Acts 12:22-23). At least twice Paul was mistaken for a god, because he performed miracles (14:11; 28:6). The Scriptures condemn any exaltation of a thing or a person to the position of a god (Rom. 1:23; 2 Thes. 2:4).

By tracing the word *theos* one can learn much about the God of the Bible. In Christ God came down among people, so the Lord's name was "Immanuel . . . God with us" (Matt. 1:23). God is seen as being eternal, as is the Lord Jesus Christ (John 1:1-2). By the same token God works miracles, as does Christ (3:2; Acts 2:22). Those who do good reveal that they believe in God (Titus 3:8).

People understand God mostly by the things said about Him. For instance, He is seen as the God of Abraham, Isaac, and Jacob (Matt. 22:32). Following on from this statement is the truth that He is the God of Israel (Matt. 15:31; Luke 1:68). Because of Christ we can say that He is also our God (Rom. 1:8). We learn from Scripture that God sustains relationships with people.

Another aspect of the relationship with God is His position as our Heavenly Father. Christ often referred to God as His Father (John 10:30). The apostles echoed this truth in their letters (Rom. 15:6; 2 Cor. 1:3; 1 Peter 1:3). Because of the Lord we can also call God "our Father" (Matt. 6:9; Rom. 8:15). This truth is found throughout the New Testament (Gal. 1:4; Phil. 4:20; 1 Thes. 1:3).

He is seen as the God of hope, joy, and peace (Rom. 15:13; 16:20). As such He is the Source and sole explanation of the peace which possesses Christians (Phil. 4:7, 9). He will guarantee the peace of Christians until they are safe at home in heaven (1 Thes. 5:23).

The Apostle Paul also referred to Christ as the God of all comfort (2 Cor. 1:3). He comforts us in our troubles, so that we may also comfort others. Likewise He is the God of love and peace, which places a benediction on our lives (13:11).

It is the genius of the New Testament that Jesus Christ is identified as God in the flesh, God incarnate. Paul said that Jesus Christ is supreme over all and He is God (Rom. 9:5). According to the Apostles Paul and Peter, Jesus Christ is our God and Saviour, one and the same Person (Titus 2:13; 2 Peter 1:2). John also joins in this teaching that Jesus Christ is God incarnate (1 John 5:20). Because there is only one God, and that God is manifested in Christ alone, all idolatry is ruled out (5:21).

ILLUSTRATIONS

Just as Scripture is full of references to God, so is literature. Many are the condemnations of atheism. Wendell Baxter said, "An atheist does not find God for the same reason a thief does not find a policeman. He is not looking for him."

H.G. Wells (1866-1946), novelist and historian, said, "Until a man has found God and been found by God, he begins at no beginning, he works to no end. He may have his friendships, his partial party loyalties, his scraps of honor. But all these things fall into place, and life falls into place, only with God."

God is not passive, He is eternally active from Creation until this present moment. Thomas à Kempis (1380-1471), who wrote *The Imitation of Christ*, said, "Man proposes, but God disposes."

C.S. Lewis (1898-1963), Oxford don and Cambridge professor, wrote: "There are two kinds of people: those who say to God, 'Thy will be done,' and those to whom God says, 'All right, then, have it your way.'"

God is a spiritual being. The classical definition of Him is found in *The Westminster Shorter Catechism:* "God is a Spirit, infinite, eternal, and unchangeable in His being, wisdom, power, holiness, justice, goodness, and truth."

One of the great writers on the love of God was Amy Carmichael (1867-1951). On this subject she wrote: "There is no need to plead that the love of God shall fill our heart as though He were unwilling to fill us. He is willing as light is willing to flood a room that is opened to its brightness. . . . Love is pressing round us on all sides like air. Cease to resist, and instantly love takes possession."

Another writer with a keen consciousness of God was G.K. Chesterton (1874-1936), who wrote concerning the power of God: "The sun does not rise because of the rotation of the earth. The sun rises because God says to it, 'Get up.'"

Will Durant has done more to popularize history than any other American writer. He too commented on the importance of God, when he wrote: "The great question of our time is not Communism versus individualism, not Europe versus America, not East versus West; it is whether man can live without God."

A great missionary statesman in Polynesia was Titus Coan, who wrote this profound prayer to God: "Lord, send me where Thou wilt, only go with me; lay on me what Thou wilt, only sustain me. Cut any cord but the one that binds me to Thy cause, to Thy heart."

Many hymns express the praise of a pious heart toward God. None is more powerful than the one penned by Frederick Faber (1814-63), an eccentric though devoted hymnist:

My God, how wonderful Thou art!
  Thy majesty how bright!
How beautiful Thy mercy-seat,
  In depths of burning light!

GOOD, GOODNESS

MEANING

In Greek the most common word for "good" or "goodness" is *agathos*. It is reflected in the English Christian name, Agatha, which was made famous by the mystery writer Agatha Christie. The Greek term is common, as it appears about 100 times in the New Testament.

Though the term is commonly found in the New Testament, secular Greek writers had a different view of "goodness." The earliest philosophers saw anything which gives meaning to life as "good." To them the concept of good was purely humanistic, and God was not involved in any way.

The Stoics, who taught about the time of Christ, believed that knowing what was good would insure that people did what is good. This viewpoint is seen in contemporary humanism. But unfortunately it is not true. People who know what is good do not always do it.

In Hellenistic times people related goodness to their gods. Those who pleased the gods were good. This is the source of our views regarding good. In Old English there was a relationship between good and God. The Old English word for "goodly" was *godlic,* and the word for "goodness' was *godnes*. It was the Jews who tied goodness to godliness. The Ten Commandments were given by Jehovah as a standard of good. Jews felt they would please God if they conformed to that standard. Thus godliness equaled goodness.

BIBLE USAGE

There are in the Scriptures two basic applications of goodness. The first is external, and it relates to things or people. It says nothing about one's relationship to God, only about one's acceptability in society.

The Bible speaks of people who are good. For instance, a good slave pleases his or her master (Matt. 25:21, 23). A good man has an unblemished reputation in his community or religious fellowship (Luke 23:50). A good man is one who is full of the Holy Spirit (Acts 11:24). Good young women are those who fulfill their responsibilities (Titus 2:5).

On the other hand, the Bible also points to *things* which are good. Good trees bear good fruit (Matt. 7:17). Still following the farming analogy, good ground is that which produces a good harvest (13:8).

Parents usually give good gifts to their children. The greatest Giver of good gifts is God Himself (Luke 11:13). In fact, James asserted that every good gift which we have comes from God alone (James 1:17).

If goodness is external and time-related, goodness in the Bible is most clearly seen when it is related to God and His people. This is internal goodness, goodness of the heart. God is the standard of all good. In fact He alone is completely good (Matt. 19:17; Mark 10:18).

Because He came from God, Jesus Christ also shared this perfect goodness (10:17; John 7:12). By the same token the Holy Spirit is also seen as being good (Luke 11:13). Since God alone is absolutely good, only the other Persons of the Trinity can share that standard of goodness.

Arising from this divine basis of all goodness is the fact that good people are God's people. A good person thinks good thoughts and does good deeds because he is related to God (Matt. 12:35; Luke 6:45). Such good people possess good consciences. Paul could claim at the end of his life that he had a good conscience before God (Acts 23:1). Such a good conscience results from obeying the teaching of God's Word (1 Tim. 1:5). A good conscience is of extreme value (1:19).

Thus goodness is closely connected with God. True goodness cannot be separated from faith in the Lord and obedience to His Word. In fact, the only source of good in the entire universe is God.

ILLUSTRATIONS

People grope around for human sources of goodness, and they make the most incredible statements. For instance, actor John Barrymore said: "The good die young—because they see it's no use living if you've got to be good." A similar statement was attributed to Finley Peter Dunne, alias Mr. Dooley: "There ain't any news in being good. You might write the doings of all the convents of the world on the back of a postage stamp, and have room to spare."

G.K. Chesterton concluded that good is ambiguous; you cannot quite grasp it: "The word *good* has many meanings. For example, if a man were to shoot his grandmother at a range of five hundred yards, I should call him a good shot, but not *necessarily* a good man."

The famed educator Maria Montessori addressed the subject of goodness when she said: "The first idea that the child must acquire, in order to be actively disciplined, is that of the difference between good and evil; and the task of the educator lies in seeing that the child does not confound good with immobility, and evil with activity."

To the Christian, however, goodness is linked to God. Francis Bacon (1561-1626), a brilliant English thinker, said: "There was never law, or sect, or opinion, did so magnify goodness as the Christian religion doth."

To the Christian goodness is personal. According to Edwin Hubbel Chapin: "Goodness consists not in the outward things we do, but in the inward thing we are." This view finds agreement in the line by William Lawson: "Goodness in the church is always individual and personal."

Robert Louis Stevenson (1850-94) was known for his spellbinding writings, but he also was a philosopher of sorts. Of goodness he said: "There is an idea abroad among moral people that they should make their neighbors good. One person I have to make good: myself." He seemed to ignore the source of that goodness in this statement, because only God can make men good.

Hugh Latimer (1485-1555) was one of the great martyrs of the English reformation. On the subject of goodness he said: "We must first be made good before we can do good; we must first be made just before our works can please God."

Along the same lines Johann Hieronymus Schroeder said: "The Cross has revealed to good men that their goodness has not been good enough."

Euripides (480-406 B.C.) was a Greek dramatist. He said concerning goodness: "When good men die their goodness does not perish." (He perceived that people remembered good deeds.) Daniel Webster (1782-1852), a statesman-orator, put a Christian twist to the same phrase: "Real goodness does not attach itself merely to this life—it points to another world."

GRACE

MEANING

The Greek word for "grace" is *charis*. It is seen in the related word *charisma*, which stands for a spiritual "gift." In its basic form *charis* means "undeserved favor," or "unearned gift." In fact, by definition a gift *is* undeserved and unearned.

In secular Greek "grace" had a very humanistic meaning. It referred to a charming person, as "a graceful woman." It also spoke of a pleasing experience, and we use it to describe "gracious dining." Another aspect of the word's secular meaning is good fortune, or a happy state of affairs. Only later was grace connected in any way to the gods. Here too it spoke of the gods making people "happy."

During the Hellenistic period of Greek history "grace" spoke of a ruler's favor. One still hears in monarchies of the Queen's gracious action in granting a pardon or a prize.

The Greek Old Testament, the Septuagint, contains 56 references to grace. The vast majority of these, 41 in all, relate grace to Jehovah's actions and His attitudes toward Israel.

BIBLE USAGE

The New Testament is essentially a "grace" book. It contains more than 150 references to grace, and most of these tell of God's gracious actions toward His people.

First, grace describes God in action. From the first His grace was manifested in the Lord Jesus Christ. This was seen in His birth (John 1:14-18) and also in His growth into manhood (Luke 2:40). Each step in the Lord's life was marked by the grace of God in action.

A second major emphasis of God's grace is our salvation. Nowhere is this seen more clearly than in the Book of Romans. Every Christian is justified by the grace of God (Rom. 3:24). In other words, a Christian now stands before God's bar of justice as innocent, because of God's grace. God's grace provides the final answer to our sinfulness in the crucifixion of Jesus Christ on our behalf (5:2-17). Thus a Christian is no longer under the Law but under Grace (6:14).

The other writings of the Apostle Paul embellish this theme of salvation through grace. To the Galatians who were bothered by legalism, Paul explained that the call of God was a product of grace (Gal. 1:15). In writing to the Ephesians Paul repeated the truth that salvation was by grace through faith plus nothing (Eph. 1:6; 2:5, 8-9). This grace of God was demonstrated by the fact that He chose us to be saved before the foundation of the world (2 Tim. 1:9). Grace came into full bloom when Christ came to earth (2 Cor. 9:8; Titus 2:11; 3:7). The Apostle Paul is, in many ways, "the apostle of grace," because his writings are so full of praise to God for His unmerited favor.

Though Paul is "the apostle of grace," other apostles also sang the praises of God's goodness. Peter referred to God as "the God of all grace" (1 Peter 5:10). Because of this characteristic, God resists proud people and gives His grace to humble ones (5:5). Peter had learned that lesson of humility the hard way, after he denied Christ before the Crucifixion. The Lord's grace was seen in Peter's restoration following the Resurrection. James reiterated this axiom of life: God resists the proud but gives grace to the humble (James 4:6).

The New Testament writers also used grace as a greeting. The Greeks would have used *chairo* (joy or gladness), but the Christians turned the phrase to *charis* (grace). Paul used this greeting to begin many of his epistles (Rom. 1:7; 1 Cor. 1:3;

2 Cor. 1:2; Eph. 1:2; Phil. 1:2). At the end of his letters he often used "grace" as a parting greeting also (Rom. 16:20; 1 Cor. 16:23; 2 Cor. 13:14; Gal. 6:18; Eph. 6:24; Phil. 4:23; Col. 4:18). In fact, almost every epistle of Paul used "grace" as a greeting.

Finally, "grace" is significant in the life of every Christian. Paul knew that he was called to the exalted position of apostleship by the grace of God (Rom. 1:5; 1 Cor. 3:10). Christians also are enabled to endure suffering by the grace of God (2 Cor. 12:9; Phil. 1:7). The spiritual gifts by which we serve the Lord are also a product of God's grace (Rom. 12:6; Eph. 4:7; 1 Peter 4:10).

ILLUSTRATIONS

Someone has said that grace can be defined with a simple acrostic: God's Riches At Christ's Expense. This is a memorable explanation of this theological definition: Grace is God's unmerited favor.

Writers have vied with one another in extolling the grace of God. Bernard of Clairveaux (1090-1153) was more than a monastic reformer. He was one of the great hymn-writers of the medieval church. Of grace he said: "Grace freely justifies me and sets me free from slavery to sin."

One of the leading revival preachers in 19th-century Germany was Christoph Blumhardt (1842-1919), who said of the grace of God: "Neither in heaven nor on earth is it possible to settle down comfortably through grace and do nothing and care for nobody else. . . . If I am saved by grace, then I am a worker through grace."

The famous English preacher Robert William Dale (1829-95) said about the powerful preaching of Moody: "Moody preached in a manner which led to the sort of effect produced by Luther. He exulted in the free grace of God. His joy was contagious. Men leaped out of darkness into light, and lived a Christian life afterward."

From about the same era Charles Finney (1792-1875) wrote concerning the grace of God: "A state of mind that sees God in everything is evidence of growth in grace and a thankful heart."

"Grace is not sought nor bought nor wrought," according to Billy Graham. "It is a free gift of Almighty God to needy mankind." To which one might add the words of Ilion Jones, a Welsh preacher: "The word 'grace' is unquestionably the most significant word in the Bible."

Though he was largely known for his emphasis on justification by faith, Martin Luther saw grace as a corollary to it. He said: "Christ is no Moses, no exactor, no giver of laws, but a giver of grace, a Saviour; He is infinite mercy and goodness, freely and bountifully given to us."

John Newton (1725-1807), a converted slave ship captain, summarized the significance of grace for all time when he wrote:

Amazing grace! How sweet the sound,
That saved a wretch like me!
I once was lost, but now am found:
Was blind, but now I see.

GREAT, GREATNESS

MEANING

The Greek word for great or greatness is *megas,* and it occurs 192 times in the New Testament. This root is seen in such English words as *"mega*phone" (an instrument to make sound greater or louder), *"mega*polis" (a combination of cities that sort of make one great city), *"mega*ton" (an explosive force equal to a million tons of TNT), and *"mega*watt" (a million watts of electricity).

The word *mega* is so common that its development is fairly predictable. Originally in secular Greek it was applied to animals which were very large. Another interesting aspect was its use to describe adults, in contrast with children.

A further development applied the word to deities. Zeus was described as being the "great god." By extension it also was used to characterize great men. A perversion of this is arrogance, when a person thinks that he or she is too great.

BIBLE USAGE

The most basic biblical use of our word refers to size. When Jesus was buried, a great stone was rolled before the grave (Matt. 27:60). The temple complex in Jerusalem was described as a great building (Mark 13:2). In the same way the Upper Room was portrayed as a great room (14:15). When the disciples encountered Jesus on the shores of Galilee, they caught a great number of fish (John 21:6).

Another frequent use of the word referred to age. Young people were called small and old people were called great (Acts 26:22). From the story of Jacob and Esau the New Testament also speaks of the older (greater) and the younger (Rom. 9:12).

Spiritual power is also described as being great. After the Christians prayed at Jerusalem, the great power of the Holy Spirit was poured out on them (Acts 4:33). This gave credibility to their testimony.

When the subject is that of sound, the word "greatness" means loudness. At the Crucifixion Jesus uttered a loud (great) cry (Mark 15:37). After a leper was healed he praised God with a loud voice (Luke 17:15). Jesus called loudly when He summoned Lazarus with a loud call (John 11:43). At the resurrection of Jesus there was great joy (Matt. 28:8). The return of Christ will be accompanied by a great trumpet blast (Matt. 24:31).

The greatness of nature yields another category of applications. As Jesus walked across the Sea of Galilee there was a strong, or great, wind (John 6:18). When the Lord commanded the storm to cease, there was a great calm (Matt. 8:26). Peter's mother-in-law was sick with a great (high) fever (Luke 4:38).

The persecution of early Christians was often a matter of degree. Jesus warned the disciples that Christians would someday face a great persecution (Matt. 24:21). Stephen reminded his persecutors that the Children of Israel had experienced a great affliction in Egypt (Acts 7:11). Following the stoning to death of Stephen a great persecution broke out in Jerusalem, and Saul of Tarsus was its chief instigator (8:1-2).

Many ideas in the Scripture are called great. Jesus reminded the Pharisees of the great commandment, that they should love the Lord their God (Matt. 22:36-38). Paul presented the teaching concerning Christ and His church, and then added that this is a great mystery (Eph. 5:32). In setting down a hymn of praise, Paul said that the mystery of godliness is great (1 Tim. 3:16). A Christian who has been born from above has many great promises on which he can rely (2 Peter 1:4).

A final use of the word pertains to great people. Jesus said that the greatest man who ever lived was John the Baptist (Matt. 11:11). The world's standard of greatness is power, but the Christian's criterion of greatness is service (20:25). Of course, the greatness of Christ far outshone any human greatness (John 4:12; Heb. 4:14).

ILLUSTRATIONS

As might be assumed, literature is full of statements concerning greatness. As William Shakespeare (1564-1616) wrote in *The Twelfth Night:* "But be not afraid of greatness: some men are born great, some achieve greatness, and some have greatness thrust upon them" (II, iv, 158).

In his *Absalom and Achitophel* John Dryden (1631-70) wrote: "Great wits are sure to madness near alli'd. And thin the partitions do their bounds divide" (line 163).

Reflecting his philosophy of history, Thomas Carlyle (1795-1881) wrote: "No great man lives in vain. The history of the world is but the biography of great men."

In his *Letter to Lady Beaumont,* William Wordsworth (1770-1850) said: "Every great and original writer, in proportion as he is great and original, must himself create the taste by which he is to be relished."

On the darker side, Lord Randolph Spencer Churchill (1849-94) spotlighted the mistakes of great men when he wrote: "All great men make mistakes. Napoleon forgot about Bluecher," the Prussian general who helped defeat him.

People have searched in vain for the key to greatness. Sir Winston Churchill said: "The price of greatness is responsibility." Thomas Fuller, a Puritan, claimed, "Great hopes make great men." Elbert Hubbard asserted, "A retentive memory is a good thing, but the ability to forget is the true token of greatness."

G.K. Chesterton (1874-1936) avowed: "There is a great man who makes every man feel small. But the really great man is the man who makes every man feel great."

A refreshing change from human greatness is the study of spiritually great people. James W. Alexander said: "The study of God's Word for the purpose of discovering God's will is the secret discipline which has formed the greatest characters."

Along the same lines A.P. Gouthey wrote: "Moses became the world's greatest jurist, not amid the luxuries of the palace of Egypt, but amid the solitude of the desert. In the desert he had time to meet and talk with God."

One of the fine Bible commentaries was initiated by Matthew Henry (1662-1714) who said about greatness: "Nothing can make a man truly great but being truly good and partaking of God's holiness." This explains the divine standard of greatness. It is not education, for God is omniscient. Nor is it achievement, for God can do everything. Neither is it fame, for God is known everywhere and is omnipresent. True greatness is spiritual submission to God, and this is expressed in service toward others.

GREETING

MEANING

In the Greek New Testament the word translated "greeting" is *aspazomai*, a very broad but meaningful term. It embraces all forms of greeting from a verbal welcome to a kiss. In fact, it is variously translated in the New Testament by "embrace," "greet," "salute" (in the *King James Version*), and "take leave of."

The original Greek use of this word was also general. Building on the basic meaning of "embrace," other forms of greeting were added as time went on. Usually they referred to some external gesture, such as offering one's hand, kissing, or expressing acclaim in some other form. The usual greeting in Greek was *chaire*, which literally meant "rejoice." In practice it also meant "welcome," "good day," "hail," "hello," and "I am glad to see you." It is a lot like our English word, "Hi." Later on the Greeks turned from personal greetings to letters of greeting, forerunners of our greeting cards.

BIBLE USAGE

The word *aspazomai* speaks generally of the social grace of greeting. In fact, Jesus said it was the least of common courtesies, and He taught that Christians should even greet those who were not particular friends (Matt. 5:47).

A slightly different turn to the word is seen in the narrative of Mark's Gospel. He mentioned that a crowd greeted Jesus eagerly, when He returned from His transfiguration (Mark 9:15). This is closer to the idea of acclaim.

A fascinating appearance of our word is in the birth narrative of Luke. When the Angel Gabriel came to the Virgin Mary, his angelic greeting troubled her (Luke 1:29). Furthermore, when Mary went to greet Elizabeth, the baby John leaped inside her womb (1:41). This says much about the joy of that special greeting.

As the Apostle Paul made his way to Jerusalem, he met with many Christians at Troas, Ephesus, Caesarea, and Ptolemais. The word for "greeting" is used to describe the "farewell" which Christians at Ephesus gave him (Acts 20:7). Again in Acts the word for greeting is used to describe a visit, when Paul stopped briefly at Ptolemais or Acre (21:7).

The most frequent use of our word is found in the New Testament epistles. Greetings are extended to special friends such as Priscilla and Aquila (Rom. 16:3, 5, 22). Churches also greet one another by reference in the apostle's letters (1 Cor. 16:19). The "holy kiss" was also used as a form of greeting (2 Cor. 13:12). General greetings were issued to "every saint" (Phil. 4:21). In the Book of Colossians Paul listed several from whom he sent greetings (Col. 4:10-14). Again in his final epistle, Paul passed on greetings (2 Tim. 4:19, 21). The same kind of greeting is given in Titus 3:15 and Philemon 23.

A general greeting to all the leaders and all the saints is included at the conclusion of the Book of Hebrews (Heb. 13:24). Peter urged Christians to greet one another with the "kiss of love," which is a fairly unusual formulation (1 Peter 5:14). In his rather cryptic epistles, John also passed on greetings to the church (2 John 13; 3 John 14). Though not using the exact word, John warned the Christians not to greet or welcome false prophets (2 John 10).

Jesus set down an interesting criterion concerning greetings. When He first sent out the disciples, He told them to bring a special greeting to each house which they entered (Matt. 10:12). The Christian greeting was one of peace. The Lord had said, "Peace be with you" (John 20:21). If this greeting was not appreciated or received, the disciples were instructed to leave immediately (Luke 10:5-6).

On the lowest level, greeting is a simple social custom. The ancient Greeks were much like the Romans and Jews. All greeted socially. However, under the exposition of Christ's teaching, greeting became an evangelistic test. Disciples were instructed to share their Gospel only with those who were receptive toward them.

ILLUSTRATIONS

Greetings remind most modern people of greeting cards. For nearly every possible event there is a suitable card. Apart from the normal birthdays, anniversaries, and wedding greetings, there are also many other memorable occasions. Depending on the neighborhood, there may be special cards for Jewish holidays, Christmas cards, or even Muslim greetings.

Recently the Soviet Union set an unusual precedent in the greeting card business. A line of Soviet Christmas cards appeared on the market in Europe. This was doubly amazing. Not only were the cards printed in English, but they came from an officially atheistic country. Apparently, profits can also be the mother of invention.

Another interesting line of greeting cards is found in England. The British driving test is very difficult and it takes many people two or three times to pass it. Thus the friends of recently licensed drivers shower the successful candidate with specially printed cards.

In his poignant poem, "When We Two Parted," Lord Byron (1788-1824) theorized concerning a future reunion, and said this about the greeting:

> If I should meet thee
> After long years,
> How should I greet thee?
> With silence and tears.

For several years our family lived in Germany, where the standard greeting was a handshake. In fact it was impolite not to shake hands. In time the extending of a hand came to be second nature. When one could not offer the right hand, one said: "The left hand is from the heart."

When Germans write to one another, the greeting is also extremely important. At the end of a letter one says: "*Gruss an Deine Mutter*" (Greet your mother). At other times one passes on greetings from another person: "*Meine Mutter laesst gruessen*" (My mother sends her greetings). It is a matter of form, but this form conveys real friendship.

In Christian circles certain German churches set aside a portion of the service for the passing of greetings. The leader asks: "Are there any greetings from other churches?" Then people from near and far stand to give greetings in the names of their home churches. It is a lovely habit which binds together Christians from various parts of the country.

Not only is this practice cultivated in church services, but it is also used in large conferences. Often I have sat through hours of "greetings" from personages great and small. Though it may be overdone, the German idea of conveying greetings does give a sense of personal regard and friendship.

GUARD

MEANING

The idea of guarding or keeping in the New Testament has similar meanings to the English words. They can mean that a person is guarded from danger, or kept from danger. Or they can mean strict obedience to a set of rules, or keeping the rules. Finally, they can also mean to preserve, to keep something from spoiling.

Three Greek words are used to describe this guarding. The most common word is *tereo*, which appears 70 times in the New Testament. Originally it meant "to observe," and only later did it come to mean "to lie in wait" or "be on guard."

A second word, *phulasso*, appears 31 times in the New Testament. It is the word used in ancient Greek to describe the work of a watchman, one who guards a city. Connected to it is the noun *phulake* (a prison or a dungeon).

The third word is *phroureo* which appears only four times in the New Testament. In each case it speaks of erecting a garrison to guard a city or a place of value. It can also refer to the siege of a city by an enemy.

All three of these words are used in the New Testament to speak of guarding or keeping. They are almost interchangeable in their usage.

BIBLE USAGE

Though their meanings are separate, we shall consider these three words in order of their frequency in the New Testament. Since *tereo* appears most frequently, it is discussed first.

In a physical sense *tereo* means to guard or keep. At the Crucifixion the Roman soldiers kept watch over Jesus (Matt. 27:36). When Paul and Silas were imprisoned at Philippi the same word was used to describe their experience. The jailer guarded them securely (Acts 16:23).

The word is also used to describe preservation, or keeping something of value. Jesus instructed His disciples to keep the commandments (John 14:21). Christians are also taught to keep themselves unspotted from the world (James 1:27). On God's part, He is keeping the inheritance He has promised us in heaven (1 Peter 1:4). In fact, the Lord keeps all of His children safely in His arms, much to our eternal comfort (1 John 5:18).

The second most frequently used word is the verb *phulasso* and the noun *phulake*. The shepherds were guarding their sheep on the night of Christ's birth (Luke 2:8). After his arrest by Herod, John was kept in prison (Matt. 14:3; Mark 6:17). In the early church the apostles were frequently kept under arrest (Acts 5:19; 12:4; 16:23-37).

This word also carries with it the meaning of protection. In Jesus' high priestly prayer, He prayed that the Father would keep Christians safe while they live in the world (John 17:11-12, 15). Paul drew confidence from the fact that all he had committed to the Lord would be kept safe until eternity (2 Tim. 1:12). Noah was preserved, kept safe, by the Lord during the Flood (2 Peter 2:5). Finally, all Christians can count on this preserving until they stand before the Lord in glory (Jude 24-25).

By the same token, this word also refers to observance of truths. As the disciples spread throughout the known world, they were charged to teach strict observance of the Lord's teachings (Matt. 28:19). The love of God is poured out on those who keep His words (John 15:10).

The third and final word *phroureo* is used only four times, but it is important to an understanding of the Lord's keeping. The Lord kept us safe until we heard the

Gospel and responded to it (Gal. 3:23). Now the peace of God keeps our hearts and minds at peace in troubled times (Phil. 4:7). The Lord keeps us and will reveal His glory in us only when Christ returns (1 Peter 1:5).

The keeping power of our Lord is awesome. It is as strong as His strength and as eternal as His person. No Christian should ever doubt this providential care of the Lord.

ILLUSTRATIONS

The world is insecure, because people have no providential Preserver. This basic insecurity is seen in the statements of worldlings. Management expert Peter Drucker said, "I was lucky. When God rained manna from heaven, I had a spoon."

Thomas Fuller (1608-61) wrote in despair: "If you are too fortunate, you will not know yourself. If you are too unfortunate, nobody will know you."

Even Socrates (470-399 B.C.) chimed in on this dismal chorus: "If all our misfortunes were laid in a common heap whence everyone must take an equal portion, most people would be contented to take their own and depart."

Turn to Christian writers, and there is a sense of God's guarding providence which is refreshing. Charles Haddon Spurgeon (1834-92) said it colorfully: "As sure as ever God puts His children in the furnace He will be in the furnace with them."

Corrie ten Boom, who recently went to be with the Lord, loved to talk about God's preservation. She said: "If a bird is flying for pleasure it flies with the wind, but if it meets danger it turns and faces the wind, in order that it might rise higher." Corrie's experiences in a Nazi concentration camp lend eloquent evidence to this statement.

William Law (1686-1761) was a devotional writer. He wrote about God's care: "If anyone would tell you the shortest, surest way to happiness and all perfection, he must tell you to make it a rule to yourself to thank and praise God for everything that happens to you. For it is certain that whatever seeming calamity happens to you, if you thank and praise God for it, you turn it into a blessing."

George Washington knew many tribulations in his military and political careers. But he trusted in the providence of God and said: "Providence has at all times been my dependence, for all other resources seem to have failed us."

The American poet Henry Wadsworth Longfellow noted the same providential care of God and said: "By going a few minutes sooner or later, by stopping to speak with a friend on the corner, by meeting this man or that, or by turning down this street instead of the other, we may let slip some impending evil, by which the whole current of our lives would have been changed. There is no possible solution in the dark enigma, but the one word 'providence.'"

The founder of the Christian Brethren movement was John Nelson Darby (1800-82), a brilliant scholar and exceptional Bible teacher. He once said about providence: "God's ways are behind the scenes, but He moves all the scenes which He is behind."

HAND

MEANING

The Greek word translated "hand" is *cheir*. It is seen in such English terms as "*chiro*practic" (manipulation by hand), "*chiro*pody" (treatment of feet by the hands), "*chiro*mancy" (palmistry), and "*chiro*graphy" (handwriting, or penmanship).

In secular Greek the hand was frequently mentioned. Aristotle called the hand "the tool of tools." Besides using it for working, the Greeks also were given to shaking hands. Since a ruler proved his power in hand-to-hand combat, a hand also symbolized power.

As Greek mythology developed, the hands of the gods assumed importance. It was the hands of the gods which allegedly protected people. When a person was unusually blessed, it was assumed that the gods had laid their hands on him.

In the Septuagint the hand often referred to God's activities in the world. More than 200 times the hand of God is mentioned in the Old Testament. It is God's hand which created the world. When blessing came on the Jewish nation, it was God's hand at work. Even in punishment, godly Jews saw the hand of God.

BIBLE USAGE

In the New Testament there are 178 appearances of the word "hand." These are divided into two broad categories. The first refers to physical hands. When Jesus met a man with a withered hand, He restored that hand immediately (Matt. 12:10-13; Mark 3:1-5; Luke 6:6-10). Indeed the hands of Jesus were often busy doing miracles of healing (Mark 6:2).

Following in the pattern of the Lord, Peter took hold of a lame man's hand, and the man was healed (Acts 3:7). Peter took Dorcas by the hand, and she was raised from the dead (9:41). Paul and Barnabas likewise healed by touches of their hands (14:3). Even Ananias, an otherwise unknown brother from Damascus, laid hands on Saul of Tarsus, and he received his sight (9:17). In fact, Luke recorded that signs and wonders were accomplished by the laying on of apostolic hands (5:12). On a more down-to-earth note, the Apostle Paul earned his keep by working with his hands (20:34).

Despite all of the good deeds which the apostles did, they were often arrested. It is ironic that their hands which had healed were shackled with chains. This is clearly seen in Peter's remarkable release from prison. As an angel burst into his cell, the chains fell from Peter's wrists, and he was allowed to go free (12:7).

The Apostle Paul was likewise seized and bound. As he proceeded to Jerusalem on his final journey, the Prophet Agabus warned Paul that his hands and feet would be bound (21:11). Later Paul was delivered by the Jews "into the hands" of the Romans (28:17).

The Bible also makes much of the hands of enemies. Jesus Christ was delivered into the hands of evil men (Matt. 17:22; Mark 9:31). Jesus used these words in informing His disciples of His imminent arrest (Matt. 26:45). This became an integral part of the Gospel we preach (Luke 24:7). In fact, at Pentecost Peter focused on this event as the climax of Christ's suffering (Acts 2:23).

Finally, the New Testament makes frequent mention of the hand of God, which tells us of the works of God in our world. He is the Creator of the world (Heb. 1:10). In His strong right hand He holds believers (John 10:29; Acts 11:21). Into God's hands Christ committed His spirit as He died on the cross (Luke 23:46). Jesus Christ has been exalted to the right hand of God (5:31; 7:56; Heb. 8:1). The entire destinies of people and the world are in the hand of God (Acts 4:28). For this reason God's hands will execute judgment on the world (10:31).

The hands of man are a miracle; they are truly "the tool of tools." The hands of the apostles were a wellspring of healing to a hurting world. The hands of Christ, which were pierced, could heal any ill and give sight to any blind eye. How good it is to know that we may find shelter in the safe hand of God. "He's got the whole world in His hands."

ILLUSTRATIONS
Human hands are wonderful. One thinks of a missionary surgeon who has given his life to people in West Africa. His skilled hands operate daily on leprosy-crippled hands, and he gives those mangled palms the ability to work again.

A fitting tribute to such surgeons was spoken by the famous preacher, John Sutherland Bonnell: "He who has healing in his hands, be he physician, surgeon, psychiatrist, pastor, or layman, may only thank God humbly that he is used in this ministry." Human hands are a wonderful creation, but God's hand created them.

On his Christmas broadcast of 1939, as war rumbled through Europe, King George VI quoted this line from Minnie Louise Haskins (1875-1957): "And I said to the man who stood at the gate of the year: 'Give me a light that I may tread safely into the unknown.' And he replied: 'Go out into the darkness and put your hand into the hand of God. That shall be to you better than light and safer than a known way.'"

Jane Montgomery Campbell (1817-78) translated a German harvest hymn, which contains this reference to the hand of God:

> We plow the fields, and scatter
>   The good seed on the land,
> But it is fed and watered
>   By God's Almighty Hand.

Another completely different reference to God's creative hand is found in William Blake's (1757-1827) poem, "Songs of Experience. The Tyger":

> Tyger! Tyger burning bright
> In the forests of the night,
> What immortal hand or eye
> Could frame thy fearful symmetry?

Along the same lines Thomas J. Higgins attributed the role of a sculptor to God: "God is the sculptor who chisels on the rough block of stone the general outline of what the finished piece will be."

The famous English poet George Herbert (1593-1633) said concerning the hand of God: "God strikes with His finger, and not with His arm." This reveals his confidence that God often deals more gently with us than what we deserve.

The Book of Common Prayer contains many beautiful paraphrases of Scripture, among which is this comforting line taken from Psalm 95:7: "For He is the Lord our God: and we are the people of His pasture, and the sheep of His hand."

Many hymns refer to the hand of God. One of the greatest of these was penned by Augustus Toplady (1740-78):

> My name from the palms of His hands
>   Eternity will not erase;
> Impressed on His heart it remains
>   In marks of indelible grace.

HAPPY (See: *Blessed.*)   **197**

HAVE

MEANING

The verb "to have" is a very common Greek word, *echo*. It has similar meanings in Greek to those in English, and it appears more than 620 times in the New Testament.

In its original form it meant to possess something, or to enjoy one's possession. The emphasis fell on material possessions, but later it came to describe character traits, as to have love, joy, peace, or hope.

Though *echo* represents no one single Hebrew verb, it is used more than 500 times in the Greek Old Testament, the Septuagint. Here it is also used for the possession of both spiritual and material benefits. It is often used to describe the possession of spiritual gifts, or even the Spirit of God.

BIBLE USAGE

The most meaningful uses of this word in the New Testament relate directly to the Lord. John made a great deal of the fact that Christians possess a relationship with the Lord. First of all, it pertains to God the Father. Only those who confess their faith in Christ possess God as their Father (1 John 2:23). Obedience to the teachings of Christ is likewise a mark of a person who has God the Father (2 John 9). Though the Pharisees claimed that they too possessed God as their Father, their lives put the lie to this claim (John 8:43-44). In short, only those who live in obedience to Christ can claim a connection to God the Father. It is a frequently held fallacy that everyone is a child of God. Actually, only those who have God as their God are truly, and biblically, children of God.

Secondly, true Christians also possess the Holy Spirit in their lives. He is called by various names, but He is the same Holy Spirit. One criterion of a Christian is that he possesses the Spirit of Christ (Rom. 8:9). The Spirit is also seen as a pledge of heaven to come. The Holy Spirit who lives in us assures us that we shall be taken to glory ultimately (2 Cor. 1:22; 5:5). He is also called the Spirit of faith (4:13). Above all else He is called the Spirit of God (1 Cor. 7:40). A Christian possesses the Spirit in all His fullness and all His roles. In emphasizing this possession there is a fullness of teaching about the nature and work of the Holy Spirit.

Not only does a Christian have the Father and the Spirit, but He also possesses in a real sense the Son. Whoever has the Son of God has everlasting, eternal life (John 5:24; 1 John 5:11-12). Having the Son also involves having an Advocate with the Father, Jesus Christ the Righteous One (1 John 2:1). Another side to this same truth is seen in a statement in Hebrews, that we have a faithful High Priest (Heb. 4:14). Whoever has Christ also has joy (John 17:13), light on the way (8:12), and peace in troubled times (16:33). The Christian also has fellowship with the Lord (1 John 1:6). There is a veritable treasure house available to a person who puts his or her trust in the Lord Jesus Christ.

The reality of this is seen in statements sprinkled throughout the New Testament. When Christians come together they have different gifts to use in ministry to the whole group (1 Cor. 7:7). They also have spiritual knowledge, that is, an experience of spiritual things (8:1, 10). They also have a deep love for one another (John 13:35; 15:13; 1 Cor. 13:1-7). Because of the finished work of Christ on the cross they have righteousness, not their own, but that righteousness which is given by God's grace (Phil. 3:9). Christians do indeed possess all the things which are necessary for spiritual life (2 Cor. 6:10).

"Having," to a non-Christian, means materialism, possessions that are here and now, which must be capable of being measured, weighed, and displayed. What a contrast exists when one considers Christians, who possess first and foremost God the Father, the Son, and the Holy Spirit. As a result, they have everything they will ever need in eternity.

ILLUSTRATIONS

It is good to remind ourselves of the importance of possessions to non-Christians. This can be seen in the statements of famous men. For instance, President John Adams (1735-1826), the second President of the United States, said, "The moment the idea is admitted into society that property is not as sacred as the laws of God . . . anarchy and tyranny commence." According to him, possessions are sacred.

Abraham Lincoln (1809-65), the sixteenth President of the United States, held a similar viewpoint: "Property is the fruit of labor: property is desirable," he asserted, "and property is good." For him property was also inviolable.

Another President, Franklin Delano Roosevelt (1882-1945), was equally emphatic about property: "The function of government must be to favor no small group at the expense of its duty to protect the rights of personal freedom and of private property of all its citizens." He too saw property as a top priority.

On the other hand, some cynics realized that possessions were dangerous. "Few rich men own their own property," claimed the atheist Robert Ingersoll (1833-99). "Their property owns them."

Edmund Rufflin (1794-1865) said it in a slightly different way: "Banks and riches are chains of gold, but still chains."

But a Christian should have a liberating view of possessions. The famous English Congregationalist preacher, John Henry Jowett (1864-1923), said this about possessions: "The real measure of our wealth is how much we'd be worth if we lost all our money."

A modern preacher, Robert Lynd, said: "No man is really consecrated until his money is dedicated."

The great second-century Christian and church father, Tertullian (160-215), had a refreshing view of possessions. In the face of persecution and suffering, he said: "Nothing that is God's is obtainable by money."

Even Benjamin Franklin (1706-90) had a spiritually sound view of possessions, about which he wrote: "Money never made a man happy yet, nor will it. There is nothing in its nature to produce happiness. The more a man has, the more he wants. That was a true proverb of the wise man, rely upon it: 'Better is little with the fear of the Lord, than great treasure, and trouble therewith.' "

Saintly hymn-writer Francis Havergal (1836-79) penned a great consecration hymn, "Take My Life and Let It Be." The fourth stanza summarizes our subject admirably:

> Take my silver and my gold,
> Not a mite would I withhold;
> Take my intellect, and use
> Every power as Thou shalt choose.

HEAD

MEANING

The word translated "head" comes from a fairly familiar Greek word, *kephale*. We see this root in such English terms as "hydro*cephalic*" (one with water on the brain), "brachy*cephalic*" (a person who's short-headed or broad-headed), and "dolicho*cephalic*" (a person with an unusually long head).

In the Greek language *kephale* had an interesting development, which gives us our English meanings. Early on it meant the head of a person or an animal. This was later enlarged to include the prow of a ship, and the top of a pillar. Sociologically it also meant the chief of a community or a city. Finally, it came to stand for the whole person. (One sees this in our phrase, "Be it on your head.")

BIBLE USAGE

In the New Testament the word is capable of several interpretations. It occurs 75 times, and the majority of these are references to a physical head. Jesus urged His disciples not to take an oath by their heads, because they could not change the color of one single hair (Matt. 5:36). (Of course, age and hair coloring can do this quite easily.)

Another reference to a human head is the gruesome death of John the Baptist. When Herod attempted to bestow a favor on the beautiful young dancer Salome, her mother asked for the head of John the Baptist. Sadly the weak king agreed to her wish and had John beheaded. Afterward the bloody head was paraded before the bloodthirsty woman, Herodias (14:1-12; Mark 6:24-28).

A more beautiful picture is an incident which occurred at the home of Simon the leper, in Bethany. As Jesus sat at dinner a woman came in and anointed His head with expensive perfume. When the devious disciple, Judas, criticized this kindness, Jesus replied that she had anointed Him for His burial. Furthermore, Jesus put that anonymous disciple into the Gospel record for all time (Matt. 26:6-13).

However, His head that was anointed in affection was soon abused by a thoughtless mob. Mocking men fashioned a crown out of long, spiked, Middle Eastern thorns; then they pressed it down upon the head of Jesus (27:29). As Mark added, some in the crowd kept beating on His head as they shouted and spat at Him (Mark 15:19).

A further reference to a physical head is found in the life of Jesus. So closely was He identified with the common people, that He had no place to call home. He had no place of His own on which to lay His head (Matt. 8:20; Luke 9:58). This sets a spartan standard for discipleship, because we are called to emulate His sacrifices.

There are also other references to the heads in the Gospels. Jesus taught His disciples that God would always care for them. He reinforced this by saying that every single hair on one's head is numbered (Matt. 10:30). The Apostle Paul emphasized the same truth when he promised protection to his shipmates, as he crossed the Mediterranean on his way to prison in Rome (Acts 27:34).

Another aspect of the biblical teaching about heads is figurative. For instance, a husband is the head of his wife, according to the New Testament (1 Cor. 11:3; Eph. 5:23). Few teachings in the Bible have been so maligned by modern people. It does not agree with the free individualism of our society, but this is nevertheless the standard of Scripture. The idea is not tyranny, but tenderness. The husband should not dominate his wife, but rather devote himself to her.

One further aspect is the teaching that Christ is the Head of His church. This is taught in the same context as the headship of the man in the home (Eph. 5:23). In fact, Paul asserted that Christ is the Head over all things, and nothing can escape His sovereign control forever (1:22; Col. 1:18; 2:10). It is important that the church not "lose its Head." If it loses touch with Christ, it is nothing but a dead organization rather than a living organism.

ILLUSTRATIONS
From a secular standpoint, many statements refer to the head. In his inimitable way, Rudyard Kipling (1865-1936) referred to one's head in his poem, "If":

> If you can keep your head when all about you
> Are losing theirs and blaming it on you. . . .
> Yours is the Earth and everything that's in it,
> And—which is more—you'll be a Man, my son!

The southern songwriter, Stephen Foster (1826-64), included many picturesque snapshots in his writings. None is more charming than this one from "Uncle Ned": "He had no wool on the top of his head, / In de place where the wool ought to grow."

We often speak of a "sorehead," as one who stays angry. Perhaps that picture came from Frederick Marryat's (1792-1848) piece, "The King's Own," where he described a mean man who was "as savage as a bear with a sore head."

Hymns often speak of the head as a symbol of the entire body. Charles Wesley (1707-88), in his beautiful way, expressed this prayer to God: "Cover my defenseless head, / With the shadow of Thy wing."

Similarly the melancholy hymnist William Cowper (1731-1800) saw through the gloom of his despondent mind and wrote this great affirmation of faith:

> Ye fearful saints fresh courage take
> The clouds ye so much dread
> Are big with mercy, and shall break
> In blessings on your head.

In a real sense Christ is the Head of His church. Roman Catholics see the Pope as the earthly head of the church, and the Church of England expresses a commitment to the Queen as head of their church. To some degree the Southern Baptists consider the President of their church as head of that large denomination, and the Scottish Presbyterians have a Moderator as their earthly head. All true believers, however, know that Christ is the Head of His invisible, worldwide church.

According to one scholar, there were 1,900 denominational groups in the world at the outset of our century. But when David Barrett put together his monumental *World Christian Encyclopedia,* in 1982, he concluded that there are no fewer than 22,000 different Christian denominations. Nevertheless, the Head of His church on earth is still the Lord Jesus Christ. An ancient seventh-century hymn expressed this great truth:

> Christ is made the sure Foundation,
>   Christ the Head and Cornerstone,
> Chosen of the Lord, and precious,
>   Binding all the church in one.

HEAL

MEANING

The word which represents healing in the New Testament is *therapeuo*. It is seen in such English words as *"therapy"* (the medical treatment of a disease), and *"therapeutic"* (a branch of medicine which deals with treatment of disease).

The original use of this word in Greek was quite different, for it meant "to serve." As such it was used to describe household servants or slaves. In Plato's time it described those who served masters as slaves, and even those who served gods in their forms of worship.

Only later did the word come to describe the healing processes, and it was then applied to the work of physicians. They were the people who "served" the sick and took care of them. Therefore the word came to mean the medical treatment of illnesses. Sometimes it was even applied to the process of divine healing.

BIBLE USAGE

There are 43 appearances of this verb in the New Testament, and 40 of them are found in the Gospels of Matthew, Mark, and Luke. As can be imagined, they refer almost exclusively to the healing ministry of the Lord Jesus Christ.

Only in the Book of Acts is the word used to describe service to God, its original meaning. The Apostle Paul, in his sermon at Mars Hill in Athens, refers to the fact that God does not need man's service. God is far greater than any service which can be rendered to Him (Acts 17:24-25).

On another occasion the word is used to describe the normal healing work of a physician. It appears in the repetition of the proverb, "Physician heal yourself" (Luke 4:23). A further general use is in the story of a woman with an issue of blood, where the comment is included that no one could heal her (8:43). Otherwise this word is reserved for the healing work of the Lord.

The Gospels refer frequently to the extensive healing ministry of the Lord. From the first Jesus traveled throughout Galilee healing every kind of sickness and every kind of disease (Matt. 4:23). This happened immediately after Christ healed Simon Peter's mother-in-law (Mark 1:30-34; Luke 4:38-40). As a result of His healing, mobs of people pressed around, hoping to be healed by His touch (Mark 3:10).

Jesus combined His preaching and teaching ministry with a healing touch (Matt. 9:35). This was in fulfillment of the messianic prophecies of Isaiah (Isa. 61:1-3). In fact, Jesus cited this healing as a proof of His messiahship when John the Baptist asked for confirmation (Luke 7:22).

The breadth of His blessing is seen in the people whom Jesus healed. He stopped the flow of blood for a woman whom physicians could not heal (8:43-48). When a Roman centurion sought His help on behalf of a paralyzed servant, the Lord restored his crippled limbs (Matt. 8:5-13). When a man appeared with a withered hand, Jesus restored full movement to it (Mark 3:1-5). Apparently His healing ministry depended on the faith revealed in any given circumstance (6:5).

When the disciples were sent out on their first missionary journey, Jesus empowered them for the task. One of the aspects of their spiritual equipment was their ability to heal the sick (Matt. 10:1, 8). Here too the impression is that of transferred messianic power. Jesus came as a preaching and healing Messiah, and He gave some of this power to His disciples as they set out on their ministries (Mark 6:13).

Jesus felt that His healing ministry was essential to His overall mission. For this reason He healed people even on the Sabbath Day, which the legalistic Pharisees could not understand (Matt. 12:10; Luke 6:7).

As one reads the Gospels, the impression becomes clearer that Jesus demonstrated His divine power through healing. Because He is divine, He is able to do anything, including healing the sick and raising the dead. In an age of inadequate medical care, this ability made Jesus stand out in stark contrast with the helpless practitioners of religion.

ILLUSTRATIONS

Healing is a subject of endless comment. "Medicine," commented James Bryce, "[is] the only profession that labors incessantly to destroy the reason for its existence."

The French Enlightenment writer and cynic Voltaire (1694-1778) jested about medicine: "The art of medicine consists of amusing the patient while nature cures the disease."

Bernard Baruch (1870-1965) was a businessman and statesman who held an optimistic opinion about medical research. He said, "There are no such things as incurables; there are only things for which man has not found a cure."

The cost of medical care has given rise to a painful strain of humor. James H. Boren said: "I got the bill for my surgery. Now I know what those doctors were wearing masks for." Similarly Francis O'Walsh added: "A hospital should have a recovery room adjoining the cashier's office."

Though wits make jokes about medicine, many people have cause to give thanks for healers, and the deepest gratitude is reserved for God, the divine Healer.

Clement of Alexandria (150-220), a second-century church father, said, "The good Instructor, the Wisdom, the Word of the Father, who made man, cares for the whole nature of His creature. The all-sufficient Physician of humanity, the Saviour, heals both our body and soul."

Another ancient church father was Origen (182-254), a contemporary of Clement. Of healing he said: "Stronger than all the evils in the soul is the Word, and the healing power that dwells in Him."

Yet another second-century Christian was Tatian (110-172), who likewise referred to God's healing. In fact, he gave some interesting insights into early medicine when he said: "Even if you be healed by drugs [I grant you that point of courtesy], yet it behooves you to give testimony of the cure to God."

The father of modern surgery was Ambroise Pare. He too gave credit for cures to God: "I dressed his wounds; God healed him." Along the same lines hymnwriter William Hunter wrote: "The Great Physician now is near, / The sympathizing Jesus."

One further witness to the therapeutic work of God was the English writer Izaak Walton (1593-1683). He said the same thing in these classical words: "Look to your health; and if you have it, praise God, and value it next to a good conscience."

HEAR

MEANING

In the Greek New Testament the word for hearing is *akouo*. It is reflected in such English words as *"acoustics"* (the science of sound), *"acoustician"* (a specialist in sound), and *"acoustical"* (sometimes used of a substance that dampens sound).

As in English, the early Greeks used this word to describe four separate things. First, it represented the sense of hearing (hearing in contrast with deafness). Second, it spoke of the act of hearing (a student was hearing the lecture). Third, it was used for the organ of hearing (the ear). Fourth, it spoke of the content of hearing (a court hearing).

In the Septuagint, the Greek Old Testament, the word hearing was almost equal to obedience. It was believed that once a person had really heard the Word of God, obedience would usually follow.

BIBLE USAGE

In the New Testament the word *akouo* fills several roles. First, it speaks of perception. Jesus pronounced a special blessing on those who heard His words (Matt. 13:16; Mark 4:23). In fact, the Lord made deaf people hear and the dumb speak (7:37), and those miracles served to confirm His claim to deity (Luke 7:22).

A second aspect of hearing is communication, when a listener hears what is said. Jesus used the illustration of a man who heard the Word and responded immediately, in His Parable of the Sower and the Seed (Matt. 13:20). However, that person gave only superficial response to the Gospel. Jesus issued a strong condemnation of those who refused to hear the Gospel message when the disciples delivered it (10:14). Only spiritually sensitive people hear the communication of God's Word (John 8:47).

Relationship defines the third aspect of hearing. Those who have a relationship with one another hear in a special way. Because God claimed Jesus Christ as His beloved Son, the disciples who followed Him were commanded to hear what He said (Matt. 17:5; Luke 9:35). Even the dead shall hear the voice of their Redeemer and respond (John 5:25). By the same token Jesus' followers hear His voice, just as sheep hear their shepherd's voice (John 10:1-8). John confirmed, in his first epistle, that the disciples had heard Jesus (1 John 1:3-5).

This relationship also holds true for subsequent Christians. At the end of his life on earth Paul wrote his final letter to Timothy, who had been his close companion. Paul reminded Timothy to pass on what he had heard, and to make provision for others to pass it on. Hearing is the foundation of Christian living and teaching (2 Tim. 2:2).

A fourth feature of hearing is attention, listening carefully to what is said. It is possible to hear casually without listening carefully. The disciples heard the teachings of Jesus Christ and listened attentively, even when they found His words hard to comprehend (Mark 14:58).

At Pentecost people from various lands listened carefully and understood the message, because God worked a miracle of communication, enabling the Christians to speak in foreign languages (Acts 2:6). Paul got a careful hearing by two attentive judges when he came to trial (24:4; 26:3). The emphasis of these passages falls clearly on careful listening to a judicial procedure.

The same word was used by Paul in his defense before the people. He recalled how the Lord spoke to him on the Damascus Road. At that time Paul listened carefully, and he comprehended the sense of the divine message (22:9). In a real sense God communicated with Paul, and he heard what God was saying.

Hearing is therefore an elastic word. It can mean that one simply hears a sound, like a bump in the night. But it can also mean the intensive listening by which we hear exactly what is being said and respond by acting accordingly. At any rate, it is important that we listen to the Lord, as He listens to us when we pray.

ILLUSTRATIONS

There are many secular references to hearing. For instance, G.K. Chesterton (1874-1936), an incredibly witty novelist, wrote in his poem "The Rolling English Road": "For there is good news yet to hear and fine things to be seen, / Before we go to Paradise by way of Kensal Green."

Poet laureate Alfred Lord Tennyson (1809-92) included something about hearing in his "Maud":

She is coming, my own, my sweet;
Were it ever so airy a tread,
My heart would hear her and beat,
Were it earth in an earthy bed;
My dust would hear her and beat,
Had I lain for a century dead.

Here Tennyson promised to hear his beloved, even if he were dead.

However, there is Someone more important to hear than even the tread of a lover. It is important for us to hear God when He speaks. E. Stanley Jones (1884-1973), a devoted missionary evangelist to India, put it in these words: "In the pure, strong hours of the morning, when the soul of the day is at its best, lean upon the windowsill of God and look into His face, and get the orders for the day. Then go out into the day with the sense of a hand upon your shoulder and not a chip."

Another great Christian was the Scottish preacher Robert Murray McCheyne (1813-43), who also spoke of hearing in an even more meaningful way: "If I could hear Christ praying for me in the next room, I would not fear a million enemies. Yet distance makes no difference. He *is* praying for me."

Perhaps the hymn-writer E. Mary Grimes (1868-1927) said it best when she wrote:

Speak, Lord, in the stillness,
While I wait on Thee;
Hushed my heart to listen
In expectancy.

Speak, O blessed Master,
In this quiet hour;
Let me see Thy face, Lord,
Feel Thy touch of power.

Another side to hearing is the truth that God hears us. In the profound *Book of Common Prayer* is this instruction to the hearers of God's words: "Hear them, read, mark, learn, and inwardly digest them." What a wonderful pattern for study of the Word of God, this is. In fact, a friend wrote a Bible study book using that line as its title.

Elsewhere in the *Book of Common Prayer* is a prayer based on Psalm 130:1-2: "Out of the deep have I called unto Thee, O Lord: Lord, hear my voice."

Hymn-writer William Whiting (1825-78) caught the same idea when he wrote: "O hear us when we cry to Thee, / For those in peril on the sea."

HEART

MEANING

Here one encounters a familiar Greek word, for the word translated "heart" is *kardia*. This is seen in such grimly familiar English terms as "*cardio*logy" (the study of the heart), "*cardio*logist" (a specialist physician who treats diseases of the heart), "electro*cardio*graph" (an electronic monitoring device for the heart), and "*cardiac* arrest" (a heart attack).

For the ancient Greeks the main meaning of the heart was the physical organ. However, under Homer it also meant the seat of emotions, as in loving with "all one's heart." For Greeks of that time, the heart was the seat of moral and intellectual life, and all emotions were embraced in this term. Later the emphasis fell on reasoning, and the heart was seen as the center of rational thought.

The Septuagint, the Greek Old Testament, considered the heart to be the moral center of one's being. The Old Testament spoke of an evil heart, when someone was taken over by Satan.

BIBLE USAGE

In the New Testament the major meaning of the heart is figurative, as the center of life, thought, feeling, and even spiritual response.

In some cases the heart refers to the whole person. The provision of God fills one's heart with joy, and makes the whole person happy (Acts 14:17). James warned rich people against fattening their hearts for slaughter (James 5:5), a warning which echoed the sayings of Jesus (Luke 21:34).

When speaking of God's knowledge of people, the Scripture says He knows their hearts (16:15). God knows if believers forgive one another from their hearts (Matt. 18:35). When we come to God in prayer, the Holy Spirit searches our hearts and suits our prayers to God's will (Rom. 8:27). In the final judgment God will judge the secrets of our hearts (2:16; 1 Cor. 14:25). When we obey God, we should do so wholeheartedly, from the bottoms of our hearts (Rom. 6:17; 1 Tim. 1:5; 2 Tim. 2:22). God wants from us wholehearted commitment which is seen in all that we do (Col. 3:17, 23).

The heart is also the seat of our thought processes, according to the New Testament. Jesus quoted Isaiah 6:9-10 to show that people understand with their hearts (Matt. 13:14-15). This same truth was reemphasized by the Apostle Paul in speaking to some Roman Jews (Acts 28:27). People who come to understand the glorious light of the Gospel understand it with their hearts (2 Cor. 4:6; Eph. 1:18). One's memory is also referred to as his heart (Luke 2:51).

Not only is the heart a description of our whole being and the rational aspect of us, but it is also the seat of our emotions. The heart is joyful when something good happens to us (Acts 2:26; 14:17). By contrast when things go wrong one's heart is consumed with sorrow (John 14:1; Rom. 9:2). Love too is felt in the heart (Matt. 22:37; 2 Cor. 7:3; Phil. 1:7). When anguish comes upon us, it also descends on the heart (2 Cor. 2:4).

A final significance of the heart is spiritual. It is the center of one's spiritual perception and purpose. The love of God is poured out in the heart of a believer (Rom. 5:5). When we trusted in the Lord, He set the seal of His Holy Spirit on our hearts (2 Cor. 1:22). The Holy Spirit also dwells in our hearts to give us a sense of our sonship; in fact He moves us to call out, "Abba [Daddy], Father" (Gal. 4:6). It is God who ultimately tests our hearts (1 Thes. 2:4).

Thus the term "heart" is full of meaning in the New Testament. It speaks of the central part of people, that point where the emotions, reasoning, spiritual instincts, and God-consciousness is. In fact, in the New Testament the heart seems to refer to the whole immaterial part of people.

ILLUSTRATIONS

There are many interesting references to the heart in literature. Of it Ansari of Herat said: "Can you walk on water? You have done no better than a straw. Can you fly in the air? You have done no better than a bluebottle. Conquer your heart; then you may become somebody."

Julius Miller marveled at the intricacy of the human heart and said: "In a normal person, the heart beats 70 times a minute, 100,000 times a day, 40 million times a year! During a single day, a ventricle pumps about 11,000 quarts [of blood], or 265 million quarts in a lifetime. If an elevator could be harnessed to this marvelous engine, you could ride from the ground floor to the fifth floor of a building in about an hour. No wonder Leonardo [Da Vinci] called it a 'marvelous instrument.'"

Robert Frost, a great American poet, said, "There never was any heart truly great and generous, that was not also tender and compassionate." A lesser-known person, Fred Russell, added this insight: "Calisthenics can build up the body. Courses of study can train the mind. But the real champion is the person whose heart can be educated."

Along the same lines is a quotation from the Salvation Army's magazine, *War Cry:* "A tourist was once staying in an inn in a valley in northern Italy where the floor was dirty. He thought he should advise the landlady to scrub it, when he perceived that it was made of mud and the more she would scrub it the worse it would become. So it is with our hearts; its corrupt nature will admit of no improvement; it must be made ever anew."

Augustine of Hippo (354-430), a great scholar and church father, often spoke of the heart. On one occasion he said: "To my God, a heart of flame; to my fellowmen, a heart of love; to myself, a heart of steel." This letter emphasized his self-discipline.

William Gladstone (1809-98), a great prime minister of England and a constitutional scholar, also spoke about the heart: "There is but one question of the hour; how to bring the truth of God's Word into vital contact with the minds and hearts of all classes of people."

Equally strong was a statement of William Penn (1644-1718), Quaker benefactor and founder of the Pennsylvania colony: "Men may tire themselves in a labyrinth of search and talk of God; but if we would know Him indeed, it must be from the impressions we receive of Him; and the softer our hearts are, the deeper and livelier those will be upon us."

An anonymous Christian struck the nail on the head when he said: "Hardening of the heart ages more people than hardening of the arteries."

HEIR

MEANING

In the Greek New Testament, the word for "heir" is *kleronomos*. It is a combination of two words: *kleros* (a lot or inheritance) and *nomos* (law). Thus the word *kleronomos* indicates the legal distribution of possessions or lots to heirs. A related word is *sunkleronomos*, which means "joint-heir."

In the original Greek culture, possessions were passed on to any person named in one's will. In fact, Greeks often built their fortunes for the purpose of passing them on to favored relatives. The Romans widened the concept to enable the distribution of possessions or wealth among close friends or loyal servants.

To the Jews, however, an inheritance was usually reserved for one's children. In fact this was preserved in the Law as the principle to be followed. The Greek Old Testament also used *kleros* to refer to casting of the lot, as was seen in the use of the Urim and Thummim (Ex. 28:30; Lev. 8:8).

BIBLE USAGE

The New Testament uses the concept of inheritance in only ten specific passages. The New Testament authors referred frequently to an heir, and their main application was in the realm of spiritual inheritance. A Christian is described as being an heir of God and a joint-heir with Christ (Rom. 8:16-17). Paul also used this concept in the narrow context of being a Jew, and thus an heir of all the promises of the patriarchs (11:1).

Because of the sacrifice of the Lord Jesus Christ, we too are drawn into this relationship and these rights (Gal. 3:29; 4:7). In the Book of Hebrews, this word is expanded to mean that we are heirs of all the promises of God (Heb. 6:17).

In Peter's profound teaching concerning Christian marriage, he developed this theme even further. A husband and wife are heirs of the promises of God, and thus are doubly related by marriage and grace. In fact, the fundamental connection in Christian marriage is that of being "joint-heirs" of the grace of life (1 Peter 3:7, 9).

But the principle of inheritance is not only used to describe heirs. In the New Testament it is also applied to the possessions which shall be inherited. These are as broad as the promises of God. First, Christians are heirs of salvation. When speaking to the Ephesian elders, Paul reminded them that they and he were heirs of the sanctifying process of God (Acts 20:32). The same truth appears again in the Ephesian letter, where Paul asserted that they shared a glorious inheritance (Eph. 1:14, 18). In the sister Epistle of Colossians, Paul again returned to the subject of salvation's inheritance (Col. 3:24).

In the Book of Hebrews there is much emphasis on the future of believers. In this connection the writer of Hebrews reminded his readers that they are heirs of the promise of God (Heb. 6:17). Furthermore, this inheritance will never lose its value, for it is eternal (9:15).

A similar statement launches the exciting Epistle of 1 Peter. There the apostle compounded the adjectives to say that our inheritance cannot be ruined or wrecked, and that it will never fade away, because it is reserved for us in heaven (1 Peter 1:4).

Another aspect of this inheritance hearkens back to the Old Testament. Our inheritance is part of God's coming kingdom glory. We shall inherit a place in God's kingdom. There we shall no longer be subjected to decay (1 Cor. 15:50). We and our fellow citizens will be saved and sanctified by the Lord (Gal. 5:21).

No matter what we have or lack on earth, we shall be rich in His kingdom (James 2:5). This kingdom promise fills us with hope. Therefore Christians will inherit the fulfillment of their hope in the Lord (Titus 3:7). This colors all our living now, because we are heirs of God's hope.

In the Westminster Abbey of the faithful (Heb. 11) are many references to our inheritance. Noah was an heir of righteousness because he believed God (11:7). This same inheritance was shared by Abraham (11:8).

In fact, Paul wrote to the Romans that they would inherit the world (Rom. 4:13). This is the ultimate hope of Christians who live by faith and not by sight.

ILLUSTRATIONS

Though many people look forward to an inheritance, it is not usually a prospect of great wealth. Literature refers to many different inheritances. In his poem, "Locksley Hall," Alfred Lord Tennyson (1809-92) declared: "I [am] the heir of all the ages, in the foremost files of time." Thus he emphasized his connections to the past.

For others, there is an inheritance of fame. In writing the epitaph for William Shakespeare, John Milton (1608-74) addressed the Bard in this reverential line:

Dear son of memory, great heir of fame,
What need'st thou such weak witness to thy name?

He regarded the greatest inheritance of Shakespeare to be his undying fame.

Shakespeare (1564-1616) drew attention to another, less joyful inheritance when he wrote his *Hamlet*. In a melancholy speech, Shakespeare put these words in Hamlet's mouth:

No more; and, by a sleep to say we end
The heart-ache and the thousand natural shocks
That flesh is heir to, 'tis a consummation
Devoutly to be wished. To die, to sleep (III, i, 56).

For Shakespeare's character, life was an inheritance of grief and sadness, and death was the only release from it.

How different it is to read lines written by godly people. The foremost revival preacher of the Great Awakening, Jonathan Edwards (1703-58), looked beyond the pain of this life and saw another inheritance, about which he declared: "The end of God's creating the world is to prepare a kingdom for His Son." Edwards looked forward to the kingdom which he would inherit with the Lord.

According to *The Book of Common Prayer*, there is another inheritance for the believer: "O Lord, support us all the day long. . . . Then in Thy mercy grant us a safe lodging, and a holy rest, and peace at the last." To the writer of that prayer, peace would be an inheritance.

The great professor and author C.S. Lewis (1898-1963) also saw a coming inheritance in the eternal realms. He wrote: "A continual looking forward to the eternal world is not a form of escapism or wishful thinking, but one of the things a Christian is meant to do. It does not mean that we are to leave the present world as it is. If you read history, you will find that the Christians who did the most for the present world were just those who thought most of the next." For C.S. Lewis, his inheritance was in the hands of his God. What safety!

HERESY

MEANING

A rather unpleasant word is "heresy." It is a direct transliteration of the Greek word, *hairesis*, and means any doctrine which diverges from the biblical standard. A related Greek word is *hairetikos*, and one can readily see the connection between this word and our word "heretic" (one who holds to and propagates a false doctrine). The verb from which these two nouns are taken is *haireomai* (to take, win, seize, or apprehend). The point of heresy seems to be that a wrong doctrine seizes someone's mind, or that someone seizes upon a false teaching.

In ancient Greek the word *hairesis* was used to describe a school of philosophy, such as the Stoics or Epicureans of Acts 17:18. As the first century passed, the first Christian heresy developed. This was gnosticism (a complicated and varied teaching that emphasized salvation through knowledge). Thus the early Christians devoted time and effort to combating the heresy of gnosticism. For instance, Origen (185-254) wrote a well-reasoned criticism of the Gnostic teacher Celsus. Heresy, then, is any teaching which diverges from the clear teaching of Scripture.

BIBLE USAGE

The root word *hairesis* appears relatively infrequently in the New Testament, showing up only ten times. Most frequently it describes a sect or splinter group. Within Judaism there were several such distinct groups, and one of these was the Sadducee party. They are referred to by Luke as a "sect" (*hairesis*, Acts 5:17).

After his conversion the Apostle Paul referred to the Pharisees also as a sect (26:5). Apparently this was not just a condemnation of their distinctive (heretical) doctrines. It was a general use of the word to describe any party.

By the same token, the Jews called Christians a "sect" (*hairesis*). They were known popularly as "the sect of the Nazarene," or followers of Jesus from Nazareth (24:5). This was obviously a critical comment, designed to demean the Lord's disciples.

Not only were there sects in Judaism, but early in the history of the Christian church the problem emerged within the fellowship. In fact, the Apostle Paul wrote the Book of 1 Corinthians to combat a party, sectarian spirit. In his introduction to the epistle, Paul challenged the Corinthians to reject "divisions" or "sects" (1 Cor. 1:10, 12-13). Paul returned to this theme later in this epistle, and again warned the Christians to reject these false, sinful divisions (11:18-19). In fact, Paul regarded such dissension within Christianity to be a sin against the Lord (12:25). He further described division and dissent as one of the "deeds of the flesh" (Gal. 5:19-20).

Though the main use of our word, *hairesis*, in the New Testament refers to dissenting groups, there is also some reference to heretical teachers. In writing to Titus, Paul attempted to correct the abuses of the faith on the Island of Crete. He called those who infiltrate the church and bring false doctrine heretics, *hairetikos* (Titus 3:10).

Only once in the New Testament is our word *hairesis* translated "false doctrine or heresy." In Peter's Second Epistle he refers to false teachers and false prophets who introduce into the church destructive teachings which deny "the Master who bought them" (2 Peter 2:1). Though this is the only direct reference to heretical doctrine, it is extremely explicit. First, its proponents are clearly marked as "false" teachers. Second, their teaching is destructive of true Christianity. Third, its main effect is to degrade the Lord Jesus Christ. Fourth, it brings destruction on those who teach it. This seems to be the clearest New Testament statement on the subject of heresy, and it should serve as a warning to any who would stray from the path of biblical doctrine.

ILLUSTRATIONS

Only twice in my ministry have I confronted real heresies. In the '60s we lived and worked in Germany. One afternoon I was teaching a Bible study, and an elderly, respected Christian man posed this question to me: "If anyone is lost eternally, will not Jesus have failed in His sacrifice on the cross?"

This heresy, called "universalism," teaches that all will be saved through the blood of Christ. (Some even insist that Satan himself will be saved in heaven.) However, the Scripture clearly teaches that those who reject Christ will be eternally lost. To assert that all will be saved is a heresy, a false teaching.

The second heresy I encountered in the West Country of England. Some in the church of which I was pastor believed that people without Christ would be lost, but that they would not suffer eternal punishment. The argument went like this: Those who reject Christ will go to a place of punishment after death. However, they will ultimately be annihilated and cease to exist. Thus they will not suffer eternal punishment in hell. This heresy, called "annihilationism," is widespread in England. It is wrong because it denies the eternal nature of punishment, and it also contradicts the biblical teaching about the immortality of the soul.

Both of these heresies divided the church. They produced a serious schism and they polarized believers. They also undercut effective evangelism designed to win people for Christ. Heresy is not a new problem, and there are many references to it.

The Puritans in England roundly condemned false teaching or heresy. John Trapp (1601-69), a Bible commentator, said, "Heresy is the leprosy of the head." His contemporary and friend Thomas Watson added, "Error damns as well as vice; the one pistols, the other poisons." A third Puritan was a pastor, John Flavel (died 1691). He said, "By entertaining strange persons, men sometimes entertain angels unawares: but by entertaining strange doctrines, many have entertained devils unaware."

The worst aspect of heresy is this: people are so ready to accept it. As Orestes Brownson put it: "Error makes the circuit of the globe while Truth is pulling her boots on." A German proverb says, "An old error is always more popular than a new truth." To which the philosopher-mathematician Blaise Pascal (1623-62) added: "Man is being filled with error. This error is natural and, without grace, ineffaceable."

Noted Bible commentator Archbishop William Trench (1807-86) drew an interesting connection between heresy and schism (division in the church). "Schism is practical heresy," he said, "and heresy is theoretical schism." In the words of John Calvin: "Heresy is a magnet to attract the unsound and unsettled mind."

HOLY

MEANING

The Greek word translated "holy" is *hagios,* which occurs in its various forms more than 275 times in the New Testament. It is reflected in the English word "*hagio*graphic" (the story of saints' lives), "*hagio*cracy" (the rule of saints), and "*hagio*latry" (the veneration or adoration of saints). Thus holiness and saints or sanctification have the same Greek word behind them.

In ancient Greek the word referred to "an object of awe or reverence." Later it came to mean something which was clean or cleansed from all contamination. The sanctuary in which one worshiped gods was also regarded as "holy." Literally the word means to be "set aside" for a special purpose, and in this case the purpose is worship. Predictably in later Greek thought, gods were regarded as being especially holy.

The Greek Old Testament, the Septuagint, made frequent use of this word. In all cases it meant something or someone who was set aside and free from contamination. God is regarded as being holy (Isa. 6:3). The ground where Moses met God was also holy (Ex. 3:5). Jerusalem was seen to be the "holy city" (Isa. 48:2; 52:1). Most holy of all places was the temple ("My holy mountain," 11:9). These places and people were set apart for special, sacred, holy use.

BIBLE USAGE

The meaning of holiness can best be seen by considering the words with which it is connected. First, God is described as being holy. In her song of praise, Mary praised God by declaring that His name is holy (Luke 1:49). Jesus, in praying to His Father, called Him "Holy Father" (John 17:11). Because God is holy, we too are committed to holiness (1 Peter 1:16). In the Revelation John also perceived that God is holy (Rev. 3:7; 4:8). God is the Source and Standard of holiness.

Christ too is holy. Before His birth an angel described Him as holy (Luke 1:35). Even the demons realized that He was "the Holy One of God" (Mark 1:24). In their proclamation the apostles repeatedly referred to Christ as the Holy One (Acts 4:27-30).

Most frequently the word "holy" is applied to the Spirit, who is called the Holy Spirit more than 60 times in the New Testament. At the baptism of Jesus the Holy Spirit descended upon Him (Luke 3:22). The Holy Spirit also caused Jesus to rejoice (10:21). In the Book of Acts, the Holy Spirit was seen to be the Source of power for the Christians (Acts 1:5, 8). At first the entire Christian church was filled with the Holy Spirit (4:31).

Angels too were called holy in the Bible. This is especially evident in the report of coming judgment (Mark 8:38; Luke 9:26). It was a holy angel who brought Peter together with the Roman seeker Cornelius (Acts 10:22).

Likewise the prophets were called holy in the New Testament. Zacharias praised God for the revelation given through God's holy prophets (Luke 1:70). Peter and John also referred to the holy prophets and their prophecies concerning Christ's coming (Acts 3:21). The holy prophets also foretold the second coming of Christ (2 Peter 3:2).

Just as the prophets were called holy, so also the New Testament applied this word to the apostles. Though Paul was himself an apostle, under the inspiration of the Holy Spirit he referred to all apostles as being holy, set apart to God (Eph. 3:5).

Christians are also called holy. Usually this is seen in the word "saints." (Saints means literally "holy ones.") Paul introduced many of his epistles by calling the Christians saints (Rom. 1:7; 1 Cor. 1:2; Phil. 1:1; Col. 1:4). The same word was used by the writer of the Epistle to the Hebrews (Heb. 6:10).

The description "holy" is also applied to places. The temple was a holy place (Matt. 24:15; Acts 6:13). Peter also remembered the Mount of Transfiguration as a holy place (2 Peter 1:18).

Any person, place, or thing which was set apart wholly for the use of God was holy. In a real sense Christians today are "saints" (holy ones), set apart to serve God. For this reason we are commanded to be holy and live in holiness.

ILLUSTRATIONS

In its profound definition of God, *The Westminster Confession of Faith* describes Him as being the "one only living and true God, who is infinite in being and perfection, a most pure Spirit, invisible, without body, parts, or passions, immutable, immense, eternal, incomprehensible, almighty, most wise, most holy, most free, most absolute."

In speaking of the Holy Spirit, Anglican churchman Thomas Arbnold (1795-1842) said, "He who does not know God the Holy Spirit cannot know God at all." In the same vein sainted Methodist Samuel Chadwick said, "The presence of the Spirit endues men with divine authority and power. . . . The Holy Ghost does not come upon methods, but upon men."

John Owen (1616-83) also commented on the Holy Spirit in saying, "God's sealing of believers is His gracious communication of the Holy Ghost unto them, so as to enable them unto all the duties of their holy calling. The effects of this sealing are gracious operations of the Spirit in and upon believers."

Holiness should characterize the lives of believers. Thomas Chalmers (1780-1847), a brilliant Scottish pastor, claimed: "The beauty of holiness has done more, and will do more, to regenerate the world and bring everlasting righteousness than all the other agencies put together."

Another outstanding preacher and theologian, Jonathan Edwards (1703-58), also commented upon holiness: "He that sees the beauty of holiness, or true moral good, sees the greatest and most important things in the world."

Contemporary evangelist Leighton Ford was practical in his statement that, "There is no detour to holiness. Jesus came to the Resurrection through the Cross, not around it." Another evangelist, Dwight L. Moody (1837-99) commented in a similar vein about holiness when he said: "It is a great deal better to live a holy life than to talk about it."

Leonard Ravenhill, a well-known authority on revival, said this about holiness: "The greatest miracle that God can do today is to take an unholy man out of an unholy world, and make that man holy and put him back into that unholy world and keep him holy in it."

HOME

MEANING

The Greek words translated "home," "house," and "household" are *oikos* and *oikia*. Though the form is changed slightly, these words are reflected in such English terms as "*eco*nomics" (the management of financial resources of a community in which we live) and "*eco*logy" (the conservation of the environment in which we live). In both cases the words relate to our larger living environment, the world that we call home.

To the ancient Greeks the words *oikos* and *oikia* were used in similar ways. However, originally *oikos* meant an inheritance passed on within a household or family, while *oikia* spoke of the house in which a family lived.

In early Greek literature these words were used to describe a dwelling place. Later they came to mean the family (household) which lived in that structure. Ultimately they meant the possessions which made up a family's household goods.

BIBLE USAGE

The words *oikos* and *oikia* were used frequently in the New Testament. Together they occur more than 200 times. In many cases they refer to the building which one calls home. Families lived in a house as home (Matt. 2:11; 7:24-27; Mark 10:29). Jesus often visited in homes (2:15; 9:33; Luke 4:38; 5:29; 7:44), as did His apostles (Acts 10:6). Churches even met in individual believers' homes (16:15, 31-34; 18:8).

Another literal application of the word is the temple in Jerusalem, which was known as the house of God (Matt. 12:4; 21:13; Luke 6:4). This view was sanctioned by quotations from the Old Testament (Isa. 56:7; Jer. 7:11).

The same word is applied to a family which lives in one house. The danger of a house (family) divided against itself was used as an example by Jesus in His teaching (Matt. 12:25; Mark 3:25). In the New Testament there are several examples of household conversions, in which entire families came to believe in Christ (John 4:53; Acts 16:31-33; 1 Cor. 16:15).

The idea of a household was also applied in a larger context. Israel was viewed by the biblical writers as a household (Matt. 10:6; 15:24). By the same token the church of Jesus Christ was also viewed as a large household of faith (Eph. 2:19-22; 1 Tim. 3:15).

Another use of the same term was as an official household. An emperor's household included his family, servants, advisers, and slaves (Phil. 4:22). This was especially true of rulers in the ancient world, and it is also reflected in the large number of people who serve rulers today.

Yet another picturesque use of the word is heaven. Jesus regarded heaven as God's home (John 14:2-3), which He will share eternally with us. Christ is the primary Heir of God's heavenly household, to which we also belong (Heb. 3:6). Because we are the household of God, we must be careful to maintain purity and spiritual cleanliness in that home (1 Peter 4:17).

There is one further reference to the house which is of importance to us as Christians. Paul often spoke about a Christian's body being his house (2 Cor. 5:1). In this connection Paul asserted that we only "tent" here on earth, because our permanent home is our heavenly body which we shall receive at the Resurrection.

Thus the words *oikos* and *oikia* are capable of many interpretations in Scripture. But they all convey the idea of a place to live, whether it be a church or a temple, where God lives, or a body or a building, where people live. Christians will never be homeless, because God is always their dwelling place.

ILLUSTRATIONS

Literature contains references to the spiritual home. The great hymn-writer Isaac Watts (1674-1748) wrote of this spiritual home:

Our God, our help in ages past
   Our hope for years to come,
Our shelter in the stormy blast,
   And our eternal home.

A more modern hymn was written by Jesse Pounds (1861-1921). Its theme underlines the longing for a heavenly home, and its title is, "The Way of the Cross Leads Home." Perhaps she was thinking of Frederick Faber's (1814-63) statement, "The music of the Gospel leads us home."

A great advocate of the Oxford Movement, John Henry Cardinal Newman (1801-90), also expressed this idea:

Lead, kindly Light, amid the encircling gloom,
   Lead Thou me on;
The night is dark, and I am far from home;
   Lead Thou me on.

Literature has many references to earthly homes. For instance, Lena Guilbert Ford (died 1916) wrote:

Keep the home fires burning,
While your hearts are yearning
Though your lads are far away
They dream of home.

Returning home is the happiest theme in literature. Joachim Du Bellay (1515-60) wrote: "Happy is the wanderer, like Ulysses, who has come happily home at last."

Along the same line John Howard Payne (1791-1852) penned these sentiments:

Mid pleasures and palaces though we may roam,
Be it ever so humble, there's no place like home.
... Home, home, sweet, sweet home!
There's no place like home!

In "Don Juan" Lord Byron (1788-1824) echoed these sentiments: " 'Tis sweet to hear the watch dog's honest bark, bay deep-mouth's welcome as we draw near home."

Robert Louis Stevenson (1850-94) compared death to coming home in his "Requiem": "Home is the sailor, home from the sea, and the hunter home from the hill."

Henry Clay Work (1832-84) was active in the temperance movement of the 19th century. In this connection he wrote this song: "Father, dear father, come home with me now. The clock in the steeple strikes one."

For a Christian, home speaks of heaven. Anglican bishop Jeremy Taylor (1613-67) wrote: "Faith is the Christian's foundation, hope is his anchor, death is his harbor, Christ is his Pilot, and heaven is his country."

As William Wordsworth (1770-1850) put it in "Skylark": "Type of the wise who soar, but never roam. / True to the kindred points of heaven and home!"

HONOR

MEANING

The word which is translated "honor" is the Greek word *time,* and the verb "to confer honor" is *timao*. These words mean several things: value, respect, honor, and even the honorarium given for services rendered. It is seen in the little-used English word *"timo*cracy" (a government which is dominated by those who love special honors).

Actually, the concept of *"timo*cracy" was developed by Plato. His student Aristotle expanded on this idea. To the early Greeks "honor" meant the value placed on a person. Soon it also came to mean people of high position.

At first "honor" related to the possessions which one had. Only later did it come to mean the honor which is conferred on a deserving person. In the great Greek city-states of Athens and Sparta honor was a matter of civic recognition.

BIBLE USAGE

Our Greek words, *time* and *timao* are variously translated in the New Testament, where they are found about 70 times. One of the most frequent uses of the word is "value." When the early Christians encountered financial need, they met it by donating the value (price) received for selling their own land (Acts 4:34, marg.).

Paul mentioned the extraordinary value of a person. Jesus Christ paid for Christians with His own life, and this established an extremely high value of every saved person (1 Cor. 6:20). For this reason Christians are bound to glorify the Lord. In Peter's writings the same word, "value," is translated "precious." Christ's blood is especially valuable or precious (1 Peter 1:19).

In a negative context, Paul warned that false abuse of the flesh in order to humiliate oneself is of no value (Col. 2:23). This demonstrates the divine judgment on man-made religion and self-abasement. It is of no value whatever. Only the work of Christ is of any real value.

If value is the first meaning of our word, the second is respect. God bestows special respect on Christians who do not appear to deserve it. They may engage in a very common ministry, but God bestows respect on them for it (1 Cor. 12:23-24). In fact, Christians should give respect to all who deserve it (Rom. 9:21; 13:7; 2 Tim. 2:20).

No New Testament writer said more about respect than Peter did. Christ is the most deserving of respect, because He is precious (1 Peter 2:7). God bestowed special respect and honor on the Lord, when He was transfigured before the very eyes of the disciples (2 Peter 1:17). This is the ultimate expression of honor on earth.

Peter also commended Christian wives, and said that they deserve the respect of their husbands (1 Peter 3:7). Some believe that Paul taught the same truth in 1 Thessalonians 4:4. In fact Peter commanded Christians to give honor to all (1 Peter 2:17).

Paul likewise wrote Timothy that true widows, who remained single in order to serve the Lord, deserved special respect and honor (1 Tim. 5:3).

The Lord Jesus referred to the commandment, "Honor your father and mother," and He reinforced this (Matt. 15:4; 19:19). Paul stated the same principle (Eph. 6:2).

There is no greater model in the practice of giving honor than the Lord Himself. Often in the Gospels we are told that Christ gave honor to His Heavenly Father, and the Heavenly Father honors the Son (John 5:23).

There are several sound reasons why we should honor other people. First, Christ set the example for us in giving honor where it is due. Second, the image of God stamped on us by our Creator qualifies each one for honor. Third, it is part of Christian humility to give honor to others. Fourth, it helps unify the church when we honor other Christians, and the same can be said about one's family. It is therefore right to give honor.

ILLUSTRATIONS

People have commented freely on the subject of honors. For instance, Mark Twain (1835-1910) said wisely, "It is better to deserve honors and not to have them than to have them and not to deserve them."

Speaking on the same subject, President Calvin Coolidge (1872-1933) commented, "No person was ever honored for what he received. Honor has been a reward for what he gave." This summarized the life of service which Coolidge lived.

The ancients also spoke of honor. Cato (234-149 B.C.) spoke of personal honor when he claimed: "I would rather men should ask why no statue has been erected in my honor, than why one has." A century earlier Aristotle said similarly, "Dignity does not consist in possessing honors, but in deserving them."

William Shakespeare (1564-1616) made frequent reference to the matter of human honors. Into the mouth of King Richard II he put these lines: "Mine honor is my life; both grow in one; take honor from me, and my life is done."

Concerning the fallen Julius Caesar, Shakespeare's character Brutus said: "As he was valiant, I honor him: but, as he was ambitious, I slew him."

George MacDonald (1824-1905) was a Scottish poet and novelist who exerted some influence on C.S. Lewis. On the subject of honor MacDonald said: "When one has to seek the honor that comes from God only, he will take the withholding of honor that comes from men very quietly indeed." In other words, what does the honor of men matter, if we have the honor of God?

This became clear to me some years ago when a popular church history book appeared in England. A friend was incensed that the noted Victorian pulpit genius Charles Haddon Spurgeon was not included in the book. It occurred to me, that the hollow honor of a historian would mean little to Spurgeon, who now enjoys the honors which God can bestow.

Honors are only valuable if they have eternal worth. The story is told that Queen Victoria frequently attended a Bible study led by one of her footmen. One evening she asked him: "When do you think the Lord will return?"

The footman was perplexed, and told the monarch that the Bible gave no specific time for the Lord's return. So we should always be ready for His return.

At this the Queen said: "Oh, I do hope that the Lord returns during my lifetime. I should love to lay at His feet the crown of the kingdom and the empire." That gracious old Queen knew to whom honor truly belongs, the King of kings.

HOPE

MEANING

The Greek word which is translated "hope" in the New Testament is *elpis*, and the verb "to hope" is *elpizo*. In the New Testament these words appear more than 80 times, and they usually refer to Christ, who is the hope of the church and the world.

Ancient Greek writers asserted that hope is engrained deeply in the nature of people. Though the ancients had no real reason for hope, they believed that all people had hope for the future. Homer said, "Hope is golden," and believed that people could find comfort through hope in times of distress. Despite the elemental uncertainty of life, people should hope in the future. Plato added that hope is the impulse which gives rise to all that is beautiful and good in the world. Ancient Greek literature had a hope without foundation, whereas a Christian's hope has the sure foundation of Christ's coming.

BIBLE USAGE

In the Scriptures there are two sources of hope: one is human and the other is divine. There are some references to human hope in the Bible. Sometimes this hope was perverted. Such was the case in Philippi where evil men hoped for gain as they exploited a demon-possessed girl (Acts 16:19).

At other times hope is misplaced or abandoned. As Paul was being transported as a prisoner across the Mediterranean Sea, the ship sailed into a fierce storm. Because the seamen had no anchor for their souls, they abandoned hope (27:20). It was only the faithful Apostle Paul who could give hope to hopeless men, because he trusted the Lord (27:25).

Indeed the Apostle Paul presented a dismal picture of people without the Lord. In writing of a Christian's future hope, Paul reminded his readers that they had been hopeless and helpless before the Gospel came into their lives (Eph. 2:12).

A farmer gives an object lesson in hope. He hopes that his seeds will germinate and produce grain (1 Cor. 9:10). By the same token the Christian life is marked by hope.

On the human level, hope is pretty precarious. But God gives us a certain hope, and the New Testament repeatedly underlines this. Christian character builds a life of hope (Rom. 5:4; 8:24-25). Even nature is marked by the hope of ultimate restoration, according to Paul (8:20-21).

To the Corinthians Paul wrote about that divine triplet of faith, hope, and love (1 Cor. 13:13). He asserted the same truths to the Galatians (Gal. 5:5-6) and the Thessalonians (1 Thes. 1:3).

In writing to the Colossians, Paul was again concerned with the subject of hope. It gave confidence to the Colossian Christians (Col. 1:23), and arose from the presence of the Lord in their lives (1:27).

The small letter to Titus is full of the subject of hope. It provides the greeting for the book (Titus 1:2). Furthermore it gives the motive for godly living, as Paul described the second coming of Christ as the blessed hope (2:12-13). It also gives assurance of eternal life (3:7).

In some ways 1 Peter is the statement par excellence of the Christian's hope. First of all, this hope is rooted in the resurrection of Christ (1 Peter 1:3). Second, the future resurrection of Christ is a cause of hope for all believers (1:21). Third, such hope is the criterion of spiritual beauty (3:5). Fourth, it is also the content of Christian testimony (3:15).

The Christian's hope is very personal. It is tied up with a personal relationship with the Lord Jesus Christ. For this reason Christians can face trouble now, because their hope is fixed on the coming of Christ.

ILLUSTRATIONS

For the sake of organization, we shall divide our illustrations between human hope and divine hope. "Where there is life there is hope," wrote John Gay (1685-1732). Then he added this dismal line: "So [he] groaned and died." For the subject of Gay's writing, hope had run out.

According to Norman Cousins, "Hope is independent of the apparatus of logic." However, hope must have a sure, safe anchor, or it is folly. Though John Bunyan (1628-88) had suffered imprisonment and persecution for his faith and ministry, he clung to his hope in Christ. Despite all his suffering he could say: "Hope is never ill, when faith is well."

Another British Baptist pastor was Andrew Fuller (1754-1815). On the subject of hope he asserted: "Hope is one of the principal springs that keeps mankind in motion." Along the same lines Robert Browning wrote in *Paracelsus:* "Love, hope, fear, faith—these make humanity."

The mother of modern nursing, Florence Nightingale, gave hope to many suffering people in her lifetime. Since her death, her inspiration has extended hope even further. On the subject she said, "The coffin of every hope is the cradle of a good experience."

Having spoken of these noble proponents of human hope, one must also turn to the real Source of hope, the Lord Jesus Christ. Don Basham concluded concerning this: "Our hope lies not in the man we put on the moon, but in the Man we put on the cross."

The same vision of hope is reflected in this statement by Gilbert Beenken: "Other men see only a hopeless end, but the Christian rejoices in an endless hope."

The Reformer of Geneva and the great theologian John Calvin (1509-64) wrote concerning hope: "The word 'hope' I take for faith; and indeed hope is nothing else but the constancy of faith."

Though John Donne (1573-1631) was the Dean of St. Paul's Cathedral, he is better known for his writings. Of the Christian's hope he said: [God] "brought light out of darkness, not out of lesser light; He can bring your summer out of winter, though you have no spring. . . . God comes to you not as the dawning of the day, not as the bud of the spring, but as the sun at noon." This is a beautiful picture of hope.

The following summary of Christian hope is attributed to the eminent Bible commentator Matthew Henry (1662-1714): "The ground of our hope is Christ in the world, but the evidence of our hope is Christ in the heart." To which James S. Stewart added: "The very disillusionment of today is the raw material of the Christian hope."

"As oxygen is to the lungs," wrote the Swiss theologian Emil Brunner (1899-1966), "such is hope for the meaning of life."

HOUR

MEANING

The Greek word which is translated "hour" is *hora*. It is also reflected in the English word "*horology*" (the study of the measurement of time, or of watches). Another word which is translated with "time" is *chronos*, which is seen in the English words "*chronicle*" (the written record of events in a time period) and "*chronograph*" (a precise time-keeping device). For the purpose of this particular study, however, we shall concentrate on the word for "hour," *hora*.

In early Greek literature this word was used to speak of specific seasons. It described the time when a vine started to produce, or when the plowing had to be started. It also was used to portray sunrise and sunset. Xenophen and Plato applied it to "the bloom of youth." In other words, *hora* was used less for a specific hour (such as 10 o'clock), than it was for more generic time ("this is our finest hour").

BIBLE USAGE

The New Testament contains 107 occurrences of this word, which qualifies it as a common word in the Scriptures. It seems to fulfill several meanings and uses, of which we shall notice only 5.

First, it spoke of an arranged time. At a feast mentioned in Christ's parable, a meal was served at an arranged hour (Luke 14:17). When Jesus had fulfilled His Father's plan for life on earth, He was aware that the hour of His suffering had come (John 12:27). In the early days of the church Peter and John went up to the temple at the arranged hour for prayer (Acts 3:1). When the Lord appears in judgment, this will be the final arranged hour (Rev. 14:7).

A second aspect of this word is the appointed hour, when people must do certain things. Jesus regarded Calvary as a specific appointment set down before the world was created (John 2:4; 8:20; 17:1). In fact, Jesus regarded His crucifixion as the hour of His glorification (John 12:23; 13:1). One can trace the progress of God's plan in Christ's earthly life by His use of the phrase, "My hour."

From a third standpoint the Bible speaks of the anticipated hour. Jesus spoke of the coming hour when true worship would cover the earth (John 4:21). He also spoke of the coming hour of general resurrection, when the dead would hear His voice and come forth (John 5:25). And He warned about a coming hour in which His followers would be persecuted (John 16:2).

Along the same lines the early church was aware of certain anticipated hours. When Paul commanded a demon to relinquish his hold on that poor servant girl in Philippi, the demon came out according to the Greek "that very hour" (Acts 16:18). When the jailer in the same city came to Christ, he took the apostles "that very hour" to his home (Acts 16:33). By the same token, when Ananias had come to Saul after his conversion, the new convert's sight was restored in that hour (Acts 22:13, marg.). There is a lovely anticipation in this word.

A fourth aspect of the word "hour" is its apocalyptic sense. It speaks of the last times. In an hour when one does not expect the Lord to return, He will come back (Matt. 24:50). No one knows what day and what hour the Lord will return (Mark 13:32). In the Book of Revelation, the exalted Lord speaks of His return "like a thief" at an unexpected hour (Rev. 3:3). The emphasis in all these passages falls on the unexpected nature of Christ's coming. We do not know the time or the hour.

A fifth and obvious use of the word "hour" is in telling time. One recalls that a sundial was the most accurate means available at the time of the writing of the New Testament. Jesus taught His disciples that there were twelve hours in the day, so one did not need to haste (John 11:9). (Incidentally, this teaching is also needed today.) In many passages the exact hour is used, which accents the historical reality of the New Testament account (Mark 15:33-34; John 1:39; 4:52; Acts 10:3, 9, 30).

It is comforting to find these references to time in the New Testament. They help put the biblical account into the world of time and space in which we live. They also help show that the New Testament is historically true.

ILLUSTRATIONS

Time is both a bane and a blessing. Dozens of literary references demonstrate this, but the best evidences are our own crammed diaries, alarming alarm clocks, and dominant wristwatches. A student went to Africa on a summer missionary project. He was determined to fit in as well as possible with the African culture. So he left his wristwatch here in America. "It was the best summer of my life," he later claimed.

Many proverbs speak of time. One example is the English phrase, "Time and tide wait for no man." From France comes this pithy remark: "There is no mortar that time will not loose." A Sanskrit proverb puts it even more clearly: "These three will be effaced by time: a debt, a sore, and a stain."

Venerable church father Augustine (354-430) said this of the tyrant time: "Time never takes time off." George Villiers, the Second Duke of Buckingham (1628-87) said similarly: "Methinks I see the wanton hours flee, / And as they pass, turn back and laugh at me." To which Sir Osbert Sitwell would add: "In reality, killing time / is only the name for another of the multifarious ways / By which time kills us." In other words, no one can outrun time.

Speaking of outrunning time, the gifted evangelist and professor Rabi Zacharias told to a group of students: "English is the only language in which a clock runs. In other languages it simply goes."

A delightful Indian Christian and speaker is Rabi Maharaj, who makes his home in Switzerland. In fact, his wife is Swiss. "My wife tells time by a precise Swiss watch," he lamented, "while I tell time by the sun."

"Time heals all wounds," someone quipped. Actually, the Roman statesman-poet Seneca said: "Time heals what reason cannot." Another writer, Jane Ace, reversed this line to say: "Time wounds all heels."

King David said, "My times are in Thy [God's] hand" (Ps. 31:15). This truth has been set to music many times, but none is more powerful than the hymn penned by the relatively unknown Anne Ross Cousin:

The sands of time are sinking, / The dawn of heaven breaks;
The summer morn I sighed for, / The fair, sweet morn awakes:
Dark, dark hath been the midnight, / But dayspring is at hand,
And glory, glory dwellest / in Immanuel's land.

"Now is the acceptable time," wrote Paul, "behold, now is the day of salvation" (2 Cor. 6:2).

HUMILITY

MEANING

The Greek word translated "humility" is a combination of two words which mean "low" (*tapeinos*) and "mind or way of thinking" (*phronesis*). Together the word for "humility" is *tapeinophronesis*. It is translated almost literally in the *Authorized Version* with "lowliness" and "lowly minded." All in all, the root word is used about 19 times in the New Testament.

Because the word is almost completely lacking in ancient Greek, it is necessary to seek ancient precedents in the Septuagint, the Greek Old Testament. There it is found 67 times, and has as its basic meanings "to bow down, make low, or humble." It seems to refer to an action rather than a state of being. In other words, it is more important that we act humbly than that we claim humility. (In fact, a claim of humility is usually a proof of pride.)

BIBLE USAGE

In order to understand the meaning of humility, it is necessary to look at this concept from two viewpoints. First, there is a reference to people of lowly position. This is factual humility, which sometimes borders on humiliation.

An example occurred in Mary's song, the so-called "Magnificat." She praised the Lord, because He had "brought down," literally "humbled," rulers. By the same token God had exalted common people out of their humiliation (Luke 1:52). This apparently refers to God's choice of Mary to be the mother of Jesus.

Yet another example of this factual humiliation is found in the Book of Romans, where the Apostle Paul urged believers to build friendships with people from the lower classes (Rom. 12:16). This is seen as an antidote to pride.

From a personal standpoint, the Apostle Paul wrote about his own depression (2 Cor. 7:6). He asserted that God comforts those who are depressed, or brought low in humiliation. Thus the Bible refers to people who feel really "low down."

Second, there is a fruitful form of humility, though it sometimes involves suffering. Because Christ was meek, Paul also was meek and humble, and he avoided any hypocrisy (10:1). By earning his way he showed humility, even though it was misunderstood (11:7). He looked with anxiety on the possibility that God might have to "humiliate" him, if he persisted in pride (12:21).

This same biblical humility is seen elsewhere in the New Testament. According to Jesus Christ there is no salvation without humility (Matt. 18:3-4). Paul presented humility as an elemental aspect of Christian character (Eph. 4:1-2; Phil. 2:3; Col. 3:12). The model for this humility was none other than the Lord Jesus Christ (Phil. 2:8).

Having been restored by the risen Lord after his shameless denial, the Apostle Peter under the inspiration of the Holy Spirit wrote a great deal on the subject of humility. Servants were to show true humility toward their masters (1 Peter 2:18). Wives were likewise exhorted to be humble (3:1, 5), as was the entire church (3:8). Elders should not be tyrants who lord it over the church, but rather they too should display biblical humility (5:5).

James likewise mentioned the true virtue of humility. He initiated the phrase that Peter used: "God is opposed to the proud, but gives grace to the humble" (James 4:6; 1 Peter 5:5; Matt. 23:12). If Christians humble themselves, God will exalt them (James 4:10).

If pride was the sin that brought Satan down from heaven to hell, humility is a characteristic of a truly converted person. Christ has given an example of such humility, and it is reflected in every true believer. As Augustine said: "Pride changed angels into devils; humility makes men into angels."

ILLUSTRATIONS

According to John Ruskin (1819-1900): "The first test of a truly great man is humility." The same truth was stated similarly by the Victorian pulpit giant Charles Haddon Spurgeon (1834-92): "Humility is to make a right assessment of oneself." "Do not be proud," Spurgeon once said, of "race, face, or grace." In other words, since we have received all that we have from God, why should we boast?

An American contemporary of Spurgeon, Dwight L. Moody (1837-99), concurred, speaking thus of humility: "Unless you humble yourself before [God] in the dust, and confess before Him your iniquities and sins, the gate of heaven, which is open only for sinners saved by grace, must be shut against you forever."

Typical of much Puritan writing on this subject is the line by William Secker who showed the contrast implicit in humility: "Pride is a sinner's torment, but humility is a saint's ornament." Another famous Puritan writer, William Gurnall, added: "Humility is the necessary veil to all other graces."

Here are two incidents from the life of John Wesley (1703-91). After the memorial service for George Whitefield a staunch supporter of Whitefield accosted Wesley, who had disagreed on some theological points with Whitefield. Asked Whitefield's supporter: "Mr. Wesley, do you think you shall see Mr. Whitefield in heaven?"

"No," retorted Wesley.

"I was afraid you would say that," lamented the lady.

Then Wesley added: "George Whitefield will be so near to the throne of God, that men like me will never catch a glimpse of him." This humility marked Wesley all his long life.

To Francis Asbury, the founder of Methodism in America, Wesley wrote these lines: "Oh, beware," Wesley warned, "do not seek to be something! Let me be nothing, and Christ be all in all."

Though it was not always true of him, after election to the presidency Dwight Eisenhower demonstrated great humility. He is credited with having said: "Humility must always be the portion of any man who receives acclaim earned in the blood of his followers and the sacrifice of his friends."

The well-known "Radio Bible Class" teacher, Richard DeHaan, wrote an excellent little book on 1 Peter, in which he gave this test of true humility. First, there is the test of precedence: "Do you feel badly when others are honored, because they outshine you?" Second comes the test of sincerity: "All too often, people say things about themselves to sound humble, when they really are not." Third is the test of criticism: "Do you react unfavorably when someone points out your shortcomings?" If you gave yourself a perfect score on this test, you failed the test of humility (Richard DeHaan, *Good News for Bad Times*, pp. 87-88).

HYPOCRITE

MEANING

The word "hypocrite" is taken directly from the Greek word *hypocrites*. Literally it means "one who plays a part." In fact, the verb *hypocrinomai* means to pretend or to make-believe. Therefore a "hypocrite" is one who pretends to be something or someone he really is not.

Actually in the Greek language this word has had a fascinating history. Early on it meant to "explain or interpret," which is the meaning that Homer gave to it. Later on it came to refer to an "answer or interpretation." In the time of Plato it gained the meaning of play-acting. Thus in the Greek theater of the day, the *hypocrites* was the person who interpreted the song of the chorus to the audience. Later he became an actor who played a part.

The implication of this word for Christianity is quite clear. A hypocrite is one who plays the part of a Christian, but does not live the part. It is a particularly negative term in biblical vocabulary.

BIBLE USAGE

There is one major thrust in all biblical references to hypocrisy; it is a warning. No matter in what context it is found, the practice is always condemned.

For instance, in the Sermon on the Mount, Jesus referred to hypocrites as candidates for the judgment of God (Matt. 7:2-5). In another place Jesus described hypocrites as those who are faithful in their speech but unfaithful in their acts (Mark 7:6). Hypocrites were able to discern natural signs but not spiritual signs (Luke 12:56). Those who were legalistic about the Sabbath also showed a degree of hypocrisy (13:15).

Especially in the Sermon on the Mount did Jesus condemn hypocrisy. When you give money, you should give in all modesty. If you call attention to the gift, this is hypocrisy (Matt. 6:2-3). If you pray, make sure it is not a show to elicit praise from people, for this is hypocrisy (6:5). If you fast, do not go around with a haggard look in order to get sympathy, for this too is hypocrisy (6:16).

In the Olivet Discourse, near the end of His earthly life, Jesus also attacked hypocrisy. The special targets of Christ's condemnation were the Pharisees and scribes (23:13, 23, 27, 29). They kept the letter of the Law, but they ignored the spirit of the Law.

The Apostle Paul made two main references to hypocrisy. In Galatians he challenged Peter and accused him of hypocrisy. Apparently Peter had fallen back into Jewish legalism and implied that this was necessary for conversion. This in Paul's mind was bald hypocrisy (Gal. 2:11-13). This was a serious charge Paul leveled at Peter, but it affected the very nature of the Gospel.

In Paul's First Epistle to Timothy, he again struck out against hypocrisy. Hypocrites who have silenced their consciences would prey on the churches of Jesus Christ in the latter days, Paul said (1 Tim. 4:2). In this passage Paul equated hypocrisy with lying, deceit, and demonic activity (4:1).

In many ways Peter's first epistle is the great refutation of hypocrisy in the church. (Could it be that he took to heart the admonition of Paul, mentioned in Gal. 2:13-14?) Peter enjoined Christians to put away hypocrisy, which keeps company with such sins as malice, guile, envy, and slander (1 Peter 2:1). Peter was also warning against hypocrisy when he said that Christians should be sincere, literally from the Greek "un*hypocrit*ical" (1:22).

From start to finish the New Testament is one in its condemnation of hypocrisy. Jesus warned against it, and illustrated His warnings by referring to the Pharisees. The apostles added the weight of their Holy Spirit-inspired epistles to this condemnation.

ILLUSTRATIONS

No one likes a hypocrite. Of them the Roman statesman Cicero (106-43 B.C.) declared: "Of all villainy there is none more base than that of the hypocrite, who, at the moment he is most false, takes care to appear most virtuous."

The eminent American author, Nathaniel Hawthorne (1804-64), added this stinging rebuke against hypocrisy: "No man, for any considerable period, can wear one face to himself and another to the multitude, without finally getting bewildered as to which may be the true." Who has not known such a pathetic creature?

Edmund Burke (1729-97), British statesman and orator, castigated hypocrisy in these words: "Hypocrisy can afford to be magnificent in its promises; for never intending to go beyond promises, it costs nothing."

If secular writers find hypocrisy loathsome, how much more do Christian writers? Many comment on the old excuse of unbelievers, that there are many hypocrites in the church. Arthur R. Adams said: "Don't stay away from church because there are so many hypocrites. There's always room for one more."

The late Billy Sunday (1862-1935) thundered away in these words: "Don't hunt through the church for a hypocrite. Go home and look in the glass." To which Sherwood Wirt, distinguished former editor of *Decision* magazine, added: "The clergyman who affects worldliness in order to 'relate' to those outside the church is only the latest in the parade of ecclesiastical hypocrites."

In the train of the Puritans many spoke out against this sin. None was more eloquent than Bible commentator Matthew Henry (1662-1714): "Hypocrites do the devil's drudgery in Christ's livery [uniform]."

One of the more famous Puritan writers was William Law (1686-1751), who concluded concerning this matter: "Solemn prayers, rapturous devotions, are but repeated hypocrisies unless the heart and mind be conformable to them."

Many years ago news reached Korea of a thrilling revival in China. The missionaries in Korea sent for a representative of the China awakening, and a lady missionary arrived in due time. "What produced the revival?" asked the host missionary in Korea.

The emissary from China answered with three questions: "Do you obey the Word of God?" The missionaries in Korea said, "Yes."

"Do you obey all the Word of God?" came the second question. This time the missionaries were somewhat reticent. No one could say an outright "Yes."

"What does God call someone who claims to obey the Word, but does not in reality?" In admitting their hypocrisy, revival came to the Korean missionary force and the churches they served.

IDOL

MEANING

The Greek word translated "idol" is similar to its English equivalent. It is *eidolon*. In its various forms it appears about 30 times in the Greek New Testament.

In ancient Greek this word meant a "figure," "picture," or "copy," and it had no religious connotations. It even meant the reflection of a person in the water. In fact, the Greeks did not consider their gods to be idols, and for this reason they had no term for idolatry.

To find the spiritual significance of this word we must turn to the Septuagint, the Greek Old Testament. Here the word *eidolon* was used to describe the images of gods or pagan deities. In fact, the Old Testament writers considered that these gods had no reality at all, but were just pieces of wood or stone. They were not alternative gods, but rather unreal gods.

BIBLE USAGE

In the New Testament idolatry is roundly condemned. The word *eidolon* has two basic meanings, both of which refer to pagan religious practice.

First, the word refers to images, which are condemned by the second commandment: "You shall not make yourself an idol, or any likeness of what is in heaven above, or on the earth beneath, or in the water under the earth" (Ex. 20:4).

In his great sermon the martyr Stephen reminded the Jewish leaders that their forefathers veered off into idolatry. While Moses was on Mount Sinai, Aaron led the people in producing a golden calf, an idol (Acts 7:41).

Paul reminded the Corinthians that they had worshiped "dumb idols" while they were still in paganism (1 Cor. 12:2). Then he contrasted life in the Holy Spirit (12:3). The same line of reasoning is followed in his first letter to the Thessalonians (1 Thes. 1:9). In fact, Paul often reasoned with the Corinthians on the basis of their conversion from idolatry (1 Cor. 5:10-11; 6:9-11; 10:7-8).

The Book of Revelation contains several statements concerning those who are barred from heaven. High on the list are those who worship man-made idols (Rev. 9:20). Thus the first meaning of the Greek word is a handmade god, an idol.

A second meaning is any false god, whether in the form of an idol or not. The Book of Acts contains many warnings against the veneration of false gods (Acts 15:20, 29; 21:25). The most depressing aspect of Athenian life was their worship of deceptive deities (Acts 17:16).

The Romans were warned not to engage in idolatry (Rom. 2:22), as were the Corinthians (1 Cor. 8:4, 7; 10:19-20; 2 Cor. 6:16). In the catalog of sin which Paul sent to the Galatians he listed idolatry among the deeds of non-Christians (Gal. 5:20). His Prison Epistles contain similar warnings against the adoration of counterfeit gods. To the Colossians, Paul wrote that they should be dead to every idolatrous thought or practice (Col. 3:5). In the companion letter to the Ephesians there is a similar statement against false gods, and a warning that no idolater will gain entrance into heaven (Eph. 5:5).

The Apostle John was concerned with the purity of the faith. In his first epistle he warned against lustful thoughts, denials of the deity of Christ, and the attacks of Satan. At the end of this strongly worded letter the Apostle John said simply: "Little children, guard yourselves from idols" (1 John 5:21).

The Ten Commandments contain a direct warning against idolatry, and the New Testament repeats it in many forms. Every major writer of the New Testament was moved by the Holy Spirit to speak out against idolatry. It is as loathsome to a

Christian as it is to a Jew.

ILLUSTRATIONS

Many writers have taken up the biblical note of condemnation against idolatry. The great German Reformer Martin Luther (1483-1546) warned of the danger when he wrote: "We easily fall into idolatry, for we are inclined to it by nature; and coming to us by inheritance, it seems pleasant."

An English evangelical writer of modern times, Arthur Wallis, echoes the sentiments of the Reformer: "An idol may be defined as any person or thing that has usurped in the heart the place of preeminence that belongs to the Lord." This is an excellent modern definition of idolatry.

While we were missionaries in Europe a Christian businessman from America visited us almost annually. He had built a business by selling model railroads, and for this he had won international acclaim. At the same time he developed the reputation of a gourmet, eating at the finest restaurants, no matter the cost. When he came to Christ he withdrew from both the business and the feasting, because he perceived that both had been idols to him. They had usurped the place of God in his heart.

Idolatry, to the brilliant evangelical preacher and writer James I. Packer, is when one imagines that God is like a person or some lower form of life.

In a church which I pastored was a fine young lawyer, who had engaged in Transcendental Meditation. "When did you first realize that it was wrong?" I asked him.

His answer was revealing: "I was taken into a room and caused to kneel down before a small statue of Krishna. At that time I began to see that this was nothing more or less than idolatry." Now that young man and his wife are training for Christian service, so that they may serve the only living God.

Not only is idolatry seen in cultic worship. Modern atheists also are in danger of idolatry. Robert Ingersoll, infamous atheist of the 19th century, once said: "Man creates god in his own image and worships this god." He almost exactly quoted the atheistic philosopher, Ludwig Feuerbach. Thus an idol can be formed in one's mind as well as in a workshop.

The brilliant philosopher Francis Bacon (1561-1626) defined the danger of idolatry in his *Novum Organun:* "There are four classes of idols which beset men's minds," he wrote. "To these for distinction's sake I have assigned names—calling the first class, Idols of the Tribe; the second, Idols of the Cave; the third, Idols of the Marketplace; the fourth, Idols of the Theater." In other words, people worship dreams, traditions, home luxuries, and the arts. Despite the passing of 400 years, these idols are still seen. Today, as then, Christians should keep themselves from idols.

IGNORANCE

MEANING

The Greek word translated "ignorance" in the New Testament is *agnoia*. One can easily see the connection to the English word *"agnostic"* (one who claims that truth about God cannot be known). Literally the word *agnoia* means "a lack of knowledge." It is made up of the word for knowing (*ginosko*) and the preface *a* which gives it a negative twist.

Ignorance was most distasteful to the early Greeks. In fact, it was synonymous with barbarism, because only the barbarians were ignorant concerning the facts of civilized life. To the Stoic philosophers, ignorance was the cause of wickedness. They believed that people who knew what was right would do it, though this is not always the case. Greeks also related ignorance to the law, and they assumed that many violations of the law were due to the ignorance of it. Only in the later Hellenistic writings did *agnoia* take on a religious meaning. It was felt that if people knew the truth, they would live in conformity to culture and civilization.

BIBLE USAGE

There are two strains of meaning for the word "ignorance" in the New Testament. First there is nonmoral ignorance. Some ignorance is involuntary, because it arises out of insufficient information or wrong leadership. Peter asserted that some people assented to the crucifixion of Christ because they did not know any better (Acts 3:17). But for others, ignorance is rooted in foolishness (1 Peter 2:15). The first aspect of ignorance received a lesser condemnation in Scripture.

The second meaning of this word is a spiritual ignorance, where people are willfully ignorant of the truth of God. Jewish leaders were ignorant of the prophetic message, despite the weekly exposition of it (Acts 13:27). In Christ God overcame the Jews' spiritual ignorance, though they did not respond in large numbers (17:30). Meanwhile the Greeks continued to worship the "unknown" (*agnostos*) God, though this was an "ignorant" worship (17:23).

In his letters Paul asserted some of the things which Christians ought to know. He did not want them to be ignorant of God's care for Israel (1 Cor. 10:1). Likewise he did not desire that they should be ignorant about spiritual gifts (12:1). The implication seems to be that Christians will act on what they know. This close bond between knowing and doing is uncommon. The Apostle Paul even extended its principle to life after death, and he alleviated the ignorance of Christians concerning the afterlife and the coming of Christ (1 Thes. 4:13-18).

The main reason why people rejected Christ, in Paul's mind, was their ignorance of the truth of the Gospel. Satan has darkened their understanding to keep them in ignorance of God's plan of salvation (Eph. 4:18; 2 Cor. 4:4). In this case ignorance of the Gospel means estrangement from God's saving grace.

The Book of Hebrews presents Christ as a faithful High Priest. One of the roles of a priest is that he should be able to deal gently with the "ignorant" who are not aware of spiritual realities (Heb. 5:2). By inference Christ is infinitely able to meet the needs of spiritually ignorant people.

The Apostle Peter likewise employed the term "ignorance" to describe preconversion life (1 Peter 1:14). Before people believe in the Lord they are ignorant of spiritual truth. In fact, when false teachers invade the sanctity of Christian churches, one of their characteristics is ignorance of spiritual truth (2 Peter 2:12-13).

Ignorance in the Bible is not just a matter of insufficient information. In biblical Greek, knowledge is closely connected with practice. What a person knows determines how he lives. Therefore a person who is ignorant of Gospel truth is lost and alienated from God. Ignorance is not just inconvenient. It is spiritually disastrous.

ILLUSTRATIONS

Many writers and thinkers have commented on ignorance and its disadvantages. According to Victor Cousin: "Ignorance is the primary source of all misery and vice." A.B. Alcott (1799-1888) wrote: "To be ignorant of one's ignorance is the malady of the ignorant."

The skeptic Christopher Marlowe (1564-93) sneered: "I count religion but a childish toy, and hold there is no sin but ignorance" (The Jew of Malta). Thomas Gray (1716-71) sounded almost as cynical when he wrote: "Where ignorance is bliss, 'tis folly to be wise" ("Ode on a Distant Prospect of Eton College").

Mark Twain, or Samuel Clemens (1835-1910), was at his best when commenting on ignorance, of which he wrote: "I would rather have my ignorance than the other man's knowledge, because I've got so much more of it."

In many ways ignorance is the mother of knowledge. Charles Kettering wrote: "A man must have a certain amount of intelligent ignorance to get anywhere." Philosopher of education John Dewey (1859-1952) also described the positive aspect of ignorance: "Genuine ignorance is . . . profitable because it is likely to be accompanied by humility, curiosity, and open-mindedness; whereas the ability to repeat catch phrases, cant terms, familiar propositions, gives the conceit of learning and coats the mind with varnish waterproof to new ideas."

In the fourth century B.C. Crates wrote: "One part of knowledge consists in being ignorant of such things as are not worthy to be known." A modern statement along the same lines came from Robert Quillen: "Discussion is an exchange of knowledge; argument [is] an exchange of ignorance."

The eminent Scottish historian Thomas Carlyle (1795-1881) concluded: "That there should one man die in ignorance who had capacity for knowledge, this I call a tragedy."

While living in Germany I often asked people how Hitler was able to slaughter 6 million Jews without a major public protest. Most people with whom I spoke said they were ignorant of Hitler's designs. This ignorance was very costly indeed.

When one reads the sayings of Galileo Galilei (1564-1642) the wellspring of his great knowledge becomes evident, for he admitted: "I never met a man so ignorant that I could not learn something from him."

Wise old Solomon wrote: "The fear of the Lord is the beginning of knowledge" (Prov. 1:7). The Christian poet George Herbert (1593-1633) stated it slightly differently: "Knowledge is folly except [God's] grace guide it."

Augustine (354-430), saintly bishop of Hippo in North Africa, stated this truth clearly when he prayed, "Our knowledge, compared with Yours, is ignorance."

IMAGE

MEANING

The Greek word translated as "image" is *eikon*. It is the basis for such English terms as *icon* (a religious painting or engraving venerated in Eastern Orthodox Churches), "*icon*ography" (the illustration of a subject by drawing), or "*icon*oclast" (the medieval zealots who broke up religious statues, or anybody who attacks cherished beliefs or practices).

In early Greek the *eikon* was an engraving of the Emperor's head on a coin. Soon it was also attached to a statue, or a metal image. Likewise it was the copy of a picture or the embodiment of a certain virtue. (We still use this idea in such English phrases as, "She is the 'image' of loveliness.")

The Jews rejected all images of God. The Ten Commandments forbade any casting of images, which was the sin into which Aaron fell at the foot of Sinai. In fact, the only image of God which is depicted in Scripture is man (Gen. 1:26). In this connection the New Testament uses the word *eikon*.

BIBLE USAGE

In the New Testament there is a literal reference to an "image." Jesus was asked about paying taxes. In answering He pointed out that tribute is paid to Caesar by the very fact that the Emperor's "likeness" (image) was stamped on the tax coin (Mark 12:16; Luke 20:24).

The Book of Revelation contains frequent "Great Tribulation" references to the beast who will demand worship during the Great Tribulation. An image of the beast will be erected as the object of idolatrous worship (Rev. 13:14). Participation in the society of the day will be limited to those who worship the image of the beast (14:9, 11). God will summarily condemn those who have bowed before the beast's image (16:2; 19:20). On the other hand, God's eternal glory will be reserved for those who do not fall down before the beast's image (20:4).

The first use of the word "image" is that of an idolatrous image. The most positive expression of an image in the Old Testament is the "image of God," as reflected in the Creation account (Gen. 1:27). Man "is the image and glory of God," according to the Apostle Paul (1 Cor. 11:7). As we have borne the earthly image of Adam, we shall also bear a heavenly image of the glorified Christ (15:49). Paul emphasized the fact that Jesus is the image of the invisible God (2 Cor. 4:4). Our transformation from a likeness to Adam to a likeness of Christ is perceived as being progressive (3:18).

According to Moses and the Apostle Paul, people were created in the image of God. The Fall defaced this image, but it did not totally erase it. When one becomes a Christian a transformation takes place. Slowly the Holy Spirit transforms Christians into the image of Christ, who is in turn the image of the invisible God (Col. 1:15; 3:10).

According to a famous German professor, "God set man in the world as a sign of His own authority, in order that man should uphold His—God's—claims as Lord" (Gerhard von Rad, quoted in *The New International Dictionary of New Testament Theology,* II, p. 287). The point is this: God created us in His image, and we are to be a living testimony to our Creator. Only one image is ordained by God to represent Him. This is the crown of His Creation, human beings. To form any other image as a representation of God is a violation of the Ten Commandments. Furthermore, it is sheer blasphemy. This was the sin which Paul condemned so strongly in the prologue to his Roman Epistle (Rom. 1:23).

ILLUSTRATIONS

The story is told that a slave once saluted General George Washington. Washington returned the salute. When queried concerning this strange behavior, Washington answered that the slave bore the image of God, and thus was worthy of respect.

A similar story is repeated concerning Abraham Lincoln, the Great Emancipator. As Lincoln entered Richmond a slave crossed his path. The President took off his hat and spoke a blessing. A perplexed southern lady looked on in absolute horror. Then Lincoln explained that he saw the image of God in that slave.

As Michelangelo (1475-1564) saw an angel in a block of stone and set about to carve it out, so God sees the image of Himself in fallen, degraded people, and He sets about to bring that image into full focus.

The image of God is the basis of salvation. In redemption God sets about to restore that image in people. German church historian Karl August von Hase (1800-90) concluded: "Only enough likeness to God remained to remind man of what he had lost, and to feel the hell of God's forsaking." In Christ this image of God is restored, because God re-creates man in His image.

William Hamilton praised the picture of God in man, when he wrote: "On earth there is nothing great but man; in man there is nothing great but mind." A similar statement is found in Shakespeare's *Hamlet:* "What a piece of work is man! How noble in reason! How infinite in faculty! In form and moving how express and admirable! In action how like an angel! In apprehension how like a god!" (ii, 2) But neither Hamilton nor Shakespeare could capture the biblical view of God's image, for they seem to have seen it without the aid of spiritual sight. Nevertheless, they both marveled at the image of God.

Louis Berkhof (1873-1957) was one of the foremost theologians of our day. Of the image of God he wrote: "The idea is that by Creation that which was archetypal [original] in God became ectypal [copied]. God was the original of which man was made a copy." The image of God, in Berkhof's mind, meant many things. It included original righteousness, the innocence of Adam before the Fall. The intellectual powers of people were also included, as was the spiritual nature of people. Futhermore man's immortality is part of that image of God, as is his dominance over nature (Louis Berkhof, *Systematic Theology,* pp 203-205).

Echoing the approach of Genesis, John Milton (1608-74) wrote in *Areopagitica:* "[He] who kills a man kills a reasonable creature, God's image." This is the original prohibition against murder, in Genesis 9:6.

Fanny Crosby (1820-1915) used the image of God as an inspiration to evangelism in her hymn "Rescue the Perishing":

Down in the human heart, crushed by the tempter,
    Feelings lie buried that grace can restore;
Touched by a loving heart, wakened by kindness
    Chords that are broken will vibrate once more.
Rescue the perishing, care for the dying;
    Jesus is merciful, Jesus will save.

IMITATOR

MEANING

The Greek word which is translated as "imitator" is *mimetes*. Basically it means to copy or imitate someone's behavior. It has many related words in English. Among these are *"mime"* (one who acts out an imitation of another person or animal), *"pantomime"* (a theater production which originally was without words), and *"mimeograph"* (a machine which makes many copies from one stencil).

In ancient Greek it referred to imitation. Aristotle used the word to describe how people imitated animals. (People learned weaving from a spider and building from a swallow.) Teachers based their whole educational procedure on imitation, as students imitated the behavior of teachers. Slowly the idea developed that people should imitate the gods, and Plato emphasized this.

BIBLE USAGE

Christians view imitation as a means of godly living. Christians are urged to imitate the Lord, and they are also to follow the examples set by outstanding Christians. Incidentally, this is particularly a New Testament concept, as the Old Testament never urged Israel to imitate God.

It is mainly a teaching of the Apostle Paul, but there are also three isolated references in Hebrews, 3 John, and 1 Peter. The reason for Paul's emphasis was his missionary zeal to lead people to faith and then on into godly living.

First, Christians are urged to imitate the Lord. In the ethical section of Ephesians, Paul urged the Christians to imitate God (Eph. 5:1). As God forgave them, they should forgive others (4:32). As God gave Christ as a sacrifice for us, we should also sacrifice for Him (5:2).

Christians are instructed also to follow Christ and imitate Him (1 Thes. 1:6). Thus the Thessalonians received the Gospel and reflected the joy of the Lord. This sensitivity to spiritual things made them imitators of the Lord.

Second, Christians were to imitate the apostles. To the spiritually fragile Corinthian church, Paul sent this message. Though many would influence them, they had but one spiritual father. Therefore they should imitate Paul (1 Cor. 4:16). As Paul conscientiously followed Christ, so they should imitate him (11:1). The word is not used, but the same idea is present in Paul's intructions to the Philippians (Phil. 3:17; 4:9). Paul presented the same challenge to the Thessalonians, to emulate his lifestyle (2 Thes. 3:7). In fact, there is an amazing little wordplay in 2 Thessalonians. Imitate our godly living (2 Thes. 3:7), Paul wrote, but do not imitate a lazy lifestyle (3:11).

Christians are called, in the third place, to imitate other Christians. The Thessalonians imitated the Judean Christians in facing persecution for the cause of Christ (1 Thes. 2:14). Christians were also called to imitate the faith and patience of other believers (Heb. 6:12). They were also encouraged to imitate the faith of those who had led them in the Christian life (13:7).

The *New American Standard Version* of the Bible translates 1 Peter 3:13, "Who is there to harm you if you prove zealous for what is good?" Another manuscript reading of this passage is reflected in the *King James* translation: "Who is he that will harm you, if ye be followers [imitators] of that which is good?" Here too the idea is that imitating a spiritual lifestyle will produce godly living.

In his powerful but short third letter, the Apostle John seems to have prepared Christians for coming conflict with evil. A word of encouragement reflects the use of our word. Christians should not "imitate" that which is evil, but rather should "imitate" that which is good (3 John 11). This is the difference between a person who follows God and one who does not.

ILLUSTRATIONS

The basic meaning of our word *mimetes* is seen in a mime. An English woman went to France to study under the famous mime artist, Marcel Marceau. All day he taught his students how to make the movements of mime, and each evening they went to see him perform. Their performances were marked indelibly by the style of the master. This is an excellent picture of a Christian who imitates the Lord by exposure to Him.

Another picture can be seen in the realm of language learning. When we went to Germany as missionaries, our daughter was only eighteen months old. She never had a lesson in German, yet she learned to speak it without an American accent. The reason was that she simply mimed the German speech forms.

Preachers often also imitate famous pulpit orators. In our day Martin Lloyd-Jones was greatly used of God at Westminster Chapel in London. Throughout the length and breadth of the British Isles many lesser lights mimed "The Doctor" to a tee. They had his Welsh accent, his mannerisms, and even his stooped shoulders.

Actually imitating a genuine man or woman of God can be good. It can lift a person beyond the narrow confines of his own spiritual life. As an African chief once said: "A good example is the tallest kind of preaching."

So concerned was he about the example which he set, that Jonathan Edwards (1703-58) framed the resolve to "never to do anything which I would be afraid to do if it were the last hour of my life."

Dr. Albert Schweitzer (1875-1965), doctor, organist, and theologian, referred to this subject when he said: "Example is not the main thing in influencing others. It is the only thing."

The same burden was formulated into a prayer by Charlene Myhre. She prayed: "Lord, let it not be that I follow You merely for the sake of following a leader, but let me accept You as Lord and Master of every step I take."

The late Pope John XXIII (1881-1963) summarized the significance of following a good example when he said: "It would be scarcely necessary to expound doctrine if our lives were radiant enough."

In his preface to the writings of Shakespeare, Samuel Johnson struck the same note: "Example is always more efficacious than precept."

Dr. Merrill Tenney taught New Testament with distinction at the Graduate School of Wheaton College. Incidentally he also taught us many important principles of ministry. One was the value of a good example. He put it this way: "The best advertisement for your church is not a large notice board, but rather the example that is set when the town drunk becomes a Christian and lives a godly life."

IMMORALITY

MEANING

In the New Testament the Greek word which is translated with "immorality" is *porneia*. It is easy to see the connection with such English words as *"pornography"* or *"porn"* (sexually explicit literature, films, and even speech) and *"pornocracy"* (a society dominated by prostitutes).

The word was coined in ancient Greek to describe the practice of prostitution, either secular or religious. This disgusting form of sexual deviance was imported from Persia. Actually, a married man in Greece could engage in extramarital sexual intercourse as much as he wished, but it was forbidden for his wife. (The word *moicheuo* was used to describe adultery, and *porneia* was usually applied to prostitution.) Corinth was a center for prostitution, homosexuality, and even lesbianism. However, the later Stoics condemned extramarital sex, and their view stood out in bold contrast with the decay of the age.

BIBLE USAGE

Whenever the New Testament mentions immorality, there is at least an implied condemnation. Nowhere does the Scripture sanction the commitment of any form of extramarital sexual acts.

Jesus spoke out against immorality. He cited immorality as the only legitimate reason for divorce (Matt. 5:32; 19:9). Such immorality is the result of human depravity (15:19; Mark 7:21). Still in all, Jesus forgave a woman who was caught in the very act of adultery (Luke 7:47, 50). Jesus based His condemnation of extramarital sexual intercourse on God's created order, which places a high priority on the sanctity of marriage.

In the Book of Acts the early Christians likewise condemned all sexual experimentation outside marriage. When the church leaders gathered at Jerusalem, they set down sexual purity as a mark of Christian living (Acts 15:20, 29). The Apostle Paul repeated this statement when speaking with the Jerusalem elders (21:25).

In fact, the writings of Paul are full of condemnation of all sexual sin. To the Romans he wrote that such sin is a mark of bald paganism, which arose out of their rejection of God (Rom. 1:24-27). For this reason "God gave them over" into judgment (1:24, 26, 28).

Because of its geographical situation, Paul warned the Corinthian church explicitly against immorality. It was a blemish on the church, in which one man had even engaged in incest (1 Cor. 5:1). Paul believed that no immoral people would enter the kingdom of heaven (6:9). He built this strong teaching on the principle of ownership: God owns our bodies so we must not engage in sexual sin (6:18-20). Christian marriage is the main bulwark against immorality (7:2). Paul used the example of Israel, where moral laxity resulted in the execution of 23,000 in one day (10:8; Num. 25:1-9). Again in 2 Corinthians there appears a condemnation of immorality (2 Cor. 12:21).

In his long lists of sins, Paul frequently included immorality (Gal. 5:19; Col. 3:5; 1 Tim. 1:10). Also he warned that no sexual sin will have a place in Christ's kingdom (Eph. 5:3, 5). To the Thessalonians Paul wrote a fairly long discourse on the subject of immorality (1 Thes. 4:1-8).

In the Book of Hebrews are both direct and indirect references to immorality. The writer indicated that immorality destroys a Christian marriage (Heb. 13:4).

Writing to the churches in Revelation, the Apostle John included a strong warning against immorality. This was God's charge against the churches of Pergamum and Thyatira (Rev. 2:14, 21). It will also be a dominant characteristic of the evil powers of the end times (9:21). For this people will be condemned (9:21; 17:2; 18:3).

Nowhere in all of the New Testament is there the slightest approval of immorality. To commit adultery is to sin against God. Though this sin can be forgiven, it cannot be tolerated, either in the church on earth or in heaven.

ILLUSTRATIONS

In our day immorality is almost a national sport. Hardly an evening passes without a dramatic presentation of pornography on prime-time television. In fact, whole cable television channels are given over to pornographic films.

Not only does the television industry broadcast pornographic films, but they are now freely available as video cassettes. From gas stations to grocery stores, one can now rent films which would have been banned from public view a decade ago.

The corner drugstore and convenience store often have pornographic magazines on sale, where they can be seen by any customer who happens to look. Pornographic presentations of heterosexual acts have almost been overtaken by homosexual pornography. As Billy Graham said, "If God does not punish America, He will have to apologize to Sodom and Gomorrah."

Recently the chief of police in Manchester, England, James Anderton, launched a public campaign against pornography. An active Christian layman, he has taken a strong stand against the debasement of sex. According to that chief constable, "Pornography is a dangerous threat to family life." Mr. Anderton took swift action to oppose the spreading fungus of pornographic book shops and cinemas in his city.

About the same time Professor Ian Donald of Glasgow University issued a similar warning. "Girls should be taught to value themselves and not enslave themselves to the lusts and deceptions of male chauvinist pigs," proclaimed the professor of midwifery. To him immorality is mental and moral slavery.

In speaking to a group of young people, former boxing champion Gene Tunney said, "Continence is the only guarantee of an undefiled spirit, and the best protection against the promiscuity that cheapens and finally kills the power to love."

A woman who had many sexual experiences once warned the young people at a certain church. She said, "If you browse around sex partners like a supermarket, you will never be satisfied with married love, and your marriage will never last." As a divorcee she spoke from bitter experience. Her promiscuous lifestyle had left her alone and aware of her own moral and spiritual bankruptcy.

Though many modern people sneer at Puritan ethics, Ralph Barton Perry put them into proper perspective when he wrote: "The Puritan Christian held, incredible as it may seem, that morals are more important than athletics, business, or art; that the good life must be founded on virtue."

The sister of President John F. Kennedy, Eunice Shriver, wrote: "Intellectual virtues can be taught . . . moral virtues are formed by acts," *The Washington Star* (July 3, 1977).

IMPUTE

MEANING

The Greek word behind the term, "to impute," is *logizomai*. Essentially it means to "reckon, calculate, evaluate, and estimate." It is a business term which means to "reckon to one's account." It is related to such English words as "*logic*," (the science of reasoning or reckoning), "*logi*stics" (the calculated way of moving supplies), "*log*arithm" (a type of mathematical calculation). In each case the basic idea is reckoning or calculating.

The ancient Greeks used the word *logizomai* to describe commercial mathematics. It was the process of charging a bill to someone's account. The word was also used in legal proceedings for attributing a debt to someone's account. By the same token, a payment could be reckoned to a person's credit.

In the Septuagint, the Greek Old Testament, there are further meanings. It is the counsel of a man. A person devises means of hurting or blessing someone. Such "devising" is *logizomai*. Morally, God charges either righteousness or evil to a person's account. The latter is the use of this word in the New Testament.

BIBLE USAGE

In some cases evil is charged to a person's account. For instance, Jesus was reckoned among the transgressors, and He was charged with evil which He had not committed (Mark 15:28). Because Christ has paid our penalty, forgiveness is available in God's grace.

Paul urged the Corinthians not to charge him with anything more than he deserved (2 Cor. 12:6). By the same token, people who are motivated by God's love do not hold sin against another person (1 Cor. 13:5).

This generous, gracious, forgiving spirit reflects God's attitude toward us. God does not reckon our sin against us, and this gives us great "blessing" (Rom. 4:8; Ps. 32:2). Paul emphasized the same truth when he stated that God does not impute Christians' sins to their accounts (2 Cor. 5:19). The basic truth is this, that since the Saviour was sacrificed for our sins, God no longer reckons them against our accounts. We shall not face judgment because of our sins. This is the good news, that our sins do not count against us anymore.

By the same token, God reckons or imputes righteousness to our accounts. This is not because we deserve it, but because Christ has covered the cost of our sin on the cross (Rom. 4:4-5). Abraham received righteousness reckoned to his account not because he was circumcised, but because he believed in the coming Messiah (4:10; Gen. 15:6). God reckons sonship to children of the whole family of faith (Rom. 9:8).

Abraham is again seen as the example for imputed righteousness in the Book of Galatians. Here again Paul pointed out that Abraham received righteousness reckoned to his account because he believed God (Gal. 3:6).

Though the Book of James is sometimes regarded as an antithesis to the Book of Galatians, both quote the example of Abraham. James emphasized the complementary aspect of this truth. Abraham acted upon his faith, and he was known as "the friend of God" (James 2:23-24).

Because God considers Christians righteous, we should also impute certain truths to our own selves. For instance, we should reckon ourselves dead to sin (Rom. 6:11). We should live as though we owe no obedience whatever to sinful desires.

Also we should consider, or reckon, ourselves to be dead to this world's values. No suffering should take us by surprise, because we are dead to the world and alive to God (8:36-37). This should be the operating principle by which we live and serve the Lord.

Because we consider ourselves alive to God, we consider all other gods to be false. Paul doubtless taught this to the Ephesian Christians, who lived in a city which was dominated by the worship of Artemis, or Diana. Doubtless Paul urged the Christians to consider Artemis to be worthless (Acts 19:27).

The Greek word "to impute" gives us an entirely new philosophy of life. We reckon that we are dead to sin, and thus sin does not dominate us. We also consider ourselves to be alive only to God, so we follow His every command. This kind of reckoning is not fantasy. It is spiritual reality.

ILLUSTRATIONS

The truth that God does not impute sin to a believer is seen clearly when we consider the statement of Dr. Martin Lloyd-Jones, former pastor of Westminster Chapel in London: "The measure of God's anger against sin is the measure of the love that is prepared to forgive the sinner and to love him in spite of his sin." Because of Christ, God can erase our sin from the account books of heaven.

A similar statement of imputed righteousness is found in the writings of the Jansenist scholar, Blaise Pascal (1623-62): "There are only two kinds of men: the righteous who believe themselves [to be forgiven] sinners, and the rest, sinners who believe themselves [to be] righteous." The difference is the imputed righteousness which comes from God through Christ alone.

The dramatic change which occurs when God imputes righteousness was described by the Victorian preacher, Charles Haddon Spurgeon (1834-92): "Sin is sovereign till sovereign grace dethrones it."

A more contemporary theologian was Louis Berkhof (1873-1957). In his Calvinistic theology he spoke of the imputed righteousness of God, and said: "The ground of justification can be found only in the perfect righteousness of Jesus Christ, which is imputed to the sinner in justification."

"People wrap themselves up in the flimsy garments of their own righteousness," said Sherwood Wirt, former editor of Decision, "and then [they] complain of the cold." Only the righteousness of Christ can protect us from the chill of God's judgment.

A rather quaint statement of this imputed righteousness is found in the writings of Puritan Henry Smith: "He hideth our unrighteousness with His righteousness; He covereth our disobedience with His obedience; He shadoweth our death with His death, that the wrath of God cannot find us."

A marvelous example of this imputed righteousness comes from the Rolls Royce factory. A traveler was motoring through Switzerland when his new Rolls Royce broke down. Immediately the factory sent out a mechanic with the necessary parts. When the businessman inquired later about the bill for this expensive service call, the factory answered: "There is no record of any Rolls Royce breaking down." By the same token, for a Christian whose sins are covered by Christ's cross there is no record of his sin in any of heaven's books. He is clothed in the imputed righteousness of Christ. "The blood of Jesus, [God's] Son, cleanses us from all sin" (1 John 1:7).

INFANT

MEANING

In the Greek New Testament several names are used for infants and children. These are discussed in the article titled *Child.* For the purposes of this article, we shall concentrate on the Greek word *nepios,* which means "infant." An infant is a young child who is not yet weaned.

The Greeks seem to have taken this word from the verb *nepeleo* (to be without power, impotent, or weak). In other words, an infant is a person who has no power and needs the assistance of parents or guardians.

Hippocrates, "the father of medicine" used the word *nepios* to describe every child from the stage of a fetus to five or six years old. It is the word used to describe a family relationship: "This is the child of those parents." Aristotle used the word to describe the entire age of childhood. In Plato's writings it portrayed a person who lived in a pretend world of fantasy, in contrast with a realist.

BIBLE USAGE

The New Testament uses the word *nepios* on two different levels. It speaks of both a physical child and a spiritual child. The word occurs 14 times.

In the New Testament Jesus made significant references to such infants. Sometimes they are capable of taking in the basic, spiritual truths much more than learned men of letters (Matt. 11:25; Luke 10:21). At Jesus' triumphal entry into Jerusalem the young ones shouted their acclaim, and Jesus again asserted that their cry was true. They saw Him more clearly than did their elders (Matt. 21:16). From other parallel passages, we learn that Jesus positively sought the loyalty of little ones. He took them seriously, even when their parents and the priests did not.

The Apostle Paul used the picture of a nursing mother to describe the tenderness of his concern for Christians. He wrote to the Thessalonians that he and his colleagues had treated them as a mother treats her infants, with love and tenderness (1 Thes. 2:7). In fact, this verse probably gives one the clearest pictures of the basic meaning of *nepios,* that of a child before weaning.

Though the word is used to describe very young children, it is also used to characterize new Christians. Paul portrayed the Law of God not as a harsh scourge to whip Christians into line, but as an instructor to teach children the rules of life (Rom. 2:20; Gal. 3:24). It is similar to the training wheels on a child's bike which keep him from a fall.

In his first letter to the Corinthians the apostle warned them that they were still "babes" in Christ, for they had not grown beyond the basics (1 Cor. 3:1). Paul wanted them to put away childish ways and live like adult Christians (13:11).

To the Galatians Paul compared the Jews to infants. They had an elemental knowledge of God's plan, but as a nation they did not mature enough to accept their Messiah (Gal. 4:1). This is not a final stage but a beginning stage of development (4:3). Paul looked for the day when the Jews would grow up and grasp their messianic birthright.

The same emphasis appears in Ephesians. Here Paul urged the Christians to grow up to spiritual maturity (Eph. 4:14-15). The signs of spiritual adulthood are knowledge of the fullness of Christ, discernment of devilish doctrines, and love for other believers (4:14-16).

The writer of Hebrews struck the same tone as the Apostle Paul. He instructed the Christians to grow beyond infancy to maturity. They should leave the elementary school of spiritual truth and enter a higher school (Heb. 5:12—6:1).

Finally Peter also spoke of spiritual infants. This time they were complimented, because they had an overwhelming hunger for the Word of God. They took to the Scriptures as a baby does to milk (1 Peter 2:2-3). The Greek word he used was not *nepios*, but rather a compound word which means "just-this-very-minute-born-ones."

It is good for a person to be born as a baby, but it is unnatural when one remains as an infant. By the same token, Christians begin as babies, but they should grow on to maturity in the faith.

ILLUSTRATIONS

There are many common characteristics between physical and spiritual infants. As Franklin P. Jones said: "You can learn many things from children. How much patience you have, for instance." Someone else added: "A characteristic of a normal child is he doesn't act that way very often." How often spiritual crybabies try the patience of Christian leaders. One German pastor lamented: "I have a whole church full of spiritual babies."

Presbyterian Life carried this insightful remark about children: "Heredity is what a man believes in until his son begins to behave like a delinquent." How often does a seemingly spiritual young Christian turn out to be a spiritual delinquent. God still loves His children, even though some seem to be delinquent.

"People who say they sleep like a baby," lamented Leo Burke, "usually don't have one." There is also a spiritual parallel here. When spiritual babies come into a house of God, they require attention. We cannot just put them on a shelf and let them go, any more than we can put a baby in a crib and just let him grow.

Maria Montessori, founder of the schools which bear her name, made this insightful comment about schooling: "The first idea that a child must acquire, in order to be actively disciplined, is that of the difference between good and evil; and the task of the educator lies in seeing that the child does not confound [or confuse] good with immobility, and evil with activity." The same holds true on a spiritual scale. Baby believers need to learn that it is good for them to be active, and bad for them to be passive pew-warmers.

Similarly the ancient writer Virgil (70-19 B.C.) concluded: "As the twig is bent the tree inclines." Alexander Pope (1688-1744) added to this line by saying: "'Tis education forms the common mind: / Just as the twig is bent, the tree's inclined." Yet another similar statement originated with Francis Xavier (1506-52), founder of the Jesuit Order: "Give me the children until they are seven and anyone may have them afterward." The principle is simple: a baby Christian also needs regular biblical instruction, if he is to grow into spiritual manhood or womanhood.

Billy Graham captured this basic principle when he wrote: "Being a Christian is more than just an instantaneous conversion—it is a daily process whereby you grow to be more and more like Christ."

INSTRUCT

MEANING

The idea of teaching or instructing is represented in the Greek New Testament by three verbs. By far the most popular word for teaching is *didasko,* which shows up no fewer than 95 times in the New Testament. This word is seen in our word, *"didac*tic" (used to describe methods or means of teaching). Its basic meaning in secular Greek is to "teach," "inform," or "instruct." It concentrates on the relationship between a teacher and his pupil. Herodotus used it to describe the chorus master in Greek theater.

A second word is *paideuo,* which is also translated "to teach," and appears about 23 times in the New Testament. This word is also reflected in English, especially in the word *"peda*gogy" (the science of teaching). The origins of this word are in the role of a tutor. The Greeks laid heavy emphasis on the moral and legal training of small children, and this was characterized by *paideuo.*

The final term in Greek was *katecheuo,* which is reflected in the word for religious instruction, *"cate*chism." This word is used eight times in the New Testament. Literally it means "to speak down," as the poets and actors spoke down from the stage to the public. Later it took the idea of teaching or instructing from a position of authority.

BIBLE USAGE

We consider the biblical uses of these words in the order of their frequency. *Didasko* carries with it the idea of public teaching. Jesus went around teaching in many places and proclaiming the Gospel (Matt. 9:35; 13:54). Often His place of instruction was a synagogue, but He also taught in the temple (Mark 12:35; Luke 21:37). In fact, He taught with some degree of regularity in the temple. He also taught in the open air, wherever people congregated to hear Him (Matt. 5:1-2; Mark 6:34).

The term *didasko* also referred to the general practice of teaching. Jesus taught by the seashore (2:13), and also in many different villages (6:6). His teaching won acclaim (Luke 4:15), and He did it almost incidentally to His travels (13:22).

After Jesus departed to heaven, the disciples took up teaching in the temple and in private houses (Acts 5:42). Sometimes they stayed in one place, as Paul and Barnabas did in Antioch (15:35). This was the means by which believers became mature disciples (Col. 1:28). Teaching was also the task which Paul committed to Timothy in the apostle's final charge (2 Tim. 2:2).

Turning from *didasko* to the second word, *paideuo,* we find a wide range of activities involved. Here, however, the emphasis falls on teaching immature believers. Paul chided the Jews because they had misused this office (Rom. 2:20). The Lord "disciplines" us to bring us to maturity (1 Cor. 11:32). The writer of the Book of Hebrews says that such discipline is part of sonship. Because we stand in the relationship of sons and daughters of the Lord, He disciplines us (Heb. 12:5-9; Prov. 3:11). Paul saw the coming of Christ as a primary motive in disciplining a disciple and bringing him or her to maturity in the faith (Titus 2:12-13).

The final word for "instruction" is *katecheuo,* which speaks of a full-time teacher. Paul was accused of teaching treacherous doctrines to the Jews, literally *"cate*chizing" them out of Judaism and into Christianity (Acts 21:21). Apollos had engaged in a *"cate*chetical" ministry even before he came to a full knowledge of Christ (18:25).

When discussing the relative merits of speaking in tongues or speaking in a known language, Paul asserted that a known language was more profitable for teaching (1 Cor. 14:19).

Paul wrote to the Galatians about their need for giving. He asserted that they should share materially with their teachers (Gal. 6:6). In other words, it is right for teachers to be paid for their ministry.

The New Testament lays heavy emphasis on the subject of spiritual teaching. It is one of the primary means of communicating both the Gospel and the instruction necessary for growing to spiritual maturity.

ILLUSTRATIONS

An elderly uncle taught me a major lesson concerning teaching and learning. He quoted his school mistress from Indiana, who told her students: "It is not for the teacher, but for life that we learn." If this was true of elementary school, it is even more true of the Christian life.

"The art of teaching is the art of assisting discovery," said Mark Van Doren. This is seen spiritually in "Discovery Bible Studies," where novices can come to grips with the Bible and see its truth firsthand.

Henry Adams said: "A teacher affects eternity; no one can tell where his influence stops." If this is presumed to be true about schoolteachers, how much more is it true of those who teach God's Word?

"The mediocre teacher tells. The good teacher explains. The superior teacher demonstrates," claimed William Arthur Ward. Then he added: "The real teacher inspires." How important it is for pastors, Bible study leaders, and Sunday School teachers to inspire.

James Hilton portrayed teaching as a war, when he said: "If I had a child who wanted to be a teacher, I would bid him Godspeed as if he were going to a war. For indeed the war against prejudice, greed, and ignorance is eternal, and those who dedicate themselves to it give their lives no less because they may live to see some fraction of the battle won." For a Christian, the war is against Satan and all his devices.

"You can teach a student a lesson for a day," began Clay Bedford, "but if you can teach him to learn by creating curiosity, he will continue the learning process as long as he lives." Augustine of Hippo struck the same chord when he said: "A free curiosity is more effective in learning than a rigid discipline."

The historian Thomas Carlyle (1795-1881) emphasized the value of trial and error when he wrote: "There is precious instruction to be got by finding we were wrong." Sometimes error is the mother of education.

The wise Puritan penman Thomas Watson claimed: "We must know God's will before we can do it aright. There is no going to heaven blindfolded." Another Puritan, Stephen Charnock, added: "A man may be theologically knowing and spiritually ignorant."

Perhaps John Milton (1608-74) best summarized the importance of instruction when he wrote: "The end of all learning is to know God, and out of that knowledge to love and imitate Him."

JOY (See: *Gladness.*)   **241**

JUDGMENT

MEANING

The word translated "judgment" in the New Testament is *krisis,* and the verb, "to judge," is *krino.* This root is seen in many English words, including "*crisis*" (a decisive time when judgment must be made) and "*critical*" (a decisive point at which judgment is seen). The elementary meaning is to make a judgment.

In early Greek the word was related to the supposed activities of the gods, who were guardians of rights and customs. They judged those actions which conflicted with their rights or customs. If people violated these basic rules of life, it was believed that the gods would punish (or judge) either the violaters or their children.

When the word was taken up in the Septuagint Greek Old Testament it took on a Hebrew flavor. In the Old Testament it was Jehovah God who judged between right and wrong. The standard for judgment was His holy Law, handed down at Sinai.

BIBLE USAGE

The idea of judgment occurs frequently in the New Testament, about 150 times in its noun and verb forms. Every part of the New Testament contains references to this important aspect of God's work. One can trace the idea right through the Scriptures.

When John the Baptist appeared as the forerunner of Christ, he came proclaiming judgment. It could come at any time, and it would be exacted by God Himself. Though the term is absent, the same idea is found in Matthew 3:7-10.

Jesus frequently referred to coming judgment. In fact, the Gospels contain a dominant emphasis on this theme. The Sermon on the Mount is replete with references to judgment (Matt. 5:22, 26, 29). Likewise the parables relating to the kingdom are full of references to the judgment of God (13:30, 47-50). To the Pharisees Jesus spoke plainly of coming judgment (12:32). Those who rejected Christ's message would be judged more severely than the residents of Sodom and Gomorrah (10:15). The same type of comparison is made between the rejecters of Capernaum and the citizens of Tyre and Sidon (11:22-24).

Not only Jesus spoke frequently of judgment. The Apostle Paul was equally explicit about it. For instance, Romans is full of judgment against those who reject the Gospel (Rom. 1:18; 2:1-11; 3:6; 5:16). Christians too will be judged for their obedience or disobedience to the will of God, at "the judgment seat of Christ" (2 Cor. 5:10).

The Apostle John likewise included many references to judgment, both in his Gospel and in his letters. For instance, he presented the powerful statement of Jesus, that only saving grace could avert God's judgment (John 5:24). John also carried the words of Jesus regarding the universal nature of judgment (5:28-29).

Likewise the Apostle Peter made much of coming judgment. God will be totally impartial in His judgment (1 Peter 1:17). God is likewise absolutely reliable as a Judge, for He cannot be corrupted (2:23). Every person must give an account to God, who will judge all (4:5-6). For these reasons Christians should keep short accounts with God (4:17).

In the Book of Hebrews judgment is a significant theme. Those who stubbornly reject the Gospel will be judged most severely (Heb. 10:26-31). In fact, there is nothing so sure as death, taxes, and judgment (9:27).

What is prophesied in the New Testament is dramatized in the Book of

Revelation. In His charges to the churches, the living Lord warns in graphic terms of judgment (Rev. 2:5, 16; 3:3, 16). At the climax of the Revelation is an account of the Great White Throne judgment, through which those who do not know the Lord will pass (20:11-15).

Judgment is a constant theme in the Scriptures. It is rooted in the holiness of God, who alone judges justly. This serves as a lever to edge people nearer to God in salvation. It is also a challenge for Christians to live godly lives.

ILLUSTRATIONS

The judgment of God is both comforting and discomforting. It comforts us to know that God will make all wrongs right. We especially thought of this while working in a violent area of Bristol, England. Newspapers dubbed the street in front of our church, "Bristol's Street of Terror." It was encouraging to know that God would someday punish those who raped innocent women, mugged passers-by, and enslaved girls in prostitution.

On the other hand, the judgment of God should be terribly discomforting to those who engage in sinful acts. Many muggers, rapists, and pimps must know that they will someday pay for their dastardly deeds.

The famous Southern Baptist preacher, Robert G. Lee, delivered a dynamic sermon with the title, "Payday Someday." Several hundred times he preached that homily, and each time many turned to Christ in faith. The judgment of God had an evangelistic impact.

Two centuries earlier Jonathan Edwards (1703-58) ignited the Great Awakening with his preaching at Northfield, Massachusetts. One of his sermons which was most effective had the title, "Sinners in the Hands of an Angry God." Witnesses testified that some of Edwards' hearers clung to the pillars of the church to avoid being drawn down into hell. Judgment fueled the flames of revival.

Judgment is not always a future event. Adolf Hitler was so consumed with hatred for the Jews that he concocted a plan to purge the German nation of God's chosen people. In the course of a dozen years more than six million Jews were gassed and incinerated in the ovens of such infamous camps as Buchenwald, Dachau, and Auschwitz. As a result Germany went down to a crushing defeat in 1945. Many saw this to be a judgment of God.

Friedrich von Schiller (1759-1805), a German professor of history, delivered his inaugural address at Jena in 1789. He asserted, "The world's history is the world's judgment." This is only partially true, because God will judge the world when history is all over and Christ returns as earth's King.

Billy Graham has been known as an honest preacher of God's judgment. He once said: "I believe the troubles that have come upon us are in part a judgment of God on us for our sins; and that unless we repent and turn to God, we are finished as a free democratic society."

The same need for repentance was stated by Professor Howard Hendricks of Dallas: "There is no fear of judgment for the man who judges himself according to the Word of God."

JUSTIFY, JUSTIFICATION

MEANING

One of the most basic truths of Scripture is that of justification. The word "to justify" is a translation of the Greek verb *dikaioo*, which means "to declare or make one righteous." The related words are *dikaiosune* (righteousness) and *dikaios* (righteous).

In secular Greek these words originally described the efforts of a tyrannical king to justify his outrageous acts. To justify meant to vindicate actions which did not really deserve vindication. Later the word came to mean that which is fair or right, and this was extended to include efforts to establish righteousness.

Pagan religion also used this idea to describe the establishment of sinlessness. To justify someone was to declare him sinless. In Egyptian mythology the role of final judgment occurred when the god Osiris weighed good deeds off against bad deeds, to establish the righteousness of a person.

The Septuagint Greek Old Testament gives us the New Testament concept of justification. On the basis of animal sacrifices God declared people forgiven and therefore righteous. As the sacrifice was offered on the Day of Atonement, Israel was acquitted of sin and declared righteous. Now on the basis of Christ's sacrifice God justifies us, and declares us righteous.

BIBLE USAGE

Throughout the New Testament there is an emphasis on justification. In fact, the primary purpose of Christ's coming was to offer Himself as the sacrifice to secure the basis of our justification.

Jesus told the Pharisees that their very words proved that they were not justified (Matt. 12:37). Only contrite persons can be justified by God (Luke 18:14).

The Book of Acts reveals that the preached Gospel is at the root of justification by faith. Because of the sacrifice of Christ sins can be forgiven, and people can be justified by God and before God (Acts 13:38-39).

If there is one major treatise on justification in the New Testament, it is the Book of Romans. First, the apostle established the fact that no one can be justified by the Law of Moses (Rom. 2:12; 3:20). Justification is possible only through the grace of God as revealed in Christ (3:24). The great thesis of Romans is that we are justified by faith alone (1:17; 3:28; 4:5; 5:1). In fact, this is the basis on which even Abraham was declared righteous before God.

Other apostolic writings also underline the primacy of justification by grace through faith in the finished work of Christ. Paul asserted that the opinion of people was not the basis of divine justification. It was rather the statement of God that conferred on him justification or acquittal (1 Cor. 4:4).

When the Galatian Christians became enmeshed in a legalistic version of the Gospel, Paul warned them that true justification came by faith alone plus nothing else (Gal. 2:16). In many ways, the Book of Galatians applies the truth of justification that the Book of Romans has stated and defined.

In the Pastoral Epistles there is also an emphasis on the justification which is accomplished by the Lord in our lives. In 1 Timothy we have an early Christian hymn or possibly even a confession of faith. It includes the statement that Jesus Christ was "justified" by the Spirit (1 Tim. 3:16). What is meant is that the Holy Spirit declared the fact that Jesus Christ was absolutely righteous and thus a perfect sacrifice for our sin.

To Titus, Paul also mentioned the subject of justification. In fact, this brief epistle is a miniature doctrinal statement by the Apostle Paul. Having said that we are not saved by our own good works, Paul asserted that justification is all of God's grace (Titus 3:5-7).

Justification in the New Testament relates primarily to the standing which we as Christians enjoy. Because of Christ's finished work, we stand acquitted, vindicated, and justified before God's judgment seat.

ILLUSTRATIONS

Many years ago a youth speaker explained the meaning of justification in a simple phrase. Justification means that I stand before God "just-as-if-I'd" never sinned.

Though Matthew Arnold (1822-88) was a professor of poetry, he also had strong theological abilities. Of justification he said: "Christ came to reveal what righteousness really is, for nothing will do except righteousness, and no other conception of righteousness will do except Christ's conception of it—His method and secret." It is, after all, the Lord Jesus Christ who makes righteousness available to us.

The great Reformed theologian Louis Berkhof (1873-1957), who wrote frequently on the subject of justification, said: "The ground of justification can be found only in the perfect righteousness of Jesus Christ, which is imputed to the sinner in justification." This adds to the concept that the righteousness of Christ is accredited to our account when we believe. (See: *Impute*.)

Henry Smith, a Puritan writer, also wrote of justification: "He [Christ] hideth our unrighteousness with His righteousness, He covereth our disobedience with His obedience, He shadoweth our death with His death, that the wrath of God cannot find us." What a glorious picture this is of the safety of God's justification.

We cannot justify ourselves. Who has not tried this? Many years ago on a snowy evening I skidded through a stop sign and was immediately taken to court by a policeman. I tried to justify myself by speaking of the slippery pavement, but nothing could justify my carelessness. By the same token, we cannot justify ourselves before God.

Thomas Watson, a Puritan preacher, said: "God does not justify us because we are worthy, but by justifying us makes us worthy." Apart from His grace we are all unworthy.

Another Puritan writer, Richard Sibbes, spoke about the relationship between justification and sanctification: "By grace we are what we are in justification, and work what we work in sanctification."

No Puritan writer is more famous than John Bunyan (1628-88), the prisoner of Beford who wrote that classic, *Pilgrim's Progress*. He drew a remarkable distinction between justification and sanctification. Christ works justification in our lives, and we stand righteous before a holy God. On the other hand, after salvation and justification, the Holy Spirit sets to work in our lives to work sanctification, by which He conforms us to the image of Christ.
(See: *Righteousness*.)

KEEP

MEANING

The word used for "keep" in the Greek New Testament is *tereo*. Not surprisingly it is common, appearing 60 times. Literally, it means "to guard a person," "to keep a possession," or "to maintain a person." In a figurative sense it speaks of "observing a body of teaching," or "obeying a law," or "fulfilling some commandment."

In ancient Greek the word *tereo* meant to take note of some fact or to keep it in view. From this abstract meaning came the literal use of keeping a prisoner or watching over another person. It even was used to describe "keeping dogs in line."

In the Greek Old Testament, the Septuagint, the word means to observe a law, or to keep the Law of Moses. Similarly it also referred to the observance of a ceremony or a special day, such as keeping the Sabbath or the Passover. In short, most of the Greek meanings are reflected in similar English usage.

BIBLE USAGE

There are three mainstreams of meaning in the word *tereo*. First, it speaks of guarding a prisoner. At the crucifixion of Jesus some Roman soldiers were ordered to keep watch over the dying Lord (Matt. 27:36). At the end of that dark day they were still keeping watch when an earthquake shattered rocks (27:54) and split the veil in the temple. The Roman guards were charged with no simple task.

Neither were the guards who were charged to keep Christians any more successful. When Peter was put in prison, an angel came to free him, in answer to the church's prayers (Acts 12:5-7). In Philippi, Paul and Silas were also put in prison, and this time an earthquake was sent by God to free them (16:23-31). The Apostle Paul was again imprisoned at Jerusalem before starting his journey to Rome (24:23). Thus the Scripture speaks first of prison in connection with the word "to keep."

Second, the Scripture points to protection as a meaning of this word. In His high priestly prayer to the Father, the Lord asks that His Father may keep the Christians from danger in the world (John 17:15). It is neither the Lord's prayer nor the Father's design to take Christians out of the world, but rather to keep them while they are in the world.

The same concept of protection is seen in the Pastoral Epistles. God will "preserve" (keep) the souls, minds, and bodies of Christians until He presents them blameless before Himself in the last day (1 Thes. 5:23). By the same token, Christians are urged to keep themselves free from sin (1 Tim. 5:22). Paul regarded the Gospel as a treasure which must be guarded, and in this sense he "kept the faith" (2 Tim. 4:7).

A third aspect of this word is practical obedience. Jesus mentioned the Old Testament imperative to keep the Law (Matt. 19:17; 23:3). For a Christian keeping God's commandment is a labor of love, not legalism (John 14:21; 15:10). It is even a proof of conversion when we do what God commands (1 John 2:3; 3:22-24; 5:3). We are not saved by keeping God's commands, but we keep them because we are saved (Matt. 28:20).

Another aspect of the same truth relates to the written Word of God. Salvation involves keeping God's Word (John 8:51, 55). As Christ kept the Father's word, so we should keep His (John 15:20; 17:6). The same emphasis abounds in John's letters (1 John 2:5).

To summarize, the word "keep" has two primary emphases for the Christian. First, we are kept safe by the faithfulness of our living Lord. Second, because we are in Him we have a Spirit-born desire to keep the Word of God.

ILLUSTRATIONS

When we lived on the south coast of England, our town had a medieval castle. Though it was mainly in ruins, there was an impressive outline yet to be seen. The innermost part of that castle was the "keep." It was there that the lord of the castle used to keep his treasury, and presumably also his prisoners.

A modern parallel is a safe. In offices, banks, and homes people today have safes. They are built so strong and locked so securely that one may safely leave treasure in them. The Lord is like a safe to us.

The Christian's security is not found in external supports, but rather in internal assurance. Dorothy Pentecost wrote: "It is impossible to have the feeling of peace and serenity without being at rest with God."

Another statement of the same truth is found in the writings of John Benjamin Figgis, who came from the strong evangelical movement led by the Countess of Huntington in 18th-century England. Of God's keeping power Figgis said: "If the basis of peace is God, the secret of peace is trust [in Him]."

A possible contemporary of Figgis was Charles Haddon Spurgeon (1834-1892), who also commented on the subject of security: "Be it ours, when we cannot see the face of God, to trust under His wings." The saints' security is in Christ alone.

This was emphasized by the Puritans, and no one said it more clearly than Richard Baxter (1615-91) in his famous book, *The Saints' Everlasting Rest*. It is well to remember that he wrote this in the midst of the turmoil of a civil war in England.

In fact, the Puritans were full of confidence in God's keeping power. For instance, Thomas Brooks wrote: "Assurance made David divinely fearless, and divinely careless [without care]." A Puritan Bishop of Norwich, Edward Reynolds (1599-1676), could also add: "Assurance will assist us in all duties; it will arm us against all temptations; it will answer all objections; it will sustain us in all conditions."

Another Puritan writer was David Clarkson, who wrote concerning the keeping of God: "Assurance and comforts are desirable, but fruitfulness is absolutely necessary. . . . The end why the Lord offers comfort and assurance of His love, is to make us cheerful in His service, and to encourage us in His work, and engage our hearts in it thoroughly."

Many hymns sound this tone, but none is greater than Martin Luther's (1483-1546) majestic anthem:

A mighty fortress is our God, / A bulwark never failing;
Our helper He, amid the flood / Of mortal ills prevailing.

A similar thought inspired Isaac Watts (1674-1748) to write these lines:

Our God, our help in ages past, / Our hope for years to come,
Our shelter from the stormy blast / And our eternal home.

KILL

MEANING

In the Greek New Testament the word for "kill" is *apokteino.* It appears 74 times in the New Testament, and is used to describe violent death, "murder, execution, and killing." The emphasis falls on the violent aspect of killing.

Homer used the word to describe any sort of violent death, and later it was even employed to describe suicide. In the history of the Trojan Wars, praise was heaped on soldiers who killed large numbers of the enemy.

In the Septuagint Greek Old Testament the word is found 150 times. In many cases it simply means to die. No distinction is made between death from natural or violent causes. In other cases, however, the word means murder, as in the description of Cain killing Abel (Gen. 4:8). Execution is its meaning in the Mosaic Law (Ex. 32:27). During the wars of Israel's history the word was also employed to portray the mass killing of enemies (Num. 31:7). Usually this word is associated with violent death.

BIBLE USAGE

In the New Testament our word usually refers to physical death. For instance, Herod had mixed feelings about the murder of John the Baptist (Matt. 14:5; Mark 6:19-20). Jesus understood that He would be killed (Matt. 16:21; 17:23). In the teachings of Jesus evil people were often seen as murderers of the just (Matt. 21:35, 38-39; Mark 9:31). Israel sinned nationally because they killed the prophets, whom God had sent to warn them (Luke 11:47). Jesus warned His disciples that men would try to kill them (John 16:2).

Not only is *apokteino* used to describe murder and execution, but it also applies to suicide. The Jews insinuated that Jesus might commit suicide (John 8:22), though this was plainly preposterous. This is an isolated incident in the New Testament, because the word usually speaks of death at the hand of another person.

There is also in the Scriptures a reference to accidental death. Evidently a tower collapsed at Siloam while it was under construction. Jesus used the accidental death of eighteen people to show that calamity does not always follow sin. He said that these people did not die because they were more sinful than any other group (Luke 13:4-5).

In the same category of accidental or catastrophic death is the scourge of plagues. Here too the word employed is *apokteino.* Sometimes animals were killed on the Sabbath, because it could not be avoided (Mark 3:4; Luke 6:9). In the end times a massive plague will kill one-third of the human race (Rev. 9:18). Thus violent death is the main meaning of the word under consideration.

There is also a secondary meaning of this word in the New Testament, a meaning that is more difficult to grasp. There is an indication that one's spiritual life can also be killed. Jesus warned His disciples about people who kill spiritual life (Matt. 10:28). Apparently this related to those who prevented others from coming to the Lord.

Paul spoke of the period prior to his conversion, and asserted that sin had killed him spiritually (Rom. 7:11). Again, it is the absence of Christ in one's life which produces spiritual death. Anyone or any thing which keeps one from Christ is a spiritual murderer.

In writing to the Corinthians, Paul mentioned that legalism can also kill spiritual life. Anyone who exalts the letter of the Law above the spirit of the Law promotes spiritual murder (2 Cor. 3:6). This was a danger in the first century.

Finally, in a prison epistle Paul returned to the subject of spiritual death. In this case it is a positive reference, because Paul boldly testified that Christ had killed the hatred which existed between Jews and Greeks (Eph. 2:16).

Though in the New Testament *apokteino* usually referred to physical death, it sometimes described spiritual death. In both cases the meaning is that of a violent death caused by another.

ILLUSTRATIONS

Death was no stranger to the early Christians. In fact, Tertullian (160-215) wrote: "The blood of the martyrs is the seed of the church." Of the original followers of Jesus, almost all died violently. Only John the Apostle is thought to have survived torture and exile to die a natural death.

The Emperor Nero kicked off the persecution of Christians. He clothed some in animal skins and then threw them to the wild beasts to be torn apart. Others he impaled on long poles, covered them with pitch, and then set them afire as lanterns for his parties.

In the time of the Reformation the early Baptists (Anabaptists) were likewise persecuted and killed. During one decade more than 5,000 Baptists were slain. One chronicler of this persecution said: "No human being was able to take away out of their hearts what they had experienced." Dr. Earle E. Cairns wrote concerning these early Anabaptists: "The Lutherans burned the Catholics; the Catholics burned the Lutherans; both burned the Anabaptists."

Following the Russian Revolution of 1917 the persecution of Christians again emerged. Aleksandr Solzhenitsyn described the year 1918: "Many courageous priests have already paid for their preaching with the blood of martyrdom" (*Gulag Archipelago*, p. 326). Since then thousands have walked the same road of sacrifice.

During the Third Reich in Germany more than 6 million Jews were slaughtered. It is less well known that at least 6,000 Protestant pastors were slain for their faith. These too were gassed and incinerated in Hitler's ovens. Dietrich Bonhoeffer (1906-45) is the most famous of them.

Sir Thomas Browne (1553-1633), the leader of religious dissenters in England, wrote: "Were the happiness of the next world as closely apprehended as the felicities of this, it were a martyrdom to live." The poet and essayist John Dryden (1631-1700) also referred to honorable death when he wrote: "All have not the gift for martyrdom."

Gustave Flaubert knew something of this when he said: "It is the truth of the doctrine that makes a martyr." To this same subject English mystic Evelyn Underhill (1875-1941) wrote: "Love makes the whole difference between execution and martyrdom." Even O. Henry (alias William Sydney Porter, 1862-1910) referred to the subject when he wrote: "Perhaps there is no happiness in life so perfect as the martyr's."

It is amazing to see the effect of martyrdom on the missionary enterprise. After John and Betty Stam were killed in China (1934), a whole wave of missionary volunteers went to that country. In 1956 five young men fell on an Ecuadorian riverside, and another wave of volunteers came. "The blood of the martyrs is the seed of the church."

KING, KINGDOM

MEANING

The Greek word for "king" in the New Testament is *basileus,* and the word for "kingdom" is *basileia.* These are reflected in such English words as the man's name *"Basil,"* and in the term *"basili*ca" (which literally means an assembly hall or royal hall).

In ancient Greek the word described a hereditary or a priestly ruler. The source of a royal office in Greek mythology was the character of Zeus, and it was assumed that both poets and kings were divinely empowered for their tasks.

Plato developed the picture of a benevolent king, who was almost godlike. His role in society was that of a shepherd who cared for his people. From this king flowed all law and order, and he was viewed as a benefactor of the whole world.

The Septuagint Greek Old Testament developed the concept of an earthly king, which began with the anointing of Saul as King of Israel. The monarchy reached its epitome in David, who in turn pointed forward to the coming of God's messianic King.

BIBLE USAGE

The New Testament contains 161 references to various kings. First of all, many earthly kings are portrayed. At the time of Christ's birth, Herod ruled as an evil force over Israel (Matt. 2:1). From his line came also Herod Antipas, who slew John the Baptist (14:1-9). In the same mold was Herod Agrippa I who had James slain and Peter imprisoned (Acts 12:1, 20) and Herod Agrippa II before whom Paul was tried (25:13-14).

In his final (and only recorded) sermon, Stephen referred to Pharaoh as the King of Egypt, who favored Joseph (Acts 7:10). A later pagan king was the Emperor of Rome, probably Nero, for whom Paul (1 Tim. 2:1-2) and Peter (1 Peter 2:13, 17) requested that prayers be made.

In the Gospels Jesus Christ is portrayed as a potential king. This is seen in His parables of the kingdom (Matt. 13:41; 16:28). His kingdom is identified with the eternal reign prophesied in Daniel (Dan. 7:14, 18; Luke 1:33). The apostles will share in this kingdom when the Lord returns (Luke 22:30).

The apostles also reflect the teaching concerning Christ's kingdom. This will be a kingdom of the righteous (Eph. 5:5), and it will be the final home of God's faithful people (2 Tim. 4:1, 18; 2 Peter 1:11).

Of the references to an eternal kingdom in the New Testament, more than 70 refer to the kingdom of God. It will be a heavenly kingdom (Matt. 6:33; 19:24). There God will exercise His sovereignty without resistance (13:43; 26:29).

The characteristics of God's kingdom are awesome. It will be an eternal kingdom, in contrast with the fading fortunes of earthly rulers (2 Peter 1:11). In that kingdom not the mighty will rule, but the righteous (Matt. 5:10; 6:33). The "poor in spirit" on earth will be welcomed and rewarded in heaven (5:3).

Satan will be forever vanquished in the kingdom of our God (Rev. 12:10-11). In God's kingdom worship will take precedence over commerce, and the Lord will be adored as He should be (Heb. 12:28). In God's kingdom all believers will partake of His glory (Rom. 8:16-17; 1 Thes. 2:12).

Just as glory will glow throughout His kingdom, so sin will be banished forever. Self-righteousness excludes people from God's kingdom (Matt. 5:20). In the millennial kingdom there will also be no place for the lawless (5:19). Humility also marks those who enter into God's kingdom (18:1-4). Though the kingdom is still hidden, in God's time it will be revealed (13:11).

Several comforting truths are connected with the kingdom. First, it demonstrates the sovereignty of our God. Second, it testifies to the ultimate triumph of our Lord. Third, it reveals the essential unity of all believers.

ILLUSTRATIONS

"The main question for any ordination candidate," claimed the late Dr. Donald Grey Barnhouse (1895-1960), "is the interpretation of the kingdom parables in Matthew 13." Many theologians feel that the kingdom of God is as crucial a topic as it is divisive.

Some believe that the kingdom of God is tied completely to the coming of Christ, and that it has no expression in the present world. This was the viewpoint of the theologian and missionary Albert Schweitzer (1875-1975), who represented liberal theological thought.

On the other hand, Professor C.H. Dodd of Oxford and Manchester believed that the kingdom of God was visible only in this age, and that it had no relevance for the end times.

Many evangelicals believe in a premillennial return of Christ, and they view the kingdom as the Millennium.

The true emphasis on the kingdom of God is not theological but ethical. German pastor Christoph Blumhardt (1842-1919) put this into proper perspective by saying: "A man who is waiting and praying for the kingdom of God has to be like a servant who always watches the hands of his master."

On the subject of God's coming kingdom Billy Graham asserted: "The longings and dreams of mankind will be fulfilled as God establishes His glorious kingdom on earth for the enjoyment of mankind." It is as though he thus interprets the statement of the catechism, that man's chief end is "to glorify God and enjoy Him forever."

Alexander Miller saw the kingdom of God as His answer to the total decay of this world. "Our Lord's primary interest was not the shoring up of the moral and spiritual values of a sagging social structure," Miller proclaimed. Then he added, "But [His aim is] the ushering in of an altogether new order: the kingdom of God."

Renowned Reformed theologian Gerhardus Vos declared: "Jesus never speaks of the kingdom of God as previously existing. To Him the kingdom is throughout something new."

During an interview with a missionary candidate, Professor Merrill Tenney of Wheaton Graduate School stumped the poor young person with this question: "Why is God going to usher in the Millennium?"

When the student couldn't answer, the professor himself gave this reason: "God will create His millennial kingdom of 1,000 years to clean up the mess that sin has made of this world." No wonder Christopher Dawson said: "The kingdom of God is not the work of man. It confounds the work of man."

KNOWLEDGE

MEANING

Few words are as important as "knowledge," which occurs more than 200 times in the New Testament. The Greek words represented are *gnosis* for "knowledge" and *ginosko* for the verb, "I know." The Greek root word is reflected in the basic English word "know" (which is simply an English form of the root word, *gnos*). More clearly this root is seen in such words as "*igno*rance" (not knowing), "*agno*stic" (one who claims that God is unknowable), and "*gnos*ticism" (a heresy which taught that one is saved by knowledge alone).

Most of the English meanings of knowledge are reflected in the history of this Greek word. Ancient Greeks used the word to describe recognition, to know something or someone by sight (I know the mayor of Chicago by sight). Later it came to mean "experience" (one knows how to swim by experiencing it). Finally it was used specifically for sexual relations (as the film title *Carnal Knowledge* inferred).

BIBLE USAGE

To be precise, the word appears 221 times in the New Testament. Many of these appearances are found in the writings of John, 82 in all. The Apostle Paul made 50 references to knowledge, and Luke in his Gospel and Acts used the word 44 times. Several levels of learning are involved in this word.

First, there is the introduction to knowledge, coming to know something or someone. Jesus told His disciples that they had the ability to know the mysteries concerning His kingdom (Matt. 13:11). Those who believe on Christ also come to know the ultimate truth, who is none other than Jesus Christ Himself (John 8:32; 14:6). Christians also enter into a knowledge of Christian love, as exemplified by the Apostle Paul (2 Cor. 2:4). But there are some things which Christians do not know this side of glory, and one of them is God's time schedule (Acts 1:6-7).

This introductory aspect also pertains to personal knowledge. Jesus knew His disciples inside out (John 1:48; 2:24). He also has intimate inside knowledge of all present-day believers (2 Tim. 2:19).

From a human perspective, belief ushers us into a knowledge of the Lord Jesus and God the Father (John 14:7; 17:3). Knowing the Lord means that we obey His commandments (1 John 2:3), overcome Satan (2:13), are distinguished from the world (3:1, 6), and enjoy eternal life (5:20).

On a second level, this biblical knowledge involves understanding. Believers are enabled to understand the parables which Jesus taught, in a way which the world cannot. By contrast, the world could not comprehend the nature and role of Christ in God's plan, so they slew Him (1 Cor. 2:8). For the same reason the vast majority of people do not believe, because they cannot understand who the Lord is (Heb. 3:10). Understanding goes beyond the introductory concept of coming to know something or someone.

A third and final aspect of this word is the idea of realization or experiential knowledge. When a woman who had suffered from a hemorrhage for a dozen years touched the robe of Jesus, she knew and realized that she was healed (Mark 5:29). In the same incident, Jesus experienced that power had gone from Him to her (Luke 8:46).

After the feeding of the 5,000 Jesus was pressed by the mob. They sought to make Him King because He had provided food for them. Jesus knew this and realized that they followed Him for the wrong motive (John 6:15).

Jesus also knew when people bore malice against Him and His disciples. When the Pharisees and Sadducees questioned Him, He knew that they were hypocrites (Matt. 22:18). After Mary of Bethany anointed Jesus, He knew that Judas misunderstood this (26:10).

Knowledge relates to faith, and a Christian knows most intimately what he believes. The model of knowledge is the Lord, who knows everything, even what people think. In the Greek New Testament, knowledge embraced everything from man's imperfect perception to God's complete comprehension.

ILLUSTRATIONS

Knowledge is as important in literature as it is in the Bible. For instance, the Greek writer, Juvenal (died 458), unleashed a whirlwind of ideas when he said: "Know thyself." The French writer Jean de la Fontaine (1621-95) decried the foolishness of a person who "knows the world and does not know himself." Alexander Pope (1688-1744) felt that self-knowledge was most important, and he wrote: "Know then thyself; presume not God to scan."

The American humorist and wit Will Rogers (1879-1935) spoke of the limit of human knowledge when he quipped: "We know lots of things we didn't use to know but we don't know any way to prevent 'em happening."

In his marvelous "Wind in the Willows," Kenneth Grahame (1859-1932), also spoke of man's limitations: "The clever men at Oxford / Know all that there is to be knowed. / But they none of them know one half as much / As intelligent Mr. Toad."

Beyond human knowledge is the knowledge which God alone gives. The godly poet George Herbert (1593-1633) saw this clearly when he penned this line: "Knowledge is folly except grace guide it."

The same insight moved John Bunyan (1628-88), who concluded: "There is knowledge and knowledge: knowledge that resteth in the bare speculation of things, and knowledge that is accompanied with the grace of faith and love, which puts a man upon doing even the will of God from the heart."

Blaise Pascal (1623-62), one of the greatest Christian thinkers, said: "Things human must be known to be loved: things divine must be loved to be known."

This truth was put in simple terms by Charles Olgivie, who commented on the elementary nature of Christian truth: "A child in a Sunday School knows more about God than all you can find in all the analects of Confucius."

One of the great prophetic preachers of our century was A.W. Tozer of Chicago. He was not only a great preacher but also a great prayer warrior. In fact, he would often lay flat out on his face in prayer and contemplation. In these times of intimate communion with God, he discerned deep truths. When he wrote these down, he titled the book, *The Knowledge of the Holy.* This was the magnificent obsession of Tozer's life.

Along the same lines, the British Anglican theologian and teacher James I. Packer sized up the skepticism and confusion of our age. In an effort to answer the pathetic plight of our times, Dr. Packer wrote his masterpiece, *Knowing God.* He concluded his book by stating: "The true priority of every human being . . . is learning to know God in Christ" (p. 314).

LAMB

MEANING
In the New Testament three different words relate to lambs and sheep. A one-year-old lamb is called *amnos,* and a smaller lamb is called *arnion.* A full-grown sheep is called *probaton.* The Scriptures include all of these words.

In secular Greek, a "lamb" (*amnos*) was used mainly for sacrifice. In fact, the basic meaning comes from the Greek Old Testament, the Septuagint, in which lambs were offered as Jewish sacrifices (Lev. 9:3; Num. 15:5). A special significance was attached to the Passover lamb (Ex. 12:5). In a figurative sense, the coming Messiah was also called "the Lamb," because He would be sacrificed for our sins (Isa. 53).

The word for "sheep" (*probaton*) originally meant any four-legged beast. But as the Greek language developed it was refined to mean an adult sheep. Like the word "lamb," "sheep" had a figurative meaning in the Old Testament. God regarded His people Israel as sheep, and He cared for them as their Shepherd (Ps. 23).

BIBLE USAGE
In the New Testament the word "lamb" often referred to the Lord Jesus Christ. He was seen to be "the Lamb of God" who would bear away the world's sin (John 1:29, 36; Isa. 53:6-7). The patience of the suffering Servant was emphasized in Philip's proclamation to the Ethiopian (Acts 8:32). The Apostle Peter portrayed Christ as the spotless Sacrifice (1 Peter 1:19). Thus the New Testament focuses on the picture of Jesus as the Lamb of God, as He is introduced in Isaiah 53.

The peculiar, diminutive word *arnion* ("small lamb") is used to describe Christians. In that post-Resurrection meeting when Jesus restored the denying disciple Peter, He instructed Peter to feed the Lord's lambs (*arnion*). Here Christians are called "little lambs" (John 21:15).

Actually, this same word for "little lambs" is used to describe the Lord Jesus in the Book of Revelation. From a human standpoint a lamb is small and defenseless, but from God's point of view the Lamb of God is important. He is seen in a position of power in heaven (Rev. 5:6, 8, 12). Because of His role in the redemptive plan of God, the Lamb will execute judgment (6:16). In glory He will be the main focus of worship (7:10). From Him will emanate a light to brighten all of heaven (21:23).

The final word which is found is *probaton* (sheep), and because sheep usually move in flocks this word is commonly found in the plural form. The Lord used this picture in parables. People will rescue a sheep, even if it means breaking the Sabbath rules (Matt. 12:11). People without Christ are like sheep without a shepherd (9:36). The Lord seeks lost people, as a shepherd searches for a lost sheep (Luke 15:4). When one is converted, Peter described it as returning to the Shepherd of our souls (1 Peter 2:25).

Jesus referred to Israel as lost sheep, because they had wandered away from Jehovah God. The disciples were sent out to gather the lost sheep of Israel (Matt. 10:6; 15:24). Likewise the disciples of the Lord were called sheep (10:16; 25:32). In the famous Good Shepherd passage, Jesus taught that many sheep remained to be found and included in the flock which is His church (John 10:14, 16).

As was mentioned, Jesus is often called a Shepherd. This is clear from His teaching about the Good Shepherd (10:11, 14). In the above-mentioned passage from 1 Peter, Jesus is also called the Shepherd and Guardian of our souls (1 Peter 2:25). Peter likewise referred to Him as the Chief Shepherd (5:4). In the Book of

Hebrews the Lord is called "the great Shepherd of the sheep" (Heb. 13:20).

It is good to know that we as Christians need not wander about in despair and doubt. We can closely follow the Good Shepherd, the Chief Shepherd, and the Great Shepherd, who is our Lord Jesus Christ.

ILLUSTRATIONS

There are two emphases which must be illustrated. First, we look at Christ as the sacrificial Lamb. Christ was the end of all Old Testament sacrifices. Under the Old Covenant, an animal was sacrificed to temporarily "cover up" sin. In the New Covenant Jesus Christ died to do away once for all with our sin. There is no limit to the sins which His blood can cover. The Lamb died so that no lambs must ever die again.

At Christmastime we often think of the shepherds and their sheep. Somehow we seldom realize that those little lambs on the Judean hillside were all marked for slaughter in the temple sacrifices of Jerusalem. In God's economy of things, Jesus was the Lamb of God. His all-sufficient sacrifice should have put to death the sacrifice of little lambs forever.

John Bunyan (1628-88) brought the sacrifice of Christ into full focus when he wrote: "As a sacrifice, our sins were laid upon Him [Isa. 53]; as a Priest, He beareth them [Ex. 28:38]; and as an Advocate, He acknowledges them to be His own [Ps. 69:5]." Along the same lines the Puritan theologian John Owen (1616-83) concurred: "He suffered not as God, but He suffered who was God."

Jesus Christ is God's sacrificial Lamb, who was slain in God's plan before the world began. As a result we can be the sheep of His pasture.

We follow Jesus as our Shepherd. The story is told of a traveler who was visiting Scotland. He dressed in a shepherd's clothes and tried to lead that shepherd's sheep. But they did not follow the stranger, for they did not recognize his voice. Likewise a Christian should always recognize his or her Shepherd's voice and follow Him.

A similar story was told by a Bible teacher. He explained that a shepherd in the Holy Land reached up and picked a few leaves, which he held behind his back as he walked along. The sheep which walked closest to the shepherd ate the leaves. This illustration urges us to stay close to our Shepherd.

In Israel we noticed that some sheep had red or blue paint sprayed on them. The shepherd explained this to us. Since the one who tended the sheep was not the shepherd, he did not recognize them. The paint blotches aided recognition. How good it is for us to know that our Good Shepherd knows us by name.

One of the finest discussions of the Shepherd Psalm was written by Philip Keller, *A Shepherd Looks at Psalm 23* (Grand Rapids: Zondervan, 1970). Here the details of the psalm are viewed through the eyes of an Israeli shepherd. This author also wrote a book about the Lamb of God in Isaiah 53.

LAMP

MEANING

The Greek word for "lamp" is *lampas,* which is remarkably similar to the English. A related word is *lampo* which means "to give light, or to shine." Both of these words speak of a light source, something which radiates light. These Greek root words also appear in different combinations. The verb for "shining forth" is *eklampo* (literally, "to shine out"). Another related verb is *perilampo,* "shine around" (the prefix *peri* means around, as in *peri*meter).

In ancient Greek this family of words spoke of radiance. For instance, the word was used to describe flashing eyes or a radiant personality. Later a more practical use of the word developed, as *lampos* came to mean a torch of pine wood or a ceramic lamp which held oil and a wick. At the same time the figurative concept developed of a hero shining forth.

The New Testament derives its meaning for these terms from the Septuagint Greek Old Testament. Dazzling light often revealed the presence of God's glory, as did the seven-branched candlestick. Thus lamps had a strong spiritual meaning in the Old Testament.

BIBLE USAGE

The word for "lamp" in all its forms appears about 30 times in the New Testament. First, there is a literal sense of the word being used to describe all manner of light. In the Sermon on the Mount, Christians are compared to a lampstand which gives light and should not be hidden (Matt. 5:15). So a lampstand is the basic meaning of this word.

In His Parable of the Wise and Foolish Virgins, the Lord described a Jewish custom. Friends of the groom went with him to bring the bride and her friends to the wedding celebration, and those who had made proper preparations were allowed to enter. One of these preparations was a lighted lamp (Matt. 25:1-13).

Another twist to the same word appears in the Lord's teaching concerning His second coming. His appearance will be like lightning, and the word for lightning is also *lampas* (Luke 17:24).

Yet another translation of the same word is found in John 18:3. When the mob went out to take Jesus prisoner, they came with lanterns and torches (*lampas*), puny people pursuing the Son of God.

A second use of these words is in picture language, and the word used here is often *lampros* (radiant, bright, or shining). Usually this is used in a figurative way. For instance, luxury is described as being radiant, glittering, or splendid (Luke 16:19). The royal garments put on Jesus in jest by Herod's men were also described as being gorgeous or radiant (23:11). The same word was used to portray the extravagance of a wealthy man who dominates a church (James 2:2). There is a close connection between this use of the word, and our reference to a "bright" tie.

This adjective *lampros* was also used to describe angelic brightness. Luke mentioned it in his reference to the angelic escort for Christ's birth (Luke 2:9). Cornelius described his angelic visitor as being radiant (Acts 10:30), and so was the angelic rescuer that Peter portrayed (12:7).

A third and final family of terms is the verb *lampo,* to light up, shine, or radiate. It is often used of spiritual radiance. At Christ's Transfiguration the disciples saw Him glow with God-given radiance (Matt. 17:2; Mark 9:2-3; Luke 9:29). This also fits in with John's vision in the Book of Revelation, where this word also describes Christ's glory (Luke 17:24).

Another aspect of spiritual radiance is seen in Christians' lives. Their righteous lives shine out in a dark world (Matt. 5:15-16). In the kingdom the righteous will shine forth as the sun, according to the promise of Christ (13:43). The Apostle Paul wrote that the source of a Christian's light is none other than the knowledge of the glory of God as seen in the face of Christ (2 Cor. 4:6). Christians are not generators of light, but are reflectors of the light which comes from Christ alone.

ILLUSTRATIONS

The radiance of glory is certainly one of the main applications of this word. It is seen in the works of Nicolas Berdyaev (1874-1948), a Russian Orthodox writer, who concluded: "The light that shines from the Crucified is a light . . . which both illuminates the obscurity of being and overcomes the darkness of nonbeing." In other words, only Christ can send a stream of light into our dark lives.

Along the same lines the Puritan minister Stephen Charnock (1628-80) also addressed the subject of light: "In nature, we see God, as it were, like the sun in a picture; in the Law, as the sun in a cloud; in Christ we see Him in His beams; He being 'the brightness of His glory, and the exact image of His person.' " Here the light of revelation is seen undimmed in the Lord alone. He is the great, eternal power source.

"In darkness there is no choice," asserted C.T. Whitmell. Then he added: "It is light that enables us to see the differences between things; and it is Christ who gives us light."

In 1966 several hundred evangelists and missionaries met in Berlin, Germany for a World Congress on Evangelism. Many participants were notable, and among them was Emperor Haile Selassie of Ethiopia. Most intriguing were two Auca Indians from Ecuador, one of whom had led the murder party which killed five missionaries in 1956. As that former murderer declared his faith in Christ, he painted a word picture: "Once my world was all in darkness," he began. "Then Jesus came into our tribe and my life. Now my life is full of light."

The great Methodist preacher and writer Samuel Chadwick spoke of the light which the Holy Spirit brought into the world: "To the church, Pentecost brought light, power, joy. There came to each illumination of mind, assurance of heart, intensity of love, fullness of power, exuberance of joy."

The above picture was taken almost directly from the Church of England service for ordination, which includes this prayer:

Come, Holy Ghost, our souls inspire,
And lighten with celestial fire.
Thou the anointing Spirit art,
Who dost Thy sevenfold gifts impart.

In 1890 General William Booth (1829-1912) wrote a book titled, *In Darkest England—and the Way Out.* He assessed the dismal state of England and especially the cities. Apart from God's grace there was no hope. Thus General Booth proposed to bring the Gospel light into every corner of "darkest England." He also set about to ameliorate the abuses of industrial society. To this end he instituted such programs as the farm colonies, a missing person's bureau, a poor man's bank, and legal aid for the poor.
(See: *Light.*)

LAW

MEANING

The Greek word which is translated "law" is *nomos*. This root word is seen in the English word, "eco*nomic*s" (literally, law relating to the household or the study of financial mechanisms). Less well known are the words "ergo*nomic*s" (the study of work efficiency) and "*nomo*thetic" (pertaining to the law-making process).

The original meaning of the Greek word *nomos* was "what is proper." With the dawn of the city-states, such as Athens and Sparta, it came to mean a legal norm. Still later, in the sixth century before Christ, it meant a divine principle or law. Socrates saw it as the norms or principles by which a city is governed. According to Plato these were generally accepted principles by which ordered, civilized society operated.

The Jews saw in this the Ten Commandments. The Law of God was described by this word in the Greek Old Testament, the Septuagint. God's Laws had several specific characteristics. They were unconditional. Their form was a prohibition. Their aim was to persuade the Jews to obey them. Despite their brevity they were also comprehensive (Gerhard Kittel, *Theological Dictionary of the New Testament*, IV, p. 1037).

BIBLE USAGE

In the New Testament two laws appear. The first law is that of the Old Covenant, and its beginning is traced back to Sinai. In fact, the word "law" appears 195 times in the New Testament, usually in connection with the Old Testament Law.

Jesus readily discussed the Law, which He summarized in the two great commandments of love toward God and love toward people (Matt. 22:36-39; Luke 10:26-27). Jesus conformed to the Law from His infancy onward (2:27). He saw His ministry as a fulfillment of the Law (Matt. 5:18; 7:12; Luke 16:17).

New Testament writers often referred to the commandments as the Law of God. Obedience to parents was called the word (or Law) of God (Matt. 15:6). However, enemies of the Cross, from Pilate to Paul's time, claimed they acted in accordance with the Law of God.

In some cases the Law was connected to Moses (Luke 2:22; John 7:23). However, the apostles asserted that salvation could never be earned by keeping the Law (Acts 15:5-11; Rom. 3:27-28). Still there is a respect for the Law of Moses as the guide to God (Heb. 10:28).

The apostles regarded the Law of God as good, but as an insufficient source of salvation (Gal. 2:19; 3:11). They asserted that people will be judged according to the light they possess. Jews will be judged according to the Law (Rom. 2:12-13).

They knew well that Christ had fulfilled all the Law. He was the one complete Sacrifice which did away with the sacrificial system of Judaism (Gal. 3:10-13). Therefore the Law is a mirror in which we see our sinfulness (Rom. 3:20), and it is a schoolteacher that instructs us Godward in Christ (Gal. 3:24).

In Christ a new Law was born. This Law commands Christians to love other Christians (John 13:34-35). It also commands that the Gospel be preached around the globe before Christ comes back (Matt. 28:18-20).

As a result of this proclamation a spiritual generation of Christians have been born into God's family. They live under a new Law. According to the Apostle Paul, this Law is stimulated by the Holy Spirit, and produces life instead of death (Rom. 8:2-4). This Law obligates Christians to bear one another's burdens (Gal. 6:2). Under "the Law of Christ" one has a new evangelistic concern (1 Cor. 9:21). This

Law gives liberty to all who obey it (James 1:25; 2:12). If followed, the Law of Christ will prepare us for His ultimate revelation in glory (2 Peter 3:2-13).

Just as the Law of Moses showed up our sinfulness, so the Law of Christ is salvation. The Old Covenant covered sin with the blood of beasts, but the New Covenant eradicates our sin through the blood of Christ.

ILLUSTRATIONS

To many people the law is a laugh. The bawdy actress Mae West once quipped: "It ain't no sin if you crack a few laws now and then, just so long as you don't break any."

"There's a different law for the rich and the poor," postulated E. Ralph Stewart. Then he reasoned: "Otherwise, who would go into business?"

Similarly, the French writer Honore de Balzac (1799-1850) in his cynical way wrote: "Laws are spiderwebs through which the big flies pass and the little ones get caught." He was paraphrasing Anacharsis (about 600 B.C.) who said: "Laws are like cobwebs, for any trifling or powerless thing falls into them, they hold it fast; but if a thing of any size falls into them, it breaks the mesh and escapes."

Law is, however, the safety net for society. William Pitt the Elder (1708-78) once said: "Where law ends, tyranny begins." In the same vein the ancient philosopher Aristotle (384-322 B.C.) acclaimed law as "reason free from passion."

President Thomas Jefferson (1743-1826) said, "Laws and institutions go hand in hand with the progress of the human mind." A later President, Woodrow Wilson (1856-1924), wrote: "The law that will work is merely the summing up in legislative form of the moral judgment that the community has already reached."

During the Second World War a Jewish chaplain called the troops' attention to the significance of God's Law when he said: "Statutory law is based upon common law; common law is based upon moral law; and moral law is based upon divine Law."

Human law seems to be inequitable, but God's Law is always fair. Swiss theologian Emil Brunner (1889-1966) saw the significance of God's Law and wrote: "Knowledge of grace presupposes the Law. Without the Law there is no experience of the grace of God. Without the Sermon on the Mount there would be no Epistle to the Romans."

Along the same lines Billy Graham concluded: "Moral law is more than a test; it is for man's own good. Every law that God has given has been for man's benefit. If man breaks it, he is not only rebelling against God, he is hurting himself. . . . The law is a mirror that shows us that we are lawbreakers and reflects our need for Christ."

The great champion of fundamental Christianity, J. Gresham Machen (1881-1937), concurred with this assessment of God's Law and wrote: "A low view of law leads to legalism in religion; a high view makes man a seeker after grace."

John Wesley (1703-91) concurred with great preachers of every age in saying: "Before I preach love and grace, I must preach sin, law, and judgment." Only then do people see their nakedness before the dais of divine justice.

LIFE

MEANING

The Greek word for "life," *zoe*, sounds familiar to English-speaking people. One sees it in our word for a "zoological" park (where live animals are kept). It is also seen in such terms as "zoology" (the study of various forms of animal life), "zoogeography" (a study of the distribution of animals), and "zoography" (descriptive zoology). It is even seen in the woman's name, *Zoe*.

In ancient Greece the word referred to the natural life which is shared by animals and people. Aristotle used it to describe the procreative processes whereby life is multiplied. In classical Greek it meant any self-movement, in contrast with mechanical movement. Plato extended the word to mean both mortal and immortal life. The Stoics felt that one should live in accordance with the life principle of the universe. For Plato life could be divided between the here and the hereafter.

To the Jews, life is tied up with their belief in Jehovah. He alone is the Creator and Source of life. Wherever life is found, God is the Source of it.

BIBLE USAGE

In either its noun form, "life," or its verb form, "to live," this word occurs no fewer than 260 times in the New Testament. There are two basic emphases in the word. The first is an emphasis on physical life, and the second is on spiritual life.

The New Testament states clearly that God is the Source of all life. In fact, all life is found in God. Paul stated this in his closely reasoned presentation to the Athenians (Acts 17:25). Even the Book of Revelation traces the breath of life back to God (Rev. 11:11).

In some cases the Bible simply speaks of life as our existence on earth. A sinner has this existence (Luke 16:25). Christ shared this life also (Acts 8:33). We have a better life because of Christ (1 Cor. 15:19; 1 Tim. 4:8).

Physical life is also contrasted with physical death. According to the Apostle Paul, we belong to the Lord in our life and our death (Rom. 8:38). In his Philippian letter Paul included an extended discussion of life and death (Phil. 1:20-26).

Though the New Testament discusses physical life, it contains many more references to spiritual life. Christ is the sole Source of this life (John 1:4; 14:6). He is called by Peter the Prince of life (Acts 3:15). Having Christ in one's life is having abundant life (John 10:10, 28; 1 John 5:11-13). Christ is the promise of eternal life (2 Tim. 1:1).

The Holy Spirit is likewise cited as a Source of this life. There is no spiritual life apart from the Holy Spirit of God (John 6:63). This spiritual life also liberates us from sin's slavery (Rom. 8:3).

It is called a new life, because it is so different from physical life. According to Paul, we are resurrected to new life (6:4). This is also God's life; it is nothing that the world can give (Eph. 4:18). Those who possess this life know peace in the midst of conflict (Rom. 8:6).

Eternal life is not a future fantasy, but a present possession. Jesus repeated this truth in His Gospel sermons (John 3:15-16; 5:24; 6:40, 47, 51, 57; 20:31). This eternal life will also carry over into eternity (Mark 10:30; Matt. 19:29). People who live for the Spirit have eternal life (Gal. 6:8). Every Christian can look forward to the prospect of eternal life with the Father (1 Tim. 1:16; 6:12). This is specially meaningful in the context of Christian marriage, where both partners are heirs of eternal life (1 Peter 3:7).

This spiritual life gives a fixed point of reference to human history. Believers will be raised to life which is eternal (John 5:29). Possession of this goal is geared to the reality of faith (3:15, 36; 4:14; 5:24; 10:28). The same truth is taught in the epistles of John (1 John 1:2; 5:11-13).

As can be seen from this summary, the Gospel and Epistles of John contain an unusual number of references to spiritual life. No matter where they are found, however, the Source is God and the means of achieving it is Jesus Christ. He is "the Way, the Truth, and the Life" (John 14:6).

ILLUSTRATIONS

Literature is full of references to life. According to James Barrie's book, *The Little Minister*, "Life is a long lesson in humility."

Corrie ten Boom often said, "It is not the duration that is important, but the donation of one's life." Alexis Carrel said it too: "The quality of life is more important than life itself." Along the same lines the Roman Publilius Syrus said: "It matters not how long you live, but how well." "Life is an excellency added to being," said the Puritan writer Thomas Goodwin (1600-80).

The famous mystical writer Meister Eckhart (1260-1327), who paved the way for the Reformation, claimed: "One person who has mastered life is better than a thousand persons who have mastered only the contents of books, but no one can get anything out of life without God."

Life on earth is important, but life in eternity is essential. "Religion can offer a person a burial service," commented Wilma Reed, "but Christ offers every person new, abundant, and everlasting life."

The Anglican bishop Jeremy Taylor (1613-67) agreed, saying: "God hath given to man a short time here upon earth, and yet upon this short time eternity depends."

John Adams also looked heavenward and said: "I cannot conceive that [God] could make such a species as the human merely to live and die on this earth. If I did not believe in a future state, I should believe in no God."

This confidence in eternal life is seen clearly in the parting words of great Christians. Dr. Martyn Lloyd-Jones (1899-1981) had a great influence on my pastoral ministry. When he came close to the end of his earthly ministry, "The Doctor" told his grieving loved ones: "Don't pray for healing. Don't hold me back from glory!"

James Burns, a Scottish divine, said on his deathbed: "I have been dying for twenty years. Now I am going to live." The sainted wife of General William Booth, Catherine Booth (1829-90), praised her Lord with these words: "The waters are rising but I am not sinking."

As the Scottish novelist and poet, George MacDonald (1759-1820), put it: "I came from God, and I'm going back to God, and I won't have any gaps [sic] of death in the middle of my life."

LIGHT

MEANING

In the Greek New Testament the word translated "light" is *phos*. It gives rise to many familiar English words such as "*pho*tograph" (literally, a writing with light), "*phos*phorous" (literally, light-bearer or a substance which glows in the dark), and "*pho*toelectric" (a cell which is switched on or off by the presence of light).

The ancient Greeks attributed many meanings to this common word. Homer used it to describe brightness of any kind, especially bright sunlight. In the writings of Aristotle it came to have a figurative meaning, the illumination of mind which comes through revelation. Later light was identified with ethical good, and darkness with evil. This viewpoint became dominant in Plato's famous book, *The Republic*. The good of the community was described with the term "light."

BIBLE USAGE

In the New Testament this word for light occurs 72 times, and almost half (33) of these are in the Gospel of John. As might be expected, the word is used both for natural light and spiritual light.

Jesus spoke of a lit lamp in His Parable of Witness (Luke 8:16). He used the same word in a parallel parable which compares a hidden witness with a hidden light (11:33). Another parable speaks of light, as a woman who lost a coin searched with a light to find her treasure (15:8).

In the historical narrative of the Gospels there is also reference to real, literal light or fire. In the night of Jesus' trial Peter warmed himself by a fire (*phos*), and this is recorded in both Mark and Luke (Mark 14:54; Luke 22:56). In the Luke passage, the *New American Standard Version* translates the word "firelight."

Just as the New Testament speaks of physical light, it also refers repeatedly to spiritual light. The Book of James refers to God as the Father, or Creator, of lights (James 1:17). Jesus is often described as light. He called John the Baptist a burning and shining light (John 5:35). In the prologue to John's Gospel, Jesus is described as the Light who came into the world to lighten every person (John 1:5-11). He referred to Himself as the Light of the world (John 8:12).

The brightness of Christ was seen most clearly in His transfiguration. He shone like an incandescent bulb (Matt. 17:2). Peter later remembered this encounter with the light of God's glory (2 Peter 1:16). Likewise John also recalled this vision of His glory (John 1:14).

When Saul of Tarsus was arrested by the Lord, he too saw a bright light. This is made clear in Luke's account of the Damascus Road experience (Acts 9:3). It is repeated in the telling of Paul's testimony before the magistrates of Judaism and before King Agrippa (Acts 22:6, 9, 11; 26:13).

Christians receive spiritual enlightenment in salvation. This is reflected in Christ's quotation of Isaiah 9:2 (Matt. 4:16). Conversion is like being exposed to evangelistic light (Eph. 5:13). Heaven is described as a place of light, where we will share the inheritance of all the saints (Col. 1:12). When one believes in the Lord, it is as if a light were turned on in his soul (2 Cor. 4:4-6). God calls us "out of darkness into His marvelous light" (1 Peter 2:9).

Thus those who have experienced the light of God's salvation become light-bearers in the world. In the Sermon on the Mount, Jesus urged His disciples to be lights in the world (Matt. 5:14-16). As an apostle, Paul became a light to the Gentiles (Acts 13:47). As a man guides a blind person, the Jews had been commissioned to guide the blind, but they had failed to exercise this role (Rom. 2:19).

As Christ comes to enlighten us, Satan sets about to keep us in the dark spiritually. In John's prologue, he reminded people that the world could not comprehend the light of Christ's coming (John 1:5). In fact nonbelievers in Christ resist the entrance of His light into the world and run from His light (John 3:19-20). According to Paul, an unenlightened mind is darkened and blinded by sin (2 Cor. 4:4; Eph. 4:18). When a person prefers sin to salvation, that person is persisting in the darkness (1 John 2:8-10).

Thus God is identified with spiritual enlightenment, just as He is the Originator of all natural light. By the same token, Satan is the source of spiritual darkness.

ILLUSTRATIONS

Literature abounds with references to light. According to the famous Puritan John Milton (1608-74), light is our vision or sight. He wrote: "When I consider how my light is spent, / E're half my days, in this dark world and wide" *(On His Blindness)*.

In his "Ode to Duty" William Wordsworth (1770-1850) derived light from the obligations of life. He wrote: "Stern daughter of the voice of God! O Duty! If that name thou love, who art a light to guide, a rod to check the erring and reprove." Here he saw duty as a means of directing people into right paths.

In his poem, "The World," Henry Vaughan (1622-95) recounted his vision: "I saw Eternity the other night, / Like a great ring of pure and endless light, / All calm, as it was bright." Here is one man's perception of eternal light.

When one turns from the speculation of writers to the surety of Christians, there is a different view of light. "You are the Light of the World," Austin Alexander Lewis wrote, "but the switch [of faith] must be turned on."

A former editor of *Decision* magazine, Sherwood Wirt, wrote these lines concerning the light of the Lord: "When Jesus healed the man blind from birth, He let him grope his way, still blind, to wash in the pool—and then the light broke. We don't need to know what we're groping toward—or why. It is enough that we have Christ's direction. The light will break in God's own time."

Many years ago Dr. V. Raymond Edman, "Prexy," visited us on the mission field. He had been blind during most of our time at Wheaton College, and shared with us the experience of regaining his sight through surgery. He believed God gave him back the light of sight.

Often Dr. Edman encouraged us with short epigrams. From others they sounded trite, but from "Prexy" they were profound. One of these is this truth: "Never doubt in the darkness, what God has shown you in the light." That statement took me and my students through many dark nights on the mission field.

The great Victorian hymn-writer Thomas Binney (1798-1874) caught the majesty of God's light in his hymn:

> Eternal Light! Eternal Light!
>   How pure the soul must be,
> When placed within Thy searching sight,
> It shrinks not, but with calm delight,
>   Can live and look on Thee.

LIKEMINDED

MEANING

The term "likeminded" is represented in the Greek New Testament by one word, *homophroneo*. This term is a combination of two Greek words. The first half is *homo* for "like" (as in "*homo*genized" milk which is made uniform or "alike" by mixing the cream into the milk). The second word is *phroneo*, meaning "I think."

The same concept is conveyed by the word *isopsuches*. This is also a combination of two words. The first is *isos* (meaning equal, as in "*isos*celes" triangles, which have two equal sides). A second word is *psuches*, for "soul" (seen in such English words as "*psycho*therapy," the healing of the mind), and "*psycho*ses" (an illness of the mind).

Historically these words have had several meanings in Greek. In the writings of Homer they convey four concepts. First, they referred to persons or things of the same kind, as all men are alike in being males. Second, the words referred to the same values or ranks, as fellow soldiers. Third, they referred to common possession, as in "share and share alike." Finally, the word referred to geometric symmetry, where two or more lines are alike in length.

BIBLE USAGE

In the New Testament these terms occur relatively infrequently. *Homophroneo* appears only once, though the phrase form "to think the same way" is found twice in the New Testament.

It is in the writings of Peter that the word *homophroneo* finds its only appearance. Christians are urged by Peter to be "harmonious," and this term is teamed up with other ones such as "sympathetic," "brotherly," "kindhearted," and "humble" (1 Peter 3:8). This oneness of thought is part and parcel of the entire concept of Christian unity, and the apostle urged it in the strongest terms upon Christians.

The same idea is found in Paul's writings. To the apparently perfect church at Philippi, Paul wrote to urge them on to oneness of purpose. In so doing he said they should be "of the same mind" toward each other (Phil. 2:2). One gets the impression that Paul was practicing preventative counseling. He wanted to forestall any division in the Philippian church.

The same verb construction is found in Romans. Paul also urged the Romans to be of the same mind toward one another (Rom. 15:5). He asserted in this connection that this unity is a product of God's gracious intervention in the Christian community.

As the first word, *homophroneo*, is used sparingly, so the second word, *isopsuches*, is used selectively. In fact, it is restricted to one reference in the writings of Paul. He commended Timothy as a "kindred spirit" (likeminded person) who would sacrificially serve the church at Philippi (Phil. 2:20).

Not only is this group of words used to describe Christian unity, but it is also used to enjoin Christians to be like the Lord. In conversion Christians are joined to Christ. They share an experience like His death and also like His resurrection (Rom. 6:5). God's gracious salvation is far different from the sin of Adam, for the benefit of salvation far outstrips the burden of sin (5:15). The God-given solution to our sin is Jesus Christ who came in flesh like ours (8:3). The likeness of Christ with us is a key to the effectiveness of His sacrifice on our behalf. We can praise God for this likeness.

Not only was Christ the perfect Sacrifice, but He is also the perfect Priest who represents us before God. The New Testament identifies Him as a Priest according to the order of Melchizedek, a mysterious man (Gen. 14:18-20). Christ is a sinless Priest. He is also a self-sacrificing Priest. Likewise He is a superior Priest, and the Scriptures find this likeness in Melchizedec (Heb. 7:15).

No other truth in all of the Scripture is more important than this one. If Christ came to be like us, we can become by faith through grace like Him. This truth is emphasized throughout Scripture in verses such as Romans 8:1-3; 2 Corinthians 8:9; and Philippians 2:5-11.

ILLUSTRATIONS
The two parallel principles emphasized in the word "likeminded" are of profound importance. The first is that Jesus Christ became like us. The all-powerful Son of God was weary as a man. Though He knew everything, He still learned obedience (Heb. 5:8). Despite His ability to be everywhere at once, He stayed in His earthly parents' humble home. Though He was eternal in His being, He grew up as a child.

This likeness which the Lord shares with us is emphasized by many Christian writers, such as the devotional author Oswald Chambers (1874-1917) who said: "Jesus Christ is not the best human being; He is a being who cannot be accounted for by the human race at all. He is not man becoming God, but God Incarnate, God coming into human flesh, coming into it from outside." Christ became like us at great expense.

Another Scottish writer was A.M. Fairbairn (1838-1912), who like Chambers wrote many devotional and theological works. Of Christ's coming Fairbairn said: "In Him [Christ], as in no other, God lived; He lived, as no other did, in God. Since Jesus lived, God has been another and nearer Being to man." Here the nearness and likeness of Christ is emphasized.

The other truth is also profound in its significance, that in Christ we can become like Him. The late German evangelist Gerhard Bergmann put this into perspective when he said: "What we need is not a concession to modern man, but a concentration on Jesus Christ."

Scottish preacher and writer William Arnot (1808-75) spoke of Christlikeness when he said: "The gentleness of Christ is the comeliest ornament that a Christian can wear."

On the same theme the unusual political and religious character, Henry Drummond (1786-1860), stated: "To become Christlike is the only thing in the whole world worth caring for, the thing before which every ambition of man is folly and all lower achievement vain."

Conversion, according to Billy Graham, is not the end, but the beginning. It is "a daily process whereby you grow to be more and more like Christ. Jesus Christ is the Man God wants every man to be like."

An old Gospel song by James Rowe (1865-1933) summarized this truth in its first stanza:

> Earthly pleasures vainly call me;
> I would be like Jesus;
> Nothing worldly can enthrall me;
> I would be like Jesus.
> Be like Jesus, this my song,
> In the home and in the throng;
> Be like Jesus all day long!
> I would be like Jesus.

(See: *Imitator*.)

LORD

MEANING

The Greek word translated "Lord" is *kurios*. It appears no fewer than 9,000 times in the Greek version of the Old Testament, the Septuagint, where it signifies Jehovah God. In the New Testament there are 717 references. This word is seen in the liturgical prayer, "Kurie elieson," "Lord, have mercy."

In the earliest Greek this word meant "to have power or authority." Later it came to describe one who is in control. As classical Greek developed, it became a title for men of importance. Since the gods of ancient Greece were neither creators nor lords of their fate, pagan deities were not called "lord" until much later.

By the time of Christ, kings had come to be called "lord." This was true of the Roman Emperor Caligula (A.D. 37-41). It was also true of Candace, the fabled queen of upper Egypt (see Acts 8:27). So too Herod the Great, Herod Agrippa I, and Herod Agrippa II were called "lord."

BIBLE USAGE

Of the New Testament references to "lord," 275 occur in the writings of Paul. Luke used the word 210 times in his Gospel and in the Book of Acts.

First, "lord" is used to describe human relationships. Jesus described the relationship of slaves to their lords (Matt. 10:24; 25:19). The Apostle Paul told slaves to obey their masters or lords as a sign of the slaves' faith in Christ (Eph. 6:5, 9; Col. 3:22). The same relationship is discussed in Galatians 4:1.

In the Parable of the Unrighteous Steward, Jesus used the relationship between slave and lord to teach the lesson of responsible stewardship (Luke 16:3, 5). In most modern translations, such as the *New American Standard Version*, the word "lord" is translated "master."

The Apostle Peter used this term to describe a husband. He lifted the statement from the Old Testament, that Sarah referred to Abraham as her "lord" (1 Peter 3:6). From this passage Peter taught mutual submission.

The second use of the word Lord refers to Christ. He is exalted because He is Lord (Phil. 2:11). Salvation is based on a confession of Christ as Lord (Rom. 10:9-10). When Thomas saw the risen Jesus, he called Him both Lord and God (John 20:28).

The Apostle Paul insisted that no one could call Jesus "Lord" unless the Holy Spirit gave that insight (1 Cor. 12:3). This identity of Jesus Christ with the Spirit is most clearly seen in 2 Corinthians 3:17-18.

The Apostle Paul often greeted the church in the name of the Lord (Rom. 1:7; 1 Cor. 1:3; 2 Cor. 1:3; Phil. 1:2). The source of strength to live the Christian life is "in the Lord," a concept seen most frequently in the Book of Philippians (Phil. 2:1, 19; 3:1, 9, 14; 4:4, 19).

Another use of the word *Lord* with Christ relates to His second coming. Paul encouraged the Thessalonians by the coming of the Lord (1 Thes. 4:13-18). The final event of this Age is called the Day of the Lord (1 Cor. 1:8; 5:5; 1 Thes. 5:2).

A third use of the word *Lord* refers to God the Father. There are many references in the New Testament to an angel of the Lord (Matt. 1:20; 2:13). The same phrase occurs in the Book of Acts, when a special emissary was dispatched to do God's work in the world (Acts 5:19; 8:26; 12:7).

The power of Jehovah God is also identified with the Lord. His name is all-powerful (James 5:10, 14). Likewise the word of the Lord is endued with exceptional authority (Acts 8:25; 12:24).

In a cosmic chorus of praise the Lord is declared to be preeminent in all the world. God is the Lord of heaven and earth (Matt. 11:25; Luke 10:21). He is Lord by virtue of creation, incarnation, and ultimate glorification.

ILLUSTRATIONS

Augustine (354-430), a wise and saintly Bishop of Hippo, understood the full impact of the lordship of Christ: "Jesus Christ will be Lord of all or He will not be Lord at all." There is no halfway house in the lordship of Christ.

Though he represents another age and a vastly different culture from Augustine's, the Southern preacher Vance Havner caught the same concept and wrote: "I came to Christ as a country boy. I did not understand all about the plan of salvation. One does not have to understand it; one has only to stand on it. . . . One thing I did understand even as a lad: I understood that I was under new management. I belonged to Christ and He was Lord."

The relatively unknown Puritan writer Paul Bayne brought home this truth: "The Lord Jesus has provided a common dole of grace and salvation for every poor soul that stands in need of it, only He will have men come and receive it; they shall have it for carrying it away."

A colorful conception of Christ's lordship was framed by Thomas Brooks (1608-80), a nonconformist Puritan pastor: "Though Christ's coat was once divided, He will never suffer His crown to be divided."

The lordship of Christ has several significant implications. In his eulogy for the Protestants slain in the Piedmont region of Italy, John Milton (1608-74) wrote: "Avenge, O Lord, Thy slaughtered saints, whose bones lie scattered on Alpine mountains cold" ("On the late Massacre in Piedmont"). The Lord was an avenging God to Milton.

At the outset of the Victorian period, Cecil Frances Alexander (1818-95) wrote of the Lord as a God of purity:

> Do no sinful action,
>   Speak no angry word;
> Ye belong to Jesus,
>   Children of the Lord.

Therefore a Christian should live under the lordship of Christ in every word and work.

Robert Burns (1759-96), a great bard of Scotland, spoke of the nearness of the Lord when he wrote: "They never sought in vain that sought the Lord aright!" ("The Cottar's Saturday Night")

In the Church of England's *Book of Common Prayer* are many glorious references to the Lord. One of these exhorts the reader to worship: "O come, let us worship and fall down: and kneel before the Lord our Maker."

Rudyard Kipling (1865-1936) enlisted the Lord to justify the British Empire, when he wrote:

> God of our fathers, known of old,
>   Lord of our far-flung battle line,
> Beneath whose awful hand we hold
>   Dominion over palm and pine—
> Lord God of Hosts, be with us yet,
> Lest we forget—lest we forget!
> ("Recessional")

LOVE

MEANING

Three Greek words were used to describe love. The first in order of importance for Bible students is *agape,* and the verb *agapao* (to love). This is a totally sacrificial love. The secret of *agape* love is not what I can get, but rather what I can give. Homer used the verb form of this word quite often, though the noun form appears only once in secular Greek literature. It is used to describe that deep and tender love which a parent has for his or her child. In the New Testament this Greek word is given a new meaning, for it is identified with God's love for us.

The second word for love is *phileo.* It is seen in several English words, such as *"phil*osophy" (literally love of wisdom), *"phil*ology" (love of words), and the city name *"Phil*adelphia" (meaning literally "brotherly love"). This is the affection which is seen between friends or relatives. It can also be seen in the Greek words which are constructed from this verb, such as *phile* (a female friend) and *philema* (a kiss). This love can describe a family or friendship.

A third Greek word for love does not appear in the New Testament. It is *eros,* and it describes sexual love, both in its legitimate and its illegitimate forms. From this word we derive our word *"erotic"* (which deals with the stimulation of sexual desires).

BIBLE USAGE

The word *agape* occurs in its various forms more than 250 times in the New Testament. In many cases it describes God's love for Jesus Christ or for us. In the account of Christ's baptism, the Father spoke from heaven and called Jesus, "My beloved Son" (Matt. 3:17). The same confirmation came when Christ's glory shone through on the Mount of Transfiguration (17:5). In the Parable of the Vineyard Owner, Jesus is portrayed as the beloved Son (Luke 20:13).

When asked the core of all commandments, Jesus Christ declared that it was unqualified love to God and to one's neighbor (Matt. 22:36-40, which He took from Deut. 6:4-5). Such unqualified love for God will certainly be rewarded. In fact, no genuine sacrifice for God ever goes unrewarded (Matt. 10:41-42). This love also extends to one's enemies, in the embrace of Christ (5:43-48).

Not only is this love used to describe our love toward God and His love for Christ, but it also portrays the love which God lavishes on Christians. As Jesus was God's beloved Son, so we too are God's beloved (Rom. 1:7). This is seen in His sovereign act of choosing us to be saved (Eph. 1:4-6; Col. 3:12).

In some cases the love of God is equated with salvation. Paul spoke of God's love being poured out in our lives (Rom. 5:5). Because God loves us, we shall never be separated from Him (8:35).

Just as God's essential nature is love (John 3:16; 1 John 4:8), so good Christians are essentially lovers. Such sacrificial love is a badge of discipleship (John 13:34-35). It is an essential part of Christian living (1 John 3:16, 23; 4:21).

Just as *agape* love is seen in Scripture, so is *phileo* (filial) love revealed in the Word of God. This describes the love of Christians for the Lord, as one sees in the post-Resurrection encounter between Peter and the Lord Jesus (John 21:15). Lest one be too hard on Peter for using the milder word for love Paul also employed it in describing love for God (1 Cor. 16:22).

Usually this love is used to describe the love of friends. In the story of Lazarus' death and resuscitation, this word is employed to describe the love of Jesus for Lazarus (John 11:3, 36). Thus *phileo* is not necessarily a lesser kind of love, for it is attributed to Jesus Himself.

This same root word is combined with *adelphos* (brother) to mean "brotherly love." It is the mark of Christian commitment to others (Rom. 12:10). Paul claimed that this love was inborn in the new birth (1 Thes. 4:9). The writer of Hebrews also enjoined Christians to brotherly love (Heb. 13:1), as did Peter in his first epistle (1 Peter 1:22).

Whether one looks at *agape* or *phileo,* love is linked inextricably to the Lord. It is He who models it in the Trinity. He also engenders love in our lives. When we display it, He is glorified.

ILLUSTRATIONS

Love in the New Testament has two main aspects. First, it often refers to human love. When writing of this, Oliver Cromwell's chaplain, Stephen Charnock (1628-80), delcared: "What is in the Word a law of precept, is in the heart a law of love."

While serving a church on the south coast of England, I met a delightful elderly couple. Their story was one of love. She had been converted from the life of a crude, profane street vendor. As soon as she turned to Christ, her husband turned into a beast and started to beat her regularly. Still this Christian lady persisted, and a dozen years afterward her husband was saved. When I knew them, they were models of devotion to the Lord and each other.

Puritan Thomas Watson declared: "Love is the queen of graces. It outshines the others as the sun the . . . planets." To which idea the medieval missionary Raymond Lull (about 1232-1316) commented: "He who loves not, lives not."

A story is often told of the aged Apostle John. He no longer could walk, and thus was carried into the assembly of believers each Lord's Day. He would raise his head and give the believers this injunction: "Beloved, love one another." When one studies John's epistles, this little story becomes believable.

An early critical commentator on the Christian church was Statius Caecilius, who said of believers: "They know one another by secret marks and signs, and they love one another almost before they know one another."

When Martin Luther's German Testament was being printed, the printer's daughter was playing in her father's shop. She picked up scraps of paper and tried to read them. One such shred contained the line: "For God so loved the world, that He gave. . . . "

Rushing to her mother the small child asked: "Mother, what did God give us?"

Never having read a Testament, the mother was baffled and exclaimed: "I do not know what God gave, but if He loves us enough to give anything, He surely will give us the very best." Through reading the Scripture that mother and many since have learned that God gave His uniquely begotten Son.

On the subject of love, the great missionary pioneer and poet Amy Carmichael (1867-1951) comforted us with these words: "There is no need to plead that the love of God shall fill our hearts as though He were unwilling to fill us. . . . [His] love is pressing round us on all sides like air. Cease to resist, and instantly love takes possession."

LUST

MEANING

The Greek word translated "lust" or "sinful desires" is *epithumia*. It comes from two Greek words, *epi* (upon) and *thumia* (sacrifice). Seemingly it means that something is sacrificed on the altar of our desire or passion. Perhaps it is our spiritual strength which is thus offered up.

In ancient Greek it originally meant evil desire. This was the meaning Plato attached to it. In fact, Plato felt that anything which was connected with this world or with physical pleasure was evil. (Thus we have our word "platonic" for a relationship which is not physical but spiritual.)

The Stoics considered *epithumia* to be an evil passion. They connected it with such evils as fear, inordinate pleasure, and pain. To them lust was one of the main causes of sin in the world. Out of it arose anxiety and greed. The uniform interpretation of this word is negative; it never speaks of a positive response.

BIBLE USAGE

The word *epithumia* is best described by the company it keeps in the Scriptures. These physical desires are forbidden, because they are evil. According to James, lust is linked in a chain of destruction with sin and death (James 1:14-15). Peter portrayed lust as the single evil which Christians must escape, and the spiritual life of Christ is the means of that escape (2 Peter 1:4).

When Paul wrote the Colossians, he too struck out at lust. According to the apostle, lust was part of a Christian's past, which he had overcome through the Lord's strength (Col. 3:5).

In the Thessalonian letter Paul allied lust with sexual perversion. Such lust should be rejected by every Christian (1 Thes. 4:4-7). The Holy Spirit would sanctify the body, and thus set it free from such lusts (5:19, 23).

Lust is also a feeling, an emotion. When one becomes a Christian, he is to crucify these lustful feelings with Christ (Gal. 5:24). Again, the Apostle Peter put these lusts in the past (1 Peter 4:3). They are part of the pagan practices which the Christian should discard at conversion (1:14; 4:2). Jesus tied these lusts to the devil himself, who is the father of such sinful desires (John 8:44).

Paul often referred to lust as being foolish. He warned rich people to beware of such foolish lusts (1 Tim. 6:9). Later Paul again warned of the danger of desires which are sinful, and he urged young Timothy to flee from them (2 Tim. 2:22; 4:3).

Such evil desires are deceptive. To the Romans Paul wrote that God allowed people to be deceived by their own lusts (Rom. 1:24, 26, 28; 6:12). This same principle was presented in Paul's Ephesian letter (Eph. 4:22).

At least three sources of lust are mentioned in the Bible. First, the human body is prone to such perversion. Before becoming Christians such lusts may have governed our lives (Eph. 2:3). John made a great deal of this in his first letter (1 John 2:16-17). Peter likewise traced the trouble back to the enemy within one's own body (1 Peter 2:11; 2 Peter 2:18).

Another source of lustful thoughts and desires is the whole world system. The secular environment in which we live presses in on us and can shape our desires. These desires may become drives which must be satisfied (Titus 2:12). Paul also warned about these in the summation of his Roman epistle (Rom. 13:14). Christians were warned to give no place to the thinking of this world (12:1-2).

As already mentioned, Jesus Christ considered Satan to be a source of such desires. In fact, the old liar and murderer was also an arsonist who set afire the lusts of this world (John 8:44). But there is no reason at all for a Christian to be beaten by these lustful, sinful desires.

ILLUSTRATIONS

In warning against these evil desires, the old pulpit master J.H. Jowett (1864-1923) warned: "An entire army of unclean forces are antagonistic to the exalted realm of the spirit." Every Christian knows experientially the truth of Jowett's assertion.

A saintly missionary once discussed with me the matter of lust, sexual desire. Candidly he admitted his temptations. When I asked him how he coped with these onslaughts, the missionary smiled and said: "Every time I am tempted by lust, I simply sit down and take out a long sheet of paper. Then I write down all I would lose if I succumbed to that temptation. My family, children, ministry, reputation, spiritual vigor, and purity would all be gone if I gave in." Then he added: "By the time my list is complete, I have long since forgotten about the supposed pleasures of my lust."

On another occasion I was visiting a godly Christian man in the hospital. He asked his wife and mine to take a walk. When we were alone, he asked: "Pastor, how can I deal with lust?" This older brother, who had lived for the Lord for many years, was still troubled by lust. Together we prayed, to combat Satan on that front.

The devastating effects of lust on Christian workers is now emerging. Increasing numbers of pastors and assistant pastors are passing out of the ministry because of lust. Fortunately, a few of them are being restored, but their number is pitifully small. This whole problem is the premise of an excellent book by Don Baker, *Beyond Forgiveness* (Portland: Multnomah, 1984).

The Bible often reinforces the importance of avoiding lust. In fact, the pattern persists in both the Old and New Testaments. For instance, when Eve was tempted to eat the fruit in Eden, she first saw it as food which would still the rumbling of her tummy (Gen. 3:6). This reminds one of the temptation of the Lord Jesus, when Satan suggested that stones could be made into bread to break His fast (Matt. 4:3). In John's first epistle this is called "the lust of the flesh" (1 John 2:16). How often our basic desire for food or drink is the trap of temptation, as one sees in an alcoholic.

In the second place, Eve noticed that the fruit looked good (Gen. 3:6). The same temptation was turned on Christ, when Satan showed Him the world's kingdoms (Matt. 4:9). This temptation is titled "the lust of the eyes" by the Apostle John (1 John 2:16). How many men are lured into trouble by a deliciously delightful woman in the office or at a party, who looks so good that she must be right.

Finally, Eve was suckered into sin by a fruit which could make her and her husband wise (Gen. 3:6). Jesus was tempted to prove the providence of God by casting Himself down and thus demonstrating divine power (Matt. 4:6). John called this the pride of life (1 John 2:16).

MAKE

MEANING

The Greek word which is translated with the verb, "to make," is *poeo*. It is reflected in such English words as *"poem," "poetry,"* and *"poet,"* all of which speak of the creative work of human beings. The word in Greek means "to make" in its simplest form, but it also means "to create," "to accomplish something," "to produce fruit from a tree," and "to perform miracles."

From the earliest times, this word was identified with creative activity. The Stoics attributed this creativity to deities, and regarded Zeus as the creator of the Bronze Age. God was regarded as Creator of the human body.

In the Septuagint Greek Old Testament this word appears no fewer than 3,000 times. Often it was used in connection with God's creative work. Likewise it spoke of God's miraculous works in history.

BIBLE USAGE

In the New Testament this word in its various forms appears about 370 times. It is often identified with creation or miraculous works. In fact, it is usually used to describe distinctively divine works.

For instance, Christ taught that He and the Father made their home in each believer (John 14:23). In the Book of Revelation this is even more clearly seen. The glorified Lord is the One who made the church into a kingdom of priests (Rev. 1:6; 5:10). Christ also promised to make each spiritual survivor a pillar in the heavenly temple (3:12). Here is true spiritual creation.

The same verb is used to describe the call and commission of Christ's disciples. "Follow Me," Jesus said, "and I will make you become fishers of men" (Mark 1:17). The Pharisees found this practice of making disciples (John 4:1) to be profoundly disturbing. The idea is this: Jesus actually made common men into uncommon disciples.

In Christ's earthly life His main ministry was making a sacrifice for our sins (Heb. 1:3). This was a unique offering, which never required repetition (7:27). In another statement, Jesus came to "do" the will of God the Father, and this verb is the same *poieo* (10:7, 9).

Another aspect of Christ's work on earth was in the realm of the miraculous. These miracles bore witness to His life, despite the determination of the Jews to crucify Him (Acts 10:39). Peter asserted that Jesus never did any sin or spoke any guile (1 Peter 2:22).

The New Testament also lays heavy weight on the works of Christ's disciples. From the first, they did miracles in God's power (Mark 6:30). Peter and John did a miracle of healing in the name of Jesus Christ (Acts 3:12). In the same name Stephen constantly performed miracles before the people (6:8). In Samaria Philip also did miracles in the name of Christ (8:6). Likewise the Apostle Paul performed miracles of healing (14:11). In each of these cases the word used to describe the performing or doing of a miracle is our verb *poieo*.

Not only did the apostles and disciples "do" (*poieo*) miracles, but they also "did" (*poieo*) the will of God. The Pharisees gave verbal assent to the will of God, but they did not do it (Matt. 23:3). This relegated them to the ranks of hypocrites.

The Apostle Paul said that people who know the will of God and fail to do it are worthy of death (Rom. 1:32). Such hypocritical behavior is destined to be punished by the Lord (2:3). This is the basis of divine judgment in the resurrection (John 5:29).

On the other hand, true Christians do the will of God. They do God's will from their hearts (Eph. 6:6), because they look to Jesus for eternal reward. Doing the will of God will always be rewarded, though we must often wait for that reward (Heb. 10:36). Because we love the Lord, we do His commandments (1 John 5:2).

This little Greek word, "to make" or "to do," is full of meaning. It embraces the entire Creation of God, and it also describes the work of Christ on earth in making a means of salvation. By the same token it presents the apostles' performance of miracles and obedience. All that we "do in word or deed" is for the glory of God (Col. 3:17, 23).

ILLUSTRATIONS

In illustrating this simple word, we concentrate on the creative activity of God. Without God there would be no Creation, since He is the source of all creativity in our world. He alone is the One who creates something from nothing.

On another level, the late President of Fuller Theological Seminary, Dr. Edward Carnell (1919-67), explained Creation clearly: "God created the world for reasons that are sufficient unto Himself. It is not necessary that we be told these reasons. As long as we know that God loves us, we have a base for hope. And when we have hope, all else can be borne in patience."

"God is the creative force who made the universe by the power of His speech," insisted Leonard Mitchell. To which the famous British Bible expositor, Graham Scroggie (1877-1958) added: "The Almighty is working on a great scale, and will not be hustled by our peevish impetuosity."

Another British evangelical, William Temple (1881-1944), an Archbishop of Canterbury, said, "The spiritual interest in the doctrine of Creation lies solely in the assertion of the dependence of all existence upon the will of God."

Though he was not an evangelical Protestant but a Roman Catholic Bishop, Fulton J. Sheen likewise extolled the creative work of God, when he said: "Why did God make the universe? God is good, and being good He could not, as it were, contain Himself; consequently, He told the secret of His goodness to nothingness and that was Creation." This theology is questionable, but the idea is absolutely enchanting.

During the middle part of our century creationists combated evolutionists on a regular basis. None was more outspoken in this conflict than Merrill C. Tenney, former Dean of Wheaton Graduate School of Theology. On Creation Dr. Tenney said: "To assert that a world as intricate as ours emerged from chaos by chance is about as sensible as to claim that Shakespeare's dramas were composed by rioting monkeys in a print shop."

Professor David Barr responded powerfully to the "God is Dead" theology of the '60s: "A dead God is the creation of men," he allowed, "but a living God is the Creator of man."

MAN

MEANING

The Greek word for "man," *anthropos,* is fairly familiar to most English readers. This word is reflected in such terms as *"anthropology"* (the study of man in his cultural setting), *"anthropoid"* (a manlike animal, such as an ape), and *"anthropomorphism"* (the attributing of manlike qualities to God, such as the "hand" of God).

Socrates used *anthropos* to describe human beings in general. In Homer's writings it drew the distinction between humans and beasts or gods, but it also distinguished between freemen and slaves. Later on the Greek idea of a three-part being—mind, soul, and body—developed.

In the Septuagint Greek Old Testament, this word was used to translate "Adam." It became a generic term for all human beings, male or female. The emphasis in the Old Testament fell on the mortality and the transitory nature of man's life (Ps. 90).

BIBLE USAGE

In the New Testament the word *anthropos* appears 550 times. Usually it is a general term for humanity. Its main role is to distinguish human beings from other forms of life.

Man is separated from the animal and plant world. Jesus insisted that service to man was far more important than aid to any animal (Matt. 12:12). Paul put forward this same line of reasoning in his presentation of the Resurrection (1 Cor. 15:39).

Similarly, there is a vast difference between humans and angels, for they represent two different kinds of life. Paul cited salvation here on earth (1 Cor. 4:9). In his statement of divine love, Paul again drew a sharp distinction between men and angels (13:1).

Though Jesus Christ was God incarnate and thus was in a very real sense man, He was not in the same class as other mortals. Paul traced his message back to Christ Himself, and not to mere man (Gal. 1:12). By the same token Paul served the Lord in his ministry and no mere human master (Eph. 6:7).

The Scriptures also sharply separate man from God, which flew in the face of contemporary Greek mythology. The Greek gods were little more than supermen. In the Bible there is frequent reference to this chasm between God and man (Matt. 10:32). Even in corrupt Judaism there was a recognition of this unbridgeable gap between God and man (John 10:33). For this reason the apostles affirmed that they must obey God rather than men (Acts 5:29).

The Apostle Paul made much of the "old man" and the "new man." The old man followed the impulses of unconverted humanity. The old man could never keep the Law of God (Rom. 2:1-3). The old man had to be "crucified," put to death, because he would never do the will of God. Thus Paul identified the old man with the crucified Christ (6:6). That old man was bound by the shackles of sin and just could not get free on his own (Eph. 4:22). In short, the old man was part of Adam's dying race (Rom. 5:11-12; 1 Cor. 15:21-23).

On the other hand the new man responds to spiritual stimulus. He has been born again, literally re-created, and thus the old life is gone (2 Cor. 5:17). Such believers share in the glory of Christ's resurrection (Rom. 6:6). As a Christian lays aside his old man, he puts on the new man (Col. 3:9-10). This new man knows no distinction between people, so there is a glorious unity among all such believers

274 (3:11).

The model of this new man is none other than Jesus Christ. He was frequently identified with humanity as the Son of man (Mark 10:45). He is simply called a Man in other places (Phil. 2:7; 1 Tim. 2:5). In the form of a man, Jesus fulfilled all God's Law and set us free from bondage (Rom. 8:2-3). As a man He took the form of a slave and carried God's plan to its ultimate conclusion, crucifixion (Phil. 2:8). Because He shared all our temptations, He can represent us faithfully before the throne of God (Heb. 4:15-16). Because God came to earth in Christ, we are represented in heaven by Him.

ILLUSTRATIONS

The Bible presents a two-sided picture of man. Because of Adam's sin, man is flawed fatally. As Augustine, a brilliant bishop of Hippo (354-430), lamented: "Man is a good thing spoiled."

A more down-to-earth description of man's dilemma was formulated by O. Donald Olsen, who said: "Mr. Average North American is typed as the installment buyer who is busy buying things he doesn't want, with money he doesn't have, to impress people he doesn't like." In other words, he is dominated by the lust of the flesh, the lust of the eye, and the pride of life.

The Christian philosopher and mathematician, Blaise Pascal (1623-62), wrote many thought-provoking books. On the subject of man he said: "What a chimera [fabled monster], then, is man! What a novelty! What a monster, what a chaos, what a contradiction, what a prodigy! Judge of all things, feeble worm of the earth, depository of truth, a sink of uncertainty and error, the glory and the shame of the universe."

Despite the disaster of the Fall, God makes man into an instrument of His glory. The Methodist minister and author of the classic on prayer, E.M. Bounds (1835-1913), set down the priority of people when he wrote: "The church is looking for better methods; God is looking for better men."

Lettie Cowman concluded: "The worker is far more important to our Lord than the work." In the same vein, Marge Ford, a valued colleague of mine, once said: "God is far more interested in what we are than He is in what we do."

A lesser-known writer, Ralph Bronkema, focused on the re-creation of man in Christ when he wrote:"Christianity is true humanity." In the same connection the poet Robert Browning (1812-89) penned this line: "Love, hope, fear, faith—these make humanity" (Paraclesus).

The famous British statesman author, Edmund Burke (1729-97), summarized the significance of man in God and wrote: "There is but one law for all, namely, that law which governs all law, the law of our Creator, the law of humanity, justice, equity."

That people can never reach their full potential without Christ is seen throughout the Scriptures. Unreconstructed humanity is inhumane. Only Christ can bring out the blurred image of God in man. As Charles E. Garman wrote: "Only as men believe in God can they believe in humanity."

MARRY, MARRIAGE

MEANING

The Greek word which is translated "to marry" is *gameo*, and the word for a "marriage" is *gamos*. This root word is seen in such English words as "mono*gamy*" (marriage to one), "bi*gamy*" (marriage to two people at the same time), and "poly*gamy*" (marriage to many at the same time).

In ancient Greece the common practice was monogamy. In the writings of Homer, the heroes were all monogamous; they were "one-women men." Only later, at the end of the golden era of Greek history, did this pattern of marriage become blurred. In the Hellenic period there was an increase in divorce, adultery, and prostitution. This coincided with a decline in Greece's cultural and political virility.

In the Septuagint Greek Old Testament this word always stands for monogamy, as God's standard of right. However, marriage was usually seen through the man's eyes. It was the man who married the woman. This was often accomplished by parental plans rather than by romantic choices. Also, neither the Old nor the New Testament gives any guidance for the formulation of a wedding ceremony.

BIBLE USAGE

In all its forms, the word for marriage occurs about 45 times in the New Testament. Marriage is a command of God, and it was instituted within the framework of Creation (Gen. 2:24). This early precedent was cited in the New Testament by the Lord (Matt. 19:4-5; Mark 10:6-8). The Apostle Paul took the subject one step further to use this statement as a basis for Christian ethics (1 Cor. 6:16-20). In another place Paul compared a Christian marriage to the relationship between Christ and His church (Eph. 5:31-32). Marriage is a fundamental teaching of the Scriptures.

For a Christian, marriage is also sharing. There is a sharing of commitment in marriage (1 Cor. 7:3). This is seen in the sacrifice of oneself for one's partner, as Christ sacrificed Himself for the church (Eph. 5:21-31). As the Apostle Peter put it, Christian spouses are joint heirs of the grace of God (1 Peter 3:7).

Because of the sanctity of marriage, adultery is banned categorically. Christ drew attention to this in the Sermon on the Mount (Matt. 5:27), and the writer of Hebrews underlined the principle (Heb. 13:4). The Scriptures summon marriage partners to strict, lifelong chastity.

Building on the teaching of the Old Testament, that God hates divorce (Mal. 2:16), Christ also decried divorce (Matt. 5:31-32). In the statements of Christ only one sin, adultery, severs the marriage bond (19:9). Paul seemed to allow also incompatibility (1 Cor. 7:8-16).

Those who opposed Jesus tried to trip Him up with hard questions about marriage. One such query dealt with marriage after the resurrection. The Pharisees, who believed in the resurrection, asked about a much-widowed woman who married seven brothers. Jesus responded that in the resurrection there will be no marriage, and our relations will be like those of the angels (Matt. 22:23-33).

Though wedding ceremonies as we now know them were unknown, there were wedding feasts in Bible times. It was at such a feast, in Cana of Galilee, that Jesus performed His first miracle (John 2:1-11). The coming of Christ to receive His church, His bride, is also compared to a wedding feast in Matthew's Gospel (Matt. 22:1-11; 25:1-13). In fact, this picture is used to describe the heavenly homecoming of Christ's church (Rev. 19:7).

Not only is the marriage relationship esteemed in Scripture, but it is used as a frequent picture of other close relationships. In Romans Paul used marriage to demonstrate the divine rejection of Israel and the reception of believing Gentiles (Rom. 9:25; Hosea 2:23). For the Corinthians Paul used marriage to paint a picture of God's love for His people (2 Cor. 11:2). The most familiar comparison is that of Christ's bride, the church, with a human bride (Eph. 5:22-32). So highly does God prize the marriage relationship, that He uses it to describe His love for the church.

ILLUSTRATIONS

Both secular and sacred authors make much of marriage. According to Ambrose Bierce (1842-1914), an American author: "Marriage [is] a community consisting of a master, a mistress, and two slaves—making in all two."

On a lighter note, Bill Lawrence said: "The honeymoon is over when he phones that he'll be late for supper—and she has already left a note that it's in the refrigerator."

"Marriage is a process," according to Francis Rodman, "by which a grocer acquired an account the florist had." Another wit remarked: "Marriage is a good deal like taking a bath—not so hot once you get accustomed to it."

According to Beverly Nichols, "Marriage [is] a book of which the first chapter is written in poetry and the remaining chapters in prose."

Though secular writers make much levity of marriage, Christians see in it a wonderful gift of God's grace. Ruth Graham, wife of evangelist Billy Graham, said: "The best advice I can give to unmarried girls is to marry someone you don't mind adjusting to. God tailors the wife to fit the husband, not the husband to fit the wife." Interestingly, Ruth Graham planned on missionary service in China, but she has spent her life as wife of a worldwide evangelist.

Robert Quillen emphasized the spiritual aspect of marriage when he commented: "A happy marriage is the union of two good forgivers." Putting it more plainly, someone gave us this advice: "Marriage is not a fifty-fifty proposition. It demands 100 percent from both partners."

Though they are not known for practical advice, many Puritan writers commented meaningfully on marriage. For instance, the historian Thomas Fuller (1608-61) suggested to young men: "Choose a wife rather by your ear than your eye."

In Matthew Henry's Commentary on Genesis 2:24 is found this remarkably moving passage concerning marriage: "The woman . . . was not made out of his head to rule over him, nor out of his feet to be trampled upon by him, but out of his side to be equal with him, under his arm to be protected, and near his heart to be beloved" (*Matthew Henry's Commentary on the Whole Bible* [McLean, Virginia: MacDonald Publishing Company, originally published 1706], I, p. 20).

Another Puritan writer, Thomas Adams (died 1653), framed the sentence: "As God by Creation made two out of one, so again by marriage He made one out of two." It is small wonder that someone described Thomas Adams as "the prose Shakespeare of Puritan theologians."

MARTYR (See: *Witness*.)   **277**

MEDIATOR

MEANING

The Greek word for "mediator" is *mesites*. It is based on the word *mesos* (in the middle). Literally, it means one who stands in the middle or presents a middle way. The Greek word is reflected in such English words as "*meso*-America" (Central America), "*mesial*" (the middle line of a body), and "*mes*encephalon" (the middle division of the brain). In each case, the idea is that of something or someone being in the middle.

Originally in Greek literature the word *mesites* referred to a middle man in business. In Homer's writings it also spoke of a no-man's land between two enemies. Later it came to refer to a peacemaker or an umpire in an athletic contest. In some cases it also referred to a guarantor or arbiter in a civil transaction. Only in the late Hellenistic period did it refer to gods as go-betweens.

In the Septuagint Greek Old Testament there is heavy emphasis on the role of a mediator. Despite the absence of the term in the Greek Old Testament, the idea is everywhere present. God is holy and thus unapproachable by human beings. Therefore, a mediator is required, and he must fulfill two functions. First, he must intercede for sinful people. Second, he must bring the sacrifice. Jesus Christ is thus the perfect Mediator.

BIBLE USAGE

There are only six references to a mediator in the New Testament. The most familiar of these is in Paul's first letter to Timothy. After stating the desire of God, that all should come to salvation, Paul introduced the means of that saving work. He is Jesus Christ, the sole Mediator between God and man (1 Tim. 2:5). This is also one of the clearest statements concerning the deity and humanity of Christ. In this connection Christ is superior to the sacrifices of animals on Jewish altars.

A second reference to the Mediator is in the Book of Galatians. Here the teaching is this: the Law of Moses mediated God's Word to the Israelites and prepared them for the coming of Messiah. Jesus came, however, as the Mediator between God and the whole human race (Gal. 3:19-21). Thus the only true Mediator is not a Law carved in stone, but the Living Word, the Lord Jesus Christ. Here Christ the Mediator stands out in superiority over the Law of Moses.

The Book of Hebrews has as its theme the superiority of Christ. Therefore it is small wonder that the writer capitalizes on the mediatorship of the Master. In proof of the truth of His assertions, God provided "an oath" or "mediator" (Heb. 6:17). In comparison with the Law of Moses, Jesus Christ is the Mediator of a far superior covenant (8:6). By this New Covenant, of which Christ is the Mediator, there is atonement for all the sins of all time (9:15). Not even the sacrifice of righteous Abel can compare to the mediation provided through the sacrifice of Jesus Christ, God's Son (12:24). In the Book of Hebrews Jesus Christ stands out as a superior Mediator over the Mosaic system of sacrifice. In fact, the sacrifice of animals was worthless after the Lamb of God was slain.

Through the mediatorship of Christ we can be admitted into salvation. He is the only Way to God (John 14:6). By the same Mediator the entire world was brought into being, and by Him it holds together (1:3; Col. 1:16). He too is the Mediator who gives us an absolutely reliable revelation concerning God the Father (John 1:18). Now in His ascended role, Jesus Christ is our great High Priest, the Mediator who is constantly calling to God on our behalf (Heb. 4:14-16; 7:25). In fact, we could never approach God at all, if it were not for our Mediator, God's Son.

ILLUSTRATIONS

Christians never cease praising God for their Mediator, Jesus Christ. Dr. L. Nelson Bell (1894-1973), missionary, statesman-doctor, and editor, said: "In our scientific age there are thousands living who owe their lives to blood transfusions. By analogy, it can be reverently said that, in a mystical sense, the Son of God is the great universal Donor, giving new life to the sinner who trusts His shed blood for cleansing."

Along the same lines, Dr. Bell's son-in-law, Billy Graham, said: "I'm going to heaven and I believe I'm going by the blood of Christ. That's not popular preaching, but I'll tell you it's all the way through the Bible and I may be the last fellow on earth who preaches it, but I'm going to preach it because it's the only way we're going to get there."

A modern apologist for the Christian faith, Os Guinness, also pointed to the sufficiency of Christ's mediation when he wrote: "At the supreme moment of His dying Jesus so identified Himself with men and the depths of their predicament and agony that no man can now sink so low that God has not gone lower." This is true mediation by identification.

Another popular preacher, L.E. Maxwell, the late founder and principal of Prairie Bible Institute in Canada, loved to talk of the Cross of Christ: "When I was saved, I accepted death as my only deliverance. Christ died in my place. I was indeed a dead man but for Christ. When I accepted Christ's death for my sin, I could not avoid accepting my own death to sin. I am committed to the Cross. My only logical standing is one of death. I have been 'born crucified.' "

Don Richardson was a missionary with the Regions Beyond Missionary union in Irian Jaya (West Irian). While there he discovered a wonderful example of a mediator. When two warring tribes could not settle their strife without bloodshed, one man gave his only son to the enemies. This conveyed a message: "If a man would actually give his own son to his enemies, that man could be trusted" (Don Richardson, *Peace Child* [Glendale, California: Regal Books, 1974], p. 206). That "peace child" was an unwitting but totally effective mediator between the two bloodthirsty tribes. Peace broke out immediately.

Jesus Christ performed perfectly the role of the Mediator. Someone described this in a word picture. When Christ was stretched out on the cross, He symbolized mediation. He was suspended between the heaven of God's holiness and the earth of man's sinfulness. His arms were spread out to receive the most diverse of people.

George Dana Boardman (1828-1903), a famous Baptist missionary to Burma, declared: "The Cross is the only ladder high enough to touch the threshold of heaven." As Jesuit court preacher Louis Bourdaloue (1632-1704) said: "In the Cross of Christ excess in men is met by excess in God; excess of evil is mastered by excess of love." With the hymn-writer one cries; "Hallelujah, what a Saviour!"

MERCY

MEANING

The Greek word which is translated "mercy" is *eleas*. It means "compassion," "pity," and "mercy." This word is contained in the liturgical prayer for mercy, "Kyrie elieson" (literally, "Lord, have mercy"). There is also a quaint old word used to describe charitable institutions, which are called "*ele*emosynary" institutions.

One New Testament scholar defined "mercy" as "the emotion roused by contact with an affliction which comes undeservedly on someone else" (Colin Brown, editor, *The New International Dictionary of New Testament Theology*, [Grand Rapids: Zondervan, 1976], II, p. 594).

This statement is supported by a study of Greek literature. Aristotle allowed that tragedy arouses pity, or mercy. Plutarch used the word to end a lawyer's speech for the defense, in which he asked for mercy from the court. Homer said the word embraced compassion and being sorry for the injured person.

BIBLE USAGE

The New Testament speaks of two sources of mercy. The first is logically the mercy of God. Part of Christ's instruction on prayer included a call for mercy (Luke 18:13). This was especially seen in the conversation between Jesus and blind Bartimaeus at Jericho (Mark 10:47-48).

When a Canaanite woman called on Jesus to release her demon-possessed daughter, she likewise pleaded for the mercy of the Lord (Matt. 15:22). In another place a sad father asked the Lord to show mercy toward his demon-possessed son (17:15).

But not just the sick and possessed were subjects of the Lord's mercy. When Mary sang her praises of the Lord's goodness she repeatedly thanked Him for His mercy toward her. In His mercy He stooped to her humble state (Luke 1:48).

Zacharias struck the same note when he sang a hymn at the birth of John the Baptist. Here too the focus of praise was the mercy of God (Luke 1:72). This was seen as part of God's covenant relationship with Israel.

But in no other connection is the mercy of God seen more clearly than in the sphere of salvation. Paul asserted the sovereignty of God in showing mercy (Rom. 9:15-18). In difficult situations Paul spoke of himself as a recipient of God's mercy (1 Cor. 7:25). This is particularly emphasized in the Pastoral Epistles, where Paul praised God for His abundant mercy in saving such a sinner as Saul of Tarsus (1 Tim. 1:13-16). In fact, Paul saw the mercy of God in all of salvation (Titus 3:5). Since we deserve nothing but hell, all salvation is sent by God's mercy.

Not only is God's mercy seen in Scripture. Christians are also commanded to show mercy. Jesus emphasized this in the Sermon on the Mount. He pronounced a special blessing on merciful people. They will receive mercy as they dispense it (Matt. 5:7).

This truth is taught in Christ's parables. When one servant was unmerciful toward a fellow servant, he came under the verbal wrath of his lord (18:33). In fact, Christ asserted that those who show no mercy will be shown no mercy (18:35). Mercy and forgiveness are closely connected in the Bible.

The Book of Acts commends mercy as a Christian virtue. When Dorcas passed away, the church at Joppa mourned greatly. They remembered her multiplied mercies toward other Christians (Acts 9:36). Even a Roman army officer, Cornelius, was commended in the Scriptures because he showed mercy toward the Jews (10:1-2).

Mercy is rooted in the nature of God, and it is seen wherever His hand moves. As a colleague of mine commented: "In mercy God withholds from us the judgment we deserve. In grace God gives to us the blessings we never deserve."

ILLUSTRATIONS

Mercy is everywhere to be seen in literature. Perhaps the most eloquent statement of mercy is found in William Shakespeare's (1564-1616) play, *The Merchant of Venice:* "The quality of mercy is not strain'd; / It droppeth as the gentle rain from heaven upon the place beneath: it is twice bless'd; / It blesseth him that gives and him that takes" (III, iv, 184).

Roland Bainton, a famous historian of the Reformation, wrote concerning the last words of Thomas Hooker (1586-1647), the founding father of Connecticut: "Gathered by his [Hooker's] bedside were his friends, who sought to comfort him, 'You are now going to receive your reward.' But the old Puritan turned and retorted, 'I go to receive mercy.'"

Speaking earlier of the same mercy, Thomas Hooker said: "Thy sorrows outbid thy heart, thy fears outbid thy sorrows, and thy thoughts go beyond thy fears; and yet here is the comfort of a poor soul: in all his misery and wretchedness, the mercy of the Lord outbids all these, whatsoever may, can, or shall befall thee."

Though he is best known for his spoof, *Don Quixote,* Miguel de Cervantes (1547-1616) had a more serious side. He wrote: "Among the attributes of God, although they are all equal, mercy shines with even more brilliancy than justice."

Perhaps the greatest American theologian ever was Jonathan Edwards (1745-1806). Of God's mercy he wrote: "You have reason to open your mouth in God's praises, both here and to all eternity, for His rich and sovereign mercy to you." This is an amazing statement to be spoken by a man best known for preaching about the wrath of God.

A famous American literary giant, Robert Frost (1875-1963), spoke of God's mercy: "Ultimately this is what you go before God for: you've had bad luck and good luck and all you really want in the end is mercy." Though we might quibble over his use of the word "luck," who would dispute his appeal to God's mercy?

Dr. Sherwood Wirt, former editor of *Decision* magazine, referred to mercy: "Mercy is unmerited favor from God Himself to an erring people who can do nothing to earn it except to hold out their hands."

None were more eloquent in their statement of sovereign mercy than the Puritans. "The mercies of God make a sinner proud, but a saint humble," according to Thomas Watson. He added: "Take heed of abusing this mercy of God. . . . To sin because mercy abounds, is the devil's logic. . . . He that sins because of God's mercy, shall have judgment without mercy." In another place Watson said: "Mercy is not for them that sin and fear not, but for them that fear and sin not."

MESSENGER (See: *Angel.*)
MIGHT (See: *Power.*)   **281**

MIND

MEANING

In the Greek New Testament are two terms which characterize different aspects of the mental process. The more common one is *nous,* which appears about 20 times in the writings of Paul. This word describes the ability to think, the understanding, the moral capabilities of human beings.

Early Greek writers were lavish in their praise of human reason. Plato called it the most excellent part of a human being, because it gave him the edge over lesser beings. Aristotle described reason as the power of thought. The Stoics believed that the whole world was ruled by a divine mind, a cosmic reason.

The other word for "mind" in the New Testament is *phronesis.* It comes from the verb *phroneo,* which means to "think," "judge," "set one's mind on something," or "have insight." This word is used to describe the activities of the *nous.* One sees it in such a phrase as "being tough-minded."

The ancient Greek writers often wrote about this word. Both Plato and Aristotle used it to describe discernment, insight, and judicious reasoning. In the Septuagint Greek Old Testament it was used to describe wisdom and intellectual cunning.

In short, the *nous* seems to be the ability to reason and think, while the *phronesis* appears to be the process of reasoning or thinking.

BIBLE USAGE

First we shall consider *nous,* which is limited largely to the writings of the Apostle Paul. It is seen to be the disposition of man, or his moral attitude. This is found in unsaved as well as saved people. When people do not accept God's enlightenment, their minds become depraved and darkened (Rom. 1:28). This is also called the understanding of man (Eph. 4:18) or a "fleshly mind" (Col. 2:18). Paul warned Timothy against people with depraved minds (1 Tim. 6:5). Such minds are darkened by sin and need God's enlightening.

When one is converted his mind is worked on by the Holy Spirit. It responds to the truth of God's Word and longs to obey Him (Rom. 7:22-23, 25). In a born-again person this mind becomes an instrument for understanding God's Word (Luke 24:45; Rev. 13:18; 17:9). Because of the presence of the Lord in our lives, our minds are kept at peace (Phil. 4:7). Thus, *nous* refers to the ability to think, understand, or comprehend.

The second word, *phronesis,* refers to the very act of thinking or understanding. It is the process of discerning or judging the merits of any movement (Acts 28:22). As we mature, this ability develops (1 Cor. 13:11). It is the assessment of a given situation or the appreciation of a person (Phil. 1:7; 4:10). This is the basic process of judging or discerning.

The word also speaks of our mind-set. Some people are "high-minded," and have an inflated view of themselves (Rom. 11:20; 12:3, 16). Unconverted people have an unregenerated mind-set and think within the framework of the world's standards (8:5-6). It is only after conversion that a person is capable of a Christian mind-set (Col. 3:1-2).

As a Christian, one is also able to achieve "like-mindedness," a unity of mind with other believers. Paul urged the Philippian Christians to be like-minded and thus preserve the unity of the church (Phil. 2:2; 4:2). He issued the same instruction to Corinthian Christians (2 Cor. 13:11). Even the Roman church received this instruction from the Apostle Paul (Rom. 12:16). This is a product of the lordship of

Christ in the church (15:5).

The mind is a gift of God and a by-product of the image of God conveyed to us at Creation. Under original sin our minds are clouded, so that we cannot comprehend spiritual truth. Try as we may, we are unable to see through spiritual realities. But when the Holy Spirit takes up His home in us, our minds are opened. We are then able to understand the truth of God, live according to the standards of God, and achieve real "like-mindedness" with the people of God. We have "the mind" (*phronesis*) of Christ (Phil. 2:5).

ILLUSTRATIONS

Frequent references to the human mind are found in literature. Often it was assumed that we are the masters of our fate. For instance, Horace (65-8 B.C.) reputedly said: "Rule your mind or it will rule you."

A contemporary of Horace, Virgil (70-19 B.C.), emphasized the importance of right thinking when he praised "a mind conscious of the right."

Writing less than a century after the birth of Jesus Christ, Juvenal (60-130) concluded concerning the mind: "Your prayer must be that you may have a sound mind in a sound body" (*Satires*, 356).

A similar assessment of the importance of the mind is found in *Paradise Lost*, the epic written by John Milton (1608-74): "The mind in its own place, and in itself can make a heaven of hell, a hell of heaven" (book 1, line 254).

One of the fathers of the Enlightenment was Immanuel Kant (1724-1804), who placed heavy emphasis on the ability of the human mind. Of it he said: "Two things fill the mind with increasing wonder and awe, the more often and the more intensely the mind of thought is drawn to them: the starry heavens above and the moral Law within me" (*Critique of Practical Reason*).

The glory of the human mind was praised by the poet Lord Byron (1788-1824) in his beautiful poem, "Sonnet on Chillon": "Eternal spirit of the Changeless mind! Brightest in dungeons, Liberty! thou art." According to him, a prisoner in body may be free in mind.

Christians see the true worth of the human mind as coming from its Creator, God. As Bible paraphraser J.B. Phillips said: "The modern intelligent mind, which has had its horizons widened in dozens of different ways, has got to be shocked afresh by the audacious central fact that as a sober matter of history, God became one of us." The incarnation of Christ is one of the greatest thoughts our mind can comprehend.

According to Richard Raines: "It does not take a great mind to be a Christian, but it takes all the mind a man has." This is seen in Katie Wilkinson's (1859-1928) great hymn:

> May the mind of Christ my Saviour
>   Live in me from day to day,
> By His love and power controlling
>   All I do and say.

James Jeans traced man's mind back to his Creator: "Mind no longer appears as an accidental intruder into the realm of matter. The universe begins to look more like a great thought than a great machine."

MIRACLE

MEANING

In the New Testament there are two Greek words which describe miracles. The first of these is *semeion* (literally "sign"). At first this word meant a visible sign which someone saw. For instance, when Constantine was embroiled in battle he saw the sign of a cross and the words, "In this sign conquer." This turned him to Christianity, and he granted toleration to the Christians in 313.

So first of all *semeion* meant a real or imagined visible sign. Later it came to mean the intervention of the deities in our world. This is the meaning which the Bible attaches to miracles, when God breaks into the natural world to accomplish some special feat.

A second word is *thauma* (which literally means "to wonder," or "to be astonished"). In this case the miracle is "in the eye of the beholder." The root word behind this Greek term is *thea* ("a vision"), or *theaomai* ("to contemplate"). It is seen in our English word "*thea*ter" (literally, "a place of seeing or viewing").

It is in this secondary meaning of astonishment that we see the root of a miracle. What causes one to be astonished or amazed is out of the ordinary. This was especially true in the Greek epic poems, which described many astonishing events. Thus *thauma* speaks of a "wonder," an amazing act, and thus a miracle.

BIBLE USAGE

The word for "miracle," *semeion*, occurs 77 times in the New Testament. The most notable miracle-worker in the New Testament is, of course, the Lord Jesus Himself. It is He who raised Jairus' daughter from the dead (Matt. 9:18-26). He too interrupted the funeral procession at Nain (Luke 7:11-17). Having raised a little girl and a young man, He also brought His friend Lazarus back to life (John 11:38-44).

Jesus also demonstrated His superiority over nature. As He slept in a boat, His disciples, who were seasoned seamen, wrestled with the wind and waves. When the Lord was awakened He simply spoke a few words and the storm was stilled (Matt. 8:26).

Immediately after this demonstration of dominance over nature, the disciples and their Lord arrived in the region of the Gadarenes. There they encountered two men who were hopelessly bound by demonic forces. Jesus freed them, thus demonstrating His dominance over demonic forces (8:28-34).

According to the Gospels, Jesus also demonstrated His superiority over man's need. When 5,000 men plus their families were fed by the Lord, He did it with only a little lad's lunch (John 6:5-13).

Not only did Jesus perform miracles, but His disciples also engaged in this ministry. On their first missionary journey, they were commissioned to do miracles in the name of the Lord (Matt. 10:7-8). This ministry was also evident in the Book of Acts (Acts 3:1-10; 8:7; 14:9-10).

By the same token, the second word, *thauma*, is also reflected in the New Testament. In fact it occurs 42 times. The miracles of Jesus moved people to amazement (John 9:30; Mark 5:30-42). People who saw the disciples work miracles were also amazed and astonished (Acts 3:11).

Not only did miracles produce this result, but also the teaching of Jesus caused people to be amazed (Matt. 7:28). Jesus exercised an authority which was totally foreign to the teachers of His time, and ours (Luke 4:22, 32).

As the apostles preached the Gospel, this too aroused amazement. The Holy Spirit enabled Galileans to communicate with people of many nations, a miracle that amazed all who were present (Acts 2:7). In fact, the Gospel continued to be a source of amazement to all who heard it (2 Thes. 1:10).

The two words which pertain to miracles are different in their emphasis. The actual miracle or sign is called *semeion*. When the word *thauma* is used, it describes the reaction of those who see a sign or a miracle, and this reaction is amazement.

ILLUSTRATIONS

In a real sense, one cannot divorce miracle from Deity. God alone is capable of overriding natural law. He can countermand the command of nature.

Many thoughtful people have tried to define miracles. The Bishop of Hippo, Augustine (354-430) argued: "Miracles are not contrary to nature, but only contrary to what we know about nature."

Another writer, E.R. Micklem, decided: "There are laws of the universe that are still waiting to be discovered by painful research. . . . I venture to suggest that if we are truly to understand the miracles of healing in the New Testament we shall have to discover the secret already at least partially revealed to those who make prayer the chief factor in their healing ministries."

As author of the book *Miracles,* C.S. Lewis (1898-1963) presented a powerful argument for the necessity of miracles. About them he said: "The divine art of miracle is not an art of suspending the pattern to which events conform, but of feeding new events into that pattern." Along the same line, the Dutch missionary speaker Corrie ten Boom said: "God raises the level of the possible."

In any case, miracles can only be understood in reference to the Lord. Profesor F.F. Bruce saw this and wrote: "We must first make up our minds about Christ before coming to conclusions about the miracles attributed to Him."

Nowhere is the miracle-working power of God seen more clearly than in conversion. Philip James Bailey brought out this point when he said: "Every believer is God's miracle."

The danger of rejecting miracles is spotlighted by Samuel Chadwick: "A ministry that is college-trained but not Spirit-filled works no miracles."

At my ordination service in 1960 this risk was held before me. When asked about God's ability to heal the sick, I gave a general, rather unenthusiastic assent. Then one pastor asked: "Does God heal instantaneously?" My confidence turned to profound embarrassment. One by one the ministerial brethren explained how God had "miraculously" healed the sick. What a profitable addition to my education that was.

An acceptable definition of "miracles" was given by Alan Richardson, a well-known British professor: "A miracle in the biblical sense is an event which happens in a manner contrary to the regularly observed processes of nature. . . . It may happen according to higher laws as yet but dimly discerned by scientists, and therefore must not be thought of as an irrational irruption of divine power into the orderly realm of nature."

MYSTERY

MEANING

The Greek word for "mystery," *musterion,* is similar to its English equivalent. This Greek word embraces such ideas as "a secret rite," "secret teaching," and "a divine mystery which is beyond human comprehension."

Its main use in Greek pertained to the so-called "mystery religions." They hid their secret teachings from most people, and revealed them only to those who had been initiated. Their teachings had very little, if any, basis in fact and were mainly mystical ideas. During the decline of the Roman Empire, there were many such Greek mystery religions. Their followers were a tolerated minority in the Roman Empire.

The biblical meaning of the word *musterion* is quite different from its secular definition. In the Scriptures the word "mystery" means those truths which are part of God's plan and can only be understood as He reveals them by His Spirit through His Word.

BIBLE USAGE

Jesus employed the word "mystery" just once according to the Gospel accounts. The disciples had been given ability to understand kingdom mysteries, which were hidden from human view and revealed only by the Spirit (Matt. 13:11; Mark 4:11; Luke 8:10).

The word "mystery" was used mainly by the Apostle Paul, who used it 21 times in his epistles. Salvation is a mystery, which God has revealed in Christ's coming. Paul reminded his readers that this mystery is now revealed even among the Gentiles. The content of this earth-shaking message is the indwelling Christ, who gives us a glorious hope (Col. 1:27). It is Christ's church which conveys this wonderful mystery to the whole world (2:2).

When pressing the priority of the Cross to the Corinthians, Paul reminded these rather weak Christians that God's eternal plan included the mystery of the Cross (1 Cor. 2:6-7). Further on in his letter to the Corinthians, Paul spoke of the mysteries which are revealed to those to whom God has given spiritual gifts (13:2; 14:2).

No book in the New Testament has more references to the mysteries of God than does Ephesians. In every instance, Paul points to some fact that is beyond the reach of unaided human reason. The climactic coming of Christ to earth is a mystery revealed (Eph. 1:9-10). By the same token Paul's Gospel message was a mystery until God revealed it (3:3, 9). Like all Bible mysteries, it had to be revealed directly by the Holy Spirit (3:5). Arising out of Paul's proclamation of the Gospel is the church of Jesus Christ. The bridal relationship between Christ and His church is likewise a mystery (5:32).

The Christian faith is nothing more or less than a mystery which can be known by revelation, not by rational discovery (1 Tim. 3:9). In the same book Paul introduced what appears to be either an early hymn or a confession of faith, perhaps a baptismal confession. Paul prefaced the confession with this phrase: "Great is the mystery of godliness" (3:16).

Many future events are unrevealed mysteries, whose details await the coming of Christ. One such event is the resurrection of the dead. Paul presented this truth by a phrase immortalized in Handel's *Messiah:* "Behold, I show you a mystery. We shall not all sleep, but we shall all be changed" (1 Cor. 15:51, KJV).

In the Greek New Testament, another reference to a mystery is connected with the coming of Christ. After the church has been taken out of the world, a period of terrible Tribulation will come. At that time "the mystery of lawlessness" will be revealed (2 Thes. 2:7).

When one reads Revelation the mystery of evil is further identified. It is compared to Babylon which plundered Israel (Rev. 17:5). The horror of this evil force is underlined in references to a prostitute and an ugly beast (17:5).

Mysteries in the Scripture fall into two categories. Some have already been revealed, and among these are the incarnation of Christ and the salvation of sinners. Others are yet to be seen, such as the general resurrection, the coming Antichrist, and the evil of the last day. It is comforting to realize that all the mysteries which bear on our salvation are already revealed to readers of Scripture.

ILLUSTRATIONS

For a long time the Bible was a hidden mystery. Few people could read it, and still fewer could afford to own one. The dominant denomination kept the Bible in a foreign language, Latin, safely out of the reach of common people. Thanks to William Tyndale (1494-1536) English people were given a Bible in their own language. Because of Martin Luther (1483-1546) Germans could read it. Jacques Lefevre d' Etaples (1455-1536) opened the Scriptures to the French. The mystery of biblical revelation was also revealed in the Reformation of the 16th century.

In fact, the entirety of divine revelation is now open to nearly everyone. The American religious leader and founder of the Disciples of Christ, Thomas Campbell (1763-1854), summarized it well: "Man cannot cover what God would reveal." How true this is of the Word of God.

Scottish theologian James Denney (1856-1917) caught the same vision when he wrote: "What Christ did had to be done, or we should never have had forgiveness; we should never have known God. But He, by taking on Himself our responsibilities and by dying our death, has so revealed God to us as to put forgiveness within our reach." The mystery of divine forgiveness is uncovered in Christ.

One of the most famous Victorian preachers of London was Joseph Parker (1830-1902), pastor of London's great City Temple. On the subject of revealed mysteries he said: "After reading the doctrines of Plato, Socrates, or Aristotle, we feel the specific difference between their words and .Christ's is the difference between an inquiry and revelation." Christ is the Revealer of God's mysteries.

One of the great writers and preachers of our day was A.W. Tozer. He not only edited The Alliance Witness, but also preached prophetically to the city of Chicago during the '50s. On the subject of mystery, he wrote: "Never forget that it is a privilege to wonder, to stand in delighted silence before the Supreme Mystery and whisper, 'O Lord God, Thou knowest!' " (The Root of the Righteous [Harrisburg: Christian Publications, 1955], p. 79)

Charles Wesley (1707-88) wrote it in hymn form:

'Tis mystery all! The immortal dies!
    Who can explore His strange design?
In vain the firstborn seraph tries
    To sound the depths of love divine!
'Tis mercy all! Let earth adore,
Let angel minds inquire no more.

NAME

MEANING

The word "name" is a translation of the Greek word *onoma*. This word is most commonly identified by its root *nom*, which is seen in the Latin word *nomen* and the English and German word "name." It is also reflected in such a combination word as "pseud*onym*" (a false name) or "hom*onym*" (a word or name which sounds the same), or "syn*onym*" (a word which means the same).

In ancient Greek culture, which was ruled by irrational demons, there were many animistic superstitions concerning names. For instance, some believed that to know a person's name was to hold some superstitious power over him.

Later on Greeks came to believe that the higher a god stood in the pantheon, the more names he had. Finally the Stoics combined all the gods into one, Zeus. Thus the name of the true God became identified with the power of that deity.

In the Septuagint Greek Old Testament the word *onoma* appears no fewer that 1,000 times. In Hebrew thinking a name is identified with character, and the name of God is the repository of God's power.

In the times of the patriarchs human names were still full of meaning. But by the dawn of New Testament times, names were much less indicative of character.

BIBLE USAGE

In the New Testament the word *onoma* and its verb form, *onimazo* (to name someone), appear 228 times. The most significant use of "name" is in relation to God or Jesus. In fact, when Jesus declared that discipleship was to be His disciples' main ministry, He commanded them to baptize in the name (singular) of the Father, the Son, and the Holy Spirit (Matt. 28:19). This is the clearest New Testament reference to the Trinity.

The name of God the Father seems to embody all that He is. His glory is identified with His name (John 12:23-28). His love is vested in the name (17:26). The perseverance of the saints is related to His name (17:12). Prayer is performed in His name (Matt. 6:9). The name of God is able to impute life to the spiritually dead (1 John 5:13). The focus of the proclamation of Christ was the name of God, His Father (John 17:26).

Just as the name of God is significant, so are the names of Christ. Before His birth Christ was the divine *Logos,* the Word of God (John 1:1-3). At His birth He was given the name of Jesus, to signify that He is the Saviour (Matt. 1:21). Because He is the God-Man, God come in the flesh, He is also called Emmanuel, "God with us" (1:23). He was called God's "beloved Son" at His baptism in the Jordan (3:17). He continually acted on behalf of His Father and in His Father's name (John 10:25). After His suffering He was exalted to heaven, where His triumph was trumpeted with a new name (Phil. 2:9-11). The Holy Spirit is poured out on Christians in the name of Jesus (John 14:26).

Salvation is seen as belief in the name of Jesus Christ (1:12; 2:23; 1 John 3:23). In the name of Jesus, and because of Him, Christians claim innumerable blessings. Salvation is mediated through His name (John 20:31; Acts 4:12). When Christians do good deeds, they should do them for the glory of the name of Jesus Christ (Col. 3:17, 23). Christians also pray in the name of the Lord Jesus Christ (John 16:24). They are also baptized in the name of Jesus Christ (Rom. 6:3; Gal. 3:27), which is never seen as a denial of trinitarian baptism (Matt. 28:19).

The sole subject of Christian proclamation is embraced in the name of Jesus Christ. This is our confession before a doubting world (Acts 8:12). Paul was commissioned at his conversion to bear that name (9:15). Missionaries go out to declare the name of Christ (3 John 7). The disciples summarized their message by referring to the name of Christ (Acts 4:17; 5:28, 40). On the basis of Christ's name Paul pleaded with the Corinthians to believe biblically (1 Cor. 1:10).

ILLUSTRATIONS

Names have provided much conversation. American humorist George Ade (1866-1944) hitchhiked on Shakespeare's rhetorical question: "What's in a name?" Ade added: "There's everything in a name. A rose by any other name would smell as sweet, but would not cost half as much during the winter months."

When commenting on the change of Samuel Goldfish's name to Samuel Goldwyn, Judge Learned Hand (who himself had an amazing name) commented: "A self-made man may prefer a self-made name."

In his usually humorous vein, Mark Twain, alias Samuel Langhorne Clemens (1835-1910), allowed: "Names are not always what they seem. The common Welsh name Bzjxxllwcp is pronounced Jackson."

English essayist William Hazlitt (1778-1830) was an ardent opponent of nicknames. He said: "The nickname is the hardest stone that the devil can throw."

When compared with all other names, the name of Jesus is the most sublime of all. The Bible attributes more than 100 names to Christ, among which are these: Advocate (1 John 2:1), Alpha and Omega (Rev. 1:8), Author and Perfector of our Faith (Heb. 12:2), Cornerstone (Ps. 118:22), Chief Shepherd (1 Peter 5:4), Sunrise (Luke 1:78), Firstborn (Rev. 1:5), Head of the church (Eph. 1:22), I Am (John 8:58), King of kings (1 Tim. 6:15), Lamb of God (John 1:29), Light of the world (8:12), Lord of Glory (1 Cor. 2:8), Mediator (1 Tim. 2:5), Morning Star (Rev. 22:16), Nazarene (Matt. 2:23), Passover (1 Cor. 5:7), Rock (10:4), Saviour (Luke 2:11), Truth (John 14:6), Word (1:1).

Few themes are so often sung as the name of Jesus. Several years ago my wife and I translated a German hymn titled, "The Wondrous Name of Jesus." Here is the first stanza:

O hear the matchless, wondrous name of Jesus,
    Sent from heaven down to earth.
It is the only hope of saint and sinner
    Ever since Creation's birth.

Many eloquent hymn-writers have also added their praise to the name of Jesus. In the 19th century Caroline Noel (1817-77) wrote the famous hymn which commences:

At the name of Jesus every knee shall bow,
Every tongue confess Him, King of glory now;
'Tis the Father's pleasure we should call Him Lord,
Who from the beginning was the mighty Word.

During the past few years many choruses have also been written that exalt the name of Jesus Christ. One of these is "His Name Is Wonderful." It contains the names Great Shepherd, Rock of all Ages, Almighty God, and King. The aim of this chorus is that its singers may bow down in adoration before the Lord.

OBEDIENCE, OBEY

MEANING

The word for "obedience" in the Greek New Testament is *hupakoe*, and the verb form "to obey" is *hupakouo*. In each case the root word is *akouo*, which means "to hear." One sees this in our English word *"acoustics"* (the science of design which helps one hear).

In secular Greek the word spoke of one standing at a door, listening intently, almost eavesdropping. Such was the reference in the writings of Plato, who used the word to describe a doorkeeper. Later on the word came to mean obedience, for after one hears and understands a command or request, he should obey it.

When the Greek Old Testament, the Septuagint, was translated, the word was used in specific connection with the Law of Moses. Children were commanded to honor father and mother, a command that was connected to a promise of long life (Ex. 20:12). Throughout the Old Testament it was assumed that Jews who heard the Law of God would obey it. Alas, this was not always true. Nevertheless, obedience and hearing are closely allied.

BIBLE USAGE

Obedience in the New Testament has two major emphases. First, there is much said about obedience to the Lord. Christians who obey the Lord are filled with the Holy Spirit (Acts 5:32). A logical expression of salvation in Christ is obedience to the Lord, and it is God who empowers believers to do this (Phil. 2:12-13). The example of obedience for all time is Abraham, who obeyed God when he was called to leave his homeland and go into the wilderness (Heb. 11:8). The proper response to a command of God is immediate, implicit obedience.

While Jesus was on earth, He was often obeyed. The elements obeyed Him, and storms stopped at His word (Mark 4:41). When He commanded, demons also submitted to His domination (1:27). He spoke authoritatively, which set Him off from the puny powers of mortal men (Matt. 7:28-29).

The motive for obedience in Scripture is faith. If one believes what God says, one will obey Him. In some cases faith and obedience are used interchangeably (Acts 6:7). In other places faith is seen as the source of obedience (Rom. 1:5). Those who do not obey the Gospel will be condemned eternally (2 Thes. 1:8).

The apostles placed a high priority on obedience to their inspired instructions. Paul identified this as a key indicator of spiritual growth (Rom. 15:18). A model believer, such as Titus, was marked by his obedience to apostolic instructions (2 Cor. 7:15). Anyone who disobeyed the word of the apostle was to be cut off from the church (2 Thes. 3:14).

Not only did Paul put a high priority on obedience, but Peter did also. Christians were marked preeminently by obedience to the Word of God (1 Peter 1:2). This liberated them from bondage to sin and conformity to pagan society (1:14).

Not only were Christians characterized by obedience to God, but they also knew the art of submission to human authorities. Despite the disgraceful nature of slavery, the Apostle Paul urged slaves to be submissive to their masters (Eph. 6:5; Col. 3:22). This was not an advocacy of the slave system, but rather an exhortation to Christian living.

By the same token, Christian children are also expected to be obedient to their parents. This is basic conformity to the Ten Commandments (Ex. 20:12; Deut. 5:16). It is also part of Christian commitment (Eph. 6:1; Col. 3:20). When a

Christian child submits to his or her parent, that child bears eloquent witness to the power of Christ.

The Apostle Peter also applies this principle to Christian wives (1 Peter 3:6-7). This is the basis for the statement in the wedding ceremony, that a wife will "love, honor, and obey" her husband. The corollary is completed by the husband's loving commitment to his wife. In no way is this teaching an approval of either mental or physical brutality against a wife.

Obedience is an attitude which comes easy to Christians. Because we have submitted to the Saviour in faith, we find it easier to submit to other people. For this reason Christians should be better spouses, citizens, children, and employees.

ILLUSTRATIONS

Many illustrations teach the principle of obedience. Some years ago Corrie ten Boom, a Dutch lady preacher, came to our campus. She illustrated her fascinating talk with all sorts of common articles. One of these was a glove, an old, almost worn-out leather glove. She held it up to show how limp it was, and then she put her hand in it. With this gloved hand she picked up a Bible and performed all sorts of actions. Her point was simple. If Christ is in us, He can do all things through us. Without Him we are as helpless as a limp glove. The secret is complete obedience to His commands.

William F. Buckley, Jr., American editor and writer, pointed out the importance of obeying God when he wrote: "I mean to live my life an obedient man, but obedient to God, subservient to the wisdom of my ancestors; never to the authority of political truths arrived at yesterday in the voting booth."

Elisabeth Elliot, missionary author and martyr's widow, also emphasized the importance of obedience when she wrote: "Throughout the Bible . . . when God asked a man to do something, methods, means, materials, and specific directions were always provided. The man had one thing to do: obey."

Another modern missionary statesman is Michael Griffith, former General Director of the Overseas Missionary Fellowship. He has written several significant books on missions, including *Give Up Your Small Ambitions*, *Cinderella with Amnesia*, and *Shaking the Sleeping Beauty*. On the subject of obedience he wrote: "Enthusiasm is easier than obedience."

D.W. Lambert came up with a similar statement when he said: "God delivers us from sin; we have to deliver ourselves from individuality, that is, to present our natural life to God and sacrifice it until it is transformed into spiritual life by obedience." In this day of self-indulgence, the entire concept of obedience appears to be out of date, but it is the secret of spiritual living.

Hymn-writer John Sammis (1846-1919) had it right when he wrote:

When we walk with the Lord
In the light of His Word,
What a glory He sheds on our way!
While we do His good will,
He abides with us still
And with all who will trust and obey
Trust and obey, for there's no other way
To be happy in Jesus but to trust and obey.

OFFERING

MEANING
The Greek word which is translated "offering" is *prosphero*. It is a combination of two Greek words: *pros* ("toward") and *phero* ("to carry, or bring"). Incidentally, the verb *phero* is seen in the English word "ferry" (a boat which bears people and things across water).

Originally this word simply meant "to bring something to a certain place." Later it assumed the meaning of setting something before a person. Because this concept is essentially religious, there are few secular references to the word.

On the other hand in the Greek Old Testament, the Septuagint, the word had a very full meaning. It was associated with the entire levitical system of sacrifices. It meant to bring something to the altar, the temple, or the priest. It also included the wave and burnt offerings.

BIBLE USAGE
There are two main ways in which an offering is described in the New Testament. In these two types of offering or sacrifice is summarized the history of God's saving work from the institution of the Jewish sacrifice system to the sacrifice of Christ.

Some Jewish leaders had an extremely perverted view of religious sacrifice. They thought that killing Christ's followers was an acceptable sacrifice to Judaism (John 16:2). This was indeed Paul's viewpoint before he was converted (Acts 26:9-11).

In the New Testament are several references to the Jewish sacrifices. If a Jew was healed from leprosy, he was required to bring a sacrifice to the priest as a token of his cleansing (Mark 1:44). This practice was encouraged by Christ.

In the Sermon on the Mount, Jesus also referred to the normal sacrifices of the Jewish religion. Jesus urged people to bring their sacrifices in clear conscience. Strained relations with other people should be rectified before a worshiper brought a sacrifice (Matt. 5:23-24).

The Apostle Paul, even after his Damascus Road conversion, continued to bring the sacrifices of Judaism. He appeared to do this in an attempt to gain entrance for the Gospel among the Jews (Acts 21:26; 24:17).

The second type of sacrifice in the New Testament is the sacrifice of Christ which terminated the old Jewish legal system (Heb. 10:5-6). In fact, the Book of Hebrews is devoted to the presentation of the perfect Sacrifice, the Lord Jesus Christ. The picture of Jesus Christ as the sacrificial Lamb is rooted deeply in the Old Testament (Isa. 53).

As the sacrifice for our sins, Christ was both perfect and eternal. He was thus able to atone for the sins of the world, which made His sacrifice infinitely superior to that of the Jewish sacrificial animals (Heb. 9:6, 14).

Hebrews 10 is one long hymn of praise to Christ for His eternal sacrifice. Jewish annual sacrifices cannot do away with the guilt of sin (10:1). They are only a shadow of the sacrifice which Christ perfected.

The Jewish sacrifices did not please God or produce forgiveness. In fact, they were the occasion of hypocrisy on the part of many priests and people. God took no pleasure in their religious mockery (10:5, 8).

Only the sacrifice of Christ could "sanctify" people, or make them holy. This aim could never be accomplished by the religious rituals of Judaism. Only the sacrifice of the Saviour once for all could do this (10:10).

Human priests had to persist in their sacrifices in order to make atonement for sin, but still the sins remained (10:11). On the other hand Christ offered Himself once (10:12), and now He makes continual intercession on the basis of that sacrifice.

The point of sacrifices is profoundly simple. The sacrifices of the Jewish religious system were temporary in their effect. Only the eternal Son of God could provide a perfect sacrifice once for all.

ILLUSTRATIONS

Sacrifice has two implications for us also. Howard Guinness, of the famous family of missionaries, spoke of sacrificial service. He said: "When the love of Christ comes into a human life, it is the greatest uplifting and ennobling power of which the world has any knowledge. It brings new birth, for it brings Christ Himself. For it no service is too great, no piece of service too humble." Howard Guinness is related to the great missionary statesman, Henry Grattan Guinness (1835-1910).

Another outstanding missionary statesman was David Livingstone (1813-73), whose body lies buried in Westminster Abbey, but whose heart is buried in Africa. Of sacrifice Livingstone said: "I never made a sacrifice. We ought not to talk of 'sacrifice' when we remember the great sacrifice which He made who left His Father's throne on high to give Himself for us."

Even the secular psychologist Carl Jung (1875-1961) knew the strength of sacrifice: "It is only through the mystery of self-sacrifice that a man may find himself anew."

Beyond doubt the greatest exposition of sacrifice is seen in the Cross of Christ. Of the Cross, Clement Alexandria (150-215) asserted: "For the sake of each of us He laid down His life—worth no less than the universe. He demands of us in return our lives for the sake of each other."

Two millennia later C.S. Lewis (1898-1963) could still sing the praise of His perfect sacrifice: "We are told that Christ was killed for us, that His death has washed out our sins, and that by dying He disabled death itself. Any theories we build up as to how Christ's death did all this are, in my view, quite secondary."

A great revival preacher and writer of nineteenth-century Germany, Friedrich Wilhelm Krummacher (1796-1868), caught the significance of Christ's sacrifice: "Jesus did not hang on the cross on His own account, but as our Representative. It was our death. . . . By His death He paid the wages of our sin for us. . . . There is no longer any cause for anxiety except in the case of those who refuse to acknowledge their sinfulness, and turn their backs on the Man of Sorrows on the cross."

According to the great theologian preacher, James Denney (1856-1917): "The simplest word of faith is the deepest word of theology: Christ died for our sins."

As the hymn-writer Lidie H. Edmunds wrote, in 1891:

It is enough that Jesus died,
And that He died for me.

OLD

MEANING

The simple word "old" represents the Greek term *palai*. This is seen in such English technical terms as "*pale*obotany" (the study of old fossil plants), "*pale*ontology" (the science of ancient life as revealed in fossils), and "*pale*ography" (the study of ancient writing).

From the time of Homer, this word has described distant events, things pertaining to an earlier time, and the past in general. Positively it speaks of those people and institutions which are venerated because of age. Negatively it pertains to that which is obsolete or worn out.

In the Septuagint Greek Old Testament the word "old" refers mainly to that which is antiquated or decaying. The term "Old Testament" is a development of the Christian era, to set the Old Testament apart from the New Testament.

BIBLE USAGE

In the New Testament what is old is best seen by comparison with that which is new. For instance, in salvation the old life of sin and defeat fades away under the glaring light of God's grace, and the Apostle Paul calls this a new creation (2 Cor. 5:17, NIV).

In His parables, Jesus often contrasted the old forms of Judaism with the new ways of His salvation. To mix Jewish religion with Jesus' revelation is like putting a new patch on an old garment (Matt. 9:16; Mark 2:21). Mixing salvation by grace with salvation by the Law is like trying to contain new wine in old wineskins, as the fermentation will burst them (Luke 5:37-38). In other words, the old religion of Judaism cannot contain Christ's salvation.

The Apostle Paul warned Corinthian Christians against relying on religious practices of the past. He called such rites "old leaven," and he urged the Christians to cling to Christ as their Passover Lamb (1 Cor. 5:7-8). Here again the principle is proved: the levitical system of sacrifice is outmoded, and Christ has become God's all-availing Offering. In the burnt offerings of bulls and goats is no salvation. It's only found in the Lamb of God who died for the sin of the whole world (John 1:29).

The contrast of old and new is also seen in sanctification, that process by which Christ conforms us to His image. The old habits of a Christian were crucified with Christ, and now we should live totally new lives (Rom. 6:6). Our behavior is transformed because we laid aside our old practices and took up new ones (Col. 3:9). In fact, our old practices were irredeemable, so Christ has given us whole new selves (Eph. 4:24). Therefore we do not obey the old commandments of Judaism, but the new law of love as seen in the Lord Jesus (1 John 2:8). Growing in sanctification is a process of putting off the old life and putting on the new life.

As a result of the sacrifice of Christ, a New Covenant has been forged between God and man. This New Covenant is the theme of the Book of Hebrews, where the author claims that the old one is obsolete and antiquated (Heb. 8:13). Christ is the perfect Sacrifice who validates the New Covenant.

In the Apostle Paul's inspired words, the Old Covenant was symbolized by Moses. It was characterized by a veiled understanding of God's dealings. On the other hand, the New Covenant of Christ is characterized by open revelation. The Holy Spirit is at work through it to conform its participants to the image of Christ. Instead of legal bondage there is spiritual freedom (2 Cor. 3:14-18).

The Old Testament was driven by the Law. People could conform to God's standard only by adhering to the Law. But under the New Testament the motivating force is the Holy Spirit and the vehicle of God's goodness is His grace offer of salvation through the sacrifice of Jesus Christ.

ILLUSTRATIONS

From a human standpoint, what is old is often cast away. Recently I put on a sweater which has 22 years and many miles on it. It still looks reasonably tidy, but its days are obviously numbered. Human creations pass away.

In the Scriptures the Law of the Old Covenant gives way to grace in the New Covenant. Puritan writer Thomas Adams (died 1653) framed this phrase about grace and Law: "The Law gives menaces, the Gospel gives promises."

Another Puritan, George Swinnock, put it this way: "The Law is a court of justice, but the Gospel a throne of grace." Oliver Cromwell's chaplain, Stephen Charnock (1628-80) was the son of a London lawyer. On the subject of grace and law Charnock said: "A legally convinced person would only be freed from the pain, an evangelically convinced person from the sin, the true cause of it."

Jumping up into our century, Swiss theologian Emil Brunner (1889-1966) said of the Old and New Covenants: "Knowledge of grace presupposes the Law. Without the Law there is no experience of the grace of God. Without the Sermon on the Mount there would be no Epistle to the Romans."

J. Gresham Machen (1881-1937), famous Presbyterian professor and New Testament scholar, summarized the relationship between Law and grace in this line: "A low view of Law leads to legalism in religion; a high view makes man a seeker after grace."

The relationship between Old and New Testaments is set down in a famous quotation by Augustine (354-430): "The New Testament is veiled in the Old Testament, and the Old Testament is unveiled in the New Testament." Someone else said: "The New is in the Old concealed, and the Old is in the New revealed" (Norman L. Geisler and William E. Nix, *From God to Us* [Chicago: Moody Press, 1974], p. 8).

In fact, Dr. Geisler has written an entire book on the theme of contrast between the Old and the New Testaments. It is called, *Christ: The Theme of the Bible.* He compares, for instance, Aaron (The Pattern of Priesthood) with Christ (The Perfection of Priesthood). Aaron entered an earthly tabernacle, but Christ went into a heavenly temple (Heb. 6:19-20). Aaron went once a year into the most holy place, but Christ went in once for all (9:24-26). Aaron went beyond the veil, but Christ ripped the veil from top to bottom (10:20). Aaron offered for his own sin, but Christ offered for our sin (7:27). Aaron offered the blood of bulls, but Christ offered His own blood (9:12).

Christ is indeed the fulfillment of the Old Testament. He fulfilled the prophets (Luke 24:27). In Him the Law, Prophets, and Psalms were fulfilled (24:44). The entire "scroll of the book" is realized in His redemption (Heb. 10:7). Christ came not to abolish the Law but to complete it (Matt. 5:17). Indeed all of the Old Testament Scriptures bear witness to Christ (John 5:39).

ONLY BEGOTTEN

MEANING

The word translated "only begotten" comes from a special Greek word, *monogenes*. Though this term appears only nine times in the Greek New Testament, it is extremely important in describing the Lord Jesus Christ. Actually the word *monogenes* is a combination of two Greek words. The first half is *mono* (literally, "only"), and it is seen in our words "*mono*rail" (a train which runs on only one rail) and "*mono*graph" (a writing which deals with one subject). The second half of our word is *genes* (seen in our English term "*gene*," which describes the process of birth). Therefore *monogenes* means "the unique one," "the unparalleled," or "the incomparable."

In ancient Greek literature the word was used to describe a unique being. The fabled bird Phoenix was called a *monogenes*, one of a kind. An only child was also called a *monogenes*. Here the emphasis does not fall on the means of birth, but on the uniqueness of the person.

This word was further used in the Septuagint Greek Old Testament. In the story of Judge Jephthah the featured character was his only daughter. She is called in the Greek Old Testament "his one and only child" (Jud. 11:34).

BIBLE USAGE

The most common use of the word *monogenes* relates to an only child. In the New Testament, an only child was usually in some special need. For instance, Jesus had an appointment at the gate of the village, Nain. As He passed by, a funeral cortege came out. A widowed mother was burying her only son (Luke 7:12). Jesus stopped the procession and then He stopped the mourning by bringing the boy back to life (7:11-17).

Soon thereafter a highly respected synagogue official named Jairus came to Jesus. He too was concerned about his only child, a little girl. In fact she was dead when the conversation was interrupted. Soon Jesus brought her back to life also (8:40-56).

Still within the Gospel of Luke is the account of a demon-posessed boy. He too was the only child of his parents (9:38). At the sight of the Saviour, the demon fled, leaving the boy free from sin's dominance.

In Hebrews 11, the Westminster Abbey of the Faithful, is a prolonged account of Abraham's life. When God put Abraham and Sarah to the test, Abraham offered up Isaac. The inspired writer called Isaac, "his [Abraham's] only begotten son" (Heb. 11:17). Abraham made the sacrifice, but God provided a lamb for the offering.

Though the original use of the word *monogenes* pertained to an only child, in the New Testament this word was invested with a wonderful new meaning. In the prologue to the Gospel of John, two references to the unique nature of Christ occur. First, John emphasized that he had seen the glory of "the Only Begotten" (John 1:14). Apparently this refers to the Transfiguration, to which Peter also referred (2 Peter 1:16-18). It was the glory which revealed that Jesus was the "Only Begotten," the Unique One.

Later on in John's prologue another reference is found. Jesus Christ came to reveal the nature of God, His Father. This too is strengthened by reference to the "Only Begotten" (John 1:18). Here the idea is that because Jesus is the unique Son of God, He alone could reveal the secrets of God's divinity.

Again in John are two references to Christ as the "Only Begotten." As the

Unique One He is singularly qualified to save people (3:16). When the subject of judgment is introduced, again the criterion of acceptance is belief in the "Only Begotten" Son of God. Only those who believe in Him can withstand the judgment of God (3:18).

The Apostle John included one further reference to the Only Begotten. God manifested His love to the world by sending the "Only Begotten" (1 John 4:9). His coming provided once-for-all eternal life to a dying race.

Whenever the descriptive term, "Only Begotten," is used in Scripture, it speaks of uniqueness. Christ was God's eternally unique solution to man's sin problem. No other answer could be found.

ILLUSTRATIONS

A magnificent little book about Christ is J. Oswald Sanders', *The Incomparable Christ* (revised edition, Chicago: Moody Press, 1971). In a section describing "the uniqueness of Christ," Dr. Sanders lined up several criteria of Christ's incomparable character.

Sanders' suggestions concerning Christ are these: first, "Nothing that Christ ever said had to be modified or withdrawn." He was uniquely truthful. Second, "He never apologized for word or action." He was uniquely courteous. Third, "He never asked for pardon." He was unique in His consistency. Fourth, "He never sought advice." He was unique in His knowledge. Fifth, "He was at no pains to justify ambiguous conduct." He uniquely did and said what He meant. Sixth, "He never asked or permitted prayer for Himself." He was always at one with the Father (*The Incomparable Christ,* pp. 3-4).

On the subject of Christ's uniqueness, William Lyon Phelps concluded: "The whole question of the Virgin Birth of Jesus need not afflict the average man. If Jesus is unique, unlike any other person, it is not illogical to believe that His birth was unique."

In further describing this unique role of Jesus, Christmas Evans (1766-1838), a famous Welsh preacher, concluded: "We can form no idea of the natural distance between God and man, but the infinite vacuum is filled up by the Messiah."

English Puritan theologian Stephen Charnock (1628-80) stated concerning Christ's uniqueness: "In nature we see God, as it were, like the sun in a picture; in the Law, as the sun in a cloud; in Christ we see Him in His beams; He being 'the brightness of His glory, and the exact image of His person.'"

In his *Systematic Theology,* Professor Augustus Hopkins Strong (1836-1921), discussed the uniqueness of Christ as "the Only Begotten God." "He [Christ] is not simply the only revealer of God," Strong stated, "but He is Himself God revealed" (*Systematic Theology* [Old Tappan: Fleming H. Revell, 1907], p. 306).

Another famous theologian, Brook Foss Westcott (1825-1901), a Bishop of Durham, wrote on the uniqueness of Christ: "In Christ the essence of God is made distinct [visible]; in Christ the revelation of God's character is seen."

No statement of Christ's uniqueness is more beautiful than Josiah Conder's (1789-1855) glorious hymn:

> Thou art the everlasting Word,
>   The Father's only Son,
> God manifestly seen and heard,
>   And Heaven's beloved One.

ORDER

MEANING

The Greek verb which is translated "order" is *tasso,* and another form is *taxis.* This family of words is seen in such English terms as *"taxi*dermy" (literally, "ordering the skin" of an animal so it looks lifelike and *"taxo*nomy" (literally "ordering names," as this is the science of classification).

In secular Greek the word referred to appointing an officer. It also was used to describe the mustering of soldiers for battle. In civilian life it was used to describe the delegation of jobs to various people.

Socrates found a larger meaning in this word, and he spoke of man in his proper place before God. Plato took this to mean that there was a divine order in the world. He thought that people filled certain roles in society by divine design.

BIBLE USAGE

The best means of understanding this word is to see the combinations in which it is found. First, the basic root word, *tasso,* is used frequently in the New Testament. Disciples went to the place where Christ designated them to work (Matt. 28:16). Likewise Paul and Barnabas were "ordered" by the brothers to go to Jerusalem (Acts 15:2). At the end of the Book of Acts Jewish leaders in Rome made an appointment to see Paul (28:23). In writing about the function of spiritual gifts, Paul urged the church to observe proper order (1 Cor. 14:40).

Another term based on this word is *apotasso,* which literally means to "take one's leave" or "depart." After completing his work at Corinth, Paul departed (Acts 18:18). From Corinth he made a brief stop in Ephesus, and then again took his leave (18:21). After a fretful delay in Troas, Paul again departed (2 Cor. 2:13). So *apotasso* means "to depart" or "take one's leave."

The term *diatasso* (literally, "order thoroughly") is translated "to order" or "command." When Jesus sent His disciples on their first journey, He gave them instructions or orders (Matt. 11:1). After Jesus brought back Jairus' daughter from the dead, He ordered that she be fed (Luke 8:55). When Paul was enduring his trial before various authorities, he was subject to the soldiers' orders (Acts 23:31). When Paul dispatched Titus to Crete, he gave Titus orders to appoint church leaders there (Titus 1:5).

Another term is *epitasso* (which means literally, "to order upon," or "to entrust someone with something"). Paul regarded his opinion concerning the Corinthian problem as "trustworthy" (1 Cor. 7:25). Furthermore, Paul regarded the Gospel as a treasure "entrusted" to him (Titus 1:3). By the same token, Paul placed his trust in Philemon, a Christian brother (Phile. 8).

Another combination word is *protasso* (here the basic word, "to order," is reinforced to mean "a strong command"). An angel commanded Joseph to take Mary and Jesus south to Egypt (Matt. 1:24). Jesus reminded some lepers He healed of the command of Moses (Mark 1:44). Cornelius was a Roman soldier, and he regarded Peter as a man under orders from God (Acts 10:33). As soon as Cornelius was converted, Peter "ordered" him and others to be baptized (10:48).

A final word is the term *hupotasso* (which means literally, "to place under," or "to be subjected to someone"). For instance, even demons were subjected to the disciples (Luke 10:17, 20). Christians are commanded to live in subjection under governments (Rom. 13:1-7). An unconverted person (8:7) and the unreconstructed world are both in rebellion against God (8:20). Part of Christian living is mutual submission to others (Eph. 5:21; Col. 3:18; 1 Peter 2:13; 3:6; 5:5). The basic assumption is that Christians are subjected to God as their Father (Heb. 12:9).

The word *tasso* speaks of order. The only order which is beneficial is God's order. Where His order is observed, there is peace. Where His order is ignored there is complete chaos.

ILLUSTRATIONS

The key to God's order is submission, as outlined in the last paragraph. To most modern people, submission is identified with failure. It is like one of those television wrestling matches, where the ultimate defeat is a submission. But in God's plan, submission is victory, and we only make progress spiritually by submitting to God.

Few men have made such a mark on the study of revival as Leonard Ravenhill. On the subject of submission to God he wrote: "Spiritual maturity comes not by erudition [learning], but by compliance with the known will of God." Submission to God's will is the key to individual spiritual progress and to the revival of the church.

Another statement of the same truth comes from the pen of T.J. Bach, a former missionary statesman. "Wherever God has placed a period," he says, "don't try to change it to a question mark."

Closely related to the concept of submission is discipline. James Alexander said: "The study of God's Word, for the purpose of discovering God's will, is the secret discipline which has formed the greatest characters." In other words, only by submission to Scripture is there any progress in Christian living.

An esteemed authority on constitutional law, Edmund Burke (1729-97), concluded: "Men are qualified for civic liberties in exact proportion to their disposition to put moral chains upon their appetites." One thinks of the many biblical injunctions to triumph over lust.

Austin Phelps (1820-90), a Congregational preacher, spoke of submission: "Character is, by its very nature, the product of probationary discipline." Along the same lines the noted Covenant preacher, Paul Rees, commented: "The highest forms of self-expression are to be found not in the lotus gardens of self-gratification but in the gymnasium of self-renunciation."

Submission is the secret of survival. If citizens do not submit to the rule of law, the result is anarchy. If marriage partners do not submit to their marriage vows, the result is either disaster or divorce. If children do not submit to their parents' discipline, the result is broken hearts and broken lives. Someone said wisely: "The cure of crime is not in the electric chair, but in the high chair." If Christians will not submit to the Word of God, a church is turned from an outpost of heaven to an outpost of hell.

When we married more than a quarter of a century ago, we selected a hymn which bore the title, "Submission." One stanza says:

Submission to the will of Him who loves me still
Is surety of His love revealed.
My soul shall rise above this world in which I move;
I conquer only where I yield.

PATIENCE

MEANING

Two words represent the English word "patience" in the Greek New Testament. The first word is *hupomone*. Its root is the verb, *meno*, which means "to remain or stay." Therefore patience has as its elemental meaning, "to endure," "persevere," or "stay."

Greek literature attributed both a positive and a negative meaning to *hupomene*. Postively, Plato and Aristotle emphasized the importance of perseverance, which they saw to be the noblest virtue. Negatively, some regarded patience as passive resignation, giving up. It is the positive aspect which is seen in the New Testament use of this word.

The second Greek word which describes patience is *makrothumia*, which basically means "long-suffering." The word *makro* is seen in "*macro*economics" (economics on a world scale). Literally the word *thumos* means "passion," "passionate longing," "anger," "wrath," or "rage." Therefore, the word *makrothumia* described one who was slow to anger. This is not passive but active. Being slow to anger does not mean that one does not care, but rather that he has his emotions under control.

BIBLE USAGE

The basic words for patience, *hupomene* and *hupomeno*, occur 48 times in the New Testament. Patient endurance is a character trait of Christians, and it will be best seen in end times (Mark 13:13; Luke 21:19). Christians will prove their faith in turbulent periods by their patience that endures.

It is this persevering patience which comes to the surface throughout the Book of Romans. For instance, a patient Christian will be rewarded at the time of judgment (Rom. 2:7; 8:25). No matter how tough the times, Christians are enabled to endure patiently by the Lord (12:12). Patience is not produced by a sheltered existence, but rather in the tumult of trouble (15:3-6).

The close connection between persecution and patience is emphasized by the Apostle Paul. He commended this among the Thessalonian Christians (2 Thes. 1:4). The Apostle Peter presented Christ as a model of patience under fire (1 Peter 2:20-23). Again the teacher of patience is persecution (2 Peter 1:6).

Likewise the Book of Hebrews characterized the Christian life as an exercise in patience. Here too patience is wed to warfare (Heb. 10:32, 36). The entire Christian life is marked by patience (12:1-2).

In the Book of Revelation the church is urged to endure, literally "to be patient." John presents himself as an example of persevering patience (Rev. 1:9). The injunction of Christ to His churches at Ephesus and Thyatira is also wrapped up with patience and endurance (2:2, 19).

The second word for patience is *makrothumia*, which literally means "long-suffering." In the Gospels Jesus gave a strong stimulus to such long-suffering. This is taught in the Parable of the Unmerciful Slave, where Jesus graphically taught the preeminence of patience (Matt. 18:26, 29).

The Apostle Paul used this word, "long-suffering," to describe the fruit of the Spirit in the life of a Christian (Gal. 5:22). As Paul prayed for Christians, he often asked God to give them patience (Col. 1:11). Christians were commanded to be patient with everybody (1 Thes. 5:14). Timothy was commended by Paul for his patience (2 Tim. 3:10).

The word "long-suffering" is also found frequently in company with teaching about the second coming of Christ. James urged his readers to wait patiently for Christ to come back (James 5:7, 10). Our model for such patience is none other than the Lord Himself (2 Peter 3:9, 15).

In short, patience is a characteristic of God in His dealings with us. Because of this divine Model we are urged to display patience in our dealings with one another.

ILLUSTRATIONS

Patience is often the butt of jokes. For instance, Oren Arnold described the prayer of the modern American: "Dear God, I pray for patience. And I want it *right now!*" Ambrose Bierce (1842-1914), an American author, added: "Patience [is] a minor form of despair disguised as a virtue."

"The key to everything is patience," asserted Arnold Glasow, "You get the chicken by hatching the egg—not by smashing it." Another wit wrote: "On second thought, patience may be a virtue, but it will never help a rooster lay an egg."

An anonymous commentator on patience produced this remark: "If you're too lazy to start anything, you may get a reputation for patience." Along the same lines, Ed Howe concluded: "A woman who has never seen her husband fishing doesn't know what a patient man she has married."

There are jokes aplenty about patience, but the Bible takes it seriously, and so do biblical Christians. A relative of ours prayed earnestly that God would give her patience. He allowed her deaf, 90-year-old mother to move in. The next years proved to be a time of tribulation, but that tribulation worked patience. Thus the Bible was proved to be true.

Missionary author Amy Carmichael (1867-1951) wrote: "We are called to be the Lord's diehards, to whom can be committed any kind of trial of endurance, and who can be counted upon to stand firm whatever happens. Surely fortitude is the sovereign virtue of life; not patience, though we need it too, but fortitude, O God, give me fortitude."

Frederick Faber (1814-63), a famed hymnist, focused on patience: "We must wait for God, long, meekly, in the wind and wet, in the thunder and lightning, in the cold and the dark. Wait, and He will come. He never comes to those who do not wait."

Christian poet George Herbert (1593-1633) said: "God takes a text, and preaches patience." According to a German proverb, "Patience is a bitter plant but it bears sweet fruit."

The Puritans often spoke of patience. George Swinnock said: "To lengthen my patience is the best way to shorten my troubles." Likewise Thomas Adams (died 1653) said: "Patience to the soul is as bread to the body . . . we must hope with patience, and pray in patience, and love with patience, and whatsoever good thing we do, let it be done in patience."

PEACE

MEANING

The Greek word for peace is *eirene,* which occurs more than 90 times in the New Testament. In English this word is reflected by such terms as "irenic" (any action which is aimed at producing peace) and "eirenicon" (a peace proposal).

In the writings of Homer, peace meant the opposite of war. It was the restoration of an atmosphere which would be characterized by civil order and would give rise to blessing and prosperity. Plato applied this word to personal life. Peace was a frame of mind or a pattern of conduct.

In the Septuagint Greek Old Testament the word *eirene* is found more than 250 times. It is a translation of the Hebrew word, *shalom.* To a Jewish writer, this word meant a state of well-being or prosperity. It was the parting wish of Aaron's priestly blessing (Num. 6:24-26).

BIBLE USAGE

In the New Testament the concept of peace is broad in its meaning. First, it speaks of civil peace. Jesus used the illustration of a man who sought peace (Luke 14:32). Stephen referred to an attempt of Moses to make peace in Egypt (Acts 7:26). Righteous people are encouraged to be peacemakers (Matt. 5:9; James 3:18).

Just as the Bible teaches that God is love, it also calls Him the God of peace. As such He gives peace to Christians and defeats Satan (Rom. 15:33; 16:20). The main sphere of peace-creation is the church (1 Cor. 14:33). This peace is communicated through obedience to God's Word (Phil. 4:9). By the same token, the God of peace makes us holy, and sanctifies us (1 Thes. 5:23). He is the seal of our blessing and the benediction of our lives (Heb. 13:20).

God is our peace, and Christ is the Prince of Peace (Isa. 9:6). At His birth angels announced the advent of peace on earth (Luke 2:14). As He prepared to leave the earth, He promised His disciples a legacy of peace (John 14:27; 16:33). Because of Christ's sacrifice there is peace among diverse peoples (Col. 1:20; 3:15). The basis of our peace is the God of peace.

Because of the sacrifice of Christ we can have peace with God (Rom. 5:1). If we trust Him, our rebellion is ended, and we have a relationship of peace with God, so we need no longer fear His wrath.

As a result of this peace *with* God we also have the peace *of* God in our hearts. Even when turmoil invades our lives we may have peace because of the indwelling Christ (1 Cor. 7:15). This is seen in the twin blessings of grace and peace (Rom. 1:7; 1 Cor. 1:3; Gal. 1:3; Eph. 1:2; Phil. 1:2; 1 Peter 1:2).

In short, life without a relationship to God is constant turmoil; there is no peace for the wicked who reject God. On the other hand, those who have placed their trust in the Lord know peace. This peace gives a spiritual unity to the church (Eph. 4:3). This peace provides a release from the trap of lust (2 Tim. 2:22). Because of this peace we can also spread peace among others (Heb. 12:14).

There is in this subject of peace a beautiful chain of blessing. God is the sole source of peace, and apart from Him is only trouble and turmoil. Jesus Christ came into this world to provide peace in two ways: He showed the world a Person at peace with God, and He died to pay the penalty of our sin and make peace between us and God. As a result we who trust Him stand in a totally new relationship of peace with God. This infuses peace into our hearts.

ILLUSTRATIONS

The world seeks peace in many places. When Neville Chamberlain (1869-1940) returned from meeting the Germans at Munich in 1938, he blithely said: "I believe it is peace for our time . . . peace with honor." Actually there was neither peace nor honor to be salvaged from Chamberlain's capitulation to Hitler.

What a difference marked the attitude of Winston Churchill (1874-1965), Chamberlain's successor. Of the same conflict Churchill insisted: "In war: resolution. In defeat: defiance. In victory: magnanimity. In peace: goodwill." He never contemplated capitulating to Hitler.

In eulogizing George Washington, Henry Lee (1756-88) praised the President as being: "First in war, first in peace, first in the hearts of his fellow citizens." Greatness in peacetime was equal, if not superior in value, to greatness in battle.

Poet laureate Alfred Lord Tennyson (1809-92) lauded Queen Victoria with these lines: "Her court was pure; her life serene; God gave her peace; her land reposed." The premier accomplishment of Victoria was peace.

Even in the first century before Christ, Marcus Tullius Cicero (106-43 B.C.) acclaimed peace as earth's greatest good, when he wrote: "Let wars yield to peace, laurels to paeans" (*De Officiis*).

Many years ago my wife was witnessing to a brilliant Catholic woman. So moral was that young mother that no Gospel approach seemed to touch her. One day my wife said in despair: "How shall I ever lead her to Christ? She is so upright." Within a few hours the breakthrough came. The neighbor arrived tearfully at our door with this question: "My son must go into the hospital for surgery. Who can give me peace of heart?" That very day she found the Prince of Peace.

Billy Graham addressed this same subject in these words: "In Christ we are relaxed and at peace in the midst of the confusions, bewilderments, and perplexities of this life. The storm rages, but our hearts are at rest. We have found peace—at last!"

Bishop John Jewel (1522-71) was a sympathizer of the Protestant Reformation. He was forced into exile by the ascension of Queen Mary in England. Of peace he said: "We [do not] eschew concord and peace, but to have peace with man we will not be at war with God."

Dwight L. Moody (1837-99) was equally emphatic in his commitment to peace through Christ's finished work, about which he said: "A great many people are trying to make peace, but that has already been done. God has not left it for us to do: all we have to do is to enter into it."

Bob Mumford, an American preacher, summarized the scriptural teaching about peace in these pithy lines: "Peace *with* God brings the peace *of* God. It is a peace that settles our nerves, fills our mind, floods our spirit, and in the midst of the uproar around us, gives us the assurance that everything is all right."

"There will be no peace," observed William Peck, "so long as God remains unseated at the conference table."

PEOPLE

MEANING
In the Greek New Testament several different words are translated "people." The most common of these is *ethnos*. We see it in such familiar English words as, "*ethn*ic" (pertaining to the culture of any group of people, such as "ethnic food"). In the writings of Aristotle, this word denoted foreign people in contrast with Greeks. Later it came to mean barbarians or subjected peoples. In the Septuagint Greek Old Testament it referred to the Gentiles or heathen.

A second word which is translated with "people" is *laos*. This word seems to refer to an organized group of people, such as an army or a crowd. It also speaks of common people in contrast with leaders. In the Septuagint Greek Old Testament it was used 2,000 times to describe Israel, God's chosen people. Here *laos* (Israel) was contrasted with *ethnos* (Gentiles).

The third word which is used frequently in the Scriptures is *ochlos*, which is translated as "crowd," "throng," or "the public." It was often used to distinguish the mass of common people from people of rank and prestige. Often this word is combined with *ethnos* or *laos*, as one sees in the phrase, "a crowd of people."

BIBLE USAGE
In the New Testament the word *ethnos* is used 162 times. This word was used mainly to distinguish the Jews from the Gentiles. The latter were the "nations" of the earth which were included in Christ's command (Matt. 28:19).

As yet these were unreached with the Gospel (4:15). Their practices stood out in bold contrast with the behavior of a disciple (20:25-26; Eph. 4:17). The Gentiles were viewed as the natural enemies of Israel and future plunderers of Jerusalem (Luke 21:24).

Because of this picture of the Gentiles, they were viewed as a primary target for missionary activity. God's sovereignty extended to the Gentiles (Rom. 3:29). The Gentiles' desperate need is described in Romans 1:18-32, especially their tendency to idolatry. Their inclusion in the missionary vision related to their inclusion in the Abrahamic covenant of blessing (Gal. 3:8; Gen. 12:1-3). The Apostle Paul emphasized the Gentiles in his proclamation, though he also included the Jews (Rom. 10:19; 11:12).

The Book of Revelation declares that the Gentiles are largely represented in the church. There will be a multinational mass of believers before the throne of God (Rev. 7:9; 11:2). The risen Lord will exercise authority over all the nations (13:7).

As *ethnos* describes the nations of the world, the second word, *laos*, speaks of God's chosen people. Christ came to "save His people from their sins" (Matt. 1:21). Still Israel was unable to take in this glorious Gospel message (13:14-15). Instead they reverted to hypocrisy and shallow superficiality (15:8-9).

The hymn of Zacharias likewise focused on the people of God. In the coming of John the Baptist, he saw the beginning of fulfillment of some Old Testament prophecies (Luke 1:68). The essence of the salvation message was to be forgiveness of sins, a message which John the Baptist proclaimed (1:77). The angelic messengers concurred with this glad hymn of praise (2:10). In each case God's people were the object of Christ's saving mission.

Later on the church assumed the title of God's people (*laos*). God has chosen Gentiles, just as He chose Israel (Rom. 9:25). A prophetic word originally aimed at Israel was used to designate the church as God's people (2 Cor. 6:17-18; Isa. 52:11). In the Book of Hebrews Israel and the church are both included under the term "the people [*laos*] of God" (Heb. 4:9; 13:12).

The third Greek word describes people as a crowd. It is *ochlos,* which was often translated as "multitude." Sometimes crowds showed anger, as at the arrest of the Lord (Mark 14:43; 15:14-15). Such crowds were easily led. In fact, some Jews accused Jesus of leading the crowd astray (John 7:12). Paul was likewise accused of misleading many people (Acts 19:26).

On the other hand, crowds often listened to Christ preach. John the Baptist preached to such multitudes (Luke 3:7, 10). When Jesus performed miracles, the multitudes marveled (Matt. 9:33). On at least two occasions Jesus also fed the multitudes who came to Him (14:19-23; 15:32-38).

It is significant that there are frequent references to crowds in the Scriptures. They demonstrate God's intense concern for people. Not only has He created them, but in Christ God reached out to re-create them.

ILLUSTRATIONS

Literature abounds with references to people. Some are more flattering than others. Lord Halifax (1633-95) lamented: "When the people contend for their liberty, they seldom get anything for their victory but new masters."

Robert Zend came to the amazing conclusion: "People have one thing in common: they are all different." Abraham Lincoln (1809-65) is famous for his remark: "God must love the common man; He made so many of them," to which writer Philip Wylie (1902-71) added: "God must hate the common man; He made him so common."

From a divine perspective people look different. The great Methodist proponent of prayer, E.M. Bounds (1835-1913), said concerning people: "The church is looking for better methods; God is looking for better men." Along the same lines, Lettie Cowman contributed this insight: "The worker is far more important to our Lord than the work."

About the priority of people, Francis McConnell once said: "Democracy is the very child of Jesus' teachings of the infinite worth of every personality." The same truth was enunciated by Theodore Parker (1810-60): "This democratic idea is founded in human nature, and comes from the nature of God, who made human nature. To carry it out politically is to execute justice, which is the will of God."

However, Thomas V. Tooher warned of the instability of human nature: "Do you want to be free? Then put your faith in God, not in man. The people gave you freedom with a vote and they can take it away with a vote."

Some time ago the British Broadcasting Corporation invited me to appear on an interview program, in which my favorite records would be played. One of those which I chose was "Eleanor Rigby" by the Beatles. It seems to epitomize the pathos of modern people in its refrain, which says: "All those lonely people, where do they all come from?" The Christian knows not only where they all come from, but also where they are going without Christ. This motivates us for mission, far and near.

PERFECTION

MEANING

The Greek word translated "perfect" is *teleios*. It's root meaning is "fulfilled purpose," which is seen in the English word *"teleo*logy" (the belief that any process is shaped by purpose). The *"teleo*logical" argument of the existence of God says that the purposeful arrangement of the universe demonstrates the existence of God.

Later on this word assumed another meaning, that of perfection. When something fulfills its purpose, it is supposedly perfect. Aristotle emphasized the aspect of ethical perfection, doing that which is right. For him self-actualization was most important. A person should realize that which is right for himself, and this is perfection. In other words, perfection is not conforming to an external standard, be it God's or man's. In this sense Aristotle stood out in bold contrast with biblical ethics, which stress conformity to God's standard.

Later, under the influence of Plato, perfection meant conformity to accepted virtues in Greek culture. When one exemplified these virtues in every way, he was perfect.

BIBLE USAGE

In its various forms *teleios* occurs about 100 times in the Greek New Testament. In each case it means "perfection," "completion," or "wholeness." For instance, in some cases it speaks of ethical perfection, behavior which is complete or whole.

An example of this ethical perfection is found in James, when he asserted that endurance in the Christian life helps make one perfect (James 1:4). Let it be added that this does not teach sinless perfection. The Bible repeatedly emphasizes that no one is sinless, but every Christian should sin less every day. James illustrated this teaching by reference to obeying God's Law (1:25). Specifically, he saw the tongue as the main battleground in achieving spiritual perfection or wholeness (3:2, 6-12). James knew that true perfection is found in God alone (1:17).

In John's epistles there is likewise an emphasis on perfection. Here the sole source of perfection is God. Only God can give perfect love, which takes away fear (1 John 4:18). No perfection exists apart from Him.

In Paul's writings there is also reference to this ethical perfection. To Timothy Paul wrote that the young man should perfect or fulfill his ministry as an evangelist (2 Tim. 4:5). No one is a perfect minister, but every Christian should fulfill his ministry.

If our behavior should be complete or whole, so should our character be brought to completion or maturity. In some ways "maturity" is the best translation of this Greek word. When writing to the Roman church, Paul urged them to sacrifice their lives for Christ's service. This service alone would be perfect or complete (Rom. 12:1-2).

Paul wrote to the Colossians, urging them to teach young Christians and thus bring them to completion or maturity in the faith (Col. 1:28). This perfection was seen in their conformity to the will of God (4:12).

Christians gain insight into the way of God as they grow in grace. This produces spiritual wisdom and maturity (1 Cor. 2:6). In fact, Paul pressured the Corinthian Christians to grow into spiritual maturity (14:20).

To the Ephesians Paul wrote that they should mature in the knowledge of God, and that this would bring them into the image of Christ (Eph. 4:13). This goal of maturity motivated all Paul's missionary work.

Besides the perfection of ethics and the perfection of character, the Scriptures also speak of perfection of doctrine. When a person professes faith in Christ, he has a basic, elementary understanding of Christian truth. He knows how to be saved, and that is about all. In time that Christian should grow on to maturity and develop a hunger for progressively deeper truth. This is what the writer of the Book of Hebrews calls perfection or maturity (Heb. 5:13—6:1).

Perfection in the New Testament is not a flawless imitation of God. Rather it is a growth into maturity which is discernible as one makes progress in the faith. Absolute perfection and completeness is found in God alone, and we shall experience it only when we are with Him.

ILLUSTRATIONS

From the first, people have realized that true perfection rests in God alone. Clement of Alexandria (155-220) was one of the earliest Christian writers. He asserted: "I know of no one man perfect in all things at once but still human . . . except Him alone who for us clothed Himself with humanity."

Along the same lines Gregory of Nyssa (330-395), a gifted teacher, instructed his students and the church: "True perfection consists . . . in having but one fear, the loss of God's friendship."

Even the pagan writer Xenophon (434-355 B.C.) came to the same conclusion: "The divine nature is perfection; and to be nearest to the divine nature is to be nearest to perfection." Christians can only achieve maturity, completeness, and perfection by conformity to Christ.

A devout Christian woman was Catherine of Siena (1347-80). Concerning perfection she concluded: "Perfection does not consist in macerating [disfiguring] or killing the body, but in killing our perverse self-will."

John Wesley (1703-91) was known for his doctrine of "Christian perfection," about which he once wrote: "What is Christian perfection? Loving God with all our heart, mind, soul, and strength."

A similar statement was made by Bishop Fulton J. Sheen, a Roman Catholic television preacher, who said: "Perfection is being, not doing; it is not to effect an act but to achieve a character."

Tom Skinner, famous black evangelist, further explained the pattern of perfection: "If you check out the life of Jesus you will discover what made Him perfect. He did not attain a state of perfection by carrying around in His pocket a list of rules and regulations, or by seeking to conform to the cultural mores of His time. He was perfect because He never made a move without His Father."

Richard Baxter (1615-91) was a famous Puritan writer. He produced a classic book on the pastoral ministry, *The Reformed Pastor* (1656), and also wrote a fine forecast of heaven, *The Saints' Everlasting Rest* (1650). On the latter subject Baxter said: "This life was not intended to be the place of our perfection, but the preparation for it."

POWER

MEANING

The Greek word for power is *dunamis*. It is seen in such English words as "*dynamic*" (a powerful person or movement), "*dynamo*" (a power-producing machine), and "*dynamite*" (an extremely powerful explosive). A related Greek word is the verb *dunamai* (to be able, or to be powerful).

In secular Greek the word meant ability or capability, as is seen in the writings of Homer. In Plato's time the words were used to describe the power of hearing or seeing. Plato applied the word to spiritual and intellectual powers, and he defined power as the mark of being. In other words, to be impotent was not to exist at all. (This has remarkable implications for powerless people today.) The Stoic philosophers saw the seat of power in an absolute, cosmic force which gives power to all else in the universe.

BIBLE USAGE

In the New Testament the words which relate to power occur more than 200 times. The Bible bases all its concepts of power on God's power, and the basic premise is that God alone is "all-powerful" or "omnipotent."

For instance, the model prayer of the Lord concludes with the statement that all rule and all power belong to God the Father (Matt. 6:13). From earliest days God was able (powerful) to perform His promises, even to the raising of Christ from the dead (Rom. 4:21-25). In fact, the power to raise Christ from the dead was seen as the greatest exercise of divine ability (8:11; Eph. 1:19-20). The same idea surfaced in the story of Abraham, who believed that God alone was powerful enough to raise the dead (Heb. 11:19).

Closely related to the power of God is the power of Christ. Before Jesus healed a blind man, He asked the poor person, "Do you believe I am able [have enough power] to do this?" (Matt. 9:28) The man enthusiastically expressed his belief, and Jesus gave him sight immediately. It is still essential that we believe in Christ's power.

Nicodemus came to Christ with one question: "What is the source of Your miracle-working power?" (John 3:2) Jesus informed him that he could never understand this, unless he were "born from above" (3:3, marg.). At Pentecost Peter backed up the truth of his message by referring to the power of Christ (Acts 2:22).

Not only did the disciples preach about the power of Christ; they also demonstrated it. When they went out on their first missionary journey, Christ gave them power to command demons and heal sicknesses (Luke 9:1). By giving them the Holy Spirit, Christ was able to endue the disciples with power for preaching and performing miracles (24:49; Acts 1:8).

When the early Christian church prayed, they were empowered to serve the Lord (4:31-33). They also performed miracles in the power of Jesus' name (4:10). Such miracles became tools of missionary advance in the life and work of Paul (Rom. 15:19). These signs were seen as a verification of apostolic power (2 Cor. 12:12). When pagans saw the power of the Gospel, they believed in Christ (1 Cor. 2:1-5; 1 Thes. 1:5).

Not only did the disciples display power, but it was also seen in the life of the church. When people came to believe in Christ, the Holy Spirit immediately filled them with power for service (Rom. 15:13). Some Christians had special gifts of miracle-working power (1 Cor. 12:10). Christians have available to them the power of the Lord Jesus Christ (Col. 1:11; 2 Thes. 1:11). As Christians demonstrate the power of God, they are also protected from Satan by God's power (1 Peter 1:5).

The greatest demonstration of divine power is the salvation of a sinner. When asked who can be saved, Jesus answered: "God has power to do anything" (Matt. 19:25-26). Paul saw the Gospel as having unlimited power, because it could save anyone who came to Christ (Rom. 1:16). Though the Law of Moses was not powerful enough to save anyone, Christ can save anyone who believes in Him (8:3). According to Paul, the Gospel is the greatest power source known to man (1 Cor. 1:18). Who knows the power of God better than a sinner who has been saved?

ILLUSTRATIONS

The power of the Gospel is the point of our preaching. Dr. Merrill C. Tenney once told us, his students: "When you want to advertise your church, don't take out a big newspaper advertisement. Get the town drunk saved, and let him be a walking demonstration of the Gospel's power." The power of the Gospel is not seen in great preaching, large churches, or glorious music. It is best seen in transformed lives.

My colleague, Dr. Timothy Warner, often speaks of "power encounters." By this he means those incidents where the power of Christ openly triumphs over the power of Satan. When a person is snatched from Satan's power, Christ is exalted. When a demon-possessed person is freed, Christ is glorified. When evil is publicly defeated by God's power, Christ is praised.

Boniface (680-754), a missionary bishop to the Germans, was told that the god Thor could defeat the Christian God. To prove the power of God, Boniface went to the religious grove of trees and chopped down the oak of Thor, the most sacred tree in that pagan religion. When Thor could not strike down Boniface, many Germans became believers. God had won that "power encounter."

By the same token St. Patrick of Ireland (390-461) faced the wrath of the spirit-worshiping Druids. He challenged the Druids to prove the power of their demons, but Patrick's God and ours proved Himself every time. This led to the establishment of the Gospel in Ireland, and through Patrick's ministry the Christian church was established. Incidentally Patrick was neither Irish nor Catholic. He was an Englishman and a Celtic (evangelical) Christian.

Christians know that the only valid source of power is the Lord. Dr. L. Nelson Bell (1894-1973), missionary physician and founder of *Christianity Today*, said: "Power in the Christian life depends upon our connection with the source of power [the Lord]."

Dr. Bell's daughter is Ruth Bell Graham, wife of Billy Graham. On the same subject of power she said: "The center of power is not to be found in summit meetings or in peace conferences. It is not in Peking or Washington or the United Nations, but rather where a child of God prays in the power of the Spirit for God's will to be done in his life, in his home, and in the world about him."

Another great proclamation of God's power originated with G. Campbell Morgan (1863-1945): "No man can do the work of God until he has the Holy Spirit and is endued with power. It is impossible to preach the Gospel save in the power of the Spirit."

PRAISE

MEANING

In the Greek New Testament three words are used to speak of "praise." The most common word is *doxa* (glory) or *doxazo* (to glorify). That word is discussed more fully in the article titled, "Glory." The word *doxa* is seen in our English term, "*dox*ology" (a hymn of praise).

The second Greek word is *eulogeo,* and it means literally "to speak well of someone or some thing." It is seen in the English word "*eulogy*" (an address in praise of a deceased friend). In early Greek literature this word meant simply, "to speak well of someone." Later on it came to mean "the advocacy of a person's cause." It is a word used frequently in the Septuagint Greek Old Testament to describe blessing, such as the blessing of Aaron (Num. 6:24).

A third Greek word for praise is *epainos.* Used sparingly in the Scriptures, the basic meaning of this word is "applause." It speaks of expressed approval or public recognition. Usually this praise was addressed to an individual or to an entire community.

BIBLE USAGE

The word *epainos* (praise), and the verb form *epaineo* (to praise) are used 16 times in the New Testament to describe praise.

In the Gospels the verb is used mainly to describe a crowd's praise for Jesus. At His birth a crowd of angels acclaimed Him as Lord and Saviour (Luke 2:13). Afterward a smaller group of shepherds praised Him (2:20). At the Triumphal Entry a great multitude praised Him (19:37). After the ascension of Christ back into heaven, the entire brotherhood praised God (Luke 24:53).

The early church continued this praise hymn to God (Acts 2:47). When a lame man was healed, he too joined the praise (3:8). The bystanders also saw the lame man praising the Lord (3:9).

A Christian should be oblivious to the praise of people, because he knows that God will ultimately praise him (Rom. 2:29; 1 Cor. 4:5). Some Christians, like Titus, were praised by all the church (2 Cor. 8:18), but they too prized the praise of God.

Though God praises obedient believers, the most obvious object of praise in the Scriptures is the Lord Himself. God's whole plan of salvation is so marvelous that it brings praise to His glory (Eph. 1:6). From the first Christian onward, salvation has brought tremendous praise to God (1:12, 14).

When the "fruit of righteousness" is seen in Christians, God is praised (Phil. 1:11). The virtues which are quoted by Paul are likewise a source of praise to God, from whom all virtue comes (4:8).

Not only is the godly life of a Christian a source of praise to God, but so is the suffering of a saint (1 Peter 1:7). When Christians suffer and thus glorify their God, they bring praise to His name.

The usual meaning of the word *doxa* is "glory." On a few occasions it is translated "praise," as we see it in our English word "*dox*ology" (a hymn of praise).

This word was used as a proof of truth. When someone made an assertion, he reinforced his statement by "giving God the praise." For instance, when the Pharisees quizzed a blind man whom Jesus healed, they ordered him to give God the glory or praise and to tell the truth (John 9:24).

By the same token the Pharisees were condemned by Christ for taking glory to themselves. They preferred the praise of men to the praise of God (12:43).

A third example of this is found in Peter's writings. Whatever a Christian does in service to the Lord should contribute to the praise and glory of God (1 Peter 4:11).

Though the word *doxa* is used frequently for "glory," it is seldom used to describe praise given by man to God. Similarly the word *eulogeo* is also used mainly to express blessing. However, it is sometimes used to describe praise. The most outstanding example is found in the story of John the Baptist's birth. After he was born, Zacharias' tongue was loosed and he praised God for the boy's birth (Luke 1:64). Here then, the word "to bless" is translated "praise."

No matter which word is used, the primary object of praise is God. Also, the most worthwhile praise is the praise of God. Human praise quickly fades; only the acclaim of God lasts forever.

ILLUSTRATIONS

Praise is heard and seen widely today. The famous initials, "PTL," stand for "praise the Lord." On British television there is a well-known program of hymns, and the title given it by secular media people is, "Songs of Praise."

Some years ago we were motoring up through the Midlands of England, when we caught a "leather-lunged" country music singer on the radio. As I reached to switch it off, she launched into a hymn. Afterward she said: "That hymn is not a lucky charm for me. It is also not just a trademark. It is a testimony, because I learned a long time ago, that God inhabits the praise of His people (Ps. 22:3, KJV).

On the subject of prayer Puritan writer Thomas Watson said: "Praise is a soul in flower." Elsewhere he added: "Praising God is one of the highest and purest acts of religion. In prayer we act like men; in praise we act like angels."

Recently a chorus has gained wide acceptance, and it emphasizes praise:

Praise the name of Jesus, Praise the name of Jesus.
He's my Rock, He's my Fortress, He's my Deliverer,
In Him will I trust. Praise the name of Jesus.

Puritan writer, John Livingstone, said about praise: "Alas, for that capital crime of the Lord's people—barrenness in praises! Oh, how fully I am persuaded that a line of praises is worth a leaf of prayer, and an hour of praises is worth a day of fasting and mourning."

A former editor of *Christianity Today*, Dr. Harold Lindsell, said: "The continual offering of praise requires stamina; we ought to praise God even when we do not feel like it. Praising Him takes away the blues and restores us to normal."

On the same subject C.M. Hanson concluded: "Praise is like a plow set to go deep into the soil of believers' hearts. It lets the glory of God into the details of daily living."

Perhaps the best-known praise hymn was written by Chester Allen (1838-78):

Praise Him! Praise Him! Jesus, our blessed Redeemer;
Sing, O earth! His wonderful love proclaim!

PRAYER

MEANING

In the Greek New Testament several words are used to describe prayer. The most common of these are *proseuche* ("prayer") and *proseuchomai* ("I pray"). The basic idea is to bring something, and in prayer this pertains to bringing up prayer requests. In early Greek culture an offering was brought with a prayer that it be accepted. Later the idea was changed slightly, so that the thing brought to God was a prayer. In later Greek, prayers appealed to God for His presence.

A second word relating to prayer is *deomai*, which is often translated in the *King James Version* with the old word "beseech." The idea in this word is to "beg" or "request." It is the intensity of the request which here is emphasized. A basic, urgent need is presented in this prayer. If anything, *deomai* is stronger than *proseuchomai*.

BIBLE USAGE

The words *proseuchomai* and *proseuche* occur about 85 times in the Greek New Testament. Prayer is primarily addressed to God, as in the model prayer which the Lord taught His disciples (Matt. 6:6-13; Luke 11:2-4). In prayer we cry to God, "Abba [literally, Daddy], Father" (Rom. 8:15; Gal. 4:6). Paul likewise emphasized the need for prayer to God the Father (Eph. 3:14).

Also in the New Testament prayer is directed to Jesus Christ. In the Gospels, many times petitions were directed to Jesus, as though they were prayers. One such is Peter's cry for help, as he sank into the sea (Matt. 14:30). In his pain Paul also prayed to the Lord for release (2 Cor. 12:8). When the glorified Christ appears in the Book of Revelation, there are further references to Him as the object of prayer (Rev. 5:8).

The New Testament teaches many things about prayer. First, it will be heard by God (John 16:24). In order to assure this hearing, prayer must be offered in faith (Matt. 21:22). It is also necessary to pray in accordance with the revealed will of God and the written Word of God (John 15:7; 1 John 5:14-15). Furthermore prayer should be accompanied by humility and sorrow for sin (Luke 18:10-14).

The Scriptures also reveal that prayer is intensive labor. Paul used the word "striving" or "agonizing" to describe it (Rom. 15:30). He urged Christians to pray persistently for him and his colleagues (1 Thes. 5:25; 2 Thes. 3:1).

Sin certainly hinders the effectiveness of prayer. This is true of tensions between people (Matt. 5:23-25). Wrong motives also hinder prayers from being answered (James 4:3). Within marriage, a man who is unkind to his wife can expect no answers to his prayers (1 Peter 3:7).

The second word for prayer is *deomai* ("beseech" or "beg"), used about 30 times in the New Testament. The most outstanding appearance is James 5:16, where the effectiveness of prayer is emphasized.

Usually this word speaks of intensive prayer. A leprous person begged Christ for healing (Luke 5:12). A desperate father pleaded for his demon-possessed son (9:38). As the end times approach, this earnest sort of prayer will become increasingly appropriate (21:36). In some cases this word can even be translated "beg" (Acts 26:3).

Often this word also involves intercession on behalf of someone else. Paul prayed for the Jews with a great intensity (Rom. 10:1). Believers engaged in active intercession for the Apostle Paul and his companions (2 Cor. 1:11). In fact, Paul felt that his very boldness in the ministry was related to these intercessory prayers (Eph.

6:18-20); Phil. 1:19). By the same token, Paul interceded on behalf of believers (1:4).

Prayer in the New Testament is a top priority. It involves the entire Trinity in the affairs of man, and it also contains the potential of power in changing people and events.

ILLUSTRATIONS

Hosea Ballou (1771-1852), an American preacher, concluded: "Between the humble and the contrite heart and the majesty of heaven there are no barriers; the only password is prayer."

Fred Beck said: "If you are swept off your feet, it's time to get on your knees." The following phrase was scrawled on the wall of an underground bomb shelter during the blitz in London: "If your knees are knocking, kneel on them." As the famous Presbyterian Pastor Louis Evans said: "The man who kneels to God can stand up to anything."

Puritan writer, preacher, and hero of faith, John Bunyan (1628-88), said concerning prayer: "Prayer is a shield to the soul, a sacrifice to God, and a scourge to Satan."

According to Richard Cook: "Most of us have much trouble praying when we are in little trouble, but we have little trouble praying when we are in much trouble."

Ole Hallesby (1879-1961) was a pioneer in theological education and a great prayer personality. He said: "To pray is nothing more involved than to lie in the sunshine of God's grace."

Another famous European preacher, Rowland Hill (1744-1833), addressed large audiences at London's Surrey Chapel. On prayer he concluded: "Prayer is the breath of the newborn soul, and there can be no Christian life without it."

Robert Murray McCheyne (1813-43) saw God move in revival power at Dundee, Scotland. A great part of this revival was prayer, about which McCheyne said: "What a man is on his knees before God, that he is—and nothing more."

Later in the 19th century Dwight L. Moody (1837-99) said of prayer: "The Christian on his knees sees more than the philosopher on tiptoe."

When we were considering a call to the pulpit of Kensington Baptist Church in Bristol, England, the church spent a half-night in prayer. They brought every aspect of our lives and the church's ministry before the throne of grace. Within days we had an unshakable conviction that the church's call was God's will for us. What followed was the most fruitful and blessed period of our lives.

Leonard Ravenhill, a revival author and preacher, wrote a book titled *Revival Praying*. Of prayer he said: "The self-sufficient do not pray, the self-satisfied will not pray, the self-righteous cannot pray. No man is greater than his prayer life."

Donald Grey Barnhouse (1895-1960), a well-known radio preacher in the middle of this century, spoke often of prayer. Once he said: "I am not sure that I believe in the 'power of prayer,' but I do believe in the power of the Lord who answers prayer."

PREACH

MEANING

The Greek word which is translated by the verb "to preach" is *kerusso*, and that which is preached is called *kerygma*. Actually, the word *kerygma* is also used as a technical theological word to denote the message of the Gospel. *Kerygma* and *kerusso* occur 68 times in the New Testament.

The original meaning of these words was a "herald at the royal court." Homer used them in this connection. They not only announced the coming of the prince, but they also carried his commands to the uttermost corners of his realm. As the government of Greece became more republican, these heralds came to serve the state rather than the court.

Certain qualities were required of heralds. They must have powerful voices, so voice auditions were often held. Also they had to be capable of calming down an unruly mob, in order to faithfully communicate the command. An honest disposition was also required, as a protection against the exaggeration of a royal decree. Furthermore, they could make no additions or subtractions from the received message. Later these heralds were also used to declare the message of a Greek deity or a religious oracle.

BIBLE USAGE

In the New Testament several men are credited with being preachers. The first preacher in the New Testament was John the Baptist. He preached in the wilderness, and his message was repentance as preparation for the coming kingdom (Matt. 3:1; Mark 1:4; Luke 3:3). In one sense, John the Baptist was an ideal herald, for he viewed himself as simply a voice that declared the message of Messiah (Luke 3:4-5; Isa. 40:3-4).

The second preacher in the New Testament was Jesus Christ Himself. Preaching was a priority ministry for the Lord (Mark 1:38). His content was defined as, "the Gospel of God" (1:14). Preaching was a mark of the Messiah, according to Isaiah (Luke 4:18-19; Isa. 61:1-2). Jesus also proclaimed the coming kingdom (4:42-43).

A third class of Christian preachers in the New Testament were the disciples of the Lord. Jesus sent out the disciples to proclaim the message of the Gospel (Matt. 10:27). The Gospel would penetrate the whole world before the end times would come (24:14). Paul's last letter to Timothy urged the young man to give attention to the task of preaching (2 Tim. 4:2).

An unexpected group of preachers were some of those whom the miracles of Jesus touched. A cleansed leper told his tale of healing far and wide (Mark 1:44-45). When a demon-possessed man was released, he proclaimed the glories of Christ throughout the whole city (5:19-20).

The content of Christian preaching gives a full view of the Gospel. The first disciples preached repentance and remission of sins (Luke 24:47). Another aspect of their declaration was the coming kingdom of God (Matt. 10:7; Luke 9:2). After the resurrection of Christ, that event became the cornerstone of Christian preaching (Acts 2:23-24; 10:42). The sacrificial death of Christ on the cross of Calvary likewise provided power for preaching (1 Cor. 1:18-23). Thus the entire life and ministry of Christ comprised the content of apostolic preaching. They were concerned, first and foremost, that people come to believe in the risen and glorified Lord.

The encouraging aspect of New Testament preaching is this: people heard and believed. Paul insisted that preaching was the only means by which people could come to faith in Christ (Rom. 10:8-17). Though others could not comprehend the wisdom of preaching, Paul found it to be the only means of persuading people to believe (1 Cor. 1:21; 2:4). Because Christ was truly risen from the grave, apostolic preaching had a "punch" (15:14).

In the New Testament, from John the Baptist to the establishment of an apostolic church, preaching was the main means of communicating the Christian message. This gives validity to the preaching ministry today.

ILLUSTRATIONS

Recently several significant books on preaching have been produced. In 1982 John Stott's significant book, *I Believe in Preaching* (London: Hodder and Stoughton), appeared. The same year Dr. Martyn Lloyd-Jones' book, *Preaching and Preachers,* was also released by Hodder and Stoughton. Though the writers' viewpoints vary, the primacy of preaching stands out in both books.

Often I have seen a young man pressed to preach. Reluctantly he takes his first assignment, and suffers greatly through it. Soon however, if the call of God is on him, he would rather preach than do anything else in the world. Preaching becomes his passion!

The dean of American preachers for many years was Andrew Blackwood. Of preaching he said: "A good sermon should be as exciting as a baseball game." (In the case of Billy Sunday, an ex-baseball player, the sermon was sometimes more exciting than a ball game.)

When asked to define preaching, Episcopal Bishop Phillips Brooks (1835-93) replied: "Preaching is truth given through personality." Evangelist Leighton Ford emphasized this truth: "When power goes out of the message it is because the Word has become not flesh but words." Bernard Lord Manning (1892-1941), a Cambridge church historian, framed these words eloquently: "Preaching is a manifestation of the incarnate Word, from the written Word, by the spoken word."

Sixteenth-century intellectual giant Desiderius Erasmus (1466-1536) spoke about training preachers in these words: "If it is possible to train elephants to dance, lions to play, and leopards to hunt, it should be possible to teach preachers to preach."

A close link between preaching and prayer was discerned by P.T. Forsyth (1848-1921), a brilliant British Congregational theologian: "A preacher whose chief power is not in studious prayer is, to that extent, a man who does not know his business. Prayer is the minister's business. He cannot be a sound preacher unless he is a priest."

Power in the pulpit is always related to personal spiritual power. An old-time southern preacher, Vance Havner, put it simply when he said: "It is not the business of the preacher to fill the house. It is his business to fill the pulpit." Similarly Dwight L. Moody (1837-99) claimed: "The best way to revive a church is to build a fire in the pulpit."

Furthermore, William Quayle, a famous teacher of preachers, placed high priority on the preparation of the messenger. He said: "Preaching is not the art of making a sermon and delivering it. Preaching is the art of making a preacher and delivering that." As John Ruskin (1819-1900) remarked: "Preaching is 30 minutes in which to raise the dead."

PREDESTINATE

MEANING

The Greek word which is translated "to predestinate" is *proorizo*. Basically this word means "to decide upon something beforehand." Its root word, *orizo*, means "to determine, or to set boundaries, or to fix some course of action." By adding the prefix *pro*, one simply says that this determination will occur in advance of the action. This basic word was used to order a meal for future consumption.

Though the word meant simply to plan in advance, in the New Testament it attracted a special meaning. Here the idea is a divine decree of God, whereby He determined in advance that something should happen. This basic word was used to describe the appointment of Jesus Christ as Judge (Acts 17:31).

A related word is "foreknowledge" (*proginosko*). One sees the English equivalent of this word in "*prognosis*" (a medical term describing the probable course which an illness will take). In the human sphere this is an educated guess. But when God is the subject of the verb, omniscience is involved.

BIBLE USAGE

The word *proorizo* is found only six times n the New Testament. In each case it speaks of God's plan for man, and the inescapable implication is that God's plan will be fulfilled. A study of this word does not display any blind fatalism, but rather the care of a loving God for His people.

The first appearance of this word is in the Book of Acts. Peter and John had been arrested and jailed for their insistence that Jesus was alive and at work. On their release they openly proclaimed that their imprisonment had been part of God's predestined or predetermined plan for their lives (Acts 4:28). A Christian can see that persecution is not without purpose, and the purpose is God's plan.

Two of the six references to God's predestination are found in chapter 8 of Romans. God predestines Christians to become conformed to the image of His Son (Rom. 8:29). When Adam fell into sin, the image of God in man was marred. In Christ a Christian is predestined to be conformed to the renewed image of Christ (2 Cor. 3:18; 1 John 3:2).

The second reference to predestination is part of an enthralling chain of events. God predestined us, and then He called us to salvation (Rom. 8:30). All those who were called were also justified, declared to be righteous. Each person who is justified will ultimately be glorified. There is no leakage in God's plan. Every person whom He predestines to salvation will ultimately be with Him in glory.

In 1 Corinthians Paul pointed to another aspect of predestination. God predestined His Son, Jesus Christ, to be offered for our sin (1 Cor. 2:7). Here again the glorification of God's children is seen to be the end result.

The remaining couple of references is found in Ephesians. God predestined believers to be adopted as sons (Eph. 1:5). In the Greek New Testament this is more than the adoption of babies, as we now know it. To a Greek, adoption involved the investing of all the father's rights and privileges in his son. When God adopted us, He gave us all the riches of heaven.

The privileges of adoption are now only partially perceived. Someday when we are with the Lord in glory, we shall fully enjoy them all. This is the inheritance to which God has predestined us (Eph. 1:11).

Predestination is not the whim of a capricious God, but rather the forethought of a loving Father. Because He chose us for salvation and conformity to Christ, we can trust Him to do what is best in all our lives.

ILLUSTRATIONS

Someone explained predestination with this simple picture. When we came to Christ, it was like walking through a gate. On the outside were inscribed these words: "Whosoever will, may come." Once we passed through the gate into the Saviour's arms, we could look back and see these words inscribed on the inside: "Chosen from the foundation of the world." We can praise Him for His sovereign and saving grace.

Joe Blinco, English Methodist preacher and evangelist, once put it in these words: "God has an exasperating habit of laying His hands on the wrong man." On a more serious note, A.B. Simpson (1843-1919), founder of the Christian and Missionary Alliance, said: "God is preparing His heroes; and when the opportunity comes, He can fit them into their places in a moment, and the world will wonder where they came from."

The story is told of a critical person, who once approached Charles Haddon Spurgeon (1834-92) and said: "Mr. Spurgeon, you are preaching the Gospel to people who have not been predestined to be saved."

Spurgeon replied calmly: "You are probably right. Please just paint a yellow cross on the back of everyone who is predestined to be saved, and I shall preach only to them." Even the critic saw the humor of that answer, for no one knows who is predestined, except God Himself. In fact, Spurgeon is reported to have prayed: "Lord, save all the elect, and then elect some more."

One of the most profound statements of this doctrine is found in *The Westminster Confession of Faith:* "All those whom God hath predestined unto life . . . He is pleased, in His appointed and accepted time, effectually to call by His Word and Spirit." In other words, God will get His man (or woman) every time!

A pastor in England preached often on the subject of predestination. Or at least one of his deacons thought he did. Every time the pastor approached the subject, the deacon would turn his back to the preacher. Only after the preacher moved on to another, more comfortable topic, would the deacon turn to face the pulpit.

As time wore on, that deacon delved deeper into the Word of God and drank in the truth of Scripture. After four years of this deep Bible teaching, the deacon was called on to pray. To everyone's amazement he said: "O God, thank You that You loved me so much, that You chose me to be Your child even before the world was." God had taught that deacon the treasures of this teaching.

When I was a young missionary, my assignment was evangelism. Often I preached in villages where never in living memory had the Gospel been heard. What a comfort it was to know that God had chosen His own. It was our privilege to proclaim to them the Gospel of grace. Only heaven will reveal the full extent of God's grace.

PRIEST

MEANING

The Greek word for priest is *hiereus*. This root is seen in many English words, such as "*hier*archy" (ruling body of clergymen), "*hier*oglyphics" (priestly engravings), and "*hier*olatry" (the worship of saints). The basic meaning of the word *hieros* is "one consecrated or filled with divine power."

Early Greek writers used this word to describe things pertaining to their pagan gods. The head of Zeus was described as being *hieros*, consecrated, or holy. The same term was used to describe an expert in the sacrificial system of religion. Men who were especially wise were set apart as priests and entitled *hiereus*.

In the Septuagint Greek Old Testament the priests were occupied with three duties. First, they served regularly in the sanctuary, whether the tent tabernacle or the temple at Jerusalem. Second, they brought sacrifices on a regular basis. Third, they discerned divine guidance through waiting on the Lord.

BIBLE USAGE

The Greek word for priest occurs 31 times in the New Testament. Almost half of these appearances are in the Book of Hebrews, where it usually refers to the Lord Jesus Christ. (A related word is *archiereus*, which means "chief priest.")

Though the priests uniformly opposed Jesus, He still showed respect to them. For instance, when He healed lepers, Jesus sent the restored men to the priests for sacramental confirmation of their healing (Matt. 8:4). This was a fulfillment of the levitical Law (Lev. 14:1-12).

Jesus also referred to priests in His parabolic teaching. In the story of the Good Samaritan, it was a priest who walked past the ambushed traveler without lifting a finger to help (Luke 10:31). No one seemed to be surprised at this callous action by the priest. Perhaps this reveals the low opinion which most people held concerning the priesthood. But despite this low opinion, many priests did come to believe in the Lord (Acts 6:7).

In speaking of the Sabbath, Jesus said that priests "break the Sabbath" by working on that day (Matt. 12:5). Jesus used this to justify His own ministry on the Sabbath. Since the Jews accepted the priests' activity on the Sabbath, they should also accept Christ's healing work on the holy day. Incidentally, Christ here seems to emphasize His role as a priest.

The Book of Hebrews makes the point that the levitical priesthood had failed to make people right with God. Those priests were only "a copy" of the perfect priesthood of Christ (Heb. 8:4-5). Despite their faithfulness in keeping the forms of Judaism, they were only a pale picture of Christ, the true Priest (9:1-9). The point is this: Human priests cannot provide a perfect sacrifice for sin (10:11).

The New Testament portrays Christ as the perfect Priest. He entered into intercession for us during the last hours before His crucifixion (John 17). Since His ascension into heaven, Christ has ceaselessly interceded for us, His people (Heb. 7:24-25). He is a Priest according to the ancient order of Melchizedek (5:6; 7:1-3, 11-15). No human frailty mars the priesthood of Christ.

In the Scriptures, however, there is another class of priests. The Bible teaches that every believer is a priest (1 Peter 2:9; Ex. 19:5-6). This means that every believer is capable of interpreting the Scriptures. It also implies that every believer is capable of an intercessory ministry. Further, it teaches that every believer can bring the offering of worship to the Lord (Rom. 15:16). This priesthood will be fulfilled ultimately in heaven (Rev. 1:6; 5:10).

In other words, there are only two classes of true priests in the world today. The first is the Lord Jesus Christ who is the perfect Priest and the Intercessor for His people. The second class of priests are Christians who engage in all the functions of priesthood here on earth.

ILLUSTRATIONS

An elderly retired missionary once joined a church which I pastored. He laid down one requirement when he joined: "Pastor," he said, "don't let me become a dumb priest." He was keenly aware that God had given him a priestly ministry of intercession and mediation, and he was eager to not let that ministry lapse into disuse. Despite severe illness, he continued to function as a priest in our midst.

There are four reasons why Christians should be encouraged to exercise a priestly ministry in the church. First, they are all equal before the Lord, and no one is excluded from this ministry (Gal. 3:28). Second, the unity of the body of Christ makes us all dependent on each other (1 Cor. 12:7). Third, no church can function well without the use of the gifts present in its priests (12:24-26). Fourth, the priesthood of believers emphasizes the glorious diversity implicit in the plan of God (12:11).

In his helpful book on the church, Professor Robert Saucy of Talbot Theological Seminary emphasizes the importance of this doctrine. According to the priesthood of believers, "All members of the church have the same direct access to God and His grace." In another place, Professor Saucy says: "The humblest believer has direct access into the throne room of God along with the minister." Referring to the work of Martin Luther, Professor Saucy claims: "One of the foundations of Reformation truth was the concept of the priesthood of all believers" (*The Church in God's Program* [Chicago: Moody Press, 1972], pp. 111, 117, 127).

Even though he was a Bishop of the Church of England, Professor J.B. Lightfoot (1828-89) insisted: "As individuals, all Christians are priests alike. . . . There is an entire silence about priestly functions [in the New Testament]: for the most exalted office in the church, the highest gift of the Spirit, conveyed no sacerdotal [sacramental] right which was not enjoyed by the humblest member of the Christian community."

Though few people know about it, there was in the 17th century a revival in Germany. One of the leading lights of that awakening was Jacob Spener (1635-1705), who wrote the book *Pia Desideria* or *Pious Desires* (1675). Part of that great revival movement, called Pietism, was a return to the Reformation doctrine of the priesthood of all believers, about which Spener wrote: "Not only ministers but all Christians are made priests by their Saviour, [they] are anointed by the Holy Spirit, and are dedicated to perform spiritual-priestly acts. . . . Indeed, it was by a special trick of the cursed devil . . . that all these functions were assigned solely to the clergy" (*Pia Desideria* [Philadelphia: Fortress Press, 1964], pp. 92-93). (See: *Chief Priest.*)

PROMISE

MEANING

The Greek words relating to the idea of "promise" are *epangelia* (a promise) and *epangellomai* (to make a promise). They contain the root word, *angel*, which means to "proclaim," "announce," or "declare." In other words, a promise is a public declaration which must come true in order to be believed.

In ancient times, the Greeks used this word to describe a simple announcement. Homer, for instance, used *epangellomai* to speak of a public pronouncement or statement of intent. In Greek literature it was never a case of pagan gods making promises to people. Instead it always involved people making promises to the gods.

On the other hand, in the Septuagint Greek Old Testament, Jehovah God was often making promises to His people. A primary example was Abraham. In response to Abraham's obedience God promised to heap blessing on him. Furthermore, God would lead Abraham's family to the Promised Land. Additionally, God would raise up from Abraham a whole people of promise, the Jews. Jehovah God is rich in promises.

BIBLE USAGE

The word for promise (*epangelia*) appears 52 times in the New Testament, and the verb form *epangellomai* occurs 15 times. First and foremost God is the Giver of promises. In fact, Paul said that the promises of God are absolutely dependable (2 Cor. 1:20). God never yet has defaulted on a promise, and He never will. "The promise of the Father" was Jesus' way of referring to the coming Holy Spirit (John 14:26). After His ascension the disciples waited patiently and prayerfully in Jerusalem until the Spirit fell on them all (Acts 2:4).

In his indictment of Jewish unfaithfulness, the martyr Stephen charged the people with ignoring the fulfilled promises of God (Acts 7:51-53).

One of God's promises was the birth of Isaac, despite the advanced age of Abraham and Sarah (Rom. 4:21). The Jews' entire national existence was an expression of God's promises. The coming of Messiah was construed by Christians as a fulfillment of the promise to Abraham (Titus 1:2).

God's promises to Abraham are often mentioned in the Book of Hebrews. Abraham waited patiently for one promise, and it was revealed (Heb. 6:15). Both the Promised Land and the promised son were received, because Abraham and Sarah waited (11:9-16). As a result, the writer of Hebrews urged Christians to cultivate patience in waiting for the promise of God (10:36).

This dominant theme of the promises of God appears throughout the New Testament Scriptures. The land of Israel was seen as the promise of God (Acts 7:17). Salvation's message, the Gospel, was likewise promised by Jehovah (13:32). Christ confirmed the promises of God (Rom. 15:8). The final facet of God's promise is the coming of the Holy Spirit (Gal. 3:14). The entire plan of salvation is considered to be a promise of God.

Most of God's promises bring benefit to people. He promised a Saviour, who would sort out the sin of the world (Acts 2:38-40; 13:23; 26:6). By the same token, He promised the Holy Spirit to stimulate us to spiritual living (Gal. 3:14). In Christ the promise of eternal life has come true (John 3:16; Titus 1:2; 1 John 5:11-13).

Just as God's promises bring blessing, so human promises often cause catastrophes. In that most evil of all treachery, the Jewish leaders promised money to Judas in exchange for the betrayal of Jesus Christ, God incarnate (Mark 14:11).

Paul warned against those who make lying professions or promises, and thus go away from the true faith (1 Tim. 6:21). False teachers often promise people freedom, but instead enslave their foolish followers (2 Peter 2:19).

From start to finish, God has always stood true to His Word. His promises to Abraham have been fulfilled in salvation for all mankind. Someone estimated that there are 8,000 promises in the Bible. It is my opinion that there are probably more, and it is my conviction that every one of them either has been or will be fulfilled.

ILLUSTRATIONS

Most Christian leaders have commented on the promises of God. An interesting remark is attributed to Billy Bray (1794-1868), a great revival preacher of Cornwall, England. According to that rough and ready revivalist: "The promises of God are just as good as ready money any day."

Billy Graham emphasized the promise of Christ's return: "Not only does the Old Testament tell us to expect the second coming of Christ, not only is the New Testament filled with the promise of it, but if we would study the historic documents of our major denominations, we would find that our founders all believed and accepted it. The most thrilling, glorious truth in all the world is the Second Coming of Jesus Christ. It is the sure promise of the future."

An editor of *The Sunday School Times* was Phillip E. Howard, father of Elisabeth Elliot. Concerning the promises of God, Philip Howard wrote: "Certainly there are promises in the Old Testament which relate to material things. But if God was faithful and merciful to Israel, whom He chose not because of their righteousness but only because of His love for them, how much more reason today to rest on the faithfulness of Him who gave His beloved Son for us! In that faithfulness is assured our right to God's promises."

According to F.R. Maltby: "Jesus promised His disciples three things: They would be completely fearless, absurdly happy, and in constant trouble." As the old song says: "I never promised you a rose garden."

Once when I was a little boy my mother came to investigate my uncharacteristic silence. She entered my parents' bedroom to find me standing on my father's large, black Bible. "Whatever are you doing?" my mother asked in horror.

My childish response was taken straight from the hymnbook. "Mother, I am 'standing on the promises.' " Actually, I thought that was the meaning of the hymn.

"God's promises are like the stars," claimed David Nicholas. "The darker the night the brighter they shine." Puritan writer Samuel Rutherford (1600-61) said concerning the promises of God: "Swim through your temptations and troubles. Turn to the promises; they be our Lord's branches hanging over the water so that His half-drowned children may take a grip on them. Let go that grip and you sink to the bottom."

Many remember a chorus, popular in days gone by, which urged us to cling to God's promises:

> Every promise in the Book is mine,
>   Every chapter, every verse, every line,
> All are blessings of His love divine,
>   Every promise in the Book is mine.

PROPHET

MEANING

The Greek word for "prophet" is similar to the English word. It is *prophetes,* and the verb "to prophesy" is *propheteuo.* Actually these words are a combination of two Greek terms: *pro* (on behalf of) and *phemi* (to say or affirm). In other words, the terms "prophet" and "prophesy" have to do with someone who speaks on behalf of another. In the Bible this is usually someone who speaks on behalf of God.

In ancient Greek the word "prophet" referred to a public proclamation. So anyone who made a public proclamation was acting as a "prophet." Later the word was connected to a religious declaration, such as the interpretation of the oracle at Delphi. Those who spoke on behalf of the oracle were called prophets. There were four characteristics of these people. First, they were not responsible for the content, which they passed on unchanged. Second, they gave advice only when asked. Third, they were relevant to the needs of the petitioner. Fourth, the prophet was called by the institution of the oracle, not by any specific pagan god.

The Septuagint Greek Old Testament had two kinds of prophets. There were speaking prophets (as Nathan, Elijah, and Elisha) and writing prophets (as Isaiah, Jeremiah, Daniel, and Amos). Two criteria were set down to prove the truth of a prophet. First, he had to speak the truth (Deut. 18:22). Second, he must not mislead the people away from Jehovah God (13:1-5).

BIBLE USAGE

The words pertaining to prophecy occur no fewer than 200 times in the New Testament. There are 5 specific cases in which these words are used.

First, they refer to Old Testament prophets. Jesus spoke often of the persecution which was poured out on Old Testament prophets (Matt. 23:31; Luke 4:24). Matthew likewise quoted the prophets frequently with regard to the birth and ministry of Jesus (Matt. 1:22; 2:17). The apostles also saw Christ as the fulfillment of messianic prophecies (Acts 3:18, 21). Likewise, Christ was the epitome of revelation, which began in the time of the prophets (Heb. 1:1-2; 1 Peter 1:10-11).

Second, John the Baptist was seen as a prophet. Christ called him the greatest prophet, the "super prophet" (Matt. 11:8, 11). Likewise the disciples classified John the Baptist as one of the prophets (16:14; 17:9-13; Mark 8:28). John the Baptist was expected as an indicator of the incarnation of Messiah (Luke 7:20).

Third, Jesus was called the Prophet. He was compared with the great prophets of the Old Testament (Mark 6:15). He was the prophet who was compared in significance with Moses, though in reality He far outshone Moses (Acts 3:22; 7:37). The Jews believed that the messianic age would be ushered in by a great prophet, and Christ filled that role completely.

Fourth, on some occasions believers were especially enabled to prophesy. This occurred during the time of Christ. For instance, when Mary visited her cousin, Elizabeth prophesied (Luke 1:41-55). At the birth of John the Baptist, his father Zacharias also prophesied (1:67-79). When Jesus was presented in the temple, Simeon prophesied that Mary would suffer anguish (2:25-33). There were special occasions when the Holy Spirit came upon believers.

Fifth, by the same token, some in the early church had the gift of prophecy. For instance, Agabus prophesied the persecution against Paul (Acts 21:10-14). At the same place Paul met the four prophetess daughters of Philip the evangelist (21:9). To the Corinthians Paul declared that certain Christians had the gift of prophecy (1 Cor. 14:3-5, 24). Actually Paul preferred this gift over the ecstatic gift of tongues. The church was built on the foundation of the apostles and the prophets, all of whom presented God's message (Eph. 2:20).

In short, the gift of prophecy existed during New Testament times. A prophet sometimes foretold coming events. If he was a true prophet, his predictions came to pass. A prophet sometimes also forcefully declared the message of God. If he was a true prophet, he led people toward God, not away from Him.

ILLUSTRATIONS

A prophet is preeminently a man of God. Concerning this remarkable class of people, Benjamin N. Cardozo claimed: "The prophet and the martyr do not see the hooting throng. Their eyes are fixed on the eternities." In fact, because their heads are in heaven, their feet sometimes float above the ground. Nevertheless their message is essential to survival in time and eternity.

Writing on the same subject, Raphael H. Levine referred to the Old Testament prophets as men of vision, when he said: "The Hebrew prophets were . . . primarily exhorters, interpreters of the will of God . . . men impelled by their vision of God as a God of justice, holiness, love, and the one and only God in a polytheistic world."

Other nations espoused a multitude of deities, but Israel followed but One, Jehovah. The messengers of Jehovah were the prophets.

Famous archeologist William Foxwell Albright (1891-1971) underlined the biblical requirements of a prophet: "Fulfillment of prophecies was only one important element in the validation of a 'true' prophet. More important still was the moral and religious content of a prophet's message." No prophet of God would or could convey an ungodly message.

Prophets were reliable not because of their intelligence. Neither was it their communication skills which made them prophets. They spoke by direct inspiration of the Holy Spirit. About this aspect the famed Dutch theologian and statesman, Abraham Kuyper (1837-1920), said: "Inspiration is the name of that all-comprehensive operation of the Holy Spirit whereby He has bestowed on the church a complete and infallible Scripture."

In our day there has been much emphasis on the need for prophetic preaching, which speaks specifically and authoritatively to the needs of our times. Once Dr. Martyn Lloyd-Jones (1899-1981) of Westminster Chapel in London was addressing a group of ministers, of which I was a part. In all seriousness he said: "Gentlemen, the day of the pastor is gone. The church today does not need mere pastors, but rather prophets who confidently can say: 'Thus saith the Lord.' "

Along the same lines David Watson wrote concerning prophetic preaching: "One of the most urgent needs of the church is to know what the Spirit of God is saying to His people *today*. There is therefore a 'particularity' about prophecy. It is a particular word inspired by God, given to a particular person or group of persons, at a particular moment, for a particular purpose" (David Watson, *I Believe in the Church* [London: Hodder and Stoughton, 1982], p. 258).

PROPITIATION

MEANING

The word for propitiation in Greek is *hilasterion,* and the verb, "to make propitiation" is *hilaskomai.* They both share the common root of *hileos,* which means "gracious or merciful." Therefore in its Greek form, the word for propitiation means to "conciliate," "expiate," "bring a sin-offering," or "obtain mercy."

In the time of Homer, the word *hilaskomai* meant to make the pagan gods happy or merciful. Later it took on the idea of a prayer to pagan deities to avoid their wrath. During the Hellenistic period of Greek history this word came to mean bringing an offering to placate angry gods.

When the Old Testament was translated from Hebrew into Greek, this word was used to describe the levitical offering system. For instance, it referred to the sin-offering as seen in Leviticus (Lev. 4; 17:11). It was also the offering brought on the Day of Atonement to provide expiation (or pay the penalty) for the sins of Israel (chap. 16).

BIBLE USAGE

Despite the deep significance and wide application of this concept, the two Greek words appear only six times in the New Testament. In some cases they refer to the idea of conciliation, whereby man attempts to be reconciled with God. But these words are also used to describe the sacrifice which Christ brought in order to pay the penalty for our sins.

First we see the human desire for reconciliation. The Lord spoke of the effectiveness of prayer. He portrayed a Pharisee who was so self-righteous that he could not obtain God's righteousness by being justified. On the other hand, Jesus told a tax collector, who was fully aware of his sin and pleaded in prayer, that God would be gracious to him, a sinner (Luke 18:13). Here one sees the first meaning of these words, a search for conciliation through the mercy and grace of God.

In the Book of Hebrews a detailed description of the temple is included, and the "mercy seat" has a central position in the holy of holies (Heb. 9:5). The "mercy seat" is literally the *hilasterion,* the place of conciliation, mercy, and grace.

A second, closely related aspect of this word is the sacrifice which Jesus brought as propitiation, or an atonement, for our sins. Here the emphasis falls on the sacrifice which Christ made, because He is our sin offering.

For instance, the Apostle Paul proclaimed that we can be acquitted of our sins because of the "propitiation" which Christ brought (Rom. 3:25). Because Christ suffered the penalty of our sins, God now can declare us righteous.

As our great High Priest, Christ not only brought the sin offering for us, but He is our sin offering. This emphasis permeates the Book of Hebrews. In fact, Christ is described as a merciful and faithful High Priest who brings a propitiation for our sins (Heb. 2:17).

Perhaps the fullest treatment of Christ's sacrifice on our behalf is found in the short Epistle of 1 John. There John declared that the incarnation reached its climax in Christ's crucifixion in our place. He thus became a propitiation for the sins of the world, and anyone who accepts His sacrifice is assured of complete cleansing (1 John 2:2).

Sometimes this sounds too legal and sterile. The Apostle John was preeminently an apostle of love, and he tied propitiation to the love of God for us. In this vein he wrote that God loved us so much that He sent His Son as the propitiation for our sins (4:10).

Our Greek words can be viewed from two standpoints. First, they can be seen as man's heart-cry for conciliation with God: "God, be merciful to me, a sinner." Second, they also refer to the sacrifice of the Lord Jesus Christ on our behalf, whereby we can be made right with God.

ILLUSTRATIONS

The Old Testament root of this word plunged deep into the Day of Atonement, in accordance with the Law of God (Lev. 16). On Yom Kippur two goats were brought to the priest. One was slain and its blood was sprinkled on the "mercy seat" as a "propitiation" for the sins of the people. The second goat became a sin-bearer. The priest would place his hands on the head of the second goat, indicating the transferal of sin to the "scape goat." Afterward the goat would be banished into the desert, never to return. It was the sin-bearer.

A Christian must not content himself with a "scapegoat." Jesus Christ has become our propitiation and sin offering. A.A. Hodge (1823-86), in his popular lectures on theology, said: "The sacrifices of bulls and goats were like token-money, as our paper promises to pay, accepted at their face value until the day of settlement. But the sacrifice of Christ was the gold which absolutely extinguished all debt by its intrinsic value. Hence, when Christ died, the veil that separated man from God was rent from the top to the bottom by supernatural hands."

This unique sacrifice of Christ should never be confused with the ineffective sacrifices of either Judaism or paganism. John F.D. Maurice (1805-72), a Church of England theologian, said: "The heathen significance of words [such as sacrifice], when applied to Christian use, must not merely be modified, but inverted." Along those same lines the famous preacher John Henry Jowett (1864-1923) concluded: "The heathen and Jewish sacrifices rather show us what the sacrifice of Christ was not, than what it was."

Animal sacrifices were annual events, but Christ died once for all. Animal sacrifices only covered sin, but Christ's blood blotted sin out. Animal sacrifices depended upon the faithfulness of human priests, but Christ was both the High Priest and the Sacrifice.

The great Australian scholar Leon Morris wrote: "The consistent Bible view is that the sin of man has incurred the wrath of God. That wrath is averted only by Christ's atoning offering. From this standpoint His saving work is properly called a propitiation" (Walter A. Elwell, editor, *Evangelical Dictionary of Theology* [Grand Rapids: Baker Book House, 1984], p. 888).

Lucy Bennett (1850-1927) summarized the significance of this truth in a beautiful hymn:

O teach me what it meaneth, / That cross uplifted high,
With One, the Man of Sorrows, / Condemned to bleed and die.
O teach me what it cost Thee, / To make a sinner whole;
And teach me, Saviour, teach me / The value of a soul.

RANSOM

MEANING

The Greek word for "ransom" is *lutron*. Both "ransom" and "redemption" come from the basic verb *luo* (to loosen). This group of words was used in Greek to speak of freeing prisoners, opening closed doors, breaking fetters, and liberating people from habits. In a very elemental sense, then, the ransom is a payment which frees a prisoner. As a ransom is paid the prisoner is redeemed from captivity.

In secular Greek literature a ransom was paid to release prisoners of war. It was also the payment given to buy a slave out of the market and free him. Even in paganism a payment was made to free someone from the supposed wrath of pagan gods.

The Septuagint Greek Old Testament used the word to describe a payment made to release a hostage. It is always a person who is ransomed in the Old Testament (Ex. 21:30; 30:12; Num. 35:31-32; Prov. 6:35). When a payment is given the hostage is freed, or redeemed.

BIBLE USAGE

In the New Testament Christ is the primary subject of the word *lutron* (ransom). It is usually Christ who is referred to as our ransom. This statement is found largely in the Gospels. The primary verse dealing with this is Mark 10:45. There Christ asserted that He "did not come to be served, but to serve, and to give His life a ransom for many." A similar statement is found in Matthew's Gospel (Matt. 20:28).

These passages are loaded with significance. First of all, Jesus thus gives eternal meaning to His death, and He does this prior to His passion. Second, the title which Jesus takes, "Son of man," is identified as a messianic name. Third, the concept of ransom implies substitution, that Jesus would die on our behalf and in our place (Isa. 53:6, 12). Fourth, the recipient of the ransom is God. It is God who lifts the punishment as a result of Christ's work on the cross. Fifth, only by the ransom of Christ could God be just and the Justifier of those who come to Him by grace through faith. The justice of God was fully satisfied in the ransom of Christ. This is one of the key passages in the entire New Testament.

Though the ransom of Christ is most clearly stated in the Gospels, it is also the subject of several references in the Epistles. Often the same root word is translated "redemption." Christians are justified, declared righteous, before God because of the redemption which Christ provided (Rom. 3:24). Now our souls are redeemed, but ultimately our bodies and a whole fallen creation will be redeemed because of Christ's death (8:23).

The basic meaning of ransom and redemption is seen in the fact that Christ's death loosed the bonds of sin and set us free (Eph. 1:7). In eternity this spiritual redemption and ransom will be fulfilled completely (1:14; Col. 1:14). The promise that we shall ultimately be completely redeemed is given by the Holy Spirit Himself (Eph. 4:30).

In many ways ransom and redemption are two sides of the same coin. Christ gave Himself as a ransom for us, so that we might be redeemed. The hymn of Zacharias praised God for redeeming His people (Luke 1:68), as did the testimony of Anna (2:38). Jesus pointed the eyes of His disciples to the ultimate accomplishment of redemption (21:28).

The sacrificed Saviour is the only source of redemption (Heb. 9:12). Consequently the Lord now has many people who have been redeemed, and these comprise the church of Jesus Christ (Titus 2:14). Christ looms above all other ransoms ever paid, being the sacrificial Lamb who provides eternal redemption (1 Peter 1:18-19).

To summarize, ransom and redemption are both parts of Christ's sacrifice on our behalf. As a ransom, Christ gave Himself to the Father to free us from the bondage of sin and the claims of divine justice. The result of this sacrifice for those who trust Christ is redemption, whereby we are freed from sin to serve the Saviour.

ILLUSTRATIONS

Once a small boy built a beautiful sailboat with his father. Actually, the dad did most of the work. One day the wind caught the little boat and propelled it out of reach. The prized possession was lost. Later the little lad spotted his boat in a secondhand store. He tried to convince the shopkeeper that the boat was his, but the man was unmoved by the boy's pleas. Finally the little boy bought back his own boat. So it was doubly his.

In the same way God originally created people. They fell into sin and slipped away from their Creator. In Christ Jesus, God bought back the people He had originally made. Now saved sinners belong to God on two counts. They are His by creation and His by redemption.

According to F.J. Taylor: "The experience of redemption which Christians now possess is but the firstfruits of that full redemption whose scope will embrace all history and nature. In Christ full redemption has already entered into the world but awaits its final consummation."

American hymn-writer Charles Gabriel (1856-1932) caught the flavor of this hope when he wrote:

When with the ransomed in glory
His face I at last shall see,
It will be my joy through the ages
To sing of His love for me.

Billy Graham explained the nature of Christ's redemptive work in this marvelous statement: "The question remains: How can God be just—that is, true to Himself in nature and true to Himself in holiness, and yet justify the sinner? The only solution was for an innocent party to volunteer to die physically and spiritually as a substitution before God. There was only one possibility. God's own Son was the only personality in the universe who had the capacity to bear in His own body the sins of the world."

Paul Rader (1879-1938) who pioneered Gospel radio broadcasting and pastored the great Chicago Gospel Tabernacle, wrote: "I stand before my neighbors on my character; but in heaven I have no standing myself at all. I stand there in the character of my Saviour."

No hymn makes this clearer than Philip P. Bliss' (1838-76) great anthem of adoration, "Man of Sorrows." One stanza puts it especially clearly:

Bearing shame and scoffing rude.
In my place condemned He stood,
Sealed my pardon with His blood,
Hallelujah, what a Saviour!

RECEIVE (See: *Take.*)
REGENERATON (See: *Born Again.*)   327

RESURRECTION

MEANING

The Greek words for "resurrection" are *anastasis* (resurrection) and *anhistemi* (I resurrect or raise from the dead). Literally these words mean, "to stand up again."

In the writings of Homer *anhistemi* means to wake up a sleepig person, or to cause him to stand up. Later on Hippocrates, "the father of medicine," employed the word to the resuscitation of the dead. This was more theoretical than practical, since only the Lord could raise the dead. By the later eras of Greek literature these words were used to speak of the transmigration of the soul. In fact, both Plato and Socrates used them to speak of the immortality of the soul. A person might be raised to immortality after death.

In the Septuagint Greek Old Testament, the word meant resuscitation. It was used, for instance, to describe the activity of Elijah in bringing back to life the son of the widow at Zarephath (1 Kings 17:17-24). It was also used to describe the bodily assumption of Enoch into heaven (Gen. 5:24).

BIBLE USAGE

The resurrection of Jesus Christ qualifies as one of the most significant events in human history, and its importance is reflected in the New Testament account. In the Gospels Jesus repeatedly predicted that He would rise from the dead. As He introduced the concept of the church, Jesus also predicted that He would be crucified and rise again (Matt. 16:21; Mark 8:31).

Immediately after His transfiguration, the Lord again returned to the subject of His death and resurrection (9:9, 31). He had been discussing His passion with Elijah and Moses on the mountain, and this subject still dominated the conversation when Jesus led His disciples down from that place of glory.

There was no question remaining in the hearts of the disciples concerning the Resurrection. They actually saw Christ after the event, though His body was of a different sort than a normal human body (John 20:19, 27). It was a glorified body, which was no longer limited to the natural laws of this world. In fact, the disciples had trouble recognizing Christ in His new form (Luke 24:16, 31). These post-resurrection appearances occurred over a period of 40 days (Acts 1:3).

Also in the Gospels one sees eloquent testimony to the Resurrection. On Resurrection Day Mary Magdalene and the other Mary dashed to the disciples with good news of Christ's return to life (Matt. 28:8, 10). This confidence also forms a foundation for the first church, as is seen in the deliberations and declarations of the disciples (Acts 1:22; 2:31; 4:33). Throughout the Apostolic Age the resurrection of Christ characterized the preaching of His followers (Acts 17:3; 1 Cor. 15:12-22). The Apostle Peter likewise introduced his first epistle with this assertion (1 Peter 1:3).

The resurrection of Christ was used as an example of new life. It meant that Christians had new desires (Col. 3:1). In baptism Christians imitate Christ's death and resurrection (Rom. 6:3-5). The Holy Spirit, who had raised Jesus from the grave (8:11), gave Christians new life. Because of this resurrection life, Christians now have spiritual power to serve the Lord (Phil. 3:10).

In fact, the resurrection of Christ is an ironclad guarantee of our resurrection. This was the basic theme of Paul, when he wrote to the Corinthians (1 Cor. 15:35-56). The same truth forms the basis of hope in Paul's presentation of the Rapture (1 Thes. 4:13-18). No earthly sorrow can dim the disciple's hope, because Jesus Christ is alive.

ILLUSTRATIONS

The resurrection of Jesus Christ has given rise to more quotable quotes than almost any other event except His birth. Congregational educationalist and theologian Horace Bushnell (1802-76) wrote: "The resurrection of Jesus Christ is absolutely the best attested fact in ancient history."

Along the same lines, Sir Norman Anderson, a lawyer and professor of law, wrote: "There is no point in arguing about the empty tomb. Everyone, friend or opponent, knew that it was empty. The only questions worth arguing about were why it was empty and what the emptiness proved."

At the end of the first century, about A.D. 93/94, Jewish historian Josephus wrote concerning Christ: "He [Jesus] appeared to them [the disciples] alive on the third day."

During the grand days of Puritanism in England, John Trapp (1601-69) wrote concerning Christ's resurrection: "Never was there as great an imposture put upon the world as Christianity, if Christ be yet in the grave."

A few years ago Frank Morison, a brilliant British lawyer, launched a study to debunk the Resurrection. He was determined to destroy once for all the basis of belief. At the end of his search, Morison met the Master who is alive. As a result that lawyer wrote *Who Moved the Stone?* (London: Faber and Faber, 1958)

Two hundred years earlier another Englishman, Gilbert West (1703-56), set about to disprove the resurrection of Jesus Christ. After intensive investigation, he too came to the conclusion that Jesus is really alive. West's masterpiece is titled, *Observations on the Resurrection.*

In the Soviet Union an atheistic lecturer chose the Easter season to attack the credibility of Christ's resurrection. A carefully reasoned address was aimed at the destruction of faith in the risen Lord. At the end an old Orthodox priest asked, if he might have the opportunity to refute the Marxist speaker. "You may only have five minutes," conceded the party functionary.

Walking to the front of the room, the aged priest shouted the familiar Eastern greeting: "Christ is risen!"

With one voice the crowd thundered back: "He is risen indeed!"

To which the old man added: "I rest my case."

A familiar theology text is William Hordern's, *Laymen's Guide to Protestant Theology* (New York: The MacMillan Company, 1955). On the subject of the resurrection of Christ Hordern concluded: "The Resurrection proclaims the fact that there is a power at work in the world which is mightier than all the forces that crucified our Lord. The Resurrection is not just a personal survival of the Man Jesus ... it is a cosmic victory" (p. 205).

In the words of Charles Wesley (1708-88): "Christ the Lord is risen today; Hallelujah!"

REVELATION

MEANING

In the Greek New Testament the word for "revelation" is *apokalypsis*, while *apokalypto* means "I reveal." One sees these words reflected in the English term, "apocalypse" (the revelation of Jesus Christ). A whole classification of literature is called "apocalyptic" (writings referring to future events). Basically the words *apokalypsis* and *apokalypto* mean "to uncover or unveil something or someone."

Herodotus was a Greek historian who wrote five centuries before Christ's birth. He said that *apokalypsis* meant the disclosure of previously hidden truth. About the time of Christ this word came to mean religious revelation. After Christ, Greek literature used this word to refer to the oracle of Delphi, who supposedly brought forth words from the pagan gods.

In the Septuagint Greek Old Testament, the word usually referred to physical uncovering. Usually, it spoke of uncovering or stripping a person.

BIBLE USAGE

In its various forms, the words for "revelation" are used about 44 times in the Greek New Testament. First and foremost they refer to biblical truth. God reveals His truth to simple people, not to the wise men of this world (Matt. 11:25). At the temple dedication of Christ, Simeon praised God for revealing His Son to both Jews and Gentiles (Luke 2:31-32).

When Christ came, the secret of salvation was finally revealed publicly (Rom. 16:25). Now the Holy Spirit carries this revelation into the consciences of all Christians (1 Cor. 2:10). For this reason He is sometimes called the Spirit of wisdom (Eph. 1:17). God also tells us when we stray from the truth (Phil. 3:15). Even the angels would like to see the revelations which we enjoy (1 Peter 1:12).

A second aspect of revelation is prophecy. In New Testament times many had visions and revelations of the Lord, which they communicated in the form of prophecies (2 Cor. 12:1). In fact, these prophets comprised a whole class of Christians (1 Cor. 14:1, 6). The Apostle Paul also received such a direct revelation from the Lord (Gal. 1:12; 2:2).

The New Testament contains several references to the revelation of Christians. When Christ comes and reveals all the true believers, even the created world will be renewed (Rom. 8:18-20). Then the full extent of our work for the Lord will be revealed (1 Cor. 3:13). Also the glory which we shall share eternally will be unveiled (1 Peter 5:1). We shall be made like the Lord Jesus Christ, when He is fully revealed (1 John 3:1-2). (See: *Coming, Second.*)

This revelation of Christians will be accompanied by a revelation of the Lord Jesus Christ. When Christ returns (Luke 17:30) in all His glory, sin will be forever unmasked. All true Christians will appear in that day with the Lord Jesus Christ (1 Peter 1:7). There will be unlimited glory for the godly when the Lord is revealed (4:13). A foretaste of this revelation was seen when the glorified Christ revealed Himself to John on the Island of Patmos (Rev. 1:1-10).

There is, however, also a shadowy side of revelation. The Bible instructs us that before Christ is revealed, the Antichrist will be revealed. This is especially emphasized in the writings of Paul. The Day of the Lord will be preceded by the coming of the Antichrist (2 Thes. 2:3). Only the presence of the Holy Spirit in the world prevents his revelation now (2:6). The appearance of Antichrist will herald his ultimate destruction (2:8).

Christians are not restricted by reason or limited by the limitations of man.

They are not bound by the cumulative wisdom of the generations. In the Scriptures Christians have a direct and reliable revelation from God, which gives them understanding of the past, comprehension of the present, and faith to face the future.

ILLUSTRATIONS

On the subject of divine revelation, noted American statesman Daniel Webster (1782-1852) concluded: "The Bible is a book of faith and a book of doctrine and a book of morals and a book of religion, of especial revelation from God."

Another notable person, British statesman and philosopher Francis Bacon (1561-1626), also praised the value of the scriptural revelation: "The knowledge of man is as the waters, some descending from above, and some springing up from beneath; the one informed by the light of nature, the other inspired by divine revelation."

One of the great minds of our century was Edward John Carnell (1919-67), who served as an early president of Fuller Theological Seminary. On the subject of revelation Dr. Carnell concluded: "Human beings cannot probe the mind of God by asking themselves what they would do if they were God. They are men and not God. And if they are virtuous men, they will wait for God to reveal Himself under conditions of His own choosing."

A rather comical story shows the necessity of revelation. One of the most bothersome pets which I ever had was a goldfish. It said absolutely nothing. Never could I cuddle and hug it. When I called it, it simply swam away. Communication was impossible. Only by becoming a goldfish could I talk to one.

God created people in His image, but sin marred that image. Besides, God is infinite and limitless, while we are finite and limited. God wanted to communicate with us, so in Christ God became man to reveal the eternal God to us.

Another aspect of revelation is found in the writings of Professor James Denney (1856-1917), a Scottish Free Church divine. On revelation he said: "What Christ did had to be done, or we should never have had forgiveness; we should never have known God. But He, by taking on Himself our responsibilities and by dying our death, has so revealed God to us as to put forgiveness within our reach."

A contemporary of Denney was the Congregational preacher Joseph Parker (1830-1902), who wrote about revelation: "After reading the doctrines of Plato, Socrates, or Aristotle, we feel the specific difference between their words and Christ's is the difference between an inquiry and a revelation."

An old, seldom-sung hymn puts it well:

The half has not been fancied
  This side the golden shore,
For there He'll be still sweeter
  Than He ever was before.

REWARD

MEANING

In the Greek New Testament the word for reward is *misthos*. Basically it means the reward one is paid for working, usually the wage for one day's work. Consequently there are several combination words connected with *misthos*. For instance, a *misthios* is a day laborer, one who is hired for casual work. A second related term is *misthotos*, a hired hand who works regularly for an employer. The third connected concept is that of a price paid for renting a room, *misthoma*.

The secular Greek writers used all of the above terms in describing the normal affairs of life. The "reward" applied to a soldier's pay. It also was used to describe the fee a doctor exacted for services rendered. Finally, it was used for the honorarium given to a priest for performing religious services.

Only later did "reward" take on an abstract meaning. In the writings of Pindar one finds reference to renown as a reward for outstanding service to the community. In the Hellenistic period of Greek literature it also referred to the reward of a moral life.

BIBLE USAGE

Jesus used the various words connected with reward in His teaching. For instance, in the story of the Prodigal Son Jesus mentioned the casual laborer, *misthios*, as the least regarded person (Luke 15:17). When speaking of the Good Shepherd, Jesus also spoke of the "hireling" (*misthotos*), an undershepherd who shares no real concern for the sheep (John 10:12-13). The rent paid for a room, *misthoma*, is seen in the account of Paul's stay in Rome (Acts 28:30).

However, the most basic meaning of reward is wages paid to a laborer for services rendered. Jesus underlined this relationship by asserting that a laborer deserves his wages (Luke 10:7). Again in addressing His disciples Jesus asserted that a reaper is worthy of his wages (John 4:36). In fact, anyone who defrauds a workman of wages is roundly condemned in Scripture (James 5:4).

The same concept of wages is applied to the Christian ministry. The Apostle Paul quoted the teaching of Jesus concerning payment for services rendered (1 Tim. 5:18). Then Paul pointed out that preachers should also be paid properly.

A second aspect of reward is spiritual reward. In the Sermon on the Mount, Jesus taught that persecution on earth would be rewarded in heaven (Matt. 5:12). On the other hand, people who serve God to gain reward on earth will have no reward in heaven, for they have already been paid (6:2, 5).

Even the most basic service for the Lord will be rewarded in heaven. Jesus asserted that the simple offering of a cup of cold water would bring eternal rewards (10:41-42).

When Jesus encountered a Samaritan woman, He took the opportunity to teach His disciples concerning spiritual rewards. In the economy of Jesus, service to the Father was sure to be rewarded (John 4:34-36). In this connection He repeated His teaching about workmen's wages (4:36).

In writing to the Corinthians Paul discussed the rewards given for spiritual service. No matter what role a person plays in building the church of Jesus Christ, the Lord will reward him (1 Cor. 3:8). In fact, the durability of one's work is a reward in itself (3:14). Only those who work willingly will be rewarded, according to the apostle (9:17-18).

There are, of course, also the rewards of unrighteousness. Though the apostle does not use the word *misthos*, he introduced the wages of sin in Romans 6:23.

(Here the word is one which applies to a soldier's pay.)

When the Jewish officials paid off Judas to betray the Lord, the disciples called the coins the wages of his wickedness (lit in Greek, "the reward of his wickedness"; Acts 1:18). Peter pointed out that some people deserve to suffer, because they have done wrong (2 Peter 2:13-15).

The close connection of wages and work is often seen in Scripture. If one serves the Lord in this life, he will receive an eternal reward. On the other hand, those who do not serve the Lord will also get their wages in eternity.

ILLUSTRATIONS

The various uses of "reward" are also seen in literature. The famous writer Virgil (70-19 B.C.) asserted: "Virtue hath her rewards and mortality her tears" (*Aeneid,* i. 461).

In his poem, "The Faerie Queen," Edmund Spenser (1552-99) spoke of the rewards of accomplishment: "Sleep after toil, port after stormy seas, / Ease after war, death after life, does greatly please." Yet he also asserted that one must do, "all for love, and nothing for reward."

Puritan writer Thomas Fuller claimed: "Praise makes good men better and bad men worse." Along the same lines Thomas Dreier declared: "One thing scientists have discovered is that often-praised children become more intelligent than often-blamed ones. There's a creative element in praise [or reward]."

During the years we spent in Germany, we saw a society which places a high priority on work and service. In speaking of service for the Lord, German Christians often said: "The greatest reward for service is the privilege of serving."

English novelist George MacDonald (1824-1905) concentrated on the rewards which the Lord gives when he wrote: "When one has to seek the honor that comes from God only, he will take the withholding of the honor that comes from men very quietly indeed." No human reward can compare with Christ's.

A lesser known Puritan, Ezekiel Hopkins, wrote these lines concerning heaven: "Where the unveiled glories of the Deity shall beat full upon us . . . we shall forever sun ourselves in the smiles of God."

Taking a leaf from the pages of English history, Thomas Adams, another Puritan, penned these lines: "He that will be knighted must kneel for it, and he that will enter in at the strait gate must crowd for it—a gate made so on purpose, narrow and hard in the entrance, yet, after we have entered, wide and glorious, that after our pain our joy may be the sweeter."

Dr. R.T. Kendall is the first American pastor of London's famed Westminster chapel. Some years ago he preached a long series of sermons on heaven. He reasoned that people need to know that their service for the Lord will be surely rewarded.

While visiting an elderly shut-in in Bournemouth, England, I was rebuked by her faithfulness. "Every time the pastor enters the pulpit," she said, "I begin to pray for him." Her faithfulness will surely be rewarded in heaven.

RICH

MEANING

The word translated "rich" in the New Testament is *ploutos*. One easily sees the connection between this term and our English word, *"pluto*crat" (which literally means one who rules because of his wealth). In Greek the word is connected to *pleroma*, the word for "fullness." In other words, a rich person is one who is "full of money or property."

In early Greek literature, the fullness of material things was contrasted with the fullness of spiritual things. It was regarded as crude to be wealthy in terms of possessions but poor in terms of immaterial things. (Sadly, many people still make this foolish exchange. They surrender spiritual wealth for financial fatness.)

Along the lines of this spiritual wealth one reads of Zeus, who was a pagan god rich in peace. But Homer spoke of wealth which made it possible for one to live without working. Socrates said that the rich were regarded as being socially sought after.

BIBLE USAGE

In the New Testament words that relate to wealth are found about 22 times. There are two basic forms of wealth in the Bible, material and spiritual.

Jesus insisted that spiritual wealth far outweighs financial wealth (Matt. 6:25-32). For this reason people should lay up treasures in heaven, where they can never be eroded or corroded (6:19-21).

Pursuing this principle, Jesus said that riches can choke out spiritual interest (13:22). This found eloquent, if sad, confirmation in a meeting between Jesus and a rich young ruler, a man who loved things more than the Lord (19:22). One rich man who followed Jesus was Joseph of Arimathea, but he followed very cautiously (27:57). Likewise Dives ended up in eternal gloom, while poor Lazarus enjoyed eternal bliss (Luke 16:19-31). In the same camp was a rich farmer who built barns but lost his soul (12:19-21). Zaccheus, however, surrendered his wealth and saw his soul saved (19:1-10).

The Apostle Paul warned against the danger of riches, which can cause spiritual shipwreck (1 Tim. 6:10, 17). The danger is not in possessing possessions, but in letting possessions possess you.

When one turns from financial wealth to spiritual wealth, he finds God to be the pattern of true wealth. God is rich in grace, so He can forgive our sins because of Christ (Eph. 1:7). In fact, the riches of His grace surpass all human comprehension (2:7). The grace of Jesus Christ is seen in this, that He left the riches of heaven to become a slave for us, that we might be made rich in Him (2 Cor. 8:9).

God is also rich in glory. Out of these riches He strengthens Christians (Eph. 3:16). In heaven He will heap these riches on His people (1:18). Because of these glorious riches, He can also meet all the needs of all His people (Phil. 4:19). Because of Christ's death the riches of His glory are advertised in us (Rom. 9:23).

Another aspect of God's riches is seen in Romans. There the Apostle Paul speaks of the riches of God's kindness, whereby He bears with us until we repent and turn to Him for salvation (2:4).

The Bible also describes several spiritually rich men. Jesus spoke of people who could be spiritually rich toward God (Luke 12:21). James promised an eternal reward to those who are rich in faith (James 2:5).

According to the Scriptures, material wealth can build a barrier between the soul and the Saviour. One who learns to trust wealth distrusts the Deliverer. On the other hand, spiritual wealth is achieved only from the Lord. Many Christians are poor in this world, but in the coming kingdom they will be rich. That is well worth waiting for.

ILLUSTRATIONS

There are abundant evidences to the trouble wealth can bring. Noel Coward (1899-1973) an urbane master of music hall melody, wrote a song titled, "Poor Little Rich Girl." The song painted a portrait of a wealthy girl who had everything but love.

A good friend is a former Chief of Chaplains of the Belgian Army. He had circulated in circles of wealth and power. When we discussed affluence, he lamented: "Money is a fine servant, but it is a terrible master."

The father of Keynsian economics was J.M. Keynes (1883-1946). He said candidly: "The moral problem of our age is concerned with the love of money, with the habitual appeal to the money motive in nine-tenths of the activities of life."

According to Richard T. Ely: "We have among us a class of mammon-worshipers, whose one test of conservatism or radicalism is the attitude one takes with respect to accumulated wealth. Whatever tends to preserve the wealth of the wealthy is called conservatism, and whatever favors anything else, no matter what, they call socialism."

Socrates (470-399 B.C.) said about wealth: "If a rich man is proud of his wealth, he should not be praised until it is known how he employs it."

President Franklin Delano Roosevelt (1882-1945) was an extremely wealthy man in his own right. Still he saw the danger of wealth and said: "The hopes of the Republic cannot forever tolerate either undeserved poverty or self-serving wealth."

When one turns from material wealth to spiritual wealth, there is a whole new tone to the writing. Dr. Warren Wiersbe wrote a short commentary on Ephesians, *Be Rich* (Wheaton, Illinois: Victor Books, 1976). In the author's preface he concluded: "Too many Christians are living like paupers when Christ made us rich! Isn't it time we stopped living on substitutes [even religious substitutes] and started drawing on the riches we have in Christ?"

In her *Sonnets from the Portuguese,* Elizabeth Barrett Browning (1806-61) wrote this provocative line: "God's gifts put man's best dreams to shame."

Some of the spiritually wealthiest people I know are materially impoverished. There was an elderly couple in Bristol, England who drove an ancient car and lived in one room. Still they were fabulously rich. Their children were serving the Lord. Their grandchildren all confessed Christ. Their whole lives glowed with the glory of their God.

It is no wonder that Francis Havergal (1836-79) could cheerfully sing:

Take my silver and my gold,
Not a mite would I withhold;
Take my intellect, and use
Every power as Thou shalt choose.

SACRIFICE

MEANING

In the New Testament the word "sacrifice" is a translation of the Greek term *thysia*. The related verb, "to sacrifice," represents the Greek word, *thyo*. This has always meant the bringing of a religious offering to a deity.

When Homer wrote, about nine centuries before Christ, these terms meant a "smoke or burnt offering." Later the term was broadened to mean the actual slaying of a sacrifice. According to Pindar, *thysia* was the very ritual of sacrifice, the religious service in which a sacrifice was brought.

In the Septuagint Greek Old Testament, this word was used to describe the Jewish sacrificial system. It also characterized the action of bringing a sacrifice. In fact, most of the major characters in the Old Testament brought sacrifices. Among them were: Noah (Gen. 8:20), Abraham (12:6), Isaac (26:25), Jacob (33:20), Moses (Ex. 17:15), Elijah (1 Kings 18:31), and David (2 Sam. 24:18). (See: *Offering*.)

BIBLE USAGE

The words pertaining to sacrifice occur about 40 times in the Greek New Testament. Jesus gave basic teaching about the priority of sacrifice. In the Sermon on the Mount He warned against bringing a sacrifice when there is sin in one's life (Matt. 5:23-24). Later on He chided some Pharisees, because they substituted sacrifices for mercy (9:13; 12:7). When sacrifices were turned into commerce and exploited for personal gain, Jesus struck out literally and expelled the animal salesmen from the temple (21:12-17). Nevertheless, the earthly parents of Jesus, Joseph and Mary, brought a sacrifice at the time of Jesus' temple dedication (Luke 2:24). Their sacrifice was sincere.

In the Book of Acts, the church moved away from the Jewish sacrificial system. The early Christians realized that Jesus Christ had brought the only perfect Sacrifice, Himself.

It was the perversion of the old sacrifices, the offering to a golden calf, that Stephen condemned in his last sermon (Acts 7:41). The Apostle Paul fulfilled his vow and brought a sacrifice when he returned to Jerusalem at the end of his missionary journeys (21:26).

The Epistles emphasize the perfection of Christ's sacrifice, and the effectiveness of His death on our behalf. The theme is sounded in Romans, where Paul proclaimed that the sacrificed Saviour made us right with God (Rom. 3:23-25).

It is in Hebrews, however, that this theme is fully developed. The priesthood of Christ is built on the idea of His atoning sacrifice (Heb. 2:17). Part of the priestly task was sacrifice, which was exemplified perfectly in Christ (5:1-9). Not only did Christ present Himself as a sacrifice, but His sacrifice was once for all (7:27). Animal sacrifices could never cleanse one's conscience, but Christ's sacrifice could (9:9-14). On the basis of His sacrifice, Christ now exercises an intercessory ministry on our behalf (10:11-12).

Because Christ sacrificed Himself on our behalf, Christians are also told to make sacrifices. They should present their bodies as living sacrifices to God (Rom. 12:1-2). Their daily lives of separation from sin are an imitation, though a pale one, of the sacrifice of Christ (Eph. 5:2). When Christians financially support the ministry, they also bring sacrifices to the Lord (Phil. 4:18). In fact, all Christians are priests designated to bring spiritual sacrifices to the Lord (1 Peter 2:5, 9).

Because of the deep significance attached to the sacrifice of Christ, the New Testament is strong in condemning sacrifices to idols. At the Jerusalem Council all of the apostolic leaders agreed to denounce sacrifices to idols (Acts 15:29). Paul insisted that idols were no gods at all; in fact they were nothing but bits of wood or stone (1 Cor. 8:1, 4, 7).

Since Christ has been sacrificed, all other religious sacrifices are out of date. The only acceptable sacrifice is the sacrifice of worship and service which dedicated believers bring to their Lord.

ILLUSTRATIONS

On the subject of sacrifice there are numerous viewpoints. One of them was expressed by the famous pulpiteer, John Sutherland Bonnell: "Take that gift God has entrusted to you, and use it in the service of Christ and your fellowmen. He will make it glow and shine like the very stars of heaven."

President Woodrow Wilson (1856-1924), was one of the few men who ever deserved to be called "a scholar and a gentleman." Realizing the strength of his character, it is not surprising that he saw service as a priority and said: "The object of love is to serve, not to win." Sacrifice and service were synonymous to President Wilson.

Another gentle President was Calvin Coolidge (1872-1933), who spoke of the sacrifice of worship when he wrote: "It is only when men begin to worship that they begin to grow." Someone said more recently: "People who do not worship God are not evil people; they are just boring people." The sacrifice of worship lifts our eyes from the gutter to the glory.

Few people today know much about sacrifice. One who did know it was the multimillionaire R.G. LeTourneau (1888-1969). He was a large man, both in girth and heart. His money had been made in the invention and production of earth-moving machinery. Some of it was spent in building roads in Latin America to open the jungle for missionary advance. His name is known mainly because of LeTourneau College in Longview, Texas. Recently, however, a legacy from LeTourneau was put to work in building large Christian and Missionary Alliance Churches at Lima. Though LeTourneau made millions, he gave nine-tenths of it to the Lord's work.

On a recent course evaluation at Trinity Evangelical Divinity School, I asked the question: "What have you learned in this introductory missions course?" Many students responded that they had learned the necessity of a sacrificial lifestyle, in order that they might serve the Lord more effectively.

Several recent writers have reminded us of the need of sacrificing to serve our Lord and others. The Bishop of Liverpool, England, David Sheppard, emphasized God's care for the downtrodden in his book, *Bias to the Poor* (London: Hodder and Stoughton, 1983).

From an American perspective, Professor Ronald Sider of Eastern Baptist College has disturbed many with his emphasis on the necessity of a sacrificial lifestyle. His most famous book is *Rich Christians in an Age of Hunger* (Downers Grove, Illinois: InterVarsity, 1978).

SANCTIFY (See: *Holy.*)

SANHEDRIN (See: *Council.*)

SAINT (See: *Holy.*) 337

SAVE, SAVIOUR, SALVATION

MEANING

The words which relate to salvation in the Greek New Testament are *sozo* ("to save"), *soter* ("saviour"), and *soteria* ("salvation"). They are reflected in the theological term "*soter*iology" (the study of the subject of salvation). Originally these words came from the root *saos*, which meant "to make safe or to deliver from a threat."

There are four elemental meanings for these words in Greek. First, they mean to save someone by the dynamic act of snatching him from danger. Homer used the word in this vein. A second meaning involved keeping someone in safety, as the envoys of a nation are kept from danger. This was employed by Plutarch. Third, it meant to benefit someone or keep him in good health. Fourth, the preservation of inner being was also described by this word. All in all, the word related mainly to the preservation of inner and outer safety.

BIBLE USAGE

In various forms these words occur 185 times in the New Testament. Usually they refer to God's work in human lives. In each case God or Christ is the Saviour. For instance, in the Pastoral Epistles, God is often referred to as Saviour. Paul prefaced the Letter of 1 Timothy with a reference to God as Saviour (1 Tim. 1:1). The preservation of public peace was seen as pleasing to God our Saviour (2:1-3). In fact, the only One who can save people is God Himself (4:10).

Likewise Paul pursued this theme in writing to Titus. God the Saviour conveyed the Gospel message to Paul (Titus 1:3). The saviourhood of God is closely identified with the saving appearance of Christ (2:10-13; 3:4).

Any saving must originate with God. To this end God sends preachers to proclaim the Gospel (1 Cor. 1:21). This salvation is all of grace, which excludes any human works (2 Tim. 1:9; Titus 3:5).

Likewise God the Son, Jesus Christ, is shown to be the Saviour according to the New Testament. This was seen in the events which surrounded His coming to earth (Matt. 1:21; Luke 2:11). In fact, He claimed that His sole purpose was to seek and save the lost (19:10; 2 Tim. 1:10). The Apostle Paul reckoned that no one was too sinful for salvation, because Christ had saved him, a persecutor of the church (1 Tim. 1:15). Now Jesus Christ is seated at the right hand of God, interceding for Christians and saving sinners (Heb. 7:25). Since His ascension Christians have patiently waited for Christ to be revealed again as Saviour (Phil. 3:20).

Though only God can save through Jesus Christ, He uses people to take the saving message far and near. Paul regarded himself mainly as an agent of salvation (Rom. 11:14). For this reason he would endure any and every hardship to bring the Gospel to people (1 Cor. 9:22). He also regarded Christian wives as agents of salvation to their unsaved husbands (7:16).

From our standpoint, the best aspect of salvation is our experience of it. The truth of Scripture is this, that we can know beyond any doubt that we are delivered by the Lord Jesus Christ. Jesus asserted that we may know now that we have eternal life (John 3:16-17). The apostles insisted that salvation is available now in the name of Jesus (Acts 4:12). When a frightened jailer asked Paul and Silas the way of salvation, they answered: "Believe in the Lord Jesus, and you shall be saved" (16:31). This assurance of salvation flows from faith and is seen in public confessions (Rom. 10:9-10). By the same token, the message which mediates salvation to Christians also signals the doom of sinners (1 Cor. 1:18).

Salvation is, from a human standpoint, the major doctrine of the New

Testament. The Bible is a book all about salvation. From the Fall to the Rapture of the church, the main work of God is saving sinners and renewing them in the image of the Lord Jesus Christ.

ILLUSTRATIONS

The greatest treasure known to people is salvation. Of this the missionary-physician Wilfred Grenfell (1866-1940) wrote: "I am conscious that for me, my only hope of salvation in this world lies in Christ."

Martin Luther's firm friend and colleague, Philip Melanchthon (1497-1560), wrote on the subject of salvation: "To know Christ is not to speculate about the mode of His incarnation, but to know His saving benefits."

Novelist Dorothy Sayers (1893-1957), a committed Christian, said about salvation: "That there is a great split today in Christendom nobody would deny; but the line of cleavage does not run between Catholic and Protestant or between Conformist and Nonconformist. It runs, as it ran 16 centuries ago . . . between those who believe that salvation is of God and those who believe that salvation is of man."

On a more simple line, ex-baseball player turned evangelist Billy Sunday (1862-1935), claimed: "It won't save your soul if your wife is a Christian. You have got to be something more than a brother-in-law to the church."

In the New Testament, salvation is linked closely to the Saviour, Jesus Christ. The late Professor Merrill Tenney said: "God doesn't just patch—He renews. God doesn't just salve sins—He saves. God doesn't just reform—He transforms men by His power."

From the standpoint of the social gospel, Washington Gladden (1836-1918) said: "To believe *on* Christ, I say: not merely to believe *in* Him, or to believe something *about* Him, but to believe *on* Him; and this means to entrust your soul to Him and to trust in Him for wisdom and strength and salvation."

Noted missionary statesman John "Praying" Hyde (1865-1912) said concerning the subject of salvation: "If every person in the world had adequate food, housing, income; if all men were equal; if every possible social evil and injustice were done away with, men would still need one thing: Christ!"

Methodist Bishop, William McDowell (1858-1937), asserted concerning salvation: "No one is 'getting along pretty well' without Jesus Christ. We are saved by a Person, and only by a Person, and only by one Person."

Scottish Puritan writer Samuel Rutherford (1600-61) wrote: "As the Lord lives, I durst promise it in His name, if we would seek Him we should see the salvation of the Lord." The proclamation was the single greatest contribution of the Puritans to England and to the American colonies. Through their preaching the Great Awakening swept through the New World and the Old.

SEAL

MEANING

The word for "sealing" in the Greek New Testament is *sphragizo*. It is largely a commercial or business term, referring to sealing a building shut. In order to guarantee property against theft, a seal was placed on it. Or sometimes it took the form of a mark or a brand, as on livestock. When a merchant bought a sack of grain, a seal would be placed on the sack until the full payment was made. This was a guarantee of coming payment.

Later the seal became a mark of royalty. Any communiqué from the crown was sealed by the king. After dabbing hot wax on the document, the king would seal it by pressing his ring into the wax. Before long, the engraved ring was called "a seal." In the religious sphere, a sacrificial lamb which was found to be suitable was also sealed, marked as suitable.

In the Septuagint Greek Old Testament, a seal was a signet ring. This ring was used to indicate a sale (Jer. 32:10). Royalty also used the seal to authenticate its orders (Es. 3:10; 8:8). Though the precise word for "sealing" is not used, Isaiah 44:5 speaks of people who had "for Jehovah" tattooed on their hands as a mark of religious sacrifice (Colin Brown, ed., *Dictionary of New Testament Theology*, III, p. 498).

BIBLE USAGE

A seal indicated ownership or authority. This word and its related terms are used 40 times in the New Testament. By and large, the New Testament use parallels that of secular Greek and the Septuagint Greek Old Testament.

Sealing means, first of all, safety. When Jesus was buried in the borrowed tomb of Joseph of Arimathea, that tomb was sealed (Matt. 27:66). The Romans thought the disciples might disturb the body, but the real danger was resurrection.

The Apostle Paul promised to put his seal on the Gentile believers in Macedonia and Greece (Rom. 15:28). He seems to mean that he wished to mark them with his teaching as a precaution against coming trouble.

In the Book of Revelation we read of an unopened book sealed with seven seals (Rev. 5:1). After they are opened by the Lamb, the Lord Jesus Christ, a prophecy of the future unfolds (chap. 6). This remarkable prophecy was sealed for safety, until the Lamb loosed the seals.

A second meaning of seal in the New Testament is identity. When God chose Israel, He gave them a seal to identify them as His people. That seal was circumcision (Rom. 4:11). Throughout history, despite deprivation and destruction, this seal has stood visibly on that people.

By the same token, the Lord has placed a seal on His church. Paul promised Timothy that this seal stood as firmly as the one on Israel (2 Tim. 2:19). It identifies the people of God, and it also separates them from the world's contamination.

The third use of this word is certainty. The certainty of our salvation is guaranteed by the Holy Spirit, who is the seal of God on our lives (John 3:33-34). Jesus Christ was guaranteed by God's seal to be the Saviour (6:27).

Along the same lines, Paul regarded his converts as the seal of his work (1 Cor. 9:2). His ministry was certified to be true, because people were actually transformed and integrated into the local churches. Even the problem children of Corinth were a seal on Paul's ministry.

A final aspect of sealing is a guarantee. When a Christian comes to believe in the Lord Jesus Christ, the Holy Spirit seals him or her as a guarantee of eternal life

(Eph. 1:13-17). The same truth is emphasized elsewhere (2 Cor. 1:22; 5:5). Every Christian, no matter how immature in the faith, has the Holy Spirit as this seal.

In the Book of Revelation this same guarantee is extended in another direction. The selected body of believers taken from times of tribulation are sealed in a special way by the Lord. They bear the name of the Lord, which is written on their foreheads (Rev. 14:1). In the glory every Christian will be thus marked and sealed (22:4).

This seal in Scripture is a source of comfort to Christians. It speaks of the security which we have in the Lord, a security which does not rest on our strength but on His Spirit.

ILLUSTRATIONS

In applying this important word, one may use the same four categories. First of all, there is a real safety in sealing. Now we use such things as dead-bolt locks to render our homes safe and seal them off from burglary.

Spiritual safety must have a spiritual security, and this is the Holy Spirit. Puritan divine John Owen (1616-83) said concerning the Spirit's sealing: "God's sealing of believers is His gracious communication of the Holy Ghost unto them, so as to enable them unto all the duties of their holy calling. The effects of this sealing are gracious operations of the Spirit in and upon believers; but the sealing itself is the communication of God's Spirit to them." God guarantees the safety of our salvation with His Spirit, the seal.

The identity of a Christian is also sealed by the Lord. Nowadays cattle farmers tattoo numbers on their cattle to identify them. In Israel one sees sheep with blotches of red or blue paint on them as identification. So the Holy Spirit in the life of a believer identifies him or her as God's own.

The third meaning of sealing is certainty, and the Holy Spirit gives spiritual certainty to Christians when He seals them. In writing about the sealing of the Spirit, William Hendricksen affirmed: "The Spirit who had given them this seal is called by His full name, 'the Holy Spirit,' to indicate not only that He is holy in Himself but also that He is the Source of holiness for believers" (*Ephesians* [Edinburgh: Banner of Truth, 1967], p. 91).

A fourth implication of the Spirit's sealing on the Christian is a guarantee of heaven to come. John Stott emphasized this in his fine commentary on Ephesians. The Holy Spirit is like an engagement ring. When a man places that ring on a woman's finger, it is a guarantee that he will marry her sooner or later.

This guarantee is also like a first installment. When one buys a home, a deposit or first installment is paid. The implied promise is that completion of the deal will provide payment for the rest, even when it is borrowed money (John R.W. Stott, *God's New Society* [Leicester: InterVarsity Press, 1979], p. 49).

The Holy Spirit is God's first installment on heaven. When a person comes to Christ, the Holy Spirit seals the deal. Living in us, the blessed Holy Spirit of God is the guarantee that God will "make good" on all His promises.

(See: *Coming, Second.*)
(See: *Behold.*)

SEEK

MEANING

The Greek term translated "seek" is *zeteo*. In its basic form it means to seek, investigate, or search for something. Homer used it to describe the striving after knowledge; it especially applied to philosophical investigation.

Later on the term took on a legal flavor, as it was used to portray a judicial investigation. From the first century before Christ onward it meant to seek, investigate, to strive for knowledge.

This word appeared more than 400 times in the Septuagint, the Greek translation of the Old Testament. Sometimes "seek" simply meant to concentrate on finding someone. Joseph sought his brothers (Gen. 37:16), and Saul sought his father's female donkeys (1 Sam. 10:2). Also in the Septuagint this word was used for seeking after God (Isa. 9:13). Conversely, God sought after His prodigal people (Ezek. 34:12-16).

BIBLE USAGE

The words based on *zeteo* occur 120 times in the New Testament. Simply speaking, they relate to seeking what was lost. In Jesus' Parable of the Pearl, a merchant sought diligently to find expensive pearls (Matt. 13:45). Luke's Gospel contains a whole cluster of parables relating to seeking. In addition to the Lost Sheep and the Lost Son Parables, Jesus told about a Lost Coin. A woman lit a torch and sought diligently to find her coin (Luke 15:8).

Another major emphasis in the Scriptures is the search for God. (Some would argue that God is not lost; we are. Still the New Testament speaks of applying effort to find God.) Christ exhorted His hearers to seek God's kingdom before anything else (Matt. 6:33; Luke 12:31). Likewise Jesus urged urgency in the search for God (Matt. 7:7; Luke 11:9). In the same vein the Apostle Paul told his Athenian hearers to seek after God (Acts 17:27). When a sinner is saved, he or she has searched seriously for God, though God really did the pursuing.

There are some references in the Scripture to show what God is seeking in His people. Jesus sought figs on a fig tree, and He seeks spiritual fruit in our lives (Luke 13:6). God is also seeking true worshipers (John 4:23). When the Lord came into this world, His primary aim was to seek and to save the lost (Luke 19:10). God seeks in His people a heart to worship and serve Him, and where this is lacking He moves on.

One kind of seeking that is condemned in the Scriptures is self-seeking. Before Christ came, people were consumed with a desire to seek righteousness on their own terms, not on God's terms (Rom. 10:3). Even among Christians Paul found many people who sought after their own interests rather than the things of God (Phil. 2:21). He contrasted this self-seeking with Christ's life of self-sacrifice (2:5-11). Paul had learned not to seek his own ends, but the building up of the church (1 Cor. 10:33).

Another perversion of this seeking was the Jewish habit of seeking a sign from God to validate the messianic message (Mark 8:12). If the people did not see a miracle, they would not believe. But despite all the miracles they saw, many still did not believe. The Apostle Paul likewise warned the Corinthians about this fundamental error (1 Cor. 1:21-23).

The whole of the Christian life can be summarized in seeking. God in His grace and mercy seeks and finds us. We have hearts which are disposed to seek after God until we find Him. After conversion, God seeks in us true worship, while we seek to please Him by what we do.

ILLUSTRATIONS

God's marvelous means of winning us for Himself are all bound up with the act of seeking. In fact Francis Thompson (1859-1907) wrote an excellent poem, "The Hound of Heaven." After studying for the priesthood, Thompson turned to medicine at the University of Manchester. Before long he became a helpless opium addict, in London. In 1888 Wilfred Meynell found him and won him for Christ. Thompson claimed that all along God had sought him like "the hound of heaven."

Another similar story is that of Augustine (A.D. 354-430). Despite the pleadings of his godly mother, Monica, he launched into a life of immorality and debauchery. Along the way he fell in with the Manichean sect, and later he became a disciple of Neo-Platonism. Finally in Milan during 386 he read the Bible, and God arrested Augustine. Consequently the church has been immensely enriched by his life and writings.

Augustine explained this searching in his testimonial book, *Confessions.* Here he recorded this powerful prayer: "Thou has created us for Thyself, and our heart cannot be quieted till it may find repose in Thee." He knew the double searching of God for the sinner and the sinner for God.

Another person who understood this seeking after God was Chicago preacher A.W. Tozer. One of the collections of his writings is titled, *The Pursuit of God.* In this compendium of essays Tozer took his readers on a quest for the holiness of God.

The son of my colleague had grown up, but not completely. In rebellion he turned his back on everything his father stood for. One time the boy even stole his father's car and ended up in jail. In sheer desperation, to escape his Christian home, the boy joined the U.S. Army. Of course God was still pursuing him, seeking him. Soon a Christian came into the boy's life, and he came to a personal faith in the Lord. Now that retired rebel is studying for the ministry.

Because God is eager to seek us, true Christians engage in evangelism to seek others. The need for going after the lost was emphasized by Myron S. Augsburger, a Mennonite evangelist. "Too many clergymen have become keepers of the aquarium," argued Augsburger, "instead of fishers of men—and often they are just swiping each other's fish."

On the same subject of seeking the lost, John Wesley (1703-91) issued a stern warning: "The church has nothing to do but to save souls; therefore spend and be spent in this work. It is not your business to speak so many times, but to save souls as you can; to bring as many sinners as you possibly can to repentance."

When Jesus lived on earth, He went around seeking and saving. Now we who are the body of Christ should be constantly involved in seeking and saving the lost. Otherwise we have no reason to remain on earth.

SELF-CONTROL

MEANING

The Greek word which is translated "self-control" is *nephoo*. In its original form it meant to be free from intoxication, or sober. It contrasted with drunkenness. In fact the ancient Greeks mistrusted "sober" people. One author condemned them by saying that the sober element in society was poor in wealth and influence.

But Philo, a contemporary of Christ, interpreted the word "sober" to mean a clear-thinking, self-controlled person. He said that sober people recognized that God is God. Furthermore, sober people see that intoxication is evil and destructive of social values. In other words, by the time of Christ the word *nephoo* had gained the meaning of "self-control." It is this meaning which shapes the New Testament's use of the term.

BIBLE USAGE

The family of words related to *nephoo* has about 10 references in the New Testament. Their importance lies not so much in the frequency of their use as in the significance of the concept.

First and foremost, the word relates to sobriety, or freedom from intoxication. When the Holy Spirit came upon the congregation at Pentecost, they appeared to be drunk. All their previous inhibitions were gone and they were free in the Spirit. The Apostle Peter thus introduced his impromptu sermon by saying that they were not drunk, but sober (Acts 2:15).

Another passage which makes pointed reference to sobriety is found in 1 Corinthians. There the Apostle Paul urged Christians to "become sober-minded," or to "sober up" (1 Cor. 15:34). The same idea is found in his injunction to the Roman Christians (Rom. 13:11-13). A similar statement is found in Paul's final appeal to the Thessalonians, where he urged them to avoid drunkenness and be sober (1 Thes. 5:6-8). Here freedom from intoxication (v. 6) is defined as self-control (v. 8).

Otherwise the Scriptures employ these terms in an abstract way, emphasizing the need for "self-control." In the Pastoral Epistles Paul set down the order of church government. In his outline of requirements for an overseer, bishop, or elder, Paul instructed Timothy to select temperate, or self-controlled, men (1 Tim. 3:2). The same requirement was imposed on the women of the church. A high spiritual standard of living was expected from Christian leaders. We ignore this principle only at the expense of the Gospel.

In his second letter the apostle turned his instruction on Timothy himself. After urging Timothy to preach well, guard the beliefs of the church, and to engage in evangelism, Paul pointed out the need for self-control (2 Tim. 4:5). Probably a lack of self-discipline paralyzes more preachers than any other single sin.

When the Apostle Paul dispatched Titus to Crete to create order out of a chaotic church, he likewise urged Titus to seek self-controlled, temperate people. Those who are older in the faith should demonstrate their maturity by self-control (Titus 2:2). Paul also pressed Titus to teach women the disciplined life (2:3-5). Not only were church leaders to exhibit self-control, but this Christian character trait should also be seen in the pew.

In the Apostle Peter's letter to suffering saints, he also enjoined self-control. Because Christians have a hope beyond the grave, they should live self-controlled lives now (1 Peter 1:13). In the light of the end times, Christians should combine a self-controlled lifestyle with prayer (4:7). Finally, Peter's prescription for combat against Satan is self-control and utter reliance on the Lord (5:7-8).

In the New Testament there is no tolerance for an undisciplined life. The reason for this is seen in the truth of the indwelling Holy Spirit, who creates order out of the chaos of an unspiritual life.

ILLUSTRATIONS

In its original use, the word *nephoo* meant freedom from intoxication to a dried-out drunkard. The danger of alcoholism was emphasized by the noted psychiatrist William C. Menninger. He said: "If alcoholism were a communicable disease, a national emergency would be declared."

Brilliant British author G.K. Chesterton (1874-1936) said: "No animal ever invented anything so bad as drunkenness—or so good as drink." To which an anonymous writer added: "People who insist on drinking before driving are putting the quart before the hearse."

Addiction goes far beyond alcohol in our society. Malcolm Muggeridge was disturbed by alcohol and drug dependence when he served as Chancellor of the University of Edinburgh. In his famous resignation speech the Chancellor lamented, "Karl Marx declared that religion is the opiate of the people. Many people today have reversed this statement and made opium [and other narcotics] the religion of the people."

In studying the subject of alcoholism, I discovered four reasons why people drink. The first is rebellion: 94 percent of the teenagers in our city of Bristol, England admitted to drinking alcohol. A second was inadequacy: one winner of a $500,000 lottery prize drank himself into oblivion because he could not cope with the pressure. The third is rejection: a rejected wife of a famous surgeon mixed alcohol and sleeping tablets and drank herself to death in the bathtub. Finally, some people drink from sheer boredom: many U.S. soldiers become alcoholics overseas, where they have little to do but sit around.

The principle of sobriety, or freedom from intoxication, is implicit in the Christian message. So is the principle of self-control. Dr. V. Raymond Edman (1900-67), during his tenure as president of Wheaton College, wrote 20 devotional books. One of them was *The Disciplines of Life*. It taught many young people the need for self-discipline in the Christian life.

When Dawson Trotman (1906-56) founded the Navigators, he laid heavy emphasis on discipleship and Scripture memory. The memorization of Scriptures was not just a good idea; it also helped to inculcate into generations of young people the disciplines of the Christian life. It built self-control.

In writing on the same subject, the noted Bible commentator Matthew Henry (1662-1714) wrote: "The first lesson in Christ's school is self-denial." It is the role of Scripture, according to Matthew Henry, to move people to "their own second and sober [self-disciplined] thoughts."

It is small wonder that the Apostle Paul compared the Christian life to the Olympics. Both demand self-discipline and self-control.

SEND

MEANING

Two Greek words convey the idea of "sending" in the New Testament. One is the word *apostello*, which is reflected in our word "apostle." It is used for the sending out of apostles or missionaries. (See: *Apostle.*)

The second word is *pempo*, which is used more generally to describe "sending." For instance, the ancient Greeks used this word to describe the sending of a person to accomplish some task. A judge was sent to preside at a trial. In the same way, an ambassador was sent to represent his ruler. Spies were sent out to gain information.

Three emphases seem to have characterized this word. First, the person being sent was emphasized. Second, the task for which he was sent became an emphasis. Third, his destination occupied a main place.

BIBLE USAGE

All three of these emphases are found in the Scripture. Most notable in the New Testament was the sending of Christ into the world. This is seen especially in the Gospel of John. Jesus knew that His earthly life was totally devoted to doing the will of His Father who sent Him (John 4:34; 5:23, 30, 37; 6:38).

Because Jesus was sent by His Father, there was a heavenly authority about His work here on earth (8:16). This same sending fired Jesus with an eternal urgency about His earthly work (9:4). At the end of His physical life Jesus returned to the Father who had sent Him (16:5).

As the Father sent Jesus, so the Holy Spirit was sent into the world (16:7). It was at the bidding of Jesus that the Holy Spirit was sent into this world (14:26). As second Person of the Trinity, Jesus also took part in sending the Holy Spirit (15:26).

The early apostles also knew that they were sent by the Lord Jesus Christ to do their task of evangelism. In fact, because Jesus was sent into the world, the apostles were also sent (20:21). By the same token Paul sent Timothy to sort out the sagging church at Corinth (1 Cor. 4:17), and also dispatched Timothy to Thessalonica (1 Thes. 3:2). Thus people were sent out in Christ's name.

A second emphasis of this word is the task for which people are sent. Jesus was sent to reveal the Father's will (John 5:30), teach the Father's truth (7:16-17), and do the Father's deeds (9:4).

John the Baptist was sent to preach and baptize (1:33). Emissaries were sent to care for churches (1 Cor. 4:17; Phil. 2:19). Concerned Christians were dispatched to take relief money to Jerusalem (1 Cor. 16:3). A team of messengers was sent out to tell the results of the Council of Jerusalem (Acts 15:25). (The Council of Jerusalem [chap. 15] concluded that salvation could be offered to the Gentiles without any Jewish strings attached.)

The destinations to which people were sent is also spoken of in the New Testament. Cornelius sent men to Joppa to persuade Peter to come with the Gospel (10:5), but the Holy Spirit had already convinced the apostle. Paul sent a messenger to Ephesus and convened a meeting of the elders (20:17). Paul was sent to Rome, where he appeared before the Emperor (25:25, 27). Probably he came up before the mad Emperor Nero.

When the glorified Christ came to John on the island of Patmos, the Lord ordered that he write God's words in a book and send them to seven churches in Asia Minor (Rev. 1:11).

This simple word *pempo* is important only because of the Sender. In many cases throughout the New Testament, the Lord is the Sender. The work which Christians do is not significant because of who they are, but because of whose they are. The Lord is the great Sender of the saints.

ILLUSTRATIONS

The sending of Christ is the single most significant event in human history. Professor Helmut Thielicke of Hamburg saw this and wrote: "To be sure, we cannot make the wind blow. But we do not need to do so, for it is already blowing. Wherever the Son of God goes, the winds of God are blowing, the streams of living water are flowing, and the sun of God is smiling."

When asked about his motives for sacrificing himself in the jungles of Africa, David Livingstone (1813-73) answered: "God had but one Son, and He sent Him as a missionary doctor."

An anonymous writer expressed the importance of Christ's coming in these lines: "Christmas is not just the birth of a baby; it is the Heavenly Father saying good-bye to His Son." Another anonymous author added: "The blessedness of Christmas is all wrapped up in the person of Jesus. Our relationship determines the measure of the blessing."

H.G. Taylor also spoke of the Father's sending of Christ when he said: "Christ came not to talk about a beautiful light, but to be that Light—not to speculate about virtue, but to be Virtue."

Puritan writer Stephen Charnock (1628-80) spoke of Christ's coming in these words: "In nature, we see God, as it were, like the sun in a picture; in the Law, as the sun in a cloud; in Christ we see Him in His beams."

By the same token the sending of the Holy Spirit has drawn comments from many people. Samuel Chadwick said concerning the sending of the Spirit: "The presence of the Spirit endues men with divine authority and power. . . . The Holy Spirit does not come upon methods, but upon men. He does not anoint machinery, but men. He does not work through organizations, but through men. He does not dwell in buildings, but in men."

A.W. Tozer, a great Chicago pastor and prophet, often spoke of the Holy Spirit. He claimed that the average Christian had very little idea about the Holy Spirit and never realized that the Spirit had been sent into the church.

Though he lived 300 years before Tozer, John Flavel (died 1691) concurred with Tozer's concern and wrote: "We preach and pray, and you hear; but there is no motion Christward until the Spirit of God blows upon them."

Just as Christ and the Holy Spirit were sent into our world to accomplish God's plan, so are Christians. Devotional writer Oswald Chambers (1874-1917) expressed this clearly when he wrote: "We are not taken up into conscious agreement with God's purpose; we are taken up into God's purpose without any consciousness at all."

Missionary leader Walter Frank expressed Chambers' idea in these words: "Our main aim must be to find out what God's doing in the world and align ourselves with His plan."

SHEPHERD

MEANING

The Greek word for "shepherd" is *poimen*. It comes from the verb *poimano* (to tend the sheep). Usually this task was delegated to a slave according to Josephus, who wrote about the time of the apostles.

Earlier, in the writings of Homer, the word was used to describe royal rulers, who cared for and "shepherded" their people. In fact Homer said: "All kings are shepherds of the people." His authority supposedly rested on his ability to care for the people. Plato picked up the same idea, and asserted that the rulers of the emerging city states must "shepherd" their people.

In the Septuagint Greek Old Testament this word is applied to leaders of every kind. The famous patriarchs of the Old Testament were shepherds, as is seen in the lives of Job, Abraham, Isaac, and Joseph. Furthermore, David was the model of a shepherd-king. From his pen came a great description of Jehovah as the Shepherd of His people (Ps. 23). The Messiah would also be the Shepherd of those who follow Him (Ezek. 34:23).

BIBLE USAGE

The words relating to shepherd occur about 38 times in the Greek New Testament. In many cases the Shepherd is Jesus Himself. He explained this role of the seeking Shepherd in the Parable of the Lost Sheep (Matt. 18:12-14; Luke 15:4-7).

In one of the most famous discourses in the entire New Testament, Jesus described Himself as the Good Shepherd (John 10:1-18). The teaching implicit in this discourse is profound. It forms the whole concept of the Good Shepherd in the New Testament. The sheep willingly follow the Shepherd, but they will not come after a false shepherd (10:5). He protects them by lying down at the door of the fold (10:7). They follow Him, because they know His voice (10:4). All pretend-shepherds are dangerous, but the Good Shepherd died for the sheep (10:7-14). There are still sheep to be brought into His fold (10:16). The entire program of Christ, from the Cross to the crown, is summarized in this discourse.

Death did not deter this ministry, because Christ took it up again in His glorified state. In fact, the Resurrection is also linked to the shepherding ministry of the Lord Jesus Christ (Heb. 13:20). This truth is seen in the writings of the Apostle Peter, who spoke of Christ as the Shepherd and Guardian of our souls (1 Peter 2:25). In instructing the elders, Peter promised that they would ultimately give account before the Chief Shepherd (5:1-4). The Good Shepherd becomes the Saviour and the Model of all spiritual ministry in the New Testament.

By the same token a shepherding ministry is passed on to the Lord's followers. In fact, when Jesus restored Peter to service after the debacle of his denial, the Lord literally instructed him to "tend My lambs and shepherd My sheep" (John 21:15-17).

In the Book of Acts, the elders of various congregations were commissioned to shepherd the sheep. As Paul paid his final visit to the church in Ephesus, he urged those elders to care for the flock as shepherds (Acts 20:28). This involved constant vigilance against false teachers, who would attack the flock like wolves (20:29).

When writing to the same Ephesian church, Paul again touched on this subject. One kind of gift which the Lord gives to His church are people who fulfill the role of shepherds or pastors (Eph. 4:11). The word "pastor" literally means "shepherd." It describes perfectly the role of an elder in caring for the church of

Christ. It should be a selfless devotion to duty, designed to prepare people for their various ministries (4:12).

At the conclusion of his first epistle, Peter intermingled the teaching concerning Christ, the Chief Shepherd, and the elders as undershepherds. As shepherds, elders should be kind, not cruel (1 Peter 5:2). Shepherds of the sheep should also be humble, not haughty (5:3). Finally, shepherds should be examples, not overlords (5:4).

ILLUSTRATIONS

No teaching from the Scripture is more comforting than the Shepherd Psalm (Ps. 23) and the Good Shepherd Discourse (John 10). Regarding the Shepherd Psalm, Augustine (A.D. 354-430) had a dream, in which he saw "Psalm 119 as a great tree, and Psalm 23 as a fair flower."

About this psalm Henry Ward Beecher (1813-87) concluded: "David has left no sweeter psalm than the short twenty-third. It is but a moment's opening of his soul; but, as when one, walking the winter street, sees the door opened for someone to enter, and the red light [of a fire] streams a moment forth, and the forms of gay children are running to greet the comer, and genial music sounds.... So in this psalm, though it is but a moment's opening of the soul, are emitted truths of peace and consolation that will never be absent from the world. The twenty-third psalm is the nightingale of the Psalms."

Charles Haddon Spurgeon (1834-92) described the Shepherd Psalm in these words: "He [David] compares himself to a creature weak, defenseless, and foolish, and he takes God to be his Provider, Preserver, Director, and indeed his everything. No man has a right to consider himself the Lord's sheep unless his nature has been renewed, for the scriptural description of unconverted men does not picture them as sheep, but as wolves and goats" (*Treasury of David*, 3 vols. [McClean, Virginia: MacDonald, no date] I, p. 353).

Who can ever forget the Twenty-Third Psalm, set to the tune "Crimond" in the Scottish Psalter (1650):

The Lord's my Shepherd, I'll not want:
  He makes me down to lie
In pastures green; He leadeth me
  The quiet waters by.

One of the finest expositions on the Good Shepherd Discourse was written by G. Campbell Morgan (1863-1945), eloquent pastor of Westminster Chapel in London. In writing on this great truth, Dr. Morgan commented: "The fold represented the whole system of the kingdom over which the Shepherd reigned. The flock referred to all those over whom He reigned. That is the picture which Jesus employed in illustration of the new order He had come to establish" (*The Gospel According to John* [London: Marshall, Morgan, and Scott, 1934], p. 173).

Morgan went on to explain that an oriental sheepfold had no door, only an opening. When all the flock were safely in the fold, the shepherd laid down before the opening. He was the door, as Christ is our Door into the fold of heaven.

SIN

MEANING

The basic general word which refers to sin in the New Testament is *harmartia*. This word is reflected in the theological study of sin, sometimes called "*harmart*iology."

In the early Greek writings of Homer, this word meant "to miss the mark." Later it came to connote an offense committed against someone or some rule. One who habitually missed the mark or committed offenses was called a *hamartinoos* (madman). In the writings of Aristotle *harmartia* came to be a collective term for all wrong or evil. It referred to any action which was not in conformity with accepted ethics.

Several other terms also described sin in the New Testament. One such word was *adikia*, a legal term meaning unrighteousness or injustice. Another term was *parabasis*, which literally meant "to walk alongside." In terms of sin *parabasis* meant "to act beside the mark," or "to miss the standard of behavior." Finally, the word *paraptoma* meant "to fall beside," "go astray," or "bump up against something." By far the most common term for sin was *hamartia*, so it occupies our attention in this study.

BIBLE USAGE

The word *harmartia* and the verb form *hamartano* (to sin) occur 173 times in the New Testament. In the Gospels they are usually related to Christ's forgiveness. Jesus actually sought out sinners, so that He might forgive them (Matt. 9:10). He rejoiced when a sinful woman came to worship Him (Luke 7:39). In fact, streams of sinners came to hear Him (15:1).

Jesus urged the disciples to deal quickly with sin among believers (Matt. 18:15-17). He also warned the disciples that blasphemy against the Holy Spirit could not be forgiven (12:31). The disciples were commissioned to confess Christ even in the midst of their sinful generation (Mark 8:38).

When the earthly ministry of Christ was introduced, He was presented as the Saviour of sinners. His very name indicated this redemptive role (Matt. 1:21). When John the Baptist pointed Him out, the rough-hewn prophet proclaimed that Jesus would be sacrificed for the sins of the world (John 1:29).

The Apostle Paul presented a clear picture of sin. The cause of man's sin was the fall of Adam (Rom. 5:12). Consequently all are infected by sin (3:23), which leads inevitably to spiritual and physical death (6:23). Paul regarded Himself as the chief among sinners (1 Tim. 1:15).

James described the anatomy of sin in the introductory paragraphs of his brief epistle. Lust leads to temptation. The temptation ripens into a sinful act, and the sinful act produces spiritual death (James 1:14-15). Sin is, by definition, doing the opposite of what one knows to be right (4:17).

John, the apostle, spoke of God's continual cure for sin. As Christians share fellowship in the light of divine revelation, the blood of Christ cleanses them from each sin (1 John 1:7, 9). The basis for this forgiveness is the sacrifice of the Saviour, which has provided a just solution to our sin (2:2). (See: *Propitiation*.) The incarnation of Christ had as its main motive the forgiveness of our sins and the destruction of the devil's work (3:5, 8). The Apostle Peter likewise pointed out that the death of Christ is an effective answer to sin (1 Peter 2:21-25; 3:18).

The Book of Hebrews illuminates a second aspect of Christ's work, His role as High Priest of our salvation. Though Christ was tempted in every way that we are, He was totally free from sin. This enabled Him to be a faithful Priest for us (Heb.

4:15). Because of Christ's separation from sin, He is able to save sinners and make intercession for saints (7:25-27).

Human literature dwells on the dark side of our sin, the destruction which it produces in this world. Scripture paints an infinitely brighter picture, because it also shows the solution to sin in Jesus Christ, God's Sacrifice.

ILLUSTRATIONS
Francis Schaeffer, a brilliant teacher and philosopher of Christianity, once said about sin: "Some psychological and sociological conditioning occurs in every man's life and this affects the decisions he makes. But we must resist the modern concept that all sin can be explained merely on the basis of conditioning."

In explaining sin, Augustine (A.D. 354-430), defined it rather simply: "Sin is energy in the wrong channel." Another church father, John Chrysostom (347-407), said of sin: "To sin is human; but to persevere in sin is not human but altogether satanic."

American philosopher, inventor, and statesman, Benjamin Franklin (1706-90) opined concerning sin: "Sin is not hurtful because it is forbidden, but sin is forbidden because it is hurtful." Rudyard Kipling (1865-1936), an English chronicler in India, concluded concerning sin: "The sin they do by two and two they must pay for one by one."

However, the diagnosis of sin is not the main thrust of the Bible, but rather the cure of sin through Christ. Dr. David Martyn Lloyd-Jones (1899-1981) wrote concerning sin: "The measure of God's anger against sin is the measure of the love that is prepared to forgive the sinner and to love him in spite of his sin."

A former pastor of Los Angeles' Church of the Open Door, J. Vernon McGee, wrote concerning sin: "When we say, 'Something should be done about Skid Row,' God is saying the same thing about us. That is why He sent His Son to help us."

Writing from the perspective of Puritanism, John Owen (1616-83) concluded concerning sin: "He that hath slight thought of sin never had great thoughts of God."

Blaise Pascal (1623-62), noted Jansenist philosopher and mathematician, wrote of sin: "There are only two kinds of men: the righteous who believe themselves sinners, and the rest, sinners who believe themselves to be righteous." Along the same lines Charles Haddon Spurgeon (1834-92) concluded: "Sin is sovereign till sovereign grace dethrones it."

R.A. Torrey (1856-1928), a companion of D.L. Moody and pastor of Moody Memorial Church, wrote: "It is absolutely certain that if a man sins, his own sin will dog him, that it will keep on his track night and day, like a bloodhound, and never quit until it catches him and brings him to book."

In the light of all this we conclude with a stanza of Horatio Spafford's (1828-88) fine hymn:

My sin, O the bliss of this glorious thought!
    My sin, not in part but the whole,
Is nailed to the cross and I bear it no more;
    Praise the Lord, praise the Lord, O my soul!

SLAVE

MEANING

The Greek word translated "slave" in the New Testament is *doulos.* Originally it meant a person who had no personal freedom, one whose will was totally subordinated to that of another person. Such persons were forever "on duty," with no free time or personal life.

In the writings of the Stoics this word was applied to religious service. Alas, many religious slaves were tied to the temple in a pitiful life of prostitution. Wherever the word is found in Greek literature, it speaks of a despised class of bondslaves, whose lives were not their own.

When the Hebrew Old Testament was translated into Greek, this word was also used to describe Israel's slavery in Egypt. Though the Jews had felt the harsh discipline of slavery, they later also held slaves. However, when Jews enslaved other Jews (for debt), those slaves had to be released after six years (Ex. 21:2) or in the Year of Jubilee (Lev. 25:30), whichever came first.

BIBLE USAGE

The word for "slave" is found 124 times in the New Testament. In each case it referred to a bondslave who was owned by his master and had no rights whatever.

Jesus often referred to slaves in His parables. Some slaves were often given large responsibilities; in fact they often managed whole households (Matt. 24:45). Sometimes Jews were sold into slavery when they defaulted on debts (18:34). No matter how hard a slave worked, he never was allowed to share in his master's leisure (Luke 17:7-10). To serve every hour of the day without reward was the slave's lot (17:10).

Paul seemed to have hinted at the dissolution of the master-slave relationship, when he wrote to Philemon about his runaway slave Onesimus. But in other letters he and the other apostles urged obedience upon slaves. In fact obedience was seen as a testimony of a slave's Christian commitment.

Slaves were to serve their masters as if they were serving the Lord (Eph. 6:5; Col. 3:22). When slaves were faithful, they reinforced the truth of the Gospel (1 Tim. 6:1). Christian slaves were not even supposed to argue with their masters (Titus 2:9). The emphasis in these passages falls not on approval of slavery, but rather on approval of Christian confession in everyday life.

The concept of slavery is given an interesting spiritual twist in the Scriptures. Jesus taught that unconverted people were slaves of sin, whom only He could free (John 8:34-36). Paul likewise spoke of people who had been slaves of sin (Rom. 6:13-17). In Hebrews one reads of unconverted people who are enslaved by the fear of death (Heb. 2:15). In writing to Titus, Paul warned him against the Cretans, who were enslaved to their own lusts (Titus 3:3).

However, a positive side of slavery is also seen in Scripture. Paul repeatedly called himself a slave of Christ (Rom. 1:1; Phil. 1:1). Not only did Paul consider himself to be a slave of Christ, but also of the church of Christ (2 Cor. 4:5).

As a slave of Christ, Christians are also slaves of love (Gal. 5:13). Timothy is praised as one who literally "slaved with Paul in the proclamation of the Gospel, as a son working with his father" (Phil. 2:22). Since Christ set Christians free from slavery to sin, they are now slaves of righteousness (Rom. 6:18). This means that they are bound eternally to serve and obey the Lord (12:11; 14:18).

The Apostle Paul presented his philosophy of Christian work in 1 Corinthians. He was adaptable, in order that he might reach all classes of society, slaves and freemen. He was also energetic, in order that he might be fruitful. In fact, he had become a slave of all people, in his magnificent mission to win them for Christ (1 Cor. 9:19-22). He admirably exemplified the Lord's teaching, that His disciples should be servants of all (Matt. 20:26).

ILLUSTRATIONS

In England William Wilberforce (1759-1833) fought slavery right up until his dying day. He had been commissioned by John Wesley to fight the curse of slavery and that Wilberforce did. In the year of Wilberforce's death, slavery was outlawed in the British Empire.

Three decades and a Civil War intervened in America before slavery was abolished. That great cause engaged such men as Jonathan Blanchard (1811-92), founder of Wheaton College; Henry Ward Beecher (1813-87); and Charles G. Finney (1792-1875), founder of Oberlin College. It was President Abraham Lincoln (1809-65) who finally rang down the curtain on the curse of slavery.

As Arthur Halley's television series, "Roots," revealed, slaves had no rights at all. Their children could be torn from their arms. Their homes were held only at the pleasure of their masters. No minute could be called their own. No money accrued to their names. They were beasts of burden, owned body and soul by slaveholders.

It is this complete commitment into which Christians enter voluntarily when they submit to the Saviour. As a freed slave could voluntarily serve his master, so Christians freed from sin should serve their Master.

In writing on this subject, Genevan reformer John Calvin (1509-64) claimed: "No one gives himself freely and willingly to God's service unless, having tasted His Fatherly love, he [the Christian] is drawn to love and worship Him in return."

The early German mystical writer, Meister Eckhart (1260-1327), knew something of this spiritual slavery, for he wrote: "If one were in a rapture like St. Paul, and there was a sick man needing help, I think it would be best to throw off the rapture and show love by service to the needy."

A spiritual follower of Meister Eckhart was the German Reformer, Martin Luther (1483-1546). Luther shared Meister Eckhart's burden for service. Luther wrote: "A Christian man is the most free lord of all, and subject to none; a Christian man is the most dutiful servant of all, and subject to everyone." This is a wonderful statement of the paradox of Christian freedom.

Several years ago an Overseas Missionary Fellowship member set about to describe the service of missionary life. She pictured it in terms of being a bondslave to the Lord. Her book was titled, *Have We No Right?* (Chicago: Moody Press, 1958) In this little masterpiece, Mabel Williamson described the sacrifice of her right to a normal standard of living, ordinary safeguards of health, private affairs, marriage, and even a home life. She was a bondslave of the Master, who also had no rights of His own. Her concluding lines are memorable:

All that He takes I will give;
All that He gives I will take;
He, my only right!

SOLDIER

MEANING

In the Greek New Testament the word for "soldier" is *stratiotes*. The root of this word is *stratos* which meant a "spreading out," or "an encampment of soldiers." It is reflected in such English words as *"strategy"* (a plan for fighting the battle), *"strategic"* (the essentials for warfare), and *"strategem"* (a plan for tricking the enemy).

Homer used these words to describe the setting up of a camp, especially a military camp. Later on *stratiotes* meant to undertake a military campaign. A related word was *stratia*, which meant "an army of people under military discipline."

As the word developed, it also came to connote a draft of men to fight a war. By the time of Alexander the Great (about 300 B.C.), military men had been elevated from the level of forced labor to positions of honor.

BIBLE USAGE

The various words relating to military life occur about 50 times in the Greek New Testament. In the Gospels the most commonly noted soldiers were centurions of the Roman army, commanders over 100 soldiers. One came to Jesus and pleaded for the healing of his servant (Matt. 8:5-13). He was a model of humility and faith, and Jesus gladly brought healing into his home.

Roman soldiers were also present at the crucifixion of Christ. Some of them staged an elaborate mockery, in which they "enthroned" Christ as a king of the Jews (Mark 15:16-20). Some of the same soldiers also gambled for the robe of Christ (John 19:23-24). But one of them, a centurion, recognized the deity of his victim, and confessed that Jesus is the Son of God (Mark 15:39).

Another reference to the military in the Gospels is found in Christ's Olivet Discourse about things to come. Here He referred to the destruction of Jerusalem under Titus in A.D. 70. Wars and rumors of war would disturb the peace of Israel, and then an invasion would rake the land with destruction (Matt. 24:6; Mark 13:7; Luke 21:9).

In the Book of Acts, Roman soldiers are often portrayed in a positive light. It was Cornelius, the Caesarean centurion, who sought the Lord. Under the guidance of the Holy Spirit Peter was dispatched to proclaim Christ to this sincere seeker (Acts 10). As a result the Gospel door was thrown wide open to the Gentile community (11:17-18).

When the story turned to the capture and execution of James and the arrest of Peter, the Roman soldiers were seen to be weaklings in comparison with the Lord. Four squads of four soldiers each were assigned to guard one preacher, Peter (12:4). They were even chained to him at night, to prevent his escape (12:6). When the Lord released him, the soldiers were left in a state of utter confusion (12:18).

In the life of Paul, Roman soldiers were often seen to be friendly. For instance, when a public riot broke out against Paul, soldiers rescued him (21:32). The reason for this rescue was Paul's Roman citizenship (23:27). During the precarious voyage from Caesarea to Rome, the Centurion Julius also intervened to save Paul's life (27:3, 42-43). Even in Rome, the soldier assigned to guard Paul allowed him to receive guests (28:16-17).

One further twist is given to the word "soldier" in the New Testament, and it is a spiritual application. Paul used a soldier as a model to illustrate Christians engaged in battle against Satan (1 Cor. 9:7). As a soldier is supported when he is in battle, so a Christian is supported when he engages in spiritual warfare.

Guarded by Roman soldiers, Paul wrote his letters to Timothy. In the first letter, Paul urged Timothy to fight manfully the battles of the cross (1 Tim. 1:18). In the second letter, Paul compared Christian commitment to military commitment. No soldier becomes embroiled in the affairs of this world, when there is a battle to be won (2 Tim. 2:3-4).

Christians are called to do battle with Satan. This is not easy, nor is it safe. However, Christ is the Captain of our salvation (Heb. 2:10, KJV), and He is well worth following.

ILLUSTRATIONS

Soldiers are often set forth as models of courage. War historian Sir William Napier (1785-1860) wrote concerning the British army: "Then was seen with what a strength and majesty the British soldier fights" (*History of the War in the Peninsula*, book xii, chap. 6).

Rudyard Kipling (1865-1936) wrote in "The Young British Soldier": "When the half-made recruit goes out to the East, / He acts like a babe and drinks like a beast, / And he wonders because he is frequently deceased, / Ere he is fit to serve as a soldier." It is not an easy road to success as a soldier, and many die in the process.

Perhaps George Bernard Shaw (1856-1950) best caught the irony of modern military life: "The British soldier can stand up to anything except the British War Office" (*The Devil's Disciple*, act III).

Human models of warfare fade when compared with divine ones. Gustav Aulen (1879-1978), a famous Swedish theologian, wrote of Christ as Captain: "Jesus Christ—Christus Victor—fights against and triumphs over the evil powers of the world, the 'tyrants' under which mankind is in bondage and suffering, and in Him God reconciles the world to Himself."

Bible commentator Henry Alford (1810-71) highlighted this spiritual warfare: "The triumphs are God's triumphs over us. His defeats of us are real victories." When the Lord subjugates us, He frees us from Satan's stronghold.

Because of the victories of our Lord, we can count on spiritual triumph too. Henry S. Haskins wrote: "The way to get the most out of victory is to follow it up with another which makes it look small." Along the same lines Corrie ten Boom, Dutch missionary-evangelist, concluded: "The first step on the way to victory is to recognize the enemy." Corrie ten Boom learned her strategy for spiritual battle in the tough arena of a Nazi concentration camp.

Many hymns illustrate this spiritual warfare. In 1749, Charles Wesley (1707-88), challenged the Methodists with these words:
Soldiers of Christ, arise,
And put your armor on.
Perhaps the most well-known of military hymns was written by Sabine Baring-Gould (1834-1924):
Onward Christian soldiers, Marching as to war,
With the Cross of Jesus, Going on before.

SON

MEANING

The Greek word for "son" is *huios,* and is generally used for any male offspring. In some cases this word also means any male descendant, such as a grandson. Another aspect of this relationship was seen in the adoption of a son by a prominent family. Sometimes these adopted sons were men on whom wealthy patrons wished to bestow their goods. This is the meaning involved when the Scriptures describe our adoption as sons of God.

Yet another use of the term son was seen in the educational process. Teachers called their pupils "sons," because they were their masters' spiritual and intellectual offspring. Apprentices to whom were committed the secrets of the guilds were also called sons and heirs of the professional skills.

BIBLE USAGE

The word for "son" occurs more than 380 times in the New Testament. About one-third of these refer to human sons, and two-thirds refer to Jesus Christ as God's Son.

Some of the more notable examples of sonship are seen in the Gospels. John the Baptist was the special son of Zacharias and Elizabeth (Luke 1:13). Jesus raised an only son from the dead, when He passed through the village of Nain (Luke 7:12-15). He likewise healed the son of a nobleman (John 4:46-53). In the Parable of the Prodigal, Jesus told the story of two sons (Luke 15:11-32). By tracing the occurrences of the word "son" in the Gospels, one can see the intimate intervention of Christ into family life.

The New Testament also uses "son" to describe descendants. For instance, Joseph was called a "son of David" (Matt. 1:20). Jews were called "sons of Israel" (Luke 1:16). This was a technical, political term in the time of the apostles, as the whole Jewish community was called "the sons of Israel" (Acts 5:21).

Christians are also called the sons or children of God. They enter into this relationship by personal faith in Jesus Christ (John 1:12). This also admits the Holy Spirit as the motivating force in their lives (Rom. 8:14). Furthermore, such a relationship gives Christians a hope for the future, because someday they will be totally transformed into the image of Christ (1 John 3:1-2).

The concept of sonship in the New Testament finds its highest expression in the Lord Jesus Christ. He is the Son of God. At His baptism the Father confirmed Christ's deity by saying, "This is My beloved Son" (Matt. 3:17). On the Mount of Transfiguration the same statement was repeated from heaven (17:5). The Apostle Peter recalled this experience when he wrote under the inspiration of the Holy Spirit (2 Peter 1:17). Paul confirmed the same connection between Christ and His Father in a quotation from Psalm 2:7 (Acts 13:33). The same quotation is repeated in Hebrews 1:5.

A second aspect of Christ's sonship is the name, Son of man. Here the humanity of Christ comes to the fore. As Son of man, Jesus had no regular resting place (Matt. 8:20). In the same role as Son of man He both healed the sick and forgave sin (9:6). When He spoke of His second coming, Christ also referred to this name, the Son of man (10:23). In His ministry Jesus was a friend of sinners, which also characterized Him as the Son of man (11:19). In challenging His disciples to confess His deity, Christ called Himself the Son of man (16:13). In fact this name, "Son of man," was only used by Christ in speaking of Himself. Others did not call Him by this name.

Third, Christ was also known as the Son of David, that is, David's successor as

King. Matthew used this term to introduce Christ's family tree (1:1). Blind men, who hoped to have healing through His touch (9:27), heard the Lord passing by and called out to Him as the Son of David. The crowds even used the name, Son of David, to denote the Messiah (12:23).

Many are called "son" in the New Testament. But only Jesus Christ carries the threefold name, Son of God, Son of man, and Son of David. Because God's Son came into this world, we can enter heaven as the children of God. Furthermore, we can now come to God in prayer and call Him "Father."

ILLUSTRATIONS

The sonship of Christ is the main focus of the Gospels. God sent His Son to be our Saviour. This truth is most eloquently expressed in one of Charles Wesley's (1707-88) lesser known Christmas hymns:

Let earth and heaven combine, / Angels and men agree,

To praise in songs divine / The incarnate Deity;

Our God contracted to a span, / incomprehensibly made man.

The magnitude of Christ's coming was grasped by the Chinese writer and Bible teacher, Watchman Nee: "God will answer all our questions in one way and one way only, namely, by showing us more of His Son."

A well-known preacher of Wales was Christmas Evans (1766-1838). Concerning the incarnation of God's Son, Christmas Evans explained: "We can form no idea of the natural distance between God and man, but the infinite vacuum is filled up by the Messiah."

Standing out in bold contrast with the simplicity of Christmas Evans is a famous New Testament professor, Bruce Metzger. He too marveled at the display of divine sonship in Christ, when he wrote: "Others had applied the name 'Father' to God, but the point is that when Jesus called God 'Father' He knew Him as the Father."

Daniel Webster (1782-1852), famous orator and statesman of early American history, also acclaimed the relationship between God the Father and God the Son: "I believe Jesus Christ to be the Son of God. The miracles which He wrought establish in my mind His personal authority, and render it proper for me to believe whatever He asserts. I believe, therefore, all His declarations, as well when He declares Himself to be the Son of God, as when He declares any other proposition. And I believe there is no other way of salvation than through the merits of His atonement." What a ringing affirmation of faith is that grand statement.

Puritan writer Thomas Manton took a slightly different line in explaining the relationship between Father and Son: "In the Scriptures there is a draft of God, but in Christ there is God Himself. A coin bears the image of Caesar, but Caesar's son is his own lively resemblance. Christ is the living Bible." To which John Penny added: "No man can know the Father any farther than it pleaseth the Son to reveal Him."

Another grand hymn of praise to God the Son was written by Josiah Conder (1789-1855):

Thou art the everlasting Word, / The Father's only Son;

God manifestly seen and heard, / And heaven's beloved One:

Worthy, O Lamb of God, art Thou,

That every knee to Thee should bow.

SPIRIT, HOLY SPIRIT

MEANING

In the Greek New Testament the word for "spirit" is *pneuma*. It comes from a root word *pneu* meaning "a sudden blast of air," "a breath," or "a blowing action." One sees it in such English words as *"pneu*matic" (an operation powered by air) or *"pneu*monia" (a respiratory disease).

The Greeks regarded air as being the essential bearer of life, which gave considerable importance to their word *pneuma*. In Aristotle's writings *pneuma* took on even more importance. It was the force which formed people and controlled their bodies. The Stoics thought that the "spirit" controlled the thought and speech processes of people. Plato considered the "spirit" to be the motivating force of all action.

In the Septuagint, the Greek Old Testament, "spirit" had two basic meanings. First, it was the breath of man which kept him alive (Ezek. 37:8). The other main use of the word in the Greek Old Testament was in reference to the Holy Spirit (Isa. 32:15-20).

BIBLE USAGE

In the Greek New Testament the word *pneuma* is found about 370 times. There are actually three main uses of this word in the New Testament.

First, it refers to the spirit of a person. Apparently this is one's essential personality, which makes him a person and distinguishes him from every other person. When Christ saves you, the Holy Spirit sets up communication with your spirit (Rom. 8:16). By the same token God breathes grace into your spirit (Gal. 6:18; Phil. 4:23). By the same Holy Spirit, the Scriptures are enabled to speak powerfully to our spirits (Heb. 4:12). At death, this essential personality, the human spirit, departs from our bodies and goes to the Lord (Matt. 27:50; Acts 7:59).

Other kinds of spirits in the Scripture are those good and evil spirits which indwell our universe. Evil spirits are usually called demons, and they fell with Satan before the world was created. Sometimes they demonize a person and actually fill that person (Matt. 8:16). They speak through human vocal cords (Mark 1:23). They even stir up trouble in the church (1 Tim. 4:1). However, the Lord is absolutely able to dispel them (Luke 4:36), and by the Lord's power Christians too can deal with them (Acts 16:18; 19:12). (See: *Demon.*)

There are also good spirits, which are known as angels. These are just as real and active as the demons. They minister to the needs of Christians (Heb. 1:7, 14). The Book of Hebrews emphasizes the point that God is the Father of all these spirits (12:9). (See: *Angel.*)

The third and most important reference to spirit in the New Testament is the information concerning the Holy Spirit. At the conception of Christ the Holy Spirit was active (Luke 1:35). The Holy Spirit descended in visible form on Christ at His baptism (Matt. 3:15-17). Through the power of the Spirit, Christ cast out demons (12:27-28). In fact, all of Christ's earthly ministry was a fulfillment of the promised presence of the Holy Spirit on the Messiah (Luke 4:18; Isa. 61:1). Before the Lord prepared to return to the Father, He promised that the Holy Spirit would come upon Christians (John 14:26; 15:26). He would convince people of the reality of redemption and judgment (16:8-9).

In the church the Holy Spirit fulfills many functions. The Holy Spirit's presence is the experience of every believer (Acts 2:2-5; 9:17; 11:15). Likewise He empowers believers to proclaim the Gospel (1:8; 4:31; 7:55). In the same connection He compels Christians to circle the globe with the Gospel (1:8; 13:1-3). The Spirit seals believers as a promise of coming glory (Eph. 1:13; 2 Cor. 1:22). He takes up residence in Christians (Rom. 8:9; 1 Cor. 6:17-20). The same Holy Spirit gives gifts to Christians for the service of the Lord (12:13).

Thus the Holy Spirit moves and motivates Christians today, and He is the sole explanation of "spiritual" life. He enlivens the body of Christ, the church, just as one's human spirit enlivens his human body.

ILLUSTRATIONS

A survey of comments on the ministry of the Holy Spirit could easily fill a book, but a few are selected to underline the importance of the Spirit's work in our world. The venerable master of Rugby School, Thomas Arnold (1795-1842), said: "He who does not know God the Holy Spirit cannot know God at all."

George Whitefield (1714-70), the Great Awakening preacher, wrote: "A young fellow came to our meeting in Plymouth, England, as he said, to pick a hole in the preacher's coat; and the Holy Spirit picked a hole in his heart."

Roy Gustafson, a contemporary evangelist and Bible teacher, said about the Holy Spirit's work: "Regardless of how sincere a soul-winner may be, he cannot add one member to the body of Christ. It would be like putting waxed apples on a tree. The Holy Spirit alone does the work."

Just as the Holy Spirit is essential to conversion, He is also necessary to living the Christian life. John Owen (1616-83), another great Puritan preacher, wrote: "God's sealing of believers is His gracious communication of the Holy Ghost unto them, so as to enable them unto all the duties of their holy calling. The effects of this sealing are gracious operations of the Spirit in and upon believers; but the sealing itself is the communication of the Spirit to them."

A notable Puritan author, William Gurnall, wrote a long treatise on spiritual warfare. When discussing prayer, Gurnall wrote: "Christ is the door that opens into God's presence and lets the soul into His very bosom; faith is the key that unlocks the door; but the Spirit is He that makes this key."

Extending this teaching concerning the Holy Spirit, Gurnall spoke also of Bible study: "God is able to interpret His own Word unto thee. Indeed none can enter into the knowledge thereof but he must be beholden unto His Spirit to unlock the door."

Another Puritan, Thomas Watson, would add to this: "We may read many truths in the Bible, but we cannot know them savingly, till God by His Spirit shines upon our soul. . . . He not only informs our mind, but inclines our will."

STONE

MEANING

One Greek word for "stone" is *petros*. It is reflected in such English terms as "*petro*leum" (oil found in the earth), "*petrol*" (the English word for gasoline), and "*petrify*" (the process by which plants are turned into stone). In the time of Homer this word and its related terms also described firmness of character. It is best known in the New Testament as the name which Christ gave to Simon. He translated the Aramaic "Cephas" into the Greek name "Petros."

A related word is *petra*, which means "rock," "boulder," or "bedrock." This is the word used for the foundation rock of the earth. It is also a name given to the Lord God Jehovah in the Septuagint Greek Old Testament. God is Israel's Rock (2 Sam. 22:2).

The third word which translates stone ·or rock is *lithos*. It is seen in such English words as "mono*lithic*" (relating to a single great rock), "*litho*graph" (a form of printing which uses engraving as on a stone), and "*litho*logy" (the study of stones). This is a stone of any sort in Greek literature. It was a building stone or some loose stone used in any special way. In the Septuagint it was found 350 times, and it referred to boundary stones, stone pillars, and even precious stones.

BIBLE USAGE

In the New Testament the word *petros* occurs 150 times, most often as the proper name of Simon Peter (*petros*). On the other hand, *petra* is found only 15 times in the New Testament. Because of the close connection between *petros* and *petra* we shall consider them together.

A most outstanding text concerning these stones is found in both Romans and 1 Peter. Jesus Christ is called "a Stone [*lithos*] of stumbling and a Rock [*petra*] of offense" (Rom. 9:33; 1 Peter 2:8). These passages quote two outstanding messianic prophecies in the Old Testament (Ps. 118:22; Isa. 8:14). The point is that the Jews missed their chance by rejecting Christ. They stumbled over the One who could have been the Rock of their salvation.

A second reference to the stone is found in Matthew. The Lord answered Peter's great confession by saying: "You are Peter [*Petros*], and upon this Rock [*petra*] I will build My church" (Matt. 16:18). It is well to remember that the rock on which Christ builds His church is not the Apostle Peter. It is the confession of Christ's deity.

The third major reference to this stone is in Paul's discussion of the Lord's Supper. As all Jews drank from the Rock in the desert, so all Christians share in the same Gospel ordinance (1 Cor. 10:3-4). Here Christ is set forth as the Rock of our salvation.

Having briefly surveyed the uses of *petros* and *petra*, we now turn to consider the uses of *lithos*. There are two rather unusual references in the Gospels. The miraculous power of God is seen in Christ's assertion that God could raise up children of Abraham from stones (Matt. 3:9). This served to show the Pharisees that their sinfulness disqualified them as true sons of Abraham.

At the Triumphal Entry Jewish leaders complained about the jubilant praise of the children. Jesus again asserted that if the children had not praised Him, the nearby stones would have (Luke 19:40).

In several places Christ is called a Stone (*lithos*). For instance, the Gospel record contains a reference to Christ as the rejected Stone (Mark 12:10; Ps. 118:22). This same picture is repeated in other places, as just mentioned (Rom. 9:33; 1 Peter

2:8). In another place Daniel is referred to, to show that Christ is the Rock which will roll over all of His enemies (Luke 20:17-18; Dan. 2:34). As Christ is the Stone, so Christians are living stones being built into a holy temple (1 Peter 2:4-5).

If Christ is the Rock of offense and the Stone of stumbling, it means that He has two roles in the world. First, He is the Rock of salvation to all who believe. Second, He is the Rock of stumbling to those who reject Him to their own destruction.

ILLUSTRATIONS

The picture of Christ as the Rock is seen in many contexts. Recently the Evangelical Free Church initiated a church-planting effort in Chicago. The name given to a new congregation was, "The Rock of Our Salvation Evangelical Free Church." When the pastor explained this name to a suburban audience, he said: "That name may not be too 'cool' in the suburbs, but it's real big in the city."

This recalled to my mind another inner city congregation, in which I served as a Sunday School teacher during college days. It was called the Rock of Ages Baptist Church. At the time I found the name strange, but it certainly put the emphasis on the right Person, the Lord who is our Rock.

A relatively new chorus emphasizes this aspect of the Lord's life and work:
Praise the name of Jesus, Praise the name of Jesus,
He's my Rock, He's my Fortress, He's my Deliverer,
In Him will I trust. Praise the name of Jesus.

In the '50s the biggest ministry in our city was Youth for Christ, and many young people attended large Saturday evening rallies. The motto which Youth for Christ displayed in those days fits in admirably with our theme: "Geared to the times: anchored to the Rock."

Matthew Henry (1662-1714) initiated the commentary project which bears his name. In the commentary on 1 Peter which Matthew Henry's colleague wrote, one finds these potent comments on the Rock of our salvation: Jesus Christ "is called a Stone, to denote His invincible strength and everlasting duration, and to teach His servants that He is their protection and security, the foundation on which they are built, and a Rock of offense to their enemies."

Once I was asked to participate in the cornerstone laying of a Lutheran Church in Germany. On that day several pastors arrived and stood out in the elements for a very formal service. One by one, we stepped forward and recited a Scripture verse before giving the cornerstone a tap with a mason's hammer. This was to me a vivid reminder of the Lord, who is the Cornerstone of our faith.

In fact, this should remind Christians not to build on false foundations. A Christian life should not be built on the false foundation of a great man, no matter how true he stood to the Scriptures. Nor should a Christian life be built on a great church of the past, where blessing was found. Neither should a Christian construct his life of faith on some spectacular past experience. Only Christ is the solid Stone and firm Foundation.

As Edward Mote (1797-1874) wrote in his famous hymn:
On Christ, the solid Rock, I stand;
All other ground is sinking sand.

STRANGER

MEANING

The Greek word for "stranger" is *paroikos*. The term is a combination of two Greek words, *para*, "alongside," and *oikos*, "house." Therefore, the literal meaning is "one who has a house alongside" others, or "a foreigner who lives alongside the people of any country." The Greek term is reflected in our word "*paro*chial" (a local district, usually a church parish).

In ancient Greek this word described aliens who were residents in a foreign land, a strange place. Slowly the term evolved to mean a neighbor who lives under the protection of a resident of long standing, a native. The early church took over this term to describe a diocese governed by a bishop, and later it came to mean a parish over which a priest had control.

The Septuagint Greek Old Testament gives us the meaning which is perpetuated in the New Testament. In the Old Testament it meant a Gentile who came to live in Israel. Philo also used it to mean a believer who lives away from his or her heavenly home; thus he or she is a stranger and an alien in the earth.

BIBLE USAGE

In the Greek New Testament this word is used only five times. Its significance rests more on the importance of the idea than on the frequency of its appearance. In each case it means a stranger or foreigner, one who lives away from his ultimate home.

After the Resurrection, Jesus encountered His disciple Cleopas and a friend on the road to Emmaus. Since Jesus was not recognized, He asked them about their obvious sadness. Cleopas replied, almost curtly, "Are You the only One visiting [*paroikos*] Jerusalem . . . unaware of the things which have happened here in these days?" (Luke 24:18) Cleopas assumed that this apparent stranger knew nothing of the Crucifixion.

When Paul was preaching at Antioch in Asia Minor, he referred to the past history of Israel. He described the people as strangers and aliens in Egypt. First they lived there as guests, then as captives, but always as aliens and strangers (Acts 13:16-17).

Not only does this term apply to social strangers, but also to strangers in a spiritual sense. In the Ephesian letter, the Apostle Paul made much of the unity of Christ's church. Because of the redemption worked out by Christ on the cross, Jews and Gentiles who believe are one in the body of Christ. Gentiles, who were strangers to the covenantal working of God, have been made one with believing Jews (Eph. 2:17-19).

Though Christians are not strangers to one another, they are strangers to the world. The Apostle Peter took this as one of his major themes. He introduced his first epistle by calling Christians "aliens" (1 Peter 1:1). Life is called a sojourn, a temporary residence for aliens (1:17). Because of this distinctive role in the world, Christians are called on to live lives which are clearly different from the world in which they are strangers (2:11). Sadly, most Christians settle down so well in the world that they do not even feel like strangers here.

The biblical example which emphasizes this truth is Abraham. Nowhere in Scripture is the life of a stranger more clearly seen than in the life of Abraham, the father of all believers. At the call of God Abraham abandoned his home and went to a place which was totally foreign. He was not even moving to a settled life, but rather to the wandering existence of a pilgrim (Heb. 11:9). This did not disturb him, because he knew that God had a city which would far outshine his homeland.

Not only did Abraham live the life of a stranger and pilgrim, but he died as a stranger and pilgrim. From the time he left Ur, he never again had a settled home on earth. The only land he owned was a burial plot for Sarah, his wife. He died wandering around as a pilgrim and a stranger (11:13).

Abraham is a picture of every Christian. From the moment of conversion a Christian is a citizen of heaven (Phil. 3:1-2). He is simply camping on earth until the time comes for him to go home to glory. Heaven is home; the earth is just an elaborate campground.

ILLUSTRATIONS

For almost half of my life I was a missionary and pastor overseas. The passport in my pocket proclaimed the fact that I was an alien. My place of birth was America, and most of my family lived there. The whole cultural orientation of my youth and childhood was American, and my thought patterns were stamped indelibly by this. When, after two decades, I finally came "home" to America, my joy was indescribable.

By the same token Christians are strangers and aliens here on earth. They have been born into a heavenly family, and their whole way of thinking is influenced by heaven's standards. When through death they go home to heaven, their joy outshines anything known on earth.

Scottish theologian and writer John Baillie (1886-1960) caught this idea and wrote: "How many preachers, during these years, have dwelt on the joys of the heavenly rest with anything like the old ardent love and impatient longing, or have spoken of the world that now is as a place of sojourn and pilgrimage?"

In exactly the same vein, the brilliant professor and author, C.S. Lewis (1898-1963), wrote: "A continual looking forward to the eternal world is not a form of escapism or wishful thinking, but one of the things a Christian is meant to do."

A Christian can have a clear picture of heaven, according to Dwight L. Moody (1837-99): "How far away is heaven? It is not so far as some imagine. It wasn't very far from Daniel. It was not so far off that Elijah's prayer, and those of others, could not be heard there. Christ said, 'When ye pray say, Our Father, who art in heaven.' Men full of the Spirit can look right into heaven."

Bishop Jeremy Taylor (1613-67), a godly English churchman, put it simply: "Faith is the Christian's foundation, hope is his anchor, death is his harbor, Christ is his pilot, and heaven is his country."

An anonymous preacher told the story of a little Swedish girl, who was out walking with her father. As they strolled along, the little one gazed at the bright blue Scandinavian sky. After a long pause in the conversation, she said: "Father, I have been thinking that if the wrong side of heaven is so beautiful, what will the right side be?"

Hymn-writer Emily Divine Wilson (1865-1942) wrote these lines as a young woman:

While we walk this pilgrim pathway,
Clouds will overspread the sky;
But when trav'ling days are over,
Not a shadow, not a sigh.

TAKE

MEANING

Two words in Greek are translated with the more general English word "take." The first word is *lambano*, which appears about 150 times in the New Testament. This word means to "take hold," or "to take under one's control." A person takes a house under his control and occupies it, or he takes a book, or money. In fact, this word was used to describe the possession of tax revenues or war booty. Its essential meaning is possession.

The second word for "taking" is *haireomai*. This term had the idea of "taking for oneself," "seizing," "comprehending," and even "selecting one alternative from among others." In the development of language, this word came to mean choosing or selecting. A pupil selected the teacher from whom he learned. Thus a related word, *hairesis*, meant a school of thought or a religious sect. We see it reflected in our word *"heresy,"* a false doctrine which is chosen by its adherents. This second group of words is seen only three times in the New Testament. For this reason we shall concentrate our consideration on the more dominant word, *lambano*.

BIBLE USAGE

Remembering that *lambano* refers to "taking under one's control," it is seen most clearly with reference to the Lord. The Lord in glory is qualified to receive praise from all creatures (Rev. 5:12). In fact all praise, honor, and glory belongs to the Lord. Therefore He takes it as His due.

The Gospel gives wonderful meanings to this word. For instance, Jesus Christ took all of our infirmities and sins on Himself (Matt. 8:17). In the same sacrificial act, Jesus laid down His life and took it up again (John 10:18). He was in total control of His fate; His death was determined by the divine counsels of God, not by the capricious acts of man. The Holy Spirit will take the truth of Christ and disclose it to Christians (16:14). Again, the initiative and independence resides with God. The glory which Christ received was part of the Trinitarian relationship. He receives this acclaim because He was, is, and always will be God (2 Peter 1:17).

Everything which people receive is contingent on God's grace. By faith they receive Christ into their lives (John 1:12). By prayer they receive good gifts from God (Matt. 7:7-8; John 16:24). The Holy Spirit comes into a Christian's life as God's good gift (7:39), and as such the Spirit empowers that Christian for witness (Acts 1:8). The Lord assured Christians of the Spirit's presence before He left the earth (John 20:22).

Building on this teaching of absolute dependence on God for all we receive, the Epistles and Acts underline the truth. At Pentecost Peter also emphasized that believers must receive the Holy Spirit by faith from God (Acts 2:38). He also tied this reception to conversion through basic belief and repentance. This same access to the Holy Spirit was confirmed in the foreign setting of Cornelius' home in Caesarea (10:47). Having received the Holy Spirit admits a Christian into a Father-and-Son relationship with the Almighty God. The Christian is then enabled to call God "Abba," literally "Daddy" in Aramaic (Rom. 8:15).

Paul asserted that not only the Holy Spirit was received from God, but also the scope of ministry came from Him. In fact, Paul treated his apostolic office as a specific gift of God (Acts 20:24). Christians are enabled to serve God effectively because of a spiritual gift, which they have received by God's grace (1 Peter 4:10-11).

The simple word "take" has two main strains of meaning in the New

Testament. First, God receives all the glory and honor, because it is due to Him. He receives only what He richly deserves. Second, we as Christians receive every spiritual blessing which we possess because of our relationship by grace through faith with the Lord, our God.

ILLUSTRATIONS

The word "take" will be illustrated from two standpoints. First, we shall see what a Christian receives from the Lord. Theologically speaking, we receive forgiveness of sins, eternal life, the indwelling Holy Spirit, and all attendant blessings which arise out of these gifts.

Practically, this word emphasizes the simplicity of salvation. It is a matter of taking and receiving. A greatly distraught woman once came into my counseling room at the church in Bristol. She was deeply disturbed because of the breakdown of her marriage. She seemed almost incapable of concentrating on the Gospel, and she refused to receive God's gift.

When I next saw her she was much more calm, and she was sincerely seeking the Lord. Still she feared that she could not become a Christian. I took a coin, which was worth about 20 cents, out of my pocket. Then I gave it to her. She took it, and immediately she understood how to receive the Lord. When I last saw her, she still had that coin taped inside her New Testament as a reminder of her conversion experience.

Arthur John Gossip said, concerning this momentous transaction: "Every time well-meaning souls insist on cheapening His message, lowering the standard, explaining away the cost, and agreeing to accept Him upon easier terms than those He states, Christ openly repudiates them, and will have none of their advice."

In a lovely picture, Roy C. Naden said: "I cast off the mooring lines at a decaying wharf and pointed the bow toward the open sea of life, trusting my new Captain to take me safely to His heavenly haven." What a picturesque analogy of receiving Christ is this.

Not only do we take Christ into our lives at conversion, but He also receives us. In the pastoral ministry we often spoke with brand-new Christians. One attitude characterized them all, and it was wonder at the grace of God. Very often this line would be heard: "Why did God ever take me?" It is no wonder that John Newton called it "Amazing Grace."

C.L. Mitton explained the grace of God in this way: "Grace is God's unmerited, free, spontaneous love for sinful man, revealed and made effective in Jesus Christ." Because grace places us under the banner of Christ, God receives us in His name.

From the circle of Puritan penmen, William Fenner explained grace: "It is a rule of divinity, that grace takes not away nature; that is, grace comes not to take away man's affections, but to take them up."

This reminds one of a simple chorus, which is a prayer:
Jesus, take me as I am, / I can come no other way;
Take me deeper into You, / Make my flesh-life melt away.
Make me like a precious stone, / Crystal clear and finely honed;
Life of Jesus shining through, / Giving glory back to You.

TEMPLE

MEANING

The Greek word translated "temple" in the New Testament is *naos*. Originally it came from the word *naio* which means "to live," or "to dwell." Therefore in its early expression, *naos* was a dwelling place of the pagan gods. This is seen in the writings of Homer.

In this elementary way, a temple was any place especially set aside for worship. Examples of this were the grotto of Zeus on the island of Crete, the cleft in the rock at Delphi, and the holy grove at Olympia. The earliest buildings set aside as temples were found in Mesopotamia, including the tower of Babel. In our hemisphere, Central America had similar centers of worship.

In the Septuagint Greek Old Testament a temple was a place of special meeting with God. In its major expression the word referred to the temple at Jerusalem. Not only did *naos* refer to the temple of Jehovah, but it also described the Tower of Babel and the idol shrines at Dan and Bethel. Another word, *hieron*, applied to the holiest place and to the priests who served there. (See: *Priest*.)

BIBLE USAGE

In the Greek New Testament the word *naos* occurs 46 times. Its most obvious application is found in connection with the temple at Jerusalem. It was at the temple that Zacharias was serving, when the Angel Gabriel gave him the news of John's impending birth (Luke 1:9).

After the birth of Jesus, He was taken to the temple to fulfill the Law (2:27). There the temple servants Simeon and Anna proclaimed their messianic joy.

Years later Jesus was incensed because of the perversion of temple worship, so He purged it of all the money changers (Matt. 21:12-13; Mark 11:15-18; Luke 19:45-48). He regarded the temple as His Father's house, which was set aside for prayer.

Questions about the temple prompted Jesus to give His Olivet Discourse (Matthew 24:1—25:46; Mark 13; Luke 21:5-36). Jesus prophesied that the temple would be destroyed (Mark 13:2), as indeed it was when Titus invaded and plundered Jerusalem in A.D. 70.

Jesus also compared the temple to His human body. He said that the temple of His body would be destroyed and reconstructed in three days (John 2:19-21). By the same token, the Apostle Paul asserted that every Christian's body is a temple of the Holy Spirit (1 Cor. 6:19). This teaching is cited to encourage Christians to live for the Lord.

Not only are individual Christians temples of the Holy Spirit, but also the universal church is a temple. Christ is the Foundation, and Christians are the temple of God. Because the Holy Spirit lives in this temple, Christians are to be holy (3:16-17). As people come to Christ and grow in grace, they emerge as a temple and a dwelling place for God (Eph. 2:22).

In his Thessalonian letters, Paul indicated that the Antichrist would try to penetrate the church, the temple of God (2 Thes. 2:4). This will be a sign of the last times and Satan's final fling against the church of Jesus Christ.

Another temple is the heavenly temple which is revealed in the Book of Revelation. Christians will be pillars of the heavenly temple (Rev. 3:12). The purpose of this temple is the worship and service of God, and we shall have eternity to engage in His service (7:15). The magnitude of this temple is indicated by the description that Christ gave John (11:1). As it was in Jerusalem, so in the heavenly temple the ark of the covenant holds the central place (11:19). The heavenly temple is the center of God's government and the origin of His commands (14:15).

The word for temple, therefore, has many meanings in the New Testament. It referred to the temple in Jerusalem, which Christ valued and some Jews devalued. The spiritual successor to that temple is twofold: the body of each believer and the collection of all believers. The church of Christ is a spiritual temple. Ultimately the heavenly temple will be seen in all its glory, where we shall worship the Lamb.

ILLUSTRATIONS

During our years in Europe we were impressed by its beautiful "temples," or cathedrals. Within London, for instance, one sees Westminster Abbey as a national church and monument. Not far away is the Roman Catholic Cathedral, Westminster Cathedral. Across the city is the third great national church, St. Paul's Cathedral. Many saw this church in the television coverage of Prince Charles and Princess Diana's wedding on July 29, 1981.

On the continent of Europe are many other significant churches. Who can forget the Kaiser Wilhelm Memorial Church in Berlin, a symbol of the raw courage of that city? In Rome, St. Peter's serves as the center of Roman Catholicism worldwide. Notre Dame in Paris has been the focus of worship for many centuries. Recently we discovered another grand cathedral in Gerona, Spain. Its beauty made the trip all worthwhile.

However, the most important temple today is the church of Jesus Christ. When our son was much younger, he asked: "Dad, why do we go to church every Sunday?" It was one of those golden opportunities to explain the primacy of worship, the importance of adoration, the devotion to God's Word, and the fellowship of believers.

It is important to remember that we are God's temple. Ernest Southcutt put it well: "The holiest moment of the church service is the moment when God's people—strengthened by preaching and sacrament—go out of the church door into the world to be *the church*. We don't *go* to church; we *are* the church."

Sir Richard Baker caught the same idea when he wrote: "His *tabernacles* did but serve to show His power, His *courts* but to show His majesty; His *altars* but to show His deity, His *house* serves to show them all; for in His house there [we] will still be praising Him, and His praise and glory is the sum of all." One recalls that the basic meaning of temple is a dwelling place, or house, of God.

The purity of Christ's church was emphasized by John Milton (1608-74), who wrote: "We read not that Christ ever exercised force but once, and that was to drive profane ones out of His temple, and not to force them in."

A clear conception of the Christian church, the temple of God, emerges when one reads this statement from evangelist and educator Myron S. Augsburger: "The Christian church is not a static institution. It is men and women who flesh out in daily life the meaning of faith, the reality of the risen Christ."

TEMPTATION

MEANING

The Greek word which is reflected in our English word "temptation" is *peirasmos.* It comes from the verb, *peiro,* "to test or try." Another possible root of this word is *perao,* "to drive across," "pass through," or "strive to overcome." Thus, "temptation" is a test which can only be survived by strength and resolution. Obviously, in the mind of a pagan Greek writer, there was no divine assistance in overcoming temptation.

This term was used in many different ways. First, the early doctors used it to describe medical tests. Second, it was also a gambling term for trying one's luck at a certain game or bet. Third, a young man employed this verb to describe his romantic "try" for a young woman, so thus it could mean to woo a young woman.

In the Septuagint Greek Old Testament this word was employed to describe the murmuring of Israel, which put God to the test. It was also used to describe the test of faith to which God subjected Abraham, when He commanded the patriarch to sacrifice his only son.

BIBLE USAGE

There are several different levels of meaning implicit in this word. Sometimes it is used in a purely secular way, and then it implies no moral or immoral testing. After his conversion, Saul of Tarsus "tried" to associate with the disciples at Damascus, but they feared him (Acts 9:26). After Israel passed through the Red Sea, the Egyptians "tried" to chase them, but drowned (Heb. 11:29). In these and other references, the word is not linked with a temptation to do evil. It is simply an attempted act.

But in the New Testament this word often reflects the source of temptation. In Jesus' confrontation with the Evil One, Satan tempted Him, and thus demonstrated the sin of tempting God (Matt. 4:7). Similarly Ananias and Sapphira also were moved by Satan to tempt the Holy Spirit (Acts 5:9).

The Apostle Paul perceived that Satan was the main source of temptation (Eph. 6:10-17). This caused Paul deep concern, because he knew that Satan tempted the church (1 Thes. 3:5). As James added, Christians are also drawn into temptation by their own lusts (James 1:14).

The source of temptation is satanic, but the object of a temptation is a Christian. In fact, Christ urged Christians to pray for deliverance from temptation (Matt. 6:13; Luke 8:13). Paul wrote the Corinthians that no temptation is unique. Satan uses the same tired old tricks on every generation of Christians (1 Cor. 10:13). James promised the Christian a reward for endurance of temptations, sometimes translated "trials" (James 1:2, 12). Peter applied this word to the tribulation which had descended on Christians in the first century (1 Peter 1:6; 4:12).

The model of endurance under temptation was given by the Lord Jesus Christ. He was tempted in every way that we are; yet He never succumbed to sin (Heb. 4:15). The temptation of Christ is chronicled in Matthew 4:1-11; Mark 1:12-13; and Luke 4:1-13.

First, Satan tempted Jesus to turn some desert stones into bread, and thus to alleviate the hunger of His 40-day fast (Matt. 4:3). Jesus answered by quoting Deuteronomy 8:3, and assserted that people should not live by bread alone, but by the Word of God (Matt. 8:4). This temptation is like the first one which Satan leveled against Eve, when he showed her that the forbidden fruit was deceptively delicious to eat (Gen. 3:6).

Second, Satan chided Christ and challenged Him to throw Himself off the temple, and thus give the angels a chance to save Him (Matt. 4:5-6). Again Jesus answered from Scripture, that it is a sin to tempt God (4:7; Deut. 6:16). This second line of temptation was reflected in Satan's second temptation of Eve, when she saw that the forbidden fruit looked luscious (Gen. 3:6).

Third, Satan showed Christ an escape route, whereby the cross could be bypassed. Christ could simply bow before Satan, and win all the kingdoms of the earth (Matt. 4:9). Again, Jesus quoted Scripture, to insist that He would never bow before Satan (4:10; Deut. 6:13; 10:20). This reminds one of the final temptation which Satan shot at Eve, when she was told that the forbidden fruit would make her wise (Gen. 3:6).

Eve and Adam failed the temptation, and with them the whole human race failed. By contrast, Christ withstood the temptations of Satan and provided a path of victory for all who would follow Him.

ILLUSTRATIONS

Some of the greatest heartbreaks to a pastor are the temptations of his people. Jim had made a profession of faith, but then he slipped back into alcoholism. Soon he was back in prison, because of the combination of intoxication and thievery which had dogged his life. He simply did not withstand temptation, even though Christians supported him.

By contrast several members of the congregation faced sexual temptations. They immediately sought spiritual support, and I had the privilege of praying for them. Often it would take strong positive action to pull them out of tempting situations, but the Lord gave them and us the victory. As a result they and our church were strengthened.

On this particular subject, one of the most helpful collections of illustrations is Lloyd Cory's *Quotable Quotations* (Wheaton: Victor, 1985).

The common nature of temptation is seen in a quote from Bishop Fulton J. Sheen (1895-1979), a Roman Catholic television pioneer: "You are not tempted because you are evil; you are tempted because you are human." Along the same line, the famed devotional writer, Thomas à Kempis (1380-1471), penned this line: "Temptations discover what we are."

J.C. Macaulay, a former pastor of Wheaton Bible Church and president of Ontario Bible College, concluded concerning temptation: "Temptation is not sin but playing with temptation invites sin."

Martin Luther (1483-1546) gave us a picture of temptation. It is not wrong for birds to fly over our heads, he allowed, but it is wrong for us to allow them to nest in our hair.

Samuel Langhorne Clemens (1835-1910), alias Mark Twain, was no theologian, but he did understand temptation, for he wrote: "There are several good protections against temptation, but the surest is cowardice."

Franklin P. Jones also wrote concerning temptation. He saw the danger of "entertaining" it, and claimed: "What makes resisting temptation difficult for many people is they don't want to discourage it completely."

THANKS

MEANING

The Greek word used for "thanks" is *eucharistia*. It is reflected in our word "eucharist," used in Roman Catholic and Episcopalian churches to describe the Lord's Table, or Communion. The word "eucharist" focuses on giving thanks for the death of Christ.

Actually, the root word in the Greek is *chair* or *char*, which means "joy." Therefore "thanks" is expressing joy because of a person, event, or thing. Originally the word meant a thankful attitude. Later it came to mean the expression of thanks. It was commonly found in ancient inscriptions to pagan deities.

In the Septuagint Greek Old Testament the word had two basic references. First, it was used as an expression of thanks to God. Second, it spoke of someone giving thanks to someone else.

BIBLE USAGE

The words, *eucharistia* (thanks) and *eucharisto* (to give thanks) appear 36 times in the epistles of Paul and 13 times in the Gospels. In the Gospels thanks is usually directed to God. A healed leper, who was a Samaritan, returned to give thanks to the Lord for healing him (Luke 17:16).

When Jesus fed the 5,000, He took a small boy's lunch. After the Lord had given thanks for the food, He broke it and multiplied it (Matt. 15:36; John 6:11). At the Last Supper, Jesus again followed this custom of giving thanks (Matt. 26:27; 1 Cor. 11:24).

The custom of giving thanks for food characterized true believers in biblical times. Paul cited this as a practice of all Christians (Rom. 14:6). Even when surrounded by unbelieving Roman seamen and soldiers, Paul still gave thanks for his food (Acts 27:35). When discussing the matter of food offered to idols, Paul again referred to the giving of thanks (1 Cor. 10:30).

Most of all, the Apostle Paul gave thanks for Christians. He thanked the Lord for the faith which was seen in Christians (Rom. 1:8). He also thanked the Lord for God's grace in the conversion of Christians (1 Cor. 1:4). Likewise Paul thanked the Lord for prayer support given by Christians on his behalf (2 Cor. 1:11). Is it not amazing, that even the carnal Corinthians gave Paul cause for thanksgiving?

Paul thanked the Lord for the wedding of faith and love, which was seen in many Christians. This was true of the Ephesians (Eph. 1:15-16). The apostle also gave thanks for faith and love as viewed among the Colossians and the Thessalonians (Col. 1:3-4; 1 Thes. 1:2-3).

Paul praised the Lord for the spiritual gifts which were given by Christians (2 Cor. 4:15). Especially was this true in Paul's prolonged praise toward God for the Philippians (Phil. 4:10-19). Paul also thanked the Lord that the Philippian Christians had engaged with him in the work of evangelism (1:3-5).

Paul likewise thanked the Lord for the response which his message had seen. Among the Thessalonians, Paul thanked the Lord that they received the Gospel so readily (1 Thes. 2:13). He also thanked the Lord for having chosen the Thessalonians to be saved (2 Thes. 2:13).

A profound truth is hidden in this word "thanksgiving." In the Scriptures, thanks is seldom given from one person to another person. Usually one person gives thanks to God for another person. Thus the glory and the thanks are due mainly to God, not to other people.

ILLUSTRATIONS

Literature is full of references to thanksgiving. For instance, Ambrose (A.D. 340-397), that Bishop of Milan through whom Augustine came to faith, wrote: "No duty is more urgent than that of returning thanks."

The venerable English preacher, John Henry Jowett (1864-1923), was also strong in his advocacy of thanksgiving. For he wrote: "Every virtue divorced from thankfulness is maimed and limps along the spiritual road."

Helen Keller (1890-1968), a shining example of triumphant living, spoke glowingly of thanksgiving: "For three things I thank God every day of my life: thanks that He has vouchsafed me knowledge of His works; deep thanks that He has set in my darkness the lamp of faith; deep, deepest thanks that I have another life to look forward—a life joyous with light and flowers and heavenly song." One recalls that Helen Keller was both blind and deaf.

Andrew Murray (1828-1917), noted South African devotional writer, urged the duty of thanksgiving on his hearers by saying: "To be thankful for what I have received and for what my Lord has prepared, is the surest way to receive more."

Christina Rossetti (1830-94), sister of the famous poet Dante Gabriel Rossetti, wrote thus concerning thanksgiving: "[Imagine being] in this glorious world with grateful hearts—and no one to thank."

Perhaps the best expression of thanks is found in the Thanksgiving Day proclamations of our Presidents. The first President, George Washington (1732-99), wrote: "[Let us thank God] for His kind care and protection of the people of this country previous to their becoming a nation. . . . for the peaceable and rational manner in which we have been enabled to establish constitutions of government for our safety and happiness."

The 16th President, Abraham Lincoln (1809-65) wrote: "It has seemed to me fit and proper that [the gifts of God] should be solemnly, reverently, and gratefully acknowledged with one heart and voice by the whole American people."

A great general turned President was Dwight D. Eisenhower (1890-1969). He proclaimed: "Let all of us . . . give thanks to God and prayerful contemplation to those eternal truths and universal principles of Holy Scripture which have inspired such measure of true greatness as this nation has achieved."

On his first Thanksgiving in office, President John Kennedy (1917-1963) issued this proclamation: "Let us observe this day with reverence and with prayer that will rekindle in us the will and show us the way not only to preserve our blessings, but also to extend them to the four corners of the earth."

Another proclamation was made by Kennedy's successor, President Lyndon Johnson (1908-73): "Let us . . . give thanks to God for His graciousness and generosity to us—pledge to Him our everlasting devotion—beseech His divine guidance, and the wisdom and strength to recognize and follow that guidance."

THINK

MEANING

There are at least two main words that characterize "thinking" in the New Testament. One of them is *dialogizomai*, seen in our English word, "*dialog*ue." It refers to conversation. The poets used it to describe the content of their poems. Philosophers used "*dialog*ue" as a method of teaching. By questions and answers pupils were brought to understand philosophical principles and concepts.

A second word for "thinking" is *dokeo*. It has to do with the thought processes, believing, accepting a concept, developing an opinion, or giving an impression. A related idea is "appearance," when one thinks something looks similar. This idea was perverted in the early church by the sect of *Docet*ism. This sect taught that Jesus Christ was not a real man, but only appeared to be human.

To summarize, *dialogizomai* speaks of opinions or thoughts which are developed and aired in discussion. On the other hand, *dokeo* deals with opinions as they develop in the mind.

BIBLE USAGE

The first word, *dialogizomai*, appears about 30 times in the Greek New Testament, and in almost every case it has a negative connotation. The scribes "reasoned" (literally, dialogued) in their hearts against Jesus (Mark 2:6; Luke 5:22). The disciples argued among one another, and this arguing was described by the same word (Mark 9:33-34).

The Apostle Paul picked up the same word. He too used it negatively to describe "futile speculation" (Rom. 1:21). This is the essence of the mental foolishness which opposes the message of the Cross of Christ (1 Cor. 1:21-25). The very reasoning of an unsaved person, according to the apostle, is useless (3:20).

Thus the frantic discussion and "dialogue" of the unsaved is fruitless. All of their collected wisdom is of no importance, according to divine revelation. There is a similar skepticism concerning the word *dokeo*.

Christ often pointed out the short circuits in the thinking of the Pharisees. They misunderstood their relationship with Abraham (Matt. 3:9). People often thought they held possessions, though these would ultimately be lost (Luke 8:18). Jesus challenged this false thinking, which assumed one's right of possession. He also queried the concept that unbelievers will be able to stand in the day of judgment (John 5:45). Finally Christ called into question their understanding, their thinking, about God's plan for Christ's life (Matt. 18:12; 21:28). In fact, the Jews were so blinded by their religious bias, that they could not come to proper conclusions concerning the Christ.

There are, however, some positive applications of the verb *dokeo*. At the end of the Council of Jerusalem, the participating apostolic leaders came to certain conclusions. They agreed (*dokeo*) to send a delegation to all the churches (Acts 15:22, 25). Furthermore, they also concluded that Gentiles could come to Christ without traveling the road of Judaism (15:28-29).

In the other epistles, Paul also used the word *dokeo* to describe thought processes. Those who rely on human knowledge or wisdom to find salvation are doomed to eternal failure according to Paul. This was especially applicable to the sophisticated Greeks (1 Cor. 8:2). Paul was firmly convinced that no Greek philosophy could pave the way to heaven. Only the Gospel of Christ's Cross can do that.

No matter which word is used for "thinking" in the New Testament, it is
inevitably surrounded with skepticism. In the Gospels, Christ confounded the best

thinking of the Pharisees and scribes. The apostolic Christians knew that the only correct thoughts were those which were subjected to the Spirit. In the epistles one sees an awareness that salvation is not thought out, but rather bought by the blood of Christ.

ILLUSTRATIONS

From the earliest days, there was a deep thankfulness for the ability to think. Aristotle (384-322 B.C.) acclaimed: "Reason is a light that God kindled in the soul."

One of the most notable Christian thinkers of all time was Galileo (1564-1642), who praised man's ability to think: "I do not feel obliged to believe that the same God who has endowed us with sense, reason, and intellect has intended us to forego their use."

According to Charles E. Garman: "Reason inspired by love of truth is the only eye with which man can see the spiritual heaven above us."

For many years it was assumed that biblical, evangelical Christians were opposed to reason. In fact, there was a real or imagined anti-intellectualism among Bible-believing people. One of the first to swim against that stream was Dr. Carl F.H. Henry, who said about reason: "Christian theology involves a revelational philosophy. The appeal to revealed truth involves not the rejection of the authority of reason, but an appeal from a limited and unenlightened reason to a reason fully informed. . . . Reason should be viewed not as a source of knowledge and contrasted with revelation, but as a means of comprehending revelation."

Reason is only reliable, however, when it is directed by God. According to W.J. Dawson: "If you would voyage Godward, you must see to it that the rudder of thought is right."

It is said of the Christian astronomer Johannes Kepler (1571-1630), that he regarded science as "thinking God's thoughts after Him." Along the same line, the noted German writer Johann Friedrich von Schiller (1759-1805) concluded concerning the use of reason: "The universe is one of God's thoughts."

The saintly Bishop Augustine of Hippo (A.D. 354-430) saw the intellect of God behind all things. He admitted: "The Almighty does nothing without reason, though the frail mind of man cannot explain the reason."

Someone compared this to modern medicine. In salvation, one receives a "heart transplant," whereby his sinful heart is replaced. As the Lord sanctifies one he receives a divine "brain transplant," in which the mind of Christ comes to control more and more of his thinking.

It is no wonder then that hymn-writer Katie B. Wilkinson (1859-1928) framed this prayer, which true Christian thinkers have echoed throughout the ages:

> May the mind of Christ my Saviour
>   Live in me from day to day,
> By His love and power controlling
>   All I do and say.

THROW

MEANING

The basic word to describe "throwing" in the Greek New Testament is *ballo*. One sees reflections of this word in our term, *ballistic* (an object which is thrown or propelled, as a "ballistic missile"). The simple Greek verb *ballo* was used to describe throwing an object. But it also meant to lay something down, or to lay an idea on one's heart.

A combination word relating to *ballo* is *ekballo*. Since *ek* means "out," this word carried the blunt idea of being "thrown out." It was used to describe the expulsion of enemies, the dismissal of a servant, and even the exorcism of an evil spirit.

Another combination word was *epiballo*. The prefix *epi* meant "upon," and the combination word meant to "throw something over," "throw oneself into a task," or "be zealous in a certain undertaking."

BIBLE USAGE

The root word, *ballo*, is used in both a literal and figurative way, and appears 130 times in the Greek New Testament. In its literal sense it was used to describe the throwing of nets or a hook in fishing (Matt. 4:18; 17:27). In farming it described the broadcasting, or throwing out, of seed (Mark 4:26). Also it described the casting of lots, like the throwing of dice (15:24).

Some of the literal uses of this word are amazing. When wine was poured into a wineskin, it was "thrown" into the skin (2:22). Jesus healed a deaf man by "throwing" His fingers into the deaf man's ears (7:33). Likewise, Thomas was invited by the Lord to "throw" his finger into the nail-prints and his hand into the spear wound in Christ's side (John 20:25-27). Any sudden motion was described as "throwing."

Frequently *ballo* was also used figuratively. As a tree that does not bear fruit is chopped down and thrown into a fire (Matt. 3:10), so those who rebel against God will be cast into "the furnace" (13:42). The same word is used to describe the throwing of a person into hell (5:29). In order to avoid this radical punishment, the Lord commanded that people throw away the offending aspects of their lives (18:9).

Having established this basic word, we shall consider its combinations. The term *ekballo* (to throw out) was often used in reference to demons. Jesus commanded the demons to leave, and they did (8:16). It was through the Holy Spirit's power that Jesus cast out demons (12:28). As Jesus healed people, He often cast out evil spirits (Mark 1:34). When the disciples were sent out on their first missionary journey, the Lord also gave them authority to throw out demons (Matt. 10:1, 8; Mark 3:15).

This same term, "to throw out," is also used about people. John warned the early church about Diotrephes, who actually threw biblical Christians out of the church (3 John 10). Paul reminded the Galatians of the time when Abraham threw out Hagar and Ishmael (Gal. 4:30). By the same token, a blind man whom Jesus healed was thrown out of the synagogue by self-righteous Jews (John 9:34).

Jesus also threw the money changers out of the temple (Luke 19:45). Likewise, He promised to cast out Satan, the prince of this world (John 12:31).

The meaning of the third word, *epiballo*, is less clear. Nevertheless, one can discern in it the concept of forceful movement. In a storm the waves threw themselves upon a small boat (Mark 4:37). In their efforts to arrest Jesus, it is said that the arresting officers "threw their hands on Jesus" (Mark 14:46).

After Jesus had been arrested, Peter denied Him. After Peter heard a rooster crow and realized his own treachery, he "threw himself down" and wept bitterly (14:72, Greek New Testament).

One common denominator unites all three of these words: it is strong, forceful action. Whether it be the simple verb of throwing, *ballo,* or the stronger verb of throwing out, *ekballo,* the idea is similar. Someone propels a person or thing away.

ILLUSTRATIONS

As the word "to throw" is used in many different ways in the Bible, it also has a multitude of meanings in everyday English. One "throws" the garbage out, and one "throws" a ball. Little children "throw" temper tantrums, and adults "hurl" insults.

Recently an ice hockey match was covered in the sports news. In sheer frustration the goalie struck out with his stick against an opposing player. Immediately the official stopped the game and threw the goalie out of the match. As the fuming hockey player left the ice, he threw his stick into the locker room. So, the word still has a lot of force left in it.

These words also have many spiritual uses. When a person comes to Christ, he or she often throws away the trappings of his pre-Christian life. A woman in our first church in England was converted from a terrible life of sin. The first thing she did was to throw out stacks on stacks of pornographic magazines. In fact, a helpful deacon took them home to dispose of them. He threw them out with his garbage. Unfortunately that week a garbage strike occurred, and the stacks of pornography remained for several days in front of the deacon's house.

A student told me that before his conversion he wore a badge with the bold phrase, "Question Authority." One night he dreamed that the Lord had taken him to heaven, but he still was wearing the offensive badge on his jacket. As he awoke, he was trying to tear off that badge. So soon he threw the badge of his rebellion away.

A well-known pastor was preaching at a Bible conference. Each day a lady came to talk with him, but she could not seem to have her problems resolved. Finally, the speaker consented to counsel her. He soon discovered that she was demonized. Only after the demon was cast out in Jesus' name could the woman find peace.

The most dramatic act of "throwing out" is excommunication. Of this Puritan Thomas Goodwin (1600-80) said: "The proper inward effect that accompanies this ordinance is inward affliction and distress of conscience by Satan, which of all afflictions is the greatest punishment."

When we were still in language school in Germany, I served as part-time pastor of a small church. Unknown to me, one of the men in the church was living in an adulterous relationship. The senior pastor, a godly brother, discovered this. After due attempts to reclaim the sinning saint, a formal excommunciation was declared. At the Lord's Table the man's name was read out, and he was barred from the table until he repented. This event is unforgettable in my ministry.

TONGUE

MEANING

The Greek word for "tongue" is *glossa*. One sees it in such English words as "*gloss*ary" (a list of words), and "*gloss*olalia" (speaking in tongues).

Most obviously this word was used to describe that part of the body we call the tongue. It was regarded by the Greeks to be an organ of speech and of taste.

As time went on the more abstract meanings began to appear. Homer used it to describe languages. We see this in our phrase, "the mother tongue." It also stood for a dialect or different form of language. Aristotle used "tongue" to describe strange or old-fashioned speech.

The Septuagint Greek Old Testament spoke against sins of the tongue, such as false witnessing. The tongue was also compared to a scourge or a sword. According to the writer of Proverbs, a tongue could hold the power of life or death (Prov. 18:21).

BIBLE USAGE

There are three aspects to the New Testament teaching concerning the tongue. First, the Bible speaks often of the physical tongue as an organ of speech. Zacharias found it hard to believe the announcement about the birth of John the Baptist; consequently his tongue (speech) was bound until the baby was born (Luke 1:20, 64).

A common occurrence in Christ's time was demon-possession. A frequent sympton of that bondage was the inability to speak, but the Lord broke such bonds (Matt. 9:32-33).

James devoted a large section of his letter to the sins of the tongue. A sinful tongue is like an arsonist who ignites fires everywhere (James 3:5). All sorts of wild animals can be tamed, but a tongue is incapable of being tamed (3:7-8). Furthermore, a tongue is prone to perversion and deceit (3:10-12). James clearly underlined the problems which the tongue poses for a Christian.

On the other hand, a tongue is also the instrument by which we praise the Lord. Peter quoted David's hymn of praise, whereby his tongue was loosened to exalt the Lord (Acts 2:26). In the Book of Philippians, Paul pointed forward to the day when every tongue will confess that Jesus is the Lord (Phil. 2:11).

If the primary meaning of tongue is the physical organ, its secondary meaning is language. At the day of Pentecost, people who represented all the various language groups were present (Acts 2:8-11). In the Revelation there are repeated references to people of every language group praising the Lord (Rev. 5:9; 7:9; 10:11; 11:9; 13:7; 14:6).

One final use of the term tongue is speaking in tongues, or "*gloss*olalia." At the Day of Pentecost, the apostolic Christians spoke in various known languages (Acts 2:4). The same was true when Cornelius received the Holy Spirit (10:46). This was construed as a fulfillment of the signs which Christ promised at the end of His earthly ministry (Mark 16:17).

In the list of spiritual gifts tabulated by Paul, he referred to these tongues. Some of these tongues, literally "languages," are understood by God alone (1 Cor. 14:2). In some cases these tongues were employed mainly in prayer (14:14). Speaking in tongues was only allowed when an interpreter was present (14:27). Paul preferred prophecy to speaking in tongues, because prophecy brought greater profit to the church (14:39).

Thus the little word "tongue" has several important meanings in the Greek

New Testament. It stands for things from the physical organ to ecstatic utterances.

ILLUSTRATIONS

Many authors have commented on the tongue, and none were more eloquent than the bard William Shakespeare (1564-1616). About the tongue he said: "He hath a heart as sound as a bell, and his tongue is the clapper; for what his heart thinks, his tongue speaks" (*Much Ado about Nothing*).

A wise old Chancellor of the German Federal Republic, Konrad Adenauer (1876-1967), summarized the significance of the tongue in these lines: "Sometimes I doubt whether there is divine justice. All parts of the human body get tired eventually—except the tongue. And I feel this is unjust." One can tell that he was a member of the legislature, the greatest "talk shop" in any democracy.

Alfred Lord Tennyson (1809-92), a poet laureate, wrote in "Break, Break, Break":

Break, break, break
  On thy cold gray stones, O Sea!
And I would that my tongue could utter
  The thoughts that arise in me.

One must ask, if the eloquent Tennyson could not express his thoughts, how can we ever do it?

Another eloquent English poet was Rudyard Kipling (1865-1936). He too spoke of the tongue when he wrote: "Words are, of course, the most powerful drug used by mankind."

Lewis Carroll (1832-98), author of *Alice in Wonderland*, showed the fickleness of speech when he wrote: "When I use a word, it means just what I choose it to mean—neither more nor less."

In a similar vein, President Abraham Lincoln (1809-65) characterized a pompous person with this cutting line: "He can compress the most words into the smallest idea of any man I have met."

The tongue is a subject of endless debate and a delight to wits of every generation. However, one use of that word has become a battleground for Christians. It is the idea of "speaking in tongues," or "*gloss*olalia."

A late English pastor and proponent of speaking in tongues, David Watson, explained it in these words: "Tongues are simply another expression of our relationship with God through Jesus Christ."

A.W. Tozer was considerably more conservative in his assessment of this phenomenon. He noted that many great men of God had never spoken in tongues, and he listed among them Augustine, Thomas à Kempis, Charles Haddon Spurgeon, and George Mueller. Therefore Tozer concluded that tongues was not the only sign of the fullness of the Holy Spirit.

Dr. V. Raymond Edman (1900-67), former President of Wheaton College, often told us: "A small percentage of speaking in tongues is Holy Spirit-inspired. Another very small sampling is satanic. The great majority of those who speak in tongues are simply giving an emotional expression." Though Dr. Edman said this in the '50s, it seems true in the '80s also.

TREASURE

MEANING

The Greek words reflected in "treasure" and "storing up treasure" are *thesauros* (treasure) and *thesaurizo* (to pile up treasure). One can easily see a connection with the English word *"thesaurus,"* which is a treasury of words.

Originally *thesaurizo* meant to store up materials, or to amass valuables. Later it was expanded to denote a chamber or chest in which treasure was kept. Throughout the ancient Middle East it was especially applied to a temple store-house, where temple taxes were stored. People were required to give a portion of their produce to the temple, and this was stored in a treasury. Finally it also meant private money boxes, the early versions of home safes.

In the Septuagint Greek Old Testament the word was used to describe wealth which was amassed. Later it also took on a more figurative meaning. Alms given to the poor were seen to be a treasure given to God. This is reflected brightly in the New Testament teaching of Christ.

BIBLE USAGE

Just as the ancient world saw both literal and figurative treasures in this word, so the New Testament contains both ideas. After Jesus was born, wise men came to the house with valuable treasures (Matt. 2:11). In the Parables of the Kingdom, the Lord also referred to such treasures. A shrewd businessman would buy a field, if it contained a treasure (13:11). Jesus also spoke of a storehouse, a treasury full of treasure (13:52). Though these references are found in parables, they emphasize literal treasures.

When Paul taught the Lord's people about the privilege of giving, he also referred to this word. Each week Christians are exhorted to collect their gifts and pass them on to the needy. The word for "collections" is *thesaurizo* (1 Cor. 16:2). This verse teaches proportional giving, regular giving, and the church's role in receiving gifts.

There is also an emphasis in the New Testament on the transient nature of treasure. In the great Westminster Abbey of the faithful, the writer of Hebrews reminded his readers that Moses gave up the treasures of Egypt for the pleasures of eternity (Heb. 11:25-26). James warned his readers that treasures will corrupt and rust, if they are not passed on in wages to the workers (James 5:3).

Much space in the New Testament is given over to a discussion of spiritual treasures. Jesus taught, as part of the Sermon on the Mount, that earthly treasures are doomed to decay, but gifts given to God will build up eternal value (Matt. 6:19-21).

The content of one's mind and heart is also seen as a treasure. A good person brings forth good from this treasury, but an evil person spews out sin (12:35). This is especially seen in the words one utters.

Paul returned to this theme when he spoke of the Gospel. To him the Gospel was an inestimable treasure. God gave it to His people, in order that they might pass it on to the world. This treasure is like a precious stone kept in a crockery pot (2 Cor. 4:7). In other words, the value is in the treasure, not the pot. The value in us is the Gospel, not our physical bodies.

Jesus Christ is seen as the repository of all treasure. In fact, Paul insisted that all the treasures of God are hidden in Christ Jesus (Col. 2:3). When one seeks basic wisdom and knowledge, Christ must be the source, for He personifies all the wisdom and knowledge of God.

Peter used this word to express warning. Some people by their evil deeds are storing up treasures of judgment (2 Peter 3:7). They will discover in eternity that all of their sins are remembered and stored up for future judgment. What a sad treasury that is!

In the Scriptures treasure has two basic meanings. First, it is material treasure which has a short life and must be left on earth. Second, it is spiritual treasure. If we serve the Lord our treasure will pay eternal dividends, but if we serve Satan our treasure of sin will pay out an eternal penalty.

ILLUSTRATIONS

"Make all you can, save all you can, give all you can," commented John Wesley (1703-91) on the subject of financial treasures.

A similar sentiment was stated by the late Chaplain of the United States Senate, Peter Marshall (1902-49): "Let us give according to our incomes, lest God make our incomes match our gifts."

A sterling example of this philosophy of life was stated by Thomas Fuller (1608-61), in his biography of Archbishop Edmund Grindal (1519-83): "Worldly wealth he cared not for, desiring only to make both ends meet."

Many people have learned the value of banking in heaven's treasury and banking on heaven's currency. The great voice of the Methodist revival in Cornwall, England was Billy Bray (1794-1868). Of God's treasury he said: "The promises of God are just as good as ready money any day."

Another aspect of heavenly treasury was seen in the life and ministry of America's great theologian and preacher, Jonathan Edwards (1745-1801). To him heaven was the only treasury worth investing in. He said: "Every saint in heaven is as a flower in the garden of God, and every soul there is as a note in some concert of delightful music."

Edward Kimball knew something about this spiritual savings account. As a Sunday School teacher he pursued and won to Christ a young shoe salesman, Dwight L. Moody (1837-99). Many years later Moody was preaching near his home in New England, and a young man came to Christ. Further investigation revealed that this young convert was none other than a son of Edward Kimball. The teacher's treasure paid interest in this life and a large dividend in eternity.

In 1978 the *Sunday Telegraph* of London carried an obituary of Sir John Laing. When the noted English building magnate died he was 99 years old, and a well-known Christian layman. Though Sir John had earned many millions, he died with only about $400 in the bank. The journalist explained: "The small net sum reflects Sir John's lifelong dedication to Christian and philanthropic work." He was wise enough to send along his treasure to heaven, where it could gather real interest for eternity.

Anna Waring (1820-1910) summarized this in her hymn:

My hope I cannot measure,
  My path to life is free;
My Saviour has my treasure,
  And He will walk with me.

TRUTH

MEANING

In the Greek New Testament the word for "truth" is *aletheia*, and was seen mainly as a contrast with a lie. Homer wrote that a lie is either the absence of truth or a partial truth. If one deceived another by telling only part of the truth, this was a lie.

In writing his *Odyssey*, Homer mentioned the role of a judge in a race. His job was to tell the truth about the winners and losers of a race.

Thucydides contrasted truth with exaggeration. Anyone who expanded or embellished the truth was really telling a lie. Thus truth is contrasted with boasting or flattery.

Plato contrasted truth with appearance. Some things may appear to be real, but actually are an illusion.

Truth is seen mainly by contrast. It contrasts with a lie of statement or understatement. Another contrast is seen between truth and exaggeration. Finally, truth stands out in contrast with appearance.

BIBLE USAGE

There are several complementary aspects of the word for truth in the New Testament. First, it speaks of trustworthiness. God's truth is contrasted with man's lie (Rom. 3:7). In fact, the entire revelation of God is summarized as "the truth of God" (15:8). Obviously God is the standard of truth by which all others must be judged.

Some people are regarded to be trustworthy, true to others and to God. Obedient Christians are true in their worship of the Lord, because they have accepted the full revelation of redemption (1 Cor. 5:8). Paul could claim that his dealings with other Christians had been marked by truth (2 Cor. 7:14). In fact, the righteousness of a Christian is expressed in truth and integrity (Eph. 5:9).

Not only are some people trustworthy, but the Lord is regarded as the Standard of all truth. In Christ's high priestly prayer, He asserted that the Word of God is truth in every sense (John 17:17). It does not simply contain truth; it is truth.

Likewise the Holy Spirit is seen to be the Spirit of Truth. It is He who leads Christians into all spiritual truth (16:13). Because the Holy Spirit is truth, the world cannot comprehend Him and His ministry (14:17).

As God the Father and God the Spirit are truth, so Christ came into our world as the personification of God's truth. In John's explanation of the Incarnation, one reads the assertion that Christ was full of grace and truth (1:14-18). Furthermore, in answer to Thomas' question concerning the nature of God, Jesus affirmed that He is the Way, the Truth, and the Life (14:6).

Because our God is true, a Christian should be marked by truth. The message by which we were saved is truth (Eph. 1:13). In fact, the Gospel is called the Word of Truth (Col. 1:5). A Christian's task is to proclaim properly the Word of Truth (2 Tim. 2:15). The entire Christian life should be lived within the orbit of God's truth (2 John 4; 3 John 3).

The Scriptures speak of truth as trustworthiness, truth as an extension of God's character, and finally truth as ultimate reality. Even the enemies of Christ were aware that His teaching was true, and that it conformed to the realities about God (Matt. 22:16; Luke 20:21). Christ modeled the truth, in which He expected His disciples to live (John 17:19).

Truth in the Scripture is tied inextricably to the person of our God. He is the

Source of all truth, and the Trinity emphasizes this aspect of God's character. No

Christian can either know or practice truth, apart from constant reliance on the One who is Truth. He is Truth, because He conforms to and indeed creates ultimate reality.

ILLUSTRATIONS

The truth is often stretched to the point of breaking. "Where have you been?" a mother challenges.

"Out," comes the child's terse answer.

"What have you been doing?" the mother follows through.

"Nothing," is the child's guarded reply. The truth is sacrificed by a series of carefully crafted answers.

Politicians often slay the truth on an altar of expedience. For instance, Adolf Hitler (1889-1945) took an expectedly cavalier attitude toward the truth. He said, "The victor will never be asked if he told the truth."

An American leader expressed the opposite attitude: "Let us begin by committing ourselves to the truth—to see it like it is, and tell it like it is." This strong defender of truth was none other than President Richard M. Nixon. His life later gave the lie to his assertion.

A distant relative of mine once sold a piece of property to my father. He was a glib man with a quick tongue. Despite his frequent forays away from the truth, he often claimed, "My word is my bond." What a travesty of truth was his life.

It is refreshing when one turns to the Christian concept of truth. John Baillie (1886-1960), a noted Scottish theologian, once said: "The New Testament does not say, 'You shall know the rules, and by them you shall be bound,' but, 'You shall know the truth, and the truth shall make you free.' " Be it noted that Jesus said this about Himself (John 8:32).

Another British Bible expositor, Alexander Maclaren (1826-1910), commented concerning truth: "If a man will not think about Christian truth he will not have the blessedness of Christian possession of God." The secret to Christ's presence is meditation on the truths of the Scriptures.

Yet another British churchman was William Temple (1881-1944), an Archbishop of Canterbury, who likewise commented on the subject of truth: "Christianity is not a drug which suits some complaints and not others. It is either sheer illusion or else it is the truth. But if it is the truth, if the universe happens to be constituted in this way, the question is not whether the God of Christianity suits us, but whether we suit Him."

Lutheran theologian Christoph Ernst Luthardt (1823-1902) was equally assertive in the cause of truth: "The truth which we need and seek is God—the living, personal God. This is the truth which is the foundation of the Christian view of the universe."

In commenting on his scientific research, Sir Isaac Newton (1642-1727) concluded: "I felt like a child playing with pebbles on the shore when the ocean of truth lay all about me."

TURN, REPENTANCE, CONVERSION

MEANING

The three words "turn," "repentance," and "conversion" all share a basic meaning in Greek. They all speak of a complete change in life or thought. Several Greek words relate to these concepts, and we shall consider two of them.

The first word is *epistrepho*, which means to turn oneself around. This may be a turning of the body, or it may refer to changing one's thoughts or attitudes. Very early in the history of Greek literature, this word came to mean turning one's thoughts to God or to piety. It is found 1,050 times in the Septuagint Greek Old Testament, and many times it spoke of Israel returning to Jehovah.

The second word is *metanoia*, which literally means "a change in mind." This term is almost absent from ancient classical Greek. It really gained its content from the New Testament. Contained in this concept are the ideas of remorse and regret for wrongdoing. When the Septuagint Greek Old Testament was translated, this word was used to depict the prophets' preaching about repentance.

BIBLE USAGE

The first word, *epistrepho*, was used in the New Testament to describe conversion. The announcement of the birth of John the Baptist was accompanied by the promise that he would "turn" many back to God (Luke 1:16).

Jesus likewise spoke often of this turning or conversion (Mark 4:12). According to Christ, unless a person turns or repents and becomes like a child, there is no salvation (Matt. 18:3). Still He knew that many would never repent and be converted (John 12:40). Jesus even spoke about Peter turning again, or "being converted" (Luke 22:32, KJV).

In the Apostolic Age, this word was widened so it included all peoples. Gentiles soon were being converted (Acts 15:19). When one turns to the Lord, a veil is lifted from his understanding (2 Cor. 3:16).

This turning involves two aspects. First there is a turning away from evil. People turn from darkness to light when they accept Christ (Acts 26:18; Eph. 5:8). There is also a turning to Christ (John 14:1, 6). As a result there is a turning to forgiveness (Acts 3:19).

The first and more generic word for conversion is *epistrepho*, and the second is more strictly a New Testament word, *metanoia* (the changed mind). John the Baptist preached the necessity of changing one's mind (Matt. 3:2, 8). Jesus likewise preached this repentance and conversion (4:17; Mark 1:15). When people did not repent, Jesus reproached them (Matt. 11:20). In fact, Jesus did not dwell upon the self-righteous, but He rather reached out to the sinners and called them to repentance (Luke 5:32).

In the Book of Acts the apostles went throughout the Mediterranean basin preaching the Gospel. Part of their proclamation was repentance, as John the Baptist had preached it (Acts 13:24). Paul also reminded people that John was a signpost, for the Baptist pointed to Christ who alone could forgive the repentant (19:4).

Repentance and conversion represent a clear change in direction. They involve a changing of one's mind about sin and a rejection of it (3:19; 5:31). This act of repentance and conversion also involves a turning to God (20:21; 26:20).

No one summarized the importance of repentance more clearly than did Peter. In his rather dramatic second letter, he spoke of the Lord's patience with the unrepentant. Then he added that the Lord had delayed His coming, so that more people would repent (2 Peter 3:9).

Whether one uses the more general term, *epistrepho*, or the specific term, *metanoia*, the emphasis of the Scriptures is clear. Conversion and repentance go hand in hand. Turning to Christ is accompanied by turning away from sin (1 Thes. 1:9).

ILLUSTRATIONS

In illustrating this concept, we shall first look at the meaning of repentance. Samuel Davies said: "The question is not, 'Shall I repent?' for that is beyond doubt. But the question is, 'Shall I repent now, when it may save me? Or shall I put it off to the eternal world, when my repentance will be my punishment?'"

A ministerial colleague in Britain is Leith Samuel. He commented on repentance: "Our Lord has laid down emphatically that a man must repent of his sins, and particularly of his critical and independent attitude toward God, or he cannot begin to live the Christian life."

Neoorthodox theologian Emil Brunner (1889-1966) described repentance: "Repentance is despair of self, despairing of self-help in removing the guilt that we have brought upon us. Repentance means a radical turning away from self-reliance to trust in God alone. To repent means to recognize self-trust to be the heart of sin."

George Whitefield (1714-70) was famous for revival preaching on both sides of the Atlantic. On the subject of repentance he said: "Let a man go to the grammar school of faith and repentance before he goes to the university of election and predestination."

Arising clearly out of repentance is conversion, about which Ralph Turnbull said: "Since the will to war is latent in human nature, only a conversion based on spiritual renewal can lead men to a new concept of living."

An anonymous writer put the essence of conversion in this sentence: "When I recognized the Master as my Guide, He steered me across a threshold into unventured expanses, all charted, as I discovered, in His Word."

One of the lesser lights in Puritanism was William Secker, but his statement on conversion is excellent: "When the wheels of a clock move within, the hands on the dial will move without. When the heart of a man is sound in conversion, then the life will be fair in profession."

Another Puritan, George Swinnock, warned against delay in being converted: "All the while thou delayest, God is more provoked, the wicked one more encouraged, thy heart more hardened, thy debts more increased, thy soul more endangered, and all the difficulties of conversion daily more and more multiplied upon thee, having a day more to repent of, and a day less to repent in."

Yet another injunction to conversion was issued by the Puritan William Guthrie, who said: "The Bible, which ranges over a period of 4,000 years, records but one instance of a deathbed conversion—one that none may despair, and but one that none may presume. . . . There be few at all saved. . . . and fewest saved this way."

UNRIGHTEOUSNESS

MEANING

The Greek word for "unrighteousness" is *adikia*. It is formed by adding the prefix, *a* (as in amoral or amillennial) to the word *dikia* (righteousness), transforming it into *adikia* (unrighteousness).

In secular Greek the word referred to unjust acts, or to deeds which caused personal injury. Rather than a general concept of injustice, this word was taken, in the writings of Plato, to mean an unjust act which injures a specific person. Such an act was not necessarily a violation of some specific law, but rather an affront against the just order of society. Among the acts which fell into this category were theft, fraud, and sexual crimes. Later this word came to mean a neglect of duty toward the pagan gods.

The Septuagint Greek Old Testament used this word to describe social sins, those deeds which violated human relations or the political order of society. Among these injustices were deceit, fraud, and lying.

BIBLE USAGE

The noun *adikia* (unrighteousness) and the verb *adikeo* (to do unrighteousness) occur 27 times in the New Testament. Basically this word speaks of harm to people. Jesus spoke of financial harm in His Parable of the Laborers in the Vineyard (Matt. 20:13). Stephen referred to the matter of personal injury in a story about Moses (Acts 7:24-27).

The epistles contain many references to *adikia* as a matter of personal injury. Paul hinted that Onesimus had caused personal damage to Philemon (Phile. 18). In writing to the Corinthians, Paul even mentioned Christians who caused offense to one another (2 Cor. 7:12). Peter explained the difference between suffering injury for doing good and suffering as an offender (1 Peter 2:20). In its most basic form, this word refers to an injury brought by one person on another. And James made it quite clear that unrighteousness could also be committed by speech (James 3:6).

There is also in the New Testament reference to unrighteousness as a principle in this imperfect, sinful world. People who practice unrighteousness still benefit from God's goodness as, for example, rain and sunshine (Matt. 5:45). By contrast Christ is completely free from all unrighteousness (John 7:18). Since God is completely righteous, He can justly judge unrighteousness (Rom. 1:18; 3:5-6).

Though unrighteousness is a dominant principle in the world, God has provided an eternally satisfying solution. By His grace Christ died to pay for all our unrighteousness (3:24). In fact, the Apostle Paul explained this as an exchange. The completely righteous One became unrighteousness for us, that we might become righteous before God (2 Cor. 5:21).

It was not only the Apostle Paul who proclaimed this. It was also a frequently recurring theme in Peter's writing. In his fascinating explanation of the sacrificial death of Christ, Peter made special reference to our unrighteousness. Here again Christ is presented as the totally Righteous One. When He went to the cross, He took all of our unrighteousness upon Himself, and thus paid our penalty. By His resurrection the validity of this sacrificial atonement was established once for all (1 Peter 3:18).

In his epistles, John too took up the subject of righteousness and unrighteousness. Having established that Christians sometimes stumble and fall into sin, John also asserted that Christ is competent to cleanse every unrighteousness (1 John 1:9). Here again the Cross is Christ's credential; it validates His claim to be the

Redeemer (2:1-2). Since all unrighteousness is sin (5:17), Christians are exhorted not to live in it.

Unrighteousness and injustice (which are the same in Greek) characterize a fallen world. They still plague Christians today. Only through the sufficient sacrifice of Christ can they be cleansed and put away. The Righteous One is the answer to the unrighteousness in our world.

ILLUSTRATIONS

If one understands unrighteousness as an injury against another person, there are many examples in modern society. One often sees a middle-aged woman cast off by her husband in favor of a younger woman. In the schools of our land pushers devote their energies to ensnaring young people in the quicksand of dope. Annually thousands of children are assaulted sexually, and the dimensions of this problem are just now appearing. It seems as though the sophistication of our society masks a whole maze of unrighteousness and injustice.

One of the great American legal experts was Oliver Wendell Holmes (1841-1935). Of this moral cesspool he once said: "Sin has many tools, but a lie is the handle which fits them all."

The deceitfulness of unrighteousness is seen in this statement by Bob Turnbull: " 'Sin' is a seldom-used word today. But whether the word turns us on or off doesn't matter; it does not alter the truth, whatever we think. If my hang-ups and negatives are called 'sin' by our Lord, then sin they are."

As the late Francis Schaeffer declared: "Some psychological and sociological conditioning occurs in every man's life and this affects the decisions he makes. But we must resist the modern concept that all sin can be explained merely on the basis of conditioning."

One of the modern trends in theology is so-called Liberation Theology. Among its advocates are Gustavo Gutierrez, Hugo Assman, and Leonardo Boff. They claim that North Americans have dealt unjustly with Latin Americans for centuries, and now it is time for the Latins to strike back. They think unrighteousness in the past must be paid by unrighteousness in the present. It is an escalating "arms race" of political and economic weapons.

Christians realize that the answer to unrighteousness is not more of the same. It is rather the righteousness of God. *The Westminster Catechism* summarized the situation in this classical statement: "Sin is any want of conformity to or transgression of the Law of God."

Archbishop William Temple (1881-1944) explained God's reaction to unrighteousness in this clear way: "God loves me even while I sin. But it cannot be said too strongly that there is a wrath of God against me as sinning: God's will is set one way, and mine is set against it. And therefore, though He longs to forgive, He cannot do so unless either my will is turned from its sinful direction into conformity with His, or else there is at work some power [the Holy Spirit] which is capable of effecting that change in me."

John Bunyan (1628-88) understood the situation when he wrote: "Sin is the dare of God's justice, the rape of His mercy, the jeer of His patience, the slight of His power, and the contempt of His love."

VINE

MEANING

In the Greek New Testament "vine" is represented by the word *ampelos*. Homer identified this as a grapevine. Working with vines was the oldest form of agriculture known to man. The vine and wine have two strong emphases in literature and culture. First, they speak of well-being, because of the success of the vineyard. Second, they speak of debauchery, because of the misuse of wine.

The Septuagint Greek Old Testament also included references to the vineyard and the wine. In fact, Jehovah was described as the Vinedresser of Israel, and Israel was His vine (Ps. 80:8-13). This exemplified the Lord's care of and concern for His people, the Jews.

But the other aspect of the subject was seen in the misuse of alcoholic beverages. For instance, when Noah got drunk, it led to the downfall of that otherwise sterling servant of God (Gen. 9:20-23). This remains as a stern warning of the danger of alcohol.

BIBLE USAGE

In the New Testament the vine is used mainly as a spiritual object lesson, which characterizes many of the 30 references to the vine and the vineyard.

Jesus told the Parable of a Vine Owner who hired day laborers to work in his vineyard. He promised each of them the same wage, but some were offended because they worked longer than others (Matt. 20:1-16). Actually the Lord taught through this parable the sovereignty and equality of His grace (Colin Brown, editor, *The New International Dictionary of the New Testament Theology* [Grand Rapids: Zondervan, 1978], III, p. 920).

In the same context is found the Parable of the Vineyard Owner. He had two sons. One promised to work in the vineyard, but did not. The other refused to work in the vineyard, but later relented (Matt. 21:28-30). Here the emphasis is on various responses to the Lord's message.

Yet another Parable of the Vineyard occurs in Matthew. A vineyard owner sought to evaluate the work of his employees. To this end he first dispatched a company of personal slaves, who were slain or beaten. Another larger group of slaves was also attacked by the ruthless work force. Finally the owner sent his son, who was also murdered. The owner himself then dealt harshly with his hired hands (21:33-41).

In the Lord's final teaching before His passion, He emphasized a picture taken from Psalm 80. The Lord Himself is the Vine, and the disciples are the branches. Only as the branches remain in the Vine do they bring forth spiritual fruit (John 15:1-5). The fruit which results from this union is described as a life of prayer, obedience to God's Word, joy in the Lord, and love for fellow-Christians (15:7-12).

Another reference to the vine is found in Christ's institution of the Lord's Supper. After celebrating the Passover meal with His disciples, Jesus took bread and broke it as an object lesson of His crucifixion (Matt. 26:26). His body would be broken for them and us. There was no confusion in the disciples' minds. They knew this was an object lesson, that Jesus did not say the bread became His body.

Afterward Christ took a cup of wine. He explained to the disciples that this was a symbol of His shed blood. Here again, Christ did not teach that the wine became His blood. He held the cup and declared that it was a symbol of His shed blood (26:28). The Apostle Paul urged the church to continue this practice in regular worship (1 Cor. 11:23-26).

In the New Testament, the vine symbolizes life in the Lord. It speaks of Him as the Source of all our strength. Any Christian who tries to produce spiritual fruit without the source of spiritual life is foolish indeed. Constant dependence is the only key to spiritual life.

ILLUSTRATIONS

In the '50s a Quaker theologian and philosopher, Elton Trueblood, wrote a slim volume, *The Predicament of Modern Man.* His theme was this: Man has cut himself off from God, and thus civilization is doomed to wilt and die. He used as his picture a vase of cut flowers. They look alive and luxurious, but their days literally are numbered. They will soon wilt, because they are cut off from their roots of life. So people who are cut off from God are doomed to wilt and perish eternally.

Though Trueblood may not have been an evangelical, he struck a biblical chord with this little book. Only as people draw their spiritual strength from the Lord do they survive and flourish. Fruitfulness is linked to dependence on God.

Professor R.V.G. Tasker, of the University of London, wrote: "The branches are not self-sustaining or independent—they have no source of life apart from the Vine." So a Christian only has life in Christ, the true Vine.

Lutheran Bible commentator Richard Lenski (1864-1936) emphasized that Jesus is the "true" Vine: "Jesus is not merely like a vine, He is more: the actual original, of which all natural vines, genuine in the domain of nature, are only images. As the real and genuine Vine in this supreme sense He exceeds all others who may in some way also be called vines, and He stands forever in contrast with all those who are not real but only spurious and pretending vines" (*The Interpretation of St. John's Gospel* [Minneapolis: Augsburg Publishing House, 1943], p. 1026).

In his newer commentary on Matthew's Gospel, my sometime colleague, Leon Morris, laid emphasis on fruit-bearing: "The emphasis is on the bearing of fruit. Pruning is resorted to ensure that this takes place. Left to itself a vine will produce a good deal of unproductive growth. For maximum fruitfulness, extensive pruning is essential. This is a suggestive figure for the Christian life. The fruit of Christian service is never the result of allowing the natural energies and inclinations to run riot" (*The Gospel According to John* [Grand Rapids: Eerdmans, 1971], p. 669).

Another aspect of Christ as the Vine is emphasized in the writings of A.W. Pink. He concentrated on the picture of God the Father as the Vinedresser: "In the Old Testament the Father is the Proprietor of the vine, but here He is called the Husbandman, that is, the Cultivator, the One who cares for it. The figure speaks of His love for Christ and His people" (*Exposition of the Gospel of John*, 2 vols. [Grand Rapids: Zondervan, 1945], II, pp. 396-397).

One emphasis shines through all of these comments: a Christian should live a life of absolute dependence on the Lord. Any attempt at independence is doomed to disaster. Fruitfulness is folly without the true Vine.

VIRGIN

MEANING

The Greek word for "virgin" is *parthenos*. It is variously used to describe a young woman without sexual experience, a daughter, a spinster, and even an unmarried man.

In English the closest related word is "Parthenon," the temple in Athens which was dedicated to the patron virgin goddess Athene. The temple was originally constructed from 447-432 b.c., but was transformed into a Christian temple in a.d. 426. As an early Christian church it was dedicated to St. Sophia. In 662 the temple was changed into a Shrine of the Virgin Mary. Thus the Greek word came full cycle. From a reference to the pagan goddess of virginity it grew to become a shrine of the premier virgin believer, Mary.

Originally the word *parthenos* meant an unmarried woman. Then Homer used it to connote sexual purity, youth, and the unmarried state. Later it was used narrowly to describe an unmarried and sexually inexperienced woman. Plato gave the word an abstract twist by speaking of "virgin freshness and beauty."

BIBLE USAGE

The word *parthenos* occurs only 14 times in the Greek New Testament. Predictably the most prominent uses of the word relate to Christ's virgin birth. Matthew mentioned many details to indicate that Mary was a virgin. She was engaged to Joseph (Matt. 1:18). She had not yet had intercourse with him (1:18). The pregnancy was unexpected and undesirable (1:18-19). Joseph was assured angelically that the baby was conceived by the Holy Spirit (1:20).

The explanation of this remarkable event is prophetically presented. This is the virgin conception (1:23), which Isaiah foresaw and foretold (Isa. 7:14). Incidentally this proves that "virgin" is the correct translation of that verse from Isaiah, and not "a young woman," as the *Revised Standard Version* has it. This statement is confirmed by Luke (Luke 1:27). Paul stated simply that "a woman" bore Christ, which may also have been an undergirding argument for the virgin birth (Gal. 4:4).

That this word means an unmarried woman can be deduced from other references in the New Testament. For instance, Anna was described as a woman who lived with her husband seven years "from her virginity" (kjv) or "after her marriage" (Luke 2:36). The daughters of Philip the evangelist were described as "virgin . . . prophetesses" (Acts 21:9).

By implication Paul claimed that he was sexually a virgin or celibate. Incidentally, the Book of Revelation also applies the word "virgin" to males (Rev. 14:4). Paul praised virginity as a significant segment of the Christian church (1 Cor. 7:25). Paul carefully avoided commanding the virgin state (7:28), but did point out that virgins have fewer worldly cares than married people (7:34). He also urged fathers not to refuse marriage to their virgin daughters (7:36-38).

There is also an abstract use of the word "virgin." The New Testament compared the Christian church to Christ's virgin bride. The idea is based on a prophetic passage, where Isaiah compared Israel to a virgin bride (Isa. 62:5). Paul told the Corinthians that God watches jealously over His church, as a man does over his virgin bride (2 Cor. 11:2). The ultimate aim of Christ is seen in terms of presenting His virgin bride in heavenly perfection (Eph. 5:25-27). This picture appears to be fulfilled in the Book of Revelation (Rev. 21:2).

The meaning of virginity is clear: it involves purity and protection from contamination. It speaks of that pristine beauty which one sees in a believing bride.

For that reason, it is an excellent picture of the church of Jesus Christ.

ILLUSTRATIONS

This subject can be illustrated from two different angles. First, it speaks of human virginity, or the single state before marriage. One of the most significant segments of the Christian community is its single people. One thinks of great missionary leaders, who turned their singleness into single-mindedness. Among them is Amy Carmichael (1867-1951), an Irish woman who founded the Dohnavur Fellowship of India.

Another stellar missionary was Frances Ridley Havergal (1900-70), who penned many hymns, such as "I Gave My Life for Thee," "Who Is on the Lord's Side?" and "Take My Life and Let it Be." Her devotional books include *Kept for the Master's Use, My King,* and *Royal Commandments.*

A third, less literary but nonetheless significant servant of the Lord was Gladys Aylward (1902-70). When missionary societies rejected her approaches, she paid her own way to China. There she developed an orphanage ministry, which was chronicled in a Hollywood film. Her visits to churches were unforgettable.

In addition to the many illustrations of single saints, due consideration must also be given to the impact of the virgin birth of Christ. This doctrine is so significant that it was included in the pamphlets, *The Fundamentals* (1910-15), which gave rise to the Fundamentalist movement.

Writing on the significance of the Virgin Birth, Professor John Frame of Westminster Theological Seminary cited four main pillars of this truth. First, the Virgin Birth is true because the Scriptures are true. Its truthfulness thus stands or falls with the veracity of Scripture. Second, the Virgin Birth attests to the deity of Christ. If Christ was not born of a virgin, His deity comes under question. Third, the humanity of Christ depends on the doctrine of the Virgin Birth. His birth was the point of entrance into the human race. Finally, in the Virgin Birth is a guarantee of the sinlessness of Christ. Had he been born of a man, He would have been contaminated by original sin ("Virgin Birth of Christ," Walter A. Elwell, editor, *Evangelical Dictionary of Theology* [Grand Rapids: Baker Book House, 1984], p. 1145).

In the face of liberal criticism and skepticism, famous Methodist theologian J.P. Cooke contended: "If the Virgin Birth is not historical, then a difficulty greater than any that destructive criticism has yet evolved from documents, interpolations, psychological improbabilities, and unconscious contradictions confronts the reason and upsets all the long results of scientific observation—that a sinful and deliberate-ly sinning and unmarried pair should have given life to the purest human being that ever lived or of whom the human race has ever dreamed" (A.H. Strong, *Systematic Theology* [Old Tappan: Fleming H. Revell, 1907], p. 676).

VOICE

MEANING

The Greek word for "voice" is *phone*. It is obviously the root of such common English words as "tele*phone*," "*phon*ograph," (literally, "voice writing"), "*phonetics*" (the science of vocal sounds), and "*phon*emics" (the units of sound in speech).

In ancient Greece this word usually related to the audible sound of the human voice. It meant both the sound of human speech and the faculty of speech. Later it came to mean a communication from a pagan god, a decree of some deity, or a message given by an oracle, such as the oracle of Delphi. Only infrequently did it mean the cry of an animal.

When the Old Testament was translated into Greek (the Septuagint), the same word was used to describe sounds of nature. It represented natural sounds, from the roar of thunder to the bleating of sheep. It also was used to describe such significant communications as God's calls to Isaiah (Isa. 6:8) and Ezekiel (Ezek. 1:28).

BIBLE USAGE

The word *phone* and its related verb *phoneo* (I call) occur about 180 times in the Greek New Testament. As in the Old Testament, the New Testament gives a wide range of meanings to these words.

This voice speaks primarily of communication. Servant girl Rhoda heard Peter's voice when he came to the door (Acts 12:14). John the Baptist described himself as "the voice of one crying in the wilderness" (Mark 1:3; Isa. 40:3). The friends of the bride and groom rejoice, when they hear the voice of the groom (John 3:29). The Lord's followers respond to His voice, as sheep respond to their shepherd's call (10:3). The basic meaning of this word is communication.

This word also speaks of speech in general. Paul described the utterances of the prophets with this word (Acts 13:27). It was also used to portray the cry of a crowd at Ephesus (19:34). Herod's speech was compared to the voice of a god, for which arrogance God punished him with death (12:21-23). The same word, *phone*, portrayed the rantings of demonized people (8:7).

Phone was used repeatedly to describe the voice of God. God's voice was heard at Christ's baptism (Matt. 3:15-17), and also at His transfiguration (17:5; 2 Peter 1:17). Christ seems to have equated His voice with God's voice, especially in terms of His call to resurrection (John 5:24-28). When Christ described Himself as the Good Shepherd, He made frequent references to His Heavenly Shepherd's voice (10:3, 16, 27). At the grave of Lazarus the Lord spoke again with the voice of God (11:43). The voice of the Lord also called Saul of Tarsus from persecution to preaching (Acts 9:4; 22:7; 26:14).

In the Book of Revelation, the voice of God is active indeed. The voice from heaven initiates the plan of God (Rev. 10:8). The same voice gives directions to John (11:12). When a blessing is pronounced on the persecuted saints, it is again the voice of God which speaks (14:13). Even the completion of God's judgment is announced by this heavenly voice (16:17). Finally the reunion of God's people in glory is announced by the heavenly voice (21:3).

The Book of Revelation uses different word pictures to describe God's voice. When God speaks, it is like the sound of mighty rushing waters (1:15). Another description compares God's voice to the clear sound of a trumpet (1:10). God speaks, and it has the weight of a thunderclap (6:1; 11:19). In another picture, the voice of God is compared to the roar of a mighty lion (10:3).

God is known to us through His communication. His voice is seen in nature, Scripture, and salvation of the lost. Because our God is a Communicator and a Creator, we too have voices with which to speak. We can communicate because He gave us this ability. Our communication is hindered only by sin; the Tower of Babel is an eloquent exposition of this truth (Gen. 11:1-9).

ILLUSTRATIONS
In this portion of our discussion, we shall first look at the communication of people about the Lord. As well-known Lutheran broadcaster Oswald Hoffmann said: "Without continued proclamation of the Good News of Christ the church would never have got off the ground. In a generation it would have become extinct."

The late President and Professor of Preaching at Northern Baptist Seminary, Charles W. Koller, claimed: "The word of man does not become the Word of God by being loudly proclaimed. No amount of noise and lather can substitute for the note of authority. God does not promise to bless the proclamation of our own clever ideas; but He does promise, 'My word . . . shall not return unto Me void' (Isa. 55:11, KJV)." Many times Dr. Koller encouraged me as a young preacher, when I preached in the church where he worshiped.

Donald Miller also emphasized the content of our communication, when he said: "The proclamation and promulgation of the Christian faith must arise out of the continued rehearsal of the events recorded in the Bible."

Not only is the voice of Christian communication important, but the direct call of God is supremely significant. The great Genevan reformer, John Calvin (1509-64) said: "There is a universal call by which God, through the external preaching of the Word, invites all men alike. . . . Besides there is a specific call which, for the most part, God bestows on believers only."

His contemporary in the conflict was Martin Luther (1483-1546), who developed a whole theology of God's calling and stated it thus: "How is it possible that you have not been called? You are already a married man or wife or child or daughter or servant or maid. . . . Nobody is without command and calling. . . . God's eyes look not upon the works, but upon the obedience in the work." Luther believed that every Christian had a high and holy calling from God. This was the basis of his teaching of the priesthood of all believers.

John "Praying" Hyde (1865-1912), a missionary prayer warrior, thus explained God's calling: "No other organization on the face of the earth is charged with the high calling to which the church is summoned: to confront men with Jesus Christ."

One of the unforgettable characters of post-war Europe was Corrie ten Boom, subject of the film and book, *The Hiding Place.* Of the call from God she said: "Jesus Christ opens wide the doors of the treasure house of God's promises, and bids us go in and take with boldness the riches that are ours."

"God's favorite word," according to Robert Sterner, "is 'Come.'"

WAY

MEANING

The Greek word for "way" or "path" is *hodos*. It is seen in the English word, "*exodus*," which means literally "the way out." In the time of Homer this word was used to describe a street, way, or path. Later it rose to fame with the invention of the Roman road system. By extension, the word also meant the course of a ship through the sea, or a journey on land or water.

Later this word took on an abstract or figurative meaning. It was used to describe "the ways and means" of achieving any given purpose. Soon the idea developed that life is one's "way" through the world. Democritus, famed for the "Laughing Philosopher," wrote: "A life without leisure is like a long road [or journey] without a place to halt."

The Greek word *hodos* appears no fewer than 880 times in the Septuagint Greek Old Testament. It described the road or path on which one walked. As one might expect, it also has the figurative meaning of "the way of life."

BIBLE USAGE

The word *hodos* appears about 100 times in the Greek New Testament. Most obviously it is used to describe the roads one travels. In fact, some of Jesus' most crucial conversations occurred on the road. On the road to Caesarea Philippi Jesus asked His disciples: "Who do people say that I am?" This question moved Peter to make his great confession of Christ's deity (Matt. 16:13-20; Mark 8:27-29; Luke 9:18-20).

Another significant reference to "way" occurred near the end of Christ's earthly ministry. At an important turning point in His life, Jesus left His ministry behind and set His face toward Jerusalem (Matt. 20:17) and Calvary.

In His parables, Jesus also referred frequently to "the way." He spoke of seed which fell on the hard surface of the road, and thus was lost to the birds (Matt. 13:4, 19). Also He taught the disciples to forage in the streets and alleys to find the lost (Luke 14:21-23).

The word *hodos* is also used figuratively in the teaching of Jesus and His apostles. In the Sermon on the Mount Jesus spoke of two ways: the broad way which leads to destruction and the narrow way which leads to eternal life (Matt. 7:13-14).

In teaching the disciples, Jesus referred to Himself as the Way, the Truth, and the Life (John 14:6). William Barclay translates that description of Jesus as "the true and living Way. In the Book of Hebrews Jesus is portrayed as "a new and living Way" into the very throne room of heaven (Heb. 10:20).

In connection with the teaching that Jesus is the Way, reference is also made to the way of salvation. Jesus' teaching was called "the way of God" (Matt. 22:16). Quoting the Prophet Isaiah, Zacharias spoke of "the way of peace" (Luke 1:79; Isa. 59:8). Paul presented Christian love as a "more excellent way" (1 Cor. 12:31).

Not only is salvation known as "the way," but the Christian life is also referred to as a walk and a way. Paul called the Gospel "the ways of the Lord" (Acts 13:10; 18:25). Peter presented the Christian life as "the way of righteousness" (2 Peter 2:21).

When one turns his back on God's way, there are also wrong ways to travel. James emphasized these in speaking of unstable ways, and erroneous ways (James 1:8; 5:20). Paul spoke about people who went their own ways (Acts 14:16). Others were spiritually ruined because they did not know God's ways (Heb. 3:10).

Thus the way was not only a road on which one walked, but it was also a life which one lived. Through Jesus Christ people are admitted into the way of salvation, which sets their feet on a new path.

ILLUSTRATIONS

Literature is replete with many references to "the way" and "the road." This is seen in a famous but anonymous Scottish folk song:

> O ye'll tak' the high road, and I'll tak' the low road,
> And I'll be in Scotland afore ye.

Alfred Lord Tennyson (1809-92), noted poet laureate, wrote concerning the road of human history: "Not once or twice in our rough island story, / The path of duty was the way to glory" ("Ode on the Death of the Duke of Wellington").

One sees how old these concepts are, when one considers the writings of Horace (65-8 B.C.), who lived prior to Christ's birth: "Remember when life's path is steep to keep your mind even." In another place he added: "We all are driven [driving] one road."

In echo of Horace, Christina Georgina Rossetti (1830-94) wrote her poem, "Up-Hill," in which she asked:

> Does the road wind up-hill all the way?
>   Yes, to the very end.
> Will the day's journey take the whole long day?
>   From morn to night, my friend.

Not only does secular literature contain references to the road of life; this concept is also found in religious literature. John Keble (1792-1866), included these lines in his well-known volume, *The Christian Year:*

> The trivial round, the common task,
> Would furnish all we ought to ask;
> Room to deny ourselves; a road
> To bring us daily nearer God.

A contemporary of Keble in the Oxford Movement was John Henry Newman (1801-90), who ultimately became a Roman Catholic Cardinal. On the subject of life's road, Newman said: "Fear not that your life shall come to an end, but rather that it shall never have a beginning."

Though little is known about Femi Ilesanmi, he made a profound statement concerning the way of life: "Being a Christian is a way of life, not a method or a technique, but a lifestyle all its own."

Many Christian hymns echo this idea. On the night of my conversion more than four decades ago these words were sung: "There'll be light in the sky from my palace on high, when I come to the end of the road." Though I was a small boy, these words helped draw me heavenward.

About the same time my father taught me a chorus with similar words:

> When the road is rough and steep,
>   Turn your eyes upon Jesus.
> He alone has power to keep,
>   Turn your eyes upon Him.

Perhaps this is the best advice a father can give his young son.

WILL

MEANING

The Greek word for "will" is *thelema*, and the verb form, "I will" is *thelo*. One sees this root word in the feminine name *"Thelma."* In its most basic form, this word refers to "a wish," "a strong desire," and "the willing of some event."

But in ancient secular Greek the word had another meaning. Homer used it to speak of "readiness," "inclination," and "desire." When one was ready for an event, or inclined to undertake a course of action, *thelo* was used. Later the word also gained a sexual meaning, as when a man has his "will" with a woman, or vice versa. In the writings of Plato the word came to speak of intention or desire.

The Septuagint Greek Old Testament contains 100 references to these words. In most cases they refer to God's will, as He revealed it to His people.

BIBLE USAGE

In the Greek New Testament these words appear 270 times. As one might expect, nearly all of these references deal with the will of God.

Perhaps the most prominent reference is found in the Lord's Prayer. There Christ taught His disciples to pray for the fulfillment of the will of God on earth as it is in heaven, without any resistance (Matt. 6:10). The primary test of one's Christianity is a willingness to do God's will (7:21).

Often the will of God stands out in bold contrast with the will of man. When these conflicts occur, one can be absolutely sure that the will of God is just and holy (Rom. 9:14-17). The whole of God's salvation plan was willed for our good. This involved the sacrifice of Christ (Gal. 1:4). It also included God's sovereign call to us, by which we are saved and sanctified (Eph. 1:5, 11). In accordance with His will, God reveals His glory to us (Col. 1:27). He also motivates us to do His will (Phil. 2:13).

It was the will of God that propelled Paul into the ministry of apostleship. He identified himself in this way, when he wrote to many churches and individuals (1 Cor. 1:1; 2 Cor. 1:1; Eph. 1:1-2; 2 Tim. 1:1).

No one ever was more conscious of the will of God than was the Lord Jesus Christ. Doing the Father's will was more important than food and drink to Jesus (John 4:34). He measured all judgment by the standard of God's will (5:30). Salvation through the Lord Jesus Christ is determined by the will of God (6:40).

There are also references to the will of people in the New Testament. A servant is bound to do his master's will (Luke 12:47).

The Apostle Paul often expressed his own will with the verb, "I desire" or "I wish." He willed to visit the Roman church (Rom. 1:13), but this did not become a reality till the end of his life. He wished that all people were single (1 Cor. 7:7), but he did not make this a rule. Another wish was that all believers had two specific spiritual gifts (14:5).

On a more general level, "the will of man" often referred to physical desires. For instance, Christians are not born by human desire, but by divine decree (John 1:13). Christians often experience confict between their righteous wishes and their unrighteous performances (Rom. 7:15-16).

The will of God is always good. No matter how it is expressed in our lives or our world, God's will is holy and thus always helpful. On the other hand, the will of people often conflicts with the will of God. And the will of Satan is always at enmity with the will of God (2 Tim. 2:26).

ILLUSTRATIONS

Human understanding of the will of God is sometimes rather weak. Even the saintly Augustine of Hippo (A.D. 354-430) confessed: "When I vacillated about my decision to serve the Lord my God, it was I who willed and I who willed not, and nobody else. I was fighting against myself. . . . All [God] asked was that I cease to want what I willed, and begin to want what [He] willed."

Godly poet George Herbert (1593-1633) emphasized the importance of aligning our will with God's: "When the will is ready [to obey God] the feet are light."

God seems to work through man's will. Though we feel that we have free will, actually our will is only free when exercised in accordance with God's will. Irenaeus (who wrote about 175-195) expressed this truth clearly: "Not only in works, but also in faith, God has given man freedom of the will."

Alfred Lord Tennyson (1809-92) stated the same principle in poetry:

Our wills are ours, we know not how;
Our wills are ours, to make them Thine.

James Jauncey was more direct: "God never burglarizes the human will. He may long to come in and help, but He will never cross the picket line of our unwillingness."

The emphasis shifts to God's will, when we read the writings of devotional author George MacDonald (1824-1905). He penned these words about the will of God: "I find doing the will of God leaves me no time for disputing about His plans."

Focusing on the all-encompassing nature of God's will, Frances J. Roberts wrote: "God's will is not a place, but a condition; not a when or where, but a how."

Corrie ten Boom's life was portrayed in the book and film, *The Hiding Place*. Less well known are the words of her sister, Betsie ten Boom, who said concerning God's will: "The center of God's will is our only safety."

Every Christian who loves the Lord and does His will can identify with this anonymous statement: "To *know* God's will is man's greatest treasure; to *do* His will is life's greatest privilege."

When we lived in England, we often sang a chorus which concluded with this thought:

There's no peace, no joy, no thrill
Like walking in His will.
For me to live is Christ
To die is gain.

George Matheson (1842-1906), a blind hymn-writer, summarized the will of God:

My will is not my own
    Till Thou hast made it Thine;
If it would reach the monarch's throne
    It must its crown resign;
It only stands unbent, amid the clashing strife,
When on Thy bosom it has leant
And found in Thee its life.

WISDOM

MEANING

The Greek word for "wisdom" is *sophia*. It is seen in the English word "philoso-*phy*," which means literally "love [*phileo*] of wisdom [*sophia*]."

In the time of Homer, wisdom was an attribute. A person might be described as being "wise." It was never an action, as saying wise words or doing wise deeds. In fact, in ancient Greece wisdom had a practical aspect also, for a wise carpenter was one who knew his trade well. In Greek culture the College of Seven Sages was distinguished by both wisdom and political discernment.

According to Socrates, wisdom was knowing how little one really knew. Aristotle equated wisdom with "philo*sophy*." The Stoics described wisdom as the application of knowledge.

In the Septuagint Greek Old Testament, wisdom was sometimes personified, as in the Book of Proverbs. It was special knowledge, mainly knowledge concerning Jehovah God. When Solomon prayed for wisdom to rule, God gave it to him. He became the wisest man on earth.

BIBLE USAGE

In the Greek New Testament, the word for wisdom is found 60 times. There are three levels of wisdom to be discovered there. First, there is human wisdom. This wisdom is usually contrasted with divine wisdom.

One of the major New Testament passages concerning wisdom is found in 1 Corinthians. God's plan to redeem us destroyed the wisdom of the worldly wise men (1 Cor. 1:19). In fact, human wisdom never could comprehend God's plan for salvation (1:21). Paul was not bound by the limits of human wisdom because the Holy Spirit conveyed spiritual wisdom through him (2:13). Human wisdom is totally inadequate to accept God's salvation (3:18-19).

There is a spiritual wisdom that is given only by the Holy Spirit. In the Old Testament, Solomon exemplified this wisdom (Matt. 12:42). When Jesus came, His wisdom also outshone the wisdom of the wisest among men (13:54). This wisdom was seen in the Lord Jesus, even when He was a small Boy (Luke 2:40, 52).

When leaders became necessary in the Jerusalem church, the apostles set about to select men who possessed this spiritual wisdom (Acts 6:3). Every Christian needs such wisdom, can ask God for it, and God will surely give it to him or her (James 1:5). It is amazing that the same spiritual wisdom which motivated Christ during His earthly ministry is available to Christians now.

Nowhere is the wisdom of God more clearly seen than in the salvation story, the Gospel. The focus for this truth is found in 1 Corinthians. Here Paul contrasted God's wisdom with the best wisdom the Greeks could muster.

By analogy, wisdom is connected to spiritual power (1 Cor. 1:17-18). People who believe in the Lord, whatever their national backgrounds, perceive the wisdom of God's salvation (1:24). Despite the apparent catastrophe of the Cross, the wisdom of God shone through that dismal day (2:2).

Paul described this reversal of man's wisdom as a mystery. In the New Testament, a mystery is a truth which has been hidden in God's mind from eternity past. It cannot be grasped by human reason, so if it is to be revealed it must be revealed by divine grace (2:6-7).

When Paul summarized this teaching, he asserted that Christ is the very wisdom of God personified (1:24, 30). In writing to the Colossian Christians, Paul again taught that Christ is the very wisdom of God, and all of God's wisdom reposes in Christ (Col. 2:3, 9-10).

The Bible pours an entirely new meaning into the Greek term *sophia*. Wisdom is not applied knowledge or superb ability. Wisdom is found solely in the Saviour. It is no wonder that the psalmist said: "The fear of the Lord is the beginning of wisdom" (Ps. 111:10).

ILLUSTRATIONS

Francis B. Thornton explained wisdom with one simple statement: "Scholars are a dime a dozen, but a man of wisdom is a rare bird." An anonymous writer told the secret of wisdom when he declared: "The wise know too well their own weaknesses to assume infallibility; and he who knows most, knows how little he knows."

When we turn to literature, we also see the frailty of human wisdom. Socrates (470-399 B.C.) said: "The beginning of wisdom is the definition of terms." Get the words right, and wisdom will follow. On the same subject of wisdom and words, Plato (427-347 B.C.) declared: "Wise men talk because they have something to say; fools, because they have to say something."

Brilliant British thinker Francis Bacon (1561-1626) asserted: "A prudent question is one-half of wisdom." Ask the right questions and you will become wise.

Samuel Taylor Coleridge (1772-1834), a skilled penman, suggested: "Common sense in an uncommon degree is what the world calls wisdom." Just follow your "horse sense" straight to wisdom.

Others warned about human wisdom. Historian and biographer Thomas Carlyle (1795-1881) cautioned, "I do not believe in the collective wisdom of individual ignorance." He knew that true wisdom was a rare commodity.

French essayist Michel de Montaigne (1533-92) maintained, concerning wisdom: "We can be knowledgeable with other men's knowledge, but we cannot be wise with other men's wisdom."

The old adage says: "A word to the wise is sufficient." Sydney Harris twisted the old line: "A word to the wise is superfluous, and a hundred words to the unwise are futile."

How different the complexion of wisdom appears when one turns to Christian writers. Famed preacher Martyn Lloyd-Jones (1899-1981) defined divine wisdom: Wisdom is "that attribute by which God arranges His purposes and His plans, and arranges the means which bring forth the results that He purposes."

A similar slant on wisdom was stated by A.W. Tozer, a famed American preacher: "Wisdom . . . is the ability to devise perfect ends and to achieve those ends by the most perfect means." To which the New Testament scholar Richard C. Trench (1807-86) added: "There can be no wisdom disjoined from goodness."

The sole source of wisdom is none other than God. "Knowledge is horizontal," declared the evangelist Billy Graham. Then he added: "Wisdom is vertical—it comes down from above."

At Christmastime much is made of the wise men who traveled a great distance to worship Christ. Several years ago this reminder showed up on a bumper sticker: "Wise men still seek Him." After all, "The fear of the Lord is the beginning of wisdom."

WITNESS

MEANING

The Greek word for "witness" is *martus,* and the verb form, "I witness," is *martureo.* In English the word "martyr" describes a person who bears witness by laying down his or her life. Actually *martus* was a legal term; it related to a witness in a formal proceeding.

In ancient Greek literature the bearing of witness was related to the confirmation of an event. One bore witness to support the truth of an event. The term was connected to the verb *merimnao* (that which requires the agreement of many minds). As many minds were brought to bear on a subject, the truth was established.

Later on a witness was seen as presenting valid legal evidence. Plato insisted that such evidence must be given freely, without coercion. In the writings of the Stoics, this word came to mean evidence for certain beliefs and convictions. Thus the root of religious testimony was planted.

BIBLE USAGE

In the New Testament the noun form *martus* (witness) appears 37 times, and the verb *martureo* (I bear witness) appears 76 times. It refers to a legal witness in its basic form. Unfortunately many legal witnesses were false witnesses. Lying witnesses slandered Jesus, in order that He might be condemned to the cross (Mark 14:55-56). By the same token, Stephen was also slandered by false witnesses, and he too was condemned to death on the basis of their untrue testimony (Acts 6:13; 7:58).

The word "witness" has yet another use; it is a general statement of truth. Paul gave witness to the religious zeal of the Jews, which zeal he had exemplified before his conversion (Rom. 10:2). On the other hand, Paul also bore testimony to the generosity of Christians (2 Cor. 8:3). In other texts he testified about the love and concern which Christians display (Gal. 4:15; Col. 4:13). Paul referred to witnesses concerning his own integrity and fidelity toward Judaism (Acts 22:5).

There is also a divine testimony or witness. God the Father bore witness to the Lord Jesus Christ (John 5:32). The Scriptures also witness to the messiahship of Christ (5:39). When the Holy Spirit came, He took the position of a witness for Christ (15:26-27). Christ came as a witness to eternal truth (1:7). This trinitarian witness is one of the themes of Revelation (Rev. 1:2, 9; 12:17).

Christians also are known as witnesses for the Lord (Acts 1:8). This testimony is empowered by the indwelling Holy Spirit (4:31-33). The Apostle Paul perceived this witness as the motivating force in all of his life and ministry, from the day of his conversion on the Damascus Road to the day of his death in Rome (23:11). When the Apostle John wrote his epistles, he viewed them as an extended witness to the incarnation of Christ (1 John 1:2-3).

Paul declared the truth of his teaching, by calling on God as his witness, when he charged Timothy to be true to the ministry (1 Tim. 5:21). Paul again professed that God was his witness when he urged Christians to quit quarreling (2 Tim. 2:14). Paul also claimed God as his witness in his final instruction to Timothy (4:1).

There is one further meaning of the Greek noun *martus,* and it is the meaning of martyrdom. In some ways, this is a particularly Christian use of the word. Paul never forgot that he had been a ringleader in the mob which made Stephen the first Christian martyr (Acts 22:20). In the Book of Revelation martyrs are seen to be those who laid down their lives for the sake of Christ (Rev. 17:6).

Every Christian is called to be a witness. This requires no special gift or

calling. It is a task entrusted to us by the indwelling Holy Spirit. From the death of

Christ until now many Christians have also been called on to witness through death. Their sacrifices for the Saviour have given a whole new meaning to this Greek word.

ILLUSTRATIONS

Our illustration of this word will comprise two concepts. First, we shall consider the idea of witnessing for Christ. J.C. Macaulay, a former pastor and college president, spoke of one's personal witness in these terms: "So long as our personal testimony exalts the glory and all-sufficiency of Christ as Saviour, rather than our character either before or after conversion, it will be helpful." Christ is the centerpiece of Christian witness, not some Christian experience.

The founder of Campus Crusade for Christ, William Bright, insisted: "The real witnessing Christian does not talk about people he has 'converted.' Witnessing is hard work unless it is done in the Spirit, and then we can't brag about it."

The Archbishop of Glasgow, Robert Leighton (1611-84), declared: "He who can tell men what God has done for his soul is the likeliest to bring their souls to God." This is a simple but profound definition of witnessing.

"To be a witness does not consist of engaging in propaganda or in stirring people up. It means to live in such a way that one's life would not make sense if God did not exist," according to Emmanuel Suhard.

Another aspect of the same truth was given by Ralph. L. Williams: "We do not stand in the world bearing witness to Christ; we stand in Christ bearing witness to the world."

The second aspect of this word is martyrdom. Thomas Browne (1605-82), a Christian physician and writer, claimed: "Were the happiness of the next world as closely apprehended as the felicities of this, it were a martyrdom to live."

An English proverb states: "It is not suffering but the cause which makes the martyr." To which Gustave Flaubert would add: "It is the truth of the doctrine that makes the martyr."

William Sydney Porter (1862-1910), better known as "O. Henry," once wrote: "Perhaps there is no happiness in life so perfect as the martyr's." As Ian Rennie said: "When a Christian is martyred, tremendous things begin to happen."

Evelyn Underhill (1875-1941) was a brilliant Christian writer. She wrote many mystical books, and on the subject of martyrdom she wrote: "Love makes the whole difference between an execution and a martyrdom."

Many Christians from the time of the apostles until the time of Emperor Constantine (A.D. 280-337) sealed their testimonies with their own blood. Of these brave believers Tertullian (160-215) wrote: "The blood of the martyrs is the seed of the church."

WOMAN

MEANING

In the Greek New Testament the word for "woman" is *gune*. This word is variously reflected in English words, such as "*gynecology*" (the medical science of feminine diseases) and "*gynecocracy*" (a society in which women rule).

The word *gune* was used to describe women in all kinds of circumstances. It spoke of single and married women, mothers and widows. In Greek society, a woman's role was defined by her relationships to men and children. She was a wife and mother. Few roles were accorded to women apart from these domestic positions.

In the time of Homer, the word *gune* emphasized contrasts. Women were contrasted with men, who had all the rights. Mortal women were contrasted with goddesses. Wives were seen in distinction from concubines.

There was little respect for women in Athens, but in Sparta they were participants in city life. In fact, one student of Greek culture wrote: "The general rule in this matter is that the further we go west the greater is the freedom of women" (Colin Brown, editor, *Dictionary of New Testament Theology* [Grand Rapids: Zondervan, 1978] vol. III, p. 1055).

In the Septuagint Greek Old Testament women sometimes appeared as leaders. Deborah was a judge, prophetesses spoke for God, and Esther was an influential queen.

BIBLE USAGE

There are in the New Testament 200 references to women in various roles. Most clearly their role is seen in the Gospels, where Christ raised them to a new level of respect in society.

Jesus often referred to women in His parables. A woman leavened the dough, and it became an example of the kingdom (Luke 13:20-21). After a woman lost one coin, she diligently sought and found it (15:8). Women will be found grinding at a mill when the Lord returns (Matt. 24:41).

Jesus entered into public conversation with women, a practice unknown in traditional Jewish society. Not only did He become a Friend of Mary and Martha (Luke 10:38-42), but He also spoke at length with a Samaritan woman (John 4:7-27). This was a double affront to culture: Jews never spoke to Samaritans and men avoided speaking to women.

In His healing ministry, Jesus also gave place to women. He healed the mother-in-law of Peter at Capernaum (Matt. 8:14-15). On His way to heal the daughter of Jairus, He also healed a woman plagued by a hemorrhage (9:18-22). Even a Canaanite woman found healing for her daughter at the feet of Jesus (15:21-28).

Among the closest followers of Jesus were several women of note. They supported Him with their material wealth (Luke 8:1-3). One woman anointed Him with expensive perfume (John 12:3). At the cross, it was the women who waited and watched (Matt. 27:55; Mark 15:40). Women also went to the grave to embalm His corpse (16:1). Women also were the first witnesses of the resurrected Lord (Matt. 28:1-10). In fact, when the men fled, the women followed their Lord.

In His preaching, women were often mentioned positively. Jesus referred to the widow of Zarephath, whom Elijah helped (Luke 4:25-26). He also told about a widow who gave her all to the Lord (Mark 12:41-44). In dealing with a known adulteress, Jesus proclaimed His power to forgive (John 8:7).

Several amazing women were included in the blood line of Jesus. Among these were Tamar, a blackmailer (Matt. 1:3), and Rahab, a prostitute (1:5). There was also Ruth, a foreign convert (1:5), and Bathsheba, an adulteress (1:6).

In the remaining portions of the New Testament, women are seen as being equal members of the church (Gal. 3:28). They are deserving of sacrificial love in marriage (Eph. 5:25; 1 Peter 3:1-7). Women were prominent in the prayers of the church (Acts 1:13-14; 12:12; 16:13-14; 17:4, 12).

After Christ came into the world, woman's role changed dramatically. She was raised from the dust to dignity, which now characterizes women in most Christian countries. The reason for this was not social progress, but the Saviour Himself.

ILLUSTRATIONS

Christian literature is full of references to the role of women. Christian Nestell Bovee claimed: "Next to God we are indebted to women, first for life itself, and then for making it worth living."

In his *Parson's Tale*, famed English poet Geoffrey Chaucer (1340-1400) wrote: "God, when He made the first woman . . . made her not of the head of Adam, for she should not climb to great lordship . . . also, certes [certainly], God made not woman of the foot of Adam, for she should not be holden [held] too low . . . but God made woman of the rib of Adam, for woman should be fellow [companion] to man."

Three centuries later Bible commentator Matthew Henry (1662-1714) refined this quotation: "The woman was formed out of man—not of his head to rule over him; not of his feet to be trod upon by him; but out of his side to be his equal, from beneath his arm to be protected, and from near his heart to be loved."

Alfonse de Lamartine wrote concerning women: "There is a woman at the beginning of all great things." To this sentiment the German writer Johann Wolfgang von Goethe (1749-1832) appended: "The society of women is the foundation of good manners."

From a Christian perspective, Arthur Gossip claimed: "It was Christ who discovered and emphasized the worth of woman. It was Christ who lifted her into equality with man. It was Christ who gave woman her chance, who saw her possibilities, who discovered her value."

The author of "The Battle Hymn of the Republic," Julia Ward Howe (1819-1910), commented on the role of women in society: "When I see the elaborate study and ingenuity displayed by women in the pursuit of trifles, I feel no doubt of their capacity for the most herculean undertakings."

Economist and philosopher John Stuart Mill (1806-73) exclaimed: "Who can tell how many of the most original thoughts put forth by male writers belong to a woman by suggestion? If I may judge by my own case, a very large portion indeed."

Charles Haddon Spurgeon (1834-92) owed much to Susannah, whom he called "Wifey." The story is told of a Saturday evening, when his sermon would not take shape. "Wifey," he called, "I can't find a word from the Lord."

Susannah then gave the great preacher a text, which he preached on the Lord's Day. How right John Stuart Mill was!

WORD

MEANING

The Greek term for "word" is *logos*. It is reflected in such English words as *"logical"* (the science of reasoning, as expressed in words), *"logistics"* (the moving, lodging, or supplying of military troops in the most logical way), and *"logo"* (a symbol which represents a word).

Coming from the Greek verb *lego* (I speak), the term *logos* originally meant "speaking," "discourse," and "recounting a story." In Homer it was the spoken word, in contrast with a fictitious myth. The Sophists (fifth century B.C. philosophers) separated the word from its content. A word, of course, does not always mean the same thing. A new slant originated with Sophocles, who believed that words had common definitions and agreed meanings. Aristotle believed that the *logos* was identical with its definition.

In the Septuagint Greek Old Testament heavy emphasis was placed on the word of the Lord Jehovah. In this connection *logos* was used more than 241 times in the Old Testament. This word of Jehovah was communicated by prophecy, command, angels, and the very act of Creation.

BIBLE USAGE

The word *logos* appears 331 times in the New Testament, and its verb form, "I speak" is found 1,320 times. The greatest emphasis falls on the word of Christ, as compared with the word of the Lord in the Old Testament.

In fact, even Christ's enemies perceived that His words were spoken with authority, an authority which came from God (Matt. 7:28-29). Jesus often emphasized this authority by introducing a statement with the phrase, "Truly, truly." This He used in speaking of the unpardonable sin (Mark 3:28-29). He also availed Himself of this assertive form when He spoke of the sign of Jonah as a visible prophecy of the Resurrection (8:12). In stating the need for salvation, He again used "Truly, truly" (John 5:24).

At the word of Jesus His disciples followed Him (Mark 2:14). He underlined this with a challenge to complete commitment (Luke 9:23). At the word of Jesus the sick were healed (Mark 1:25; 9:25; Luke 4:18). Bystanders remarked that even the demons obeyed His voice (Mark 1:27).

Not only was the word of Jesus powerful, but He Himself was called the Word. He is the incomparable expression of God. Indeed Christ was God's final word to the world. The Gospel of John is opened with an extensive prologue presenting Christ as *Logos*, the Word.

As the Word, Christ was eternally present with the Father (John 1:1-2). This gives credence to the concept of the Trinity. Through the Word, God created everything which exists in the world (1:3). When Christ came into the world He brought light and life, so spiritual enlightenment is derived from Him (1:4-9). Despite the momentous nature of Christ's coming, His own people rejected Him (1:11). Nevertheless, any revelation which we have of God has its source in the Word, Jesus Christ (1:14, 16, 18). As the Word, Christ is God's greatest Communicator to mankind.

Not only did Christ speak the Word and personify the Word, but the scriptural Word of God is full of Him. Through the word of the Cross, people hear about salvation and are saved (1 Cor. 1:18, 21). In other places the Gospel message is known as the Word of God (14:36). Paul also coined the term, the Word of reconciliation, another synonym for the Gospel (2 Cor. 5:19). In Philippians Paul presented the Gospel as the Word of life (Phil. 2:16).

But it is the introduction to the Book of Hebrews which summarizes this idea best. God spoke in times past by the prophets, and they brought the Word of the Lord. Then in a later time God spoke through His Son (Heb. 1:1-4).

ILLUSTRATIONS

Words are, according to Rudyard Kipling (1865-1936), "the most powerful drug used by mankind." Entertainer Eddie Cantor declared: "Words fascinate me. They always have. For me, browsing in a dictionary is like being turned loose in a bank."

Another evaluation of the worth of words came from the pen of Edward Thorndike, who said: "Colors fade, temples crumble, empires fall, but wise words endure."

A leading light of the Enlightenment was philosopher John Locke (1632-1704), who said: "We should have a great many fewer disputes in the world if words were taken for what they are, the signs of our ideas only, and not for things themselves."

If human words are so important, one may assume God's words are infinitely more weighty. The controversial Anglican turned Catholic, William Chillingworth (1602-44), concluded: "I am fully assured that God does not, and therefore that men should not, require any more of any man than this: to believe the Scripture to be God's Word, to endeavor to find the true sense of it, and to live according to it."

No single group of Christians were more adamant in their allegiance to the Word of God than the Puritans. One of them, John Penry, said: "We hold that neither man nor angel is anywise to add or detract anything, to change or to alter anything from that which the Lord hath set down in His Word."

John Owen (1616-83), a famed Puritan penman, argued: "We say not that the Spirit ever speaks to us *of* the Word, but *by* the Word." In writing about the Christians' spiritual armor, William Gurnall claimed: "Bless God for the translation of the Scriptures [into English]. The Word is our sword; by being translated, the sword is drawn out of its scabbard."

Not only is the written Word important to us as Christians, but we also give full attention to the Living Word, the Lord Jesus Christ. William Temple (1881-1944), an evangelical Archbishop of Canterbury, asserted: "[Jesus] does not have to rely on the authority of the past or on other teachers. . . . .He acts with the manifest authority of God; He is the creative Word of God. In Him we are to see what is the purpose of God in making the world and in making us."

Several hymns set this theme to music. One is the familiar worship hymn by Mary Lathbury (1841-1913), the first stanza of which says:

Break Thou the Bread of Life, dear Lord, to me,
As Thou didst break the bread beside the sea;
Beyond the sacred page I seek Thee, Lord,
My spirit longs for Thee, Thou Living Word.

A lesser-known hymn, penned by Josiah Conder (1789-1855), comes from the British Isles:

Thou art the everlasting Word, / The Father's only Son;
God manifestly seen and heard, / And heaven's beloved One.

WORLD

MEANING

The Greek word for "world" is *kosmos,* and is seen in many English terms. For instance, the *"cosmos"* is the whole world or universe. A matter of *"cosmic"* significance, is something which is important for the whole world. When one speaks of a *"cosmo*politan" city, it means a city which has citizens from many parts of the world. (Actually *"cosmo*politan" is comprised of two words: *cosmos* [world] and *polis* [city].) This is a real "world-class city."

In early Greek literature the word *cosmos* spoke of building or establishing a culture or city. Anything which was made up of parts was called a *cosmos* as, for instance, a group of rowers or a troop of soldiers.

The verb form of this word, *cosmeo,* meant to adorn or beautify. It is seen in our English word, *"cosme*tic," a substance which adorns or makes one more beautiful.

By the time of Plato, the word *cosmos* had taken on the meaning of a world or universal viewpoint. It was the universe, inhabited by people. Aristotle felt that this world was eternal, and that it had neither beginning nor end.

BIBLE USAGE

The word *cosmos* appears 188 times in the New Testament. It has three distinct shades of meaning. First, it is a neutral dwelling place for the world's peoples. It was created by God, and its peoples were arranged by Him (Acts 17:24-26). Jesus Christ was the divine Agent in that creative act (John 1:3, 9). This origin, by God's Creation, is assumed throughout the New Testament (Matt. 25:34; John 12:31; Rom. 1:20; Rev. 13:8). Just as the world had a beginning in Creation, so it will also have a conclusion (Matt. 24:35). The world is the home of all peoples (4:8; Acts 17:26). There is neither condemnation nor approval attached to the world as a residence for people.

Another aspect of the world is the indication that the world is fundamentally opposed to the things of God. In contrast with Christians, the world is largely immoral (1 Cor. 5:10; Col. 2:20). In the Book of Hebrews, the world is seen as being hostile to faith (Heb. 11:7, 38). James called the world "an enemy of God" (James 4:4). Peter referred to it as being ungodly, that is not dominated by God's view of things, and used Noah's world as an example (2 Peter 2:5). John, in his epistles, claimed that the world and its value system is passing away (1 John 2:15-17). Thus the world's view of life does not coincide with God's view.

In one sense the world is neutral, and in another sense it is opposed to God. Finally, it is the object of God's saving acts. God loved the world and gave His Son for it (John 3:16, 19; 1 John 4:9). Jesus came as the Light into a dark world (John 1:9; 8:12; 9:5). Though not everyone in the world will be saved, the death of Christ is sufficient for the whole world (1:29; 1 John 2:2). In fact, several passages refer to Christ as, "the Saviour of the world" (John 4:42; 1 John 4:14).

Because God had a world view in His redemptive plan, Christians are commissioned to live for the Lord in the world. We are left in this world to demonstrate His love (4:19). Though the world is antagonistic to faith, we are protected by His presence (John 17:11, 18, 21). In Jesus' parting commission to the disciples, He sent them out into all nations to make disciples (Matt. 28:18-20). This command encompasses the entire world, and every creature in it (Mark 16:15; Acts 1:8). In one sense, the worldwide missionary commission is a logical outworking of God's creative act, whereby He made the world. It also reflects God's redemptive act, in which He sent Christ to die for the whole world. God has a worldwide view of things.

ILLUSTRATIONS

Nearly everyone has something to say about the world. President Woodrow Wilson (1856-1924) said: "We are citizens of the world; and the tragedy of our times is that we do not know this." The same sentiment was echoed by William Lloyd Garrison (1805-79), an abolitionist editor: "My country is the world. My countrymen are all mankind." As early as the fourth century before Christ, Diogenes (412-323) wrote: "I am a citizen of the world."

Another statement along the same lines came from the pen of a well-known Christian mystical writer, Francois Fenelon (1651-1715): "All wars are civil wars, because all men are brothers. . . . Each one owes infinitely more to the human race than to the particular country in which he was born."

This concept has been catapulted into our consciousness by modern writers. Marshall McLuhan, for instance, declared: "The world has become a global village." Adolf Keller expressed the slightly suppressed fear of the world, when he wrote: "It is five minutes to twelve on the clock of the world's history."

The world is one of God's arenas of activity. Jonathan Edwards (1703-58) expressed this: "The end of God's creating the world was to prepare a kingdom for His Son." In his poem, "God's Grandeur," Gerard Manley Hopkins wrote: "The world is charged with the grandeur of God."

A 19th-century German Lutheran theologian and preacher, Christoph Ernst Luthhardt (1823-1902), summarized the world's importance in this line: "The view we entertain of God will determine our view of the world."

Theodore T. Munger declared: "The unrest of the weary world is an unvoiced cry after God." One of Billy Graham's associate evangelists, John Wesley White, concurred: "The world hopes for the best, but Jesus Christ offers the best hope."

Many Christians have been charged with a vision to reach our world. In 1966, several hundred missionaries met at Wheaton, Illinois for a congress on "The Church's Worldwide Mission." Later that year a more widely representative group met in Berlin for "The World Congress on Evangelism." Again in 1974 preachers and evangelists met at Lausanne, Switzerland for "The International Congress on World Evangelization." The emphasis in all of these meetings was on reaching our world with the Gospel. Alas, it is often more simple to discuss evangelism than to do it.

Today there is a growing movement among students to evangelize the world. It echoes "The Student Volunteer Movement," which set the goal of world evangelization in one generation. The contemporary movement is called "The World Christian Movement." Ralph D. Winter and Steven C. Hawthorne have edited a massive volume titled *Perspectives on the World Christian Movement* (Pasadena: William Carey Press, 1981).

WORSHIP

MEANING

The Greek word for "worship" is *proskuneo*. Originally it meant "to kiss reverently," which involved stooping down to kiss. Early Greek writers spoke of stooping to kiss the ground, as an expression of thanksgiving for a safe arrival. (This is the gesture Pope John Paul II makes on arriving in a foreign land.)

Later on, *proskuneo* came to mean prostration, throwing oneself on the ground to show awe or respect before some deity. This was seen not only with regard to pagan gods or goddesses. It also was practiced when appearing before rulers, such as Alexander the Great. The idea was one of reverence, and this attitude of submission was signaled by falling prostrate on the ground.

In the Septuagint Greek Old Testament such worship was reserved for Jehovah God. In fact, it was considered sacrilege for a Jew to express worship toward any other pagan god or person. One recalls that Daniel's friends refused to bow to their ruler's idol (Dan. 3:1-12).

BIBLE USAGE

The word *proskuneo* appears no fewer than 60 times in the Greek New Testament. Such worship is always reserved for the Lord. Consequently Christ never refused to accept worship. When a healed leper threw himself at the Lord's feet, Jesus responded by healing the man instantly (Matt. 8:2-3).

Jairus, a synagogue official, likewise bowed in worship before the Lord. Consequently Jesus raised his daughter from the dead (9:18-25).

When Jesus walked on the water, His disciples were astonished. As soon as the Lord boarded their boat, the storm ceased, and the disciples worshiped Him as God's Son (14:33; Mark 6:51).

Similarly a Canaanite woman worshiped Christ in an effort to find help for her demonized daughter. Jesus claimed He had come to Israel, but He responded to the woman's worship by releasing her daughter (Matt. 15:25-28).

That Christ received worship was a proof of His deity. He had asserted strongly that only God is worthy of worship (4:9-10). He also received worship after His resurrection. Many who met Christ fell down and worshiped Him (28:9, 17). Even a former doubter, Thomas, confessed Christ's deity (John 20:28).

Not only did Jesus accept worship, but He also taught the essentials of worship. The Samaritan woman was preoccupied with the place of worship, but Jesus taught her that true worship was spiritual, not spatial (4:20-24).

When some Greeks came to Jerusalem to worship at the Feast of Passover, they sought to see Jesus Christ. Though they engaged in worship as Jewish proselytes, they would learn to worship the Messiah (12:20-21). The same truth is seen in the visit of the Ethiopian treasurer to Jerusalem (Acts 8:27-39).

Jesus taught and received worship. And the worship of Him will occupy Christians throughout eternity. In the Book of Revelation, one sees 24 elders in an attitude of worship toward the Lamb. They worship Him because of His sacrifice on the cross (Rev. 4:10-11). His dominion also drives them to worship (5:13-14; 7:11-12; 19:4). So does His eternality (11:16-17).

The temple will be restored as a center of true worship, according to the revelation of the risen Lord (11:1). Not only will Israel worship the Lord, but there will be a worldwide worship, when Christ will be revealed to all eyes (14:7; 15:4).

Also in the Book of Revelation there is a perverted worship. During the Great Tribulation some will bow down and worship the beast (the Antichrist), and the dragon (Satan) (13:4). These worshipers are those whose names are not recorded in heaven (13:8). All who fail to worship the beast will be killed (13:15). This is the source of martyrs in the Great Tribulation. On the other hand, none of these who worship the beast will have a heavenly home (14:9-11).

Thus worship in the New Testament is a two-edged sword. On one hand, those who worship the Lord will live forever in heaven. Those who submit to any other worship are doomed to eternal damnation. It is eternally important to watch what we worship.

ILLUSTRATIONS

According to Kenneth E. Kirk (1886-1954), a late Bishop of Oxford: "Worship depends not upon our own activities, but upon the activities which God brings to bear upon us; to them we are forced to react as worshipers."

In old English "worship" really meant "worthship." This is reflected in a remark attributed to Eric Mascall: "Every act of worship is its own justification. It is rendering to God that of which He is worthy." Harold C. Bonell declared: "To worship means to recognize supreme worth."

A German pietistic hymn-writer, Gerhard Tersteegen (1697-1769), declared: "The true inner life is no strange or new thing; it is ancient and true worship of God, the Christian life in its beauty and in its own peculiar form. Wherever there is a man who fears God and lives the good life, in any country under the sun, God is there, loving him, and so I love him too."

Puritan Stephen Charnock (1628-80) emphasized the significance of worship: "We may be truly said to worship God, though we want [lack] perfection; but we cannot be said to worship Him if we want [lack] sincerity."

Another Puritan, Thomas Goodwin (1600-80), underlined the importance of worship by showing that each worshiper is important: "In public worship all should join. The little strings go to make up a concert as well as the great."

"What we worship determines what we become," asserted Harvey F. Ammerman. He added, "If we worship material possessions, we tend to grow more materialistic. If we worship self, we become more selfish still. That is why Christ continually endeavored to direct men's worship."

C. Neil Strait expanded on this idea: "Worship is, in part, listening to what God might say to us, through music, through words, through fellowship. It is also our response to what He speaks. Worship has occurred when life responds with an openness to how God could change our lives."

One well-known worship hymn was written by John S.B. Monsell (1811-75). Its first stanza sets the tone:

O worship the Lord in the beauty of holiness,
  Bow down before Him, His glory proclaim;
With gold of obedience, and incense of lowliness,
  Kneel and adore Him, the Lord is His name.